Industrialising Africa

This book is part of the Peter Lang Political Science, Economics, and Law list.
Every volume is peer reviewed and meets
the highest quality standards for content and production.

PETER LANG
New York • Bern • Berlin
Brussels • Vienna • Oxford • Warsaw

Horman Chitonge

Industrialising Africa

Unlocking the Economic Potential of the Continent

PETER LANG
New York • Bern • Berlin
Brussels • Vienna • Oxford • Warsaw

Library of Congress Cataloging-in-Publication Data

Names: Chitonge, Horman, author.
Title: Industrialising Africa: unlocking the economic potential
of the continent / Horman Chitonge
Description: New York: Peter Lang, 2019.
Includes bibliographical references and index.
Identifiers: LCCN 2018054670 | ISBN 978-1-4331-6558-0 (hardback: alk. paper)
ISBN 978-1-4331-6559-7 (ebook pdf) | ISBN 978-1-4331-6560-3 (epub)
ISBN 978-1-4331-6561-0 (mobi)
Subjects: LCSH: Industrialization—Africa. | Africa—Economic conditions—21st century.
Africa—Economic policy. | Economic development—Africa.
Classification: LCC HC800.Z9 I533 2019 | DDC 338.96—dc23
LC record available at https://lccn.loc.gov/2018054670
DOI 10.3726/b15988

Bibliographic information published by **Die Deutsche Nationalbibliothek**.
Die Deutsche Nationalbibliothek lists this publication in the "Deutsche
Nationalbibliografie"; detailed bibliographic data are available
on the Internet at http://dnb.d-nb.de/.

29 Broadway, 18th floor, New York, NY 10006
www.peterlang.com

TABLE OF CONTENTS

TABLES

FIGURES

PREFACE

In 2011 *The Economist* magazine published a volume with a cover page entitled, *Africa Rising: A Hopeful Continent* (https://www.economist.com/leaders/2011/12/03/africa-rising). Although this article cautioned against inflated optimism about the prospects of sustained economic growth in Africa, it argued that "some fundamental numbers are moving in the right direction." Of of these fundamental numbers cited was that six out of the ten fastest growing economies between 2000 and 2010 were in Africa. The article further argued that foreign direct investment flows grew significantly over the same period, that the arrival of China improved the state of infrastructure in many African countries and that the appetite for technology grew in leaps and bounds. What caught my attention in the article was the line that, "Africa could break into the global market for light manufacturing and services such as call centres." When I finished reading this article I decided to look at the manufacturing profile of different African countries. My interest in this was to find out if the manufacturing activities in African countries were contributing to the growth that *The Economist* article highlighted. So, I started looking at the sectoral composition of output for African countries, which is reported in the *African Statistical Year Book*, published annually by the African Development Bank. I particularly focused on the industrial sector because manufacturing is reported under this sector. I then discovered that the industrial sector performance was actually not that bad in most countries.

When I closely looked at the manufacturing sector, it became apparent that this sector in many African countries was actually declining or stagnating, during the time when most countries were reporting GDP growth rates of over 5 percent. The decline of the manufacturing sector was occurring even in countries listed by *The Economist* magazine as among the top 10 fastest growing economies in the world. Figures on employment ratio in the industrial sector as a whole reflected a similar trend of either declining or remaining stagnant at the time when the continent was reporting high growth rates. This made me to pause and ask the question, where is the growth coming from? Is it agriculture or services?

When I explored this question further, it then became apparent that the growth reported in most of the countries on the African continent was largely buoyed by higher commodity prices on the global market. In other words, the continent is still specialising in the supply of raw materials to the industrial centres of the world. For those who are familiar with the colonial history of Africa, Africa's specialisation in the exporting of raw materials was a part of the colonial plan, designed specifically to keep the colonies from competing with the industrialised countries in manufactures. While this made sense during colonial rule because African economies at that time were controlled by colonial regimes, it does not make sense now when African countries have officially attained independence. Why should African countries, after attaining independence, continue to operate under the same structure which was not meant to benefit Africa and its peoples? It could either be that the post-colonial African states are in fact not yet independent in the true sense of the word, or that African leaders do not see anything wrong with operating under the colonial economic structures, even if these structures do not serve Africa's interests. With all these questions in mind, I decided to explore the issues further and this book draws from that research.

I started this research by looking at what African countries did immediately after attaining independence. My frustration with this work was that I could not find any documents on the industrial strategies which African countries adopted after independence. Online resources could not help because the documents I was looking for were not available. To understand why industrialisation has been so elusive on the continent as a whole, I started to focus on the strategies for industrial development, particularly manufacturing, which most of the African countries adopted after independence. After inquiring from many people where I could find documents on the industrial policies and strategies, I was told that the only place where you can find this kind of material is the Nordic Africa Institute (NAI) in Uppsala, Sweden. So, I decided to go to the NAI and I was impressed by what I found there. I decided to spend a full month in the library going through the documents, particularly the industrial development sections of the National Development Plans (NDPs). My other challenge in this regard was that I could not read the NDPs for African countries colonised by France, Portugal or Spain. So, I ended up focusing on the NDPs of former British colonies. Here also we have an example of an incomplete decolonial project, with Africa still separated by not only the colonial borders, but language as well.

In the NAI library, every African country has a dedicated section with different types of literature from government reports, academic books, research reports, media articles, videos, documentaries, etc. For my research, the basement, where they keep all the materials on Africa before the year 2000, proved to be an invaluable resource. Although I could not find the industrial policy documents on every African country, I found the different volumes of the NDPs for all African countries from the first NDPs to the last ones, before development planning was interrupted by the introduction of the Structural Adjustment Programmes (SAPs) during the 1980s.

In each NDP I looked at, there was a section on industrial development, clearly stating the objectives and targets for various industrial activities. After a review of the NDPs for several countries, I realised that most African countries prior to the onset of SAPs were in principle determined to decentre the colonial economic logic and structure by seeking earnestly to build industrial capabilities in their respective countries. Reading through these documents, particularly the preface to the NDPs, I got the sense that the African leaders of that time understood clearly that they had to defy the colonial economic logic in order to give Africa the chance to grow its industrial sector and economies. And many African countries made a good start, with significant progress in the first ten years.

On the basis of what is articulated in the NDPs, it is apparent that the leaders of that time realised that one of the ways through which African countries could defy the colonial economic logic and re-orient their economies was by implementing an aggressive industrial development strategy. In other words, industrialisation was a central component of the decolonisation project in Africa during the 1960s. So, what I have done in this book is to examine the past and present state of industrial development strategies, and on the basis of this, identify a few prerequisites for industrialising the continent. One of my major conclusions is that industrialising Africa today should be treated as a decolonial project, which requires the dismantling of the colonial economic structures and defying the colonial economic logic. The book argues that African states will have to play a central role in initiating the process of re-orienting African economies from the colonial designs to a structure where Africa can reap the benefits of the abundant natural and human resources. The book acknowledges that undoing the colonial economic structure is not an easy thing as the past experience has shown, but it can be done, and the pressure is on African leaders to take bold decisions and actions. Through the analysis of the key themes on industrial development in Africa, the book offers a new and critical perspective on what it will take Africa to attain significant levels of industrial development.

ACKNOWLEDGMENTS

This work would not have been possible without the contribution of many people. I would like to first thank my family, my wife Dr. Millicent A. Chitonge and my children Chilufay and Alinda who gave me the time and support to work on this project. I would like to convey my sincere thanks to the staff at the Nordic Africa Institute (NAI), where the research for this book started, and I would like to particularly thank Dr. Patience Musasa and Ms Eva-Lena Svensson for facilitating my fellowship at the NAI; Ms Iina Soiri (NAI director) and Professor Victor Adetula (NAI head of research) for accepting my application for a visiting fellowship at the NAI. I wish to convey my sincere thanks to the NAI Library staff, who assisted me with fetching the documents I required from the basement, particularly Mr. Mattias Akesson. I would also like to express my gratitude to the University of Cape Town's University Research Committee (URC) for a sabbatical grant that supported my fellowship at the NAI.

Some chapters of this book were written while I was a visiting fellow at the University of Zambia (UNZA) in the Department of Geography and Environmental Studies, and I would like to thank the department for hosting me and giving me the space to work. The final review and editing of the chapters in the book was done while I was a visiting scholar at the African Studies

Centre, Tokyo University of Foreign Studies, and I would like to express my sincere thanks to the Director, Professor Takeuchi Shinichi and the members of staff, for providing me with a conducive work environment.

ABBREVIATIONS

3ADI:	Africa Agribusiness and Agro-industries Development Initiative
ACET:	African Centre for Economic Transformation
ACFTA:	Africa Continental Free Trade Area
ADLI:	Agriculture Demand-Led Industrialisation
AEO:	African Economic Outlook
AfDB:	African Development Bank
AI:	Artificial Intelligence
AIA:	Alliance for the Industrialisation of Africa
AIDA:	Accelerated Industrial Development for Africa
ANZSIC:	Australia and New Zealand Standard Industrial Classification
APCI:	Africa Productivity Capacity Initiative
ARN:	Africa Rising Narrative
AU:	African Union
BBC:	British Broadcasting Corporation
CIDL:	Classic International Division of Labour
CSC:	Commodity Supper Cycle
DEPTH:	Diversification, Export, Productivity, Technology and Human well-being

DESA:	Department of Economic and Social Affairs (UN)
DRC:	Democratic Republic of Congo
DTI:	Department of Trade and Industry (South Africa)
EAC:	East African Community
ECOWAS:	Economic Community of West African States
EDBs:	Economic Development Boards
EDPs:	Economic Development Programmes
EEIT:	East and Southern Europe Investment Trust
EIU:	Economist Intelligent Unit
EM:	Enterprise Mauritius
EY:	Ernest and Young
FAO:	Food and Agriculture Organization
FDI:	Foreign Direct Investment
FIR:	Fourth Industrial Revolution
GDP:	Gross Domestic Product
GEM:	Global Entrepreneurship Monitor
GEMA:	Global Entrepreneurship Monitoring Association
GNP:	Gross National Product
HDI:	Human Development Indicators
H-O-S:	Hecksher-Ohlin-Samuelson
ICT:	Information and Communication Technology
IDB:	Industrial Development Board
IDDA I:	Industrial Development Decade for Africa One
IDDA II:	Industrial Development Decade for Africa Two
IDL:	International Division of Labour
IESA:	Industrial Extension Services Agency
IFAD:	International Fund for Agriculture Development
IGC:	International Growth Centre
ILO:	International Labour Organization
IMF:	International Monetary Fund
IOT:	Internet of Things
IPC:	Industrial Policy Council
ISA:	Industrial Services Agency
ISG:	International Study Group
ISI:	Import Substitution Industrialisation
ISIC Rev 3:	International Standard Industrial Classification Revision 3
ISIC Rev 4:	International Standard Industrial Classification Revision 4
LICs:	Low Income Countries

LPA:	Lagos Plan of Action
MCCI:	Mauritius Chamber of Commerce and Industry
MEXA:	Mauritius Export Association
MGI:	Mackenzie Global Institute
MITI:	Ministry of International Trade and Industry (Japan)
MNC:	Multinational Corporation
MVA:	Manufacturing Value Added
NACE:	Statistical Classification of Economic Activities in the European Union
NAICS:	North America Industrial Classification System
NDC:	National Development Councils
NDP:	National Development Plan
NGO:	Non-government Organisation
NIDL:	New International Division of Labour
NIE:	New Institutional Economics
NRRCs:	Non-resource Rich Countries
ODI:	Overseas Development Institute
OECD:	Organisation for Economic Cooperation and Development
PIACs:	Presidential Investment Advisory Councils
PRB:	Policy Regulatory Body
QAS:	Quality Assurance Services
R&D:	Research and Development
RRCs:	Resource-Rich Countries
SADC:	Southern African Development Community
SAPs:	Structural Adjustment Programmes
SMEs:	Small and Medium Enterprises
SNA:	System of National Accounts
SOEs:	State-Owned Enterprises
SSA:	Sub-Saharan Africa
UNCTAD:	United Nations Conference on Trade and Development
UNDP:	United Nations Development Programme
UNECA:	United Nations Economic Commission for Africa
UNIDO:	United Nations Industrial Development Organization
USA:	United States of America
VAT:	Value Added Tax
WDI:	World Development Indicators
WEF:	World Economic Forum
YEPs:	Youth Entrepreneurship Programme

· 1 ·

INDUSTRIALISING AFRICA

The Key Arguments

Introduction

Industrialising the African continent has been on the African development agenda since the 1960s, when African countries succeeded in dislodging colonial regimes from the continent. Although industrialisation has been on the cards for 60 years in most countries, there is wide agreement among scholars of different ideological alignment that industrialising the continent has been elusive so far. Various indicators of industrial development are arrayed to support the view that efforts to create an extensive industrial base and build strong industrial capabilities have produced disappointing results in most (if not all) African countries. Some scholars have even questioned whether Africa can industrialise at all (see Newman et al, 2016b). The flip side of this, is to ask whether industrialisation is important for Africa, and what kind of industrialisation Africa needs today.

Analysts who question Africa's ability to industrialise may be justified given the skimpy industrial profile on the continent, especially manufacturing since the 1980s. As illustrated in this book, Africa's manufacturing share in total output (Gross Domestic Product, GDP), which is a basic measure of industrial development, averaged only 10 percent in 2015, and this is falling in many countries. Africa's share in global manufacturing was less than 1 percent in the same year. While there is growing optimism that the industrial sector in Africa will be radically transformed as the "Fourth Industrial Revolution" (FIR) takes root, there are doubts if African countries have laid a solid foundation for reaping the dividends of FIR[1] (EIU, 2018).

It is argued in this book that laying the foundation for any genuine industrialisation on the continent would require decentring the colonial economic logic, which has robbed Africa of its immense industrial and economic potential. In the context of the growing awareness around the FIR, debates on industrial policy and capability in Africa have started to feature more prominently. Industrialisation has featured strongly in debates on Africa's development, especially after the end of first *commodity super cycle* of the 21st century.[2] In these debates, industrial development in Africa is widely perceived to be the missing link in Africa's economic growth and development prospect, with weak industrial growth often cited as a sign that the continent has failed to transform the structure of its economies.

The direct offshoot of the failure to industrialise is evident in the low capacity to create productive jobs, which in turn explains the painfully slow pace of reducing poverty rates, amidst rising income and wealth inequality in most countries (see Page, 2015). In most African countries the lack of productive jobs has become a political imperative, with many African governments battling to find a workable solution to this challenge. The 2012 Economic Report on Africa, for instance, argues that Africa's failure to create adequate jobs to cater for the growing labour force is mainly attributed to the inability to create sustainable industrial production capacity. The failure to industrialise has forced most African economies to continue relying heavily on commodity production for export (UNECA, 2012). But the dramatic fall of commodity prices on the global market in 2015 has reignited the debate on the need for Africa to industrialise as a means to promote sustained and inclusive economic growth and social transformation.

A growing number of studies have highlighted the point that without significant levels of industrialisation, it will be difficult for African countries to generate adequate jobs to cater for the steady growing labour force, reduce poverty and inequality and transform the structure of African economies (McMillan and Rodrik, 2011; Gelb et al, 2014; Oqubay, 2015; World Bank, 2015; Newman et al, 2016b; UNECA, 2016b; UNIDO, 2016). The recent sharp decline of commodity prices on the global market has rejuvenated the view that unless African countries confront the colonial economic logic which consigned African economies to specialise in the production and export of raw materials to the world, industrialisation will continue to be elusive. It is argued in this book that decentring this economic logic entails transforming the structure of African economies from commodity mono-economies to diversified economies, supported by a broad industrial base. This can only be achieved through a complete overturn of the colonial economic rationale which still dictates the nature and scale of economic activities in African economies today.

The sharp decline of commodity prices on the global market in 2015 has not just brought to the fore the debates on the role of industrial development in Africa's economic growth and development; it has also put considerable pressure on the current accounts of most African countries, pushing some countries back to the International Monetary Fund (IMF) to negotiate for balance of payment support[3] (World Bank, 2015). Given past experiences of African countries with the World Bank and the IMF, there are now worries about what the effects of the IMF and the Bank's second generation "shock therapy" (Structural Adjustment programmes—SAPs) will be on Africa's industrial development prospect.

Critics of the *Africa Rising Narrative*, which emerged on back of rising commodity prices since 2003, feel well-vindicated now. They have been arguing that the growth episode experienced in most African countries since the beginning of the new Millennium is unlikely to be sustained because it is predominantly based on higher prices of commodities (see Arbache and Page, 2009; Rowden, 2013; UNECA, 2016). Others pointed out that though the recent economic growth reported in most countries in Africa can be attributed to a number of factors, "rising commodity prices, and natural resource discoveries" have accounted for the larger share of the growth observed (Newman et al, 2016a:3). Some of the concerns which analysts have expressed about the recent growth in Africa include the inability to promote inclusive growth and faster decline in poverty rates (ILO, 2017). The 2012 *Economic Report on Africa* elaborates on this:

> The failure of economies to generate adequate employment is partly because recent growth has been driven by the capital-intensive extractive industries (mining and oil exploration). These activities also have limited forward and backward linkages with the rest of the economy. African countries therefore need to diversify their sources of growth towards developing pro-poor sectors if they are to make inroads into reducing high unemployment and poverty rates (UNECA, 2012:39).

The downside of relying solely on extractive industries, in the African context, is that these activities use less labour per unit of capital because they rely on heavy and modern machinery in the production process, leading to a situation where larger sections of the labour force remain in the low-productivity activities in small-scale agriculture and the urban informal sector. While productivity in the extractive industries such as mining can be as high as 100 times that of agriculture (see McMillan and Rodrik, 2011), the mining and other extractive industries accounts for only a tiny proportion of the labour force as illustrated in Chapter 6. Thus, the capacity to create jobs through extractive industries is low compared to the secondary sector activities, particularly manufacturing (see UNECA, 2016a).

Africa's Failure to Transform the Colonial Economic Structure and Logic

The failure of African countries to industrialise is attributed to the failure to restructure the colonial economic structure and decentre the rationale that underpins it. African economies are locked in the colonial economic architecture, where the colonies were structured to be suppliers of raw materials and act as small (perhaps growing) markets for finished products. This structure puts countries that rely on the export of raw materials at a huge disadvantage, and industrialising Africa would require overturning this structural set up. Simple as that may sound, close analysis of the situation reveals that it has been difficult for African countries to decentre the colonial logic and economic set up. During colonial rule, since the colonies were structured to serve the interests of the metropoles (see Rodney, 1972), it made sense to operate within this set-up. In independent Africa, it does not make sense to entertain the colonial economic structure and logic which does not advance Africa's interests. Therein lies the fundamental challenge of industrialising Africa.

The outcome of continuing to operate under the colonial economic set up has been that of strengthening the economic and political power of the former colonial centres, while at the same time weakening Africa in general. This idea has been articulated more clearly by Friedrich List (1909:295) who is sometimes referred to as the father of "infant industry" (see Chang, 2003), when he argues that the British empire understood well the fact that a nation grows in wealth and power by importing raw materials and exporting manufactured goods. He argues that this policy was openly professed by all English policymakers. For example, "The Minister of George I,...openly declared, on the occasion of the prohibition of importation of manufactures of India, that it was clear that a nation could only become wealthy and powerful if she imported raw materials and exported manufactured goods" (List, 1909:295). By ingraining this logic in their economic engagements, the British government made sure that all the colonies contributed to making Britain wealthy and powerful.

In Africa this set up has been reproduced and still dominates and dictates economic activities. If we look at the export diversification index (EDI), which is a rough estimate of how far a country has gone in disrupting and defying the colonial economic logic, the picture is quite revealing. In most countries, the EDI has declined since the 1980s, manifested by few (if any) manufactured products in the export basket (see ACET, 2014; AEO, 2017). As shown in Chapter 3, in countries where manufactured products constitute a sizable component of the export basket, this is dominated by semi processed natural-resources (see UNIDO, 2016a).

There have been several reasons offered to explain the failure of African countries to decentre the colonial economic logic and these include institutional deficiencies, loss of policy autonomy during the time of SAPs, and the failure to discipline markets (see Soludo and Ogbu, 2004). Other analysts have attributed Africa's failure to disrupt the colonial economic logic to the anti-state ideology that dominated economic policy starting from the 1980s (Olukoshi, 2004), while others have put the blame on the hostile posture that developed economies have adopted towards Africa's efforts and plans to industrialise (see Lagos Plan of Action, 1980). What is common in most explanations is the failure among African states to consistently implement strategies aimed at defying and transforming the colonial economic structure and logic. Consequently, African countries have persistently failed to find strategies which would lead to building industrial production capabilities as the foundation for a high growth path.

This book seeks to illustrate that creating industrial capabilities is a product of three key factors: a) a strong awareness of the disadvantages of operating under a colonial economic logic, b) following from that, a strong commitment to decentre the colonial economic structure and c) consistent and deliberate actions by the state, aimed at building capabilities tailored towards realising the African potential. Industrialisation, wherever and whenever it has occurred, has never happened by chance; it has always been a result of deliberate and dedicated strategies and actions (UNECA, 2016a). To contextualise the current industrialisation challenges on the African continent, the book has discussed the past industrialisation strategies and outcomes. Drawing from the assessment of the past industrial development efforts in Africa, the book has identified some of the policy gaps which need urgent attention to spark sustained industrial growth on the continent in the 21st century. It is argued in the book that to achieve the objective of industrialising the continent, African countries should first learn to defy the colonial economic logic under which most African countries still operate. In pursuing this line of argument, the book seeks to move the debate on industrial development in Africa from a discussion of the industrial sector performance to the broader arguments around what Africa needs to do to achieve meaningful and sustained levels of industrial development.

Elusive Industrial Development in Africa

One of the important factors that explains Africa's failure to disrupt the colonial economic logic is that of weak African states. This is itself a product of continuing to operate under the colonial economic logic and structure, which were designed to weaken African states through relations of dependence and domination. As illustrated later, the role of the state in taking deliberate action to defy the colonial logic at the national and regional levels is crucial. With specific reference to creating industrial production capabilities, there is ample evidence showing that any country which has successfully industrialised has relied on various instruments of the state to drive the process. In a sense, the struggle to industrialise has always involved the state, and more so today as late-industrialisers face a stiffer gradient to climb. Alice Amsden captures this well in the passage below:

> States in modern history have always intervened to spur economic activity. Even with the First Industrial Revolution, whose guiding principle was laissez-faire, is now being reassessed by historians with this axiom in view. In the…Second Industrial Revolution in Germany and the United States, state intervention intensified…. The instruments of intervention have been cumulative. Not only have states in late-industrialising countries intervened by protecting infant industries. They also have intervened by providing private investors with a *battery of incentives* that, simplified, boil down to subsidies. The subsidy, which includes tariff protection and financial incentives, epitomizes the *struggle to industrialise* after the Second World War (Amsden, 1989a:12–13, emphasis added).

The point Amsden is making in the passage cited above is that industrialisation requires deliberate and calculated actions, spearheaded by the state, to transform the structure of an economy into what a country or region envisions. In other words, industrialisation has never happened by strictly abiding to a country's static comparative advantage; what an industrial policy seeks to do is to identify a set of industrial activities which a country uses to achieve specific goals and national interests (see Wade, 1990; UNECA, 2016a). This cannot be done by sticking to a static conception of comparative advantage. Oqubay (2015) makes a similar argument in his assessment of industrial policy and prospects in Ethiopia.

Despite the strong awareness of the importance of industrialisation in Africa, since the early independence days in the 1960s, industrial development on the continent has remained elusive in many African countries as the data presented in chapters 3 and 6 show. Unfortunately, the progress made during the 1960s and 1970s was reversed, especially between 1980 and 2000, such that today the levels of industrial activities in many countries are still below the levels reached in the mid-1970s. In many countries, manufacturing share in GDP is only recovering to its 1970 level, while manufacturing share in export has dropped to less than 3 percent, below the 1970 level (Newman et al, 2016b). This elusive nature of industrialisation in Africa has been attributed by some analysts to the abundance of natural resources which is said to have created a *comparative disadvantage*, making industrialisation less likely (Wood and Berge, 1997; Collier, 2000).

Given the elusive nature of industrialisation in Africa, this book discusses the prerequisites for industrial development in Africa. One of these prerequisites is the realisation that industrialisation is a product of deliberate, planned and well-coordinated actions, usually by public institutions. This prerequisite is much more important in Africa today given the large penalty which late industrialisers face. The other preconditions for industrial development in Africa, discussed in this book, include the need to create institutions with the capacity to coordinate industrial activities, the need to provide, what I refer to as *secondary public services*, particularly, *industrial services* and also the need to defy conventions around *static comparative advantage*, which entrench the colonial economic logic.

Given the failure of individual African countries to decentre the colonial economic logic and structures, one can sympathise with the Lagos Plan of Action's (LPA, 1980) emphasis on locating the project of defying the colonial economic logic at the continental level. The main reason why a collective project has higher prospects of decentring the colonial economic logic is that defiance can be a costly strategy if undertaken by an individual country. In a fundamental sense, defiance is a game of numbers, and this is why a strategy at the regional or continental level has a better prospect of succeeding than a national strategy. Proponents of this view argue that one of the reasons why African countries have failed to decentre the colonial economic logic is because they have acted as individual countries, which makes it hard to implement a defiance strategy (see Olukoshi, 2012).

Industrialisation: The New Consensus

Starting from the 1980s, the mainstream view on industrialisation has been that there is no place for industrial policy in economic development (UNECA, 2016a). But today there is an emerging consensus that *selective industrial policy* is indispensable to creating and sustaining conditions for successful industrialisation (Lall, 2004, UNECA, 2016a). In Africa, this emerging consensus on industrialisation has given rise to a wider agreement about what Africa needs to do in order to industrialise. One of the points of agreement is around *selective industrial* policy, which emphasises the idea that a country or region needs to pick a number of strategic industrial activities on which to focus at a particular time (Soludo and Ogbu, 2004).

In line with this new consensus, there is now a growing body of literature that is emphasising the importance of industrialisation in Africa as the solid ground for economic growth and diversification as well as poverty reduction and the creation of inclusive economies (Weiss, 2000; Lall and Kraemer-Mbula, 2005; Matambalya, 2015; Page, 2015; UNECA, 2016; Zamfir, 2016; Newman et al, 2016a). The United Nations Economic Commission for Africa (UNECA) has been consistent in its call to industrialise Africa as the basis for genuine structural transformation and the building of resilient economies. In addition to the earlier annual *Economic Reports on Africa*, which focused on diversification and structural transformation (see UNECA, 2011), UNECA's last three annual reports have all focused on industrialisation, with the 2016 report highlighting the need to factor environmental sustainability in the current industrial plans and strategies (see UNECA, 2016b).

In this growing literature on industrialisation in Africa, there is a convergence of views, across the ideological iron curtain, that African economies remain vulnerable to external shocks due to their over-reliance on commodity export. For Africa to overcome this challenge, it has been argued, African economies should shift from relying on commodities to building a diversified production base, supported by a strong manufacturing sector. This essentially entails defying the colonial economic logic which assigned African economies the task of supplying raw materials to the global economy.

But Why Industrialise Africa?

Several analysts have tried to explain why industrialisation is central to economic growth and development in Africa, and why African economies will find it difficult to diversify from commodity-based economies if industrialisation does not take root (Ciarli and Di-Maio, 2015; Matambalya and Cisse, 2015; Newman et al, 2016b; UNIDO, 2016a). UNECA explains the importance of industrialisation in Africa in more emphatic terms, arguing that there cannot be economic transformation, creation of productive jobs, reduction of poverty and inequality in Africa without industrialisation:

> African countries need to industrialise to increase incomes, create employment, raise value-added activity and diversify their economies. Industry has traditionally been a central source of generating employment—in developed and developing countries. In Africa, though, high rates of economic growth over the past decade have not translated into the structural transformation of the economy required (UNECA, 2016b:53).

The theoretical arguments supporting the importance of industrialisation are provided in Chapter 2. Here it suffices to say that industrialisation is now widely seen as a non-negotiable item on Africa's economic growth and development agenda (Timmer et al, 2012), and the question is not about whether Africa should industrialise, it is about what the continent should do to achieve this goal.

However, the new consensus is still defined narrowly, focusing on finding a trade and industrial formula that works. In other words, the new consensus on industrialisation is still focusing on the economic dimension of industrial development (Soludo and Ogbu, 2004). This book demonstrates that as a central pillar of Africa's development strategy, industrialisation touches on many issues including agrarian transformation, decolonisation of African economies, state capacity, entrepreneurship and the broader question around technology and the provision of public goods. When seen in this broader framework, it is clear that industrial policy alone is not a panacea for Africa's growth challenges. Industrial policy must be supported by complementary policies in education, financial and macroeconomic policies, and effective institutions with the capacity to implement the outlined strategy consistently in a coherent manner. In this regard, African governments are well aware of what needs to be done, but the challenge continues to be around how to translate this awareness and ideas into action.

Is There a Penalty for Late Industrialisers?

While there is an emerging consensus around the importance of industrialisation in developing countries, including countries in Africa, there is also a body of literature that is cautioning against the popular optimism about industrialisation's role in employment creation and poverty reduction. For example, Rodrik (2015) and Felipe et al (2017), using the concept of premature de-industrialisation, which they argue is occurring in poor countries at low levels of GDP per capita, contend that the job creation power of the manufacturing sector has significantly declined when compared to the experience of early industrialisers, when the sector had a high employment creation capacity.[4] One of the reasons cited in support of the idea of premature de-industrialisation is that manufacturing employment share in total employment in all economies is *peaking* at much lower levels than before, making it more difficult for late industrialisers to achieve higher manufacturing employment share (see also Tregenna, 2009; 2016). Drawing from the experiences of a large number of countries, these studies have concluded that the late industrialisers should look not only at manufacturing as the engine of growth and employment creation but adopt a broader development approach to supplement the limited employment creation capacity exhibited in the manufacturing sector (see Felipe et al, 2017:21). The impact of the phenomenon of premature deindustrialisation on the prospect of industrial development in Africa is discussed in Chapter 10. Here it suffices to note that this finding suggests that there is a penalty which the late industrialisers have to face. Though coming from a different starting point, Amsden (1989b) makes a similar point that late industrialisers face a steeper uphill in their quest to industrialise. It is primarily because of the larger penalty of being a late industrialiser that the state must play a much stronger role than ever before. Some analysts are now advocating for high value addition activities in the service sector as a remedy for the penalty arising from pre-mature deindustrialisation (Basbay, 2018). The high value-added industrial services strategy in Africa encounters several challenges including low skills and low industrial activities as illustrated later in Chapter 6.

Manufacturing Is Still the Engine of Growth

While this emerging literature highlights the huge penalty that comes with being a late industrialiser (penalty which many countries in Africa will have to face and navigate through), there is strong evidence to support the view that manufacturing is still the engine of growth, especially for economies at early stages of development. For instance, a study conducted by McKinsey Global Institute (MGI) argues that,

> Manufacturing still matters a great deal, but its importance is as a driver of productivity growth, and trade. Manufacturing continues to make outsize contributions to research and development, accounting for up to 90 percent of private R&D spending in major manufacturing nations. The sector contributes twice as much to productivity growth as its employment share, and it typically accounts for the largest share of an economy's foreign trade; across major advanced and developing economies, manufacturing generates 70 percent of export (Manyika et al, 2012:17).

Although the phenomenon of de-industrialisation is becoming more pronounced in industrial countries, the role of the manufacturing sector in developing economies remains critical not just for employment generation, but as an avenue for learning to compete, for technological catch-up and indeed for defying the colonial economic logic. Certainly, in the African context, manufacturing should not be valued for employment creation alone, but as a means to *learn by doing*, a means to build competitive industrial capabilities. Building competitive industrial capabilities is largely about creating the right "mind-set" which allows people to experiment with new ideas and techniques. To the extent that manufacturing acts as a conduit for innovation and technological dispersion, its role in promoting growth and structural transformation in Africa cannot be over-emphasised.

Industrialisation and Comparative Advantage

The colonial economic logic is implicitly tied to the basic economic concept of *comparative advantage*. The concept is largely associated with David Ricardo (2001 [1817]) who developed it to explain his theory of free trade. In the free trade theory, comparative advantage simply refers to the relative advantage one gains from specialising in producing goods and services at a lower cost relative to other producers. An example makes this clearer. Assume that firm A and B both produce iPads and shoes. If firm A produces more iPads than firm B using the same amount of resources, while firm B produces more shoes than firm B with the same amount of resources, then firm A can be said to have a comparative advantage in the production of iPads over firm B, and firm B has a comparative advantage in the production of shoes over firm A. In theory, firm A can produce iPads at a lower cost than firm B when it specialises in iPad production, in the same way that firm B can produce shoes cheaply by specialising in shoe production. The two firms can then exchange iPads for shoes, and it is understood that the outcome is often a win–win situation in the sense that they can both get what they want at a lower cost than if they produced both goods by themselves. Both gain in the sense that workers in firm A can obtain shoes cheaper than if they produced shoes on their own, just as workers in firm B can acquire iPads cheaper than if they produced the iPads on their own.

The fundamental question is, what makes firm A produce iPads cheaper than firm B, and firm B produce shoes cheaper than firm A? There are several factors which give rise to comparative advantage between firms or countries including availability of natural resources. But the most important factors are accumulated manufacturing capability, skills and technology. Details about the factors that influence comparative advantage are beyond the scope of this book, the interest here is to illustrate the concept.

The situation is much more complicated when applied to countries, but the basic idea is that countries gain by specialising in producing the goods and services over which they have a comparative advantage, and then trade the goods they produce with other countries. Here, the fundamental question is, how then do countries acquire comparative advantage relative to others? If conceptualised in static terms, comparative advantage is mainly attributed to differences in factor endowments and their relative prices. The theory of factor proportions which was developed by two Swedish economists Eli Hecksher (1919) and Bertil Ohlin (1933), and later by Paul Samuelson (1948) (giving rise to the famous Hecksher–Ohlin–Samuelson (H-O-S) theorem) draws from the factor endowment theory. According to this theory, a country should specialise in producing and exporting goods and services in which it has a relatively abundant factor (factor profusion principle). In other words, a country has comparative advantage in goods produced from factors that it has in abundance relative to other countries.

Of course, the assumption here is that a country with a relatively abundant factor can utilise the factor at a lower cost than a country that is less endowed in a particular factor. For example, countries in Africa situated within the tropics are expected to have a comparative advantage in palm oil production relative to countries located in temperate zones where it is difficult to grow palm trees. Thus, the view of comparative advantage rests on factor abundance and their price prior to trade (see Jones, 1957). But once trade is brought into the equation, the notion of comparative advantage makes more sense if seen from a dynamic perspective (see Krugman, 1987).

The other critique of the static comparative advantage approach from which the factor proportion theory draws is that it leaves factor prices as the only policy instrument, when in actual fact, a country can build an advantage by developing the technical and innovative know-how (see Amsden, 2001). When we introduce trade into the factor proportion theory, it is possible to conceptualise comparative advantage in dynamic and not static terms. The advantage of dynamic comparative approach is that it can change depending on what a country does: meaning that factor endowment is not a fixed term in a model (Krugman, 1981; Redding, 1999).

Seen from a dynamic perspective, comparative advantage does not only depend on factor endowment, but on other things such as the technology and accumulated skills over time. In other words, the differential cost margins on which the static view of comparative advantage is built can be altered as countries and firms acquire new skills, accumulate experience, acquire new production techniques and capabilities, even by changing the way production is organised and managed (see Kaldor, 1957). Young (1991) in his study of the effects of *learning by doing* finds significant dynamic aspects from the spill-over effects of trade and technical exchange which alters the comparative advantage of countries over time (see also Redding, 1999). In this sense, comparative advantage is not something fixed; countries can (and in fact do) change the texture of their comparative advantage by developing new abilities, acquiring new techniques and know-how, and by learning to build industrial capabilities. As the former Japanese Minister of International Trades and Industry explained, dynamic comparative advantage should be seen as something which a firm or country can create and not something that is permanently fixed by nature, geography, geology, history, culture or initial level of income.

In most of the discussions on the role of trade in promoting economic growth, comparative advantage is depicted in static and not dynamic terms.

Paul Krugman (1987) illustrates that competitive advantage is like a *moving band*, determined by what you do in the moment and guided by where you intend to be in the future. Using a simple model (which he calls unconventional) he demonstrates that defying comparative advantage through various means such as temporary protection of local industries, selective industrial strategies, etc., may actually *permanently* alter a country's comparative advantage, as a result of accumulated experience through learning by doing (Krugman, 1987). It is for this reason that the state becomes important in creating conditions where building of capacity by firms can be enhanced through strategic policy interventions.

In the African context, we now know for instance that although it was believed for a long time that because of low formal employment, labour costs in Africa would give African countries a comparative advantage in labour-intensive industrial activities such as textile, leather and agriculture processing, the evidence points in the opposite direction: African labour costs are not that different from industrialising countries in Asia (see Gelb et al, 2014). What this suggests is that factor cost alone cannot be relied on to build dynamic comparative advantage; the key lies in being able to create and upgrade capabilities and skills. It is in this sense that industrialisation in less industrialised countries can be promoted by defying current static comparative advantage to build dynamic comparative advantage through "learning by doing" (Arrow, 1962).

As we see later, while in theory it sounds good that each country specialises in what it has an endowment advantage, in reality, it matters what a country makes (Chang, 2016), and it matters hugely what a country exports (Hausmann et al, 2007). It is in this sense that defying current static comparative advantage can be in the interest of poor nations who want to industrialise.

Industrialisation as an Act of Defying Static Comparative Advantage

Because of poor industrial performance in Africa over the past decades, some countries have resigned themselves to gliding along the natural contours of their static comparative advantage. In other words, some countries have resigned themselves to the dictates of geography and history. Consequently, Africa's industrial presence (manufacturing particularly) on the global stage has remained quite insignificant, giving rise to the subtle pessimism which is sometimes framed in terms of the continent having no comparative advantage in manufacturing. And the question which this begs is, can the continent change the structure of its comparative advantage? The obvious answer is yes, as long as one conceptualises comparative advantage as something dynamic as opposed to something static. Indeed, the history of industrialisation attests to the dynamic nature of comparative advantage, with countries being able to reconfigure their comparative advantage in many things depending on what they did and wanted to achieve.

One of the weaknesses of the H-O-S theorem is that it provides a rigid framework that leaves little room for countries to change their fortune. In a sense, the concept of static comparative advantage from which the H-O-S theorem builds is a colonial tool that colonising countries used to discourage competition from the colonies and the developing world today. As Amsden (2001) has observed, the H-O-S model leaves limited policy options for uncompetitive countries (which often tend to be developing countries) and blocks the opportunity for these countries to develop their "know-how." Sticking to static notions of comparative advantage prevents countries from learning to go against the current, to restructure their initial comparative advantage.

For example, a conception of comparative advantage as a static condition would lead to the argument that it is futile for African countries to try and produce computers which other, better technologically-endowed, countries are already producing because the former have no comparative advantage in computers. But African countries will only create the capability to produce computers by learning to do so, even if in the initial stages these countries have no comparative advantage, what so ever. The Japanese deputy minister for the Ministry of International Trade and Industry (MITI) in the 1970s elaborates on this drawing from the Japanese experience:

> The MITI decided to establish in Japan industries which require intensive employment of capital and technology, industries that in consideration of comparative cost of production should be the most inappropriate for Japan, industries such as steel, oil-refining, industrial machinery of all sorts, and electronics. From a short-run, static viewpoint, encouragement of such industries would seem to conflict with economic rationalism. But, from a long-range viewpoint, these are precisely the industries where *income elasticity of demand is high, technological progress is rapid, and labour productivity rises fast*. It was clear that without these industries it would be difficult to employ a population of 100 million and raise their standard of living to that of Europe and America with light industries; whether right or wrong, Japan had to have these heavy and chemical industries (cited in Wade, 1990:25).

What the former MITI official is basically saying is that a country does not progress by sticking to its static structure of comparative advantage; a country progresses when it defies its static condition of comparative costs to establish conditions of new dynamic comparative advantage. Put in more simpler terms, comparative advantage should not be conceptualised as something cast in stones, as most economists trained in general equilibrium theory naturally do (see Krugman, 1981). If Japan had strictly followed its static structure of comparative costs at the time it was seeking to industrialise, it would have never established steel, automobile, industrial machinery factories it did during the 1920s and 1930s. Japan established these industries even if a static and short-run analysis indicated that it had no cost advantage in heavy duty machinery and electronics. It was a long-run analysis which provided the justification for Japan to establish these industries even if it did not have the comparative advantage in any of them at that time. In other words, the long term vision provided the rationale for the country to take deliberate decisions and actions to establish these industries as a way of changing its future course of development.

If we agree that the structure of a country's comparative advantage can be changed, then the important thing developing countries should be focusing on is how to re-configure their current structure of comparative advantage to create dynamic structures which serve their interest in the long run. Of course, creating dynamic comparative advantage takes time and commitment, but the good thing is that it can be done, and countries can do it by learning or beginning to do it. The process of industrialisation always involves going against one's existing cost disadvantage to create new cost advantages. There is no country that started with a superior comparative advantage in manufacturing of cars or electronics; all countries that enjoy this advantage today embarked on a journey to create and build the advantage they currently enjoy, and in most cases, this involved going against what, at some time, was recognised as the country's comparative advantage.

The Challenge of Industrialising Africa

Learning to defy static comparative advantage as noted earlier has been quite difficult for many countries on the African continent. This is primarily because African ideas and ways of doing things have always been subordinated to those from outside, such that new ideas, good practices, discoveries of unique ways of doing things and organising society and production have always come from outside Africa. In this configuration, anything African is not properly valued. Consequently, the continent is always a *follower* and *consumer* of ideas and techniques developed elsewhere; in a way, Africa is always playing *catch up*.

What this has entailed is that Africa always looks elsewhere for new inventions, for innovations, for inspiration, for techniques and for models of industrial development. Being a follower, it has always been impossible for Africans to lead the way. This is because by the time Africans learn to do what others are doing, the inventors or originators of the ideas or technology have mastered the inventions so much that it becomes difficult to compete with them. As long as Africa is following behind what others have discovered, it will be difficult to compete with them, difficult to create new ideas over which Africa will an advantage of reaping what Joseph Schumpeter calls the *entrepreneur's profit*. The only new discoveries one often hears of on the continent are resources; for example, oil and gas reserves in Ghana in 2009, oil and natural gas in Uganda 2011, Natural gas in Mozambique 2007 and the list can go on. While these are important, it is new ideas and techniques which count as the world moves to a digital economy where skills and knowledge define and shape the distribution of power and wealth (UNECA, 2016a).

In terms of new ideas and techniques, the story on Africa has been quite disappointing, and this is reflected in the low levels of industrialisation and high dependence on extractive sectors as noted above. Just to cite one example, in terms of patents and Research and Development (R&D), most African countries have negligible scores and occupy the bottom of the list (see Lall and Kraemer-Mbula, 2005:30–31; UNIDO, 2016b).

Industrialising Africa Is a Decolonial Project

But the fact that African countries today have comparative advantage in the export of commodities (natural resources) is by no means accidental, nor is it a reflection of an inherent inadequacy on the part of Africans; much of this has to do with the way Africa is inserted in the global economy. Today's structure of industrial production is based on the international division of labour (IDL) which is largely determined by what has been referred to in the development literature as *geography* and *geology*—in other words—nature (see Amirapu and Subramanian, 2015). But countries that have industrialised successfully have worked hard to overcome the constraints which geography and geology impose on them. However, the constraints (or opportunities) of *geography* and *geology* in Africa have always been interpreted as fate; little can be done to change them. Since this has been the dominant narrative, for sure, Africans have not faired well on the road to overcome the constraints of geography and geology.

Extroversion of Africa: A Sign of an Incomplete Decolonisation

Extroversion is partly a result of Africa being defined from outside, primarily through the colonial project, which not only defined what Africa should produce, but also where these products should go. In other words, the African world view is outwardly orientated, resulting in what Hountondji (1997) and Bayart (2000) have referred to as the *extroversion of Africa*. This outward orientation of African economies has serious consequences not only on the development of a vibrant industrial sector, but on many other sectors of African societies. To a large extent, the extroversion of Africa's production structures (for both knowledge and commodities) is an integral component of the colonial and imperialist project (Mamdani, 1996; Hountondji, 1997). The existing forms of extroversion are a clear sign that the project of decolonising the continent remains an incomplete one (see Chitonge, 2018). The fact that African economies continue to fulfil the colonial mandate of being suppliers of raw materials to the world is a sign of the failed attempt to disrupt the colonial economic logic and structures. In this sense, extroversion is manifested in the failed industrialisation in Africa—the failure to decolonise African economies so that they can be re-oriented to serve African interests.

In contemporary Africa, extroversion whether it relates to knowledge (modes of thought) or commodity production (extractive enclaves) constitutes a lingering sign of an incomplete decolonisation project, which if completed would have confronted and disrupted the colonial economic logic and structures which are still dominant. The imperial project thrived by affirming a single epistemology, a single mode of being and thinking, a single culture, a static structure of comparative costs etc., while at the same time devaluing and dismissing other epistemologies, other modes of being, knowing and doings, etc. Therefore, disrupting the colonial/imperial rationality, requires a radical project that uncovers the injustice and the internal contradiction of this project. Like industrialisation, disrupting the colonial rationality requires a project of defying the conventions which undermine the African modes of being, African system(s) of thought, African knowledge(s) and African rationality. Seen from this perspective, genuine industrialisation in Africa is likely to occur when the projects of defying the norms around comparative advantage couched in static terms are flouted.

Africa's Attempts at Defying the Colonial Economic Logic

However, there is a trade-off involved in deciding to promote activities in an area where an economy or firm does not have comparative advantage. In some cases, the opportunity cost of defying comparative advantage can be so prohibitive (high) that countries decide to glide along the static structure of comparative advantage. A good example of this is the current situation where most African countries have continued to rely solely on the export of primary commodities. If Africa is to upgrade and expand its industrial base, it has to learn to defy the current structure of its comparative advantage and be prepared to pay the hefty price this involves. As noted above, African countries will have to create viable industrial activities even in areas where they may seem to have no comparative advantage now. This will involve disrupting the colonial economic logic that allocate Africa the task of supply raw materials to the world.

While the opportunity cost of adopting a strategy of defying comparative advantage is undeniably high at the beginning, in the long term, the gains from building dynamic comparative advantage based on cumulative learning by doing outweigh the costs. Many industrialised nations adopted this approach as a way of increasing their share of global manufacturing. In such an approach, the dynamic gains and effects from the use of technology initiate industrialisation (see Krugman, 1981; Redding, 1999). Ha-Joon Chang makes a similar point in his debate with Justin Lin, pointing out that while comparative advantage is important to consider in any industrial policy setting, it serves a poor country well "to defy its comparative advantage in order to upgrade its industry" (Lin and Chang, 2009:489). The trade-off involved in adopting this strategy must be broadly understood, including the gains from upgrading and capacity building in an economy.

In Africa, the strategy of defying comparative advantage is not something new; the ISI strategy which was prevalent in most newly independent African countries during the 1960s and 1970s (see Tribe, 2000; UNECA, 2014; Matambalya and Cisse, 2015) operated under the idea of producing imported goods locally, including those in which many countries had no comparative advantage at all. For most countries at that time, this was done for various reasons including the imperatives of decolonising the economies to reduce dependence on the former colonial powers (on which they depended for manufactured goods) as a way to realise economic independence (Mendes et al, 2014; see Chapter 5 of this book). The economic reasons which underpinned ISI in Africa and elsewhere were elaborated by Raul Prebisch (1950) and Hans Singer (1950) and resonated with the ideological positions of most newly independent countries not just in Africa (see Chitonge, 2015).

With hindsight, it is clear that the ISI strategy narrowly focused on defying comparative advantage through the replacement of imported consumer goods by locally produced goods and ignored the export side of the equation. Defying comparative advantage, broadly conceptualised, implies that countries that export primary products should build capabilities to begin to export manufactured goods by supporting local firms to become competitive (see Amsden, 1989b). Examples from Cambodia, Vietnam, Taiwan, Indonesia and China clearly illustrate that this can be done when a country carefully selects strategic industries which have the potential to break into the competitive international markets (Lall, 2004; UNECA, 2015; Newman et al, 2016a).

As we shall see in Chapter 5, there is a much stronger consensus that if a country is to defy comparative advantage, it does not help to simply focus on replacing imported consumer goods with locally manufactured ones; it pays to promote sectors through which a country can build competitive capabilities, over time, to take a share of the global export markets for capital goods and other high-tech activities. Such a move would not only, with time, build productive capabilities in manufactured goods and services in which a country initially had no comparative advantage (Krugman, 1981). In countries where this strategy has been successful, it took regular assessment of the outcomes and repositioning of the selected interventions. Amsden (1989b) singles out the ability to assess the interventions aimed at defying current and creating future comparative advantage regularly as an important factor that explains the success of industrialisation among several late industrialisers.

The Regional Integration and Industrialisation

One of the factors that can contribute immensely to reversing Africa's position of disadvantage is that of regional cooperation between African countries. This is an idea that was strongly articulated by some African leaders during the 1960s, but got side-lined, especially during the 1980s when Africa lost its sovereignty over policy making. Although the idea of collective self-reliance was at the centre of the development strategy envisioned in the LPA, there has been little progress to overcome the colonial design of balkanising the continent, with fragmentation being more visible even today in the area of industrial development and trade. This is another manifestation of a strong grip of the colonial economic logic on the continent (see Olukoshi, 2012).

In recent years, the regional dimension to Africa's strategy for industrialisation has been emphasised, highlighting the importance of industrial strategy and policy at the regional economic community (REC) level. The UNECA has strongly argued for a regional approach to industrial development in Africa. In this regard, there have been growing calls for Africa to increase intra-Africa trade as a means to build the capability for countries on the continent to compete at the international level (UNCTAD, 2015). Three RECs in Africa now have industrial policy at the regional level. The *Economic Community of West African States* (ECOWAS) was the first region to launch a regional industrial policy in 2010. This was followed by the *East African Community's* (EAC) industrialisation policy launched in 2012 and the *Southern African Development Community* (SADC) in 2013.

Before these regional initiatives, there were several continent-wide moves (especially starting from the mid-1990s) aimed at re-igniting industrialisation at the continental level. The LPA, for instance, declared 1980 to 1990 as the *First Industrial Development Decade* for Africa (IDDA I), and called upon all member states to promote "intra-African industrial co-operation, in all its various forms, as an instrument for self-reliance and acceleration of industrial development…for Africa, taking into account…the discouraging attitude of developed countries" (*Lagos Plan of Action*, 1980:19). The first concrete step towards promoting industrial development at the continental level was the *Alliance for the Industrialisation of Africa* (AIA) launched in 1996, intended to boost the implementation of the *Second Industrial Development Decade for Africa* (IDDA II) which started in 1989.[5] The IDDA II was meant to provide a framework for African leaders to develop industrial strategies and mobilise support for the outlined plan of action.

More recently and perhaps the most ambitious industrialisation initiative at the continental level is the *Accelerated Industrial Development for Africa* (AIDA) which was launched in 2007, with elaborate implementation plans launched in 2009 and 2010 (see AU, 2007). The AIDA initiative developed seven key focus areas which include upgrading production and trade capacities; promoting infrastructure and energy for industrial development; developing industrial policy and institutional capacity; strengthening human resource development for industry; industrial innovation systems, and R&D and technology development; financing and resource mobilisation; and sustainable development initiatives (see AU, 2007).

In addition to AIDA, the AU in collaboration with Food and Agricultural Organization (FAO), International Fund for Agricultural Development (IFAD) and UNIDO developed another initiative called the African Agribusiness and Agro-processing Development Initiative (3ADI), which has been running parallel with AIDA since 2010 (see FAO/UNIDO, 2010). In all these initiatives, there is a belief that African industrialisation can be enhanced through cooperation at the regional and continental level. The recently launched Africa Continental Free Trade Area (ACFTA) is also premised on the idea that this will promote industrial growth as African countries trade among themselves, and in the process build the capacity to compete at the global level (UNECA, 2018). It remains to be seen if AIDA, 3ADI and ACFTA will deliver on industrial development. Little progress will come out of these initiatives if there is no attempt to understand and disrupt the colonial economic logic on the continent.

Technology Matters

Arguing that Africa should find its unique path to industrialisation sounds contrary to conventional mainstream economic wisdom which asserts that late industrialisers have an advantage because they do not have to break "new ground" as it were; they can literally pick technology from the shelves (the so called *off-the shelf* technology) to build their industrial capacity (see Grossman and Helpman, 1990; Lin and Chang, 2009; Felipe et al, 2017). Along the same lines, it has been argued that developing countries should actually "take advantage of their backwardness, by importing modern technology and institutions developed elsewhere" (Lin and Chang, 2009:484). According to this view, less industrialised countries like those in Africa must gravitate along their natural endowment gradient, imitating and adapting technologies developed in rich countries rather than being at the frontier of innovation because poor countries have no resources to finance high-tech innovation; they have no comparative advantage in the high-tech segments of global value chains.

But there is now empirical evidence suggesting that the issue of technology spill-over is not simply a matter of picking technology off the shelves; if diffusion of technology were that simple, then technology would play little role in accounting for the income and welfare differentials we are seeing between countries (Amsden, 1989a; Wade, 1990). We know that technology disparity accounts for the larger portion of productivity and income gap within and between countries (Gelb, et al, 2014).

Apart from technological lags between the poor and rich countries, use of technology in the latter is constrained by several factors including inadequate cumulative experience and the capacity to acquire and use even simple technology. Most importantly, the cost of importing such technology in countries where international investors only participate in the extractive sectors is prohibitive. This is one of the reasons why many low-income countries have relatively low levels of industrial capacity and capabilities, particularly in high value-added manufacturing activities. It is not accidental that African countries have so much natural resources but add little value to the resources by way of processing them, and as a result, get little out of them (UNIDO, 2016a). One way of breaking out of the vicious circle of low industrial capacity is to force oneself to learn to build capabilities, by going against the current script.

Africa in the International Division of Labour (IDL)

In trying to explain the weak industrial performance in Africa, political economy analysts move beyond the analysis of industrial capabilities in individual African countries and try to situate African economies in the global context (see Arrighi, 2002). One of the most commonly used theories in this regard is the theory of IDL, which seeks to explain the logic behind the way production is organised at the global level. The IDL approach focuses on understanding the reasons why poor countries tend to be mostly exporters of primary commodities while richer countries dominate the export of manufactured goods and high-value services (Singer, 1950, 1984). The explanations given for this vary, although the different views converge in two key related concepts of division of labour and comparative advantage.

The concept of division of labour was elaborated by Adam Smith (2005 [1776]) who linked it to the idea of specialisation in the process of production. Adam Smith saw specialisation as a positive development in society because, for him, when people specialise in doing the same tasks over time, the result is improved productivity and efficiency, and general welfare in society. For Adam Smith, the improvement in the process of production resulting from specialisation was the cause and source of the "wealth of nations." Taking the idea of specialisation and division of labour further, David Ricardo (2001 [1817]) applied the concept to the international arena, observing that nature endows nations differently. As such some nations, due to their natural endowment, are inclined to produce certain goods more efficaciously and economically, thereby creating comparative advantage in particular products (see discussion on comparative advantage earlier in this chapter). Effectively this situation gives rise to the IDL and international trade, where by countries tend to specialise in producing certain goods and services which they export to buy what they cannot produce. This idea that countries focus on producing goods in which they enjoy a relative cost advantage formed the basis of what is known as Classic International Division of Labour (CIDL) (see Jenkins, 1984; Starosta, 2016).

In a fundamental sense, classical political economists like Smith and Ricardo conceived IDL as a consequence of natural endowment, though it has later been argued that technology and human capital can significantly alter a country's endowment structure and therefore comparative advantage. Jenkins (1984) classifies the different versions of IDL into two broader categories which he refers to as *neo-Smithian* and *neo-Ricardian*, with the former stressing the importance of the connections in world markets, while the latter putting emphasis on the spatial variation in the rates of profits as the central feature which determines the morphology of IDL.

The CIDL has been debated over the years resulting in various strands of the theory, with some analysts arguing that the recent deepening of integration in the world economy requires that adjustments to CIDL be made to account for the new phenomenon observed (Mittelman, 1995). Several political economists have challenged the classic understanding of IDL and have framed the debates differently.

Industrialisation in the Core-Periphery Framework

Some of the major restructuring of CIDL theory occurred after World War II, when analysts framed the debates in terms of the division of the world into periphery and centres. Analysts who use this framework to analyse how global production is organised argue that the peripheral areas of the global economy have been allocated the task of producing raw materials while the centres have specialised in the production of manufactured goods and high value addition services. This version of IDL gained currency during the 1950s-1960s when structuralism and dependency theories became popular. One significant difference from the classic formulation of IDL is that the post-war formulation does not employ the concept of comparative advantage to explain the difference in the levels of industrialisation between countries. Instead, it deploys the *core–centre* and periphery–metropole framework (Wallerstein, 1974), or satellite and metropolitan countries (Frank, 1970) to explain the differences. Emmanuel Wallerstein (1974) who is one of the proponents of the core-periphery framework, draws from his *world system theory* to argue that the capitalist system from the beginning has always been a global system in which the world has been divided into *core*, semi-*periphery* and *periphery* areas, depending on the specific levels of specialisation in the production process that regions engage in. He argues, for instance, that North Western Europe, particularly England, emerged as a core of the modern world system by specialising first in agricultural production using higher skilled labour, while Eastern Europe emerged as the periphery specialising in the supply of raw materials such as raw cotton, gold, grain and sugar. Countries around the Mediterranean Sea constituted the semi-periphery region of the world economy of the 17th century, and they specialised in the production of relatively high-skill-oriented products such as silk and spices.

While it might seem here as if the division of labour between the regions is actually following the naturally occurring comparative advantage in line with the factor endowment in each region or country, the main determinant of this division of labour between regions and countries, according to this framework, is actually not factor endowment per se, but the strength of the nation-states that emerged in the 16th and 17th centuries:

> The key fact is that given slightly different starting-points, the interest of various local groups converged in northwest Europe, leading to the development of strong state mechanisms, and diverged sharply in the peripheral areas, leading to very weak ones[states]. Once we get a difference in the strength of the state machineries, we get the operation of "unequal exchange," which is enforced by strong states on weak ones, core states on peripheral areas (Wallerstein, 1974:401, emphasis in original).

In this framework, the differences in industrial capabilities and the way production tasks are distributed between nations are determined not purely by economic but by political factors.

It is interesting to note that in this framework, it is the nature of the state that is central to shaping the activities a country is assigned to undertake in the global economy; it is not a matter of how naturally endowed a country is. A similar approach is adopted here where it is argued that the state is crucial in reshaping industrial capabilities including dynamic comparative advantage. In the Wellersteinian framework it is argued that political factors play a major role in influencing economic outcomes at the global level, such that the strength of states is central to understanding the different development capabilities as well as the role that states play in the global system, and the position states take in the IDL.

States in the World Economy

If the strength of the state is so central, the key question is, how then do some states acquire their strength relative to others? As noted above, the strength of a state, according to this view, is correlated not with any cultural factors, but with its initial role in the world economy.

> One cannot reasonably explain the strength of various state-machineries at specific moments of the history of the modern world-system primarily in terms of a genetic-cultural line argumentation, but rather in terms of the structural role a country plays in the world-economy at that moment (ibid).

What initiates the growth in the strength of the state machinery is said to be a convergence of various political and social interests, but mainly those of the producers and the merchants who advocate for stronger state institutions to protect their interests. This is a similar view articulated by Polanyi (1944) in his explanation of the emergence of nation-states in Western Europe, where the lobbying of the merchant class for protection against foreign imports led to the creation of stable and strong political institutions (see also Mittelman, 1995). List (1909) also validates the view that stronger nations perpetuate their position in the global system through their economic power.

According to Wallerstein, the idea that the "strength of the state machinery in core states is a function of the weakness of other states' machinery" (ibid, 403) creates a structure in which the position a state occupies in the world system is determined not by its factor endowment, as neoclassical economic theory suggests, but by the relative strength of the state itself. In other words, stronger states in the world economy use their political strength to advance their economic power and interests. What this entails is that the specialisa-

tion that initiates the division of labour at the international level creates a momentum which re-enforces the same dynamism leading to stronger states becoming even stronger by means of accumulating the economic advantage acquired through political influence. This economic advantage gained from the political strength is used to further consolidate political influence, and the circle goes on until there is a disruption in the world system, giving rise to a new power configuration or world order (ibid).

In this framework, the weaker states, like colonies, can only have a chance to contest for a better or stronger position in the world economy when a disruption of the existing world order occurs. It is only then that poor or less industrialised nations can have a chance of moving up the ladder in the current world economy.

While it is clear that stronger states often use their political influence to accumulate economic power, what is not clear in this model is whether the weaker and poor (less industrialised) states can initiate the disruption of the current world order, so that they can contest for better or stronger positions in the system. In the case of defying the existing IDL, it would be in the interest of the weaker states to disrupt the existing order if they are to have any prospects of improving themselves. The agency of states in both defying comparative advantage and in taking up more advantageous position in the IDL is crucial. There is no doubt that given a positive prospect of re-arranging the current structure of comparative advantage and the accompanying division of labour, many African states would grab the moment with both hands. Indeed Africans initiated the liberation struggle to contest the configuration of global political and economic power. Our argument here is that though there was a partial victory where political freedom was secured in Africa, the struggle remains an incomplete one especially at the level of knowledge and economic structures.

On the contrary, states that are currently favoured by the existing structure of global comparative advantage and the division of labour would not be willing to relinquish or freely share their position of advantage and power; they would do anything possible to remain in the position of strength. Due to these differences of interest, tension can (and often) emerge between and among nations in the world economy, in their bid to keep the status quo. Poor or weaker states may also seek to disrupt the current IDL to move themselves up the ladder, and this has happened in several cases including the rise of the Asian tigers and now China.

The equilibrium in the world economy created by the *push* and *pull* forces lasts up to a point when the pull by poor nations and the corresponding push to keep things in balance. If left at the current equilibrium, poor (less industrialised) nations will remain in a position of weakness and poverty while rich nations will maintain their position of strength. Since both groups of nations are looking to protect and enhance their national interests, it is actually in the interest of the poor nations to pull harder to have a chance to reposition themselves in this harsh world economy environment.

The prospect of the weaker states disrupting the current equilibrium in this tug of war is slim if the weaker nations glide along the structures of current power and comparative advantage configuration. The chances of overturning the current configuration of power and privileges increase if poor countries confront the current power configuration together.

We see aspects of this in the African context where there is now strong emphasis on cooperation as a means to build capabilities for industrialisation in a world where breaking into the viable industrial global circuits is no mean achievement (LPA, 1980; UNECA, 2015). As noted earlier, the regional approach to industrialisation in this context offers higher prospects of successful industrial development in Africa when compared to individual country strategies. But coordinating industrial policy and strategy at the regional level is much more complicated, and from the experience of regionalism in Africa so far, this remains a major challenge which African regional economic blocks will have to learn to navigate more astutely to have a good chance of reversing their position of disadvantage.

Satellite-Metropole Framework

The idea behind the core-periphery framework is to emphasise the unevenness in the distribution of production tasks, economic power, industrial capabilities and the wealth of nations. Andre Gunder Frank (1970), who is one of the main proponents of dependence theory, argues that it is most fruitful to think of the global economic system as consisting of satellite and metropolitan economies. He uses this framework to emphasise the unevenness in the distribution of tasks between the different segments of the global system. Frank (1975), however, starts his analysis from a basic economic principle, arguing that we need to start with capital accumulation on a global scale and then trace how this unfolds and subsequently affects different regions of the world. He argues that this gives us a better chance to grasp the underlying dynamic and structure of unevenness in global production and development in general. Using the *satellite–metropole* framework, he argues that the configuration of countries into metropole and satellite ensures that the surplus is drawn from the latter into the former, mainly through trade, and sometimes open coercion. According to this view, as long as the satellite–metropole structure remains in place, the underdevelopment of poor countries (all of them former colonies) cannot be reversed (Frank, 1970). The stronger the interaction between satellite and metropole economies, the more deeply entrenched is underdevelopment in the former group of countries.

> ...contemporary underdevelopment is in large part the historical product of the past and continuing economic and other relations between the satellite underdeveloped and...metropolitan countries. Furthermore, these relations are an essential part of the structure and development of the capitalist system on a world scale as a whole (Frank, 1970:5).

In this framework, the uneven industrial development we see in the world economy today is a product of the satellite–metropole structures and relations, which perpetuate the condition of weak industrial development in satellite economies and stronger industrial power in the metropoles. Though this is not framed in terms of the unbalanced power relations as Wallerstein's World System theory does, there is an implicit imbalance of power between the satellite and the metropole, particularly in terms of economic capability, resulting from accumulation of economic surplus dynamics. Like Wallerstein's model, Frank's model also affirms the idea that comparative advantage is created not out of any configuration of factor endowment, but through the prolonged period of expatriation of surplus value from the weaker economies.

Writing specifically on the relationship between Africa and Europe, Samir Amin (1972) sees the same dynamic at work since the 17th century. He argues that in the relationship between,

> Europe and Africa since the mercantilist period (1600 AD), Africa has been cumulatively weakened to the point which makes economic growth and development impossible as long as the structures which perpetuates Africa's subordinate position in the relations continue (Amin, 1972:107).

Accordingly, Africa's weak industrial development performance can be attributed to the relationships in which Africa's position has, for a long time, remained the same, namely, the supply of raw materials to feed European (and now Chinese) industries, in such a way that the European nations (and now the Chinese) always capture the largest value in the engagement. In this way, it has been argued, Africa's prospect of industrialising has been constrained by this one-sided relationship.

From the beginning of this relationship, it has been argued that "Europe assumed the power to make decisions within the international trading system" (Rodney, 1972:77) and consigned Africans to the lowest segments of the global value chain. Walter Rodney, for instance, sees the imbalance of economic power between African countries and the European colonisers as pivotal in Africa's current role in the global economy:

> But with colonialism, the capitalist determined what types of labour the workers should carry on in the world at large. Africans were to dig minerals out of the subsoil, grow agricultural crops, collect natural products, and perform a number of other odds and ends such as bicycle repairing. Inside Europe, North America and Japan, workers would refine the minerals and the raw materials and make bicycles (Rodney, 1972:177).

The emphasis among political economists is on the point that the lack of industrial development in Africa is the result of a lopsided global economic structure which constrain the growth of industrial capabilities in weaker economies. According to this view, it is not because African countries have no comparative advantage in manufacturing that industrialisation has been elusive, it is primarily because the dominant international economic system dictates and shapes industrial dynamics in Africa.

Rodney, Amin, Frank and Wallerstein have emphasised the view that global structures which determine the division of labour between countries effectively dictate what countries can produce and export. The argument that most African countries have no comparative advantage in manufactured goods, except in the production of primary products using cheap labour-intensive technologies, is therefore seen as a ploy meant to subject African countries to the logic of uneven development—the colonial economic logic. The solution they offer is more radical than the strategy of defying comparative advantage. Amin (1990) for instance proposes a de-linking strategy as the most effective way of responding to underdevelopment and poverty, not only in Africa, but in other parts of the underdeveloped world.[6]

The New International Division of Labour (NIDL)

But some analysts have contested the idea that the world is divided into two groups of countries, resulting in some countries specialising in the supply of raw materials, while the other group of countries concentrate on supplying manufactured goods to the global economy. Scholars who contest this view of the world economy argue that this was the situation which prevailed prior to the 1970s; after the first oil crisis, the global economy today, so they argue, has undergone significant restructuring in the way production is organised such that the resulting configuration of the global economy cannot simply be accounted for in terms of the OIDL. Frobel et al (1980), for instance, argue that significant relocation of production tasks which used to be associated with Western Europe and North America has occurred to such an extent that the IDL, starting from the 1980s, looks very different today. They argue that analysis of

> ...contemporary world economy has already indicated that the old or classical international division of labour is now open for replacement. The decisive evidence for this hypothesis is the fact that developing countries have increasingly become sites for manufacturing—producing manufactured goods which are competitive on the world market (Frobel et al, 1980:12).

Drawing from their case studies on global manufacturing production in 103 countries from all parts of the globe, Frobel et al (1980) conclude that that manufacturing is no longer a preserve of industrial countries; manufacturing activities and capacity have relocated to countries which were formerly not involved in industrial production for export. They attribute this restructuring of global production to four major factors including the fragmentation of production, the presence of cheap labour in developing countries, the increase in technology which has enabled goods to flow relatively cheaper and faster, and finally the rationalisation of investment decisions by multinational corporations, seeking to maximise profits. A similar view is advanced by Mittelman (1995) who argues that the old version of IDL does not hold in the current global situation:

> The familiar imagery of a core, semi-periphery, and periphery no longer applies to a new structure that envelopes both vertically integrated regional divisions of labour based on the distinctive comparative advantages of different locations, and horizontally diversified networks which extend their activities into neighbouring countries as part of corporate strategies of diversification and globalisation. The old categories do not capture the intricacy of the integration of the world economy as well as the ways it constrains all regions and states to adjust to transnational capital. The global transformation now underway not only slices across former divisions of labour and geographically reorganises economic activities, but also limits state autonomy and infringes sovereignty (Mittelman, 1995:273).

Here Mittelman (1995) follows Frobel et al (1980) in suggesting that in this new restructuring of the global economy, the state's role is undermined by the presence of large transnational corporations. They attribute the shifts in the structure of global production configuration to the innovation of capital itself:

> This new international division of labour is an "institutional" innovation of capital itself, necessitated by changed conditions, and not the result of changed development strategy by individual countries or options freely decided upon by so-called multinational companies (Frobel et al, 1980:46).

With specific reference to industrialised countries, Frobel et al (1980) argue that the state in industrialised countries while it has tried to stop the flow of industrial activities into developing countries through various incentives such as "grants, loans and tax concessions" has "so far failed to yielded any noticeable success in making domestic industrial sites attractive again" (ibid, 4).

Although the evidence suggests that manufacturing activities have indeed shifted from industrialised countries, the flow has not gone to all developing countries, less still to Africa as we shall see in chapters 3 and 6 when we look at the status of the manufacturing sector in Africa. If we look at the global share of manufacturing value added today, although countries in East Asia have made significant inroads in what was dominated by a few Western countries, evidence today still shows that close to two-thirds of global manufacturing value added is in industrialised countries (see UNIDO, 2016). More importantly in terms of the unevenness which the division of labour theory emphasises, the flow of surplus value, skilled labour and wealth has continued to be overly concentrated in the early industrialisers such that little restructuring in the global wealth map has occurred outside of East Asia (Hutchinson, 2004).

As Starosta (2016) has observed, the NIDL while it brings out valuable insights in how the global economy has been reconfigured has overlooked the basic idea that despite the relocation of manufacturing capacity to some parts of the developing countries, particularly East Asia, the world is still polarised between countries with a massive concentration of capital and influence, and countries that still remain dependent on industrialised countries for capital, technology, highly specialised skills, manufactured goods and special services. In the case of Africa, the dominant economic activities have remained export of raw materials. In this sense, effects of the NIDL have not touched Africa yet.

Most importantly, Frobel et al's (1980) analysis seems to undermine the role of the state and industrial policy in the new global manufacturing order, when there is overwhelming evidence that countries that have made progress in developing manufacturing capabilities have done so through the state playing a central role not just in attracting foreign capital but also in creating conditions to ensure that manufacturing capabilities are developed and constantly upgraded (Johnson, 1982; Amsden, 1989a; Wade, 1990). In a recent analysis of why some countries succeed in implementing industrial policy and build industrial capacity while others fail, Whitfield and Buur (2014) emphasise the role of the state as central to explaining the difference in country performance. Thus, in as much as the relocation of manufacturing activities may seem to be beyond the control of states, there are certain decisions and actions by states which are critical in shaping the shift in the spatial global industrial configuration. Ultimately, states, through various instruments, have a critical role to play in ensuring a successful project of defying comparative advantage which lays the foundation for industrial growth.

ISI as a Tool for Defying the Current IDL

Prior to the 1980s, the idea of defying comparative advantage was attractive to many low-income countries including many African countries, such that many of them embarked on strategies which sort to reverse their positions of disadvantage. This involved going against the current to compulsorily break through the vicious circle generated by weak industrial growth and low investment. Using this strategy to industrialise has not been easy, but it offers a starting point for any country that is serious about upgrading its industrial capabilities and increasing income and welfare levels among its people. Such a strategy cannot, as illustrated later in this book, focus merely on replacing imported goods with locally made consumer goods. As the experience of ISI in Africa and other places has demonstrated, a strategy of defying comparative advantage can only be effective when it incorporates plans to build capabilities for learning to create new ideas, techniques and methods of producing and organising production. But to create such capabilities successfully, sustained effort and commitment from those in-charge of public policy is required. Since creating local enterprises with the capabilities to compete globally brings many benefits to the state (including the political dividend), it is in the state's interest in this is big, and this is why the state should not only support the initiatives aimed at building industrial capabilities but also initiate, promote and sustain them. The following chapters in this book illustrate the important role the state needs to play in a strategy of defying comparative advantage to disrupt the current IDL. There are various ways through which the state can accomplish this as chapters in this book illustrate.

Notes

1. The Fourth Industrial Revolution is characterised by the spread of what is often referred to as the *digital economy* underpinned by advances in technology such as computer-aided designs (CAD), additive manufacturing (3-D printing), robotics, artificial intelligence (AI), cloud computing, smart platforms, wireless communication, and the internet of things (IOT)etc. The earlier stages of industrial revolution include the first industrial revolution which was built on harnessing the steam engine, the second industrial revolution introduced the use of electricity in the manufacturing process, and the third industrial revolution was characterised by the advance of information and communication technology (ICT, see Banga and te Velde, 2018).
2. A commodity supper cycle (CSC) is simply a prolonged period of high prices for commodities (commodity boom) on the global market. This is different from the normal business cycle which tends to be shorter. The first CSC in the new millennium was reported to have started around 2002 when prices for commodities started to rise until the May/June 2015 when commodity prices generally began to taper off.
3. For instance, Ghana, Angola, Zambia, Mozambique, Nigeria, Liberia, Egypt by 2017 had initiated the process of accessing support from the IMF. Several other countries such as Kenya, Zimbabwe and Sudan have looked east (China) for assistance.
4. There are several factors proposed in the literature to explain the falling employment elasticity of manufacturing growth, including *technological dispersion*, which creates stiff competition for manufacturing employment across nations (Felipe et al, 2017), *rapid productivity growth* in the manufacturing sector compared to other sectors (Rodrik, 2015) and *changing consumer taste* (Dasgupta and Singh, 2006).
5. The *First Industrial Development Decade for Africa* covered the period from 1980 when it was launched as an outcome of the *Lagos Plan of Action*, but was side-tracked by the implementation of SAPs during the 1980s. Towards the end of the 1980s, after realising the weaknesses of SAP, the Organisation of African Unity decided to re-launch phase two of the *Industrial development decade for Africa* (IDDA II) in 1989.
6. De-linking is explained as a collective action that disrupts the logic of capitalism and establishes socialist relations of production and accumulation. Amin (1990) emphasises collective effort in the delinking strategy and argues that it is practically impossible for single countries to delink, but that acting together, the global South can create its own system of value creation and distribution, separate from the current global system.

References

African Centre for Economic Transformation (ACET, 2014). "Growth with Depth—African Transformation Report." Available at: www.acetforafrica.org.pdf? Accessed 18 November 2014.

African Development Bank/Organisation for Economic Cooperation and Development/United Nations Development Programme (AEO, 2017). *African Economic Outlook 2017: Entrepreneurship and Industrialisation*. Abidjan: AfDB/OECD/UNDP.

African Union (2007). "Action Plan for Accelerated Industrial Development of Africa." AU Conference of Ministers of Industry, 1st Extra-Ordinary Session, 24–27 September, Midrand, South Africa.

African Union and United Nations Economic commission for Africa (AU/UNECA, 2018). "African Continental Free Trade Area: Questions and Answers." Available at: https://www.google.com/search?q=African+Continental+Free+Trade+Area%3A+Questions+and+Answers&ie=utf-8&oe=utf-8&client=firefox-b-a. Accessed 14.05.2018.

Ake, C. (1981). *A Political Economy of Africa*. Lagos: Longman Nigeria.

Amin, S. (1972). "Underdevelopment and Dependence in Black Africa: Historical Origin." *Journal of Peace Research*, Vol. 9, No. 2. 105–120.

Amin, S. (1990). *Delinking: Towards a Polycentric World*. London: Zed Book.

Amirapu, A. and Subramanian, A. (2015). "Manufacturing or Services: An Indian Illustration of a Development Dilemma." Centre for Global Development (CGD) Working Paper No. 409. Washington, DC: CGD.

Amsden, A. H. (1989a). *Asia's Next Giant: South Korea and Late Industrialization*. New York: Oxford University Press.

Amsden, A. H. (1989b). "Diffusion of Development: The Late-Industrializing Model and Greater East Asia." *American Economic Review*, Vol. 18, No. 2. 281–286.

Amsden, A. H. (2001). *The Rise of 'The Rest': Challenges to the West from the Late-Industrialising Economies*. London/New York: Oxford University Press.

Arbache, S. J. and Page, J. (2009). "How Fragile is Africa's Recent Growth?" *Journal of African Economies*, Vol. 19, No. 1. 1–24.

Arrighi, G. (2002). "The African Crisis: World Systemic and Regional Aspects." *New Left Review*, Vol. 15 (May-June). 5–32.

Arrow, K. (1962). "The Economic Implications of Learning by Doing." *Review of Economic Studies*, Vol. 29, No. 3. 155–173.

Banga, K. and te Velde, D. W. (2018). "Digitisation and the Future of Manufacturing in Africa." Supporting Economic Transformation (SET) Working Paper. Available at: https://progs.odinet.org.uk/iedg/Economic%20Transformation/SharedDocuments/Future%20of%20manufacturing%20project/set.odi.org. Accessed 12.03.2018.

Basbay, M. (2018). "Is Manufacturing Dead?" TRT World Research Centre Discussion Paper. London: TRT World. Available at https://researchcentre.trtworld.com/images/files/discussion_papers/IsManufacturingDead.pdf. Accessed 12/02/2019

Bates, R. (1981). *Markets and States in Tropical Africa: The Political Basis of Agricultural Policies*. Berkeley: University of California Press.

Bayart, F. (2000). "Africa in the World: A History of Extroversion." *African Affairs*, Vol. 99. 217–267.

Bertil, O. (1933). *Interregional and International Trade*. Cambridge: Harvard University Press.

Chang, H. (2003). "Kicking away the Ladder: The 'Real' History of Free Trade." Foreign Policy in Focus (FPIF) Special Report. Available at: www.personal.ceu.hu/corliss/CDST_Course_Site/Readings_old_2012_files/Ha-Joon%20Chang%20-%20Kicking%20Away%20the%20Ladder-The%20"Real"%20History%20of%20Free%20Trade.pdf. Accessed 21. 03.2015

Chang, H. (2010). "How to 'do' a Developmental State: Political, Organisational and Human Resource Requirement for the Developmental State," in O. Edigheji (ed.), *Constructing a Developmental State in South Africa*. Cape Town: HSRC Press. 82–96.

Chang, H. (2016). "Making Things Matters: This is What Britain Forgot." *The Guardian*, 18 May 2016.

Chitonge, H. (2015). *Economic Growth and Development in Africa: Understanding Trends and Prospects*. London/New York: Routledge.

Chitonge, H. (2018). "Trails of Incomplete Decolonisation in Africa: The Land Question and Economic Structural Transformation." *African Studies Monograph*, Special Issue No. 57, 19–41.

Ciarli, T. and Di-Maio, M. (2015). "The Theoretical Arguments for Industrialisation-driven Economic Growth and Development," in F. Matambalya (ed.), *African Industrial Development and the European Union Co-operation: Prospects for a Re-engineered Partnership*. London/New York: Routledge. 30–68.

Collier, P. (2000). "Africa's Comparative Advantage," in H. Jalilian, M. Tribe and J. Weiss (eds.), *Industrial Development and Policy in Africa: Issues of De-Industrialisation and Development Strategy*. Cheltenham: Edward Elgar. 11–21.

Dasgupta, Sukti and Singh, Ajit(2006). "Manufacturing, Services and Premature Deindustrialisation in Developing Countries: A Kaldorian Analysis." United Nations University-World Institute for Development Economics Research (UNU-WIDER) Research Paper No. 2006/49. Helsinki: UNU-WIDER.

De Vries, G., Timmer, M. and de Vries, K. (2015). "Structural Transformation in Africa: Static Gains, Dynamic Losses." *Journal of Development Studies*, Vol. 56, No. 6. 674–688.

Department of Trade and Industry (DTI, 2016). *Industrial Policy Action Plan (IPAP) 2016/17–2018/19*. Pretoria: DTI.

Eli, H. (1919). "The Effects of Foreign Trade on Distribution of Income." *EKonomics Tidskrift*, Vol. XXI. 497–512.

Felipe, J., Mehta, A. and Rhee, C. (2017). "Manufacturing Matters…But It's the Jobs that Counts." Asian Development Bank Paper Series No. 420.

Food and Agricultural Organisation/United Nations Industrial Development Organisation (FAO/UNIDO, 2010). *African Agriculture and Agro-Industries Development Initiative(3A-DI): A Programme Framework*. Rome: FAO/UNIDO.

Frank, A. G. (1975). "Development and Underdevelopment in the New World: Smith and Marx versus the Weberians." *Theory and Society*, Vol. 2, No. 4. 431–466.
Frank, G. A. (1970). "The Development of Underdevelopment," in R.I. Rhodes (ed.), *Imperialism and Underdevelopment*. New York: Monthly Review Press. 4–17.
Frobel, F., Heinrichs, J. and Kreye, O. (1980). *The New International Division of Labour: Structural Unemployment in Industrialised Countries and Industrialisation in Developing Countries* (trans. Pete Burgess). Cambridge: Cambridge University Press.
Gelb, A., Meyer, C. and Ramachandran, V. (2014). "Development as Diffusion: Manufacturing Productivity and Sub-Saharan Africa's Missing Middle." Centre for Global Development (CGD) Working Paper No. 357, Washington, DC: CGD.
Grossman, G. and Helpman, E. (1990). "Comparative Advantage and Long-run Growth." *The American Economic Review*, Vol. 80, No. 4. 796–815.
Hausmann, R., Hwang, J. and Rodrik, D. (2007). "What You Export Matters." *Journal of Economic Growth*, Vol. 12, No. 1. 1–25
Hirschman, O. A. (1958). *The Strategy of Economic Development*. New Haven: Yale University Press.
Hountondji, P. (1997). "Introduction: Centering Africa," in P. Hountondji (ed.), *Endogenous Knowledge: Research Trails*. Dakar: CODESRIA. 1–42.
Hutchinson, F. (2004). "Globalisation and the Newer International Division of Labour." *Labour and Management in Development Journal*, Vol. 4, No. 6. 1–24.
International Labour Organisation (ILO, 2017). *World Employment Social Outlook: Trends 2017*. Geneva: ILO.
Jenkins, R. (1984). "Divisions over International Division of Labour." *Capital & Class*, Vol. 8, No. 1. 28–57.
Johnson, C. (1982). *MITI and the Japanese Miracle: The Growth of Industrial Policy*. Stanford: Stanford University Press.
Jones, R. W. (1957). "Factor Proportions and the Hecksher-Ohlin Theorem." *Review of Economic Studies*, Vol. 24, No. 1. 1–10.
Kaldor, N. (1957). "A Model of Economic Growth." *Economic Journal*, Vol. 67, No. 268. 591–624.
Krugman, P. (1981). "Trade, Accumulation and Uneven Development." *Journal of Economics*, Vol. 8. 149–161.
Krugman, P. (1987). "The Narrow Moving Band, the Dutch Disease, and the Competitive Consequences of Mrs. Thatcher." *Journal of Economics*, Vol. 27. 41–55.
Lagos Plan of Action (LPA, 1980). *The Lagos Plan of Action for the Economic Development of African: 1980–2000*. Addis Ababa: OAU.
Lall, S. (2004). "Selective Industrial and Trade Policies in Developing Countries: Theoretical and Empirical Issues," in C. Soludo, O. Ogbu and H. Chang (eds.), *The Politics of Trade and Industrial Policy in Africa*. Trenton/Asmara: Africa World Press Inc. 75–110.
Lall, S. and Kraemer-Mbula, E. (2005). "Is African Industry Competing?" Queen Elizabeth House (QEH) Working Paper No. 122. Oxford University, London.

Lin, J. and Chang, H. (2009). "Should Industrial Policy in Developing Countries Conform to Comparative Advantage or Defy it? A Debate Between Justin Lin and Ha-Joon Chang." *Development Policy Review*, Vol. 27, No. 5. 483–502.

List, F. (1909). *The National System of Political Economy* (trans. by Sampson S. Lloyd). London: Longmans, Green & Co.

Mamdani, M. (1996). *Citizen and Subject: Contemporary Africa and the Legacy of Late Colonialism*. Princeton: Princeton University Press.

Manyika, J., Sinclair, J., Dobbs, R., Kassey, L., Mischke, J., Roxburgh, C., George, K., O'Halloran, D. and Ramaswamy, S. (2012). *Manufacturing the Future: The Next Era of Global Growth and Innovation*. Washington, DC: McKinsey Global Institute.

Matambalya, F. and Cisse, M. (2015). "Leveraging African-European Union Co-operation for Africa's Industrialisation: An Introduction," in F. Matambalya (ed.), *African Industrial Development and the European Union Co-operation: Prospects for a Re-engineered Partnership*. London/New York: Routledge. 1–29

Matambalya, F. (2015). "The Urge to Industrialise African Countries: Which Lessons can be Learnt from the Empirics of the Process?" in F. Matambalya (ed.), *African Industrial Development and the European Union Co-operation: Prospects for a Re-engineered Partnership*. London/New York: Routledge. 69–86.

McMillan, M. and Rodrik, D. (2011). "Globalisation, Structural Change and Productivity Growth." National Bureau of Economic Research (NBER) Working Paper No. 17143.

Mendes, A. P., Beterlla, M. A. and Deixeira, R. F. A. (2014). "Industrialisation in Sub-Saharan Africa and Import Substitution Policy." *Brazilian Journal of Political Economy*, Vol. 34, No. 1. 120–138.

Mittelman, J. (1995). "Rethinking International Division of Labour in the Context of Globalisation." *Third World Quarterly*, Vol. 16, No. 2. 273–295.

Naude, W. (2010). "New Challenges for Industrial Policy." United Nations University (UNU)/World Institute for Development Economic Research (WIDER), Working Paper No. 2010/107.

Newman, C., Page, J., Rand, J., Shimeles, A., Soderbom, M. and Tarp, F. (2016a). *Made in Africa: Learning to Compete in Industry*. Washington, DC: Brooking Institute Press.

Newman, C., Page, J., Rand, J., Shimeles, A., Soderbom, M. and Tap, F. (2016b). "The Pursuit of Industry: Policies and Outcomes," in C. Newman, J. Page, J. Rand, A. Shimeles, M. Soderbom and F. Tap (eds.), *Manufacturing Transformation: Comparative Studies in Industrial Development in Africa and Emerging Asia*. London: Oxford University Press. 1–24.

Olukoshi, A. (2004). "Democratisation, Gloabalisation and Effective Policy Making in Africa," in C. Soludo, O. Ogbu and H. Chang (eds.), *The Politics of Trade and Industrial Policy in Africa*. Trenton/Asmara: Africa World Press Inc. 43–73.

Olukoshi, Adebayo (2012). "The African Union and African Integration: Retrospect and Prospect" in *Reflections on Africa's Development: Essays in Honour of Abdouile Janneh*. Addis Ababa: ECA. 35–56.

Oqubay, A. (2015). *Made in Africa: Industrial Policy in Ethiopia*. London: Oxford University Press.

Page, J. (2015). "Structural Change and Africa's Poverty Puzzle," in L. Chandy, H. Kato and H. Kharas (eds.), *The Last Mile in Ending Extreme Poverty*. New York: Brooklyn Institute Press. 219–248.

Polanyi, K. (1944). *The Great Transformation: The Political and Economic Origins of Our Times*. Boston: Beacon Press.

Prebisch, R. (1950). *The Economic Development of Latin America and Its Principle Problems*. New York: United Nations Economic Commission for Latin America and Caribbean.

Redding, S. (1999). "Dynamic Comparative Advantage and the Welfare Effects of Trade." *Oxford Economic Papers*, 51. 15–39.

Ricardo, D. (2001 [1817]). *On the Principles of Political Economy and Taxation*. Ontario: Batoche Books.

Rodney, W. (1972). *How Europe Underdeveloped Africa*. Washington, DC: Howard University Press.

Rodrik, D. (2013). "Unconditional Convergence in Manufacturing." *Quarterly Journal of Economics*, Vol. 128, No. 1. 165–204.

Rodrik, D. (2015). "Premature Deindustrialisation." National Bureau of Economic Research (NBER) Working Paper No. 20935. Available at: http://www.nber.org/papers/w20935. Accessed 16.09.2017.

Rowden, R. (2013). "The Myth of Africa Rise." Available at: http://www.twincities.com/ci_22327262/rick-rowden-myth-africas-rise

Samuelson, P. A. (1948). "International Trade and Equalisation of Factor-Price." *Economic Journal*, Vol. 58, 163–184.

Singer, W. H. (1950). "The Distribution of Gains Between Investing and Borrowing Countries." *American Economic Review*, Vol. 40, No. 2. 473–485.

Singer, W. H. (1984). "The Terms of Trade Controversy and the Evolution of Soft Financing: Early Years in the UN," in G. Meier (ed.), *Pioneers in Development*. New York: World Bank. 273–301.

Smith, A. (2005 [1776]). *An Inquiry into the Nature and Causes of the Wealth of Nations*. Pennsylvania: Pennsylvania State University Electronic Classics Series.

Soludo, C. and Ogbu, O. (2004). "A Synthesis of Major Themes in the Political Economy of Trade and Industrialisation in Africa," in C. Soludo, O. Ogbu and H. Chang (eds.), *The Politics of Trade and Industrial Policy in Africa*. Trenton/Asmara: Africa World Press Inc. 1–42.

Starosta, G. (2016). "Revisiting the New International Division of Labour Thesis," in G. Charnock and G. Starosta (eds.), *The New International Division of Labour: Global Transformation and Uneven Development*. London: Palgrave-Macmillan. 79–103.

The Economist Intelligent Unit (EIU, 2018). *Who is Ready for the Coming Wave of Automation? The Automation Readiness Index*. London: EIU.

Timmer, P., McMillan, M., Badiane, O., Rodrik, D., Binswanger-Mkhize, H. and Wouterse, F. (2012). "Patterns of Growth and Structural Transformation in Africa: Trends and Lessons for Future Development Strategies." International Food Policy Research Institute (IFPRI) Thematic Research Note 02. West Africa Office.

Tregenna, F. (2009). "Characterising De-industrialisation: An Analysis of Changes in Manufacturing Employment and Output Internationally." *Cambridge Journal of Economics*, Vol. 33, No.4. 433–466.

Tregenna, F. (2016). "Deindustrialisation: An Issue for Both Developed and Developing Countries" in J. Weiss and M. Tribe (eds.), *Routledge Handbook of Industrialisation and Development*. London/New York: Routledge. 97–115.

Tribe, M. (2000). "The Concept of 'Infant Industry' in a Sub-Saharan African Context," in H. Jalilian, M. Tribe and J. Weiss (eds.), *Industrial Development and Policy in Africa: Issues of De-Industrialisation and Development Strategy*. Cheltenham: Edward Elgar. 30–57.

United Nations Conference on Trade and Development (UNCTAD, 2015). "Promoting Entrepreneurship for Development." Note by UNCTAD Secretariat, Geneva, Switzerland.

United Nations Economic Commission for Africa (UNECA, 2011). *Report on Africa 2011: Governing Development in Africa—the Role of the State in Economic Transformation*. Addis Ababa: ECA.

United Nations Economic Commission for Africa (UNECA, 2012). *Economic Report on Africa 2012: Unleashing Africa's Potential as a Global Growth Pole*. Addis Ababa: UNECA.

United Nations Economic Commission for Africa (UNECA, 2014). *Report on Africa 2014: Dynamic Industrial Policy in Africa—Innovative Institutions, Effective Processes and Flexible Mechanisms*. Addis Ababa: UNECA.

United Nations Economic Commission for Africa (UNECA, 2015). *Report on Africa 2015: Industrialising Through Trade*. Addis Ababa: UNECA.

United Nations Economic Commission for Africa (UNECA, 2016a). Transformative Industrial Policy for Africa. Addis Ababa: Economic Commission for Africa.

United Nations Economic Commission for Africa (UNECA, 2016b). *Economic Report on Africa 2016: Greening Africa's Industrialisation*. Addis Ababa: UNECA.

United Nations Industrial Development Organisation (UNIDO, 2016a). *Industrialisation in Africa and Least Developed Countries: Booting Growth, Creating Jobs, Promoting Inclusiveness and Sustainability*. Vienna: UNIDO.

United Nations Industrial Development Organisation (UNIDO, 2016b). *Industrial Development Report 2016: The Role of Technology and Innovation in Inclusive and Sustainable Industrial Development*. Vienna: UNIDO

Wade, R. (1990). *Economic Theory and the Role of Government in East Asian Industrialisation*. Princeton: Princeton University Press.

Wallerstein, I. (1974). "The Rise and Future of the World Capitalist System: Concepts for Comparative Analysis." *Comparative in Society and History*, Vol. 16, No. 4. 387–415.

Weiss, J. (2000). "Introduction: Africa and Industrial Development," in H. Jalilian, M. Tribe and J. Weiss (eds.), *Industrial Development and Policy in Africa: Issues of De-Industrialisation and Development Strategy*. Cheltenham: Edward Elgar. 1–21.

Whitfield, L. and Lars, B. (2014). "The Politics of Industrial Policy: Ruling Elites and their Alliances." *Third World Quarterly*, Vol. 35. 126–144.

Wood, Adrian and Kerstie, B. (1997). "Exporting Manufactures: Human Resources, Natural Resources, and Trade Policy." *Journal of Development Studies*, Vol. 34, No. 1. 35–59.

World Bank (2015). *Africa's Pulse: Analysis of Issues Shaping Africa's Future*. Washington, DC: World Bank.

Young, A. (1991). "Learning by Doing and the Dynamic Effects of International Trade." National Bureau of Economic Research (NBER) Working Paper No. 3577.

Zamfir, L. (2016). *Africa's Economic Growth: Taking off or Slowing Down?* Brussels: European Parliament Research Services, PE573.891.

· 2 ·

INDUSTRIALISATION, ECONOMIC GROWTH AND THE TRANSFORMATION OF SOCIETY

Introduction: Industrialisation and Social Change

Industrialisation in economic literature has often been used synonymously with development. In development economics particularly, industrialisation has been granted an elevated podium, and this is reflected in the phrases such as the "engine of growth," the spark of "economic take-off," or a sector with the "power of dispersion." For many people, industrialisation is believed to be a sign that development is deepening in a society, a sign of a society transitioning from low- to middle income status (UNIDO, 1980; Chenery et al, 1986; Syrquin and Chenery, 1989; Wade, 1990); from agrarian to industrial society (Singer, 1950; Hirschman, 1958). Not only that, industrialisation is also widely associated with the rise of consumerism and one could call it the "middle-class bulge." Yet, the industrial sector, as explained later in this chapter, is only one of the many sections of the economy.

Even within the industrial sector, it is often the manufacturing sector which has traditionally been regarded as the engine of growth, with manufacturing-to-GDP ratio widely seen as a key indicator of a country's not only industrial development, but also economic standing and stature in the world. This view is articulated well in the *Transformative Industrial Policy for Africa*, which argues that,

> Throughout the history of capitalism, the manufacturing sector has been seen as the engine of economic development. Very few countries have developed their economies without developing a strong manufacturing base—so much so that the term 'industrialised country' and 'developed country' are often used interchangeably (UNECA, 2016b).

One of the major reasons why manufacturing is widely believed to be centrally important in a developing economy is that manufacturing growth exerts a pulling effect on other sectors (Hirschman, 1957; Kaldor, 1966; Tregenna, 2009). Part of this strong association of development with manufacturing comes from the relatively strong correlation between manufacturing value added (MVA) and other indicators of economic development such as GDP per capita, wage employment, levels of education, technological advancement and utilisation, savings, fixed capital and human capital formation (Tregenna, 2015). For instance, in their study of 108 countries, Syrquin and Chenery (1989) find a relatively strong correlation between MVA and the growth of savings and investments in general.

Similarly, Albert Hirschman (1958:108) in trying to describe the role of manufacturing in the transformation of the economy, cites a Danish economist who argued that the industrial sector is critical to the process of economic growth and development because it possesses "the power of dispersion," suggesting that the manufacturing sector, in particular, has the power to spread the positive momentum not just in the economic sector, but in all sectors of society, including the way people organise social and political life. The social side of the industrialisation story has often been overlooked in the literature especially in more recent years when the analysis has been solely directed at the economic dimensions, particularly MVA.

But in actual fact, industrialisation, where it takes root, induces societal-wide changes, including the way people relate to one another and organise themselves. Simon Kuznets (1966:6) highlighted this when he argued that economic growth does not only induce accumulation of capital and the refinement of the techniques needed to further improve production, it also leads to changes "in the system of views that dominate and govern the behaviour of men." Rodrik (2015) makes a similar point when he observes that industrialisation does not only lead to changes in the economic sphere; it brings about much deeper transformation of society including rapid urbanisation, creation of new social groups such as trade unions, professional bodies—all of which feed into the making of the political and social fabric of society.

A close look at the history of industrialisation reveals that there are many societal changes induced by the growth of industries, particularly manufacturing, leading to significant transformation of societies. The modern state itself is perceived to be a product of industrial capitalism (see Polanyi, 1944; Chitonge, 2015). Therefore, industrialisation is widely believed to play a central role in bringing about wider changes in society beyond the economic structural shifts and the accompanying institutional and technical adjustments. Hans Singer captures this more clearly:

> ...the most important contribution of an industry is not its immediate product (as is per force assumed by economists and statisticians) and not even it effects on other industries and immediate social benefit..., but perhaps even further its effects on the general level of education, skill, way of life, inventiveness, habit, store of technology, creation of demand etc. And this is perhaps precisely the reason why manufacturing industries are so universally desired by underdeveloped countries; namely, that they provide the growing points for increased technical knowledge, urban education, the dynamism and resilience that goes with urban civilisation, as well as the direct Marshallian external economies (Singer, 1950:476).

According to this view, industry (particularly manufacturing) is not just a driver or engine for economic growth, but a sector which initiates broader changes including the way people relate to the world around them. Most importantly, the point that Hans Singer is making is that industrialisation, where it occurs to a significant level, creates a virtuous circle with multiple benefits beyond the economic sphere. The broader social transformative power of the industrial sector is mediated through the cumulative acquisition of skills, technology, innovativeness and a positive mind-set that comes with the dynamics of industrial production. While there are many indirect contributions that industrialisation makes to society, this chapter focuses on the economic dynamic and its impact on the broader process of economic development.

Industrial Classification

As noted above, the strong emphasis put on manufacturing in economic development literature (especially in development economics, see Kaldor, 1957;1966; Kuznets, 1966; Chenery et al, 1986) may help explain the tendency to conflate industry with manufacturing. But the two terms do not mean the same thing, and it is important to distinguish them. Under the *International Standard Industrial Classification* (ISIC) of all economic activities, a four-digit system is used to classify various economic activities. The four-digit system used in ISIC correspond to the four levels of classification, ranging from the broadest category which is a *section* to the most refined classification which is a *class*. In between the section and class, economic activities are further classified into *divisions* and *groups*. In ISIC Rev 4, the different sections are identified by letters; for example, letter A represents activities under agriculture, forestry and fisheries, *B* represents mining and quarrying activities, C represents manufacturing, *D* covers electricity, gas, steam, and air conditioning supply, *E* covers water supply, sewerage etc., *F* represents construction. Letters G–*U* constitute what in the System of National Accounts (SNA) is broadly referred to as the tertiary sector or services (the service sector). *Sections* are further divided into *Divisions*; for instance, under Section A (which is agriculture, forestry and fisheries), there are three divisions: *division* 01 (crop and animal production), division 02(forestry logging) and division 03(fishing and aquaculture). These three divisions are further classified into *groups*: for instance, *group 011* is for all activities involving the growing of non-perennial crops, while *group 012* covers the growing of perennial crops. These groups are further divided into *classes*, which refer to more specific activities. For example, class *0112* is specifically for activities related to growing rice, while *class 0114* is for activities related to growing sugarcane only.

As for what in SNA is referred to as the industrial sector, ISIC Rev 4 divides this into four sections: i) Manufacturing: Section C, subdivided into *divisions 10–33*); ii) Electricity, Gas etc.: Section D, with only one *division 35*); iii) Water supply, sewerage etc.: Section E, subdivided into *divisions 36–39*); iv) and construction: Section F, subdivided into *divisions 41–43*). Section B (mining and quarrying, which under the SNA is sometimes classified as part of the industrial sector, is under the ISIC Rev 4 categorised as part of the primary (extractive) sector, together with Agriculture.[1]

Within the industrial sector, the manufacturing subsector is further divided into groups and classes, such as food and beverages, tobacco products, leather and leather products and footwear, chemical and chemical products, paper and paper products etc. Under ISIC Rev 4, the manufacturing sector has several (23) *divisions*, about 70 *groups* and over a hundred *classes*. For example, division 20 (Manufacturing of chemical and chemical products) is further divided into two groups (201: manufacture of basic chemicals including fertiliser etc., and 202: manufacture of other chemical products). Under the more refined classification, the group (manufacture of chemicals) is further divided into the manufacture of basic chemicals (class 2011), separated from the manufacture of fertiliser and nitrogen compounds (class 2012). The ISIC system is built on the principle of grouping together all economic activities that are produced from similar processes (see DESA, 2008).

Harmonising Different Classification Systems

It is important to note that this classification is intended to provide a framework for collecting and reporting statistical data, and for improving comparability between countries (see DESA, 2008). The ISIC system is largely drawn from the SNA framework which is used to estimate gross domestic product (GDP) and related output indices including the gross national product (GNP). Unlike the ISIC, SNA divides the economy into three broad categories or sectors: *Primary sector* (which consist of agriculture, forestry and fisheries, and sometimes, mining and quarrying, also known as the extractive sector), *Secondary sector* (which consists of manufacturing, construction, water, electricity and gas, and other industries in general, also known as the secondary or industrial sector) and the *Tertiary sector* (which comprises of all services provided in the economy from financial to personal services, communication and tourism). As the types of economic activities expand, the lines between sectors are in some instances becoming blurred such that it has been suggested that the division between manufacturing and services is no longer a useful distinction (see Manyika et al, 2012). However, it can be argued that such distinctions remain important in providing an indication of what activities are taking place in specific areas of the economy, for purpose of assessing changes in the structure of the economy over time.

Although the SNA has been standardised to ensure comparability, there are differences between countries in the classification of economic activities (see de Vries et al, 2015). For example, some countries include mining under the secondary (industrial) sector, while others include it under the primary (extractive) sector. Which sector the mining activities are classified under can lead to different sectoral composition figures in an economy, which in turn may give different impressions about the structural changes taking place in the economy over time.[2] When mining and quarrying are reported under the primary sector, this often tends to exaggerate the composition of the primary sector in the economy, giving a different picture of what is actually is happening to the economy as a whole.

While the purpose of the ISIC is to help maintain continuity of how economic activities are classified over time and comparability between countries, the harmonisation process has mainly focused on matching the different classification systems from the developed regions of the world. For example, ISIC Rev 4 focused on harmonising the three classification systems from Europe (NACE), North America (NAICS) and Australia and New Zealand (ANZSIC), and it is not clear if the developing countries in Asia, Latin America and Africa have their own systems of classification. What is noted in ISIC Rev 4 is that member countries in the ASEAN and Africa (AFRISTAT) regions were consulted in the process of compiling ISIC Rev 4 (see DESA, 2008). It seems that there is a preference to use the economic structure and models of the developed countries when classifying and estimating economic activities everywhere, assuming that the economies of less industrialised countries would have the same structure and engage in similar economic activities. But such an assumption is rather shaky and it needs to be interrogated more given that developing countries are exhibiting different economic structural composition and activities.

ISIC Revision 4

The United Nations Department for Economic and Social Affairs (DESA) has been responsible for putting together an international system that promotes the standardisation of statistical information to enhance the comparability of data between different countries. ISIC I, which was launched in 1948, has been revised several times (in 1956, 1965, 1979 and 2008) to ensure that the framework captures the changing economic activities and structure (ibid). So far, four revisions have been carried out, with the current (ISIC Rev 4) being the fourth. The revision of the classification system has been necessitated by the emergence of new activities as economies expand and become more sophisticated. For example, ISIC Rev 4 has provided space for capturing the fast-growing information and communication activities which in some economies constitute quite a significant share of the economy. The growth of this sector has expanded in such a way that some of the activities fall under industrial sector "proper" while others fall under the traditional service sector (see ibid).

The other revision incorporated in ISIC Rev 4 includes the reporting of informal economic activities as well as the productive activities of Non-Governmental Organisations (NGOs) which were excluded in earlier ISIC versions. The inclusion of informal economy activities can have a large bearing on African and other developing regions' economies, which tend to have larger informal activities even within the broader industrial sector (Elkan, 2000). For example, education in ISIC Rev4 stands as an independent section, just like real estate services, information and communication, as well as professional and scientific services which were all grouped together in ISIC Rev 3.1 (see DESA, 2008). As noted above, the expansion of the classification system has been necessitated by the emergence of new economic activities which require to be classified separately to reflect the changing structure of the global economy. However, although ISIC Rev 4 was approved in 2008, many countries are still operating under the ISIC Rev 3.1 classification and most of the analysis in this book will use ISIC Rev 3.1.

What is important to note is that ISIC does not report the value of goods produced in an economy; it provides a framework for capturing data on economic activities; it is a classification system and not a database (ibid). The United Nations Industrial Development Organisation (UNIDO) provides statistics on industrial activities based on ISIC's four-digit classification system.

In this book, manufacturing will not be used synonymously with industry; the manufacturing sector will be used to refer to activities which fall under section C, divisions 10–33 in ISIC Rev 4. The term "industrial sector" will be used to refer to the broader sector which includes *Sections* C, *D*, *E* and *F* in ISIC Rev 4.

Industrial Strategy: The "Old Consensus" and the Mainstream View

As noted earlier, pioneers of development economics strongly believed in industrial growth as the source for economic growth momentum and development. This belief galvanised into what has been referred to as the "old consensus" (see Killich, 1980). Over the years, this strong belief in the manufacturing sector seems to have been lost as the "old consensus" of the 1950s and 1960s was gradually abandoned, during the 1970s. The weakening of the old consensus and the strong belief in guided industrial development has been attributed to the resurgence of orthodoxy policy prescriptions, which in the words of Albert Hirschman (1984:89) have been "politically naïve, socially explosive and economically counterproductive from any longer-run point of view." In Africa, the resurgence of neo-liberal ideology sponsored by international donors and financial institutions resulted not only in the loss of policy autonomy on the part of African governments, but the ascendency of the view that industrial policy and strategy are redundant (Soludo and Ogbu, 2004).

Mainstream neoclassical economic view on industrialisation has consistently argued that there is no need for industrial policy or guided industrial strategy since markets can perform the task of guiding investments and allocating resources to viable industries. This view, which became mainstream at the beginning of the 1980s, argued for measures to make markets more efficient at allocating resources by allowing competitive markets and the supporting institutions to develop instead of developing industrial policy which brings in state intervention (see Wade, 1990; UNECA, 2016a).

The Counter-Argument

But this view has been contested by analysts who argue that industrial development in low-income countries (LICs) would be hampered without deliberate and strategic policies. This view was strongly supported by the pioneers of development economics who argued that left to the markets, industrialisation in LICs would not only be too slow, but can lead to perverse patterns of industrial growth (see Rosenstein-Rodan, 1943; Scitovsky, 1954). Analysts who support "guided industrial development" (the old consensus) argue that upgrading of industrial capabilities in LICs would have limited success without intervention from the state to promote the technology transfer needed to become competitive (see Lall, 2004). Those who see the central role of industrial policy have argued that leaving industrial development to markets alone would result in suboptimal investment patterns due to the divergence between *social* and *private* returns on investment (Scitovsky, 1954; Rosenstein-Rodan, 1957). A 1980 UNIDO report provides three reasons to justify the role of the state, especially in the case of industrial development:

> In general, the prerequisites for making public industrial sector an effective instrument of economic development in developing countries are (a) the formulation of long-term strategies and the establishment of machinery to co-ordinate the activities of the sector, (b) introduction of multidimensional system of performance measurement..., (c) the recruitment and training of the best qualified staff for the sector (UNIDO, 1980:14).

One of the main contentions about industrial policy has been that the private sector cannot generate sufficient investments needed in LICs where market failures are rampant (Wade, 1990). Because of these and other shortcomings associated with an unguided industrial strategy, there is now an emerging view that a strong case can be made for a selective industrial policy (Lall, 2004). Accordingly, there is a growing consensus that whenever a country is formulating industrial policy, it is important to have clear goals that policy is intended to achieve. Admittedly, clearly outlined industrial objectives should be used as goalposts to guide the actions of all key stakeholders, and this is where the importance of an industrial policy lies. Analysts who support this view recognise the important role the state must play not only in formulating industrial policy and strategy, but also in ensuring that the different actors in the all sectors understand and embrace the identified objectives.

Those who argue for an unguided industrial approach emphasise the importance of following a country's comparative advantage manifested in competitive markets. As alluded to in Chapter 1, apart from being contested, the strategy of strictly abiding to a country's comparative advantage has proved to be quite disabling for many less industrialised countries. It is actually countries that have gone against their existing comparative advantage which have managed to muster significant industrial skill, capability and share of the global markets (see Krugman, 1987; Amsden, 1989; Redding, 1999; Lin and Chang, 2009).[3] It is in this sense that Arkebe Oqubay's (2015) view that strong state action in terms of guiding industrial activities and providing incentives to all actors including private sector becomes crucial to any strategy of industrial development, not just in Ethiopia. Therefore, in order for African countries to achieve meaningful levels of industrialisation, it is imperative that they actively develop and implement targeted industrial policies and strategies, tailored towards defying the current comparative advantage which is underpinned by the colonial economic logic.

In a critique of the strategy of strictly adhering to comparative advantage, Chang (2003) has observed that the now industrialised countries are being disingenuous by giving the impression that they actually developed their industrial capabilities by remaining faithful to their static comparative advantage. Chang (2003) argues that the actions of the now industrialised economies are akin to "kicking away the ladder" which they used to get to where they are today. The key message in this debate is that the critical component that assists a country to muster some comparative advantage in high-value-added activities, such as skills, innovation and technical competence, can only be acquired by deliberately carrying out activities in specific nodes where these capabilities can be generated, and the action of the state is indispensable in this regard. There is no other way to do this apart from getting one's hands dirty, and of course one must choose carefully where to start from. The debate on the role of the state in industrial development is discussed in more detail in Chapter 7.

Balanced Growth (General) vs. Unbalanced (Selective) Industrial Policy Strategy

The other strand of the debates around the question of industrialise policy is between those who advocate for a *balanced growth* strategy that paid equal attention to all segments of the economy (see Rosenstein-Rodan, 1943, 1957; Nurkse, 1953; Scitovsky, 1954), and those who argue that industrialisation does not have to follow a balanced growth; that the industrial strategy should be selective, targeting those sectors and subsectors with the highest potential to upgrade and expand industrial capabilities at a given time (see Hirschman, 1958; Krishna and Perez, 2005). This debate though in recent years has not been formulated in terms of balanced or unbalanced growth, surfaces in policy strategies which emphasise the need to be selective in the process of identifying and supporting sectors with strong potential to generate linkages to other sectors as drivers of industrialisation and economic growth (see Lall, 2004).

Why Is Industrialisation Important to Africa?

In the African context, the importance of industrialisation has been highlighted by UNECA, which has consistently argued that the continent's lack of industrialisation is the main reason why economic development and the necessary structural transformation have not occurred in most African economies. In one of its annual economic reports on Africa, UNECA (2014:55) argues that there is now "a strong consensus that an expanding prosperous industrial sector is crucial to the structural transformation of African economies." The importance of industrial development was broadly stated in an earlier UNECA publication, which observes that,

> Industrial production creates job opportunities at high skill levels, and facilitates dense linkages among service and agricultural sectors, rural and urban economies, and consumer, intermediate and capital-goods industries. In addition, the prices of manufactured exports are less volatile and less susceptible to long-term deterioration than those of primary goods, making industrialisation particularly strategic

> in highly commodity-dependent developing countries. The move to industries is a critical tool in creating jobs, reducing poverty and developing outlaying regions. Finally, it [industrialisation] can spur technological advances and innovation as well as productivity gains. In short, it can play the leading development role more suitably than any other sector (UNECA, 2012:109).

This emphatic endorsement of the role industrialisation plays in the development process of an economy is supported by the view that the less industrialised countries can transition from being dependent on export of primary commodities to a diversified export base by promoting industrial growth. This view is reiterated in a recent policy document which gives several reasons why industrialisation is important to Africa including that "the manufacturing sector has faster productivity growth than agriculture and services" and "the manufacturing sector acts as the 'learning centre' of the economy in the sense that it plays the leading role in diffusing technological progress" (UNECA, 2016a:31). Other analysts have also come to similar conclusions arguing that "industrialisation remains the main avenue for sustained development in Africa" (Lall and Kraemer-Mbula, 2005). Page (2015) makes a similar observation, noting that promoting industrial growth can stimulate productivity growth in agriculture, which will be central to solving what he calls "Africa's poverty puzzle."

The Role of Industrialisation in Economic Development

The early development economists started by illustrating that industrialisation was crucial to the development process in any developing country. Several thinkers in the post-World War II era, coming from different ideological dispositions and schools of thought, agreed that industrialisation is essential for improving living standards and the welfare of people in LICs. Whether these thinkers are classified as neoclassical, Keynesians, structuralists, Marxist or neo-Marxist, institutionalists using heterodox theories, they seem to have converged on the point that industrialisation is an essential ingredient in the development strategies of LICs. What has been hotly debated is how LICs should industrialise, including the choice and sequencing of policies. While there are several views on the question of how to industrialise, the sections below expand on some of the key reasons advance by scholars to support the view that industrialisation is essential for development, especially in LICs.

Productivity and Growth

One of the popular views often cited to illustrate the dynamic role of industrialisation in economic growth is productivity. Simply put, productivity is the rate at which a firm produces goods and services per unit of input or variable factor (labour and capital). A firm that is producing more output per unit of variable factor than other firms can be said to enjoy higher productivity, if it uses comparatively smaller amounts of variable factor to produce the same output. In other words, productivity is the measure of how efficient a firm or sector uses its available resources in the process of producing goods and services. There are several factors which affect the productivity of a particular firm including skill levels, type of technology, accumulated experience, morale of workers, demand conditions, structure of the product market, the state of infrastructure, firm size and availability of capital. In short, factors which influence productivity can be internal to a firm (e.g., morale of workers) or external (e.g., state of infrastructure and macroeconomic conditions). Productivity usually varies between sectors in the same economy, as is the case with agriculture and manufacturing or services. In the industrialisation literature, large productivity differentials between sectors is widely taken as a sign of inefficiency in the allocation of resources in the economy, and this condition often reflects the level of development in an economy (see McMillan and Rodrik, 2011).

In a standard production function, productivity is accounted for by three parts: physical capital, human capital and a residue which is a product of how human and physical capital are combined in the production process—this is widely referred to as technology. While the residue in a standard production function is commonly attributed to technology effects, it can include other things, such as the way production is organised, which is broader than just technological sophistication. For example, the way a particular plant is laid out can affect productivity in many ways. It is important here to note that the 'unmeasured' productivity residue accounts for the larger productivity differential between sectors, firms and economies (see Gelb et al, 2014).

Cross-country empirical evidence shows that industrial activities enjoy higher productivity than other sectors (primary and tertiary). Available evidence suggest that the average productivity for African economies is the lowest in the world, being only a third of the global productivity per worker (Table 2.1).

Table 2.1: Labour Productivity per Worker (in 2011 USD) by World Regions, 2000–2018.

	2000	2005	2010	2015	2016	2017	2018
Africa	10,229	11,391	12,759	13,006	12,976	12,883	12,966
Asia and the Pacific	11,923	14,454	19,166	23,952	25,022	25,683	26,890
East Asia	13,096	16,642	22,984	30,070	31,614	32,625	34,362
Europe and Central Asia	53,066	58,773	61,882	65,178	65,627	65,743	67,005
Latin America	29,654	28,970	31,426	32,094	31,841	31,363	31,623
North America	90,599	99,631	104,731	108,552	108,660	108,139	110,068
South East Asia	15,334	17,795	20,390	23,917	24,578	25,064	25,901
World	**24,242**	**26,760**	**30,306**	**33,758**	**34,418**	**34,550**	**35,477**
Ratio of Africa's Productivity per Worker to Other Regions (%)							
Asia and the Pacific	85.8	78.8	66.6	54.3	51.9	50.2	48.2
East Asia	78.1	68.4	55.5	43.3	41.0	39.5	37.7
Europe and Central Asia	19.3	19.4	20.6	20.0	19.8	19.6	19.4
Latin America	34.5	39.3	40.6	40.5	40.8	41.1	41.0
North America	11.3	11.4	12.2	12.0	11.9	11.9	11.8
South East Asia	66.7	64.0	62.6	54.4	52.8	51.4	50.1
World	**42.2**	**42.6**	**42.1**	**38.5**	**37.7**	**37.3**	**36.5**

Source: Author. Based on data from the International Labour Organisation (ILO, 2018).[4]

It is also apparent from Table 2.1 that the average productivity per work in Africa has been falling since 2000, relative to other regions and the global average. Data presented in Chapter 6 also show that productivity in the industrial sector is the highest, higher than that of the services and agricultural sectors. It is this feature of the industrial sector, particularly the manufacturing sector, which makes analysts believe that the industrial sector is the engine of growth.

The aggregate labour productivity figures presented in Table 2.1 mask the disparities between countries in Africa. If we disaggregate the labour productivity of African countries by income levels measured in per capita terms, it is evident that low and lower middle income countries have very low labour productivity, while the middle and higher income countries have labour productivity rates close to the global average (Table 2.2).

Table 2.2: Labour Productivity in Africa by Income Category (in 2010 USD), 2000–2017.

	2000	2010	2015	2017	Change (%), 2000–2017	Annual Growth (%)
Africa Average	10,229	12,759	13,006	12,883	25.2	1.5
Low Income Countries	1,073	1,283	1,417	1,429	33.2	2.0
Lower Middle Income Countries	4,866	6,918	7,476	7,347	51.0	3.0
Upper Middle Income Countries	21,035	23,294	22,296	22,852	8.6	0.5
World	**24,242**	**30,306**	**33,758**	**34,550**	**27.0**	**1.6**

Source: Author. Based on data from the International Labour Organisation (ILO, 2018).

For LICs (which constitute about half of the countries) the productivity of labour was less than 20 percent of the labour productivity rates in middle-income countries. This is an indication that the larger section of the labour force is engaged in low-productivity activities, mainly subsistence agriculture and informal urban activities (see Fox and Thomas, 2016). Given this level of productivity, the challenge for Africa is immense. What is worrying is that, while productivity per worker grew between 2000 and 2005, there is a reversal in the later period from 2005 to 2015 (Table 2.3).

Table 2.3: Labour Productivity Growth (%) by World Regions, 2000–2018.

	2000–2005	2005–2010	2010–2015	2015–2018
Africa	11.4	12.0	1.9	-0.3
Asia and the Pacific	21.2	32.6	24.9	12.3
East Asia	27.1	38.1	30.8	14.3
Europe and Central Asia	10.8	5.3	5.3	0.7
Latin America	-2.3	8.5	2.1	-1.5
North America	9.7	5.1	3.6	1.4
South East Asia	16.1	14.6	17.3	8.3
World	**10.4**	**13.2**	**11.4**	**1.9**

Source: Author. Based on data from the International Labour Organisation (ILO, 2018).

When compared to labour productivity trends in other regions, Africa's productivity growth rates have been the lowest since 2010. This may be a reflection of low levels of industrial development, particularly manufacturing, employing only a tiny section of the labour force (see Chapter 3).

In the early stages of economic development, it is the manufacturing sector that exhibits high efficiency in the allocation and use of resources (Chenery et al, 1986). But as economies grow, the productivity gaps between sectors are expected to shrink, eventually converging within narrow margins as a result of pressure induced by the most efficient sectors. The narrowing of productivity occurs as different sectors compete for scarce resources in the economy—for example, labour. Productivity growth in an economy is seen as crucial to the process of sustained economic growth. The importance of the industrial sector in this regard is that it can induce the growth of productivity in the agriculture and services sectors through backward and forward linkages (Hirschman, 1958). In other words, a highly productive industrial sector can induce efficiency in other sectors as it interacts with them through procuring of inputs and supply of manufactured products.

In African countries, available evidence suggests that average productivity in the industrial sector has consistently been the highest, with productivity per worker in agriculture in 2010 being only 5 percent that of industry, and productivity in service slightly better at more than half (58 percent) of industry (see Timmer et al, 2012; de Vries et al, 2015). Such huge productivity differentials between sectors, as noted above, are taken as an indication of underdevelopment, reflected through pronounced dualism in the economy (McMillan and Rodrik, 2011).

Evidence from other developing regions such as Latin America, South Asia and Eastern Europe show similar patterns but relatively smaller productivity gaps between sectors (Timmer et al, 2012). One of the reasons why industrialisation is seen as critical to sustained economic growth, especially at the early stages of economic development, is that the industrial sector has the potential to induce productivity growth in other sectors, especially the productivity of labour. In most developing countries, it is labour which is often inefficiently allocated and used in the economy, thereby affecting total factor productivity.

Why Is Productivity Higher in the Industrial Sector?

There are several factors which explain why productivity in the industry sector as a whole is higher than in the primary and tertiary sectors. One explanation which is commonly advanced is that, to a large extent, productivity is determined by the level or intensity of capital employed in a particular sector (see Nurkse, 1953; Lewis, 1954; Kaldor, 1957). The capital–labour ratio in industries tends to be consistently high, such that the industrial sector is characterised by the "deepening of capital structure" (Kaldor, 1957:592; Wade, 1990). Productivity in the Kaldorian model is attributed largely to capital intensity, such that "technical innovations which are capable of raising the productivity of labour require the use of more capital per man—more elaborate equipment and/or more mechanical power" (Kaldor, 1957:595).

Here the key issue is to explain why there is high capital intensity in the industrial sector compared to the service and the agricultural sectors. One of the explanations is that industrial production requires large capital overheads in terms of physical equipment relative to the other sectors. Kaldor (1957) gives an example of road construction where in one case bulldozers are used, while in another case the road is constructed using shovels and picks. A firm that is constructing roads using caterpillars and bulldozers has high capital intensity compared to a firm using wheelbarrows and shovels to construct roads. Ragnar Nurkse (1953) uses a similar example of shovels to illustrate the point that capital, converted into equipment, increases the efficiency of labour when it accumulates in the right proportions.

Thus, the more capital applied in production, the more labour-saving improvements can be achieved (deepening of capital), effectively substituting labour for capital in cases where labour is a scarce factor. In situations where capital is a scarce factor, the more labour applied to the limited capital (widening of capital) leads to a situation where the effects of diminishing returns set in, with the marginal productivity of labour declining as more labour is added. Thus, the labour-intensive strategy often recommended for LICs has its limit; a certain proportion of capital needs to be available to make use of the abundant labour more efficiently. Little capital thinly spread over copious labour leads to inefficiency in the use of variable factors and this in turn, impacts on total factor productivity. Although labour can also be a substitute for capital, it is often a poor substitute, such that low levels of capital negatively impact on total factor productivity (Kaldor, 1957).

But in the case of countries at the early stages of development, where capital is often a scarce factor and labour is in abundant supply, capital accumulation induces rapid growth in factor productivity especially in the modern sector (see Lewis, 1954). It is capital that enables a firm to acquire production equipment, which contributes to productivity growth. A road constructing company using bulldozers will achieve higher productivity in the sense that it can finish the same work in a shorter period of time, and perhaps cheaper, using less labour than a firm using shovels. Of course, the implication is that bulldozers cost more than shovels; that the capital intensity is higher when one uses bulldozers compared to shovels.

The other way of expressing the same point is that in industry, because of high capital intensity, factors (both labour and capital) tend to be more efficient in the production process, especially in the initial development phases when the features of dualism are strong in the economy. But in underdeveloped economies, wage differentials and large productivity gaps between sectors persist, pulling down the economy-wide productivity rate (see McMillan and Rodrik, 2011). While productivity differentials exist between sectors and firms in developed countries, they are more prevalent and wider in underdeveloped economies. For example, in an economy where more than half of the labour force is engaged in subsistence agriculture, using rudimentary tools such as hoes to cultivate, the productivity of labour would be relatively lower than in an economy where there is more use of machines, such as tractors and harvesters.

One of the reasons that explains why productivity in the agricultural sector in Africa remains the lowest is because labour, due to lack of improved equipment, operates way below its optimum capacity, often under-utilised leading to the phenomenon of underemployment (see Mhone, 2001). On the other hand, in industrial sectors where modern equipment is used in the production process, total factor productivity is higher due to the technical improvements induced by the use of sophisticated tools. However, the technological differentials between countries is not just a matter of capital availability; there are other factors which influence the technological gap including skill levels, the size of firms and markets needed to use certain technologies efficiently. Although there is a suggestion that technological dispersion is faster within the manufacturing sector across countries, a situation that is expected to lead to the phenomenon of *unconditional* productivity convergence within the sector, regardless of country circumstances, policies or geography (see Rodrik, 2013), there is little empirical evidence to show that manufacturing productivity is unconditionally converging across countries.

Even if unconditional convergence in the manufacturing sector were a reality, it would bring little relief to most African countries where the manufacturing sector is only a tiny section. While achieving high productivity is crucial for the economy, it makes little impact if the affected sector only accounts for a small portion of the economy in terms of both labour and output. High productivity can make a difference if the manufacturing sector, in particular, expands and induces productivity growth in other sectors. Unfortunately, this has proved to be extremely difficult to realise in Africa. The industrial sector in most African countries accounts for less than 10 percent of the total labour force on average (see Chapter 3 and also Tregenna, 2015), meaning that only 1 in 10 people are engaged in activities where productivity is relatively high and growing. While the services sector enjoys a much higher productivity rate than agriculture, it is on average only half of the productivity levels in industry. Further, most of the people in the services sector are employed in the retail and hospitality subsectors where productivity is low, though higher than in agriculture (Fox et al, 2013; Timmer et al, 2014). The sectoral productivity dynamics in Africa are discussed in more detail in Chapter 6.

Productivity Growth Outside the Industrial Sector

The other factor often cited to justify the focus on industrial development is that it can contribute to higher economy-wide productivity if it absorbs a considerably higher proportion of the labour force initially involved in low-productivity activities. But in the African context, the industrial sector, particularly manufacturing, has not absorbed, and is still not absorbing, people in low-productivity sectors such as agriculture and urban informal activities. Available evidence reveals that the industrial sector, as a whole accounts for about 7 percent of the total labour forces on average (see Chapter 3), leaving the majority of workers either in subsistence agriculture or informal work (Fox and Thomas, 2016). This is not surprising, given the elusive nature of industrialisation on the continent. Generating massive employment for the largely under-employed workers in subsistence agriculture and informal sector is not just an economic challenge but also a political imperative for most countries in Africa.

Since majority of the people in most African countries are still employed in agriculture and urban informal sector, it is only logical that the process of development, in pursuing an aggressive industrialisation strategy, needs to take into account measures aimed at improving productivity and upgrading production capabilities in the sectors where the largest proportion of the labour force works. In this sense, UNECA's (2014) call for African governments to implement measures to improve productivity in the subsistence agricultural sector as part of the strategy of industrialisation makes a lot of sense. Improving productivity in agriculture can have many effects on industrialisation (see chapter 8). Arthur Lewis (1954) in his two-sector model was very aware of the importance of improving productivity in the subsistence sector as an indispensable ingredient of effective industrial strategy. He argued that "industrial and agrarian revolution always go together" and that "economies in which agriculture is stagnant do not show industrial development" (Lewis, 1954:433).

Not only that, but it has also been illustrated that productivity in agriculture can contribute to industrialisation as the demand for manufactured goods resulting from increased income in the rural sector enlarges the market for industrial goods. This view is central in the agricultural demand-led industrialisation (ADLI) framework (Adelman, 1984), and is discussed in more detail in Chapter 8. Growing productivity outside the industrial sector is also essential because it helps sustain domestic demand in the economy, which can lead to further expansion of industrial activities and capabilities. This is crucial in the early stages of industrialisation when local firms are building capacity to compete at the international level.

Capital Accumulation, Productivity and the Vicious Circles

But in this story, productivity, as we have seen above, is largely influenced by the intensity of capital, which in turn influences the accumulation of technical capabilities in an economy and the productivity of labour. If capital is so decisive, it is important to examine what influences capital accumulation and investment in an economy. This is a question that has received considerable attention in the literature on economic growth on both sides of what is sometimes referred as the "iron curtain"[5] (see Streeten, 1959:170). The dominant view has been that poor countries have low capital and this, in a fundamental way, affects levels of productivity, primarily because capital is too thinly spread over labour. It has thus been argued that because productivity is essentially a function of human and physical capital, the low levels of productivity in Africa "reflect, at a minimum, low levels of education and investment" (WEF, 2017).

Using our road construction example above, productivity is low in LICs because workers have little capital to access caterpillars or bulldozers; they also have low levels of accumulated human capital. But the low levels of accumulated human and physical capital are themselves a reflection of low capital in general. In other words, the condition of low productivity can be explained by low income, low savings, slow capital formation, and investment, which leads to the famous vicious circle recognised by Nurkse (1953) when he observed that "a country is poor because it is poor."

The circularity of this relationship between productivity and income lies in the fact that poor countries are poor because they have low income, and low income drags productivity down, which in turn keeps income low. "The low real income is a reflection of low productivity, which in its turn is due largely to the lack of capital. The lack of capital is a result of the small capacity to save, and so the circle is complete" (Nurkse, 1953:5). The crucial question is how does one break out of this vicious circle of low income, low productivity to create a virtuous circle of dynamically growing productivity and higher income? Many countries battle to find answers to this question, although the theory is clear on mechanisms for increasing capital formation in an economy.

There are two main routes a country can take: one is to induce saving from the little there is so that a country builds its stock of capital slowly. The other is to induce the flow of capital from other countries, often by attracting foreign direct investments (FDIs) from international corporations which have accumulated enough capital. However, there are advantages and disadvantages for both routes, but this is not a place to go into the details of the merits and demerits of the two routes. It is important, though, to note that the most preferred route by most developing counties is attracting FDI by any means, and many countries in Africa have been outdoing each other in the bid to woo foreign investors into their countries (see Chitonge, 2017).

FDI and Productivity

The World Bank's *Doing Business Index* (DBI), which ranks countries according to the measures put in place to facilitate establishment of business enterprises, has influenced the investment environment reform agenda in many African countries (Page, 2014). Indeed, there has been an increase in the flow of FDI into Africa since 2000, but it is important to look at which sector attracts the largest share of FDI on the continent. Has the growing flow of FDI contributed to improving productivity in African economies in any significant way?

Analysis of FDI flows into Africa clearly shows that capital is going into activities linked to the extraction of natural resources, with a few resource-rich countries capturing the lion's share of total FDI between 2000 and 2010 (see AEO, 2013; EY, 2017).[6] What is surprising in all this is that despite the increased FDI flows into some countries over the past decade, productivity levels in most of these countries have either remained the same or worsened. What is more worrying in this regard is that productivity outside of the extractive enclaves, particularly mining and oil industries, is falling far behind (see AEO, 2013). Since FDI has been flowing mainly into the extractive sector, which has weak linkages to the rest of the economy, the productivity effects in most African economies have been limited. Further, although African countries have been doing everything they can to attract FDI, Africa has remained a capital scarce continent as manifested in low productivity rates.

Analysis of sectoral productivity dynamics confirms the view that capital's (especially FDI) contribution to improving productivity in an economy largely depends on which sector capital is flowing into. If capital is flowing into the enclave extractive subsectors of the economy which have little or no linkages to other sectors, the economy-wide productivity effects tend to be insignificant. In some cases, it may even decline as the rising capital intensity in the extractive sector leads to retrenchment of the largely unskilled workers who often end up in low-productivity activities in informal retail or subsistence agriculture. Thus, the issue is not just about how much capital flows into a country, but also the type of inflows and what capital does when it comes to a country.

Hans Singer (1950) in his famous paper on investment in developing countries offers a friendly caution against an unscrupulous courting of FDI:

> ...the import of capital into under-developed countries for purposes of making them into provider of food and raw materials for the industrialised countries may have been not only rather ineffective in giving them the normal benefits of investment and trade but may have been positively harmful. The tea plantations of Celyon, the oil wells of Iran, the copper mines of Chile, and the cocoa industry of the Gold Coast[Ghana] may all be more productive than domestic agriculture in these countries; but they may well be less productive than domestic industries in those countries which might have developed if those countries had not become specialized to the degree in which they now are to the export of food and raw materials, thus providing the means of producing manufactured goods elsewhere with superior efficiency (Singer, 1950:476).

What Singer is suggesting is that not all capital that comes into a country contributes to the economy's productivity growth; some capital can in fact reduce the overall productivity in an economy. Newman et al (2016a) have also recommended the need for African countries to screen FDI to ensure that only investments which contribute to building local capabilities in the economy, especially in industrial sectors, are promoted. They also emphasise the need to retain the profits made once the initial investment is afloat. But in most African countries, the state agencies tasked with attracting FDI have solely focused on recruiting investors, with less attention given to what capital does and where it goes when it comes into the country.

Ultimately, like many other aspects of economic activities, there are two sides to the investment capital story; the demand side has often been taken for granted in most less developed countries. It is on the demand side where issues of what type of FDI is needed and what the expected gains from such inflows are needed to be scrutinised so that they fit in the long-term development vision. But what we are seeing in most LICs is a scramble for foreign capital (mostly Chinese capital in the case of Africa), without considering the benefits of this or at least make an effort to force capital to do what a country wants to achieve. The ability to discipline capital so that it fits into a country's broader and long-run plan is important in the context of industrialisation (Amsden, 1989).

The question about where a poor country can get the capital needed to create and sustain competitive capability in the economy and what type of capital can contribute to realising this objective is a critical one which should not be ignored. But it is important to note that capital is not the only factor in the industrialisation story; there are other aspects which need to be considered. There is a common view that money can buy anything; but that is only true to a certain extent. Massive lamps of capital poured into an economy with weak institutions, low skills level, inadequate infrastructure, weak regulatory systems, high levels of corruption, weak leadership and unstable political and economic environment will achieve little in terms of inducing productivity growth. In more recent models of economic growth, the emphasis has been on the point that capital takes different forms including disembodied as well as embodied forms.

Industrialisation and Employment Creation

Apart from the industrial sector being the driver of productivity growth in an economy, the sector is also seen to have high potential for mass employment creation compared to the agricultural or service sector. For instance, it is argued that "Industry has traditionally been a central source of generating employment—in developed and developing countries" (UNECA, 2016b:53). Industry's potential to absorb labour is believed to exist in two ways: one is through a direct path of labour-intensive industrial activities, and the other, indirectly through strong intersectoral linkages, with both agriculture and services. Literature on industrialisation suggests that countries with low levels of industrial development find it difficult to create real jobs. This is true in most African countries which have experienced decent growth since the beginning of the new millennium, but have failed to create adequate employment, largely due to the poor performing industrial sector, particularly manufacturing.

In most African economies there is now an urgent need to ensure that the economy creates more real jobs to cater for the growing youth population, especially in urban areas where open unemployment is becoming a common phenomenon. Some authors refer to the failure to create jobs as a "time bomb" which has a strong potential to induce social and political destabilisation in society (see UNECA, 2012). The ILO reports that its social unrest index (SUI) which measures the reported levels of discontent within the population has increased in most African countries (ILO, 2017). Although lack of employment is not the only factor that influences the level of discontent captured by the SUI, it contributes significantly to a country's level of discontent within the population (ibid). High unemployment among the youth who are increasingly becoming more educated across Africa is also noted to be one of the urgent challenges facing African countries (see Filmer and Fox, 2014).

The employment challenge in Africa has broadly been attributed to lack of structural transformation (McMillan and Rodrik, 2011), and to the lack of robust growth of the industrial sector which is believed to have the capacity to absorb the large numbers of the youth entering the labour market (Fox and Thomas, 2016). Newman et al (2016a:15) from their study of 8 African economies conclude that the "failure to industrialise is clearly a major part of Africa's employment problem." However, the biggest challenge in Africa regarding employment has not been open unemployment, but under-employment which is a result of low levels of productivity and low incomes (see Mhone, 2001). As Chitonge (2012) has observed, in terms of unemployment, most African countries appear not to have a huge problem since unemployment figures are not too far from the global average.[7] Labour participation on the continent, except in North Africa, was the second highest in the world in 2017, suggesting that most people are engaging in activities of some sort (ILO, 2017). The high employment and participation ratios in Africa could be explained by the fact that most people have little or no social protection such that they have to engage in some activity as a way to survive. In such circumstances, open unemployment is not an option (Chitonge, 2012).

Employment Creation Potential in the Industrial Sector

While manufacturing has traditionally been perceived as a 'job spinner' in the economy, the employment creation potential of the manufacturing sector is now debatable in the context of the emerging phenomenon of pre-mature de-industrialisation (see chapters 1 and 10). For instance, Newman et al (2016b) argue that agriculture can be more labour intensive in the early stages of economic development when capital is still a scarce factor. However, the fact that the industrial sector often enjoys steadily rising productivity over time means that the opportunity to create wage employment with higher productivity is high.[8] It is this feature of the industrial sector which gives it a high potential to contribute significantly to the creation of productive jobs than any other sector in the economy.

However, the responsiveness of employment creation to manufacturing growth (manufacturing employment elasticity) can be expected to be lower than in the agricultural sector where formal employment is low and wages are more flexible, especially in Africa. What gives the industrial sector an advantage in terms of job creation is its ability to absorb more labour, without leading to declines in productivity and wages. This can be partly explained by the high capital-labour ratio in the industrial sector, which often rises when capital accumulation reaches a critical threshold, making it possible for output per worker to even increase or remain constant with additional workers, suggesting that marginal productivity of labour is high. It is for this reason that the industrial sector is seen as critical in generating employment.

The other reason why industrial activities tend to contribute more to the creation of jobs is the strong backward and forward linkages to other sectors. As Hirschman (1958:112) observed, the backward linkage between agriculture and industry provide "powerful stimuli to the development of agriculture." Although there is contestation about which sector should initiate the transformation of the economy, there is wide agreement that where industrial development has taken off, the industrial sector, through the growing demand for agricultural produce and services from the growing industries and urban population, indirectly induces the growth of jobs in these other sectors. This was strongly argued by Kaldor (1966:112) when he observed that,

> It is the rate of growth of manufacturing production (together with ancillary activities of public utilities and construction) which is likely to exert a dominating influence on the overall rate of economic growth: partly on account of its influence on the rate of growth of productivity in the individual sector itself, and partly also because it tends, indirectly, to raise the rate of productivity growth in other sectors.

The anticipated growth in productivity can lead to more jobs in manufacturing since with rising productivity, the labour required to produce the same or even more agricultural goods declines, enabling more jobs to be transferred to the industrial sector without negatively affecting the level of agricultural production. This in turn may lead to growth in employment generation capacity in industries. But as we have seen in later years, at some point, the success of the manufacturing sector, particularly growth of productivity, leads to low labour-intensity, which in turn leads to low job creation capacity (see Tregenna, 2009).

Here we see a virtuous circle in operation, in contrast with the vicious circle of low capital, low income and low productivity mentioned earlier. The virtuous circle created by a rapidly growing industrial sector has been widely reported in many industrialised economies including the emerging Asian countries. Singer (1950), for instance, argues that the fact that these trends are largely absent in many less industrialised countries is a sign that these countries have missed out on the momentum that industrialisation generates. In many developing countries, the failure to industrialise has limited the opportunities for change, particularly the opportunity to put many people into real jobs and reduce abject poverty.

Jobless Growth in Africa

In most African countries, the performance of the industrial sector with regard to employment creation has been disappointing, especially in later years despite the decent growth experienced over the last 15 years. With the sluggish growth in most countries following the decline of commodity prices on the global markets after 2015, "Many African economies are struggling to provide sufficient job opportunities to meet the needs of the burgeoning workforce" (WEF, 2017:24). As noted earlier, total employment in the manufacturing sector has remained low, averaging 7.1 percent for resource-rich countries in 2013 and just 5.8 percent for non-resource-rich countries (see Table 3.5). Formal wage employment in the manufacturing sector is even much lower reported at 3 percent in 2010 (Filmer and Fox, 2014).

There are several reasons which help explain this seemingly jobless growth in Africa. The first is that there has been lack of growth in labour-intensive industrial activities such as textile, apparel and furniture, leather and footwear, and agro-processing which often signals the start of an industrial turnaround in developing economies (Newman et al, 2016b). When these activities grow, they tend to create sustained demand for labour, thereby creating real jobs in the economy to absorb the labour force from low-productivity activities, mainly subsistence agriculture and informal trading. But in Africa, most of these activities have recorded a steady decline starting from the 1990s mainly due to competitive pressure from China, India and Turkey.

The other reason why the industrial sector has not contributed much to creating employment at the time when most economies in the continent experienced relatively high and stable growth rates is that majority of the countries in Africa have experienced perverse structural economic transformation whereby the labour force is moving from low- (and sometimes from high) productivity activities to other low-productivity activities, mainly in the informal retail and trading, and household enterprise (McMillan and Rodrik, 2011; Filmer and Fox, 2014; Newman et al, 2016a). This general trend is captured well in a UNIDO report, which observes that,

> While people have moved out of rural areas and the share of agriculture in employment and value added has dropped since the 1960s, the primary beneficiaries have been urban and often informal services, not manufacturing. African labour has tended to move from agriculture to services, and while services have had much higher productivity than agriculture, their productivity gains over time have been very limited (UNIDO, 2016:9).

But this trend points to the lack of momentum in the manufacturing and other industrial sectors. While many Africans are willing to move from subsistence agriculture and informal trading, there are no opportunities in the high-productivity segments of the economy. Further, as illustrated in Chapter 6, segments of the services sector like insurance, real estate, tourism, banking and business services such as accounting and market research are relatively small and require highly skilled labour which most Africans who are moving from subsistence agriculture do not have. As a result, whereas the contribution of these high-value-added activities to productivity is positive, their contribution to job creation has been small.

Although the labour data in Africa are quite scanty, making it difficult to analyse trends in various subsectors, available estimates suggest that only 16 percent of the total labour force are in formal wage employment (Fox and

Thomas, 2016), and industry's share in total employment remains low for the continent, declining and stagnating in most countries.

While the ratio of manufacturing employment is different across countries (see Table 3.5), one thing that is common to many countries is that the share of manufacturing in total employment is generally low, with only a handful of countries (Congo, Algeria, Swaziland, Tunisia, Senegal, South Africa, Egypt and Mauritius) reporting manufacturing share in total employment of over 10 percent in 2013. What is worrying is that most of the countries are experiencing declining share of manufacturing in total employment (see Table 3.5). These trends point to the fact that the continent has not experienced positive structural transformation which is marked by the shift of labour from low to high-productivity sectors (McMillan and Rodrik, 2011; Timmer et al, 2014).

> Had Africa's economies gone through patterns of structural change that were more in line with those counterfactual economies—faster decline in the share of labour force in agriculture and more rapid increase in the employment share of industry—poverty reduction would have been greater (Newman et al, 2016a:18).

But the fact that Africa has not gone through positive structural transformation calls for more context-specific explanations of what is happening. Employment creation in the industrial sector and the broader economy is low, because of the low growth of economy-wide productivity, particularly in agriculture and informal sectors where majority of Africans work today. Even if many countries have reported relatively decent growth rates between 2000 and 2015, this has not generated the momentum to create jobs and reduce poverty because the growth is mostly occurring in the extractive sectors which are actually more capital-intensive with low employment responsiveness to growth (see UNECA, 2012).

For the continent to make progress towards creating jobs, African countries will have to learn how to disrupt the economic structures established under colonial rule. This is the crux of the matter. We can speak about sound macroeconomic management, business-friendly environment, good governance and all that, but they are not enough; Africa has to learn to undo the colonial economic structure as the prerequisite for industrialisation. The "standard advice, such as improving the business environment and education—though still needed and extremely useful—is not enough, given the challenges most countries in the region face" (WEF, 2017:35).

Industrialisation and Agriculture in Africa

The other crucial factor that explains the low employment elasticity of growth in Africa is the fact that productivity in agriculture has remained low and declining in most countries. The challenge this poses in terms of industrialisation and structural transformation is that, if agriculture which employs more than half of the workforce is experiencing declining productivity rates, this is expected to have a negative impact on industrialisation because it reduces domestic demand for industrial products which is an important stimulator of industrialisation in the early stages when domestic demand matters a lot (see Adelman, 1984). If productivity and therefore wages and income in agriculture grow, this can increase domestic demand for manufactured products which can stimulate the further growth of local industries, including agriculture itself, through backward linkages. But since the agriculture sector in most African countries is still locked in low-productivity activities, the stimulant for industrial growth is subdued. Rising productivity and income in agriculture played a crucial role in East Asia where "agrarian transformation served as the basis for economies to industrialise, paving the way for a more diversified base to emerge. Increased incomes for farmers created buoyant demand in rural areas for farm inputs, for processing and marketing services as well as for consumer goods and services" (UNECA, 2012:120).

There is consensus in the literature on industrial development, supported by historical evidence, that growth in the agriculture sector is the bedrock of structural transformation (Lewis, 1954; Adelman, 1984; Mundle, 1985; Kay, 2002, Feizhou and Camille, 2009). "It is now largely accepted that growth in the agriculture sector which contributes to poverty reduction and makes internal demand more dynamic, has been the precondition for transforming economies that are now industrialised or undergoing industrialisation" (NEPAD, 2014:15).

In the case of East Asia, sustained productivity growth among small-scale farmers is what triggered structural transformation and spurred rapid growth in the industrial sector (Pingali, 1997). In the case of most African countries where productivity in agriculture has remained low and is declining, the situation constitutes a major impediment to industrialisation, poverty reduction and inclusive growth (Filmer and Fox, 2014). Increased productivity in agriculture is not just good for increasing demand for industrial products, but also in reducing the size of the labour force engaged in agriculture.

It has been estimated that 10 percent increase in agricultural labour productivity results in between 1.3 and 2.8 percent reduction in the share of agriculture in the labour force, meaning that increased productivity in agriculture can also lead to further relocation of labour into other sectors (Yeboah and Jayne, 2017). But the relocation of labour from agriculture cannot happen if the industrial sector is not able to absorb the surplus labour, and this is why industrialisation cannot be pursued as an isolated policy; it has to be well-integrated in the broader development plan.

Although there are now indications that the employment creation capacity of manufacturing has declined steadily in all economies including the less industrialised countries (Rodrik, 2015), the potential of the industrial sectors to contribute towards achieving mass employment generation is still a valid proposal for developing countries at the early phase of industrialisation. While in the past industrial share in total employment peaked at between 25 and 30 percent before dynamics of deindustrialisation set in, the estimated highest industrial employment share is currently between 15 and 18 percent.[9] Even if we go with the 18 percent as the manufacturing employment share ceiling, this would mean that African countries have the chance to increase their current manufacturing share in total employment by 150 percent, which can make a huge dent on under-employment, poverty and overall productivity.

The good news for the later industrialisers is that MVA, despite the declining employment creation capacity of the manufacturing sector, has remained stable in most post-industrial countries, signifying a rise in labour productivity. Achieving high levels of industrial employment has been an enduring challenge in majority of African countries, mainly because of the lack of momentum in the agriculture sector.

As Page (2015) has rightly observed, the stress put on industrialisation should not be interpreted to mean a disregard for improving productivity in the agricultural sector in particular, as some industrial enthusiasts tend to suggest (see Chitonge, 2016). The fact that Africa still has more than half of its labour force in agriculture, primarily in subsistence agriculture (see Fox and Thomas, 2016), means that the agricultural sector should form an integral part of the industrial strategy because agriculture remains the largest user of one of the critical factors of production—labour. The industrialisation process cannot ignore the agriculture sector; agriculture must be part of a rounded story of industrialisation.

Industrialisation and Technology Dispersion

Apart from playing a central role in driving productivity growth and creation of jobs, industrialisation is also seen as critical to technology diffusion and adaptation. As the 2012 *Economic Report on Africa* and the *Transformative Industrial Policy Document* (UNECA, 2012; 2016a) observe, the industrial sector, particularly manufacturing, often acts as a conduit for technological upgrading and growth of innovation in an economy. The literature on economic growth in general and industrialisation in particular is almost unanimous on the view that industrialisation is a conduit for capturing spill-over effects through tapping into and developing new technologies (Tregenna, 2009; 2015).

In the industrial sector, technology is often associated with modern machinery, equipment and communication systems. Because of its heavy reliance on sophisticated equipment to manufacture goods, the industrial sector is traditionally seen as the driver of technological advances. Improvement in technology is realised mainly though firms seeking to find new production techniques and methods of production. In this sense manufacturing is often at the frontier of innovation, imitation, adaptation and learning by doing. In other words, "although innovation, imitation, learning and selection are found in all sectors of the economy… these factors are stronger in the manufacturing sector which is why industrialisation is essential to growth…" (Ciarli and Di-Maio, 2015:49).

In the current global context where value chains are widely dispersed across the globe (see UNECA, 2016a), usually through large multinational corporations which control the core value chains, it is important that firms in less industrialised countries adopt and adapt the latest technology for them to remain competitive. In a rapidly changing world of technology, this requires constant upgrading of production methods and techniques, and the manufacturing sector can play an important role in importing and adapting the latest technology.

The concern in Africa is that most of the manufacturing on the continent are occurring in low-value-added activities, linked to natural resources using low technology. Although there are reports of diversification into telecommunication and media, this is only happening in the bigger economies mainly South Africa, Nigeria, Egypt, and Kenya (see EY, 2017). Current estimates suggest that almost 90 percent of manufacturing exports from Africa are natural resource based, using low and medium tech, resulting in African countries being locked in the low-valued-added segments of global value chains (see

UNIDO, 2016:10–11). The challenge for African countries is to defy this configuration of global manufacturing by creating capacity to participate in high-value-added activities. Developing and upgrading capacities is not something one learns in economics or business studies; it is a practical skill that accumulates through engaging in the actual activities.

Traditionally, development economics theory has focused on modelling technology in a typical production function, using growth accounting techniques. In the earlier models, technology was regarded as an exogenous factor which could not be entirely accounted in the earlier standard growth model. For example, in the famous Robert Solow (1956) model, technology or technical change is external to the model in the sense that the model could not account for changes in technology. Later models (see Romer, 1986; Lucas, 1988; Rebelo, 1991), have endogenised technology such that it can now be explained as an integral part of a standard growth model, mainly through the decisions made by firms or governments to invest in research and development (R&D) and other innovative activities which lead to technological advancement and new production techniques. In this way, technology is fully accounted for in a growth model as an outcome of rational and deliberate action of economic actors. It is not by accident that countries which are industrialised, with a well-developed manufacturing sector, lead the innovation and technology development ranking table, including the emerging digital economy (see EIU, 2018). These countries also spend a relatively higher proportion of their national income on R&D, sometimes in joint ventures between the public and private sector.

Industrialisation and Technology Spill-Over Effects

However, it has been noted that although firms factor into their business models returns to investment in R&D, not all the returns can be internalised by a single firm, leading to large externalities in the form of technology spill-over to other firms. In this sense technology (investment in R&D) has a feature of being an impure public good (I have referred to this as secondary public goods), mainly because the *social rates of return* often exceeds the *private rates of return* (see Jones and Williams, 1998). Scitovsky (1954:144) explains the nature of this dynamic in more simple terms: "The output of the individual producer may depend not only on his input of productive resources but also on the activities of other firms. This...may be called 'direct interdependence among producers,' but is better known under the name of 'external economies and diseconomies.'" Therefore, not all companies that benefit from modern technology paid the cost involved in the invention of the technology in question.

Positive external economies can also accrue to a firm that uses inputs produced from another company using modern technology that enables it to produce at a lower cost than otherwise (see Krugman, 1981). What this essentially means is that firms can produce using technology developed by other firms, that is, without paying the cost (full or partial) involved in developing the technology. It is also possible that firms could be negatively affected by the activities of other firms in the process of developing or applying technology, thereby experiencing diseconomies or negative externalities.

Earlier economists such as Scitovsky (1954) and Young (1928) emphasised the importance of external economies and used this to justify state intervention in promoting industrialisation. Due to the socialised nature of returns to investment in technology research, there have been calls for public investment in technology in order to optimise social returns (Young, 1991).

There is a view that less industrialised countries in Africa and other developing regions can benefit either through importing technology or allowing MNCs to bring the technology when they invest in these countries (Lall and Kraemer-Mbula, 2005). Foreign investments are encouraged because of the potential external economies through technology diffusion that this may generate. This is one of the reasons why many less industrialised countries jostle for FDI, regardless of where it goes, assuming that the investments will eventually induce catch-up effects by tapping in the technology from other countries. The South African Industrial Action Plan has specifically identified attracting foreign firms with high manufacturing technology capabilities as a way of promoting technology transfer, which is expected to improve the diffusion of technology to other sectors (see DTI, 2016).

However, although many less industrialised countries are desperately seeking to attract technology, technology transfer is not as simple as picking a spanner from the shelves of industrialised countries; it requires developing the capacity to absorb and adapt the technology to the local context (Lin and Chang, 2009). For sure, there have been technological spill-over into many African countries through the investments and trade with multinational companies, but the impact of technology on industrial production has remained muted, mainly the scope of the small size of industrial sector in most countries. There are two pathways through which technology has filtered into the continent: through acquiring of production equipment by local firms—embodied technology, and through the establishment of subsidiaries of MNCs in the continent which bring the technology and techniques with them. But the industrial sector in most African countries is dominated by low and medium technology, with little high-tech involved (see Chapter 3). As noted earlier, the evidence of unconditional convergence in manufacturing on grounds of technological dispersion in Africa is absent (see de Vries et al, 2015).

In most African countries, especially the resource-rich countries, the most sophisticated technology has gone into the exploitation of natural resources such as minerals, oil and related products. It is common to find the latest equipment in oil or mineral extraction in Nigeria, as one would find in Australia or China. This is why productivity in the mining sector in many African countries is many times higher than the economy-wide productivity. For example, it has been reported that labour productivity in mining in Malawi is 136 times that of agriculture, suggesting that if mining was to employ all the workers in Malawi, the country would have the same labour productivity as the United States (McMillan and Rodrik, 2011:6).

Most MNCs which have established subsidiary companies in Africa are not in manufacturing or the broader industrial sector; they are heavily concentrated in the extractive industries which are often poorly linked to other sectors, giving rise to enclavity, a feature that is often attributed to the colonial economic logic (see Mhone, 2001). Outside of South Africa, Egypt and Tunisia technology in the manufacturing sector has been transferred only through the importation of equipment for production, mostly by local firms. In some industries such as agro-processing, we are seeing some of the latest equipment in maize milling, juice extraction, grading of agricultural produce, vegetable oil extractors, etc. But even there, the scale of production remains low, though growing fast in response to the growing urban population.

But there is another way of looking at technology in the form of skills or techniques which are not embodied in any physical or fixed capital. Kaldor (1957) makes this clear when he distinguishes what he calls "technical progress" (advance of technology embodied in physical capital) and "technical innovation" which refers to improvements in the organisation of production, factory lay-out and the way of combining factors of production. He argues that productivity can grow even with the same stock of physical capital as long as the disembodied technological innovation filters into the production process. Arrow (1962) expanded on this and attributed the larger part of the disembodied technology to experience—which he called "learning by doing." He argued that the "technical change in general can be ascribed to experience, that is the very activity of production which gives rise to problems for which favourable responses are selected over time" (Arrow, 1962:156).

It is probably in this latter sense that technology and innovation have greater externalities to areas where industrial production has significantly developed. It essentially involves the spreading of ideas and practices about how to organise not only production but also the firms and all the structures that support it, including incentives for workers. This is a type of innovation that may be more mobile and can spread faster than embodied technology which may require modification to adapt to the local context. Young (1991) makes a similar observation that technical innovation in terms of how to organise production, aside from physical equipment, has substantial spill-over effects as innovative ideas in one firm or industry spread to other industries even across borders. The imitating firms, in a bid to adapt the ideas to suit their circumstances can make minor or major moderations which can lead to new techniques and organisational models. But all these techniques can be learnt by actively engaging in the production process; nothing can replace experience. Since industry involves the repetitive acts in the process of production, it is widely believed that "industrialisation is not only a response to changing demand and supply conditions but also a principal means of acquiring modern technology" as well as technical capabilities (Chenery et al, 1986:2).

In most African countries, it can be argued that the process of acquiring technology to develop the technical capabilities has been hampered because of the small size of the industrial sector. While the learning curve is quite steep, especially in the services sector where local firms are interacting with international companies through franchised hotels, the rate of diffusion has been slow. There is great optimism that as some of the Africans in diaspora, who have had experience of working with MNCs in high-efficiency firms (some of them as top executives), return to establish businesses in Africa, there will be quicker and wider spread of the technical innovation to other sectors including manufacturing (see Chapter 9). We are already seeing this in cases where local firms that supply franchised international companies are learning to adopt the management techniques via the supply contract requirements. How far this will spread to the manufacturing sector and contribute to its growth remains to be seen. What is clear though is that the learning needs to be enhanced through deliberate policy and programmes aimed at deepening industrial capabilities on the continent.

Industrialisation and Income Growth

The link between income and industrialisation is simple and often taken for granted in economic literature. The income impact of industrialisation operates through two aspects discussed above, productivity and employment growth. The common view is that industrialisation, where it is widespread (particularly, growth in the manufacturing sector), leads to higher income for the simple reason that productivity in the industrial sector is higher than that in the rest of the economy. In the neoclassical framework, since productivity of labour is what determines wages, a higher productivity in the industrial sectors entails higher wages, and if this sector absorbs a significant portion of the labour force, the higher wages in this sector raise the overall income levels in the economy. Simon Kuznets (1955, 1966) who studied the effect of economic growth on income levels and distribution, singles out the shift of labour to the high-productivity manufacturing sector as the key drivers of income growth and decline in inequality. High productivity in manufacturing also has a strong equalising effect on income distribution. The explanation for this is that, during the early stages of economic growth, when majority of the population are in agriculture where wages and income are low, average income is low and income inequality is high. As economic growth through industrialisation progresses, the structural change in the economy, induced primarily by the demand for labour occasioned by high productivity in the industrial sector, would naturally lead to a shift in factor allocation (particularly labour) from the low- to high-productivity segments of the economy. As more and more labour shift to sectors of the economy with high productivity, their wages rise, at least, pushing the general income levels in the population up, leading to fall in inequality.

Kuznets (1955) analysed sectoral income per capita differentials using mainly data for the United States and observed that income in the agriculture sector is lower than in industry and service sectors, and that the proportion of labour in agriculture had been declining over time relative to the share of industry and services. This is illustrated in more detail using data from a group of 12 industrialised countries where the trends he described in 1955 seem to be confirmed (see Kuznets, 1966:88, 106).

However, Kuznets' analysis has been contested from different angles, particularly the idea that income inequality declines with economic growth and industrialisation. Thomas Piketty (2105), in particular, contends this position arguing that the decline in income inequality observed in the industrial countries between 1913 and 1948 is accidental; it had nothing to do with the process of economic growth. He argues that this decline was as a result of the two major wars, and that recent income distribution trends, starting from the 1980s, show growing inequality across countries, including developed countries: "In fact, Kuznets himself was well aware that the compression of high US incomes between 1913 and 1948 was largely accidental. It stemmed in large part from multiple shocks triggered by the Great Depression and World War II and had little to do with any natural or automatic process."

But Kuznets' analysis of income trends in industrialised countries and the accompanying model of structural change have had strong influence among analysts of economic structural transformation and industrialisation (see Chenery et al, 1986). With specific reference to the industrial sector, there is wide agreement that the movement of labour and other factors from low- to high-productivity activities leads to overall income growth and that this dynamic is the most effective way of raising general income in an economy (McMillan and Rodrik, 2011; Timmer et al, 2012; Newman et al, 2016a). In this story, the industrial sector, especially manufacturing, is seen as the driver of the income growth dynamic because of its higher productivity and also its capacity to absorb larger proportions of the labour force (Chenery et al, 1986; Ciarli and Di-Maio, 2016). A strong confirmation of this view can be found in Murphy et al (1989:1003) who argue that,

> Virtually every country that experienced rapid growth of productivity and living standards over the last 200 years have done so by industrializing. Countries that have successfully industrialized—turned to production of manufactures taking advantage of scale economies—are the ones that grew rich, be they 18th-century Britain or 20th-century Korea and Japan.

The failure to establish a diverse manufacturing sector in LICs is thus used to explain why incomes are low in these countries. Newman et al (2016b) also attribute the low capacity in creating productive jobs and the slow reduction in poverty in many African countries to the poor performance of and the failure to deepen industrial development and structural transformation. As shown in Chapter 3, employment levels in the industrial sector in all African countries remain low. In the case of manufacturing, employment share for 2013 ranges from the insignificant less than 1 per cent in Mozambique, Chad and Sierra Leone, to the moderate levels of 10 percent in South Africa, and a handful of countries such as Swaziland, Tunisia and Mauritius reporting manufacturing employment of above 15 percent (see Table 3.5). With this level of employment in the most productive sector, the potential for industrial jobs to contribute to income growth and poverty can be expected to be quite high, provided that industrialisation occurs. But productive jobs have to be created for people in low-productivity activities to be relocated to high-productivity activities. As Chitonge (2016:9–10) has argued,

> [P]eople involved in subsistence agriculture would be happy and willing to move to capitalist sectors (as is evident from the people migrating to urban areas…in search of jobs), the challenge is that the capitalist sectors are not creating enough jobs to absorb those who are looking for employment. The [challenge] therefore is not that people engaged in subsistence agriculture are held back by cultural or other factors as Collier (2006) suggests; the challenge is that the modern sectors are not restructuring well enough to generate sufficient jobs.

The potential of the industrial sector to create jobs and raise income which is widely acknowledged in the literature would need to be realised at a much larger scale if structural transformation in Africa is to take root. This in turn calls for strategies to find a game changer that can spur industrialisation.

While the evidence is clear that most African countries which have some deepening of industrial sector have higher incomes in general, the distribution of this income is a totally different story. What is important though is to ensure that more and more people participate in industrial activities as a way to promote inclusive economies which are so critical in maintaining political and social stability on the continent. Given that most people are employed in the low-productivity sectors where wages are low, industrial development stimulated by rising productivity in the economy can contribute to increased income as more people get to work in the sectors where productivity is not only higher, but is also growing. In this sense, a growing industrial sector has the potential to spread the benefit of growth more widely, and in the process promote inclusive growth which is urgently needed in Africa where the growth witnessed over the past decade is accruing to a small section of the population in formal employment (see Chitonge, 2015). A recent report on the impact of the growth experienced over the last decade observes that even if growth rates across the continent have been positive "not all Africans are benefiting from the growth" (AfDB, 2013:13). But industrialisation's capacity to create real jobs in African economies will not be realised if there are no radical plans to disrupt the current colonial economic structures.

Industrialisation and Structural Transformation

Industrialisation is also seen as key to promoting positive structural transformation and diversification of economies in Africa. In other words, industrial policy is a critical tool for decolonising African economies. The industrial sector, manufacturing in particular, is widely believed to play a central role in the diversification of economies because of the wider activities that the manufacturing sector connects with. The wider range of activities under manufacturing include simple processing of agricultural products, light manufacturing for household goods (involving low to medium technology and techniques) and heavy manufacturing of capital goods using complicated technology and skills (see DESA, 2008). Given the broad range of manufacturing activities, it is often argued that a developing industrial sector, led by growth in manufacturing, provides the opportunity to broaden both the production and export bases, as the economy diversifies from being an agrarian or commodity dependent to the production of a wide range of manufactured products. The advantages of a more diversified economy include the ability to withstand the external shocks associated with commodity exports. In this sense, the diversification of a country's export base is some form of protection or security from the volatility associated with commodity prices, which often has negative impact on economic growth in countries whose main exports are commodities.

Historical evidence supports the view that it is countries with large components of manufactures in total export that exhibit more resilience and sustained economic growth and income per capita growth (ACET, 2014). A diversified economy is able to export a diverse range of goods and services to the global market such that when prices in some of its exports decline, it is compensated by the steady or rising prices in the other export goods. But for countries whose exports are primary commodities (which is the case for most African countries), when prices of these commodities fall, export earnings decline, which negatively affects public revenue and the exchange rate for the local currency. The other disadvantage of relying heavily on commodities is that the prices of commodities, relative to the prices of manufactures (terms of trade), decline over time, giving rise to unfavourable terms of trade for commodity exporters (see Prebisch, 1950; Singer, 1950). Although the evidence to support this view has been disputed (see Singer, 1984), it is commonly acknowledged that prices of commodities are volatile and have a tendency to decline over time (Jacks, 2013; Ciarli and Di-Maio, 2015). The effects of commodity price volatility are well-known in most African countries, and often mark the turning points in Africa's economic growth trajectory. The most recent experience is the sharp decrease in commodities on the global market in 2015 after over a decade of higher prices (WEF, 2017).

Against All Odds

A game changer for Africa's industrialisation will have to be radical enough to break out of the current low employment growth trap. Although this does not mean replicating what has been done elsewhere, African countries can learn from the radical steps that countries which have managed to overcome the counter-forces of low capital, low skills, low productivity and low growth have taken, namely that they created capabilities to compete on the international market, not by sticking to comparative advantage, but by actually defying static comparative advantages. There are many examples of this in the past if one looks carefully at countries which have managed to build industrial capabilities. For instance, "It has long been understood that Switzerland's prowess in watches, say, or Belgium's in chocolates cannot be explained by the normal forces of comparative advantage" (Hausmann et al, 2007:2). If African countries stick to their current comparative advantage, they will always have no comparative advantage in manufacturing and other sectors, and the consequences of this scenario are well known in Africa. For industrialisation to be an engine of growth and employment creation on the continent, African countries would have to create dynamic comparative advantage in these activities by defying the status quo. Doing this means going against the current, and one must be prepared to deal with the high opportunity cost this involves. As noted in Chapter 1, defying comparative advantage means that a country is fighting for a share on the global market against countries which have already established themselves as leaders in the industry. For sure, engaging in such a battle requires careful planning, perseverance and unflinching commitment. The game changer for Africa will be to engage in deliberate acts of decolonising African economies by transforming the current economic structures which are underpinned by an imperial economic logic.

Notes

1. We come back to this point later in this chapter and in Chapter 3 where we look at the composition of the industrial, including manufacturing, sector in Africa.

2. Interestingly Simon Kuznets (1966:87) also noted the point that mining is sometimes included under the primary sector or extractive industries often reported together with agriculture, though he preferred to "put it under industry because of the large scale of its productive unit, its close connection with manufacturing…."
3. Redding (1999) gives an example of South Korea's Pohang Iron and Steel Company (POSCO), which at the time the company was established in 1973 had no semblance of comparative advantage in steel and iron, since the country had no raw materials for steel production. By the mid-1990s, POSCO which, twenty years earlier, had no comparative advantage in iron and steel had transformed itself into a competitive producer able to out-compete with Japanese and American producers, and became the 11th largest producer of steel in the world with 80 plants. Chang (in Lin and Chang, 2009) also gives the example of Japanese cars which had to be protected from foreign competition for a long time until the auto industry was able to compete with other global car makers.
4. Figures for 2018 are estimates.
5. This was widely used to refer to the ideological divide between capitalist and communist/socialist views. But the use of the iron curtain image is quite misleading because there are actually several divides even within the two blocks. For example, within the capitalist views, there were (and still are) serious divisions (curtains) between the neoclassical and the Keynesian views or between what was then called mono-economics and development economics (see Singer, 1984).
6. For example in 2016, five countries (South Africa (20.6 percent), Morocco (12 percent), Egypt (11.7 percent), Nigeria (7.5 percent) and Kenya (5.9 percent)) account for almost 60 percent of total FDI flow to the continent (see EY, 2017:10–11). Even if there is a considerable amount of FDI going into real estate, construction and transport (ibid), the bulk is in resources extraction.
7. In 2016, unemployment rate in 2017 was 8 percent compared to 6.4 percent for the global average (see ILO, 2017).
8. Current estimates show that productivity in manufacturing is six times higher than that in agriculture (see Newman et al, 2016b:11), though industry employs only a tiny section of the population, less than 5 percent in most countries, with 7 percent as the average for the region (see Timmer et al, 2014:6).
9. For example, the industrial share in total employment in the United States peaked at 25 percent in the 1950s, though it has declined to less than 10 percent in 2014 (Rodrik, 2015).

References

African Centre for Economic Transformation (ACET, 2014), Growth with Depth—African Transformation Report, Accra: ACET available at http://africantransformation.org/wp-content/uploads/2014/02/2014-african-transformation-report.pdf access 18.06 2016

Adelman, I. (1984). "Beyond Export Led Growth." *World Development*, Vol. 12, No. 9. 937–949.

African Development Bank (AfDB, 2013). "Annual Development Effectiveness Review 2013: Towards Sustainable Growth for Africa." Available at: www.afdb.org. Accessed 23.10.13.

African Union (AU)/African Development Bank (AfDB)/Economic Commission for Africa (ECA) (AU/AfDB/ECA, 2017). *African Statistical Year Book 2017*. Addis Ababa: AU/AfDB/ECA.

Amsden, A. H. (1989). *Asia's Next Giant: South Korea and Late Industrialization*. New York: Oxford University Press.

Amsden, A. H. (2001). *The Rise of 'The Rest': Challenges to the West from the Late-Industrialising Economies*. London/New York: Oxford University Press.

Arrow, K. (1962). "The Economic Implications of Learning by Doing." *Review of Economic Studies*, Vol. 29, No. 3. 155–173.

Chang, H. (2003). "Kicking away the Ladder: The 'Real' History of Free Trade." Foreign Policy in Focus (FPIF) Special Report. Available at: www.personal.ceu.hu/corliss/CDST_Course_Site/Readings_old_2012_files/Ha-Joon%20Chang%20-%20Kicking%20Away%20the%20Ladder-The%20"Real"%20History%20of%20Free%20Trade.pdf. Accessed 21. 03.2015.

Chenery, H., Robinson, S. and Syrquim, M. (1986). *Industrialisation and Growth: A Comparative Study*. Washington, DC: World Bank.

Chitonge, H. (2012). "Social Protection Challenges in Sub-Saharan Africa: Rethinking Regimes and Commitments." *African Studies*, Vol. 71, No. 3. 323–345.

Chitonge, H. (2015). *Economic Growth and Development in Africa: Understanding Trends and Prospects*. New York/London: Routledge.

Chitonge, H. (2016). "Zambia at 50: The Persisting Challenges of Economic Structural Transformation." Development Southern Africa, DOI:10.1080/0376835X.2016.1231053.

Chitonge, H. (2017). "Capitalism in Africa: Mutating Capitalist Relations and Social Formations" *Review of African Political Economy*, DOI:10.1080/03056244.2017.1372280.

Ciarli, T. and Di-Maio, M. (2015). "The Theoretical Arguments for Industrialisation-driven Economic Growth and Development," in F. Matambalya (ed.), *African Industrial Development and the European Union Co-operation: Prospects for a Re-engineered Partnership*. London/New York: Routledge. 30–68.

Collier, Paul (2006). "African Growth: Why a 'Big Push'?" *Journal of African Economies*, Vol. 15, Supplement 2. 188–211.

De Vries, G., Timmer, M. and de Vries, K. (2015). "Structural Transformation in Africa: Static Gains, Dynamic Losses." *Journal of Development Studies*, Vol. 56, No. 6. 674–688.

Department of Economic and Social Affairs (DESA, 2008). *International Industrial Standard Classification of All Economic Activities*, Revision 4. New York: United Nations Department of Economic and Social Affairs.

Department of Trade and Industry (DTI, 2016). Industrial Policy Action Plan (IPAP) 2016/17–2018/19. Pretoria: DTI.

Economic Outlook for Africa (2013). *African Economic Outlook 2013: Structural Transformation and Natural Resources* (Special Thematic Edition). Available at: http://www.undp.org/content/dam/rba/docs/Reports/African%20Economic%20Outlook%202013%20En.pdf. Accessed 13.08.2015.

Elkan, W. (2000). "Manufacturing Microenterprises as Import Substituting Industries," in H. Jalilian, M. Tribe and J. Weiss (eds.), *Industrial Development and Policy in Africa: Issues of De-Industrialisation and Development Strategy*. Cheltenham: Edward Elgar. 23–29.

Ernest and Young (EY, 2017). "EY's Attractiveness Programme for Africa." May 2017. Available at: https://webforms.ey.com/Publication/vwLUAssets/ey-attractiveness-program-africa-2017-connectivity-redefined/$FILE/ey-attractiveness-program-africa-2017-connectivity-redefined.pdf. Accessed 22.05.2018.

Feizhou, Z. and Camille, B. (2009). "Land Reform Throughout the 20th Century in China," in H. Binswanger-Mkhize, C. Bourguignon and R. van den Brink (eds.), *Agricultural Land Redistribution: Towards a Greater Consensus*. Washington, DC: World Bank. 119–136.

Felipe, J., Mehta, A. and Rhee, C. (2017). "Manufacturing Matters…But It's the Jobs that Counts." Asian Development Bank Paper Series, No. 420.

Filmer and Fox (2014). *Overview: Youth Employment in Sub-Saharan Africa*. Washington, DC: World Bank.

Fox, L., Haines, C., Huerta-Munoz, J. and Thomas, A. (2013). "Africa's Got Work to Do: Employment Prospect in the New Century." International Monetary Fund (IMF) Working Paper 13/201.

Fox, L. and Thomas, A. (2016). "Africa's Got Work to Do: A Diagnostic of Youth Employment Challenges in Sub-Saharan Africa." *Journal of African Economies*, Vol. 25, No. 1. 16–36.

Gelb, A., Meyer, C. and Ramachandran, V. (2014). "Does Poor Mean Cheap? A Comparative Look at Africa's Industrial Labour Costs." Centre for Global Development (CGD) Working Paper No. 325. Washington, DC: CGD.

Hausmann, R., Hwang, J. and Rodrik, D. (2007). "What You Export Matters." *Journal of Economic Growth*, Vol. 12, No. 1.

Hirschman, O. A. (1958). *The Strategy of Economic Development*. New Haven: Yale University Press.

Hirschman, O. A. (1984). "A Dissenter's Confession: 'The Strategy of Economic Development' Revisited," in G. M. Meier and D. Seers (eds.), *Pioneers in Development*. New York/London: Oxford University Press. 87–111.

International Labour Organisation (ILO, 2017). *World Employment Social Outlook: Trends 2017*. Geneva: ILO.

International Labour Organisation (ILO 2018). Labour Productivity: ILO Modelled Estimates (ILOstat) available at http://www.ilo.org/ilostat/faces/oracle/webcenter/portalapp/pagehierarchy/Page3.jspx?MBI_ID=49 accessed 18/10/2018.

Jacks, D. (2013). "From Boom to Bust: A Typology of Real Commodity Prices in the Long Run." National Bureau of Economic Research (NBER) Working Paper No. 18874. Available at: http://www.nber.org/papers/w18874. Accessed 21.03.2016.

Jones, C. and Williams, J. (1998). "Measuring the Social Returns to R & D." *Quarterly Journal of Economics*, Vol. 110. 1127–1170.

Kaldor, N. (1957). "A Model of Economic Growth." *Economic Journal*, Vol. 67, No. 268. 591–624.

Kaldor, N. (1966). Causes of the Slow Rate of Growth in the United Kingdom. Cambridge: Cambridge University Press.

Kay, C. (2002). "Why East Asia Overtook Latin America: Agrarian Reform, Industrialisation and Development." *Third World Quarterly*, Vol. 23, No. 6. 1073–1102.

Killich, T. (1980). "Trends in Development Economics and their Relevance to Africa." *Journal of Modern African Studies*, Vol. 18, No. 3. 367–386.

Krugman, P. (1981). "Trade, Accumulation and Uneven Development." *Journal of Economics*, Vol. 8. 149–161.

Krishna, K. and Perez, C. (2005). "Unbalanced Growth." *Canadian Journal of Economics*, Vol. 38, No. 3. 832–851.

Krugman, Paul (1987). "The Narrow Moving Band, the Dutch Disease, and the Competitive Consequences of Mrs. Thatcher." *Journal of Economics*, Vol. 27, No. 1–2. 41–55.

Kuznets, S. (1955). "Economic Growth and Income Inequality." *American Economic Review*, Vol. 45, No. 1. 1–28.

Kuznets, S. (1966). *Modern Economic Growth: Rate Structure and Spread*. New Haven: Yale University Press.

Lall, S. (2004). "Selective Industrial and Trade Policies in Developing Countries: Theoretical and Empirical Issues," in C. Soludo, O. Ogbu and H. Chang (eds.), *The Politics of Trade and Industrial Policy in Africa*. Trenton/Asmara: Africa World Press Inc. 75–110.

Lall, S. and Kraemer-Mbula, E. (2005). "Is African Industry Competing?" Queen Elizabeth House (QEH) Working Paper No. 122. Oxford University, London.

Lewis, W. A. (1954). "Economic Development with Unlimited Supplies of Labour," *Manchester School*, Vol. 20, 139–191.

Lin, J. and Chang, H. (2009). "Should Industrial Policy in Developing Countries Conform to Comparative Advantage or Defy it? A Debate Between Justin Lin and Ha-Joon Chang." *Development Policy Review*, Vol. 27, No. 5. 483–502.

Lucas, R. (1988). "On the Mechanics of Economic Development." *Journal of Monetary Economics*, Vol. 22, No. 1. 3–42.

Manyika, J., Sinclair, J., Dobbs, R., Kassey, L., Mischke, J., Roxburgh, C., George, K., O'Halloran, D. and Ramaswamy, S. (2012). *Manufacturing the Future: The Next Era of Global Growth and Innovation*. Washington, DC: McKinsey Global Institute.

McMillan, M. and Rodrik, D. (2011). "Globalisation, Structural Change and Productivity Growth." National Bureau of Economic Research (NBER) Working Paper No. 17143.

Mhone, G. (2001). "Enclavity and Constrained Labour Absorptive Capacity in Southern African Economies." A paper prepared for the discussion at the UNRISD on The Need to Rethinking Development Economics, September 7–8, 2001, Cape Town South Africa.

Mundle, S. (1985). "The Agrarian Barrier to Industrial Growth." *Journal of Development Studies*, Vol. 22, No.1. 49–80.

Murphy, K., Shleifer, A. and Vishny, R. (1989). "Industrialisation and the Big Push." *Journal of Political Economy*, Vol. 97, No. 5. 1003–1026.

Naude, W. (2010). "New Challenges for Industrial Policy." United Nations University (UNU)/World Institute for Development Economic Research (WIDER), Working Paper No. 2010/107.

New Partnership for African Development (NEPAD, 2014). *Agriculture in Africa: Transformation and Outlook*. Johannesburg: NEPAD.

Newman, C., Page, J., Rand, J., Shimeles, A., Soderbom, M. and Tap, F. (2016a). "The Pursuit of Industry: Policies and Outcomes," in C. Newman, J. Page, J. Rand, A. Shimeles, M. Soderbom and F. Tap (eds.), *Manufacturing Transformation: Comparative Studies in Industrial Development in Africa and Emerging Asia*. London: Oxford University Press. 1–24.

Newman, C., Page, J., Rand, J., Shimeles, A., Soderbom, M. and Tarp, F. (2016b). *Made in Africa: Learning to Compete in Industry*. Washington, DC: Brooking Institute Press.

Nurkse, R. (1953). *Problems of Capital Formation in Underdeveloped Countries*. London: Basil Blackwell.

Oqubay, A. (2015). *Made in Africa: Industrial Policy in Ethiopia*. London: Oxford University Press.

Page, J. (2014). "Industrial Policy in Practice: Africa's Presidential Investors' Advisory Councils." WIDER Working Paper No. 2014/117.

Page, J. (2015). "Structural Change and Africa's Poverty Puzzle," in L. Chandy, H. Kato and H. Kharas (eds.), *The Last Mile in Ending Extreme Poverty*. New York: Brooklyn Institute Press. 219–248.

Piketty, T. (2015). *Capital in the 21st Century*. Cambridge: Belknap Press of Harvard University Press.

Pingali, P. (1997). "From Subsistence to Commercial Production Systems: The Transformation of Asian Agriculture." *American Journal of Agricultural Economics*, Vol. 17, No. 2. 628–634.

Polanyi, K. (1944). *The Great Transformation: The Political and Economic Origins of Our Times*. Boston: Beacon Press.

Prebisch, R. (1950). *The Economic Development of Latin America and Its Principle Problems*. New York: United Nations Economic Commission for Latin America and Caribbean.

Rebelo, S. (1991). "Long-Run Policy Analysis and Long-Run Growth." *Journal of Political Economy*, Vol. 99, No. 3. 500–521.

Redding, S. (1999). "Dynamic Comparative Advantage and the Welfare Effects of Trade." *Oxford Economic Papers*, Vol. 51. 15–39.

Rodrik, D. (2013). "Unconditional Convergence in Manufacturing." *Quarterly Journal of Economics*, Vol. 128, No. 1. 165–204.

Rodrik, D. (2015). "Premature Deindustrialisation." National Bureau of Economic Research (NBER) Working Paper No.20935. Available at: http://www.nber.org/papers/w20935. Accessed 16.09.2017.

Romer, P. (1986). "Increasing Returns and Long-Run Growth." *Journal of Political Economy*, Vol. 94, No. 5. 1002–1037.

Rosenstein-Rodan, N. P. (1943). "Problems of Industrialisation of Eastern and South-Eastern Europe." *Economic Journal*, Vol. 53, No. 210/211. 202–211.

Rosenstein-Rodan, N. P. (1957). "Notes on the Theory of the Big Push." Economic Development Programme Project C/57–25. Centre for International Studies. Cambridge: Massachusetts Institute of Technology.

Scitovsky, T. (1954). "Two Concepts of External Economies." *Journal of Political Economy*, Vol. 62, No. 2. 143–151.

Singer, W. H. (1950). "The Distribution of Gains Between Investing and Borrowing Countries." *American Economic Review*, Vol. 40, No. 2. 473–485.

Singer, W. H. (1984). "The Terms of Trade Controversy and the Evolution of Soft Financing: Early Years in the UN," in G. Meier (ed.), *Pioneers in Development*. New York: World Bank. 273–301.

Solow, M. R. (1956). "A Contribution to the Theory of Economic Growth." *Quarterly Journal of Economics*, Vol. 70, No. 1. 65–94.

Soludo, C. and Ogbu, O. (2004). "A Synthesis of Major Themes in the Political Economy of Trade and Industrialisation in Africa," in C. Soludo, O. Ogbu and H. Chang (eds.), *The Politics of Trade and Industrial Policy in Africa*. Trenton/Asmara: Africa World Press Inc. 1–42.

Streeten, P. (1959). "Unbalanced Growth." *Oxford Economic Papers*, Vol. 11, No. 2. 167–190.

Syrquin, M. and Chenery, H. B. (1989). "Three Decades of Industrialisation." *World Bank Economic Review*, Vol. 3, No. 2. 145–181.

The Economist Intelligent Unit (EIU, 2018). *Who is Ready for the Coming Wave of Automation? The Automation Readiness Index*. London: EIU.

Timmer, M., de Vries, G. and de Vries, K. (2014). Patterns of Structural Change in Developing Countries. Groningen Growth and Development Centre (GGDC) Working Paper No. 149.

Timmer, P., McMillan, M., Badiane, O., Rodrik, D., Binswanger-Mkhize, H. and Wouterse, F. (2012). "Patterns of Growth and Structural Transformation in Africa: Trends and Lessons for Future Development Strategies." International Food Policy Research Institute (IFPRI) Thematic Research Note 02. West Africa Office.

Tregenna, F. (2009). "Characterising De-industrialisation: An Analysis of Changes in Manufacturing Employment and Output Internationally." *Cambridge Journal of Economics*, Vol. 33, No.4. 433–466.

Tregenna, F. (2015). "Deindustrialisation, Structural Change and Sustainable Economic Growth. UNIDO Research, Statistics and Industrial Policy Branch Working Paper No. 2/2015. Vienna: UNIDO.

United Nations Economic commission for Africa (UNECA, 2012). *Economic Report on Africa 2012: Unleashing Africa's Potential as a Global Growth Pole*. Addis Ababa: UNECA.

United Nations Economic commission for Africa (UNECA, 2014). *Report on Africa 2014: Dynamic Industrial Policy in Africa—Innovative Institutions, Effective Processes and Flexible Mechanisms*. Addis Ababa: UNECA.

United Nations Economic Commission for Africa (UNECA, 2016a). Transformative Industrial Policy for Africa. Addis Ababa: Economic Commission for Africa.

United Nations Economic commission for Africa (UNECA, 2016b). *Economic Report on Africa 2016: Greening Africa's Industrialisation*. Addis Ababa: UNECA.

United Nations Industrial Development Organisation (1980). World Industry Since 1960: Progress and Prospects. Vienna: UNIDO.

United Nations Industrial Development Organisation (UNIDO, 2016). *Industrialisation in Africa and Least Developed Countries: Booting Growth, Creating Jobs, Promoting Inclusiveness and Sustainability*. Vienna: UNIDO.

Wade, R. (1990). *Economic Theory and the Role of Government in East Asian Industrialisation*. Princeton: Princeton University Press.

World Economic Forum (WEF, 2017). *The Future of Jobs and Skills in Africa: Preparing the Region for the Fourth Industrial Revolution*. Geneva: WEF.

Yeboah, K. Felix and Thomas, J. S. (2017). "Africa's Evolving Employment Trends: Implications for Economic Transformation." *Africa Growth Institute*, Vol. 14, No. 1. 18–22. 1–25.

Young, A. A. (1928). "Increasing Returns and Economic Growth." *The Economic Journal*, Vol. 38, No. 152. 527–542.

Young, A. (1991). "Learning by Doing and the Dynamic Effects of International Trade." National Bureau of Economic Research (NBER) Working Paper No. 3577.

· 3 ·

INDUSTRIAL DEVELOPMENT IN AFRICA

An Overview

Introduction: Industrial Development Trends in Africa

Analysis of various indicators of industrial development suggests that, except for a small number of countries (South Africa, Mauritius, Egypt, Swaziland, Morocco and Tunisia), industrialisation has been elusive on the African continent. Although significant progress towards industrialising the continent was made during the first two decades of independence in several countries, the levels of industrial development were relatively low even in countries that had a relatively strong and broad industrial base. In this regard, talk of de-industrialisation in Africa (Jalilian and Weiss, 2000) is misleading given that modern industrial development on the continent has not materialised to any significant level. There is now wide agreement among analysts that industrialisation in Africa has been and continues to be weak, and this has contributed to the poor economic development outcomes such as low income levels, persisting high rates of poverty, rising inequality and low levels of productive and wage employment (see Page, 2015; UNECA, 2016b; WEF, 2017).

One of the basic indicators of weak industrialisation in Africa is the prevalence of informal employment (mainly self-employed and family non-wage work) which averages 80 percent of total employment and 90 percent of new jobs being created (see ILO, 2016:33). In most countries, 3 out of 4 jobs are in informal employment, with the ratio of informal employment share rising to 84 percent in Zambia, 86 percent in Zimbabwe, 89 percent in Tanzania and 94 percent in Uganda, just to mention a few examples (ibid). It is therefore not surprising that majority of workers in Africa earn below the international poverty line of US$1.90 per capita per day, with 66 percent of workers in Malawi, 70 percent in Zimbabwe, 77 percent in Burundi, 78 percent in Madagascar, 73 percent in the DRC, 68 in Mozambique and 69 percent in Liberia earning below this threshold in 2015 (UNDP, 2016). In countries where significant levels of industrial development have been realised, manifested by a vibrant manufacturing sector, informal employment and the proportion of working poor are significantly lower than in countries with extremely low levels of industrial development (ILO, 2017). As noted in Chapter 2, industrial development is a good predictor of other measures of development. Countries or regions where significant levels of industrialisation have occurred, whether during the 18th, 19th or 20th centuries, are marked by high levels of formal employment and significantly higher average income in the population (see Murphy et al, 1989).

Low levels of industrial development in Africa are also visible from many other aspects including heavy dependence on a narrow band of commodities for export, slow economic structural transformation, low standards of living and heavy dependence on low technology. In a document outlining the action plan to accelerate industrial development in Africa, the African Union (AU, 2007) attributes the existence of high levels of poverty to the poor performance of the manufacturing sector in particular. As highlighted in Chapter 2, manufacturing is widely seen as the engine of growth in the process of economic growth and development, and the share of manufacturing in total output (Manufacturing Value Added, MVA) and in employment are widely used as indicators of a country's or region's level of industrial development (see UNIDO,1980; 2016b; Tregenna, 2016). Figures on some of these indicators are presented in this chapter to assess the status and trends in the level of industrial development on the continent.

The chapter provides an overview of industrial development in Africa as a context in which the discussion on industrialising Africa should be situated. Focus in this chapter is on manufacturing, and how this relates to the dynamics in other sectors over time. Statistical indicators of industrial development from MVA, share of manufactures in total output, employment and export,

MVA per capita, and recent trends in industrial production are presented to illustrate the point that industrialisation is still a huge challenge in Africa at the moment. One of the worrying trends emerging from the analysis of the available data is that the industrialisation momentum seems to have weakened even at the time when most countries on the continent experienced decent growth. This weakening of industrial performance over the last decade and half is more evident even in countries which have traditionally had stronger industrial profiles such as South Africa, Mauritius, Namibia, Swaziland, Egypt and Morocco.

The Data Sources and Challenges

It is important to note, at the beginning, the challenge of data in this exercise. Although the availability and quality of data in many African countries has improved significantly (Young, 2012), there are still many challenges, especially with manufacturing and labour data (Fox and Thomas, 2016). Many analysts who have attempted to analyse industrial development trends in Africa acknowledge the challenge regarding data, mainly when it comes to consistency in the data reported over time.[1] For example, in a paper assessing structural transformation in Africa, de Vries et al (2015), using data from World Bank's *Word Development Indicator* (WDIs),[2] find huge discrepancies in the data on employment. A similar concern was raised by Fox and Thomas (2016), Filmer and Fox (2014), and Tregenna (2009).

Data on employment and poverty are particularly problematic not only because different countries conduct their surveys in different years, but also because of the inconsistencies between surveys, which give rise to not only large errors in the data reported between surveys, but also issues of comparability across surveys within the same country. De Vries et al (2015:675) give an example of agriculture employment figures in Ethiopia reported to be at 22 million in 1994 but dropped to only 3 million in 2004! Tribe (2000:81) finds similar discrepancies in his review of manufacturing data on 35 sub-Saharan Africa countries. He gives the example of Mauritius, where it is reported that the share of manufacturing in total export rose from 27 percent in 1980 to 90 percent in 1993; such big jumps do raise suspicion about the credibility of the data. When analysing employment trends in Zambia Chitonge (2016) finds similar discrepancies in the figures on formal employment for manufacturing and services sectors between the 2005 and 2012 labour force surveys.

It is also important to acknowledge that the data constraint is not only unique to Africa as some critics often imply; the problem with data quality affects many parts of the world (see Srinivasan, 1994; Tregenna, 2009), though the challenges faced in Africa might be of a different nature. Hence, the common disclaimer that the data presented here must be cautiously interpreted, applies. Having said that, there is no doubt that despite gaps in the data that we have, the challenges regarding industrial development in Africa overall are evidently clear.

Data presented in this and the following chapters are drawn from different sources, but mainly from the World Bank's World Development Indicators (WDIs) online databank, the African Statistical Year Book (ASYB), the International Labour Organization (ILO) online database, the United Nations Industrial Development Organization (UNIDO) database, and the Human Development Index (HDI) data by the United Nations Development Programme (UNDP). The reason for using these different sources of data is mainly that there is no single source of data that covers all the different aspects of industrial development in Africa. Combining information from these different sources gives a clearer picture of the status of and trends in industrial development in Africa.

Africa in this book refers to the whole continent, including North Africa which is usually reported under a different region, either under the North Africa and Middle East or simply Arab States. The politics of the unity of the continent is discussed in Chitonge (2015) and interested readers can consult that text. Here Africa refers to the 54 countries which form the African union.[3] The ASYB has been reporting data on 54 African countries and provides the average not only for sub-Saharan Africa, but for the whole continent. In most cases, the average for the continent is not weighted mainly because the original data did not weight the mean by relevant measures.

Overall the data presented in this chapter highlight not only the differences, but also the similarities between countries in terms of the different aspects of industrial development. When closely analysing the state of industrial development on the African continent, there are surprising similarities between countries. For example, MVA per capita values for resource-rich (RR) and non-resource-rich (NRR) countries are surprisingly similar (see Table 3.3).[4]

Industrial Performance in Africa

Although majority of countries on the continent manifest weak industrial development, a close analysis shows that different countries are at different levels of industrial development. There are a few countries where the industry sector constitutes a significant sector in the economy, but in most countries the industrial sector is relatively small and weak. If we look at industrial share in output (GDP), we find a significant difference between the resource rich (RR) and the non-resource rich (NRR) countries. As illustrated in Table 3.2, industrial share in total output is on average 8.7 percentage points higher in RR countries than in NRR countries. Among RR countries, 10 countries reported industrial share in total output of over one-third in 2015. In the case of the NRR countries, only three countries (Egypt, Uganda, Swaziland) reported industrial share in total output of over 35 percent in 2015 (see Table 3.2).

One possible explanation for the higher industrial share in total output among RR countries is that industrial activities in this group are boosted by the processing of natural resources. The abundance of natural resources in RR countries tend to enlarge the industrial sector as natural resources are often partially processed (for example sorting, grading of coffee or cocoa beans or the smelting of mineral ores) before being exported. For this reason, industry-to-GDP ratio is not a good measure of industrialisation. A good indicator of industrialisation is manufacturing-to-GDP ratio, and if we use this indictor, we see that there are only a few countries with MVA above 10 percent (see Table 3.3). When we look at this indicator, it becomes evident that most countries on the continent face similar challenges, with relatively low levels of manufacturing across economies. Even in countries such as South Africa, Mauritius, Kenya, Cote d'Ivoire, Cameroon, Egypt and Tunisia which are traditionally known to have a well-developed industrial sector including manufacturing, their ratios are far from the average of industrialised countries or emerging economies.

Although there seem to be a positive correlation between the MVA per capita and the GDP per capita as Figure 3.1 shows, the correlation is weaker except for NRR countries where the correlation is stronger[5] (Figure 3.1).

Figure 3.1: MVA per Capita and GDP per Capita by Country Resource Status, 2015.

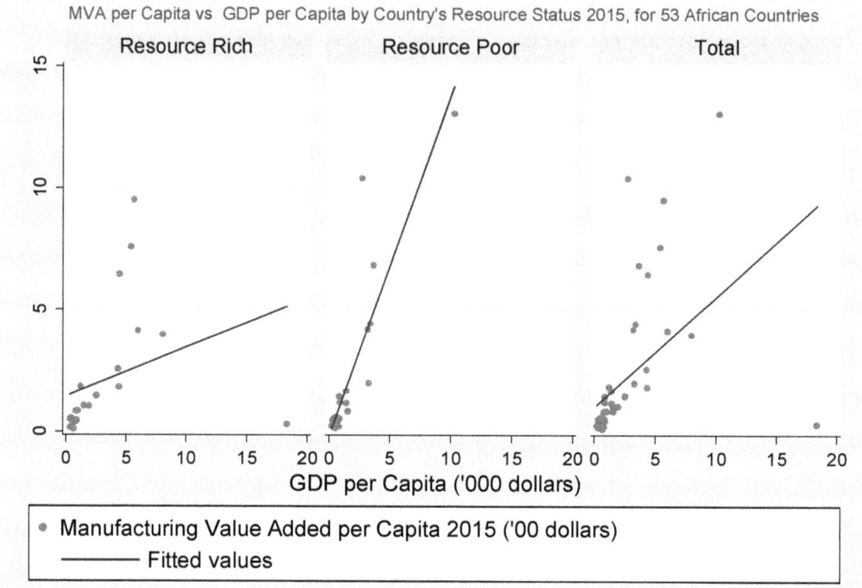

Source: Author. Based on data from the African Statistical Year Book (ASYB, 2017)and UNIDO (2016b).

The stronger correlation between MVA and GDP per capita observed among NRR countries can be attributed to the fact that industrial activities in these countries are concentrated in the manufacturing sector, while in the RR countries the activities are boosted by production of natural resources which do not fall under manufacturing. It is commonly believed that countries which rely on natural resources often have little incentive to develop manufacturing sector because they enjoy high rents from extractive industries. The reason for this is that a "relative abundance of natural resources tends to shift emphasis away from manufacturing to the primary [extractive]sector since the resource costs of exporting primary products is less" (UNIDO, 1980:48). This is why although the industrial share in total output is significantly higher in RR than in NRR countries (see Table 3.3), the MVA gap between the two sets of countries is smaller. The reason for this is that "countries with modest [natural] resources have little choice but to emphasise industry at the outset of their development process" (ibid).

Overall, we see in Figure 3.2, there is a positive correlation between MVA per capita and GDP per capita, though the correlation is weak and the levels of MVA per capita in most African countries are very low, with only a handful of countries having MVA per capita of over US$500 in 2015 (Figure 3.2).

Figure 3.2: MVA per Capita and GDP per Capita by Country, 2015.

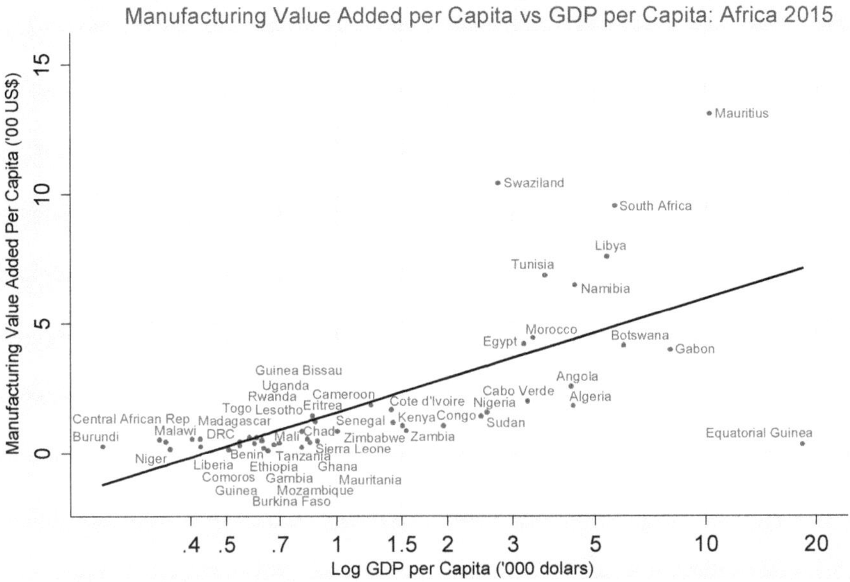

Source: Author. Based on data from the African Statistical Year Book (ASYB, 2017).

The overall picture emerging out of this is that industrial development on the continent is still generally weak, characterised by low levels of manufacturing share in both GDP and employment. The African Union (AU, 2007: 1) captures the industrial performance of African countries well when it observes that,

> Africa is the least developed region of the world in terms of industrialisation. It accounts for a negligible share of global industrial output and manufactured exports. Only in few of the countries is the manufacturing value added /GDP ratio above 20 percent. In a large number of African countries, the manufacturing sector's contribution to GDP is less than 15 percent and in some cases lower than 5 percent. The output of the sector is heavily concentrated on low technology products such as food, textiles, clothing, footwear, etc. The majority of African countries are yet to be involved in any significant sense in the medium-and high-technology segments of global manufacturing that have been characterized by dynamism and rapid growth in recent years. The African economy is heavily dependent on the production and export of primary products and consequently suffer from the associated risks of this dependence.

In fact, as shown in Figure 3.3, only Swaziland reported a manufacturing-to-GDP ratio of over 20 percent in 2015. The average for lower-middle and upper-middle income countries was just over 10 percent in 2015, while the average for lower income countries was less than 10 percent (Figure 3.3). The rest of the countries have had MVA of less than 10 percent since 2000 (see Figure 3.3).

Figure 3.3: Trends in the Share of Manufacturing Value Added in Total Output by Income Status, 2000–2014.

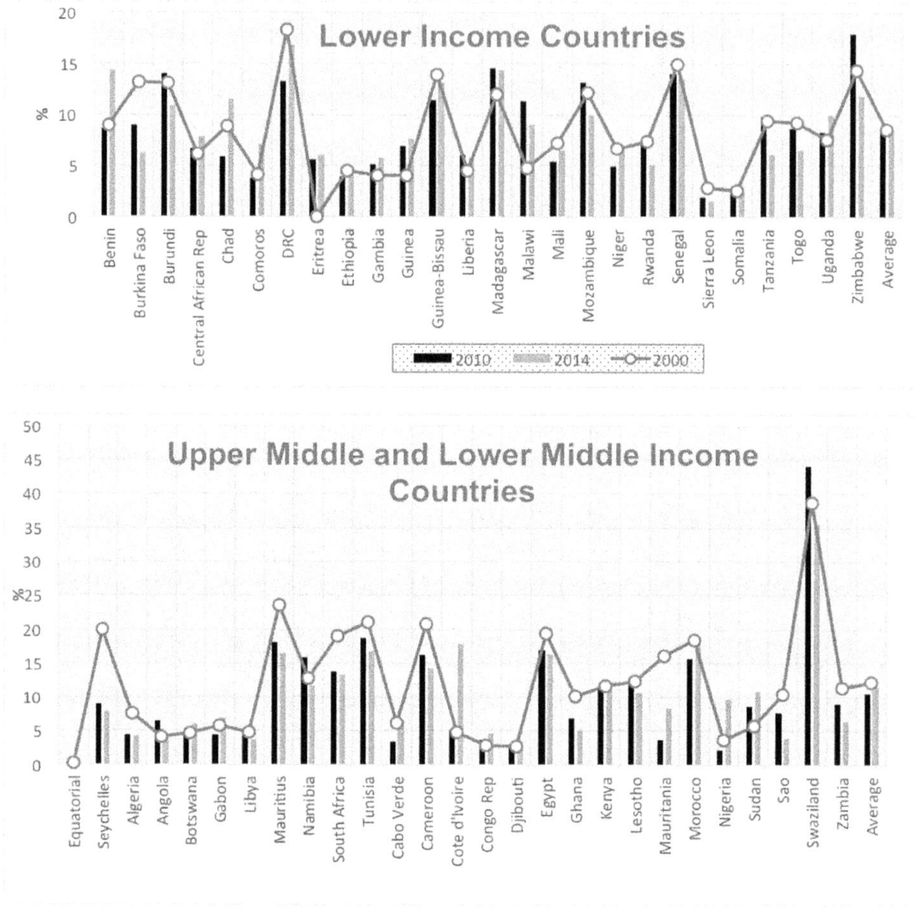

Source: Author. Based on data from the African Statistical Year Book (ASYB), various years and World Development Indicators.

The challenges of industrial development in Africa should be quite evident from the data presented above. While the summary by the African Union, cited above, was made more than 12 years ago, the picture has not changed much, with industrial development indicators in a number of countries stagnating while in others declining. Although several countries reported growth of MVA between 2000 and 2015, many countries experienced declining manufacturing share in total output, particularly in RR countries (see Table 3.3).

Given that most countries in Africa experienced stronger growth between 2000 and 2015, it is essential to look at how this growth has impacted on the industrial sector, particularly manufacturing. Such an exercise would not only provide some insight about the structural challenges facing African countries but also useful information for formulating policy interventions required to address the challenges. In this regard, it is essential to understand the nature and scope of the challenge before one can begin to think of ways to respond.

We see a similar picture of weak industrial development emerging when we look at the share of manufacturing in total employment. Apart from a few countries (Congo, Swaziland, Senegal, Egypt, Mauritius and Tunisia) which reported manufacturing share in total employment of above 10 percent, the rest of the countries have less than 10 percent, with almost half of the countries reporting less than 5 percent (see Figure 3.4)

Figure 3.4: Trends in Manufacturing Share in Total Employment by Resource Status, 2000–2013.

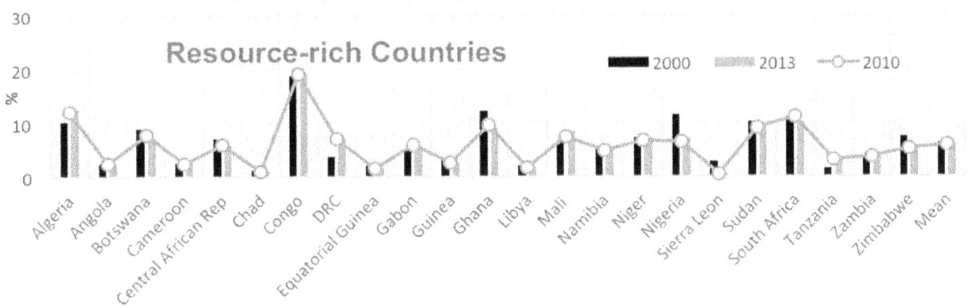

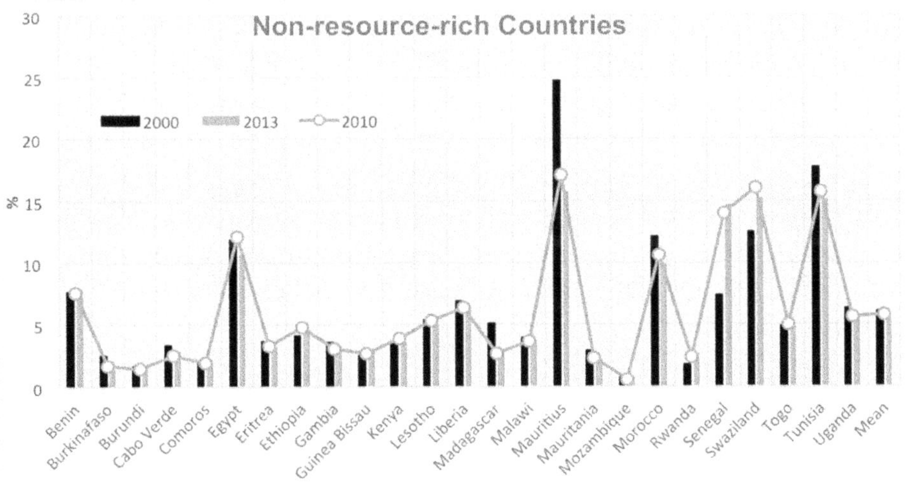

Source: Author. Based on data from the African Statistical Year Book (ASYB), various years and World Development Indicators.

In terms of manufacturing employment, there is actually little difference between the RR and NRR countries. The average for the two groups is almost the same.

The Broader African Development Context

To put the industrial development indicators presented above into context, it is essential to look at the broader development context of countries in Africa. In the World Bank classification of countries, a country's level of development is determined by its GDP per capita. Classifications that combine several indicators (e.g., the UNDP's HDI)[6] produce a slightly different ranking of countries as shown in Table 3.1. For example, Angola, which is classified as an upper middle-income country under the World Bank classification system is classified as a low human development country under the HDI system. On the other hand, Kenya, which is classified as a low-income country under the World Bank classification, is classified as a medium human development country. There are many other countries like South Sudan which on the basis of GDP per capita is classified as lower middle income, but under the HDI classification, it falls under the lower human development category.

Under the World Bank classification, countries are divided into four categories based on the level of income per capita. *Upper Income Countries* are countries with GDP per capita (in 2011 US dollars) of more than US$12,476; while *upper middle-income countries* are countries with GDP per capita of between US$4,036 and 12,475; *lower-middle income* countries are countries with GDP per capita between US$1,026 to 4,035; and the lower income countries are countries with GDP per capita of less than US$1,025. According to this classification, two African countries (Equatorial Guinea (with GDP per capita of US$12,820) and Seychelles (US$14,680)) fell in the upper income category in 2015.

Table 3.1: Country Classification by Income Group and HDI, 2016.*

	Lower Income Countries					Upper & Lower Middle Income Countries			
	Population (Millions)	Surface Area (km² '000)	GDP per Capita (USD)	HDI Classification		Population (Millions)	Surface Area (km² 000)	GDP per Capita (USD)	HDI Classification
Benin	10.9	114.8	840	Low			**Upper Middle Income**		
Burkina Faso	18.1	274.2	640	Low	Algeria	39.7	2,381.7	4,850	High
Burundi	11.2	27.8	260	Low	Angola	25	1,246.7	4,180	Low
C. African Rep.	4.9	623	330	Low	Botswana	2.3	581.7	6,460	Medium
Chad	14	1284	880	Low	Gabon	1.7	267.7	9,200	Medium
Comoros	0.8	1.9	780	Low	Libya	6.3	1,759.5	4,692	High
Dem. Repub. of Congo	77.3	2344.9	410	Low	Mauritius	1.3	2	9,780	High
Eritrea	5.2	117.6	891	Low	Namibia	2.5	824.3	5,190	Medium
Ethiopia	99.4	1104.3	590	Low	South Africa	55.4	1,219.1	6,080	Medium
Gambia	2	11.3	460	Low	**Mean†**	**16.1**	**938**	**6,040.2**	
Guinea	12.6	245.9	470	Low					
Guinea-Bissau	1.8	36.1	590	Low			**Lower Middle Income**		
Liberia	4.5	111.4	380	Low	Cabo Verde	0.5	4	3,280	Medium
Madagascar	24.2	587.3	420	Low	Cameroon	23.3	475.4	1,320	Low
Malawi	17.2	118.5	340	Low	Cote d'Ivoire	22.7	322.5	1,420	Low
Mali	17.6	1240.2	760	Low	Djibouti	0.9	23.2	1,945	Low
Mozambique	28	799.4	590	Low	Egypt	91.5	1,001.5	3,340	Medium
Niger	19.9	1267	390	Low	Ghana	27.4	238.5	1,480	Medium
Rwanda	11.6	26.3	700	Low	Kenya	46.1	580.4	1,340	Medium
Senegal	15.1	196.7	980	Low	Lesotho	2.1	30.4	1,280	Low
Sierra Leone	6.5	72.3	620	Low	Mauritania	4.1	1,030.7	1,370	Low
Somalia	10.8	637.7	…	…	Morocco	34.4	446.6	3,030	Medium
Tanzania	53.5	947.3	920	Low	Nigeria	182.2	923.8	2,790	Low
Togo	7.3	56.8	540	Low	Rep. of the Congo	4.6	342	2,540	Medium
Uganda	39	241.6	700	Low	São Tomé & Príncipe	0.2	1	1,760	Medium
Zimbabwe	15.6	390.8	860	Low	South Sudan	12.3	644.3	1,067	Low
Mean†	**15.6**	**390.8**	**860**		Sudan	40.2	1,879.4	1,920	Low
					Swaziland	1.3	17.4	3,280	Low
	High Income Countries				Tunisia	11.3	163.6	3,930	High
Equatorial. Guinea	0.8	28.1	12,820	Medium	Zambia	16.2	752.6	1,490	Medium
Seychelles	0.1	0.5	14,680	High	**Mean†**	**30.0**	**512.6**	**2 038.4**	

Source: Author. Based on data from the 2017 African Statistical Year Book (ASYB) and 2017 Human Development Report (UNDP, 2017).

*Ellipses indicate missing data. †Mean is unweighted.

Table 3.1 divides countries into four groups, upper-middle, upper lower-middle, lower-middle, and lower income countries. In GDP per capita terms, there are significant differences between these four groups of countries, with the GDP per capita for the lower income countries being only a third of the upper lower-middle income countries and only a seventh of the upper-middle income countries.

Apart from the 2 upper income countries, 9 countries were classified as upper-middle income countries in 2015, 17 lower-middle income countries and 26 low income countries. It is interesting to note that all countries which were classified as low-income countries (with GDP per capita less than US$1025) are all categorised as low human development countries under the HDI system. This may be a reflection of the heavy weighting given to income in the construction of the HDI.

Trends in the Industrial Sector

If we look at the share of industry in total output for 2015, it is apparent that the figures for most countries are within the global average for developing countries which was around 30 percent in 2015 (see UNIDO, 2016b). Only smaller countries such as Sierra Leone, Comoros, Gambia, Liberia, Sao Tome and Principe, Djibouti and Cabo Verde reported industrial share in total output below the global average for developing countries. As noted earlier, the share of industry in total output is also quite low for NRR countries such as Ethiopia, Madagascar, Malawi, Rwanda, Burundi, Burkina Faso and in the two countries experiencing prolonged internal conflict—Somalia and Central African Republic.

The average industry-to-GDP ratio for all the 54 countries on the continent was estimated at around 29 percent in 2015, representing an 11 percentage point decline from 40 percent in 2008. Declining share of industry in GDP should be a big concern because it reflects the relative slowdown in industrial activities at the time when the continent's GDP grew at an average of 4.2 percent per year over the same period.

Table 3.2: Industrial Sector's Share in Total Output Trends (%), 1980–2015.*

	Resource-rich Countries						Non-resource-rich Countries				
	1980	1990	2000	2010	2015		1980	1990	2000	2010	2015
Algeria†	57.7	48.2	58.1	62.1	38.9	Benin	12.3	13.2	14.2	13.7	25
Angola	...‡	40.9	72.1	59.9	43.4	Burkina Faso	20.5	21	15.7	25.4	20.2

	Resource-rich Countries						Non-resource-rich Countries				
	1980	1990	2000	2010	2015		1980	1990	2000	2010	2015
Botswana	50.7	61	54.5	45	33.1	Cabo Verde	17	21.4	17.4	18	20.5
Cameroon	25.6	29.5	36	30.3	28.5	Comoros	13.2	8.3	11.7	11.4	10.8
C. African Repub.	20.1	19.7	14.7	20.2	15.1	Cote d'Ivoire	19.7	23.2	20.3	27.2	31.7
Chad	8.9	17.7	11.7	13.7	56.1	Egypt	36.8	28.7	33.5	37.5	36.2
Democ. Repub. of Congo	35	29	23.4	23.2	42	Ethiopia	...	11.1	12.4	14.3	17.7
Equa. Guinea	...	10.6	87.7	92.5	60.1	Gambia	14.9	13.1	9.2	12.3	15.8
Gabon	60.4	43	60.4	59.4	52.8	Kenya	20.9	19	17.5	19.8	19.5
Ghana	12.3	16.9	28.4	18.6	27.6	Lesotho	26.5	34.4	28.5	31.9	32
Guinea	...	33.3	35.5	47.2	28.9	Mada-gascar	16.1	12.8	15.6	12.2	18.6
Mali	13.2	15.9	21	17	19.8	Malawi	22.5	28.9	14.5	22.7	16.3
Namibia	55.8	38	28	19.6	31	Mauritius	26.2	32.8	31	27	21.7
Nigeria	49.7	30.3*	52.2	41.5	20.4	Maurita-nia	26	28.8	36.9	43.9	28.6
Niger	22.5	16.2	17.8	16	19.9	Mozambi-que	34.4	18.4	24.5	23.4	21.6
Rep. of the Congo	46.6	40.6	73	75.4	42.5	Morocco	31	33.4	29.2	29.7	29.2
Sierra Leone	21.9	19.2	15.8	20.7	4.8	Rwanda	21.6	24.6	14.5	15	18.3
Sudan	...	15.3	17.2	33	39.1	Senegal	20.1	22.2	23.6	22.4	23.4
South Africa	48.4	40.1	31.8	30.8	29.2	Seychelles	2.5	15.6	16.3	31.2	21.5
Tanzania	...	17.7	19.2	25.5	26.4	Swaziland	8.4	30.2	43.2	44.1	46.5
Zambia	42.1	51.3	25.3	26.8	35.3	Togo	24.8	24.5	22.5	19.6	15.7
Zimbabwe	11.8	29	33.1	20.4	26.8	Uganda	4.5	11.1	22.7	25.5	35.3
						Tunisia	36	33.6	33	32.3	27.2
Average§	**34.3**	**28**	**37.1**	**36.3**	**32.8**	**Average§**	**20.7**	**22.2**	**22.1**	**24.4**	**24.1**

Source: Author. Based on data from the African Statistical Year Book (ASYB), various years and World Development Indicators.

* Countries with incomplete data are excluded.

†Algeria and Sudan, which were omitted in the IMF list of resource rich countries in 2010, are included here.

‡ Ellipses indicate missing data.

§Averages are unweighted.

It is interesting to note that countries with a large industrial share in total output are mainly RR countries like Algeria, Angola, Botswana, DRC, Equatorial Guinea, Gabon, Libya, Congo Republic and Zambia. Only a few NRR countries such as Swaziland, Cote d'Ivoire, Mauritania, Egypt and Lesotho reported industry-to-GDP ratio of above 30 percent in 2015 (see Table 3.2). The share of industry in total GDP in most RR countries is clearly boosted by the inclusion of mining and extraction of natural resources such as oil and natural gas in the industrial sector, most of which fall outside of manufacturing.

Mining, which in the ISIC 4-digit classification includes mining of coal, extraction of metal ores, crude petroleum, natural gas, and quarrying, has certainly contributed to the higher industrial share in GDP in RR countries like the DRC. If mining is excluded from the industrial sector in most RR countries, the industrial share in total output figures would be much lower as evident from the small share of manufacturing. It is also interesting to note the influence of mining, particularly petroleum, in the industrial sector of most of the countries with a high industry-to-GDP ratio. Majority of them including Algeria, Angola, Chad, Equatorial Guinea, Congo, Gabon, Libya, Nigeria and Sudan have recorded decline in industrial share in total output ranging from Algeria's 20 percentage point decline, between 2000 and 2015 to Angola's almost 30 percentage decline.

The sharp decline in the price of oil experienced in 2015 could account for much of this sharp drop in the industrial activities on the continent. Industrial figures after 2015 are likely to confirm this. Declines in industrial shares are also reported in non-oil-exporting countries such as South Africa, Lesotho, Namibia, Swaziland, Tunisia, Uganda, Mauritius and Kenya, but the range of decline among these countries is smaller. Few countries (Burkina Faso, Cote d'Ivoire, DRC, Ghana, Tanzania, Zambia and Zimbabwe) however reported an increase in the share of industry in the reference period. It is also evident that countries where industrial share in total GDP grew between 2000 and 2015 are largely RR countries dependent on metal ores (DRC, Tanzania, Zambia and Ghana) and agricultural commodities for Cote d'Ivoire and Burkina Faso.

If we look at the structure of industry in most African countries, it is apparent that most of them are engaged in the production of commodities with a few exceptions such as South Africa, Mauritius, Tunisia, Lesotho, Swaziland, Senegal and Namibia. The other components of the industrial sector are construction, water, electricity and gas, whose share in GDP, apart from construction, tends to be quite low ranging between 1.5 and 3 percent. Thus, it is usually the mining activities which push the industrial sector figures in most countries up, and it is important to bear this in mind when analysing the industry-to-GDP ratios in Africa.

Although mining is a high-productivity subsector (see Chapter 6), its role in industrialisation so far has been weak mainly because of its capital-intensive and enclave nature, with little connection to other sectors of the economy (McMillan and Rodrik, 2011; AEO, 2017). This is why when growth is driven by rising commodity prices, it has limited impact on other sector in terms of employment, income in the general population and economy-wide productivity. As noted earlier countries with abundant natural resources tend to focus on exploiting and exporting natural resources, and pay less attention to developing manufacturing capabilities, while countries with little natural resources have no choice but to engage in manufacturing activities of some sort.

Trends in the Manufacturing Sector

The manufacturing sector in most African countries has remained small, with little growth momentum over the past decade. Manufacturing share in GDP figures confirm the observation made earlier that industrialisation in general and manufacturing in particular has been elusive on the continent. If we look at the period from 2000 to 2014, only a handful of countries reported manufacturing share in total output of above or close to 15 percent; namely, Egypt, Swaziland, Morocco, Cameroon, Tunisia and Mauritius (see Figure 3.3 above). Over two-thirds of countries on the continent have manufacturing-to-GDP ratio of less than 10 percent, with several countries including Sierra Leone, Somalia, Equatorial Guinea, Congo Republic, Djibouti, Gambia, Ethiopia, Angola and Libya reporting manufacturing share in total output of less 5 percent in 2015 (see Table 3.3 below). In other words, manufacturing activities in most of these countries are only a tiny appendage of the economy.

If we look at middle income (lower and middle) and the lower income countries in Africa, there is a difference between these two groups of countries, with the former reporting 3 percentage points of MVA higher than the latter, on average (figure 3.3). Interestingly, most of the countries in the lower and middle-middle income country category are also RR countries, while majority of the countries in the lower income category are NRR countries. This seems contrary to the view that countries with abundant natural resources neglect to build their manufacturing sector because of the rents from extractive industries (see UNIDO, 1980; Sachs and Warner, 1997). This view, which is often referred to as the *resource curse* or *resource pessimism* is counter-intuitive in the sense that countries with abundant natural resources should use the available resources as the foundation for building strong and diverse manufacturing base.

Some analysts have, for instance, pointed to the development of manufacturing sector in the US, Norway and Australia which initially relied heavily on the exploitation of natural resources (Kaplan et al, 2011). There is no reason why African countries cannot utilize the diverse set of natural resources to build their manufacturing capabilities. Although manufacturing activities have remained low in most African countries, the explanation for this cannot be entirely attributed to the abundance of natural resources, but largely to the colonial economic logic and structures which have continued to dictate economic activities in Africa.

Current trends in the manufacturing sector in Africa are worrying because the sector seems to be losing steam if the figures we see between 2000 and 2015 in most countries are anything to go by. More than half of the countries reported declining manufacturing-to-GDP ratio, with significant declines in countries such as Mauritius, Cameroon, Seychelles, Algeria, Libya, Tunisia, Ghana and Zambia, where manufacturing has been relatively larger in the past (see Table 3.3). Only a few countries (Nigeria, Republic of Congo, Sudan, Cote d'Ivoire, Malawi, Guinea and Comoros) reported substantive increase in manufacturing share in total output between 2000 and 2017 (see also Figure 3.3 above).

Table 3.3: Manufacturing Share in GDP (%), 2000–2017.*

Upper and Lower Middle Income Countries					**Lower Income Countries**				
	2000	2010	2017	Change (%), 2000–2017		2000	2010	2017	Change (%), 2000–2017
Algeria	7.5	4.3	5	**-33.**	Benin	9	8.6	12	**33.3**
Angola	4.1	6.4	4.1†	**0.0**	Burkina Faso	13.2	9	6	**-54.5**
Botswana	4.7	4.2	5	**6.4**	Burundi	13.1	14	9	**-31.3**
Cabo Verde	6.1	3.4	8	**31.1**	C.. African Rep.	6.1	6.7	7	**14.8**
Cameroon	20.8	16.2	15	**-27.9**	Chad	8.9	5.9	3	**-66.3**
Cote d'Ivoire	4.8	5	13	**170.8**	Comoros	4.1	3.8	8	**95.1**

Upper and Lower Middle Income Countries					Lower Income Countries				
	2000	2010	2017	Change (%), 2000–2017		2000	2010	2017	Change (%), 2000–2017
Djibouti	2.7	2.4	4	**48.1**	Dem. Rep. of the Congo	18.3	13.3	20	**9.3**
Egypt	19.4	16.9	16	**-17.5**	Eritrea	...	5.6	5	**-10.7**
Equat. Guinea	0.2	0.2	0.1†	**-50**	Ethiopia	4.5	3.9	6	**33.3**
Gabon	5.8	4.3	3	**-48.3**	Gambia	4	5.1	5	**25.0**
Ghana	10.1	6.8	4	**-60.4**	Guinea	4	7	11	**175.0**
Kenya	11.6	11.4	8	**-31**	Guinea-Bissau	13.9	11.4	11	**-20.9**
Lesotho	12.3	12.8	16	**30.1**	Liberia	4.5	6	3	**-33.3**
Libya	4.8	5	3.7†	**-22.9**	Madagascar	12	14.5	14.4*	**20.0**
Mauritania	16.1	3.7	6	**-62.7**	Malawi	4.8	11.3	9	**87.5**
Mauritius	23.5	18	16.5	**-29.8**	Mali	7.2	5.4	6.6*	**-8.3**
Morocco	18.4	15.7	16	**-13.**	Mozambique	12.2	13.2	9	**-26.2**
Namibia	12.8	15.8	11.6	**-9.4**	Niger	6.7	4.9	6	**-10.4**
Nigeria	3.7	2.2	9	**143.2**	Rwanda	7.4	7.2	6	**-18.9**
Rep. of the Congo	2.9	3.7	8	**175.9**	Senegal	14.9	14	11	**-26.2**
São Tomé and Príncipe	10.4	7.7	7	**-32.7**	Sierra Leone	2.8	1.9	2	**-28.6**
Seychelles	20	8.9	6	**-233.8**	Somalia	2.6	2.5	2.5*	**-3.8**
South Africa	19	13.8	12	**-36**	Tanzania	9.4	9.9	6	**-36.2**
Sudan	5.7	8.6	10.8	**89.5**	Togo	9.2	8.7	4	**-56.5**
Swaziland	38.7	44.1	31	**-19.9**	Uganda	7.6	8.3	8	**5.3**
Tunisia	21.1	18.7	15	**-0.47**	Zimbabwe	14.4	17.9	8	**-44.4**
Zambia	11.4	9.1	8	**-29.8**					
Average‡	**12.2**	**10.6**	**11.2**	**-7.8**	**Average‡**	**8.6**	**8.5**	**7.6**	**-11.1**

Source: Author. Based on data from the African Statistical Year Book (ASYB, various years) and the 2017 World Development Indicators (online database).

*Ellipses indicate missing data.

†2014 figures are used for countries missing 2017 data.

‡Averages are unweighted.

Unlike the broader industrial sector, the average share of manufacturing in total output for the region increased marginally from 10.3 to 11.2 percent between 2000 and 2017. While this is a positive development, the rate of increase is very low to suggest any meaningful turnaround of Africa's manufacturing fortunes (ACET, 2014). Moreover, the average figures for the region hide the disparities between countries.

When we look at individual countries, we can classify countries into four groups. One group reported very low MVA of less than 5 percent in 2017, and this group of countries include Algeria, Djibouti, Ethiopia, Libya, Somalia and Sierra Leone. Then we have another group with MVA of above 5, but less than 10 percent. This is the largest category with 27 countries including the RR countries such as Chad, Angola, Congo, Gabon, Nigeria, Tanzania and Zambia, and the NRR countries such as Malawi, Rwanda, Namibia, Seychelles, Togo and Uganda. The third group of countries had MVA ratio of above 10 percent, but below the regional average of 11.1 in 2014; they include Sudan, Zimbabwe, Lesotho, Mozambique and Burundi. Apart from Sudan and Zimbabwe which are RR countries, the rest of the countries are traditionally classified as NRR countries. The fourth group of countries is made of 16 countries with manufacturing share in total output of above the region's average. This group of countries has RR countries like Cameroon, South Africa, DRC and Equatorial Guinea, as well as NRR countries such as Cote d'Ivoire, Senegal, Swaziland, Mauritius, Morocco, Tunisia, Egypt and Guinea Bissau. The continent's MVA-to-GDP ratio of 11 percent was below the global average reported in 2014 at 16 percent, and far below the average for emerging economies at 24 percent (UNIDO, 2016b).

The overall picture that emerges from the available data is that the manufacturing sector in Africa has not significantly contributed to the growth reported over the last decade and half in most countries. This view is confirmed by the relatively low share of manufacturing in total output, when compared with other regions where MVA ratios are high (see Newman et al, 2016b). A recent study of industrial development on the continent drawing from eight cases studies of Africa countries summarises the overall trends in these words:

> By any measure [,] Africa's industrial sector is small relative to the average for the developing world as a whole. The share of manufacturing in GDP is less than one-half of the average for all developing countries, and in contrast with developing countries as a whole it is declining. Manufacturing output per capita is about 10 percent of the global developing country average. Per capita manufactured exports are slightly more than 10 percent of the developing country average, and the share of manufactured

exports in total exports is strikingly low. Moreover, these measures have changed little since the 1990s (Newman et al, 2016a:6).

We will come back to the long-term trends in manufacturing in the next chapter when we look at the performance of the industrial sector from the early 1960s. Here we focus on the current status of the industrial sector with emphasis on manufacturing.

Figures for 2017 confirm the observation made in the passage cited above that manufacturing share in total output is small and that in half of the countries (27 out of 54) it declined between 2000 and 2017, and in another 6 countries, it marginally changed (ether declining by less than 1 percentage point or remaining unchanged) over the same period. The share of manufacturing in GDP in all the countries in 2015 was less than 20 percent except for the Swazi Kingdom (Eswatini) which reported 34.7 percent. Countries like South Africa, Mauritius, Zimbabwe, Seychelles, Cote d'Ivoire, Lesotho and Namibia which are traditionally known to have a relatively developed manufacturing base are actually losing ground (see Table 3.3).

Significant decline in manufacturing share in total output was reported in a large number of countries including Seychelles, Equatorial Guinea, Algeria, Cameroon, Ghana, Mauritania, Sao Tome and Principe, Zambia, Sierra Leone, Tanzania and Burkina Faso, all reporting a drop of over 30 percent between 2000 and 2017. Mauritius also registered a huge drop of 29 percent. While one has to be cautious in labelling such drop in MVA as signs of de-industrialisation, falling manufacturing activities in low-income countries are a strong sign of the declining momentum in the sector. In the context of a rapidly growing labour force on the continent, declining activities in the manufacturing sector are a cause for great concern. As noted in Chapter 2, a growing manufacturing sector is known to provide the opportunity for developing countries to raise income and productivity in the population through the expansion of productive jobs. Falling manufacturing activities on the continent should therefore be seen as a disappointing outcome in terms of job creation.

However, there are several countries that recorded a rise in the share of manufacturing in total output including Cote d'Ivoire, Botswana, Malawi, Sudan, Congo Republic and Nigeria. The largest improvement is reported in Nigeria with a notable 143 percent increase between 2000 and 2017. It is not clear what explains this huge jump in manufacturing activities, perhaps the rebasing of the Nigerian economy in 2012/13 financial year led to a better estimation of output in the various sectors of the economy including manufacturing.[7]

When we look at other key measures of industrialisation, particularly the MVA per capita, it is also apparent that most countries in Africa are not performing well on this measure (Table 3.4; see also Figure 3.2).[8]

Table 3.4: Trends in Manufacturing Value Added (MVA) per Capita (in 2010 USD), 2000–2015.*

Resource-rich Countries					Non-resource-rich Countries				
	2000	2010	2015	Change (%) 2000–2015		2000	2010	2015	Change (%) 2000–2015
Algeria	145	182	207	**42.8**	Benin	55	53	55	**0.0**
Angola	95	258	302	**217.9**	Burkina Faso	43	39	49	**14.0**
Botswana	309	415	487	**57.6**	Burundi	18	23	26	**44.4**
Cameroon	70	81	54	**-22.9**	Cabo Verde	186	185	200	**7.5**
C. African Rep.	186	185	200	**7.5**	Comoros	35	42	40	**14.3**
Chad	33	42	47	**42.4**	Cote d'Ivoire	259	172	167	**-35.5**
Dem. Rep. of the Congo	92	56	69	**-25.0**	Djibouti	22	30	35	**59.1**
Equat. Guinea	326	443	468	**43.6**	Egypt	9	32	42	**366.7**
Gabon	273	397	485	**77.7**	Eritrea	51	21	22	**-56.9**
Ghana	25	27	28	**12.0**	Ethiopia	8	12	18	**125.0**
Guinea	1	14	17	**1600.0**	Gambia	29	27	25	**-13.8**
Libya	49	33	38	**-22.4**	Guinea Bissau	73	60	61	**-16.4**
Mali	27	50	62	**129.6**	Kenya	105	110	118	**12.4**
Namibia	457	648	644	**40.9**	Lesotho	68	131	145	**113.2**
Niger	19	17	21	**10.5**	Liberia	77	85	95	**23.4**
Nigeria	122	121	116	**-4.9**	Madagascar	61	65	56	**-8.2**
Rep. of the Congo	53	106	129	**143.4**	Malawi	28	46	46	**64.3**
Sierra Leone	7	10	8	**14.3**	Mauritania	592	759	256	**-56.8**
Sudan	122	148	143	**17.2**	Mauritius	1,107	1,192	1307	**18.1**
South Africa	865	952	971	**12.3**	Morocco	344	406	421	**22.4**
Tanzania	584	685	703	**20.4**	Mozambique	122	86	97	**-20.5**
Zambia	110	85	84	**-23.6**	Rwanda	17	29	32	**88.2**
Zimbabwe	93	107	120	**29.0**	São Tomé and Príncipe	92	95	103	**12.0**
					Senegal	84	149	255	**203.6**
					Seychelles	1,207	856	917	**-24.0**

	Resource-rich Countries				Non-resource-rich Countries				
	2000	2010	2015	Change (%) 2000–2015		2000	2010	2015	Change (%) 2000–2015
					Somalia	2	2	...	..
					Swaziland	1,134	1,073	1,041	-8.2
					Togo	38	39	45	18.4
					Tunisia	29	48	56	93.1
					Uganda	50	65	61	22.0
Average†	**163**	**202**	**216**	**32.9**	**Average†**	**209**	**211**	**214**	**2.7**

Source: Author. Based on data from the African Statistical Year Book (ASYB), various years.

*Ellipses indicate missing data.

†Averages are unweighted.

While MVA per capita grew between 2000 and 2015 in most countries except in a few countries such as the DRC, Libya, Mauritania, Senegal, Zimbabwe, Eritrea, Seychelles and Cote d'Ivoire, MVA per capita levels are very low in almost all countries. As noted by Newman et al (2016a), the average level of MVA on the continent is less than 10 percent of the average for developing countries. In countries such as Chad, Equatorial Guinea, Liberia, Niger, Sierra Leone, Burundi, Rwanda, Burkina Faso, Ethiopia, Malawi, Rwanda and Mali, MVA per capita for 2015 was below US$50 (see also UNECA, 2016). The average MVA per capita for the continent reported in 2015 (US$206) was less than a fifth of the global average (US$1 262) in 2013, and less than a quarter of the average for Latin America (see UNIDO, 2016b: 231). Based on these figures, there is no doubt that the challenges of industrialisation on the continent are substantial.

Trends in Manufacturing Employment

The challenge of industrialisation on the continent is also reflected in the manufacturing employment trends. First, employment levels in manufacturing are comparatively low in all countries. Only four countries (Congo Republic, Mauritius, Tunisia and Swaziland) had the manufacturing share in total employment above 15 percent, which is the global average. The average of 7 percent for the RR countries and 4.8 percent for the NRR countries in Africa is agonisingly low (see Table 3.5).

Table 3.5: Trends in Manufacturing Share in Total Employment Trends (%), 2000–2013.*

Resource Rich Countries	Manufacturing Employment (%)			Change %	Non-Resource Rich Countries	Manufacturing Employment (%)			Change %
	2000	2010	2013	2000–2013		2000	2010	2013	2000–2013
Algeria	10.2	12.1	12.7	24.5	Benin	7.7	7.6	7.4	-3.9
Angola	2.5	2.4	2.4	-4.0	Burkina Faso	2.5	1.7	1.5	-40.0
Botswana	8.9	7.9	7.2	-19.1	Burundi	1.7	1.5	1.5	-11.8
Cameroon	2.6	2.4	3	15.4	Cabo Verde	3.4	2.5	2.8	-17.6
C. African Rep.	7.1	6	5.9	-16.9	Comoros	1.9	1.9	2.2	15.8
Chad	1.2	0.9	0.9	-25.0	Egypt	11.9	12.1	10.7	-10.1
Dem. Rep. of the Congo	3.8	7	7.2	89.5	Eritrea	3.7	3.3	3.2	-13.5
Equat. Guinea	2.1	1.5	1.6	-23.8	Ethiopia	4.1	4.8	4.5	9.8
Gabon	4.9	5.9	5.8	18.4	Gambia	3.6	3.1	3.3	-8.3
Ghana	12.2	9.6	9.1	-25.4	Guinea Bissau	2.5	2.7	2.8	12.0
Guinea	3.1	2.7	2.6	-16.1	Kenya	3.7	3.9	3.6	-2.7
Libya	2.1	1.8	1.8	-14.3	Lesotho	5.4	5.3	5	-7.4
Mali	6.7	7.4	8.5	26.9	Liberia	6.9	6.4	6.5	-5.8
Namibia	5.3	4.9	4.8	-9.4	Madagascar	5.1	2.7	2.6	-49.0
Niger	7.3	6.8	7.2	-1.4	Malawi	4	3.7	3.6	-10.0
Nigeria	11.5	6.6	7.3	-36.5	Mauritania	2.9	2.3	2.2	-24.1
Rep. of the Congo	18.8	19.1	19.3	2.7	Mauritius	24.7	17.1	15.7	-36.4
Sierra Leone	2.8	0.5	0.4	-85.7	Mozambique	0.7	0.6	0.7	0.0
Sudan	10.3	9.2	9.6	-6.8	Morocco	12.1	10.6	9.9	-18.2
South Africa	11.2	11.1	10.1	-9.8	Rwanda	1.8	2.4	2.7	50.0
Tanzania	1.5	3.2	3.3	120.0	Senegal	7.4	14	14.7	98.6
Zambia	3.9	3.8	4.1	5.1	Swaziland	12.5	16	15.2	21.6
Zimbabwe	7.5	5.2	4.9	-34.7	Togo	4.9	5	4.9	0.0
Mean†	**6.4**	**6.0**	**6.1**	**-1.2**	Tunisia	17.7	15.7	15.1	-14.7
					Uganda	6.3	5.6	5.7	-9.5
					Mean†	**6.1**	**5.8**	**5.7**	**-6.7**

Source: Author. Based on data from the African Statistical Year Book (ASYB), various years.

*Countries with incomplete data are excluded.

†Means are unweighted.

The concern here is that in almost 80 percent of the countries, manufacturing employment declined between 2000 and 2013, with large decline reported in several countries including Chad, Equatorial Guinea, Burkina Faso, Madagascar, Ghana, Nigeria, Sierra Leone, Zimbabwe and Mauritius (see Table 3.5). Only in a handful of countries (Algeria, DRC, Libya, Senegal, Tanzania, Rwanda and Swaziland) did employment in the manufacturing sector rise over the same period. This is more apparent in Figure 3.3 presented above.

The low levels of manufacturing employment highlight the urgent need to create productive employment across the continent (see Fox and Thomas, 2016). This has been a challenge for the continent since the 1980s, largely because of the low capacity exhibited by the manufacturing sector against the background of a steadily growing labour force. As noted in Chapter 2, Manufacturing has traditionally been known to have the potential to create low and semi-skilled employment in large numbers, though this potency has not been actualised in many African countries. The fact that the manufacturing sector in Africa is actually shedding jobs highlights a huge employment challenge which is linked to problems of structural transformation.

Manufacturing employment, as highlighted in Chapter 2, has been widely affirmed to be critically important in promoting inclusive growth, sustained income growth and improving living standards, mainly because of its ability to generate a higher proportion of productive jobs when compared to other sectors. Even in the context of the emerging phenomenon of premature de-industrialisation which has affected manufacturing job creation capacity in many economies even in low-income countries, "manufacturing remains critically important to both [developing] and industrialised countries. In [developing countries], it helps countries move from a low-income, agriculture-based economy towards rising incomes and, with them, rising living standards. In the industrialised world, it remains a key source of innovation and competitiveness…" (UNIDO, 2016b:1992). In this sense, manufacturing is critical to structural transformation as we highlight in Chapter 6.

While it has been reported that manufacturing employment has been falling consistently in all regions, including the newly industrialising countries over the last 25 years, a phenomenon attributed to de-industrialisation in post-industrial countries such as Japan, Germany, the United States, France and Switzerland (UNIDO, 2016b),[9] the levels of employment in manufacturing in Africa are extremely low, and that presents huge potential for growth. If we look at manufacturing share in total employment on the continent, we see that it is even below that of the de-industrialising post-industrial countries like the United States with manufacturing employment at 9.8 percent in 2014. For the continent as a whole manufacturing share in total employment has remained stubbornly low at just 7 percent on average, since 2000 (see Figure 3.4).

Like figures on industrial share in total output there is great variation among African countries. However, the common thing among African countries is the low share of manufacturing in total employment, with almost half of the countries reporting less than 5 percent manufacturing employment ratio, and only three countries (Congo Republic, Mauritius and Swaziland) have more than 15 percent share. In countries such as Sierra Leone, Chad and Mozambique, manufacturing employment is almost non-existent at less than 1 percent in 2013. These figures are well below the countries that are de-industrialising such as Germany (19.4 percent), Japan (17 percent), South Korea (16.4 percent), Switzerland (13.5 percent) and the United States (9.8 percent) in 2014 (see UNIDO, 2016b:191). Given the low level of income and development in Africa, we should be seeing higher levels of employment in manufacturing.

But the manufacturing employment ratio reported in Africa can be deceptive mainly because the absolute numbers of people employed in manufacturing are actually very low, consisting only a few thousands in some countries. What is worrying in the context of the industrialisation debates on the continent is that manufacturing employment has remained stagnant at low levels in most countries, reflecting the lack of dynamism in the sector. In countries that saw increase in the share of manufacturing employment between 2000 and 2013, such as Tanzania, Zambia, Guinea Bissau, Gabon, Ethiopia, Congo and Rwanda, the increase was quite small and from very low initial levels (see Table 3.5). Only Swaziland, DRC and Algeria experienced relatively high growth, with manufacturing share in total employment in DRC doubling over this period, though from a very low 3.8 percent to 7.6 percent.

de Vries et al (2015) observe that what is striking is that though economic growth in the continent picked up momentum since the early 2000s, employment in the manufacturing sector did not grow in the region as a whole, except in a few countries. While there is great variation between countries, the common experience is stagnation of the manufacturing sector at very low levels which are reflected in the low income per capita, persistently high levels of poverty and low wage employment ratio.

The low levels of wage employment, especially in the industrial sector which we have seen in this chapter, should be a cause for concern, mainly because industry and manufacturing have higher productivity and income compared to agriculture and services where majority of the people on the continent work (Filmer and Fox, 2014; UNECA, 2016a). Now, if only 7 percent of the workforce is participating in high-productivity activities while majority (85 percent) on average are engaged in informal urban and rural activities (see Fox and Thomas, 2016), it implies that only a small section of the population is capturing the growth dividends in the economy. This is the reason why although growth has improved in most economies, poverty has remained stubbornly high, leading to what has been referred to as the "poverty puzzle" (Page, 2015). The slow reduction in poverty is observed by the World Bank (2013:14) which reported that "despite the continent's growth turn around and progress in the fight against poverty during the last decade, poverty in Africa remains unacceptably high, and the pace of reduction unacceptably slow."

Part of this slow response in poverty to economic growth can be explained by the structure of African economies which have a tiny but relatively highly productive industrial and manufacturing sector, employing only a tiny section of the population, leaving the majority in the low-productivity, low-income segments of the economy. With this structure, it is not surprising that poverty has remained high and productive jobs are being created at a snail's pace in almost all countries. It is in the context of this predicament that the strategies and efforts aimed at deepening industrial development on the continent have to be prioritised if any headway in improving the income of the people and reducing poverty will be made.

Manufacturing Export Trends

The other common measure of industrial development used to assess a country or region's capability to manufacture goods competitively at the global stage is the MVA per capita. If we look at the Africa relative to other regions of the world, African's performance on this measure is again an outlier as Table 3.6 shows.

Table 3.6: Trends in Manufacturing Export per Capita by Regions of the World, 1995–2013.

	($USD)					Share in Global Manufacturing Export (%)				
	1995	2000	2005	2010	2013	1995	2000	2005	2010	2013
Africa	41	62	110	207	212	**1.1**	**1.2**	**1.4**	**1.8**	**1.5**
Asia the Pacific	346	566	1,291	2,509	3371	8.9	11.1	15.9	22.0	24.3

	($USD)					Share in Global Manufacturing Export (%)				
	1995	**2000**	**2005**	**2010**	**2013**	**1995**	**2000**	**2005**	**2010**	**2013**
Europe	83	127	302	483	620	2.1	2.5	3.7	4.2	4.5
Industrialised Countries	3,218	4,015	5,967	7,579	8,929	82.5	79.1	73.4	66.4	64.4
Latin America	213	309	460	632	733	5.5	6.1	5.7	5.5	5.3
World	**3,901**	**5,079**	**8,130**	**11,409**	**13,866**					

Source: Author. Based on data from the United Nations Industrial Development Organization (UNIDO, 2016b).

We see that Africa's MVA export per capita was only a tenth of the global average, a fifth of the Asia and Pacific Region and one-seventh of Latin America. This is a reflection of low competitive manufacturing capacity on the continent, with most countries having little manufactured products in their total export. What this suggests is that although African countries are engaging in manufacturing activities, these activities are heavily concentrated in the low value-added sections of global value chains, which accounts for the extremely low MVA export per capita. This is also confirmed by the figures on the continent's impact on world MVA and world trade which remain insignificant (see Table 3.8).

Looking at trends in the manufacturing sector between 2000 and 2014, it is clear that the sector in most countries is clearly not growing, with half of the countries reporting declining manufacturing activities, while in another quarter of the countries, manufacturing activities have stagnated, over the reference period. Thus, in the context of the critical role assigned to the manufacturing sector in the process of economic development (see Murphy et al, 1989), structural transformation, diversification and productivity growth (see Chenery et al, 1986), the implications of the observed industrial development trends in Africa are quite clear. There is almost unanimity on the view that much of the growth reported in Africa since the beginning of the new millennium can be largely attributed to the high prices of commodities (McMillan and Rodrik, 2011; Page, 2012; ACET, 2014; Timmer et al, 2014; de Vries et al, 2015; Newman et al, 2016a; UNECA, 2016).

For industrial development to complement the current economic dynamic in African, a new formula for growing the industrial sector must be found, and the role of the manufacturing sector is critically essential. This has been highlighted in Chapter 2. The critical role of the manufacturing sector becomes more evident when we consider the current patterns of industrial development against the levels of productive employment and poverty.

It is also interesting to note that the little manufacturing activities reported in the continent is highly concentrated in the processing of natural resources, mainly agro-processing, dominated by food and beverages. This production structure which is prevalent in Africa explains why the continent has remained principally an exporter of commodities, most of them in raw form. This export profile brings several challenges which are well known in Africa. Therefore, when looking at the industrial sector in Africa, particularly manufacturing, it is essential to see what type of manufactured goods are being produced and exported.

The Manufacturing Sector Scope in Africa

While we have seen above that the manufacturing sector in most African economies is small and it is not growing as fast as one would expect, it is important also to look at the types of manufactured products on the continent. As noted earlier, African countries have different manufacturing capabilities, though most countries' manufacturing is largely composed of low-tech activities, dominated by the processing of natural resources, especially food. In the ISIC classification, all agro-processing manufactures such as food and beverage, tobacco, textiles, clothing and apparel, wood and wood products, paper and paper products, printing and publishing, and furniture fall under the low-tech category, while petroleum refinery, rubber and plastic products, basic metals, non-metallic mineral products and fabricated metal products are classified as medium-tech goods. In the high-tech category, we have the manufacturing of chemicals and chemical products, machinery and equipment, electrical machinery and electrical parts, precision instruments and motor cars, etc.

The Dominance of Food and Beverages

A close look at manufacturing activities in Africa reveals that most of the activities are concentrated in the low-tech manufacturing, mainly agro-processing, which in turn is dominated by food, tobacco and beverages. A

UNIDO (2016a) report confirms this, observing that up to 90 percent of manufactured export from Africa is based on the processing of natural resources. As Table 3.7 shows, food alone accounts for a surprisingly large share of manufactured exports in most countries. In countries like Eritrea, Ethiopia, Malawi, Tanzania and Zambia, food alone accounted for more than half of total manufactured exports in 2010.

Table 3.7: Trends in the Share of Food in Total MVA for Selected African Countries (%), 1990–2015.*

	1990	1995	2000	2010	2015
Cameroon	63.1	38.2	43.0	0.0	…
Egypt	21.6	19.6	19.2	15.0	…
Eritrea	59.4	77.1	28.2	51.9	…
Ethiopia	61.6	50.7	54.2	46.4	29.8
Kenya	46.7	46.0	28.6	31.4	37.3
Malawi	87.4	89.3	107.6	67.0	…
Morocco	35.2	32.7	0.0	0.0	…
Nigeria	…	16.4	…	…	…
Senegal	60.3	45.2	32.8	35.9	…
South Africa†	20.5	25.2	18.7	16.9	…
Swaziland	63.2	…	…	…	…
Tunisia	17.5	15.3	15.7	9.1	…
Uganda	43.5	54.5	…	…	…
Tanzania	92.6	71.4	80.2	54.8	…
Zambia‡	44.08	44.4	59.6	68.7	…

Source: FAOStats DataBank Online Resource (http://www.fao.org/faostat/en/#data/MK).

*Ellipses indicate missing data.

†Figures for South Africa are estimates by the author based on data from the Department of Agriculture, Forestry and Fisheries (DAFF, 2012).

‡Figures for Zambia are from the World Development Indicators (online resource).

The dominance of food and natural resource processing is a characteristic feature of an economy in the early stages of industrial development (Syrquin and Chenery, 1989a). But if this structure of the economy persists, it is a sign of the failure to deepen industrial development. The main concern here is that the processing of food and natural resources is a low value addition activity, which largely explains the low MVA per capita in most African countries. The dominance of food processing in the manufacturing sector also suggests that these economies find it difficult to participate in the high value-added activities, which often require medium- to high-tech manufacturing activities.

In 2017, almost half of MVA originated from resource-based manufacturing using low-tech (UNIDO, 2017). In 1993, similar figures were reported where food beverages, tobacco, textile and leather, and wood products accounted for over 60 percent of MVA (see Tribe, 2000:84). In countries such as Gambia, Congo, Central African Republic, Cameroon, Burundi, Burkina Faso, Botswana, Togo and former Zaire (now DRC) food processing alone accounted for more than half of manufacturing output (ibid, 82–84). Figures for 2015 suggest that in most of the countries manufacturing activities are dominated by low-tech manufacturing (see Table 3.8 below). In some countries, up to 70 percent of manufacturing activities are involved in food production, mainly for domestic consumption, and this pattern has not changed since the 1980s (see Tribe, 2000). In their analysis of manufacturing trends in nine African countries, Balchin et al (2016) also found that food and beverage accounted for the bulk of total manufacturing ranging from 40 to 70 percent.

Industrial theory suggests that the manufacturing sector in countries at the initial stages of industrialisation tend to be dominated by light manufacturing, predominantly food, textile and clothing (see Syrquin and Chenery, 1989a). But, gradually countries build capacity to engage in high-tech manufacturing, such as production of heavy-duty machinery and other intermediate products to be used as inputs in the manufacturing process. Therefore, it is normal at the beginning of industrial development for the share of food and beverages, to dominate the manufacturing sector. Simon Kuznets (1966) who analysed the historical data on the structural changes of industrialised economies in Europe, America and Australia, found similar patterns showing that as industrial development progresses, the share of food and beverages in total manufacturing output declines with time. The explanation provided for the declining share of food and beverages as income rises is that firms begin to produce capital (producer) goods in the manufacturing sector as a country accumulates sufficient capital and technology to engage in capital-intensive and high-tech manufacturing. In their study of patterns of industrial development in several countries, Syrquin and Chenery (1989b:155–156) observed that,

> Over the course of the transition there is a significant shift in value added from primary production to manufacturing and nontradables. Early industries are established at low income levels to satisfy the essential demands of the population (food textiles and clothing). They are characterised by simple technologies and low income elasticities of demand.

This shift is explained in detail by Kaldor (1966) who proposed four phases of industrial transition from light to heavy duty manufacturing. He developed a four-stage transition model in which an economy moves from an initial stage where the production of consumer goods, primarily food, textiles, beverages and other light manufactures, for the domestic market, dominates. In the second stage, when the capacity for production of consumer goods exceeds domestic demand, an economy seeks market for consumer goods beyond national borders. In the third stage, as the demand for food rises (at home and abroad), so does the demand for equipment used in the processing of food and other consumer products, and firms may begin to manufacture capital goods. This eventually leads some firms to shift attention to the production of machinery and other equipment, first to supply the domestic market, and later the international market. At this stage, manufacturing enters the fourth stage characterised by the export of both consumer and high-tech producer goods.

But Kuznets (1966:142) argues that such an interpretation is a "misleading over-simplification" since the increase in heavy duty (high-tech) manufacturing is only modest and it is partly to do with the shift in the technology which substitutes the use of natural input by manufactured or synthetic intermediates. This caution is important to bear in mind, especially when we consider economies that are trying to industrialise at different times and in different contexts like countries in Africa today.

Interestingly, this point has been largely ignored in economic growth analysis. What has been emphasised is the idea that the manufacturing structure changes from resource-based to high-tech production as income rises, and it is often assumed that all economies would have to pass through the same dynamics as if history and social systems are time-invariant variables. The influence of this conventional view is more evident in the structural transformation debates where the process of economic change from a predominantly agriculture-dominated to manufacturing and service-dominated economy is reduced to that of "marching through the sectors" (see Chapter 6).

In mainstream industrial theory, the explanation given for the high composition of food and other essential goods in the manufacturing output in low-income countries is that the demand for food relative to other manufactures is high in the population, and given that incomes are low, it is rational to direct attention to the production of food which enjoys a growing demand. It is only when countries have accumulated enough capital, skills and technology that manufacturing shifts to the production of capital goods for export (Chenery et al, 1986a). In this sense, the dominance of food processing in the manufacturing sector is usually seen as a transition phase, which is a sign of an economy at an early stage of development. For African economies whose manufacturing sectors have been dominated by food and beverage for a long time, this is a sign of the failure to break from the structural constraints imposed by the colonial economic architecture and logic. The debilitating effects of the colonial economic design is evident in the fact that six decades after the end of colonial occupation, African countries are still struggling to find a way to break loose from the colonial economic engineering.

In the industrialisation literature, the apparently strong linkage that food production and the agro-processing activities have with the agricultural sector is seen as a potential driver of industrial development during the early stages. Intuitively, countries at the lower levels of development are often preoccupied with meeting the essential needs before they can even think of producing luxury and non-essential goods. For instance, it has been argued that only countries that have experienced substantial income rise will have the sufficient demand for non-essential goods (Pingali, 1997). The challenge for many African countries is that they fail to move beyond the dominance of natural resource-based manufacturing, such that for the past six decades, all what most Africans countries have been trying to do is produce enough food to feed the people, and in some cases without much success. In several countries food imports have in fact been rising in recent years (Rakotoarisoa et al, 2012). Perhaps countries should start by manufacturing the tools used in the production and manufacturing of food.

Importance of High-Tech manufacturing

Why should we be concerned about food and beverage constituting the largest share of manufactured products? There are several reasons why a manufacturing structure dominated by food and beverages is problematic. The obvious one is that such a structure is an indication of a narrow production base, using low technology. While focusing on producing food is certainly good for meeting domestic demand in countries where urbanisation is proceeding at a fast rate, it is not good in terms of export earnings, which are important for maintaining a healthy current account and macro-economic stability in general. Other than that, the manufacturing of food, beverages and other light manufacturing goods is associated with low productivity because they occur in the low value-added segments of global value chains. It is also difficult for countries producing food for the domestic market to build capacity to compete in international markets. Available evidence suggests a strong correlation between expanding exports and competitive capacity. For example, Songwe and Winkler (2012), in their study of export diversification in Africa, found that increased export is associated not only with rising productivity but also with great capacity for employment creation. They argue that, "One of the primary challenges facing Africa's resource rich countries is how to diversify production beyond the natural resources. Natural resource-based products have dominated exports for the past 50 years, but reliance on such products has not made African countries richer" (ibid, 2).

Recent reports that the food and beverage component of the manufacturing sector has been increasing above the average for the sector due mainly to the rising domestic demand from the growing urban population (Balchin et al, 2016) may be a sign of African manufacturing being locked into the low value-added gear. The concentration of manufacturing on food and beverage also suggests that manufacturing at this stage is largely for the domestic and not export markets. Without entering into export markets, it will be difficult for African economies to increase productivity and contribute to resilience in the economy (ibid). The challenge for African countries is not only that manufacturing is dominated by processing of food and other natural resources, but also that productivity is still low.

> Productivity in Africa's manufacturing still is far below that of developed countries (around 40 percent of that of the United States for the most advanced countries in the continent), and most of the firms in manufacturing are small and informal. Egypt, Morocco and South Africa stand out for their higher specialization in manufacturing and higher labour productivity (UNIDO, 2016a:10).

Although there are claims of technological convergence in the manufacturing sector, with technology use rapidly spreading throughout the globe (Rodrik, 2015), only a few countries (Kenya, Egypt, South Africa and Morocco) use high-tech in their manufacturing activities. Given the widespread use of low-tech manufacturing in Africa, it is not clear how African countries are preparing themselves to become active players in the Fourth Industrial Revolution where high-tech manufacturing through digitisation, 3D printing, artificial intelligence and robotics is gradually dominating manufacturing production lines in developing economies (see Bangà and te Velde, 2018).

The dominance of resource-based manufacturing output in Africa is a reflection of countries in the continent failing to engage in high value-addition activities which require medium and high technology. The platinum mined in Zimbabwe and South Africa should be processed into semi-finished products before exporting it to China and Germany. This would increase South Africa and Zimbabwe's proportion of the value generated from the platinum value chain, which is captured and retained in the country. There are now promising examples of African countries adding significant value to their resources before exporting them. In the case of coffee and tea in Uganda, it has been reported that the country now packs and brands coffee before exporting to the world markets (see UNECA, 2015). In other sectors, most African companies would argue that they do not have the technology to process the resources into, at least, semi-finished products. But this is where the industrial policy should come in to assist firms so that they can develop and upgrade the capacity to engage in high value-added activities. The South African government has recognised the importance of the state assisting firms to build export capacity in the country and several measures have been outlined to put this into practice (DTI, 2016). The big question is, will these good ideas get implemented on the ground? As argued in Chapter 7, the state has to play a more active role in ensuring that African countries build and upgrade their industrial capacities by providing tailored interventions to strategic nodes of the industrial system.

While the manufacturing sector in most countries is dominated by processing of food and natural resources, most of the food produced is consumed locally, except for a few cash crops, which are exported, often in unprocessed or semi-processed form. With this manufacturing structure, it is not surprising that in most African countries, the three top exports are dominated by metal ores, crude oil and natural gas or agricultural products such as coffee, cocoa beans (raw), tea, cut flowers, tobacco, cane sugar (raw), live animals, hard wood and cashew nuts.

A recent study has confirmed the over-reliance on a narrow band of commodities for export, observing that,

> about 26 percent of Africa's countries rely on one or two resource commodities for at least 75 percent of their exports, while about 60 percent rely on up to five commodities. With falling commodity prices, a narrow export base increases current account pressures for countries such as Angola, Chad, Congo, Eritrea, Guinea-Bissau, Nigeria, Libya, Sierra Leone and South Sudan which almost exclusively depend on a single commodity export (AEO, 2017: 78).

In oil-rich countries, such as Angola, Sudan, Chad, Libya, Gabon, Nigeria, Congo and Equatorial Guinea, more than three-quarters of total export by value comes from a single product—petroleum (ibid). In the mineral-rich countries such as Niger (uranium ore), Guinea (aluminium ore), Zambia (copper and cobalt) export of metal ores usually accounts for up to three-quarters of the export revenue, with manufacturing accounting for a negligible proportion. Countries that mainly depend on agriculture such as Malawi (tobacco), Burundi (coffee), Guinea Bissau (cashew nuts), Burkina Faso (cotton) also show the same over-dependence on one or two agricultural produce which accounts for over 70 percent of total export revenue. Although the manufacturing sector is dominated by the food processing industries, many countries still rely on imports to meet their basic food requirement, with the continent spending about US$63 billion annually on food beverages and tobacco imports (ibid).

There Is No Single Industrial Path

As in many other fields of study, the modernisation theory has been quite influential in industrial studies. The dominant form in which the modernisation theory has manifested itself in industrial literature is in the idea that today's less industrialised countries will have to go through the stages of industrial growth similar to those traversed by the now industrialised and industrialising nations. We find a classical example of the modernisation theory in Rostow's (1959) stages of economic growth in which the vanguard economy of Britain has "beaten the path" of industrialisation, which late industrialisers have to pass through, but faster than the early industrialisers because the path is already 'beaten, and the stumps and sarsens have all been cleared.

But this approach of following in the footsteps of the 'path-breakers' has caused more harm to the industrialisation prospects of less industrialised countries through a series of knock-on effects. One channel through which the negative effects of the modernisation framework has been mediated is the strong adherence of late industrialised to the gospel of static comparative advantage, which has entailed that countries should do things the way the British, French, Germans, and now the Chinese did it. But as Obrien and Keyder remind us,

> there is more than one way of transition from an Agricultural to Industrial economy and from rural to urban society. Economic theory lends no support to assumptions... that there is one definable and optimal path to higher per capita incomes and still less to the implicit notion that this path can be identified with British industrialisation as it proceeded from 1870 to 1914 (cited in Syrquin and Chenery, 1989b:7).

Thus, experience of industrialisation from other countries and regions can only present useful lessons, but not blueprints to be replicated. The challenge for African countries seeking to industrialise today is to identify possible paths to industrialisation after a careful consideration of local and international conditions. An industrial path a country or region charts must be created by starting to remove the stumps and boulders and plotting its own trajectory, which might be totally different from paths traversed by other countries or regions. Identifying and charting a successful industrial path requires one to know where he or she is and the ultimate finishing line.

Technology in African Manufacturing

Crucial to a successful African strategy of industrialisation is a gradual transition from low-tech to medium and hi-tech activities, especially for export goods and services. Although the manufacturing share in total export among Africa in 2013 was relatively high, with the average of 47 percent for the continent, the share of medium- and high-tech manufactures in total export was small in most countries (see Table 3.8). The average for the continent was only half the global average, and well below that of other developing regions. There were only five countries (South Africa, Cote d'Ivoire, Mozambique, Tunisia and Morocco) with over 40 percent medium- and hi-tech manufactures in total export. Even in these countries, the bulk of this involves the processing of natural resources into semi-finished products as alluded to earlier. While the composition of medium- and hi-tech manufactured goods in Africa's export grew slightly overall between 2009 and 2013, this growth came from a few countries and even there, the initial levels remain relatively low. This is reflected in the region's almost negligible impact on world MVA, with all countries, expect for South Africa, reporting less than half a percent (Table 3.8).

Table 3.8: Use of Technology in Manufacturing for Selected African Countries.

	Manufacturing Export per Capita (USD)		Medium and Hi-tech Share in Total Export (%)		Manufacture Export Share in Total Export (%)		Country Impact on World MVA (%)	
Resource-rich Countries								
	2008	**2013**	**2008**	**2013**	**2008**	**2013**	**2008**	**2013**
Algeria	407.2	377.6	0.7	0.8	18.3	22.4	0	0.08
Botswana	2,407.1	3,573.4	4.8	3.4	94	95.4	0	0.01
Cameroon	59.3	65.1	24.7	14.3	54.6	33	0	0.04
C.. African Rep.	17	5	4.7	14	59.6	60.1	0	0
Gabon	788.8	642.8	6.6	10.1	12.2	18.2	0	0.01
Ghana	32.3	79.8	18.1	33.3	19.6	16.4	0	0.02
Namibia	1,117.8	1,713	13.8	25.8	49.9	69.1	0	0.01
Niger	35.8	67	3.9	6	51.4	89.3	0	0
Nigeria	30.3	35.1	73.2	19.4	5.6	6.7	0	0.09
Rep. of the Congo	433.8	625.3	67.8	85.9	18.3	26.6	0	0.02
South Africa	1,016.9	1,208.9	51.1	43.7	69.1	67	0.01	0.52
Tanzania	31.3	33	22.9	22.4	42.5	36.8	0	0.02
Tunisia	1,523.1	1,317.7	39.2	46.8	81.9	84.9	0	0.08
Zambia	126.5	182.8	12.6	23.2	30.9	25	0	0.01
Non-resource-rich Countries								
Burundi	3.3	3.8	44.8	28	19.9	18.9	0	0
Cabo Verde	25	75.6	0	1.1	63.8	54.5	0	0
Cote d'Ivoire	235.5	268.4	16.7	45.6	44	45.1	0	0.03
Egypt	212.7	228.2	24.5	31.6	61.8	65.1	0	0.22
Eritrea	0.4	0.4	14.7	14.7	34.6	34.6	0	0
Ethiopia	9.1	13.3	23.3	13.3	10.7	15.7	0	0.01
Gambia	1.9	0.6	10.7	5.6	28.8	10.3	0	0
Kenya	59.8	58.1	17.7	21.6	49.6	48.7	0	0.03
Madagascar	61.8	42.5	2.1	4.4	79.6	55.6	0	0.01
Malawi	10.8	22.6	15.3	12.8	17.3	30.1	0	0
Mauritius	1,583.3	1,468.5	12.4	3.5	80.6	96.3	0	0.02
Morocco	491.4	534.8	31.6	44.5	74.9	80.4	0	0.12
Mozambique	14.2	44.6	35.9	44.8	12.2	28.7	0	0.02

	Manufacturing Export per Capita (USD)		Medium and Hi-tech Share in Total Export (%)		Manufacture Export Share in Total Export (%)		Country Impact on World MVA (%)	
Rwanda	11.2	27	3.6	4.4	57.2	63.4	0	0.01
Senegal	144.5	117.2	17.3	15.2	81.5	62.1	0	0.02
Swaziland	888.8	888.8	29	29	92.9	92.9	0	0.01
Uganda	14.6	17.3	14.8	13.8	34.4	38.2	0	0.01
Africa Average	**122**	**128**	**31**	**34**	**43**	**47**	**1**	**1**

Source: Author. Based on data from the United Nations Industrial Development Organization (UNIDO, 2016b).

The significance of high-tech manufacturing activities is that they have great potential to improve productivity (UNIDO, 2016b), particularly of labour, and increase the diffusion of technology in the economy. Although the use of high-tech in manufacturing requires huge capital outlay which most LICs in Africa may not have, it is imperative to gradually build high-tech manufacturing capacity in the high value-added activities such as machinery for special purposes and motor vehicles and vehicle parts. It has been observed that a rising share of high-tech manufactures such as chemicals, pharmaceuticals and heavy-duty machinery is a good indicator of "industrial depth" (Wade, 1990: 44). Given its multiplier effect in the economy, building capacity for high-tech manufacturing should be part of the long-term strategic plan to re-position African countries into global manufacturing. Investments that contribute to the creation of high-tech manufacturing capacity should be undertaken with the aim of deepening industrial development over time.

To facilitate investments in this area, the state can use various types of incentives to support and encourage firms to begin the process. Where private firms are not suited to undertake such incentives, the state can initiate the process of developing high-tech manufacturing capacity by establishing state-owned enterprises to lead the way. Building technical and innovative capacity in the industrial sector, particularly manufacturing, should not be done in an enclave manner as in the colonial times. The capacity built in industry should be a strategic asset with the critical "power of dispersion."

A high ratio of low-tech manufacturing translates into low MVA per capita which is evident in most African countries as indicated earlier in this chapter. Only a few countries (South Africa, Tunisia, Seychelles, Namibia, Swaziland and Mauritius) had MVA per capita of more than US$500 in 2015.

Low levels of MVA do reflect not only low levels of industrial development on the continent, but also the low technology employed in manufacturing (AEO, 2017). This is clear when we look at the ratio of medium- and high-tech manufacturing in total manufacturing output and in total manufactured export. In most countries on the continent such as Algeria, Botswana, Congo, Zambia, Malawi, Uganda, Rwanda, Senegal, Ghana, Nigeria, Niger, Mauritius, Madagascar, Gabon and Ethiopia, this was less than half of the global average of 58 percent in 2013. Only a handful of countries such as Egypt, South Africa, Morocco, Tunisia and Swaziland report a significant share of medium- and high-tech manufacturing (see Table 3.8).

The importance of medium- and hi-tech in total manufacturing is that this adds more value to intermediate products, captures and retains a high proportion of the value in the global value chains and can therefore be an effective mechanism for raising income and creating productive jobs. Sections of value chains where the highest value is added involve the use of medium- and hi-tech manufacturing techniques and methods. It has for instance been recognised that countries benefit more from manufacturing by increasing the share of medium- and high-tech manufacturing relative to the low-tech resource-based manufacturing (UNIDO, 2016b:180).

Manufacturing activities that create more value including the newly emerging areas of artificial intelligence, robotics, use of nanotechnology, 3D printing and design, discovery of new materials, augmented reality all involve the use of high-tech in the production of goods and services. In this regard the performance of African countries is evidently below average when compared to other regions. Two of the key indicators of a country's use of hi-tech are the share of MVA in total export and the MVA export per capita. As Table 3.9 shows, Africa's MVA share in total export was the lowest when compared to other regions of the world and only half of the global average. The situation is even worse when we consider MVA export per capita which in 2013 was only a tenth of the global average.

Table 3.9: Share of Manufacturing in Total Export and MVA Per Capita by Region, 2009–2013.

	Share of Manufacturing in Total Export (%)		MVA per Capita		MVA per Capita Change
	2009	**2013**	**2009**	**2013**	**Change 2009–2013**
Africa	43	47	122	128	4.9
Asia and the Pacific	84	81	438	559	27.6

	Share of Manufacturing in Total Export (%)		MVA per Capita		MVA per Capita Change
	2009	**2013**	**2009**	**2013**	**Change 2009–2013**
Europe	91	90	1,021	1,206	18.1
Industrialised Countries	90	87	4,180	4,751	13.7
Latin America	69	64	768	836	8.8
World	**86**	**83**	**1,104**	**1,262**	**14.3**

Source: Author. Based on data from the United Nations Industrial Development Organization (UNIDO, 2016b).

African countries should start by identifying the most promising areas of medium- and hi-tech in their economies, which they can use to influence the performance of other sectors. The idea that these kinds of activities can only be embarked on by developed countries because they have money is one of the reasons why most countries on the continent have failed to realise higher levels of industrialisation. It is only when African leaders can envision themselves and their countries being path-breakers in specific areas of manufacturing, management, and technology development that we are likely to see industrial progress.

The cost of delaying the starting of a radical shift in re-orientating economic and industrial policy has been growing with time, such that African countries have foregone a great deal. Given the status of industrial development on the continent, it is clear that the challenges are huge and radical actions are needed urgently to find a way to create productive jobs at a faster rate to meet the demand from the steadily expanding labour force. The potential for an expanding industrial sector to contribute to creating real employment and spread the benefits of economic growth is well known. On the other hand, the failure to sustainable growth of the industrial sector can only lead to further frustration of the youth, which is a recipe for instability. As noted above, low levels of industrial development in most African countries have contributed to the failure to create adequate productive jobs even in economies which have been growing at double digit figures in the past 15 years.

Manufacturing Sector Dynamics

In their study of patterns of industrialisation and development, Syrquin and Chenery (1989a) examine the impact of manufacturing on income levels. The main finding of their study is that as industrialisation progresses, the industrial sector, manufacturing in particular, goes through three structural shifts. At the early stages of industrial development, which they call "early industries," production is mainly characterised by the production of essential goods such as food, beverages, textile and clothing to meet the essential needs of the people (Syrquin and Chenery, 1989a:156). The manufacturing sector at this stage is characterised by a heavy dependence on resources using low or simple technology, with a low manufacturing share in GDP of roughly between 7 and 8 percent. The other characteristic feature of the economy at this stage is a low-income elasticity of demand which is generally associated with the demand functions for food and basic needs (see Singer, 1950). But as income rises, mainly driven by the inter-sectoral linkages which increase the use of industrial material as intermediates by other industries, the structure of manufacturing shifts to the production of intermediate goods using medium-range technology (see Kaldor, 1966). The products mainly associated with this phase of industrial development, which they refer to as "*middle industries*," include chemicals, petroleum and rubber products, wood and wood products and non-metallic minerals (Syrquin and Chenery, 1989a).

Medium-tech industries, unlike the low-tech industries, according to Syrquin and Chenery (1989a), are associated with higher income elasticities of demand and the use of sophisticated technology in the production processes. As incomes rise further, the composition of the manufacturing sector shifts more towards the production of capital goods (mainly machinery) and some intermediate products such as paper and paper products, basic metals, vehicles and durable consumer goods (ibid). At this stage the share of manufacturing in total output rises to around 24 percent, with an income characterised by low share of consumption in total output and a rise in saving rates in the population. At this level, "food consumption drops by about 20 percentage points, while non-food consumption…goes up. The shift from consumption to investment takes place at a lower income level; the decline in food consumption is spread over a wider income range" (ibid, 154). Syrquin and Chenery (1989b) then make the general observation that the transition from early to middle industries occurs at the income level (GDP per capita) of US$1500 (in 1980 dollars), while the transition from middle to late industries is said to take place around national income per capita of U$3000 (in 1980 dollars). The main driver of this transition is final demand in the economy which changes from being predominantly food and other necessities to more durable non-essential products.

This view was earlier articulated in a popular UNIDO (1980) report on the progression of industrialisation, giving the specific levels of per capita income at which structural change in industrial production and the economy in general occurs. A more recent UNIDO report uses a similar framework to classify countries and to provide policy directions to member countries. In a 2016 Report, it was observed that the "manufacturing structure of industrialised countries tends to be made up less of primary and secondary goods, with more emphasis on medium-and high tech sectors…while traditional industries contribute a high share in [developing and emerging economies]" (UNIDO, 2016b:177). In the case of Africa, the report concludes that "Africa exhibits the lowest regional medium-and high-tech share among the other regions, and manufacturing there is highly dependent on resource-based products" (ibid, 180–181).

Implications of the Current Structure of the Manufacturing Sector in Africa

We have already discussed the challenges associated with specialising in the manufacturing of food and export of commodities. Some of the common challenges associated with such a production structure include the problem of secular decline in the prices for commodities relative to that of manufactured goods (Singer, 1950), the volatility of prices for commodities on the global market and also stifling of growth of the non-tradition exports as a result of the infamous Dutch Disease. In this sense, what one exports matters a lot, and there is now evidence showing that "countries that specialise in the types of goods that rich countries export are likely to grow faster than countries that specialise in other goods" (Hausmann et al, 2007:2). Obviously rich countries would not like competition and would do anything possible to protect their interest, including "kicking away the ladder" they used to climb to where they are now, just to prevent the poor countries from catching up with them (see Chang, 2003).

In 2013, the average manufacturing export per capita in Africa at US$193 was only about 10 percent of the global average, 2.7 percent of the average for industrialised countries, less than 8 percent of Europe's and 22 percent of

Latin America's. This is a reflection of the low value of manufacturing export in the continent. Although manufacturing export in total exports when compared to other regions is roughly around half, the value of these exports is low as the manufacturing per capita figures show. This confirms the view that most African countries' manufactured exports are mainly composed of food and other processed raw materials, which has been the case from as early as the 1980s (see Tribe, 2000; UNIDO, 2016a). This is also confirmed by the low levels of MVA per capita, reflecting the small share of manufacturing in total output but also by the fact that the figures for the African continent lag far behind those of other developing regions.

Unfortunately, manufacturing has continued to be a marginal activity in most economies on the continent, with MVA remaining stagnant, for the past three decades. Not surprisingly, the agricultural sector also has not seen any increase in productivity over the years, leading to a double deficit in manufacturing and agriculture with serious consequences for poverty reduction and employment creation at the time when most of the economies have actually reported decent growth.

Unlocking the African Potential

The current status of industrial development on the continent presented above highlights the need to think holistically, and with a long-term perspective. Development approaches in the past have emphasised one thing over the other. For example, there have been times on the continent when improving productivity in agriculture was seen as the key to unlocking the African growth potential (especially at the start of the SAPs during the early 1980s), while at times, industrialisation was seen as the magic bullet for putting Africa on the sure path to catching up with the rest of the world. But these strategies have not yielded much as the discussion above highlight. When growth gained momentum across most African countries in the post-crisis period (2010 onwards), there was great optimism among analysts, partly generated by the *Africa Rising Narrative* sparked by the 2011 article in *The Economist* magazine. But those who were critical enough to ask the question about sources of growth, questioned the foundation of the celebrated growth mainly because they did not see a solid basis for sustained growth.

In this case, if the less industrialised countries ever want to industrialise and develop, they must create their own ladders; they should not look for the old ones used by countries that have industrialised. Waiting for the industrialised countries to lend them ladders is not a wise strategy and it has never worked anywhere. It is therefore important to realise that for African countries to unlock their economic potential they have to learn to build their own ladders which will enable them climb the rocky cliffs of the industrialisation process. In most African countries, this would entail replacing the colonial scaffolds and pillars which were not meant to raise African industrial activities to any great heights. Keeping the colonial scaffolds has made industrialisation on the continent appear like an impossible task. As argued in chapter 1, this is partly a result of the failure to decolonise not just the economic structure, but the economic logic, which has perpetrated the myth that Africa can develop by specialising on the production of primary commodities over which it has relative comparative advantage.

With very low and declining productivity in agriculture in most countries (de Vries et al, 2015) and a stagnating industrial sector, the fundamentals of a solid growth trajectory in African economies are still missing. These fundamentals cannot be created by donor partners or development agencies outside of the continent; they must be created by Africans themselves when they appreciate and identify where they want their economy to be in future. Industrial development will be crucial for generating the momentum around which to rally other forces within the economy. But this will be difficult to realise without paying equal attention to the dynamics in the broader economy including agriculture and now the informal urban sector where majority of the people work. As Arthur Lewis (1954) observed, manufacturing only flourishes when agriculture is doing well. This is not an argument for a "balanced growth," but for strategic thinking, which aims to identify the key movers in the economy. The task here is not replicating what others have done or borrowing their ladders; the real task is for Africa to build its own ladders, designed to navigate the challenges it faces. Designing Africa's own ladders would increase the chances of climbing to the peak of the global industrial pyramid.

Notes

1. For a general discussion of the challenges of data in Africa see Deverajan (2013) and Jerven (2013).
2. The World Bank compiles the WDI based largely on data supplied by the country's statistical office.

3. There are actually55 countries now that the Saharawi Arab Republic has officially been recognised by the AU, though yet to be given national sovereign status by the United Nations.
4. The IMF (2013) classifies a country as RR if the export of natural resources such as minerals, oil, metals and unprocessed timber accounts for over 25 percent of total export. The World Bank (2015:49) using 10 percent of GDP rents from natural resources as the threshold for RR countries comes up with a different list with only 17 countries being classified as RR: Cameroon, Central African Republic, Ghana, South Africa, Tanzania, Zimbabwe, Sierra Leon and Sudan are excluded from the list of RR countries. Given this discrepancy in the classification of countries, here the IMF list, though it is based on the 2010 data, looks more realistic. There are a number of countries which have started to export these natural resources after this classification (e.g., Cote d'Ivoire, Burkina Faso, Liberia, Madagascar, Uganda), such that the list of RR countries in Africa is currently estimated at 26 countries and this might go up as more countries discover natural resources (IBIS, 2015).
5. The adjusted regression coefficient R^2 for resource rich countries was 0.0971, while for non- resource rich countries it was 0.8312, and for all countries, it was 0.2399.
6. The HDI takes into account other indicators including life expectance, years of schooling as well as GNP (see UNDP, 2016).
7. Newman et al (2016b:4) report similar figures for Nigeria—1.9 percent share of manufacturing in GDP for 2013, based on the Groningen database. The figures reported here are based on the Africa Statistical Year Book compiled by the African Development Bank in conjunction with the African Union and the Economic Commission for Africa. Such sharp rise in figures raises questions of data quality and consistency in the measurement of the sector. It could be possible that the manufacturing sector in Nigeria was underestimated in previous years. Without discounting the challenges with the data, the overall picture is clear from the data, which is that manufacturing accounts for a small share in total output.
8. The MVA per capita is a basic measure of a country's or region's level of industrialisation, taking into account the size of population.
9. It has been reported that manufacturing employment in industrialised countries declined from 91 million jobs in 1991 to 63 million jobs in 2014, representing a decline from 21.8 percent share in total employment to 13.2 percent over the same period (UNIDO, 2016b:190). But manufacturing employment has declined even in developing countries. For China, manufacturing employment declined from 14.9 percent in 1995 to 11.5 percent in 2014 (ibid, 192). However, although employment has been declining steadily, productivity has been increasing, which suggests that labour is becoming more efficient as labour-saving technology enhances productivity growth (See Kaldor, 1957; Tregenna, 2009), and also reducing the employment elasticity of manufacturing growth (Rodrik, 2015).

References

African Centre for Economic Transformation (ACET, 2014). *Growth with Depth—African Transformation Report*. Accra: ACET. Available at: http://africantransformation.org/wp-content/uploads/2014/02/2014-african-transformation-report.pdf. Accessed 18.06 2016.

African Development Bank/Organisation for Economic Cooperation and Development/United Nations Development Programme (AEO, 2017). *African Economic Outlook 2017: Entrepreneurship and Industrialisation*. Abidjan: AfDB/OECD/UNDP.

African Union (2007). Action Plan for Accelerated Industrial Development of Africa. AU Conference of Ministers of Industry, 1st Extra-Ordinary Session, 24–27 September, Midrand, South Africa.

Balchin, N., Gelb, S., Kennan, J., Martin, H., te Velde, D. and Williams, C. (2016). "Developing Export-based Manufacturing in Sub-Saharan Africa." Supporting Economic Transformation (SET) Report, London.

Banga, Karishma and te Velde, Dirk Willem (2018). "Digitisation and the Future of Manufacturing in Africa." Supporting Economic Transformation (SET) Working Paper, available at https://progs.odinet.org.uk/iedg/Economic%20Transformation/SharedDocuments/Future%20of%20manufacturing%20project/set.odi.org accessed 12.03.2018.

Chang, H. (2003). "Kicking away the Ladder: The 'Real' History of Free Trade." Foreign Policy in Focus (FPIF) Special Report. Available at: www.personal.ceu.hu/corliss/CDST_Course_Site/Readings_old_2012_files/Ha-Joon%20Chang%20-%20Kicking%20Away%20the%20Ladder-The%20"Real"%20History%20of%20Free%20Trade.pdf. Accessed 21.03.2015.

Chenery, H.B., Robinson, S., and Syrquim, M. (1986). *Industrialisation and Growth: A Comparative Study*. Washington D.C.: World Bank.

Chitonge, H. (2015). *Economic Growth and Development in Africa: Understanding Trends and Prospects*. New York/London: Routledge.

Chitonge, H. (2016). "Zambia at 50: The Persisting Challenges of Economic Structural Transformation." Development Southern Africa, DOI:10.1080/0376835X.2016.1231053.

De Vries, G., Timmer, M. and de Vries, K. (2015). "Structural Transformation in Africa: Static Gains, Dynamic Losses." *Journal of Development Studies*, Vol. 56, No. 6. 674–688.

Department of Agriculture Food and Fisheries (DAFF, 2012). 2010. *Abstract of Agricultural Statistics*. Pretoria: DAFF.

Department of Trade and Industry (DTI, 2016). *Industrial Policy Action Plan (IPAP) 2016/17–2018/19*. Pretoria: DTI.

Deverajan, S. (2013). "Africa's Statistical Tragedy." *Review of Income and Wealth*, DOI: 10.1111/roiw.12013, 2013.

Filmer, D. and Fox, M. (2014). *Overview: Youth Employment in Sub-Saharan Africa*. Washington, DC: World Bank.

Fox, L. and Thomas, A. (2016). "Africa's Got Work to Do: A Diagnostic of Youth Employment Challenges in Sub-Saharan Africa." *Journal of African Economies*, Vol. 25, No. 1. 16–36.

Hausmann, R., Hwang, J. and Rodrik, D. (2007). "What You Export Matters." *Journal of Economic Growth*, Vol. 12, No. 1. 1–25.

IBIS (2015). *Natural Resource Watch Report on Sub-Saharan Africa*. Copenhagen: IBIS.

International Labour Organization (ILO, 2016). *World Employment Social Outlook: Trends 2016*. Geneva: ILO.

International Monetary Fund (IMF, 2013). "Boom, Burst or Prosperity? Managing Sub-Saharan Africa's Natural Resource Wealth. New York: IMF.

Jalilian, H. and Weiss, J. (2000). "De-industrialisation in Africa: Myths or Crisis," in H. Jalilian, M. Tribe and J. Weiss (eds.), *Industrial Development and Policy in Africa: Issues of De-Industrialisation and Development Strategy*. Cheltenham: Edward Elgar. 137–176.

Jerven, M. (2013). "Comparability of GDP Estimates in Sub-Saharan Africa: The Effect of Revision in Sources and Methods Since Structural Adjustment." *Review of Income and Wealth*, DOI: 10.1111/roiw.12006, 2013.

Kaldor, N. (1957). "A Model of Economic Growth." *Economic Journal*, Vol. 67, No. 268. 591–624.

Kaldor, N. (1966). *Causes of the Slow Rate of Growth in the United Kingdom*. Cambridge: Cambridge University Press.

Kaplan, D, R. Kaplinsky, and M. Morris, (2012). *'One thing leads to another'—Commodities, linkages and industrial development: A conceptual overview*. (MMCP Discussion Paper No. 12). Cape Town, South Africa and Milton Keynes,

Kuznets, S. (1966). *Modern Economic Growth: Rate Structure and Spread*. New Haven: Yale University Press.

Lewis W. A. (1954). "Economic Development with Unlimited Supplies of Labour." *Manchester School*, Vol. 20. 139–191.

McMillan, M. and Rodrik, D. (2011). "Globalisation, Structural Change and Productivity Growth." National Bureau of Economic Research (NBER) Working Paper No. 17143.

Mkandawire, T. (2001). "Thinking About the Developmental States in Africa." *Cambridge Journal of Economics*, Vol. 25, No. 3. 289–313.

Murphy, K., Shleifer, A. and Vishny, R. (1989). "Industrialisation and the Big Push." *Journal of Political Economy*, Vol. 97, No. 5. 1003–1026.

Naude, W. (2010). "New Challenges for Industrial Policy." United Nations University (UNU)/World Institute for Development Economic Research (WIDER), Working Paper No. 2010/107.

Newman, Carol, Page, J., Rand, J., Shimeles, A., Soderbom, M. and Tap, F. (2016a). "The Pursuit of Industry: Policies and Outcomes," in Carol Newman, J. Page, J. Rand, A. Shimeles, M. Soderbom and F. Tap (eds.), *Manufacturing Transformation: Comparative Studies in Industrial Development in Africa and Emerging Asia*. London: Oxford University Press. 1–24.

Newman, C., Page, J., Rand, J., Shimeles, A., Soderbom, M. and Tarp, F. (2016b). *Made in Africa: Learning to Compete in Industry*. Washington, DC: Brooking Institute Press.

Page, J. (2012). "Aid, Structural Change and the Private Sector in Africa." United Nations University (UNU)/World Institute for Development Economic Research (WIDER) Working Paper No.2012/21.

Page, J. (2015). "Structural Change and Africa's Poverty Puzzle," in L. Chandy, H. Kato and H. Kharas (eds.), *The Last Mile in Ending Extreme Poverty*. New York: Brooklyn Institute Press. 219–248.

Pingali, P. (1997). "From Subsistence to Commercial Production Systems: The Transformation of Asian Agriculture." *American Journal of Agricultural Economics*, Vol. 17, No. 2. 628–634.

Prebisch, R. (1950). *The Economic Development of Latin America and Its Principle Problems*. New York: United Nations Economic Commission for Latin America and Caribbean.

Rakotoarisoa, M., Lafrate, M. and Paschali, M. (2012). *Why Has Africa Become a Net Food Importer: Explaining Africa's Agriculture and Food Trade Deficit*. Rome: FAO.

Rodrik, D. (2015). "Premature Deindustrialisation." National Bureau of Economic Research (NBER) Working Paper No.20935. Available at: http://www.nber.org/papers/w20935. Accessed 16.09.2017.

Rostow, W. W. (1959). *The Stages of Economic Growth: A Non-Communist Manifesto*. Cambridge: Cambridge University Press.

Singer, W. H. (1950). "The Distribution of Gains Between Investing and Borrowing Countries." *American Economic Review*, Vol. 40, No. 2. 473–485.

Singer, W. H. (1984). "The Terms of Trade Controversy and the Evolution of Soft Financing: Early Years in the UN," in, G. Meier (ed.), *Pioneers in Development*. New York: World Bank. 273–301.

Songwe, V. and Winkler, D. (2012). "Export and Export Diversification in Sub-Saharan Africa: A Strategy for Post-Crisis Growth." Africa Growth Initiative (AGI) Working Paper No.3. Brookings: World Bank.

Srinivasan, T. N. (1994). "Data Base for Development Analysis." *Journal of Development Economics*, Vol. 44. 3–27.

Syrquin, M. and Chenery, H. B. (1989a). "Three Decades of Industrialisation." *World Bank Economic Review*, Vol. 3, No. 2. 145–181.

Syrquin, M. and Chenery, H. B. (1989b). "Patterns of Development: 1950 to 1983." Discussion Paper No. 41. Washington, DC: World Bank.

Timmer, M., de Vries, G. and de Vries, K. (2014). Patterns of Structural Change in Developing Countries. Groningen Growth and Development Centre (GGDC), Working Paper No. 149.

Tregenna, F. (2009). "Characterising De-industrialisation: An Analysis of Changes in Manufacturing Employment and Output Internationally." *Cambridge Journal of Economics*, Vol. 33, No.4. 433–466.

Tregenna, F. (2016). "Deindustrialisation: An Issue for Both Developed and Developing Countries" in J. Weiss and M. Tribe (eds.), *Routledge Handbook of Industrialisation and Development*. London/New York: Routledge. 97–115.

Tribe, M. (2000). "The Concept of 'Infant Industry' in a Sub-Saharan African Context," in H. Jalilian, M. Tribe and J. Weiss (eds.), *Industrial Development and Policy in Africa: Issues of De-Industrialisation and Development Strategy*. Cheltenham: Edward Elgar. 30–57.

United Nations Development Programme (UNDP, 2016). *Human Development Report: Human Development for Everyone*. New York: UNDP.

United Nations Economic Commission for Africa (UNECA, 2015). *Report on Africa 2015: Industrialising Through Trade*. Addis Ababa: UNECA.

United Nations Economic Commission for Africa (UNECA, 2016b). *Economic Report on Africa 2016: Greening Africa's Industrialisation*. Addis Ababa: UNECA.

United Nations Economic Commission for Africa (UNECA, 2016a). Transformative Industrial Policy for Africa. Addis Ababa: Economic Commission for Africa.

United Nations Industrial Development Organisation (1980). World Industry Since 1960: Progress and Prospects. Vienna: UNIDO.

United Nations Industrial Development Organization (UNIDO, 2016a). *Industrialisation in Africa and Least Developed Countries: Booting Growth, Creating Jobs, Promoting Inclusiveness and Sustainability*. Vienna: UNIDO.

United Nations Industrial Development Organization (UNIDO, 2016b). *Industrial Development Report 2016: The Role of Technology and Innovation in Inclusive and Sustainable Industrial Development*. Vienna: UNIDO.

United Nations Industrial Development Organization (UNIDO, 2017). *World Manufacturing Production: Statistics for Quarter II, 2017*. Vienna: UNIDO.

Wade, R. (1990). *Economic Theory and The Role of Government in East Asian Industrialisation*. Princeton: Princeton University Press.

World Bank (2013). *Africa's Pulse: An Analysis of Issues Shaping Africa's Economic Future. Vol. 8 (April 2014)*. Washington, DC: World Bank.

World Bank (2015). Africa's Pulse: An Analysis of Issues Shaping Africa's Economic Future. October 2015, Volume 15. Available at https://openknowledge.worldbank.org/handle/10986/2272212/06/2016.

World Economic Forum (WEF, 2017). *The Future of Jobs and Skills in Africa: Preparing the Region for the Fourth Industrial Revolution*. Geneva: WEF.

Young, A. (2012). "The African Growth Miracle." *Journal of Political Economy*, Vol. 120, No. 4. 696–739.

· 4 ·

INDUSTRIALISATION AND DEVELOPMENT PLANNING IN AFRICA

Introduction: The African Industrialisation Aspirations

Africa's desire to industrialise the continent did not start with the *First Industrial Development Decade* (1980 to 1990), proclaimed in the Lagos Plan of Action (see LPA, 1980:15). In most countries, plans to industrialise started immediately after independence, during the early 1960s. But the history of industrialisation in Africa is punctuated by episodes of optimism, disillusionment and resurgence. The period after independence was characterised by buoyant optimism that African countries would industrialise rapidly and 'catch up' with industrialised countries. Kwame Nkrumah was one of the leaders with a strong conviction that African countries needed to industrialise rapidly to 'catch up' with developed countries. This conviction is evident in the famous adage that "we will achieve in a decade what took others a century…" (cited in Ayittey, 1999:7). Nkrumah was not alone; Julius Nyerere also envisioned Africa catching up with developed countries by "running while others walk" (see Mkandawire, 2011). These early visions and aspirations to industrialise the continent were the first conceited efforts to disrupt the colonial economic set up. Indeed significant progress in disrupting the colonial economic logic was made during the first decade of independence in many countries (Bates, 1981; Mkandawire and Soludo, 1999). A background paper prepared for the joint conference of the African ministers of finance, which compared GDP per capita growth rates for the periods 1960–1973 and 1980–2000, concluded that growth was much higher during the first decade of independence, with more countries reporting higher growth (UNECA/AU, 2011). As shown in this chapter, African countries during this period adopted the principles of development planning and many formulated and implemented National Development Plans (NDPs), in which the industrial strategy was embedded.

But this moment of optimism, created mainly by the initial success and also by the euphoria of having succeeded with political decolonisation, manifested in the dislodgement of colonial regimes from African soil, was followed by a long period of disillusionment and hopelessness as the challenges of industrialising the continent became apparent, and in some countries intractable. During the period of disillusionment, development planning was abandoned in most countries, and with it, industrial policy; leaving the industrialisation project to forces of the market as SAPs reigned large (Soludo and Ogbu, 2004). The implementation of SAPs during the 1980s and 1990s led to a phenomenon which some analysts have referred to as the *deindustrialisation* of Africa (see Noorbakhsh and Paloni, 2000), when the initial progress made during the 1960s was slowly reversed. As illustrated in Chapter 3, industrial capacity in most African countries today is still below the levels reached in the mid-1970s before the first oil crisis.

It has now become apparent that African countries have to reboot their industrialisation strategies; they have to come up with a game changer if industrialisation is to be realised. This is the dominant view in the current period which I refer to as the resurgence *period,* when industrialisation is featuring strongly on Africa's development agenda, at country, regional and continental levels. The rise of interest in industrialisation in Africa is evident in the number of countries which have now formulated separate industrial policies and strategies (see UNECA, 2014). It is yet to be seen if African countries and the continent at large will, this time around, find a game changer to make industrialisation a reality.

Given the revived interest in industrial policy on the continent, this chapter looks at the earlier efforts by African countries to promote industrial growth. Most countries developed the five-year (in some countries seven-year, and others ten-year) NDPs in which they elaborated the development goals of the nation, including industrial development. Since in the earlier period African countries did not develop separate industrial policies (industrial policies were embedded in the NDPs), this chapter examines the NDP documents, focusing on the industrial strategy component.[1] Chapter 5 examines the actual implementation of the industrial strategies developed in the NDPs. Because of the language challenge, this chapter focuses on the experience of 18 African countries whose NDPs are in English. While most African countries designed several NDPs prior to the onset of SAPs, in this chapter the focus will be on the first two or three NDPs.

Development Planning and Industrial Policy

The decline in industrial activities in Africa since the mid-1970s has had a cumulative effect which is now being manifested in the failure of most African economies to generate sufficient productive jobs to absorb the growing labour force, especially the youth (see WEF, 2017). The challenge posed by the inability to generate productive employment has brought back industrialisation on the development agenda in most African countries as the only option for transforming African economies, promoting inclusive growth and reducing poverty. Starting from the mid-1990s when it became clear that the SAPs were not going to deliver sustained growth and reduction in poverty, many African countries, starting with Ghana in 1996, revived the practice of long-term national development planning, expressed in terms of Vision 2020 and Vision 2030. In some countries, the long-term plans are complemented by medium term (five year) plans. A quick glance at the planning documents in different African countries suggests that industrial policy and strategies are back on the agenda (see UNECA, 2014). With the return of development planning (what I refer to as the *second-generation development planning*) there is a revival of hope that things may just begin to look up again. While critics remain sceptical about the potential of these plans to contribute to Africa's prospect of disrupting the persistent colonial economic logic, there is wider agreement among analysts that Africa has no option but to industrialise (see UNECA, 2012; ACET, 2014; UNIDO, 2016; Newman et al, 2016). This agreement is buoyed by an emerging consensus that industrial policy occupies an important place in the development of developing countries (see Lall, 2004). It has been argued for instance that these "days, contrary to the heydays of market fundamentalism in the 1980s and 1990s, few people would deny that there are instances where state interventions in industrial development is justified" (UNECA, 2016a:28).

Development Planning in Africa

Development planning in most countries in Africa did not start at independence; various colonial governments carried out different types of planning for development. In a study that reviews the experience of development planning in Africa, Waterston (1965) argues that different forms of development planning were attempted in many of the former colonies, including those in Africa. Green (1965) focusing on the African development planning experience alludes to the fact that development planning in most African countries started during colonial rule. But most of the planning prior to independence took the form of "capital budgets" focusing on public investments, excluding private investments, and operated within the annual budget cycle. Commenting on the Ghanaian experiences, Ewusi (1981) observes that prior to the Seven-Year Development Plan (1963–1970) all the plans were capital budgets which covered the public sector only. As Killick (1983) acknowledges, development planning after World War II involved comprehensive planning for both private and public entities, not just planning for public resources. He further argues that comprehensive development planning in post-colonial Africa, while it built on the foundations laid during colonial rule, was articulated by independent African states as they sought to achieve rapid development in their societies. "With active encouragement of the World Bank and other aid agencies, most newly independent states hastened to prepare medium-term development plans, often building upon foundations laid in the colonial period" (Killick, 1983:47).

The Plight of African Industrialisation During the Colonial Period

At this point, it is important to note that although during colonial rule there were some industrial activities that emerged in different parts of the continent, it was not the intention of the colonial government to industrialise the colonies as argued in Chapter 1. The colonial economic logic was deeply entrenched in the idea that African countries' main role in the international division of labour was that of supplying raw materials to the global economy. For example, Ewusi (1981:4) in his review of the colonial industrial activities in Ghana reports that "most of the firms established before 1950 were in the wood and cork industries, exporting mainly logs of timber. The 1960 Directory of Industrial Establishment indicated that 45.5 percent of the total number of establishments in the manufacturing sector were in the timber exporting industry." In terms of the overall development project, it has been observed that "unlike their colonial predecessors, they [the new African states] were deeply committed to the development of their local economies" (Bates, 1981:13).

The low priority given to industrial development during colonial rule should not be surprising. Industrialising the African continent at that time would have gone against the colonial economic logic of maintaining a steady supply of raw materials to the industrial centres of the world, and that of ensuring the continued dependence of the colonies on imported manufactures. In his famous book, *How Europe Underdeveloped Africa*, Walter Rodney (1982) explains why industrialising Africa was actually diametrically opposed to the colonisers' interest and the colonial project as a whole (see Chapter 1). Andrew Kamarck (1967) when commenting on development projects in Africa during colonial rule argued that the colonial administration had little interest in developing the continent, and whatever benefit may have accrued from the colonial project was actually accidental, something that economists refer to as positive externality; it was not intended to benefit the colonies. He argues that if one looks at the railway lines developed during the colonial period in all African countries, while they might have opened access to remote areas, they were not meant for the benefit of the local people living on the sides of the railway line. The primary intention was to transport the raw materials for export. A comment by the first Zambian President Dr. Kenneth Kaunda highlights the neglect of infrastructure which most of the colonies in Africa (and perhaps in other colonies) experienced:

> The structure which we inherited from the colonial era resulted in many situations which have to be put right: an education system which was so far below requirement that at the time of independence only a handful of people had anything like sufficient training to enable them take their places in the service of government; a transport system which is linked in a situation of subservience to Southern Africa…, and trade so organised that we seemed irrevocably linked to supply from Southern Africa not only for raw materials but also for ordinary consumer goods of everyday life (Republic of Zambia, 1966:i).

Industrialisation and the infrastructure which goes with it, in the big colonial scheme of things, was thus not a development priority. From a colonial perspective, it is clear that establishing a flourishing industrial sector in Mali or Chad would have undermined the entire project of maintaining control and dependency of the colonies, except in colonies that had large settler population (such as South Africa, Zimbabwe, Namibia, Kenya and Algeria) where the European immigrants took the colonies as their permanent place of residence. In non-settler colonies, the development of infrastructure was tailored to serve the settlers and not the indigenous Africans. Even in settler colonies, the infrastructure developed was largely meant for a minority settler population, with the South African policy of separate development and later apartheid being a classic example of a vicious form of colonialism.

Commenting on the industrial history of Ghana, Ackah et al (2016:48) argue that,

> The industrial sector that was inherited from the colonial rulers was one that had been underdeveloped mainly because the regime was more interested in extracting raw materials from the Gold Coast (Ghana) while at the same time creating an economic system heavily dependent on manufactured products from Britain.

Thus, the neglect of industrial development in Africa was by no means an accident; it was an outcome of a calculated set of actions in the service of the grand imperial scheme.

In the education sector which is a crucial aspect of any genuine development project, including industrial development, we also find evidence of deliberate disregard of the interest of African people. Estimates suggest that as late as 1958, there were only 8000 Africans (south of the Sahara) graduating with secondary school certificates, and only 10 000 were studying at universities, with more than half of these being in only two countries: Ghana and Nigeria (see Berg, 1964:561). Given this, one may be justified to argue that in "these figures lie the most severe indictment of colonial rule" in Africa (ibid).

But this has to be situated in the broader scheme of things in which colonialism, as a political and economic project, was implemented. What seems to be negligence actually forms part of a rational colonial strategy of maintaining power and control over Africa. Educating a lot of Africans in technical and high-skilled fields would have created competition between Africans and the few colonial officials and settlers. Hence, it was not in the interest of the colonial officials to embark on mass education and skilling of Africans. In fact much of the education burden during colonial rule was borne by missionaries whose strategy and interest was primarily evangelisation through education. Part of the colonial government's disregard of educating Africans can also be attributed to the racist ideologies which were supported by the belief, quite pervasive among colonialists, that an African was only good for manual work (see Hill, 2005).

Thus, the neglect of African communities in all aspects of life no doubt served the interests of colonial regimes across Africa. This was also true about promoting a vibrant industrial sector on the continent, something that would compete with the mother countries for the share of markets for manufactures. As noted in Chapter 1, the fact that African economies have been assigned the role of supplying raw materials in the international division of labour is intricately part of the self-interest of the stronger nations, underpinned by a colonial rationality. For Africa to make progress, it must disrupt this rationality, by restructuring their economies so that they can process most of the raw materials into finished manufactured goods.

The Structure of Colonial Economies in Africa

In setting up economic activities in Africa, the colonial regimes were interested in securing the source of cheap raw materials, and all the investments were directed towards that objective, with little attention paid to the lop-sidedness of the structure of the economy created by this pattern of investment. It is no wonder that one of the characteristic features of most African economies has been a high degree of sectoral fragmentation which has made the linkages between different sectors weak, resulting in extreme conditions of enclavity (see Mhone, 2001). A good example of this is the extractive sector, whether it is oil or minerals. Most of the colonial economic activities operated as enclaves, with no connection to other activities in the economy, and in most cases with only a skeleton of basic industrial activities. Despite over eight decades of colonial rule,

> At independence, Tanzania [for example] was virtually without industry. In the years 1960–62 the manufacturing sector accounted for only 3.4 percent of total gross domestic product. In 1963, only twenty-two thousand people were employed in manufacturing, a very small proportion of the total work force. Most manufactured goods were imported; even by comparison with her East African neighbours, Tanzania's industry was woefully under-developed (Republic of Tanzania, 1969:59).

If the bigger vision of colonialism was to ensure that the colonies did not have industrial capacity to compete with the colonial powers, it makes sense then to argue that industrial development during the colonial period was not on the agenda.

The example cited above is not unique to Tanzania; the picture is representative of most African countries at the end of colonial rule. The colonialists had a strong belief, which is pervasive even today, that industry was too sophisticated for Africans. After all, the dominant theory decreed that

Africa did not have comparative advantage in manufacturing, and therefore, the continent had to stick to the primary sector where it had comparative advantage. Interestingly, Africa has continued to internalise this idea, with most African governments performing exceptionally well in terms of remaining loyal to this maxim. In this sense, Colin Leys (1982:102) is perhaps right when he argues that the underdevelopment of Africa and African technology is "*shaped* and *developed* by colonialism" (emphasis in original).

Apologetics of colonialism fail to see the poor state of industrial development in Africa as a direct consequence of the colonial economic logic. Even today, it is possible to find historians who choose to celebrate what they see as the "net" positive outcomes of colonialism in Africa (see Gilley, 2017). As Myrdal observes, the "'colonial theory' was only too often apologetic writing that attempted to absolve the colonial regimes from responsibility for the conditions of underdevelopment" (cited in Meier, 1984:7). But from an African perspective, the fragmented structure of the economy creates huge disadvantages. As argued in the next chapter, when most of these countries became independent, it proved to be difficult to restructure these economies. While colonialism should not be the only excuse for African countries' failure to successfully restructure their economies six decades after independence, the way these economies were set up continues to constrain efforts aimed at transforming them. The overall influence the colonial economic structure continues to exert on African society in general cannot be over-emphasised.

The extroverted nature of these economies points to a mechanism which perpetuates a situation where Africa benefits little from their resources and labour. Reversing this situation would require re-orientating African economies in such a way that Africans realise greater value from African resources and labour. This can be done by ensuring that Africa does not just dig the copper and coltan from the soil and export it raw to Switzerland or China, but that it adds and captures as much value as is possible before shipping it to other continents. Achieving this has been an enduring challenge in Africa, but it is something that can and must be done. The precondition for achieving this is radical restructuring which would enable these economies to have some internal coherence as the basis for interacting with the rest of the world. This is the tangible outcome of a process of economic decolonisation. With careful planning and committed leadership, African economies can be successfully decolonised.

Foundations of Development Planning in Africa

Planning is a common activity that one can find in different fields including in the military, urban development, schools, hospitals and in various spheres of government. Here the focus is on economic development planning, with specific reference to the African *experiences*. Development planning as an applied field of economics is often seen as a technical field in which economic models of growth forecasting and accounting are used to determine the allocation of resources and setting of economic targets. But that is a very economistic way of thinking about development planning, and as some scholars have observed, viewing development planning from that angle almost makes economic planning an impossible mission (see Leys, 1982). In the first place, development planning is a process that involves bringing together different ideas to reflect the overall political, social and economic objectives of a country (see UNECA/AU, 2011). In this sense, development planning is not just an exercise in economic modelling and growth forecasting.

A broader approach to development planning should have four basic features: First, it should start with the broader national goals—the *social and political dimension*. Second, within the identified social and political goals the development planning process should come up with practical strategies to realise the identified goals/objectives—the *implementation aspect*. Third, the planning process should have a mechanism to bring the different threads of a development plan together—the *coordination aspect*. Fourth, the planning process, while it should identify priorities within an economy, its planning framework should cover the entire economy in an integrated manner—the *consistency dimension* (see Killick, 1976).

The Rationale Behind Development Planning

In development economics, there are three major reasons advanced to support development planning. First, there is the common argument, especially among the pioneers of development economics, that the ubiquity of market failures, especially in developing countries, makes it difficult for development to proceed without systematic planning (Nurkse, 1953; Lewis, 1984). The second is that, because of underdeveloped markets in developing countries, any genuine development efforts to be successful, would require coordination of investments in various sectors (see Scitovsky, 1954). Scitovsky (1954:150) expands on this, arguing that in developing countries, markets are inadequate in communicating the right signal to investors, and as such "centralised investment planning" is necessary to generate greater impact in the economy. He stresses the point that the price mechanism fails to give adequate signal to private actors to optimise their investment decisions. Hence the price mechanism is seen to be less suitable to guide the medium- to long-term investment decisions, which many developing countries have to undertake. Scitovsky (ibid) explains the disadvantage of relying on price signals to guide long-term investments:

> In an economy in which economic decisions are decentralised, a system of communication is needed to enable each person who makes economic decisions to learn about the economic decisions of others and coordinate his decisions with theirs. In the market economy, prices are the signalling device that informs each person of other people's economic decision; and the merit of perfect competition is that it would cause prices to transmit information reliably and people to respond to this information properly. Market prices however, reflect the economic situation *as it is* and *not as it will be*. For this reason, they are more useful for co-ordinating current production decisions, which are immediately effective and guided by short-run considerations, than they are for co-ordinating investment decisions, which have a delayed effect and —looking ahead to a long future period—should be governed not by what the present economic situation is but by what the future economic situation is expected to be. The proper co-ordination of investment decisions, therefore, would require a signalising device to transmit information about present plans and future conditions as they are determined by present plans; and the pricing system fails to provide this (emphasis added).

Scitovsky has a footnote at the end of this extract where he acknowledges the point made by Kenneth Arrow that future markets provide the signals about how the future economic conditions will be and thus serve the purpose of a *signalling device*. He accepts this argument, but argues further that in developing countries where even present price signals are imperfect, it is unlikely that the price system would communicate properly to countless individuals making investment decisions about what the economic situation and prices would be in ten or fifteen years' time. The conclusion he draws is that some kind of planning is essential in economically backward countries where decentralised decisions of private investors are not likely to lead to investment patterns that can lead to coherent industrial development. What the pioneers of development economics were actually arguing for was the importance of an industrial development strategy.

It is important here to note that what these pioneers of development economics had in mind was not the Soviet Union-type command economy, but one in which centrally planned investment, preferably by the state, or some *supra*-national planning agency like the East and South-Eastern Investment Trust (EEIT) proposed by Rosenstein-Rodan (1943), would provide the mechanism to coordinate the investment of both private and public sectors. For Scitovsky (1954) and Nurkse (1953) the main objective of supporting a planned economy was to secure what they referred to as *balanced growth*, in which the different parts of the economy grow at relative rates to avoid creating disequilibrium in the economy. This is not a point to go into the balanced growth debate; the focus here is on the rationale for adopting development planning and the influence the ideas of the early development economists had on African leaders who were earnestly looking for means to quickly "catch up" and reduce dependence on the former colonial powers.

Third, it has been argued that without proper planning involving the state, it would be difficult to mobilise adequate resources required for development. Rosenstein-Rodan (1943, 1957) strongly argued for coordinated efforts aimed at mobilising sufficient resources for investment to kick-start the development process, an idea which was referred to as the *Big Push theorem*.

There is no doubt that some of these ideas motivated the various development plans which independent African states developed and implemented during the 1960s. In Ghana, for instance, Arthur Lewis who is regarded as one of the leading pioneers of development economics and planning, was influential in the designing of various development policies including the first NDP (see Kanbur, 2016). A review of the development plans in Africa does point to the fact that the ideas of the early development economists played an important role in shaping both the planning processes and the actual content of the development plans. The appeal of development planning in many African countries was not only based on the economic justification, but also on the view that planning offered the fastest means of catching up with the developed countries, perhaps inspired by the example of the former Soviet Union's rapid growth through the first five-year planning period (see Leys, 1982:100).

First-Generation Development Plans in Africa

African countries designed and implemented different development plans from the 1960s to the 1980s when development planning was abandoned (in most countries). Even though a number of countries such as Swaziland, Botswana, Lesotho and Egypt produced fourth and fifth NDPs, by the mid-1980s (see Table 4.1), most countries stopped formulating NDPs when structural adjustment programmes were introduced (see Soludo and Ogbu, 2004). Olukoshi (2004) argues that development planning and notions of a developmental state were swept away by the strong anti-state ideology that came with the neoliberal counter-revolution in the 1980s. The anti-state ideology was probably more strongly deployed in Africa than in any other parts of the world such that African states were demonised for being blotted, inefficient, over-extended, lethargic and inefficient (see Mkandawire, 2001). It is not surprising that by the early 1990s, most African states were hollowed out, with little capacity to formulate and implement any meaningful policy, later on the complex industrial policy. The strong liberal economic thinking that dominated economic policy during this time did not see the role for industrial policy (Lall, 2004, UNECA, 2016a). It is only in recent years that development planning is being entertained in Africa in the form of Vision 2020 and 2030.

Development Plan: A Rallying Instrument

While different countries in Africa had different experiences with development planning in terms of implementation and outcomes, it is quite striking that all the 18 NDPs reviewed for this study, especially the first and second NDPs, were built on the strong belief that developing a country was a task that required everyone's effort and sacrifice, for the betterment of the nation. The view that developing a country is a collective undertaking to which every citizen was encouraged to contribute practically is a common thread that runs in all the early NDPs. For example, the preface to the first NDP of Botswana stipulates that, the "National Development Plan sets out in detail the task to be tackled. Every Motswana should play a part" (Republic of Botswana, 1968:i). In Ghana, we find a similar statement by the then president Kwame Nkrumah:

> It [the Seven-year National Development Plan] stets out clearly the effort and sacrifice which will be required of each of us to enable that plan to succeed. I, for my part, am determined that the plan shall succeed but my determination must be supported by the combined efforts of the whole nation, including Members of Parliament, our Public Servants, our farmers and working people (Republic of Ghana, 1964:ii).

The first Sudanese NDP strongly highlights the importance of wider public participation and commitment from all citizens as the prerequisite for successful implantation of the NDP: "the highest standard of devotion and efficiency from the public services, widespread understanding and participation from the people and sacrifices borne equally by all citizens are essential if the efforts and resources of the entire nation are to be mobilised in support of the Plan..." (Republic of the Sudan, 1962:2). Similar statements are found in the prefaces of the NDPs of most countries included in this study. In this sense, development planning falls within the realm of development economics which broadly deals with the issues of how to achieve economic growth and improve the living standards of the people.

However, there is a marked difference in the way development planning was viewed in South Africa during the 1960s and 1970s, and this should not come as a surprise.[2] In South Africa the emphasis was rather on the technical side, estimating what resources (financial and human) would be required to achieve the desired or possible growth rates in the economy.

> The purpose of these programmes is to determine the maximum growth rate which, based on certain assumptions and given the political and social economic framework of the country, could be attained in the next six years without causing excessive pressure on the available factors of production and/or the balance of payment (Republic of South Africa, 1974:v).

It is apparent that in the South African context, development planning followed a conventional route where the focus was on estimating the resources needed against the targets set. It seems that what was then called the *Economic Development Programmes* (EDPs) in South Africa were largely seen as a technical tool for assessing the capacity of the economy under different scenarios. Reading through the EDPs from 1960s to the end of the 1980s, it is apparent that these programmes were less perceived as a rallying point for the nation, which was an overriding characteristic of the NDPs in the other African countries. This, however, should be expected given that the apartheid government which was in power at that time had a narrow constituency to which it was politically accountable. There was no necessity to explain to the nation what the rationale behind the EDPs was and what the role of the people in the programme was. Apart from that, the technical approach adopted is reflective of economic and development planning capacity in much of the developed world where this was the playground for planning economists (see Killick, 1976).

Review of the NDPs in African countries suggests that there was a strong sense among African leaders, at that time, that developing African economies could only be successful if all people participated. It is evident that African leaders strongly believed that developing these countries was not just a matter of experts doing their best; everyone, including the efforts of the small farmer in remote villages, were seen as essential to the national project at hand—the development of the country. This strong sense of development as a collective national task, requiring the participation of ordinary people, could be attributed to the strong spirit of collectivism engendered by the ideology of nationalism, which was strong during the liberation struggle and in the period immediately after independence. It is also evident that the two main objectives dominant in all the NDPs, regardless of the economic ideological a country adopted, were the general improvement of the living conditions of the people and improved economic performance, expressed in terms of increased income (see Table 4.1).

Table 4.1: National Development Plans (NDPs) in Selected African Countries, 1960–1990.

Country	Year of Independence	Plan Type	Plans	Economic System	Main Objective of NDP
Botswana	1966	rolling 5-year	1968–1973, 1970–1975, 1976–1979, 1979–1985	mixed	Guide the economic and social development of Botswana
Cameroon	1960	5-year	1966, 1971, 1971–1976	mixed	Improve the standard of living of the citizens
Egypt	1958	5-year	1960–1965, 1982–1987, 1987–1992	socialist	Improve the standard of living of the citizens
Ethiopia	N/A*	5-year	1957–1961, 1963–1967, 1968–1973, 1974–1979	mixed/ socialist	Accelerate the socioeconomic development process
Gambia	1967	5-year	1975–1980, 1981–1985	mixed	Maximise the rate of national economic development
Ghana	1957	7-year	1955–1961, 1963–1970, 1975–1980	socialist	Modernisation of agriculture and rapid expansion of industrial activities
Kenya	1963	6-year	1964–1970, 1970–1974, 1974–1978, 1979–1983	mixed (African socialism)	Greater welfare for all of the country's people
Lesotho	1966	5-year	1970–1975, 1975–1980, 1980–1985, 1986–1990	mixed	Economic emancipation of the country

Country	Year of Independence	Plan Type	Plans	Economic System	Main Objective of NDP
Liberia	1847	4-year	1967–1970, 1976–1980	market (ODP)	Accelerate the nation's social and economic development
Malawi	1964	4-year, then 10-year	1962–1965, 1965–1969, 1971–1980	market-led	Accelerate the pace of national development
Nigeria	1960	6-year	1962–1968, 1970–1974, 1975–1980	market-led	Transform the national economy into a modern, diversified and virtually self-sustaining system
Sierra Leone	1961	10-year, then 5-year	1962–1972, 1974–1979	mixed	Transform the economy from primarily productive to diversified
South Africa	1994† (1910)	5-year with annual reviews	1964–1965, 1966–1968, 1969–1970, 1972–1977, 1970–1972, 1974–1979, 1978–1987	mixed	Aid the formulation of the country's economic development policy
Sudan	1960	10-year, then 5-year	1961–1971, 1970–1975, 1974–1979, 1978–1983	mixed/ socialist	Increase the national income growth rate
Swaziland	1968	5-year	1969–1974, 1973–1977, 1978–1983, 1989–1990	mixed	Improve citizens' living conditions
Tanzania	1963	5-year	1961–1964, 1964–1969, 1969–1974, 1976–1981	socialist	Improve general standard of living
Uganda	1963	5-year	1961–1966, 1969–1971, 1971–1975	mixed	Transform the base of the economy and modernise it
Zambia	1964	5-year	1966–1970, 1971–1976, 1979–1983	mixed	Radically improve the standard of living of the population

Source: Author. Based on data from various NDPs.

**"Year of independence" does not apply to Ethiopia because the country was not formally colonised.

†For South Africa, the actual date of independence is 1910 when the country became a republic. However, 1994 is widely referred to as the year of independence because that's when the majority of South Africans became politically free in the true sense.

Indeed many ordinary people sacrificed a lot in the liberation struggle, and after dislodging colonial regimes from African soil, they were being called upon once again to contribute to fighting the evils of underdevelopment marked by what was, in the early days of independence, referred to as the unholy trinity of *diseases*, *poverty* and *illiteracy* (Mkandawire, 2003).

Whether this call from the leaders for the people to sacrifice for the development of their countries was mere rhetoric is a different debate. What is clear is that the call for people to make their contribution reflects the thinking dominant at the time, that ordinary people had a role to play in the development of a country. This is in clear contrast with the development strategies and initiatives being adopted in Africa today, which have emphasised the role of international experts and the 'clever' bureaucrats as the only actors on the development stage. It seems as if African policymakers have come to believe that development can be done without the population in rural areas engaged in subsistence agriculture and in survivalist businesses in urban areas. The reasons for adopting this stance are not clear, but one of them is the carry-over from SAP years whose influence is still lingering in many policy corridors in Africa today.

The other common feature found in all the second and third NDPs is a consistent pattern of starting with a review of the previous plan. In most reviews, what seems common among all the plans is the honest recognition of the challenges of implementing the plans. In most of the plans there is a candid acknowledgement of the challenges faced in implementing the first NDPs and some reasons why the targets outlined were not met. In the case of Tanzania, the second NDP clearly acknowledges that most of the targets set in the first NDP were not met because the plan was not implemented as envisioned over the plan period. The reviews in most second and subsequent NDPs also indicate that the subsequent plans were formulated drawing from the lessons learnt in the process of implementing the previous plans. In cases where the review of the previous planning and implementation process was open and thorough, it is evident that valuable lessons were learned and efforts were made to avoid repeating the same mistakes. A good example of this is the second NDPs in Kenya and Tanzania, where the mistakes made in the previous plan were acknowledged and measures were taken not to repeat them.

Industrialisation Strategies in NDPs

In all the NDPs for the 18 countries reviewed, the industrial strategy formed an integral part. But there is great variation in how countries approached industrial development, which is largely a reflection of a country's capacity at the time of independence. In some countries, the section on industrial development was only a small section with little detail regarding the goals and the means to achieve them. In other countries, the industrial section constituted a substantial portion of the NDPs. For example, the section discussing industrial policy in Botswana's first NDP was only two pages, with no clear targets set over the plan period, while the section covering industrial development in Cameroon's first NDP constituted the bulk of the plan, with details on industrial activities identified to be central to the development of the country. A close look at the structure and content of the first NDPs for most of these countries reflects not just the difference in the planning ability, but also the administrative capacity which the colonial regimes left behind in these countries (see Mkandawire, 2010).

Scope of the First-Generation NDPs

The NDPs themselves covered a wide range of development issues from land tenure reforms and infrastructure development to finance, international aid and government services. While the content, philosophy, priorities and objectives of these plans differ markedly between countries, there are striking commonalities. For instance, the structure of most NDPs is surprisingly similar, perhaps reflecting the stamp of British administrative legerdemain across the board. All the plans started with the preface by the president or King (in the case of Lesotho and Swaziland), except in the case of Malawi, in which the philosophy, rationale and objectives of the plan were stated in brief by the minister of planning. Secondly, in most of these plans there is recognition of the important role that planning plays in a country's development and the role of the state in coordinating the development activities, with the plan broadly seen as a statement of intent. In Gambia for example, the NDP is defined as,

> An attempt to take a substantive step forward—involving...much more specific definitions of national objectives, priorities, and where possible targets, establishing a frame for maximising integration, coordination and executive ability in the public sector...It should be seen and judged, not as a programming exercise, but primarily as a national statement of firm intent (Republic of the Gambia, 1975:1).

Egypt's first NDP links the need for planning to the national goal of transforming the country through coordinated efforts in the allocation and use of available resources: "The need to undertake planning depends on the need for the National Economy to organize itself better and to ensure the transformation of the labour force available in the form of non-wage labourers qualified as a truly effective force of skilled workers" (United Arab Republic, 1958).

In this light, the NDPs were also seen as instruments for affirming a country's control over its resources and destiny. This comes out more clearly in Nigeria's first NDP:

> The basic objective of planning in Nigeria is not merely to accelerate the rate of economic growth and the rate at which the level of living of the population can be raised; it is also to give her an increasing measure of control over her own destiny. The present First National Plan is therefore seen as the first in a series which will bring Nigeria to the take off stage (Republic of Nigeria, 1962:3).

In this context, the development plans should not be seen as just technical documents elaborating what the countries wanted to achieve over the plan period, they also represented a statement of intent and, most importantly, an expression of sovereignty, signalling that an African-run government was in-charge and capable of determining its own future.

NDPs: Mere Shopping Lists?

As illustrated above, in most newly independent African countries during the 1960s, development planning was seen as an important exercise in which the country identified priorities to focus on and direct national attention and resources over a given period of time. For countries emerging out of colonial rule, with meagre resources, developing a plan, outlining how the little available resources could be used and which sections of society should be prioritised, was an attractive exercise such that all independent African states saw it necessary to formulate NDPs for their respective countries. Being able to systematically decide which sector should receive more attention in the context of the scarce resources gave the newly independent countries the opportunity not only to rationalise the resources but also to have a long-term sequencing of development projects. This comes out more clearly in Tanzania's second NDP:

> ...although this Second Plan is an improvement on the First, planning is always the same in one important respect. It involves making decisions about the allocation of scarce resources; it means choosing between many desirable activities, because not everything can be done at once. It is vital that this should be clearly understood.

> There are many things which are urgently needed in Tanzania and which the plan does not provide for (Republic of Tanzania, 1969:ix).

For most African countries coming out of colonial rule, scarcity of resources against the background of huge developmental challenges arising from decades of colonial rule was a real test of character they had to face. In this context, planning provided a means for identifying priorities and allocating the scarce resources to the most urgent needs. While in some countries such as Ghana, rapid industrial growth was a top priority, in other countries industrialisation was seen as something that will develop naturally as the economy grows.

Although the statements in most NDPs show that the drafters understood what they wanted to achieve by formulating these documents, NDPs in most African countries have been criticised for showing lack of understanding of planning in general, with critics pointing out that most of these plans were merely a "shopping list" of incoherent projects (see Green, 1965:249–250). Claude Ake (1981) was particularly critical of these plans arguing that while it is good to develop a plan as a roadmap for action, most African countries lacked a clear strategy on how to realise their outlined goals. He argues that this is primarily because in most countries the term *development* was taken to mean becoming like the industrialised countries (usually the former colonial powers), while in others, it simply meant expanding gross domestic product.

While it is quite true that most of the NDPs are scanty on the concrete strategy of how to realise the goals they set, especially when it comes to industrialisation, most of them contain relatively elaborate measures to be taken to realise the outlined goals. This is true for majority of the 18 NDPs reviewed for this study. Each of them has a section explaining where the funds for the plan would come from and the actions to be taken to achieve the broader development goals. Most NDPs have a list of projects clearly identified to be implemented during the plan period as a means to realising the identified development goals. An example of an NDP with clear strategic plans is Lesotho's second NDP. Like many other NDPs of that period, Lesotho's second NDP identified poor infrastructure as one of the priority areas with high potential to contribute immensely to the strategy of improving economic growth performance by raising productivity in agriculture. In this sense, the plan's strategy is consistent, because infrastructure as a priority area received the second largest resource allocation in the plan, reflecting its importance in the overall development strategy for the country.

> The Second largest component in the overall Second Five-Year Plan is physical infrastructure.... Lesotho's transport and communication system inherited at independence was highly inadequate, severely restricting administrative and social services and inhibiting agricultural production for the money economy (Republic of Lesotho, 1975:66).

Another good example is Kenya, which maintained a consistent strategy in the first, second and third NDPs, by focusing on rural development, arguing that the "government believes that it is only through an accelerated development of rural areas that balanced economic development can be achieved, that the necessary growth of employment opportunities can be generated and that the people as a whole can participate in the development process" (Republic of Kenya, 1969:1). In Zambia's second NDP, there is also a clear strategy outlined which focused on building infrastructure neglected during colonial rule, and then investing in rural areas to enable rural farmers transport their agricultural produce to the market and inputs to reach the farmers (Republic of Zambia, 1971).

The Implementation Challenge

However, there are numerous examples in the NDPs reviewed here where the strategy to achieve the identified goal is not clearly outlined. In some cases, the resources allocated to the particular line item did not reflect the envisioned level of priority in the plan. A close look at the first-generation NDPs suggests that, in most of the countries, outlining the strategy and the goals for development was not a problem; the main problem was actually implementing the plans. This is a challenge which has been highlighted in many studies on NDPs in Africa (see Green, 1965; Waterston, 1965; Mkandawire and Soludo, 1999; UNECA/AU, 2011). In most cases, due to various reasons, the larger portions of the plans were actually not implemented. There are a number of countries such as Ghana, Nigeria, Uganda, Ethiopia, Sudan, Liberia and Sierra Leone, where the implementation of these plans was interrupted either by military take-over of government or by the eruption of civil wars. In the case of Ghana, the first NDP was planned to run for seven years from 1963 to 1970, and a subsequent NDP to follow immediately thereafter, but the second NDP only appeared in 1977, under a military ruler—General I. K. Acheampong, *Chairman of the Supreme Military Council*. However, even in countries that had stable governments, the implementation of plans proved to be a challenge such that in most cases, the initial plans were actually abandoned or drastically deviated from. For example, Tanzania's second NDPs, which reviewed the first NDP, acknowledges that the first NDP (1964–1969) had to be deviated from due to the adoption of the *Arusha Declaration* in 1967, two and half years after the first NDP was adopted.

> By resolution of the *Arusha Declaration* we have decided that our Government and our people must work for economic growth in *a manner which will bring benefit to all; and we have decided on the policy of Socialism and Self-Reliance*. It is in the light of these accepted objectives that Government has examined the achievements and failures during the First Plan Period, and used the accumulated experience in drawing up the Second Plan (Republic of Tanzania, 1969:viii, emphasis in original).

One of the reasons given for this is the fact that in 1967, the *Arusha Declaration* was launched and it came with a new national vision which was not articulated in the first NDP. In other words, the first NDP was interrupted by the launching of the *Arusha Declaration*, which may be perceived as a lack of consistency in the overall planning process (see Killick, 1976). We see a similar turn of events in Zambia where the president in 1969 announced what is known as the *Mulungushi and Matero Economic Reforms* outside of the first NDP.[3] There are other examples of plans not being followed or totally abandoned in the middle of the plan period. Only a few countries, such as Kenya, Botswana, Egypt and Swaziland, maintained some form of consistency in the implementation of NDP between the first and second plans. For instance, in Egypt's first NDP, it is reported that 80 percent of the projects aimed at promoting industrialisation and 70 percent of agriculture projects were successfully implemented between 1960 and 1965 (see UNECA/AU, 2011).

The fact that most countries did not stick to the plan raises a fundamental question about how much weight should be attached to an NDP if the plan is frequently abandoned mid-way. This issue has been extensively debated in the past, and two major positions stand out. There is one view that the development plans are formal documents meant to guide development efforts in the country by applying technical tools and the science of economic planning. On this side of the debate are mainly economic planners who put emphasis in the planning process, setting out clearly defined objectives and quantifiable targets that can be realised through the help of forecasting techniques. A good example of this is Jan Drewnowski who defines economic planning as,

> a policy which sets its objectives in the form of quantitative targets to be reached at a determined time. An economic plan is a set of targets to be reached in a given time. An economic plan is national when its targets cover all the national economy. It is a partial economic plan when its targets cover some parts of the economy only. Targets

> set in the plan must of course be feasible. To make sure that they are so, they must be derived by confronting policy objectives with available resources of the economy and their possible uses (cited in Green, 1965:250).

This is of course a narrow definition of planning. One of the major limitations of this definition is its focus on targets as something that a plan must be judged by. The implication of this is that once the plan is formulated, the implementation has to strictly adhere to the plan in order to realise the objectives and the set targets. In a way this approach would result in a less flexible implementation programme over the plan period such that the plan becomes a blueprint that has to be followed to the letter, even if the context has changed or goals shifted.

The other view of planning adopts a different approach, which sees the plan as a flexible guide to realising national objectives. The best example of this view is elaborated by Adebayo Adedeji who argues that a plan, being a compromise document,

> ....is honoured more in the breach than in the observance. Partly, because of political pressure and inter-departmental rivalries and partly because resource projections tend...to diverge widely from actual revenue, there is little discernible relation between what is contained in a Plan and what in fact gets done. Thus, it will be a great mistake to regard a plan as a blue print for action. Rather...a Plan...is a document assessing a country's problems, stating broad conclusions about the scale and direction of development efforts and indicating some of the main projects, programmes, and policies to be executed (ibid).

The two views provide different pictures of what constitutes a plan. While in the first the plan is narrowly conceived, the conception of a development plan in the second may be characterised as overly broad to the point of being vague. In the context of a developing country, it is perhaps more realistic to think of an NDP as a statement of broader national objectives, with both short- and long-term objectives defined by the political, economic, social and historical context. The usefulness of the second view is that it adopts a broader approach, taking into account not just the economic resources available, but also the political factors which shape and influence the formulation of the plan as well as its implementation. This is critical to any meaningful planning process (see Killick, 1976).

However, the second view goes to the extreme of even suggesting that the content of a plan has nothing much to do with what gets done on the ground. If that is the case, then what is the point of having a plan in the first place? Clearly, development plans do influence what gets implanted though they are rarely implemented in a rigid manner by strictly abiding to every letter stated in the plan. If the plan is perceived as a statement to guide national activities aimed at realising national goals, then the goals can be adjusted or totally abandoned in the course of the plan period depending on the circumstances, as the examples of the *Arusha Declaration* in Tanzania and the *Mulungushi/Matero Reforms* in Zambia suggest. In fact, Tanzania's first NDP clearly embraces the idea of a flexible plan that can be adjusted in the course of its implementation as circumstances dictate: "The plan therefore is a flexible one, and periodically we shall examine progress in the light of new circumstances, making adjustments as required" (Republic of Tanganyika and Zanzibar, 1964:viii). Thus, while the components of the plan should be strictly implemented to realise the set objectives, its implementation should be flexible enough to allow for the unseen and unplanned for events which often arise in the course of executing the plan. In other words, the nation should not be enslaved by a plan, but rather the plan should be in the service of national objectives.

Development Planning as an Assertion of Sovereignty

Development planning in Africa in the early days was largely seen as an instrument for affirming a country's sovereignty and this should not be surprising. As Green (1965:45) has highlighted, in most countries, planning was seen as "as a logical historical development from the national independence effort, now to be channelled into the rapid improvement of standards of life and of economic capacity. The national plan is both a symbol of that effort and a means of bringing it about." Tony Killick agrees with this view observing that, "In Africa during the 1960s, 'having a plan' became almost a sine qua non of political independence" (Killick, 1983:47). Without doubt, in the newly independent African states, development planning was an expression of independence, demonstrating that African leaders were in the driving seat.

A close look at any of the NDPs developed in Africa during the 1960s shows that the plans were not just a mechanism for chasing and realising economic growth and improvement of living standards of the citizens; they were much more than that. For countries emerging from the grip of foreign occupation and facing the prospect of neo-colonialism, being able to plan how the country's resources were to be used was a very practical sign of demonstrating the condition of being independent; the ability to make own decisions. Of course, the formulation of the plans in most newly independent African countries was supported by the former colonial powers through various mechanisms, particularly the secondment of economic planners who provided technical support to the planning commissions or departments (see Kanbur, 2016). Commenting on development planning in Cote d'Ivoire, Killick (1983) observes that although planning had undergone radical changes to improve its relevancy in the post-independence circumstances, it continued to rely heavily on French expatriate personnel.

Even though expatriates played an important role in the design of the development plans in Africa, the key objectives around which the plans were crafted came from the African political leaders, who were keen to demonstrate that they were in-charge and free to choose priorities in the national scheme of things. During colonial rule this function was far removed from all Africans, especially the nationalist leaders who were fighting for independence; they were not consulted on any plans designed for the colonies or protectorates. Drawing up budget plans and the allocation of national resources was a privilege of a few colonial officers who determined what was important for the colony and how the resources were to be mobilised and used.

After dislodging the colonial regimes, it was a logical sequel for the leaders of the newly independent African countries to affirm their hard-won independence by demonstrating that they were in-charge, not just of the state machinery, but also through the decisions taken on how to use national resources. In a sense, being able to take charge of identifying national priorities and how resources were to be allocated was a fundamental means of expressing the state of being independent. The significance of the development plans in this context was to assert control over the nation as a whole, including the foreign private enterprises which dominated the economies of most countries at the time of independence. In the case of Ghana, for instance, Ewusi (1981) argues that foreign enterprise, particularly in the industrial sector, were dominant both in terms of output and the number of firms.

Although the nationalist leaders who came to power had no direct and full control over the activities of the foreign companies which operated in their countries, being able to plan for the entire nation and point out to everyone, including foreign companies, the direction in which the economy was to be stirred was a symbolic act of being in-charge over the affairs of the country, which is a basic expression of national sovereignty.

As noted earlier, some of the African leaders who took over from the colonial governments understood that while they were in-charge in terms of political power, they did not have full control over economic power of their respective countries, and national planning was one way of asserting control over the economy. This was particularly important to leaders such as Kwame Nkrumah, Julius Nyerere, Leopold Senghor, Abdel Nasar, Kenneth Kaunda, Jomo Kenyatta who adopted strong ideological positions towards colonialism and neo-colonialism. A good example of this can be found in Kenya's first President, Jomo Kenyatta, who argued that,

> ...we intend...to lessen our dependence on foreign capital and to enable Kenya's own citizens to profit directly from investments in their country's development.... Only when we have made important strides in these and other ways can it be truly said that Kenya's political independence is being followed by economic independence (Republic of Kenya, 1964:ii).

The idea that political independence did not automatically translate into economic independence is something that subsequently became apparent to most African leaders when they took over from the colonial officials. In an attempt to realise economic independence, most African countries embarked on various schemes such as the nationalisation of strategic sectors of the economy, indigenisation and the formulation of development plans as means to rid themselves of undue colonial influence. Most of these and similar measures were envisioned not only to speed up the rate of economic development, but also to reduce dependence on foreign capital and to exercise control over the economy. In this sense, these measures were aimed at decolonising African economies. As illustrated in the next chapter, the import substitution industrialisation (ISI) was particularly aimed at disrupting the colonial economic logic, in an attempt to enlarge economic independence of post-colonial African states.

Socialism and NDP

It is sometimes argued that during the 1960s and 1970s, most developing countries, including the newly independent African countries, took a hostile posture towards foreign capital and sometimes openly rejected foreign investments (see te Velde, 2006). In Ghana, the "fear of foreign domination...led to the enactment of an indigenisation decree restricting ownership of some manufacturing activities only to Ghanaians" (Ewusi, 1981:10). A close look at the reality on the ground shows that while there were African leaders who were suspicious of foreign investors and the operations of big multinational corporations (MNCs), the official policy encouraged foreign investments, with many countries stating clearly that they had no option but to attract foreign investments to achieve some of the goals set out in the NDPs. All the NDPs, especially the earlier ones, have a section where they discuss financing of the plan, and in most cases, there is a clear indication that since the countries could not mobilise all the resources needed, the shortfall was to be covered by foreign private investment and aid from international donors. Even countries that had a strong socialist leaning like Ghana openly acknowledged that private foreign investments were an important part of the development plan, especially with regard to industrial development:

> Foreign investment as the private sector arm of our industrial development can play an important role in our economy. It has valuable contribution to make to our economy and to the attainment of certain specific objectives. Among these will be production of consumer goods, the local processing of Ghanaian raw materials and the utilisation of Ghanaian natural resources in those lines of economic activity where a large volume of investment is required. Foreign investment enterprise will contribute personal initiative, managerial ability and technical skills towards the development of the country (Republic of Ghana, 1964:xii).

We find similar views in Tanzania where the second NDP projected that 30 percent of investments over the plan period would come from foreign private investors (Republic of Tanzania, 1969). Similarly, Egypt's first NDP, while strongly affirming that the country was adopting a socialist philosophy, encouraged private capital to operate in partnership with the state, arguing that the objective was "to construct a democratic, social and cooperative society where public capital and private capital will collaborate for the benefit of all the inhabitants" (United Arab Republic, 1958). In many other countries such as Kenya, Zambia and Nigeria, African governments used tariff barriers to stem off competition from outside as a means of attracting foreign investments into the country (see Bates, 1981). It has thus been observed that despite many African leaders' commitment to socialism, "all admit the need for private foreign investment, though with varying degree of enthusiasm" (Berg, 1964:552).

For critics, African leaders' embrace of private capital in a socialist state seems to be a contradiction that makes the whole socialist enterprise unclear (see Berg, 1964). But at the beginning of the process of economic development, it was perhaps inevitable that even countries that envisioned and espoused a strong socialist ideology had to leave room for private investments to complement public resources. The pronouncements on socialist strategy did not foreclose the participation of the private sector. What a socialist state entails is the control of strategic means of production by the state, something that has been referred to as the democratisation of development (see Bates, 1981). What is critically central in a sociality strategy is, not necessarily, the absence of private investment, but that the state is in control of the major means of production; that the state directs and coordinates the activities of all key actors, including private enterprises.

In practice, most socialist states have allowed some level of private enterprise in partnership with public enterprises. Complete absence of private enterprise is rare, except in fully blown communist states where every productive activity is undertaken by the state. Thus, most countries that embraced socialism as their guiding philosophy were in fact mixed economies. For instance, Nkrumah, after asserting that Ghana will be developed according to socialist principles, openly declared that "We in Ghana have a mixed economy in which *we have assigned* to both public and private enterprise legitimate and important roles to play in our development" (Republic of Ghana, 1964:i, emphasis added). The crucial phrase in this citation is the "we have assigned", signifying that the state was in control and assigned specific roles to private enterprises.

As noted above, for most African countries, this was not only a way of following the dictates of socialism, but perhaps even more importantly, a way of asserting the independence of the state, expressing the freedom to coordinate economic activities in the country. In some cases, the strong emphasis put on demonstrating this independence led to the concentration of power in the political leaders, most of whom were strong charismatic leaders. Ake (1981) was particularly critical of African leaders who used the façade of asserting economic independence to create an elite network of politicians bent on enriching themselves at the expense of national development.

Post-Colonial African States' Approach to Big Business

The evidently strong need to show foreign private companies that a post-colonial African state was in-charge of the economic activities was largely provoked by the colonial regime's laissez faire attitude, especially towards big foreign companies which formed alliances with colonial governments. Colonial Africa's economic history, prior to World War II, is littered with private chartered and concession companies across the continent, which operated freely in most cases, with little accountability to the colonial government. Some of the examples include the Imperial British East African Company (IMEAC), the British South African Company (BSAC), the Royal Niger Company (RNC), Company du Congo pour le Commerce et l' Industrie, Portuguese Mozambique Company, Comet Speciale du Katanga, Comte Nationale du Kivu, Compagnie des Chemins de Fur du Congo Superieur aux Grand Lacs Africains, Societe Generale, United Africa Company and many others (see Rodney, 1982).

Prior to World War I, the colonising powers had thought that Africa was going to be what Kamarck (1967) refers to as the "new America" and literally divided up the continent among these concession companies, some of them owning extensive rights which independent African countries were forced to "buy back" after independence. A dramatic example of this is the case of the BSA which administered the then Northern Rhodesia Territory until 1924, and claimed ownership of all mineral rights. After independence BSA insisted that the Zambian government had to "buy the rights back" when the country sought to nationalise mining assets and rights towards the end of the 1960s (see Faber and Potter, 1971).

Although most of these companies had gone bankrupt by the time most African countries were becoming independent (ibid), the practice of foreign companies operating in Africa had grown deep in the structures of colonial governments. Even after independence, there was a dominant presence of some of the MNCs such as Unilever, General Motors, British Petroleum, Standard Bank, Barclays Bank, General Electric, Firestone, Cadbury and their subsidiaries. These companies continued to operate forming strong alliance with the former colonial governments. Because of their close association with the colonial governments, these companies were suspected of being purveyors of neo-colonialism relying on their large economic power and influence. If these companies were to operate independently as they did during colonial rule, this would undermine the autonomy of the newly independent African states. One way to reduce their influence in the country was for the state to take a stronger and direct control of the economy. The principles of free enterprise which most of the leading former colonial powers embraced were being entrenched in the colonial divorce documents—the Lancaster Constitutions which were drafted by the British to protect the interests of British investors. Therefore, although most post-colonial African states needed foreign investments to complement domestic resources for development, they looked at these investments with suspicion, fearing that they could be conduits of neo-colonialism.

Dealing with Big Capital

However, while African states prior to the 1980s did not trust these MNCs and did everything they could to tame them, they allowed many of them to operate hoping that they would contribute (as we have seen in the quote from Ghana's NDP above) to the development of Africa, particularly industrial development which was regarded as an urgent matter. But as Ake (1981:137–138) observes, "The power of the multinationals within the African economy as well as the world economy has made it very difficult for African governments to domesticate them and make them a real asset to the enterprise of building a coherent economy capable of self-sustaining." With hindsight, it is clear that these MNCs and the whole lot of foreign investments have contributed little to the objective of improving the living standards of the African people, and much less to industrial development. As we have seen in the preceding chapter, industrial development has remained weak and only a small component in most African economies.

As noted in Chapter 2, the type of foreign investment that flows into a continent is a major factor in explaining this disappointing contribution of foreign investments. As Singer (1950) warned, not every investment is desirable, and most African countries have failed to be selective in what they attract and accept as investments. Nyerere also acknowledged that the blanket acceptance of foreign investment is a mistake that needed to be corrected:

> In 1964 we had not worked out at all clearly the implication of our socialist belief. As a result, we were simply trying to attract investment of any type, and the role of the public enterprise appeared to be that of filling in gaps left by the private investment. All this changed in 1967 when the Arusha Declaration was adopted, the N.D.C. [National Development Corporation] was then given its very heavy new responsibilities, and other parastatal organisations were created (Republic of Tanzania, 1969:ix).

Given the level of industrial development on the continent today, it is clear that the type of investment a country attracts matters a lot, and that the state has to play a critical role in deciding what type of investment a country wants. Coming up with a selective investment strategy is one area where most African countries have consistently performed below average and the outcomes have continued to constitute a serious indictment on these governments (see

Lall, 2004). The large share of investments up to date has been going to (just like in the colonial era) the extraction of raw materials, and this trend intensified when the commodity prices on the global market spiked starting from 2002, with a temporary dip in 2009 and 2015 (EY, 2017; WEF, 2017). African governments, especially in the New Millennium, as they try to outcompete each other to attract foreign investment, have failed to engage with big international capital on their own terms, despite being in position of strength in terms of the rich natural resources which most countries possess. Contrary to this softening attitude towards big capital, in the earlier development strategies we find strong ideological orientation across African countries, rooted within the decolonisation discourse following the successful dislodgement of colonial regimes.

Industrialisation Under African Socialism

As noted earlier, although African countries during the 1960s did not develop separate industrial policies, they all had a section in NDPs on industrial development. In most countries, the section on industry included a strategy on how to expand the industrial sector, with some specific industrial activities identified as priority areas. While all countries outlined their industrial strategy in the NDPs, the most comprehensive industrial plan can be found in Kenya (1st and 2nd NDP), Cameroon (1st NDP), Liberia (2nd NDP) and Swaziland (2nd NDP). Apart from being elaborate, the industrial strategy in these NDPs had a clear plan on how the identified priority areas were to be financed and what the state was expected to do. A set of institutions were established to facilitate the process of industrial development. However, for the industrial plan and strategy to be successful, it should be situated in the broader rationale and philosophy behind the NDP. A detailed discussion of the industrial strategy in the NDPs is presented in Chapter 5; here we look at underlying principles.

Underlying Principles of the NDP

Notably, all NDPs reflect a particular set of ideologies which informed and shaped the various components of the plan, including the industrial component. Popular ideologies found in most NDPs include socialism and its ancillaries including indigenisation, rural development and developmentalism. In an article that is largely dismissive of the notion of African socialism, Berg

(1964:549)[4] begins with this observation: "It is hard these days to find an African statesman who does not advocate 'a socialist path' to economic development." Jitendra Mohan (1964) also makes a similar observation that though there are different connotations attached to the term socialism, leaders of independent African states embrace the notion of socialism, qualified by adjectives such as African, Arab, Senegalese, Fabian, Malagasy, Algerian, Pragmatic, empirical socialism as a way of conveying something unique and original. Because of the amorphous shape of African socialism, critics are quick to dismiss it as containing nothing fundamentally African: that, like capitalism, it is also an "imported ideology" (Berg, 1964:554).

Indeed the different versions of African socialism tended to create confusion and a sense of disarray which actually undermines the cogency of the idea proponents of African socialism were trying to put across. But in all these diverse doctrines, it is possible to find a common denominator. Nkrumah (1964), although he disagrees with the term *African socialism*, arguing that there is no such thing as African socialism but only scientific socialism, identifies two common elements in all the different formulations: "The terms 'Socialism' has become a necessity in the platform diction and political writing of African Leaders. It is a term which unites us in the recognition that the restoration of Africa's humanist and egalitarian principles of society call for socialism" (Nkrumah, 1975:200).

Nyerere (1975:194–195) offers a philosophical understanding of African socialism, which he interprets as an "attitude of the mind" rooted in the,

> ...sense of the security it gave to its members, and the universal hospitality on which they could rely. But it is too often forgotten, nowadays, that the basis of this great socialistic achievement was this: that it was taken for granted that every member of society—barring only the children and the infirm—contributed his fair share of effort towards the production of its wealth. Not only was the capitalist, or the landed exploiter, unknown to traditional African society, but we did not have that other form of modern parasite—the loiterer, or idler, who accepts the hospitality of society as his "right" but gives nothing in return! Capitalistic exploitation was impossible. Loitering was an unthinkable disgrace.

Although there are a variety of conceptual approaches to African socialism, some of which are contradictory to each other, the common idea was that the economic system in post-colonial Africa had to be rooted in the social practice and values of traditional African society.

Even though different African leaders who developed the concept of African socialism had different understanding of African social practice and basic values, the notion of mutual responsibility between individuals and communities, arising from a deep-rooted sense of a human-centred world view, stands out in most formulations. Apart from being a way of thinking about Africa, free from colonial influence, the African socialism discourse that developed was an expression of the desire to self-define, rather being defined by *others*, as was the case during colonialism. African socialism, seen from this angle, could be understood as a direct offshoot of self-determination; being able to say who I am and what I want to be. If this project of self-definition had succeeded, it could have been a radical way of decolonising not just the political sphere, but the economic, cultural and most importantly, as Ngugi (1986) argues, the mind. African socialism constituted an important element of re-affirming African values and world view, centred on the reciprocity between an individual and community:

> Our first step, therefore, must be to re-educate ourselves; to regain our former attitude of mind. In our traditional African society we were individuals within a community. We took care of the community, and the community took care of us. We neither needed nor wished to exploit our fellow men (Nyerere, 1975:195).

Unfortunately this decolonial project across Africa has remained an incomplete scheme, such that colonial rationality and world view continue to dominate many spheres of African life even today as evident not only in the untransformed structures of the economy, but also in the life orientation including curricula, knowledge production and aspirations. As Gitendra Mohan observes,

> African Socialism is a three-fold affirmation. It affirms Africa's "originality," its "distinctiveness," its "personality." It affirms Africa's "independence," ideologically as well as politically. And it affirms Africa's "open mindedness," its rejection of the "tyranny of concepts," and indeed of "ideologies," its adaptability and flexibility… (Mohan, 1966:228).

The biggest tragedy that befell the decolonial project was the unquenchable longing among African leaders, even those who espoused African socialism, to emulate their former colonial masters. Even if the physical occupation of the continent ended six decades ago, there is still an insatiable appetite in Africa to imitate and be like the West; the West, in a sense, has remained an indelible reference point in everything Africa and Africans do. As Fanon (1963) observed, in the consciousness of the post-colonial African leaders, the only image that looms large was that of being like the former colonial masters.

Whether we talk about the political structures, the economic undertaking and indeed the academic enterprise, the aspiration among Africans has always been to be like or at least catch up with the former colonial masters. This is how deep the colonial rationality has gone, such that even the most attractive act of defining oneself as an expression of being free has been overshadowed by the enticing images of Western civilisation and epistemology. It is therefore not surprising that there has been little success recorded in the direction of transforming colonial economies since the colonial logic is still the dominant frame of reference and provides a framework for assessing progress. As is widely known, African socialism, though it proved to be an attractive concept, did not survive the onslaught of the colonial epistemological warfare, which has become more entrenched.

Rationale for African Socialism

The task here is not to go into the details of African socialism but to highlight the reasons why socialism in general was so popular and attractive to African leaders during the 1960s, and why it was seen to offer a better way of organising society, in terms of realising the industrial development dream. In the NDPs reviewed for this study, socialism was openly acknowledged in some but implicitly affirmed in others. The importance of this, in this context, is that the ideology underpinning the NDP influenced the nature of industrial strategy that a country formulated and implemented. The fact that socialism, in all its shapes and colours, was an appealing ideology in Africa during the 1960s and 1970s is less disputed, though it must be noted that not all independent African states adopted socialism as their strategy for realising economic development and independence. There were countries such as Malawi, Cote d'Ivoire, Swaziland, Lesotho, Liberia, Sierra Leone and Nigeria that did not openly adopt socialism as the national philosophy.

However, features of socialist development can be discerned in most NDPs including in countries which did not openly declare socialism as their preferred development ideology. For instance, while the Nigerian government did not officially adopt socialism, it is acknowledged that the Federal Government decided to adopt a development strategy in which the state played an important role in not just providing social services, but also actively coordinating and managing industrial development by means of "direct execution of a number of capital projects by the Government of the Federation, Statutory Corporation and the numerous local and native authorities" (Republic of Nigeria, 1962:3). Similarly, though Botswana did not openly adopt the philosophy of African socialism, its first NDP acknowledged that the fostering of the "spirit of self-reliance" through the creation of village structures constituted the core values of the independent nation (see Republic of Botswana, 1968).

As Berg (1964) observed, it was difficult to find an African leader who did not embrace socialism in one form or another. Some leaders used the rhetoric of socialism while others embraced it with genuine commitment and resolve. There are several reasons why socialism in general proved to be so attractive to the newly independent African states looking for magic bullets to accelerate industrial development. Some of the key factors are briefly discussed below.

Control of the Development Process by the State

First, socialism appealed to African leaders because it provided an opportunity for African states to assert their independence as stated earlier. Because socialism, in principle, allows the state large latitude in the economic and social life of a country, it provided a good justification for post-colonial African states to affirm sovereignty and ensure control not just of political affairs but also economic activities which were central to the notion of economic independence. Although the state being in control of economic affairs of a country did not entail a total banning of private enterprise, it did signal to private actors in the economy, both foreign and local, that there was someone in-charge and that everyone had to play by the rules outlined by the state.

Controlling private actors is easier in a setting where the state has more powers to intervene in the economy than in a market system where the role of the state is rather limited. We find a good example of this in Swaziland's first NDP, where it is stated that, "Government welcomes foreign capital for investment in the private sector and will provide reasonable terms. [But] The private sector for its part will be expected to co-operate in the attainment of the government's principal objectives" (Republic of Swaziland, 1969:15). While private actors were welcomed with open arms, they were expected to fit into the grand scheme of things, laid out by the state. This is more emphatically stated in Ghana's first NDP: "Our government has always insisted that the operations of all economic enterprises in Ghana should conform to the national economic objectives and be subject to the rules and regulations which are made in pursuance of our socialist policies" (Republic of Ghana, 1964:xii).

Although what this entails is not elaborated on in the plan, it was expected that the private investors would play an important role in contributing to the national development objectives set out by the state. How much the private actors followed the policy prescription depends very much on the capacity of the state to ensure that all actors act within the prescribed policy and plans. It is not easy to accomplish this in a market economy where actors only respond to the promptings of supply and demand forces, spurred by the desire for profit. Indeed the purpose of formulating NDPs is, in a fundamental way, rooted in the belief that the state can provide not only coordination of the different activities in the economy, but also a supervisory function on various actors in the economy. Where development planning is effectively implemented, the state has a role in deciding even the kind of investments and where these investments should be channelled by private investors.

Experience from African countries shows that implementing this was difficult for many countries, such that the execution of the plans faced many challenges (see Killick, 1983). Nonetheless, for the newly independent African country seeking to chart a new chapter in their respective countries, after emerging from colonial rule, having a state that played a more active role beyond creating a market-friendly environment proved to be attractive to most African leaders. This perhaps is why none of the countries openly advocated for a market economy. As Berg (1964:554) observes, "It is hardly surprising that 'decolonisation' and the reduction of the role of private enterprise should seem related."

The second major reason why socialism proved to be more attractive to African leaders is that most of them associated capitalism with colonialism, and the two (colonialism and capitalism) were seen as two sides of the same coin. Senghor explains this when he argues that "'there is naturally, in the mind of proletarian nations, complete identification between capitalism and colonialism, between the political system and the economic system.' Hence the rejection of capitalism by 'the most conscious leader'" (cited in Mohan, 1966:221–222). Berg (1964:550) makes a similar observation that all African leaders view capitalism with suspicion as the "economy of the colonisers" and see the two as mechanisms for oppressing African societies.

While in the context of the strong anti-colonial sentiments of the 1960s and 1970s it is not far-fetched that African leaders were reluctant to embrace capitalist development strategies on the grounds that it was associated with the colonial system, this was not the only factor why capitalism was less attractive to many African leaders. There are several other factors which contributed to capitalism being less attractive to African leaders at that time, including the fact that capitalism promotes inequality, that it leads to the exploitation of one group of people by another, that economic growth under a capitalist system is slow, that it perpetuated the dependence of Africa on the former colonial powers and that it was unnatural to the African way of life (Berg, 1964). However, the main reason was the idea that going the capitalist way would slow the process of development due to the low levels of capital and the reluctance of foreign investors to commit large resources to Africa. Wade (1990) in his review of East Asian economies argues that post-World War II, there was a popular belief that a free market approach would slow down the pace of development, particularly industrialisation. The socialist route which created larger spaces for the state to act was preferred because it enabled countries to mobilise resources for investment in a way that made the state effectively the development pacemaker. After observing that African countries could not successfully pursue the "capitalist way" because they lacked capital, Senghor speaks about the "weaknesses of the capitalist camp, the impotence of its methods, the senility of its institutions. Its solutions cannot satisfy us" (cited in Mohan, 1966:222).

Given the urgent need to improve the living conditions of the majority of the African people, it is not surprising that most African leaders at that time opted for a system that allowed them to dictate the pace of development in their countries. There were also some concerns about the risks that came with the capitalist system, especially the fluctuations in the global markets over which developing countries have no control whatsoever. This concern is articulated in Lesotho where the market-oriented development strategy is rejected as a recipe for disaster:

> The alternative to planned development would simply be to surrender the economic future of the country to exogenous and entirely uncontrollable forces which have so far been inimical to the promotion of domestic sources of income and employment. The government is decisively opposed to such a fatalistic attitude. Its intention is to build up a development momentum, which may eventually get the country out of the trap of economic backwardness (Kingdom of Lesotho, 1970:xiv).

While it made sense then to embark on a growth trajectory where the government had more control over the growth process, these leaders failed to realise that they were operating in an international system that was dominated by capitalist relations and institutions. As such, they were in fact not in control even if they marshalled the state apparatus to influence economic activities in their respective countries.

Reducing Dependency on Former Colonial Powers

Third, socialism proved to be attractive to African leaders because it offered a means of reducing dependence on former colonial powers. To the extent that socialism created space for the state to undertake productive activities in the economy, it was possible for the state to embark on development projects tailored towards promoting the production of some of the goods imported from abroad. The strategy of ISI which almost all African countries adopted immediately after independence (see Chapter 5) could only be successfully undertaken if the state exercised significant influence in the way investment resources were allocated in the country. Initiating a process of replacing some of the imported goods required the state to play an active role in investing in strategic sectors of the economy, including the establishing of new manufacturing enterprises, meant to produce previously imported goods locally. Again, it was easier to undertake these kinds of activities under socialism than under capitalism, where the private sector is expected to lead the way, guided by market forces. In effect, if strictly followed, this would mean that African countries had to continue to depend on former colonial powers for manufactured goods since they did not have comparative advantage in most of the manufactured goods they imported. The socialist model proved to be attractive in this regard because it did provide not only the space for the state to invest in strategic sections of the economy as a way of decentring the colonial economic logic, but also a means for the state to take over certain enterprises through nationalisation. This gave the state more control over the economy, and for the newly independent states in Africa seeking to affirm their independence and authority, the promise of a socialist route was hard to resist.

Nation-Building

Fourth, in a bid to strengthen the state and create capacity for nation-building, socialism appeared to offer the best opportunity. Nation-building was one of the key objectives of the nationalist movements across Africa which came to power during the 1960s. Creating a unified nation in a context where decades of colonial rule left fragmented communities divided along ethnic lines (see Killick, 1983) required a strong state which could create stability to overcome the weak lines of ethnic cleavages, aggravated by the divide and rule tactics of colonial regimes all over Africa. Most African leaders at that time sought to cultivate the spirit of national unity through the idea of national solidarity, which was another hallmark of African socialism. Various philosophies were deployed towards this end, all riding on the idea that African social practice was communitarian by nature and the strong ties this entailed provided the magic glue for unifying fragmented communities into a nation. In ethnically divided societies, nation-building has remained a challenging task which many African countries are still struggling with even today. In countries where the ideology of socialism was strongly developed, national unity has tended to be stronger, though this view needs to be empirically tested.

Consolidate Political Power

The fifth reason why socialism proved to be attractive to most African leaders is that it offered an avenue through which they could consolidate their political power. As Mohan (1966:223) observes,

> The new ruling class, which regards itself as the guardian of the "national interest," is thus led into claiming and asserting "the supremacy of political action," "the primacy of politics," "the need for political action and political direction all along the line."

In most countries this led to the emergence of one-party state systems, justified in the name of promoting national unity and overcoming the tendencies towards division and strife which multi-partism was alleged to engender (see Mkandawire, 2003). Socialism made it easier for some of these leaders to usurp power from the people such that they became pre-occupied with how to keep that power rather than using it to serve the people. Eventually, the emphasis on staying in power under the pretext of promoting national unity diverted the attention of most African leaders from the noble task of building successful economic and industrial projects (Ake, 1981). In this sense, socialism was largely abused.

Elements of excessive concentration of power in some of the African leaders are evident in some of the NDPs, especially the second and third NDPs. Nonetheless, some African leaders were aware that the primary task at hand was to improve the welfare of the people as a way to consolidate the achievement and meaning of independence, not just the amassing of power. For example, Uganda's second NDP correctly observes that broad-based prosperity is what gives meaning to independence and also constitutes a cornerstone for national stability: "We are all desirous of seeing prosperity and greatly expanded social services in our country, both of which can constitute a strong base for our independence. A high degree of prosperity and social services within the reach of the masses is a cornerstone of a nation's stability" (Republic of Uganda, 1966:ii).

Rural Development in the NDPs

As noted above, in most NDPs, there were apparent efforts made to identify priority areas for development. One such area that is common in most NDPs is rural development. As one would expect, there are variations in the way this was understood and articulated, with some NDPs approaching rural development from a narrow perspective of improving productivity in the agricultural sector (subsistence sector in particular). Others took a broader perspective that approached rural development from an integrated development viewpoint. For example, while in Lesotho, Sudan and Uganda, the focus was on improving productivity in the rural sector, countries such as Liberia, Kenya, Zambia, Ethiopia and Tanzania took a broader approach, where rural development was conceived as a strategy beyond the need to improve the productivity of subsistence farmers. It was conceptualised broadly to include the provision of infrastructure and other social services. A more elaborate approach can be found in Ethiopia's third NDP:

> Over time it will be desirable to integrate all the various inputs to rural development—agricultural programmes, credit, marketing, extension services, co-operatives, nutrition programmes, environmental sanitation, water supply, rural electrification and other infrastructure, community development activities, support for small-scale and cottage industries, etc (Republic of Ethiopia, 1973:III.1).

In general, all the NDPs which were formulated during the 1970s seem to have a strong emphasis on rural development, particularly integrated rural development. This was conceived in such a way that the interventions to the rural sector were to be closely coordinated to create synergies. Kenya's second NDP highlights the importance of an integrated approach to the rural sector:

> The key strategy of this Plan is to direct an increasing share of the total resources available to the nation towards the rural areas...rural development should not be seen as a special programme but as the underlying strategy of the whole Plan. A raising of the levels of education and health in rural areas, an emphasis on the improvements of the secondary road system, higher expenditure on rural water supplies, an extension of rural electricity amenity scheme and an improvement of social services in rural areas, all represent the planned efforts of the Government to raise the general standard of rural life. In addition, there are other integrated schemes aimed at raising

> the level of agricultural income and developing of non-agricultural enterprises more rapidly in the rural areas (Republic of Kenya, 1970:2).

The emphasis on rural development in all the NDPs should not come as a surprise. It is only logical that the focus of any genuine development strategy should be directed to the sectors where majority of the people live and work. The rural sector houses majority of the people in most African countries even today. Accordingly, for any significant progress to be made, including progress in industrial development, it is imperative to pay attention to the rural sector where majority of the people (63 percent in 2016) work and earn a living (see Fox and Thomas, 2016; UNECA, 2016b).

During the 1970s, integrated rural development became a central theme in development discourse and policy spearheaded by the World Bank president at that time, Robert McNamara, who in his famous 1973 *Nairobi Speech* advocated strongly for integrated rural development, making it the main development policy for the World Bank during the 1970s (see Chitonge, 2015). Most African countries were persuaded to formulate integrated rural development strategies and many incorporated them into NDPs. In some countries such as Zambia, Tanzania, Kenya and Cameroon, the emphasis on rural development was said to be in response to the neglect of the rural sector during colonial rule. Aware of the deplorable conditions in rural areas, post-colonial African states during the first decade of independence sought to focus more on rural areas as a strategy for reducing inequality in the standards of living between the urban and rural communities. Zambia's first NDP, for example, singles out the urban–rural disparities as a key area of concern: "A constant preoccupation of my government is the disparity in the standard of living between the rural masses and the comparatively limited industrial sector" (Republic of Zambia, 1966:vi).

In the first decade of independence, it was clear to government leaders in Kenya, Zambia and Ghana that without improvement in the rural sector, it was going to be difficult to promote sustainable industrial development; developing the rural sector in general was seen as an indispensable part of the balanced growth strategy where industry developed at the same pace with agriculture and services. In Kenya's 2nd NDP, it is clearly stated that the growth of the manufacturing sector would be determined by the growth in the agricultural sector (see Republic of Kenya, 1970). Liberia's 2nd NDP also strongly affirms the need for an integrated approach:

> The cornerstone of the diversification strategy is integrated rural development. This involves the design and implementation of comprehensive programs for raising agricultural productivity, improving associated rural economic activities such as market-

ing and providing social and physical infrastructure so as to enhance the quality of life in the villages where most Liberians live (Republic of Liberia, 1976:1).

However, despite the strong emphasis on rural development in the NDPs, the reality on the ground suggests that little has been achieved to date. Rural areas across the continent have remained the most underdeveloped in every sense of the word. Development literature on Africa highlights what has been referred to as the *urban bias* (see Berg, 1964; Arrighi and Saul, 1968; Bates, 1981). In his famous work on *States and markets in Africa*, Bates (1981) illustrates how rampant the urban bias phenomenon had developed in Africa during the 1970s, epitomised by the transfer of rural resources through agricultural marketing boards to urban sectors. He argues that this bias certainly stifled the growth of the agricultural sector which in turn impacted negatively on industrial development.

The discussion in this chapter has focused on the dominant features of the NDPs in Africa, and has highlighted some of the common features found in most of these documents and how this shaped the industrial strategy in various African countries. One of the things that stand out is that while the plans in the NDPs are convincing, the implementation and the outcome of these strategies do not have much to show. This has led to some critics arguing that most of these were simply a list of dreams without clear strategy (see Ake, 1981; Killick, 1983). As illustrated in this chapter, most NDPs identified both the key national goals as well as devised strategies of how to realise these goals including industrial development goals. The biggest challenge has been implementation of these strategies, especially where plans were interrupted or abandoned in the middle of the plan period. The next chapter looks at industrial development strategies in these NDPs.

Notes

1. Formulating separate industrial policy, in most countries, only in the 2000s. There are still a number of African countries which have no separate industrial or trade policy (see UNECA, 2014).
2. The first National economic development plan was formulated in 1964, and reviewed every two years.
3. The Mulungushi Reforms were announced in April 1968 at the Mulungushi Conference Centre a few kilometres outside of a mining Town called Kabwe. The reform's main thrust was the requirement from 24 international companies to offer a controlling share to the state. The others include the restriction of the issuance of trading licences to Zambians only and the restriction of borrowing by expert business people (see Kaunda, 1968). These

reforms came into effect in January 1969. The Matero reforms were later announced in one of the low-cost towns in Lusaka called Matero, and they mainly focused on acquiring a controlling share by the state in the mining companies, which were excluded in the Mulungushi Reforms.

4. Elliot Berg is renowned for his leading role in the study that culminated in the publication of the famous Berg Report in 1981, forming the basis on which Structural Adjustment Programmes (SAPs) in Africa were formulated.

References

Ackah, C., Adjasi, C. and Turkson, F. (2016). "Industrial Policy in Ghana," in C. Newman, J. Page, J. Rand, A. Shimeles, M. Soderbom and F. Tap (eds.), *Manufacturing Transformation: Comparative Studies in Industrial Development in Africa and Emerging Asia*. London: Oxford University Press. 48–69.

African Centre for Economic Transformation (ACET, 2014). *Growth with Depth—African Transformation Report*. Accra: ACET. Available at: http://africantransformation.org/wp-content/uploads/2014/02/2014-african-transformation-report.pdf. Accessed 18.06.2016.

Ake, C. (1981). *A Political Economy of Africa*. Lagos: Longman Nigeria.

Amin, S. (1972). "Underdevelopment and Dependence in Black Africa: Historical Origin." *Journal of Peace Research*, Vol. 10, No. 2. 105–120.

Arrighi, G. and Saul, J. (1968). "Socialism and Economic Development in Tropical Africa." *Journal of Modern African Studies*, Vol. 6, No. 2. 141–169.

Ayittey, G. (1999 [1992]). *Africa Betrayed* (2nd Ed.). New York: St Martin's Press.

Bates, R. (1981). *Markets and States in Tropical Africa: The Political Basis of Agricultural Policies*. Berkeley: University of California Press.

Berg, E. (1964). "Socialism and Economic Development in Tropical Africa." *The Quarterly Journal of Economics*, Vol. 78, No. 4. 549–573.

Chitonge, H. (2015). *Economic Growth and Development in Africa: Understanding Trends and Prospects*. London/New York: Routledge.

Ernest and Young (EY, 2017). "EY's Attractiveness Programme for Africa." May 2017. Available at: https://webforms.ey.com/Publication/vwLUAssets/ey-attractiveness-program-africa-2017-connectivity-redefined/$FILE/ey-attractiveness-program-africa-2017-connectivity-redefined.pdf. Accessed 22.05.2018.

Ewusi, K. (1981). *The Process of Industrialisation in Ghana*. Accra: Institute of Statistics, Social and Economic Research, University of Ghana.

Faber, M. L. and Potter, J. G. (1971). *Towards Economic Independence: Papers on the Nationalisation of the Copper Industry in Zambia*. Cambridge: Cambridge University Press.

Fanon, F. (1963). *Wretched of the Earth*. New York: Groves Press.

Fox, L. and Thomas, A. (2016). "Africa's Got Work to Do: A Diagnostic of Youth Employment Challenges in Sub-Saharan Africa." *Journal of African Economies*, Vol. 25, No. 1. 16–36.

Gilley, B. (2017). "The Case for Colonialism." *Third World Quarterly*, DOI: 10.1080/01436597.2017.1369037.

Green, R. (1965). "Four African Development Plans: Ghana, Kenya, Nigeria and Tanzania." *Journal of Modern African Studies*, Vol. 3, No. 2. 249–279.

Hill, J. (2005). "Beyond the Other? A Postcolonial Critique of the Failed State Thesis." *African Identities*, Vol. 3, No. 2. 139–154.

Kamarck, A. (1967). *The Economics of African Development*. New York: Praeger.

Kanbur, R. (2016). "W. Arthur Lewis and Roots of Ghanaian Economic Policy." Charles H. Dyson School of Applied Economic Management, Working Paper No. 06, Cornell University, New York.

Kaunda, K. (1968). "Zambia's Economic Reforms." *African Affairs*, Vol. 67, No. 269. 295–304.

Killick, T. (1976). "The Possibility of Development Planning." *Oxford Economic Papers* (New Series), Vol. 28, No. 2. 161–184.

Killick, T. (1983). "Development Planning in Africa: Experiences, Weaknesses and Prescriptions." *Development Policy Review*, Vol. 1, No. 3. 47–76.

Kingdom of Lesotho (1975). *Kingdom of Lesotho Second Five Year Development Plan, 1975/76–1979/80*. Maseru: KoL.

Kingdom of Lesotho (1970). *Lesotho First Five Year Development Plan, 1970/71–1974/75*. Maseru: KoL.

Lall, S. (2004). "Selective Industrial and Trade Policies in Developing Countries: Theoretical and Empirical Issues," in C. Soludo, O. Ogbu and H. Chang (eds.), *The Politics of Trade and Industrial Policy in Africa*. Trenton/Asmara: Africa World Press Inc. 75–110.

Lewis W. A. (1954). "Economic Development with Unlimited Supplies of Labour." *Manchester School*, Vol. 20, 139–191.

Lewis, Arthur (1984). "The State of Development Theory." *The American Economic Review*, Vol. 74, No. 1. 1–10

Leys, C. (1982). "African Economic Development in Theory and Practice." *Deadalus*, Vol. 111, No. 2. 99–124.

Meier, G. (1984). "The Formative Years," in G. Meier and D. Seers (eds.), *Pioneers in Development*. New York/London: Oxford University Press. 3–26.

Mhone, G. (2001). "Enclavity and Constrained Labour Absorptive Capacity in Southern African Economies." A paper prepared for the discussion at the UNRISD on The Need to Rethinking Development Economics, September 7–8, 2001, Cape Town South Africa.

Mkandawire, T. (2001). "Thinking About the Developmental States in Africa." *Cambridge Journal of Economics*, Vol. 25, No. 3. 289–313.

Mkandawire, T. (2003). "African Intellectuals and Nationalism." A Paper Presented at the Conference on the 30th Anniversary of CODESRIA, Dakar, Senegal.

Mkandawire, T. (2011). "Running While Others Walk: Knowledge and the Challenge of Africa's Development." *Africa Development*, Vol. XXXVI, No. 2. 1–36.

Mkandawire, T. and Soludo, C. (1999). *Our Continent, Our Future: African Perspectives on Structural Adjustment*. Dakar: CODESRIA.

Mohan, J. (1966). "Varieties of African Socialism," in R. Milliban and J. Sauville (eds.), *The Socialist Register, 1966*. London: Merlin Press. 220–266.

Newman, C., Page, J., Rand, J., Shimeles, A., Soderbom, M. and Tap, F. (2016). "The Pursuit of Industry: Policies and Outcomes," in C. Newman, J. Page, J. Rand, A. Shimeles, M. Soderbom and F. Tap (eds.), *Manufacturing Transformation: Comparative Studies in Industrial Development in Africa and Emerging Asia*. London: Oxford University Press. 1–24.

Ngugi, W. T. (1986). *Decolonising the Mind: The Politics of Language in African Literature*. London: James Currey.

Nkrumah, K. (1975 [1964]). "African Socialism Revisited," in G. M. Mutisco and S. W. Rohio (eds.), *Readings in Africa Political Thought*. London: Heinemann. 200–209.

Noorbakhsh, F. and Paloni, A. (2000). "The De-Industrialisation Hypothesis, Structural Adjustment Programmes and the Sub-Saharan Dimension," in H. Jalilian, M. Tribe and J. Weiss (eds.), *Industrial Development and Policy in Africa: Issues of De-Industrialisation and Development Strategy*. Cheltenham: Edward Elgar. 107–129.

Nurkse, R. (1953). *Problems of Capital Formation in Underdeveloped Countries*. London: Basil Blackwell.

Nyerere, J. K. (1975). "Ujamaa-The Basis of African Socialism," in G. M. Mutisco and S. W. Rohio (eds.), *Readings in Africa Political Thought*. London: Heinemann. 191–199.

Olukoshi, A. (2004). "Democratisation, Gloabalisation and Effective Policy Making in Africa," in C. Soludo, O. Ogbu and H. Chang (eds.), *The Politics of Trade and Industrial Policy in Africa*. Trenton/Asmara: Africa World Press Inc. 43–73.

Organisation of African Unity (LPA, 1980). *The Lagos Plan of Action for the Economic Development of African: 1980–2000*. Addis Ababa: OAU.

Republic of Botswana (1968). *National Development Plan, 1968–73*. Gaborone's: RoB.

Republic of Ethiopia (1973). *Strategy Outline for the Fourth Five-year Plan: 1974–1979*. Addis Ababa: Planning Commission.

Republic of Gambia (1975). *Five Year Plan for Economic and Social Development, July 1975–June 1980*. Banjul: RoG.

Republic of Ghana (1964). *Seven-Year Plan for National Reconstruction and Development*. Accra: Office of the Planning Commission.

Republic of Kenya (1964). Development Plan 1964–1974. Nairobi: National Planning Commission,

Republic of Kenya (1969). *Development Plan: 1970–1974*. Nairobi: Planning Commission.

Republic of Kenya (1970). *Development Plan 1970–1974*. Nairobi: National Planning Commission.

Republic of Liberia (1976). *National Social and Economic Development Plan, July 1976–June 1980*. Monrovia: RoL.

Republic of Nigeria (1962). *National Development Plan: 1962–1968*. Lagos: Ministry of Economic Development.

Republic of South Africa (1974). *Economic Development Programme for the Republic of South Africa, 1974–1979*. Pretoria: RSA.

Republic of Swaziland (1969). *Post Independence Development Plan*. Mbabane: Ministry of Finance and National Planning.

Republic of Tanganyika and Zanzibar (1964). Five year Plan for Economic and Social Development (Vol. 1): general Analysis: Dar Es Salaam: Planning Commission.

Republic of Tanzania (1969). *Second Five-Year Plan for Economic and Social Development*. Dar Es Salaam: Planning Commission.

Republic of the Sudan (1962). *The Ten Year Plan on Economic and Social Development: 1961/62–1970/71*. Khartoum: Ministry of Finance and Economics.

Republic of Uganda (1966). *Uganda's Second Five Year Plan*. Kampala: Ministry of National Planning.

Republic of Zambia (1966). *The First National Development Plan: 1966–1970*. Lusaka: Office of the National Development and Planning.

Republic of Zambia (1971). *Second National Development Plan: 1972–1976*. Lusaka: Ministry of Planning and National Guidance.

Rodney, W. (1982). *How Europe Underdeveloped Africa*. Washington, D.C.: Howard University Press.

Rosenstein-Rodan, N. P. (1943). "Problems of Industrialisation of Eastern and South-Eastern Europe." *Economic Journal*, Vol. 53, No. 210/211. 202–211.

Rosenstein-Rodan, N. P. (1957). "Notes on the Theory of the Big Push." Economic Development Programme Project C/57–25. Centre for International Studies. Cambridge: Massachusetts Institute of Technology.

Scitovsky, T. (1954). "Two Concepts of External Economies." *Journal of Political Economy*, Vol. 62, No. 2. 143–151.

Singer, W. Hans (1950). "The Distribution of Gains Between Investing and Borrowing Countries." *American Economic Review*, Vol. 40, No.2. 473–485.

Soludo, C. and Ogbu, O. (2004). "A synthesis of Major Themes in the Political Economy of Trade and Industrialisation in Africa," in C. Soludo, O. Ogbu and H. Chang (eds.), *The Politics of Trade and Industrial Policy in Africa*. Trenton/Asmara: Africa World Press Inc. 1–42.

te Velde, D. W. (2006). "Foreign Direct Investment and Development: An Historical Perspective." Background Paper for World Economic and Social Survey for 2006.' ODI (Commissioned by the UNCTAD).

UNIDO (2016). *Industrial Development Report 2016: The Role of Technology and Innovation in Inclusive and Sustainable Industrial Development*. Vienna: UNIDO.

United Arab Republic (1958). *General Five Year Framework Plan*. Cairo: UAR.

United Nations Economic Commission for Africa (UNECA, 2012). *Economic Report on Africa 2012: Unleashing Africa's Potential as a Global Growth Pole*. Addis Ababa: UNECA.

United Nations Economic Commission for Africa (UNECA, 2014). *Report on Africa 2014: Dynamic Industrial Policy in Africa—Innovative Institutions, Effective Processes and Flexible Mechanisms*. Addis Ababa: UNECA.

United Nations Economic Commission for Africa (UNECA, 2016a). Transformative Industrial Policy for Africa. Addis Ababa: Economic Commission for Africa.

United Nations Economic Commission for Africa (UNECA, 2016b). *Economic Report on Africa 2016: Greening Africa's Industrialisation*. Addis Ababa: UNECA.

United Nations Economic Commission on Africa/African Union (UNECA/AU, 2011). "Development Planning in Africa: Key Issues, Challenges and Prospects." A Background Paper prepared for the 4th Joint Annual Meeting of the AU Conference of Ministers of Economy and Finance and the UNECA Conference of African Ministers of Finance, Planning and Economic Development, 24–27 March 2011, Addis Ababa, Ethiopia.

Wade, R. (1990). *Economic Theory and the Role of Government in East Asian Industrialisation.* Princeton: Princeton University Press.

Waterston, A. (1965). *Development Planning: Lessons from Experience.* Baltimore: John Hopkins Press.

World Economic Forum (WEF, 2017). *The Africa Competitive Report 2017.* Geneva: WEF.

· 5 ·

INDUSTRIAL DEVELOPMENT STRATEGY IN NATIONAL DEVELOPMENT PLANS

Introduction

The preceding chapter has discussed the rationale behind the post-colonial development planning approaches in Africa, prior to the introduction of SAPs in the 1980s. This chapter looks closely at the industrial strategies which independent African states designed and implemented before the commencement of SAPs. There are two main aims for analysing the industrial strategies in Africa during this period. The first is to look at the strategies adopted, the justification behind them, their viability and the practical implications of the programmes. The second is to assess the economic and political context in which the programmes were formulated and implemented.

Often, when we speak about industrial policy in Africa prior to the 1980s, the first thing that comes to mind is the *Import Substitution Industrialisation* (ISI). While the ISI was a popular strategy for industrial development in almost all African countries (all the countries reviewed in this study implemented some form of ISI), it was not the only component of industrial policy at that time. There are other aspects of industrial policy which are usually overlooked in the literature. To get a sense of what these strategies were and what they were intended to achieve, it is essential to examine the motivations behind these strategies and what they were expected to deliver. Here, focus is not on assessing the outcomes of the national development plans (NDPs), but rather on understanding the thinking behind them and whether they amounted to a programme to steer African economies from the colonial economic logic. This has been done by looking at the overall objectives stated in the NDPs, and also by focusing on the sections in the NDPs dealing with industrial development. But this exercise is particularly challenging in countries where development planning was either interrupted or abandoned as a result of civil war, military takeovers and other forms of political instability (see Killick, 1983). Given the critical importance attributed to the manufacturing industry in economic development, the focus here will be on the trends in the manufacturing sector up to the point when SAPs interrupted national development planning in most African countries. As noted in the preceding chapter, industrial policy, including manufacturing, was treated as an integral part of the broader process of development.

From Annual Budget Plans to NDPs

By the time most African countries attained political independence, African leaders strongly believed that planning for development was an indispensable exercise on the long road to economic independence. As noted in Chapter 4, development planning in most of these countries started during colonial rule, though the development plans before independence did not have the national character and did not prioritise industrial development. It has been observed that the "colonial Government had never encouraged the introduction of vigorous industrial policy in African colonies. This type of policy would come into conflict with the main mission of European rulers to provide the metropolis with a market for manufactured goods and supply of cheap raw material" (Mendes et al, 2014:122). Drawing from the Ghanaian experience, Ewusi (1981) argues that prior to independence, the dominant industry in Ghana was the extraction and export of raw timber which accounted for over 45 percent of total manufacturing output in 1960. Many African countries such as Tanzania, Botswana, Gambia, Uganda and Sierra Leone did not have noticeable manufacturing capacity at independence. Most African leaders who took over the post-colonial economy were aware of the lopsidedness of the economic structure they inherited, and in response, devised means to speed up industrial development as part of the plan to modernise African economies. Development planning, by means of five-, seven- or ten-year plans was one of the popular ways through which industrial development was implemented. African leaders were attracted to development planning because it offered the fastest route to development through the "big push" strategy (see Killick, 1980; Leys, 1982). Not only that, but development planning was attractive to African leaders during the 1960s because it presented a practical way of expressing the spirit of independence (see Ogujiuba et al, 2011). By the end of the 1960s every independent African state had developed a development plan and the culture of planning was slowly developing in many countries. Specific strategies and programmes were devised to enhance industrial growth as part of the broader development process.

Prior to independence, long-term development plans were not common. The emphasis was on the short-term plans which focused mainly on allocating national resources and setting targets in the economy. The most common instrument used, particularly in British colonies, was the *capital expenditure programme*, which was basically a list of stand-alone projects. The Minister of Finance and Economics in Sudan highlighted this in his radio broadcast statement on the inaugural of the first Ten-year development plan:

> It is a pleasure, indeed an honour to speak to you tonight about the first plan for economic and social development…In fact it is the first comprehensive and balanced plan, since most of our development efforts in the past was not in essence more than collections of capital works of various nature put together without an underlying theme or defined targets joining them together. Our development efforts in the past lacked coordination and did not take into close consideration the characteristics of our National Economy… (Republic of the Sudan, 1962:3).

The Nigerian first NDP also makes a similar observation that although there were development plans in the past, the 1962 NDP was the first development plan which gave "a sense of direction to the economy, a sense of priority and urgency and to enlist the support and co-operation of all sections of the community to work for a better future" (Republic of Nigeria, 1962:5). Green (1965) also acknowledges that while economic planning was initiated in the colonies immediately after the Second World War, what existed before independence were mainly annual budgets and economic development survey reports, which gave an indication of the projects to be prioritised. The 1962 development plan for Nyasaland [now Malawi] distinguishes between a development plan and a development survey report:

> The Latter is a submission of experts on what may be done in a country studied. It sets out to define and analyse problems, to draw conclusions, to recommend solutions, to moot objectives and to suggest a scale of priorities. Thus, a development survey

> report describes what should be done regardless of the size of available resources. A development plan on the other hand is an outline of what can, and is intended to, be done with a specific amount of resources within the stated period. It is a compilation of projects agreed upon by the government… (Nyasaland, 1962:1).

While the importance of planning had almost become mainstream in development economics, especially in the newly independent states (not just in Africa), supported by the dominance of Keynesian demand management approaches which emphasised state intervention to avoid an economy being locked in low equilibrium, there were still some diehard neoclassic economists who did not see the need for planning as we noted in chapters 2 and 4. They strongly believed that the market was efficient enough to allocate resources in the economic, and as such planning and industrial policy, in particular, was not necessary (see Chenery et al, 1986). As Lall (2004) observes, this view became the "new" consensus of the 1980s, when the dominant economic views became hostile to the very idea of an industrial policy because it promoted state intervention.

But prior to the 1980s, most African countries were convinced beyond doubt that to achieve their dream of rapidly transforming their countries from simple agrarian economies into sophisticated industrial economies, planning was an indispensable apparatus. This belief might have been inspired by the success of economic planning in Russia during the inter-war period (see Leys, 1982). Thus, "In the 1960s most of the newly independent African states, diverse as they [were], adopted development planning to effect deep-seated changes in their economies and societies. This was not surprising, given the major theoretical and policy propositions of the pioneers of development economics" (UNECA/AU, 2011:1).

Industrial Policy in the NDPs

As noted earlier, leaders of the newly independent African states strongly believed that formulating and implementing NDPs was the quickest way of catching up with developed countries. The idea of development planning as a tool for speeding up the process of economic development is acknowledged in the 2nd NDP for Tanzania, which argued that the "publication of a Five-Year Plan does not create more resources; all it does is enable the nation to allocate the resources it possesses in a manner which will bring the people as quickly as possible towards the goals they have set for themselves" (Republic of Tanzania, 1969:x). In this regard, there was a wide perception that allocating resources and coordinating development ventures in the economy if left to markets would slow the process of development (see Mohan, 1966). Planning was therefore seen as deliberate and warranted intervention by the state to direct and speed up the process of economic development. In this arrangement, industrialisation was believed to be the means for transforming African economies and societies rapidly. Nigeria's first NDP articulates this view succinctly:

> In no country in the world is economic and social development free from some form of deliberate effort to *speed up the process*. Governments everywhere play a vigorous role in shaping the design of a nation's economic development. In some countries the role of government is all-pervading and directly and extensively interferes with the lives of the people. In other countries, the influence of government is limited to policy measures within which all economic and other actions take place... (Republic of Nigeria, 1962:2 *emphasis added*).

While there is a recognition in this statement that there are different types of planning and the levels of government involvement in the economy, which is framed as a matter of choice, there was a strong belief among African leaders that some form of planning is essential in order to speed up the pace of development, especially for countries at the early stages of economic development. In other words, African leaders of that time realised that without planning, it would be difficult to realise the objectives of economic and social development within a reasonable period of time.

The Rationale for Industrial Policy

Most of the sectoral plans elaborated in the NDPs suggest that planning played a key role in providing space for the state to actively participate in the economy. Therefore, the role of the state in post-colonial Africa economies was not limited to just filling the gaps left by the private sector. The state allotted itself the responsibility of marshalling the entire economy towards the intended social and economic objectives. Arthur Lewis explains why planning and an active role for the state in the economy is necessary in developing countries.

> Planning in backward countries imposes much bigger tasks on governments than does planning in advanced countries. The government has too many things which can in advanced countries be left to entrepreneurs. It has to create industrial centers, to put through an agricultural revolution, to control the foreign exchanges more strictly, and in addition to make up a great leeway of public services and/or ordinary

> economic legislation. And all this has to be done through a civil service that is usually much inferior to that of an advanced country. Why then do backward countries take more readily to planning? Because their need is also so obviously much greater. And it is also this that enables them to carry it through in spite of error and incompetence (cited in Meier, 2001:16).

In a sense, most African leaders during the first decade of independence were loyal students of development economics. Pioneers of development economics did not only limit the role of the state to creating an environment in which private enterprise could flourish; they advocated for stronger state involvement in economic activities. In his famous article on how depressed areas can achieve rapid industrialisation, Rosenstein-Rodan (1943:204) observed that "Active participation of the State in economic life is a new factor which must be taken into account as a new datum."

The reason given for recommending active state involvement in the early stages of industrialisation is that the private investors do not have the capacity to mobilise investments to a critical threshold to generate larger economy-wide effects. It was also argued that private investments in developing countries did not only lack scale but also exhibited strong tendencies towards fragmentation of investments, which made it hard to achieve sustainable levels of industrial growth. Rosenstein-Rodan (1943), for instance, argued that the most important component of any industrialisation programme (which is skilling or training of the labour force) can only be suitably carried out by the state. And in terms of coordinating industrial development, he argued that "Complementarity of different industries provides the most important set of arguments in favour of a large-scale planned industrialisation" (ibid, 205). His preference for large-scale industrial development approach is justified in this way:

> If the industrialisation of international depressed areas were to rely entirely on the normal incentive of private entrepreneurs, the process would not only be very much slower, the rate of investment smaller and (consequently) the national income lower, but the whole economic structure of the region would be different. Investment would be distributed in different proportions between different industries, the final equilibrium would be below the optimum which a large E.E.I.T. could achieve (ibid, 206–207).

Although Rosenstein-Rodan was not writing about industrialisation in Africa and was thinking about a *supra*-national industrial development corporation (IDC) of sorts (i.e., E.E.I.T), his idea resonated with the aspirations of the leaders of the newly independent African states (see Killick, 1980). To African leaders who were looking for the quickest route to catch up with the rest of the world, the appeal of planned investment in which the state set the "pace" of industrialisation and development was quite strong, especially if we put this in the context of African leaders' mistrust of foreign private investment as a conduit for neo-colonialism (see Chapter 4).

The other argument often advanced in support of planned industrialisation in Africa was that private investments only went into the extractive industries, mainly minerals and crude oil. This is a trend observed not just in Africa but in most developing countries. For African countries during the early days of independence, faced with the challenge of inadequate private investments going into industrial development, the state was forced to mobilise resources, particularly for manufacturing industries.[1] Further, the market mechanisms in most African countries were poorly developed primarily because majority of people in the 1960s were actually outside of the monetary economy. In such cases, the market only reached a small section of the population, mostly in urban areas. These factors made the idea of development planning and industrialisation attractive to African leaders such that most of them developed (often) ambitious plans to build industries in the shortest time possible (Bates, 1981).

The "Big Push" Strategy

Although the strategy of industrialising through an active state has not worked well in Africa, the idea of planned industrialisation advocated by the pioneers of development economics had a strong appeal to and great influence on African leaders. In the case of Ghana, some of the leading development economists of the 1950s such as Arthur Lewis, Nicolas Kaldor, Albert Hirschman and Dudley Seers actively contributed to the debates leading to the formulation of the first NDP (see Republic of Ghana, 1962). Development economics itself as a young sub-discipline was developing the argument that in developing countries, because of missing markets, the state had a responsibility not just to mobilise investment capital but also to undertake investments in critical areas of the economy, including the manufacturing sector (see Hirschman, 1981). Hirschman (1958:33) in particular argued that mainstream development strategies and theories, because they were constructed to understand economic challenges in advanced economies, "will have minimum relevance in any radically different environment." He goes on to advise that the "economics of development [developing economies] dare to borrow too extensively from the economics of growth [advanced economies], like the underdeveloped countries themselves, it must learn to walk on its own feet, which means that it must work out its own abstractions."

This set of ideas which came to be known as the "*Big Push*" were embraced by many prominent development economists who believed that there was a minimum level of investment needed to create viable industrial enterprises, and that the private sector may not have sufficient incentive to invest up to required levels to generate meaningful levels of industrial production. Rosenstein-Rodan (1957:1) explains the idea behind the *Big Push* strategy:

> There is a minimum level of resources that must be devoted to a development programme if it is to have any chances of success. Launching a country into self-sustaining growth is little like getting an air plane off the ground. There is a critical ground speed which must be passed before the craft can become airborne. Proceeding bit by bit will not add up in its effects to the sum total of the single bits. A minimum quantum of investment is a necessary (though not sufficient) condition of success. This is in a nutshell the contention of the theory of the big push.

In the early days of development economics, this was the central argument used to justify the need to plan and coordinate industrialisation through an industrial policy and action plan.

The main role of development planning was envisioned to be primarily to reduce the gulf between the *social* and *private returns* to investments, which tend to increase if investments are left to private actors. The argument was that since private investors rely primarily on price signals, their decisions always lead to a less optimal position. Proponents of the *Big Push* argued that this view is more relevant in the context of developing countries where markets are less developed and price signals often fail to provide the best guidance (see Scitovsky, 1954). In most developing countries, it was argued, markets were "even more imperfect than in developed countries. Price mechanism in such imperfect markets does not provide the signal which guide a perfectly competitive economy towards an optimum path" (Rosenstein-Rodan, 1957:3).

After an analysis of American (USA) foreign direct investments in the 1940s, the Gray and Rockefeller reports conclude that, "it must be frankly recognised that investment abroad cannot be expected to solve the problem of financing development alone" (cited in Nurkse, 1953:84). In addition to the poorly developed markets, giving rise to weak market mechanisms in developing countries, it was also observed that the price mechanism can only give signals about current economic situation and is less effective in signalling what the economic situation would be in the medium to long term. On the basis of this, the state was strongly recommended to take a leading role in planning and directing industrial development.

Planned Industrialisation: A Strategy for Overcoming Double Dependence in Africa

The quest for industrialisation in Africa during the 1960s should be seen in the broader context of the urgency to 'catch up' with the rest of the world. African leaders at independence were aware of the fact that Africa needed to embark on a project of defining a new strategy for transforming their economies and societies. Industrialisation was widely believed to be the quickest avenue for realising this dream. The manufacturing sector, in particular, was seen as strategically placed in the bigger scheme of reducing the double dependence on export of primary commodities and on the importation of intermediate inputs, capital goods and finished manufactures from industrialised countries. The double dependence burden was clearly articulated in Uganda's second NDP:

> Just as Uganda is dependent on agriculture for a large proportion of its income so it is dependent on imports as a source of supply for most manufactured goods. Not only heavy machinery, complicated equipment and luxuries but also simple consumer goods are imported (GATT, 1966:2).

This captures well the typical structure of a colonial economy, and the logic behind this is not hard to see if one locates this in the broader colonial project. The challenges which flow from this structure of the economy are quite straight forward:

> In addition to its high dependence on export in general (export form nearly one half of the monetary gross domestic product), its total export earnings depend on a narrow range of products. Three quarters of Uganda's exports are furnished by two agricultural commodities, coffee and cotton, the marketing of which is subject to considerable uncertainty (ibid, 5).

Since most African countries during the 1960s inherited similar economic structures, characterised by heavy dependence on the export of a narrow range of primary commodities (often raw materials) on one hand, and heavily dependent on importing even the simplest manufactured good on the other hand, the pressure to industrialise was palpable. The challenge posed by the situation in which African countries, like Uganda, found themselves is that the lopsided economic structure created extreme pressure on the current account and the local currency from the burden of importing both capital goods as well as consumer goods, including food products. The pressure becomes even more given the volatility of commodity prices on the global market. The impact of importing consumer and capital goods on the current account is articulated in Tanzania's 2nd NDP:

> The potential importance of the growth of manufacturing is particularly great in relation to the balance of payments. Development demands heavy imports of capital goods and transport equipment. As the pace of development accelerates, demand for such goods rises faster than the overall growth of the economy and the growth in primary commodity export earnings. If the economy remains dependent on imports as a source of supply for all manufactured goods, scarcity of foreign exchange will place a serious brake on the speed of development (Republic of Tanzania, 1969:60).

As we shall see later in the chapter, many African countries used this argument as the rationale for implementing the ISI strategy. During the mid-1970s, as the first oil shock effects filtered into the real economy, many African countries came face to face with the challenge described above. The shock arising from falling demand for and consequently decline in the price of commodities on the global market, which was (and still is) the main (if not the only) foreign currency earner for most African countries, created huge pressure on the external account. The worsening balance of payment situation during the 1970s made it difficult for many countries to import even the basic intermediate goods needed for agricultural production. In this context, the strategy of replacing imported consumer goods with locally manufactured goods was widely believed to be the only option, and many countries adopted this as we shall see later in the chapter.

Political Justification for Industrialisation in Africa

Apart from economic considerations like the impact on foreign exchange rate and the current account which heavy reliance on imports have, there are other non-economic factors which made industrialisation appear the sensible thing to do. For African countries during the 1960s, reducing dependence on developed former colonising countries as a way to consolidate their newly won independence was one of the major factors that justified the ISI strategy. The reasoning was that if they produced locally some of the goods they were importing, this would lessen the foreign exchange pressure as the dollars that could have been spent on importing juice and chocolate from Switzerland and Belgium would now be available to cover the cost of importing intermediate and heavy-duty goods required in manufacturing and agriculture. While this made sense, developing countries were told, for over a century, that "their comparative advantage lay in exporting agricultural commodities" (Lewis, 1984:129), and should therefore leave manufacturing activities to industrialised countries which had comparative advantage in manufacturing. But, as argued in Chapter 1, for an industrial development project to be successful, it requires deliberate actions targeted at building the industrial capabilities which would enable countries to transition from static to dynamic comparative advantage. To achieve this, some kind of planning was (and is still) deemed indispensable.

While there have been questions raised about the implementation of projects in the NDPs and whether planning itself makes any sense if there are huge gaps between the plans and what gets implemented on the ground (see Killick, 1983), there is one thing that was clear to most African leaders after independence, which is that they had to industrialise, and planning was the best instrument they identified. This is a point where there has been (even today) wide consensus across the ideological "iron curtain". At the moment, the new consensus does not question whether Africa should industrialise or not; it is taken for granted that Africa has to industrialise. A more controversial question is how African should industrialise (see Wade, 1990). In other words, that Africa should industrialise is a widely accepted view; few would argue that Africa does not need to industrialise. The question of how to industrialise is obviously a practical one that involves making choices based on the available options. As one would expect, opinions and preferences are bound to differ, and this is evident in the industrialisation debates in Africa whether one is looking at the situation in the 1960s or today.

Coordinating Industrial Activities through Public Enterprises

Reading through the first-generation NDPs, one gets the sense that African leaders and policy makers who formulated these plans were thinking of making a quick start by marshalling national resources towards the identified developmental objectives, which they thought were urgent. This comes out more clearly in Kenya's first NDP, where planning is seen as a tool for coordinating the economic activities in the country:

> Planning is intended to co-ordinate activities in the private and public sectors, to ensure that actions in each sector complement those in the other and to influence development in both sectors for the common good (Republic of Kenya, 1964:3).

It is not easy to say how much of this thinking can be attributed to the *Big Push* theory (see Murphy et al, 1989; Krishna and Perez, 2005). What is clear is that most NDPs embraced the idea that coordination of investments was indispensable to rapid industrialisation in Africa. Given the context in which the NDPs were formulated, it can be argued that coordination of investment was not embarked on because the markets were thin or missing and therefore not able to issue the right signals (via prices) to investors. The principal factor was the belief that the state had to play an active role, not just for economic reasons articulated in the concept of the *Big Push*, but also for political reasons, mainly to ensure that the government was in the driving seat of the development enterprise. During the 1960s, putting the state in the driving seat was justified on the grounds that it helps to overcome market failures which were rampant in developing countries (see Scitovsky, 1954; Singer, 1984).

Further, in most African countries, like many other developing countries, capital investment funds were scarce, especially in the industrial sector. Since most of the foreign investments went into extractive industries, mainly mining, this left a huge gap in the industrial sector. Several NDPs reviewed here suggest that most of the foreign direct investments shied away from manufacturing and other industrial sub-sectors. It was partially because of the gap left by the private investors in the industrial sector that many African countries during the first decade of independence established state-owned enterprises (SOEs) to address the challenge of lack of private investments (Bates, 1981; Olukoshi, 2004). In this sense, most African states had no option but to set up industries because few or no private sector investor was willing or had the capacity to establish these industries. There has been a great deal of debate about the role of SOEs, but in terms of the reasons for establishing SOEs, they were seen as an important component of the strategy of initiating industrial development in Africa.

However, by the mid-1970s, it was becoming apparent that the problem of operating SOEs efficiently was so endemic that SOEs became barriers to any prospect of realising the identified developmental goals. Nonetheless, for our purposes here, it is evident that African leaders after independence widely adopted the idea that coordinating industrial development would not only create efficiency in the economy, but also quicken the process of industrial development. It was in view of this goal that the first five-year plans set ambitious targets of establishing a wide range of factories in various sectors.

The target of creating a large and diverse industrial sector over a short time reveals the ambitiousness of some of the leaders at that time. From experience, we know that industrial development is rarely achieved in a decade; it takes long time to transform society. The fact that these leaders saw their industrial sectors expanding at a fast pace is a reflection of their enthusiasm and also optimism which was not in short supply after accomplishing the mammoth task of dislodging colonial regimes from African soil. As noted earlier, different African countries pursued different industrial development strategies. It is beyond the scope of this book to discuss all the different strategies. To get a sense of the efforts of industrialisation in Africa during the 1960s, it is essential to look at the common strategies: that is, strategies that are found across countries. In the next section, several examples of these strategies are discussed. But before discussing the strategies in detail, a few remarks about industrial development approaches, drawing from the NDPs, are warranted to foreground the strategies.

The Agriculture-Industrial Disconnect

The role of agriculture in industrial development has been a contested topic. Some analysts argue that governments of the newly independent African states, in their quest to catch up with the industrialised countries, neglected and, in some cases, ransacked the agriculture sector in the pretence to develop the industrial sector. It is argued that agriculture was seen as a sector for backward nations; modernising nations were supposed to focus on industrial development. Bates (1981), for example, argues that in many African countries, capital was diverted from agriculture into industry in such a way that it was impossible for the agriculture sector to develop in any significant way. The broader context to this debate is the famous *urban bias* which, apparently, was rife in most African countries just after independence (Arrighi and Saul, 1968). One of the main channels through which African governments demonstrated preference for industrial development was via the National Agriculture Marketing Board (NAMBs), which were often used as cash cows for the inefficiently run SOEs. In some cases, African states are alleged to have manipulated the pricing of agricultural commodities, while in other cases, politicians simply instructed top officials of the NAMBs to release money to bankroll state-owned industrial enterprises:

> When either the Development Corporation or the Finance Corporation sought funds, its directors often simply bypassed the Marketing Board and approached the Ministry directly; the Ministry would then issue a directive to the Board, instructing

> it to loan the requisite funds to the corporation requesting them. The result was the creation of a spate of new industrial firms—including printing companies, cement works, a glass factory, textile plants, a leather works, and a plastic company—financed in large part by loans secured from the marketing agencies. The resources secured from the Marketing Board were obtained on exceptionally generous terms. Indeed, investigations reveal that in many instances the two corporations simply failed to repay the Marketing Board… (Bates, 1981:21).

Neglect of the agricultural sector was highlighted in the Berg report, which provided several examples to illustrate this. One example identified in the report is the overvalued exchange rate, which negatively affected the agricultural sector (see World Bank, 1981). What Bates describes in the passage cited above comes close to capturing the bias towards industrialisation among African leaders during the first decade of independence. However, the apparent bias against agriculture could be attributed to the strong influence of the two-sector model, which tended to portray agriculture as a sector in secular decline (see Chapter 6).

The other reason why the industrial sector was preferred in most countries was the strong belief that industry was synonymous with modernity (urbanism), while agriculture represented the traditional, rural, backward life (Bates, 1981).

While the neglect of the agriculture sector in most African countries cannot be denied even today, this is actually puzzling because in almost all of the first NDPs reviewed here, agriculture is identified as the foundation of African economies and that development will be difficult without modernising this sector. All the NDPs reviewed in this book alluded to the fact that agriculture is important because that is where most of "our people derive a living," a motto that is stated in all the NDPs. From countries less endowed with minerals such as Ethiopia, Malawi, Lesotho, Swaziland, Kenya, to the resource-rich countries such as Nigeria, Zambia, Ghana, Zimbabwe, Sudan and Botswana, the importance of agriculture is strongly acknowledged. So it is quite surprising that actions on the ground point in the opposite direction.

Although agriculture was widely recognised as a priority sector, the implementation of the NDPs, particularly the allocation of resources, suggests that it was the industrial sector that mustered political support. This perhaps is more evident in the fact that during the 1970s and 1980s, agriculture was in most countries looted in the name of securing resources for industrialisation (Bates, 1981). It seems as though African policy makers believed that industrial development could take off even when the agriculture sector was in shambles. Historical evidence, however, as we shall see in Chapters 6 and 8, show that a thriving agriculture sector provides an impetus for industrial development. Thus, the neglect of agriculture in many African countries has no strong theoretical basis, and the irony this creates is difficult to understand. The interesting thing is that even in Arthur Lewis' (1954) two-sector model, agriculture is recognised to provide a strong impetus for industrial development in the initial stages. As argued in Chapter 6, there cannot be any meaningful industrialisation on the continent without first improving productivity in the agricultural sector. But the actions of most African states are not aligned with this view. As a result, the linkages between agriculture and industry have remained weak at best, though there are signs that through the rapidly growing agro-processing subsector on the continent, these linkages will be consolidated (ACET, 2014). Even if industrialisation has all the positive attributes discussed in Chapter 2, in the African context, the growth of the agricultural sector is crucial to making industrialisation a reality.

Foreign Aid Dependence

The other general observation to make regarding the pre-SAP industrial strategies in Africa, as expressed in the NDPs, is the overwhelming dependence on foreign aid. A close reading of the NDPs of Lesotho, Swaziland, Botswana, Liberia, Sierra Leone, Malawi and Ethiopia reveals a strong belief among the leaders of these countries that economic development, including industrialisation, could be achieved through international aid. In some countries, there was a strong expectation that the large chunk of the required funds for the programmes outlined in the NDPs would come from development partners. In Swaziland, for instance, the larger chunk of funding (65 percent) for the first NDP was expected to come from aid, mainly from the British Government and "other friendly countries" (Republic of Swaziland, 1969). While there is nothing wrong with international aid, it is doubtful that aid would leverage adequate resources for an African "*Big Push.*" As things turned out, the aid which have flowed in to Africa since the 1960s has little to show in terms of industrialisation (see Collier, 2006). In as much as African countries' development plans and strategies for industrialisation are concerned, a clear strategy on how to mobilise resources to fund these programmes should be an important part of the plan, and should not be left to the whim of international aid. Even if aid could provide adequate resources to support industrialisation in Africa, in the context of the need to re-orient African economies from the colonial logic, it is unlikely that a flourishing industrial sector would be in the interest of the donor countries who provide aid to Africa.

Seeds of Defiance

While African post-colonial economies continued to depend on aid from the former colonial masters, the 1960s were dominated by strong sentiments against neo-colonialism and the seeds of defying the colonial economic logic were sown in many countries. Although the strong anti neo-colonial views expressed by many African leaders after independence may seem contradictory with the practice of continuing to receive aid from former colonial masters, receiving aid from Western countries was justified on the grounds that the colonisers took a lot from Africa which they had to share with independent Africa. However, receiving aid from former colonisers compromised the anti-neo-colonial principle, for the simple reason that aid made it difficult for African leaders to see the subtle continuation of relations that undermined African interests, especially in the area of industrial development. For this reason, it is perhaps not surprising that the seeds of defiance sawn during the liberation struggle were never natured to fruition. This is one of the reasons why the decolonisation project has remained incomplete, especially in the economic and knowledge production spheres.

In terms of industrial development, there is ample evidence showing that many African leaders did earnestly seek to embark on a development path with the intent to disrupt the colonial economic logic. Several countries sought to do this by developing local industries which could locally produce most of the imported goods, partly as a way of reducing dependence on developed countries, and partly to assert the newly won independence. Part of this defiance strategy was rooted in the decolonial discourse, framed around the principle of "going back to African roots"—*African socialism*.

With specific reference to industrial development, it has been observed that African leaders were "convinced that industrialisation strategies should form a critical part of their attempts to achieve more rapid and self-reliant development and they [were] therefore committed to specific policies to accelerate industrial growth" (ODI, 1986:1). Elements of this defiant strategy are more evident in the *Lagos Plan of Action* (LPA, 1980) which saw the production of intermediate and capital goods by African firms as the most effective way of reducing dependence on industrialised countries and promoting *collective* self-reliance. One of the common strategies adopted across the continent, including South Africa, was the famous import substation industrialisation (ISI). Within the ISI strategy, the creation of SOEs or parastatal companies in all strategic sectors of the economy, including manufacturing, was a key component.

SOEs: Africa *Big Push* Strategy

The creation of SOEs in most African countries during the 1960s and 1970s was primarily seen as the practical way to speed up the process of industrial development, following on the *Big Push* framework. The creation of SOEs was supported by several factors, including the belief that the state should give direction and shape to all economic development activities in the country. This view, as we have seen above, emphasised the importance of coordinating investment and development activities. Many countries including those that did not openly advocate for statist approach to economic development embraced this idea. For example, even if Nigeria and Kenya in principle did not advocate for strong state involvement in the economy, they both established SOEs in many areas of the economy, including agriculture marketing, food and agricultural processing, finance, construction, textile and transport sectors.

It is important here to note that some of the SOEs were carry-overs from the colonial days, particularly in the agricultural sector, where the state heavily intervened through the infamous agriculture marketing boards. However, most of these colonial projects were reformed and new ones were added to invigorate the development momentum in the country, with a strong focus on industrial growth.

Although different countries deployed SOEs as an instrument of industrialisation differently, this was a popular strategy across Africa during the 1960s and 1970s. For example, the Nigerian government was clear that the state had a responsibility to coordinate and direct the activities of the private enterprises towards the identified national economic and social goals. Nigeria's first NDP clearly affirms an important role the state had to play in the economy, particularly in sectors where the private sector was not keen to invest. In these circumstances, the creation of SOEs was widely believed to be the quickest way to build industrial capabilities, and this was based on the understanding that without state involvement, the upgrading of industrial capacity would be limited (Lall, 2004). This is clearly stated in Kenya's second NDP: "Government aims to increase its own participation in the growth of industry, both in terms of the promotion of new projects and in the financing of them" (Republic of Kenya, 1970:305). We discuss the role of the state in industrialising Africa in Chapter 7.

SOEs in Africa were not just used as instruments for filling in the gaps created by the absence of private sector investment, but also to direct industrial activities into strategic areas. This also made sense in terms of influencing the pace of industrialisation as stated earlier. In the development plans of most African countries, "state enterprises were seen in every African country as a necessary part of the process of industrialisation, diversification, the development of productive forces and national economic independence" (Ake, 1981:96). Therefore, SOEs in the early days after independence served the strategic role of guiding the development of the industrial sector, in particular promoting the effort to build manufacturing capacity and capabilities. In countries which developed strong ideological positions, parastatals played an important role throughout the economy, not just in the industrial sector. SOEs were as pervasive as the state itself in several countries, with wide-ranging operations from the dairy produce boards and bus transport companies, to the retail chain stores spread throughout the country.

But the performance of these SOEs has left a bad name for public enterprises in Africa, and those that still survived the onslaught of SAPs' privatisation campaign have only remained a reminder of the giant state-owned companies, which dominated African economies during the 1970s and early 1980s. Most of these enterprises were large ventures with sizeable capacity, which gave them large and often a monopoly of the domestic markets (see Ogujiuba et al, 2011). Some analysts have blamed these public giants for the failure to industrialise in Africa because they prevented the emergence of genuine African entrepreneurs (see Chapter 9). They argue that these SOEs gave rise to what has been referred to in the literature as the *bureaucratic bourgeoisie* who were only interested in enriching themselves by looting state resources (see Arrighi and Saul, 1968; Ake, 1981). We come back to this point in Chapter 9, where we discuss the role of entrepreneurship in African's industrial development story.

Despite the poor performance and the corruption which are often associated with the SOEs during the 1970s and 1980s, their role in fostering industrial development in many African countries should not be overlooked.

As shown in Table 5.1, the creation of parastatals, boosted the growth of the manufacturing sector in many African countries until the early 1980s when foreign exchange crisis brought these enterprises to their knees.

Table 5.1: MVA-to-GDP Ratio for Selected African Countries, 1973–1981 (%).

	Share of MVA in GDP		**Contribution to African MVA**	
	1973	**1981**	**1973**	**1981**
Angola	6.94	3.99	3.43	0.94
Benin	7.92	6.65	0.47	0.30
Botswana	5.31	11.84	0.17	0.62
Burkina Faso	13.83	13.86	1.13	1.10
Burundi	10.83	11.54	0.52	0.55
Cameroon	10.16	11.36	3.26	3.96
Cabo Verde	6.07	6.10	0.04	0.05
Cen. African Rep.	12.92	13.13	0.58	0.42
Chad	11.51	7.53	0.67	0.34
Comoros	7.07	5.34	0.06	0.03
Equa. Guinea	5.49	5.28	0.06	0.02
Ethiopia	10.73	10.74	3.51	3.34
Gabon	6.21	9.41	0.99	2.03
Gambia	6.48	2.52	0.11	0.04
Ghana	12.95	14.09	7.18	5.10
Guinea	4.37	3.76	0.52	0.44
Guinea Bissau	1.37	1.53	0.02	0.02
Ivory Coast	12.97	15.59	4.89	6.97
Kenya	11.77	13.34	4.14	4.88
Lesotho	5.69	5.11	0.11	0.11
Liberia	4.88	5.63	0.34	0.34
Madagascar	11.65	10.05	2.40	1.61
Malawi	12.23	12.55	0.82	0.96
Mali	9.66	8.64	0.56	0.55
Mauritania	5.04	6.29	0.22	0.25
Mauritius	13.91	2.43	0.89	1.47
Mozambique	9.85	7.35	4.77	2.11

	Share of MVA in GDP		Contribution to African MVA	
	1973	1981	1973	1981
Namibia	6.43	6.65	0.88	0.94
Niger	10.61	6.69	0.77	0.64
Nigeria	4.74	8.17	19.28	32.40
Rep. of the Congo	7.14	7.63	0.04	0.51
Réunion	3.86	3.63	0.52	0.51
Rwanda	3.97	13.45	0.19	0.83
Senegal	13.37	13.75	2.57	2.03
Sierra Leone	7.17	6.46	0.52	0.41
Somalia	9.48	9.67	0.50	0.46
Sudan	15.30	7.83	8.09	4.25
Swaziland	2.19	23.86	0.47	1.03
Togo	9.23	6.87	0.58	0.37
Uganda	7.37	4.29	2.54	1.22
Tanzania	11.09	5.79	3.01	1.47
Zaire	8.26	6.18	3.87	1.72
Zambia	18.57	16.93	4.53	3.34
Zimbabwe	25.1	26.7	9.1	9.3
Mean	**6.9**	**3.9**	**3.4**	**0.9**

Source: Author. Based on data from the Overseas Development Institute (ODI, 1986: 2).

The rapid decline of industrial capacity utilisation which most of industries in African countries experienced in the decade 1970 to 1980 is a clear indication of the negative effects of the foreign exchange crisis which started in some countries as early as 1975. In Ghana for instance, the average manufacturing capacity utilisation among firms declined from 40 percent in 1978 to 25 percent in 1985 (Tribe, 2000:90). While in the period between 1963 and 1973, only one country (Reunion) experienced declining MVA growth, in the period 1973–1981, 14 countries reported negative MVA growth (ODI, 1986). For countries such as Sudan, Angola, Uganda, Tanzania and Mozambique, MVA declined by half between 1973 and 1981, with the average MVA for the region falling by more than 40 percent over the same period (Table 5.1).

Manufacturing trends between 1980 and 1990 were even worse, leading to some analysts suggesting that de-industrialisation occurred during this decade (see Noorbakhsh and Paloni, 2000). When the rates of industrial growth prior to and after the 1980s are compared, they point to the fact that the gains made during the first decade of independence began to be eroded during the 1980s and the continent is yet to recover from this crisis (Newman et al, 2016).

It is important to reiterate the point that the establishment of SOEs should be seen as a strategic step which was intended not just to fast-track industrial development, but also as a means to consolidate control over strategic sectors of the economy, which during colonial time was largely in private hands, with strong links to the former colonial centres (see Ake, 1981). Seen from this angle, SOEs were meant to serve economic as well as political objectives (see Ogujiuba et al, 2011). If one looks at SOEs as purely economic entities, it is easy to miss their strategic role in the broader scheme of things, underlined by the urge to decolonise and set Africa on an independent path to growth and prosperity. One practical way in which this path was set to be realised was through the import substation industrialisation.

National Development Corporations

Apart from SOEs, evidence from the NDPs suggests that there were two other institutions which were central in the industrial development schemes. One of such institutions was the *National Development Corporation* (NDC). In most countries, state investments in the productive sectors were handled by a statutory body, usually the NDC. The role of the NDCs was generally to encourage investment in new productive ventures, not only in the industrial sector, but in the entire economy. In Kenya, for instance, the role of the Development Finance Company was described as "to stimulate the flow of private investment by providing loans or share capital to fill marginal gaps in private projects" (Republic of Kenya, 1964:81).

In several countries, the NDCs, in particular, functioned more like industrial credit institutions, aimed at promoting the growth of industrial enterprises. In most countries the NDCs were also used as vehicles for promoting the indigenisation policy by supporting the business ventures of indigenous Africans business men and women as highlighted later in this chapter. For instance, the *Malawi Development Corporation* was given the task of increasing the participation of local business people in industry, not just in commerce (Republic of Malawi, 1964).

In countries such as Nigeria, Kenya and Ghana, there were dedicated financial institutions that provided financial support to both public and private enterprises as well as joint ventures between the state and the private sector. In Nigeria's 3rd NDP for instance, two statutory industrial finance institutions were created to promote the development of industrial and commercial activities—the *Nigerian Industrial Development Bank* and the *Nigerian Bank for Commerce*. The roles of these institutions were to "play a more stimulating role in the manufacturing activities…operating more as industrial promoters than as banks" (Republic of Nigeria, 1975:154).

Industrial Development Corporations

The other critical institution dedicated specifically to promote industrial activities, particularly manufacturing, was the IDC. Again, this type of institution is found in almost all of the NDPs reviewed here. In Swaziland, for example, the *National Industrial Development Corporation of Swaziland* was established in 1971 by the Industrial Development Act, with the aim of promoting and facilitating industrial investment and development (Republic of Swaziland, 1973:101). In Kenya the IDC, which was inherited from colonial times, was reformed and dedicated to the provision of loans for industrial development, particularly to Kenyan industrial players.

> The Industrial Development Corporation was established in 1955, with Government capital to encourage medium and large scale industry. In 1960 it began to operate a fund to provide loans for African industrialists. Now that the Development Finance Company of Kenya is providing substantial finance for large scale industry, the Industrials Development Corporation will be devoting its major efforts towards the encouragement of Africans in small scale industry and commerce (Republic of Kenya, 1964:81–82).

Kenya is one of the countries where the system of support aimed at promoting industrial development was advanced in such a way that it did not just provide loans to support the setting up and upgrading of industrial enterprises. Industrial development was promoted through the provision of what was called "industrial extension service, designed to operate much as the agricultural extension service does" (ibid, 82). The idea of providing industrial extension services (similar to the provision of extension services in agriculture), which was proposed in Kenya in the 1960s, has now been identified as one of the practical ways in which African countries can support industrial development on the continent (UNECA, 2015). How far these ideas were implemented in Kenya during the 1960s is not easy to assess, but the main point is that such strategies demonstrate that serious thought was given to the idea of industrialisation in the respective countries.

As we have seen earlier, one of the reasons given to justify the establishment of these statutory institutions was to facilitate the growth of the industrial sector, especially in areas where there was not enough private sector involvement. Further, creating state institutions to support industrialisation made it possible for the state to play the coordinating role in industrial development. In countries that had a strong socialist leaning, such as Tanzania, Zambia and Sudan, all industrial development institutions were established and owned by the state.

Undoubtedly, the mechanisms which were elaborated in the NDPs had the potential to stimulate industrial development. As noted above, one of the main reasons for government's involvement in the industrial development activities was to respond to sluggish industrial growth, and most of the interventions outlined in the NDPs were meant to speed up the growth of the industrial sector. This is explicitly stated in Botswana's second NDP:

> The slowness of industrial development to date must be partly attributed to the lack of entrepreneurial initiative. For this reason the Government has established the Botswana Development Corporation (BDC), the function of which will be to identify business opportunities in industry, commerce and agriculture; undertake the related detailed feasibility studies and interest potential investors in specific projects. The BDC...will manage Government's investments in industry and commerce, promote indigenous industrial and commercial entrepreneurs, and issue commercial loans to private enterprise (Republic of Botswana, 1969:61).

It is possible to deduce from such statements that the private sector was small, and therefore the state had to step in to stimulate the development of industry, by supporting entrepreneurs, both local and foreign, and by actively engaging in industrial production through SOEs. We know for instance from the early World Bank Mission and other analyses that the private sector in Africa during the 1960s was almost non-existent, especially in manufacturing and other industrial activities outside of primary commodities (see Kamarck, 1967).

In such circumstances, most African governments after independence had no choice but to get involved in not just providing support to stimulate industrial growth, but in establishing enterprises in various sectors of the economy. For example, through such initiatives, the government of Sudan set up public-owned industrial enterprises in a wide range of activities including tannery and cardboard manufacturing, sugar, canning, onion, milk powder factories. Two main reasons are given for the state's decision to embark on some of these projects:

> The specific reasons for public investment in just these types of manufacture are in some cases the size of the investment (as with sugar production) and in others the… lack of interest, or rather hesitation so far on the part of the private sector. The later explanation is particularly applicable where the public investment will open up new fields of industry, e.g., the cardboard factory, the onion dehydration factory and others (Republic of the Sudan, 1962:117).

Here we see similar a reason to the ideas of the *Big Push* that often private investments fail to mobilise the huge capital outlay required to start new industrial ventures, especially in developing countries where many private investors are interested in extractive industries. In the example of Sudan cited above, the question of the size of the investments required is definitely a good reason why the state had to step in and establish some of the factories. Many African countries had similar ventures.

ISI Strategy in Africa

The ISI model of industrialisation, which was popular in Africa and other developing countries in Asia and Latin America during the 1960s and 1970s, was effectively a way of building *ladders* for industrialisation. When analysed in the context of the colonial economic structure and logic, the ISI was a practical way of defying static comparative advantage. It was a practical way of implementing a strategy of *learning by doing*, with the aim of building industrial capabilities and competitiveness (see Amsden, 2001). If we take Chang's (2003) view that developed countries created their own ladders, but after climbing to the top of the industrial summit, they kicked away the ladders which they used to climb, perhaps not primarily as an act of sabotage but to protect their own interest, then developing countries seeking to have a share of the global manufacturing cake (market) will have no choice but to create their own ladders. As noted in Chapter 1, since the industrial and international economic landscape has changed, developing countries will have to create new ladders to successfully negotiate the more rugged landscape of industrial development (see Naude, 2010).

African leaders during the early 1960s seemed to have understood this simple fact quite well, and many of them started to construct their own ladders, perhaps not perfect ones, but nonetheless ladders which had the potential to build the manufacturing capabilities as part of the broader strategy of decentring the colonial economic logic. This is apparent when one reads through the earlier NDPs. What is interesting in most NDPs is that despite coming from different starting points, they all came to the same conclusion that achieving industrial development in Africa would involve a radical re-orientation of African economies to deconstruct the colonial economic structures. In this regard, the ideological heterogeneity which we see among the African countries made little difference when it came to the doctrine of ISI—all countries found it attractive.

Rationale for the ISI Strategy in Africa

The ISI model in Africa was premised on four major arguments: reducing dependence, reducing pressure on current account, learning to overcome the disadvantage of specialising in export of primary products and building manufacturing capabilities. The need to reduce dependence on industrialised countries, as we have seen earlier, was a real one, given that African countries during this period were just emerging from colonial rule, with little manufacturing capacity in most of the goods they were consuming, especially in the urban sector. Relying on industrialised countries for consumer goods, in a big way, reduced their independence, especially in the economic sphere. In Nigeria, Uganda and Botswana's NDPs, the governments stated clearly that the reason why they implemented the ISI was to reduce dependence on imported manufactured goods which limited the development of local industries.

But there was another level of dependence in terms of reliance on the export of a few commodities to industrialised countries, which in most cases turned out to be the former colonial powers. Uganda, as highlighted in earlier, complained about a high dependence on two crops which rendered the economy vulnerable to external shocks when the prices of the two commodities fell. Most African countries viewed the dependence on imported manufactured goods from industrialised countries and the dependence on the export of primary products to former colonial powers as something that restricted their independence. For most countries, ISI was seen as an effective mechanism for achieving economic independence.

The view that heavy dependence on imported manufactures from industrialised nations and export of primary good to the same countries reduces the country's independence is a view clearly articulated in the NDPs of several African countries including Uganda and Kenya. In Lesotho, Swaziland, Botswana and Zambia, the dependence was largely expressed in terms of over-dependence on South Africa for supplies and access to external markets. In Tanzania and Sierra Leone, the objective of reducing dependence on imported goods was linked to the idea of *self-reliance* which also fed into the politics of consolidating economic independence of African countries, by relying on domestic resources. This was particularly emphasised in Tanzania where the *Arusha Declaration in 1967* identified *self-reliance* as one of the key objectives of the development plan for the country. In this regard, the thinking was that if some of the imported goods were produced locally, this would increase the use of local resources to satisfy most of the country's needs, a situation that would promote self-reliance and independence.

The Foreign Currency Objective

Reducing the proportion of imported goods, particularly consumer goods, was also regarded as a desirable thing because it eased pressure on the current account and foreign reserves, and many African countries cited this as the reason for adopting the ISI strategy. Here the reasoning was purely economic. If most of the goods imported were produced locally, especially non-durable consumer goods and food stuff, it would save the importing country foreign exchange, which could be used to import capital goods and other intermediate goods not available in the country. In countries where these goods were imported from other countries, it meant that the country had to secure more foreign currency to pay for the imported goods, both consumer and capital goods. The pressure this situation created on the current account was quite significant given that most of the countries relied on a limited number of commodities for foreign exchange earnings, and in moments of commodity price shock on the global market, these countries felt the pinch much more, in terms of the balance of payment challenges.

In Ghana for instance, it was argued that establishing local factories to produce both consumer goods and intermediate inputs needed in other sectors would significantly ameliorate the balance of payment situation (Republic of Ghana, 1964:16). It was thus argued that the surest way of dealing with the balance of payment challenges is for a country to increase the value and scope of its exports, which could increase and stabilise export earnings and the exchange rate for the local currency.

During the 1970s most African countries embraced the view that to reduce the pressure on the current account, they had to start producing some of the imported goods locally, a situation which was expected to improve the current account balance, but also build capacity for manufacturing by dedicating the available foreign exchange to securing capital goods. In this sense, ISI was meant to kill two birds with one stone. To stem off the pressure created by the foreign currency shortages, most countries followed the strategy of restricting the importation of goods through various mechanisms, including the restriction on the issuance of import permits (by means of import quotas). For most countries in Africa with little and volatile foreign currency reserves, the idea of "saving" foreign currency by reducing imported consumer goods was economically appealing and politically popular.

The Infant Industry Argument

The other reason for adopting ISI in Africa was the famous *infant industry argument* (IIA). The IIA is perhaps one of the most popular justifications for ISI not just in Africa, but in other parts of the world, including the developed world. Wade (1990), Johnson (1982) and Amsden (1989) have shown how this policy was vigorously implemented in East Asia, starting with Japan, up to the late industrialisers such as Vietnam, Singapore and Thailand. The IIA rests on the principle that industries in developing countries, because of various factors such as poor infrastructure, low technology, low skills levels, are unable to compete fairly with goods produced in developed countries where the production environment including the cost of borrowing, infrastructure and support services is well-developed (see Tribe, 2000). If the goods produced in developed countries are freely allowed, so the argument goes, into developing countries with young and struggling manufacturing industries, they would stifle and eventually wipe out local industries that produce the same goods. In order to promote growth of manufacturing industries in developing countries, the young (infant) industries have to be protected from foreign-produced goods. List (1909) made a compelling argument for infant industry strategy as a tool used by all industrialised nation to increase their wealth and power. Giving the example of England, he argued that "the protective commercial policy adopted by the English nation at the expense of the Hansards, the Belgians, and the Dutch helped England attain to manufacturing supremacy, and that from the latter, aided by her Navigation Acts, arose her commercial supremacy" (List, 1909:21).

Free trade proponents often argue that if local industries in poor countries cannot compete with other international producers, it means that they are producing in a field where they do not have competitive advantage and would do well to shift to some industry where they are able to compete favourably. They would argue that protecting these infant industries brings inefficiency in the system and in the long run reduces the welfare of the people in that country (see Lin and Chang, 2009).

But critics of free trade argue that no country in the world has ever developed significant industrial capabilities without protecting embryonic local industries up to the point where they are able to compete without support (see Amsden, 1989, 2001; Lall, 2004). This is the point that Chang (2003) has made using the image of kicking away the ladder, pointing out that the now developed countries used different tactics of protecting young industries as a ladder for climbing the industrial cliff, and when they reached the top, they then kicked away the ladder and expected the developing countries to catch up with them.

The idea of protecting young industries from outside competition was also attractive in Africa prior to SAPs, and many governments adopted it (Ake, 1981; ODI, 1986; Ogujiuba et al, 2011). The level of protection differed between countries, but the common form of protection was both tariff and non-tariff mechanisms, including import quotas.

However, the crucial issue about infant industry protection as a strategy for industrial development is that it should be a temporary measure. The reasoning is quite simple and pragmatic. If an industry remains at infant stage for a long time (say over 30 years), then one has to be worried about the potential of the infant to grow and become a player on the global scene. The period it takes to mature, of course, differs, depending on the type of industry and also the local and international context in which the industry is located. But at some point, infant industries should be able to graduate; supporting them when they are weak should not be a permanent feature; protection should enhance and support the learning process.

One of the critiques labelled against ISI in Africa is that the protection of infant industries was seen as something permanent. As such ISI in Africa failed to foster learning and growth to a point where manufacturing industries could compete without government support (Tribe, 2000; Ogujiuba et al, 2011). Some critics of ISI in Africa have argued that in fact Africa had no infant industry to protect, so the whole strategy was actually misconceived (Collier, 2000).

The performance of ISI in Africa has been quite disappointing, but the strategy itself was widely adopted in many African countries immediately after independence. The strategy had great promise and indeed a number of industrial entities with sizable capacity developed in many countries (Bates, 1981). Bates (1981) referred to the period before the SAPs as the watershed for African industrial development, which saw a rapid development of relatively strong industrial capacity in many countries. While the learning and growth processes did not materialise as planned, it is evident that African countries were trying to create their own ladders which they could use to navigate the rough terrain of industrial development in the 20th century.

Terms of Trade Argument

A more sophisticated reason for adopting ISI in Africa is the terms of trade argument which was largely developed in the context of Latin America by Singer (1950) and Prebisch (1950). In Africa, the appeal of this argument was based on the fact that most African countries export primary commodities, and by specialising in exporting these exports, they were at a disadvantage since the price of commodities relative to that of manufactures tends to decline (see Chitonge, 2015). It was therefore thought that to overcome this disadvantage, African countries had to try and build their manufacturing capabilities so that they could also benefit from exporting manufactured goods. We have seen earlier how specialising in the export of primary commodities creates problems for countries in Africa, and it seems that this was one of the views which made the ISI strategy more attractive to African leaders during the 1960s and 1970s.

ISI as a Decolonisation Strategy

The ISI model was, in simple terms, based on the idea that countries should produce some (perhaps most) of the goods that they imported. In this sense, the ISI model was fundamentally an *inward looking* strategy, at least during the initial years of the strategy. To the extent that ISI was an inward oriented strategy, it defied the principles of static comparative advantage and instead encouraged efforts aimed at building new capabilities, particularly in the manufacturing sector. Seen from this perspective, the ISI model was a defiant strategy that did not follow the dictates of the classic trade theory and the principles of comparative advantage (see Chapter 2). As a strategy aimed at defying comparative advantage, the ISI challenged the idea that international trade leads to a win-win outcome, when we all specialise in what we have comparative advantage over others. In other words, the ISI strategy was a rejection of the idea that overall welfare in society increases through international trade which is boosted when nations produce according to their comparative advantage.

The relationship between international trade and welfare is highly contested in both mainstream economic and political economy literature, with some scholars contending that the situation is much more complex than what the trade theory tend to suggest (Jones, 1957). It has for example been argued that "specialisation" following a country's comparative advantage, which the trade theory advocates for should not be taken as an outcome of a simple process of exchange, because there are many other factors which can actually alter the welfare outcomes in either direction (see Krugman, 1987). A few empirical studies illustrate that trade can lead to negative welfare outcomes in some circumstances.

Krugman (1981) and Redding (1999), for example, successfully show that under certain circumstances, international trade tends to raise welfare in some countries while at the same time reduce welfare outcomes in others. In Krugman's (1981) model it is the initial capital stock differentials which are critical to the effects of trade on welfare between trading countries. In Redding (1999) it is actually the spill-over effects in the form of accumulated experience from learning by doing which affect a country's capacity to build new advantages over others, which in turn influences the level of welfare accrued from trade. Using evidence from this type of analysis, it has been argued that "comparative advantage now must be interpreted with care, because it reflects not only natural ability but also the (endogenous) benefit from cumulative experience" (Grossman and Helpman, 1990:814).

A similar set of debates emerged within the new discipline of development economics which highlighted the disadvantage developing countries face by specialising in exporting commodities while relying on imported manufactured good (see Prebisch, 1950; Singer, 1950; Lewis, 1984). With regard to ISI, Lewis (1984:125) observes that development economists from the late 1940s had not just doubted the wisdom of specialising on the export of primary products, but "were happily engaged in their traditional occupation of showing why, if not controlled, imports will be excessive." These debates clearly influenced the development of ISI on the African continent, in some countries directly through the advice given by some of the economists (e.g., in Ghana) while in others indirectly through the diffusion of ideas.

Indigenisation and Industrial Development

The other important strategy, related to the ISI, which many African countries adopted is that of indigenisation. Indigenisation, as a strategy for industrial development, had two components. There was indigenisation that focused on replacing expatriates in the public sector, especially in the civil service and in top parastatal management positions. The other component of the indigenisation strategy focused on providing support to local entrepreneurs to promote their participation in commerce and industries. In most NDPs, indigenisation was broadly conceived as an affirmative action as well as a means of reducing foreign influence in the country. Liberia's 2nd NDP raised the issue of foreign ownership of industries as a national concern:

> Despite the efforts of Government at indigenisation, the greater part of the modern sector of the economy has remained under foreign ownership. The mining sector… the modern manufacturing sector, and the organised retail and wholesale trade sector are all predominantly foreign-owned (Republic of Liberia, 1976:1).

Again, there are different ways in which indigenisation was formulated and implemented in different African countries. But the common thinking behind the strategy was that indigenous Africans had been side-lined in the key economic activities in the country during colonial rule, and so they had to be supported by the post-colonial state to increase their role in the economic activities of the country. As the passage from Liberia's NDP cited above suggests, indigenisation was partially aimed at reducing the role of foreign private enterprises in the country for fear of neo-colonial influence through big foreign private firms which were often associated with the former colonial powers. Indigenisation, therefore, was a popular strategy because it was seen as an effective way of reducing inequality between local and foreign actors (Green, 1965).

In Sierra Leone's first NDP, for example, it is stated that:

> In view of government's policy to encourage African enterprise, it seems equitable, therefore, to demarcate the principal areas in which foreign enterprise will not be encouraged in the private sector: retailing and merchandizing, fishing, the purchase and exploration of domestic agricultural produce whether monopolised by marketing boards or not, motor transportation. Government's objective in connection with its policy of encouraging African enterprise is to gradually reduce the area of foreign participation in these activities (Republic of Sierra Leone, 1962:6).

Similar statements are also found in Kenya, Ghana, Nigeria, Zambia, Cameroon, Liberia, Sudan and Swaziland's NDPs. The idea was that African business people would be given preference just as their European or American counterparts were given favours during colonial rule. Kenya's first NDP adopted a much clearer position and strategy for realising indigenisation:

> One of the major approaches to increasing African participation in the economy... is the promotion of small scale industry and commerce under African ownership and management. The approach will be a threefold one. First, the Government will encourage African-owned manufacturing organisations by providing training in management and technical skills, an advisory service and loans. Second, Africans will be aided in commerce, also through the provision of loans and advice.... Finally, Africans will be encouraged to enter larger scale ventures as they gain the knowledge and experience required to manage them (Republic of Kenya, 1964:81).

Apart from that, as clearly suggested by the extract from Sierra Leone's NDP, the ultimate goal was to localise ownership with the understanding that locally owned capital will be easy to control and discipline in cases of mischief.

In Kenya the participation of Africans in commercial and industrial activities was not limited only to activities such as retail and transport, but included food processing as well as manufacturing of light and heavy duty products. Indigenisation was a politically popular strategy which most African countries, including South Africa and Zimbabwe, embarked on immediately after wrestling power from colonial regimes. However, the outcome of such interventions leaves much to be desired, especially as far as industrial development is concerned. We have not seen many of the African captains of industry taking up the commanding heights of the private sector. It has been observed that most of them have developed parasitic tendencies relying on privileged access to state resources instead of developing the appropriate entrepreneurial acumen (Arrighi and Saul, 1968). Ake (1981) was also critical of indigenisation, arguing that state capitalism that promoted the growth of bureaucratic bourgeoisie created a national bourgeois class that combined both political and economic power, sometimes in partnership with foreign capitalists whom they were trying to act against.

Cottage Industries

The other common strategy that is found in all NDPs from the first to the third and fourth plans is that of promoting small rural industries. In some NDPs, these industries are conceptualised as craft industries, making traditional African craft, while in others they were given a much broader meaning to include small businesses involved in the production of goods for sale.

In more recent years, this area has been elevated to that of the small and medium enterprise (SME). But during the 1960s, the idea of craft industries dominated the thinking, and craft making was seen as one way of promoting Africans' participation in the process of industrialisation and the creation of employment.

> The main objective of the Government programme for the development of small scale industries are the creation of employment opportunities, mobilisation of local resources, mitigation of rural urban migration, and more even distribution of industrial enterprises in different parts of the country (Republic of Nigeria, 1975:155).

In Swaziland, the government created the Small Enterprise Promotion Office (SEPO) as a vehicle for promoting small enterprises. In Zambia, the promotion of small scale industries was linked to the plan to bring development to rural areas. In countries like Tanzania and Ethiopia, the craft industrial development strategy was linked to the agriculture sector through cooperatives.

As a strategy for industrial development, the cottage industry policy has received little attention and there has been little success in using this as a model for industrial development in Africa. In the earlier industrial strategies, the small industry route was adopted on the basis that this type of activities has less initial capital requirement and would involve many people in both rural and urban areas. Thus, the strategy itself made sense, in view of the fact that many African countries at that time had low formal employment (just like today as we have seen in Chapter 3). Today there is now more attention in many African countries directed towards stimulating the growth of SMEs as a viable industrialisation route in Africa (AEO, 2017). In the past, the contribution of the small industries has been insignificant, and it remains to be seen if the current efforts to promote the growth of SMEs will be given the support that is required for this to contribute to industrial development.

There are other strategies which African governments during the 1960s and 1970s articulated in the bid to promote industrial development, but the ones discussed above are among the key strategies. This chapter focused not so much on whether they achieved their set objectives, but on highlighting the industrial strategies adopted.

Outcomes of Industrial Strategies

There have been extended debates about whether these strategies were realistic or were merely wishful thinking, inspired by independence euphoria. How realistic these aspirations were at that time has to be assessed against the steps taken to realise what they had envisioned in the broader international political and economic context. Perhaps, one of the major shortcomings of the industrial strategies of the 1960s in Africa, as Ake (1981) has observed, was its failure to take into account the international political economy context in which African leaders sought to industrialise their countries. The focus was so much on taking charge of the domestic arena as if that was the only thing that mattered for Africa's industrial development. Yet it was clear that the fate of Africa was inextricably linked to the international division of labour which any industrial plan in Africa has to confront. As indicated in Chapter 1, for any industrialisation strategy to be successful it has to be, in effect, an act of defying the current configuration of comparative advantage, which requires that African countries consider the global economic situation.

Matambalya (2015) uses an example of industrial development in England, to argue that industrial development in England was a culmination of defiant actions which started during the reformation, spearheaded by the English Monarchy which defied and rebelled against the Church, when the King of England declared independence from the Vatican in 1534. He argues that not only did this mean that the revenues previously collected by the Vatican started to accrue to the King, but the

> reformation process unleased several changes that facilitated the emergence of an industrial society: creating a conducive environment for learning and generation of knowledge and development of skills, strengthening national identity and unity… smoothening the process of domestic market integration (DMI), agricultural revolution, improvement of infrastructure, securing access to abundant supplies of mineral and raw materials, technological evolution (Matambalya, 2015:70).

While the 16th-century English context and situation were very different from that of Africa in the 1960s, the central point is that any successful industrialisation would require African countries freeing themselves from the inhibitive forces of conventions, particularly the current international division of labour which works so much against African interests.

While the industrial strategies adopted during the first two decades of independence in Africa have produced mixed outcomes, one thing that is clear is that these strategies demonstrated the desire to disrupt the colonial economic logic by seeking to re-orient African economies from specialising on exporting primary commodities to economies with diversified production and export structures. Although some countries registered initial success in this regard, diversification of African economies remains a big challenge even today.

Note

1. See Nurkse (1953) for a general comment on the flow of investment in to developing countries. He argues that foreign investments in most developing countries concentrate in the extractive sector because this is where companies can make quick money. If there is no deliberate policy to guide investment in other sectors, the situation can lead to a mono-economy or enclave economy, which is a dominant feature in most developing nations.

References

African Centre for Economic Transformation (ACET, 2014). *Growth with Depth—African Transformation Report*. Accra: ACET. Available at: http://africantransformation.org/wp-content/uploads/2014/02/2014-african-transformation-report.pdf. Accessed 18.06.2016.

African Development Bank/Organisation for Economic Cooperation and Development/United Nations Development Programme (AEO, 2017). *African Economic Outlook 2017: Entrepreneurship and Industrialisation*. Abidjan: AfDB/OECD/UNDP.

Ake, C. (1981). *A Political Economy of Africa*. Lagos: Longman Nigeria.

Amsden, A. H. (1989). *Asia's Next Giant: South Korea and Later Industrialisation*. New York: Oxford University Press.

Amsden, A. H. (2001). *The Rise of 'The Rest': Challenges to the West from the Late-Industrialising Economies*. London/New York: Oxford University Press.

Arrighi, G. and Saul, J. (1968). "Socialism and Economic Development in Tropical Africa." *Journal of Modern African Studies*, Vol. 6, No. 2. 141–169.

Bates, R. (1981). *Markets and States in Tropical Africa: The Political Basis of Agricultural Policies*. Berkeley: University of California Press.

Chang, H. (2003). "Kicking away the Ladder: The 'Real' History of Free Trade." Foreign Policy in Focus (FPIF) Special Report. Available at: www.personal.ceu.hu/corliss/CDST_Course_Site/Readings_old_2012_files/Ha-Joon%20Chang%20-%20Kicking%20Away%20the%20Ladder-The%20"Real"%20History%20of%20Free%20Trade.pdf. Accessed 21.03.2015.

Chenery, H., Robinson, S. and Syrquim, M. (1986). *Industrialisation and Growth: A Comparative Study*. Washington, DC: World Bank.

Chitonge, H. (2015). *Economic Growth and Development in Africa: Understanding Trends and Prospects*. New York/London: Routledge.

Collier, P. (2000). "Africa's Comparative Advantage," in H. Jalilian, M. Tribe and J. Weiss (eds.), *Industrial Development and Policy in Africa: Issues of De-Industrialisation and Development Strategy*. Cheltenham: Edward Elgar. 11–21.

Collier, P. (2006). "African Growth: Why a 'Big Push'?" *Journal of African Economies*, Vol. 00, Supplement 2. 188–211.

Economic Commission for Africa and the African Union (ECA/AU, 2011). "Planning in Africa: Issues, Challenges and Prospects." United Nations Economic Commission for Africa (UNECA) Working Paper No. E/ECA/COE/30/8. Addis Ababa: ECA/AU.

Ewusi, K. (1981). *The Process of Industrialisation in Ghana.* Accra: Institute of Statistics, Social and Economic Research, University of Ghana.

General Agreement on Trade and Tariffs (GATT 1966). *Uganda Development Plan.* Geneva: GATT.

Green, R. (1965). "Four African Development Plans: Ghana, Kenya, Nigeria and Tanzania." *Journal of Modern African Studies*, Vol. 3, No. 2. 249–279.

Grossman, G. and Helpman, E. (1990). "Comparative Advantage and Long-run Growth." *The American Economic Review*, Vol. 80, No. 4. 796–815.

Hirschman, O. A. (1958). *The Strategy of Economic Development.* New Haven: Yale University Press.

Hirschman, A. (1981). *Essays in Trespassing: Economics to Politics and Beyond.* Cambridge: Cambridge University Press.

Johnson, C. (1982). *MITI and the Japanese Miracle: The Growth of Industrial Policy.* Stanford: Stanford University Press.

Jones, R. W. (1957). "Factor Proportions and the Hecksher-Ohlin Theorem." *Review of Economic Studies*, Vol. 24, No. 1. 1–10.

Kamarck, A. (1967). *The Economics of African Development.* New York: Praeger.

Killick, T. (1980). "Trends in Development Economics and their Relevance to Africa." *Journal of Modern African Studies*, Vol. 18, No. 3. 367–386.

Killick, T. (1983). "Development Planning in Africa: Experiences, Weaknesses and Prescriptions." *Development Policy Review*, Vol. 1. No. 2. 47–76.

Krishna, K. and Perez, C. (2005). "Unbalanced Growth." *Canadian Journal of Economics*, Vol. 38, No. 3. 832–851.

Krugman, P. (1981). "Trade, Accumulation and Uneven Development." *Journal of Economics*, Vol. 8. 149–161.

Krugman, P. (1987). "The Narrow Moving Band, the Dutch Disease, and the Competitive Consequences of Mrs. Thatcher." *Journal of Economics*, Vol. 27. 41–55.

Lall, S. (2004). "Selective Industrial and Trade Policies in Developing Countries: Theoretical and Empirical Issues," in C. Soludo, O. Ogbu and H. Chang (eds.), *The Politics of Trade and Industrial Policy in Africa.* Trenton/Asmara: Africa World Press Inc. 75–110.

Lewis, W. A. (1954). "Economic Development with Unlimited Supplies of Labour." *Manchester School*, Vol. 20. 139–191.

Lewis, A. (1984). "The State of Development Theory." *The American Economic Review*, Vol. 74, No. 1. 1–10.

Leys, C. (1982). "African Economic Development in Theory and Practice." *Deadalus*, Vol. 111, No. 2. 99–124.

Lin, J. and Chang, H. (2009). "Should Industrial Policy in Developing Countries Conform to Comparative Advantage or Defy it? A Debate Between Justin Lin and Ha-Joon Chang." *Development Policy Review*, Vol. 27, No. 5. 483–502.

List, F. (1909). *The National System of Political Economy* (trans. by Sampson S. Lloyd). London: Longmans, Green & Co.

Matambalya, F. (2015). "The Urge to Industrialise African Countries: Which Lessons can be Learnt from the Empirics of the Process?", in F. Matambalya (ed.), *African Industrial De-*

velopment and the European Union Co-operation: Prospects for a Re-engineered Partnership. London/New York: Routledge. 69–86.

Meier, G. (2001). "Introduction: The Old Generation of Development Economists and the New," in G. M. Meier and J. Stiglitz (eds.), *Frontiers of Development Economics: The Future in Perspective*. New York: Oxford University Press. 13–49.

Mendes, A. P., Beterlla, M. A. and A. Deixeira, R. F. (2014). "Industrialisation in Sub-Saharan Africa and Import Substitution Policy." *Brazilian Journal of Political Economy*, Vol. 34, No. 1. 120–138.

Mohan, J. (1966). "Varieties of African Socialism," in R. Milliban & J. Sauville (eds.), *The Socialist Register, 1966*: London: Merlin Press. 220–266.

Murphy, K., Shleifer, A. and Vishny, R. (1989). "Industrialisation and the Big Push." *Journal of Political Economy*, Vol. 97, No. 5. 1003–1026.

Naude, W. (2010). "New Challenges for Industrial Policy." United Nations University (UNU)/World Institute for Development Economic Research (WIDER), Working Paper No. 2010/107.

Newman, C., Page, J., Rand, J., Shimeles, A., Soderbom, M. and Tap, F. (2016). "The Pursuit of Industry: Policies and Outcomes," in C. Newman, J. Page, J. Rand, A. Shimeles, M. Soderbom and F. Tap (eds.), *Manufacturing Transformation: Comparative Studies in Industrial Development in Africa and Emerging Asia*. London: Oxford University Press. 1–24.

Noorbakhsh, F. and Paloni, A. (2000). "The De-Industrialisation Hypothesis, Structural Adjustment Programmes and the Sub-Saharan Dimension," in H. Jalilian, M. Tribe and J. Weiss (eds.), *Industrial Development and Policy in Africa: Issues of De-Industrialisation and Development Strategy*. Cheltenham: Edward Elgar. 107–129.

Nurkse, R. (1953). *Problems of Capital Formation in Underdeveloped Countries*. London: Basil Blackwell.

Nyasaland (1962). *Development Plan, 1962–65*. Zomba: Government Printers.

Ogujiuba, K., Nwogwugwu, U. and Dike, E. (2011). "Import Substitution Industrialisation as Learning Process: Sub-Saharan African Experience as Distortion of the 'Good' Business Model." *Business and Management Review*, Vol. 1, No. 6. 8–21.

Olukoshi, A. (2004). "Democratisation, Gloabalisation and Effective Policy Making in Africa," in C. Soludo, O. Ogbu and H. Chang (eds.), *The Politics of Trade and Industrial Policy in Africa*. Trenton/Asmara: Africa World Press Inc. 43–73.

Overseas Development Institute (ODI, 1986). "Industrialisation in Sub-Saharan Africa." ODI Briefing Paper, London: ODI.

Prebisch, R. (1950). *The Economic Development of Latin America and Its Principle Problems*. New York: United Nations Economic Commission for Latin America and Caribbean.

Redding, S. (1999). "Dynamic Comparative Advantage and the Welfare Effects of Trade." *Oxford Economic Papers*, Vol. 51. 15–39.

Republic of Botswana (1969). *National Development Plan, 1968–73*. Gaborones: RoB.

Republic of Ghana (1964). *Seven-Year Plan for National Reconstruction and Development*. Accra: Office of the Planning Commission.

Republic of Liberia (1976). National Social and Economic Development Plan, July 1976-June 1980. Monrovia: RoL.

Republic of Kenya (1964). *Development Plan 1970–1974*. Nairobi: National Planning Commission.

Republic of Kenya (1969). *Development Plan: 1970–1974*. Nairobi: Planning Commission.

Republic of Kenya (1970). *Development Plan: 1970–1974*. Nairobi: Planning Commission.

Republic of Liberia (1976). *National Social and Economic Development Plan, July 1976–June 1980*. Monrovia: RoL.

Republic of Malawi (1964). *Development Plan, 1965–69*. Zomab: Malawi Government.

Republic of Nigeria (1962). *National Development Plan: 1962–1968*. Lagos: Ministry of Economic Development.

Republic of Nigeria (1975). *Thirds National Development Plan, 1975–1980*. Lagos: Ministry of Economic Development.

Republic of Sierra Leone (1962). *Ten Year Plan of Economic and Social Development for Sierra Leone, 1961/72–1971/72*. Free Town: Sierra Leone Government.

Republic of Swaziland (1969). *Post Independence Development Plan*. Mbabane: Ministry of Finance and National Planning.

Republic of Swaziland (1973). *Second National Development Plan, 1973–1977*. Mbabane: Ministry of Finance and National Planning.

Republic of Tanzania (1969). *Second Five-Year Plan for Economic and Social Development*. Dar Es Salaam: Planning Commission.

Republic of the Sudan (1962). *The Ten Year Plan on Economic and Social Development: 1961/62–1970/71*. Khartoum: Ministry of Finance and Economics.

Rosenstein-Rodan, N. P. (1943). "Problems of Industrialisation of Eastern and South-Eastern Europe." *Economic Journal*, Vol. 53, No. 210/211. 202–211.

Rosenstein-Rodan, N. P. (1957). "Notes on the Theory of the Big Push." Economic Development Programme project C/57–25. Centre for International Studies. Cambridge: Massachusetts Institute of Technology.

Scitovsky, T. (1954). "Two Concepts of External Economies." *Journal of Political Economy*, Vol. 62, No. 2. 143–151.

Singer, W. H. (1950). "The Distribution of Gains Between Investing and Borrowing Countries." *American Economic Review*, Vol. 40, No. 2. 473–485.

Singer, W. H. (1984). "The Terms of Trade Controversy and the Evolution of Soft Financing: Early Years in the UN," in G. Meier (ed.), *Pioneers in Development*. New York: World Bank. 273–301.

Tribe, M. (2000). "The Concept of 'Infant Industry' in a Sub-Saharan African Context," in H. Jalilian, M. Tribe and J. Weiss (eds.), *Industrial Development and Policy in Africa: Issues of De-Industrialisation and Development Strategy*. Cheltenham: Edward Elgar. 30–57.

United Nations Economic Commission for Africa (UNECA, 2015). *Report on Africa 2015: Industrialising Through Trade*. Addis Ababa: UNECA.

Wade, R. (1990). *Economic Theory and the Role of Government in East Asian Industrialisation*. Princeton: Princeton University Press.

World Bank (1981). *Accelerated Development in Sub-Saharan Africa: An Agenda for Action (The Berg Report)*. New York: IBRD/World Bank.

· 6 ·

INDUSTRIALISATION AND STRUCTURAL TRANSFORMATION IN AFRICA

Introduction: Industrial Structure in Africa

The previous two chapters looked at the strategies adopted by African countries to promote industrial development during the 1960s and 1970s. Some of the key strategies adopted included the import substitution industrialisation, creation of state-owned industrial enterprises, indigenisation and the promotion of cottage industries, particularly in rural areas. As data on the current status of industrial development presented in Chapter 3 show, the implementation of these strategies did not deliver the anticipated rapid industrialisation in most countries. Although it has been argued that the implementation of these strategies was interrupted when SAPs were introduced in most African countries during the 1980s (Mkandaire and Soludo, 1999; Olukoshi, 2004; Soludo and Ogbu, 2004; Oqubay, 2015), it has also been observed that the implementation of the strategies encountered several challenges even before the introduction of SAPs (see Killick, 1980, 1983). It is difficult to speculate about what would have happened to industrial development in Africa if these strategies had not been interrupted by SAPs. What we know today is that industrial development in Africa remains weak and at very low levels in most countries. Low levels of industrial development on the continent are evident in the lack of structural transformation, which is manifested in the fact that most African economies are still operating under the same economic structures constructed during colonial rule. As argued in Chapter 1, the dominant feature of the colonial economic structure and logic was the specialisation of African countries in the production of raw materials for export, and little has changed up to this day.

As data presented in this chapter show, most African economies' exports are still dominated by unprocessed or semi-processed raw materials, with little value addition taking place within the continent. Recent estimates suggest that up to 90 percent of exports from Africa are natural resource-based, mostly semi-processed goods (UNIDO, 2016). This production and export structure presents many challenges, some of which have been mentioned in previous chapters. One of the most serious challenges that this production structure presents is around the ability and capacity of African economies to create productive jobs. The inability to create productive employment in Africa is occurring when "Africa's working-age population continues to expand quickly. The working-age population in Africa is expected to grow close to 70 percent between 2015 and 2035, or approximately 450 million people" (WEF, 2017:35). In this context, the importance of transforming African economies in such a way that they can create enough productive jobs to accommodate the steadily growing labour force cannot be over-emphasised.

This chapter examines the link between industrialisation and economic structural transformation in Africa. Recent data on structural transformation in Africa are presented and analysed to see if there are any signs of African economies undergoing significant positive structural changes. The evidence on structural transformation trends in African countries presented in this chapter point to a deviation from the "orthodox path" which has been referred to as "marching through the sectors" (UNECA, 2016b). What we have seen in most African countries is that these economies are effectively becoming *service economies* without any significant levels of industrial growth, contrary to what mainstream theory envisages (see Rodrik, 2015). It has thus been observed that the "African pattern of structural change is very different from the classic pattern that has produced high growth in Asia, and before that, the European industrialisers" (Rodrik, 2014:9). The key question which this raise is around the practical and policy implications of the observed trends on structural transformation in Africa. To examine these trends, the chapter takes a long-run perspective of structural transformation, focusing on the changes in the sectoral composition of African economies over time.

Economic Structural Transformation Back on the Policy Radar

Economic structural transformation debates in Africa are back on the agenda. Like debates about industrialisation in general, structural transformation debates have been ignited by strong growth experienced in most African countries between 2000 and 2014. What has sparked the debate is the inability of African economies to create productive employment and the slow decline of poverty rates at the time when most economies in the continent have been experiencing a sustained spell of descent economic growth. Oqubay (2015:9) observes that many "scholars and policy makers are concerned that Africa's growth is insufficient to improve living standards for a rapidly growing population…to achieve industrialisation and economic transformation, and to ensure a more equitable development structure." A recent report by the World Economic Forum (WEF, 2017) singles out the failure to create adequate productive employment as one of the major challenges which many African economies are facing in the post-crisis period (i.e., post-2009).

For analysts interested in the African growth story in the 21st century, the lack of positive structural change raises two related questions: First, what has been the force driving the growth reported in many African countries in recent years (What is the source of the growth)? Second, will this growth be sustained for a longer period? Arbache and Page (2009) sparked the debate by raising questions about the sustainability of the growth reported in most African countries prior to the 2008/09 global financial and economic crisis. Questions about the sustainability of growth in African countries were being asked in view of the highly episodic growth experienced by many African countries in the past (see Ndulu and O'Connell, 2008).

During the 2008/09 financial and economic crisis, many analysts were convinced that the decent growth reported in most African countries from 2002 onwards, was going to be halted by the 2008/09 financial crisis. But when Africa's growth proved to be resilient in the face of the global financial crisis, with growth rebounding to pre-crisis levels just a year later in 2010 (Brixiova and Ndikumana, 2011; World Bank, 2015), analysts started to show more interest in the African growth story. This is evident in a series of studies conducted just after the crisis, seeking to analyse the dynamics of the growth reported in Africa (McMillan and Rodrik, 2011; Devarajan and Fengler, 2012; Page, 2012; Timmer et al, 2012; McMillan and Harttgen, 2014, De Vries et al, 2015).

Although some of the authors dubbed the growth reported in Africa, "an African miracle" (see McMillan and Harttgen, 2014), most of the studies concluded that this growth was fragile, and that positive structural transformation was not occurring in most economies. Some analysts suggested that though African economies are undergoing structural change in terms of the composition of labour and output, the sectoral shifts observed so far represent *perverse* structural change (McMillan and Rodrik, 2011, Timmer et al, 2012; Rodrik, 2014). In other words, the growth reported on the continent is not contributing much to positive economic structural change.

While some analysts have acknowledged that the structure of African economies has been changing as evident in the substantial growth of the service sector's share in total output (see Table 6.1), it is widely believed that the growth reported in the continent has been driven by high commodities prices on the global market and, this has, contributed little to positive economic structural transformation (see UNECA, 2012, 2016b; Page, 2015). Studies conducted so far have answered the two questions about the sources of growth in African economies and the sustainability of the African growth momentum in the new millennium. The attention for analysts has now shifted to explaining the reasons for the lack of positive structural transformation, and how this positive structural change can be promoted and sustained.

In trying to answer the question of why the growth experienced in most African countries in recent years has not led to positive economic structural change, most analysts point to over-reliance on commodity production and export in most African economies (Timmer et al, 2012; Rodrik, 2014; de Vries et al, 2015; Page, 2015). The United Nations Economic Commission for Africa (UNECA) identified narrow export based on commodities as one of the factors that explain the lack of positive structural transformation. Although most African economies have been reporting decent growth rates over the past decade and half, this growth has been without "depth." The fact that high commodity prices account for the larger share of the growth reported in Africa is linked to the apparent failure to create enough productive jobs to absorb the growing labour force. Several editions of *Economic Report on Africa* (ERA) by UNECA have highlighted the fact that the growth seen in most African countries is not resulting in African economies transforming the structures set up during colonial rule (see UNECA 2012, 2016b).

Drawing from this diagnosis, there is almost consensus among analysts that to achieve sustained economic growth, African governments must work hard to transform the structures of their economies, and that industrial growth is one of the viable ways through which this can be done. As pointed out in Chapter 2, the failure to diversify African economies from the export of raw materials is a clear sign these countries are still operating under the colonial economic structures and rationale. In this sense, the failure to structurally transform African economies from commodity export is a permanent reminder of an incomplete decolonial project in Africa (see Chitonge, 2018). For Africa to industrialise, African countries have to carry the decolonisation project, which started with the liberation struggle for independence, to its logical conclusion, which includes economic decolonisation. The economic sphere is one area where decolonisation is desperately needed if Africa is to make progress, not only because the economic structure determines the material conditions of the continent, but also because the material conditions determines how the continent interacts with the rest of the world.

Industrialisation and Structural Change

As noted in Chapter 2, industrialisation, particularly manufacturing, is widely acknowledged to be critically important in the process of structural transformation. In other words, industrialisation is one of the important mechanisms through which positive structural transformation can be realised (see UNECA, 2016a). Economic structural transformation is here understood to mean the sustained shifts in the sectoral composition of output and labour over time, underpinned by the shifting of labour from low to high productivity activities.

Understood from this angle, structural transformation can be positive (contributes positively to increase in productivity and employment) or perverse (negatively impact on productivity and job creation in the economy). Seen from this perspective, structural transformation occurs in all economies over time, to the extent that the sectoral composition of an economy rarely remains the same. Therefore, different types of structural transformation can occur, and the concern should be on what type of transformation is occurring in an economy, and what contribution it makes to sustainable economic growth and societal-wide changes including raising levels of well-being in the general population (Tregenna, 2016).

In this regard, the desired type of structural transformation is one which is characterised by a shift of labour from low- to high-productivity activities. For example, a shift of labour and other factors from subsistence agriculture to informal trading in rural and urban areas has little impact in terms of positive structural transformation. As long as factors are shifting from low- to low-productivity activities, this type of transformation can have negative outcomes for the overall economy (see McMillan and Rodrik, 2011). It is in this context that industrialisation, to the extent that the industrial sector (manufacturing in particular) is characterised by higher productivity, can play an important role in promoting positive structural transformation.

The challenge for Africa, therefore, is not that there has been no structural transformation in the economies, but that most economies are experiencing structural transformation characterised by the movement of factors (particularly labour) from low (and sometimes high) to low-productivity activities. As we shall see later, this type of structural change often has negative social and economic outcomes.

Structural Change: "Marching Through the Sectors"?

Debates on the role of industrialisation in structural transformation have widely acknowledged that in countries where manufacturing has not grown to become a significant segment of the economy, economies often portray and experience signs of perverse structural transformation, characterised by labour moving from high to low-productivity activities.

The dominant approach to conceptualising, measuring and analysing structural transformation is rooted in the idea that has recently been referred to as "marching though the sector" (see UNECA, 2016b), which effectively views structural transformation as a linear process of economic structural change. This process is widely perceived to occur in three continuous phases: the first is dominated by agricultural-led growth in the initial stages, this is followed by industrial sector-dominated (export-led) growth, which eventually gives way to a service-dominated economy. Within this framework, a service-dominated economy is seen as a feature of a maturing, post-industrial economy, characterised by growing demand and rising prices for services relative to products in the primary and secondary sectors.

But this conventional view of structural change is being challenged by emerging evidence of the prevalent phenomenon observed in many developing countries which some analysts are calling *premature deindustrialisation*, a phenomenon which is defined by low-income countries experiencing steady expansion of the service sector with a stagnant or declining industrial sector (see, Tregenna, 2009, 2016; Basbay, 2018). Evidence in many developing economies points to a situation where the service sector is becoming the leading sector in terms of its share in total output, and, in some cases, labour (see Choudhury and Chatterjee, 2015; Rodrik, 2015; Treganna, 2016; Basbay, 2018). This suggests that these economies have effectively become *service economies*, with a thin layer of industrial and manufacturing sector.

Trends in Sectoral Composition of African Economies

In the case of Africa it is evident that the service sector has become the largest sector, on average accounting for more than half of total output in 2015 (Table 6.1).

Table 6.1: Sectoral Share of Output Resource Status of African Countries (%), 1980–2015.

		Non-resource-rich Countries	Resource-rich Countries	All Countries
Agriculture	1980	30.9	23.6	27.2
	1990	30.4	25.7	28.1
	2000	29.6	20.3	24.9
	2010	26.2	16.8	21.5
	2015	23.4	17.4	20.4
Industry	1980	18.3	36.4	27.4
	1990	21.4	31.0	26.2
	2000	20.6	38.5	29.6
	2010	22.7	37.0	29.9
	2015	22.7	32.6	27.7
Services	1980	43.4	41.2	42.3
	1990	47.1	43.3	45.2
	2000	49.2	41.2	45.2
	2010	51.0	42.7	46.9
	2015	53.0	50.1	51.5

Source: Author. Based on data from the African Statistical Year Book (ASYB), various years.

Figures on individual countries suggest that in 2015 the service sector was the largest in more than two-thirds of countries in Africa (see Appendix I and II). In countries such as Mauritius, Seychelles, Cabo Verde, Gambia, Zambia, Senegal, Namibia, Botswana and South Africa, the service sector accounts for two-thirds or more of the total output (ibid). Overall, the rise in the share of services in total output started in the 1990s, but picked up momentum between 2010 and 2015. This rise in the share of the service sector in the economy has been attributed to a number of factors include the significant growth of the communication sector buoyed by the mobile revolution, business services and tourism (UNECA, 2016a). While the growth of the service sector is seen as normal in developed countries, the expansion of the service sector without a significant manufacturing sector is sometimes seen as an anomaly in economic growth theories (see Basbay, 2018).

In this context, it is important to assess how well the conventional theory of structural change (marching through the sectors) explains the experience in low-income countries. Buera and Kaboski (2009) explored this question and based on their empirical review of the data available, they concluded that the theories of economic structural transformation fail to explain the changes we are observing in many developing countries. In other words, while the theory of structural change explains the patterns of structural change occurring in developed economies, the theory does not explain why low-income countries, like most countries in Africa, are 'skipping' the phase of industrial growth (Basbay, 2018). In this sense, developing countries seem not to conform to the mainstream theory of structural transformation.

As noted above, recent trends in most developing countries suggest that structural changes in these countries are not exhibiting the same structural change patterns observed in the now industrialised countries; many countries are skipping the industrial phase, going straight into services. In other words, what we are seeing in most of these countries is a significant growth of the service sector without substantial growth in the industrial, particularly manufacturing, sector, contrary to what mainstream theory predicts. In fact, industrial share in Africa in total output and labour has either remained stagnant or declined since the 1970s as evident in the data presented in Chapter 3. In terms of manufacturing, we see a trend where manufacturing share in total output and employment have started to declined at extremely low levels of GDP per capita (see also Tregenna, 2016). Given this pattern of economic structural change, it is important to understand the patterns we are observing in Africa, and what this means in terms of realising positive structural transformation.

Social and Economic Structural Change

The starting point for analysing structural change is that sustained economic growth induces some form of change, not just in the structure of the economy, but also in the broader structures in society, including the structure and nature of the family, which evolve with the growing economy. In this sense, structural transformation can be an unsettling process which "brings disruption to the traditional ways" in such a way that there are always losers in the process: "old skills become obsolete, old trades are ruined" (Hirschman, 1958:6). Simon Kuznets (1966), based on his analysis of industrialised countries, made some observations on how changes in the economic sector induce change in other sectors of society. But Kuznets' analysis focused mainly on economic changes, with less attention given to the impact of the changing economic structures on social relations and structures. An important study that highlighted the social impact of structural change in the economy, particularly deindustrialisation, is Bluestone and Harrison's (1982) research on the devastating effects of falling industrial activities on workers and their families in the USA. But before going into the analysis of the patterns of structural change in African economies, it is essential to broadly outline what is meant by economic structural transformation and what parameters are used to study the change over time, and how such changes relate to industrialisation.

Theories of Economic Structural Transformation

The concept of economic structural transformation is derived from the basic idea that as economies grow, certain changes occur in the composition of the economy. As noted in Chapter 2, it is not just economic structures that shift as economies grow, but the social, cultural and religious aspects of societies change over time, in response to the changing employment patterns and the lives of people. The related idea of economic structural change is evident in Rostow's (1960 theory of stages of economic growth, where he talks about the changes through which the economy, and society in general, goes as it grows.[1] Like "the marching through the sectors" perspective, Rostow's five stages of economic growth were conceived in a linear manner, such that an economy is expected to graduate from one stage to another and may not skip a stage in the process of change.

In theories of economic structural change, structural transformation has been widely understood in terms of the shift of labour from one sector to another. This is a view which is still dominant among many economists even today (UNECA, 2016b). This view of structural transformation is elaborated in Arthur Lewis' (1954) two-sector model.

Literature on economic structural transformation shows that the two-sector model has a strong influence on the conceptualisation and measurement of economic structure change across the globe. In this framework, positive structural transformation is understood to be constituted by the shift of labour from low- to high-productivity activities, within or between sectors. A common indicator of positive structural transformation is the narrowing of productivity gaps between major sectors and subsectors in the economy. In cases where labour moves from high- to low-productivity sectors in the economy, this is often characterised as perverse structural change, mainly because the net result of this kind of change is increasing productivity gaps between sectors (McMillan and Rodrik, 2011; Timmer et al, 2012; de Vries et al, 2015).

Conceived broadly, structural transformation can be seen as a process of "spreading economic opportunities in a balanced way across all segments of the population and regions of the country…" (Dhin, 2014:19). The emphasis here should be on spreading the economic opportunities both in terms of the different groups of people in society and geographically. This understanding of structural transformation highlights three fundamental features: (a) the process has to be broad-based, (b) the geographical spread of economic activities (de-concentration of economic activities) and (c) the creation of economic opportunities. Viewed from this angle, structural transformation can be seen as a process that goes beyond the sectoral shifts in the composition of labour and total output.

It is also important to distinguish between structural transformation that produces static and dynamic effects. Dynamic structural transformation occurs when labour, particularly, shifts to a sector where labour productivity is changing, meaning that the receiving sector is not experiencing static trends in productivity. What determines the dynamism is the fact that productivity in the receiving sector is changing over time—preferably growing (productivity can also be declining in the receiving sector). Static structural transformation occurs when labour moves to a sector where productivity is not changing (whether low or high). In terms of structural transformation, it is positive dynamic structural change that matters in the long run (see Timmer et al, 2012).

Role of Industrialisation in Structural Change

Inter-Sectoral Linkages

As alluded to earlier in this chapter, there is wide agreement that industrialisation is central to the process of economic transformation for the simple reason that the industrial sector is assumed to promote the growth of sophisticated technology which makes it possible to rapidly expand employment opportunities without lowering productivity and wages. The growth of industries is therefore associated with the growth of the capacity in the economy to absorb labour from sectors where productivity and wages are low (Chenery et al, 1986). In economies where positive structural transformation has occurred, labour moves from the low-productivity activities (mainly traditional agriculture in the initial stages of economic development) to the sectors with high productivity (mainly industry and services). Expansion of industrial activities is seen to be vital to the process of structural transformation in an economy in terms of creating demand for agricultural produce via backward linkages, such that agricultural produce are used as inputs in the manufacturing sector (see Adelman, 1984). This is particularly true in economies where food processing industries expand as more people move from rural to urban areas, leading to more people becoming dependant on purchased rather than self-grown food.

Albert Hirschman (1958) who explored the idea of inter-sectoral linkages observed that the industrial sector acts as an engine of growth by creating demand for agricultural products, which it uses as input in the manufacturing processes. He argued that while industry is linked to both agriculture and service sectors, its linkage is stronger with the agricultural sector than with services, especially in the early stages of economic development. According to Hirschman (1958), economies where inter- and intra-sectoral linkages are weak, the process of structural transformation is slow and often undetermined, since the different parts of the economy are pulling in different directions, without coherence. Here, Hirschman (1958) was not arguing for a *balanced growth* approach where investment in different sectors is given the same priority to avoid a situation where inadequate supply of inputs in one sector creates a constraint for growth in other sectors, and the economy at large (see Nurkse, 1953). Hirschman (1958) proposed an *unbalanced growth* approach to economic development, emphasising the view that not all sectors or subsectors should receive the same attention; some sectors because of their "power of dispersion" (the strong potential to stimulate growth in other sector) should be prioritised so that, through the backward and forward linkages, they can stimulate growth in other sectors as they grow. In this sense, stronger sectoral linkages are central in a positively transforming economy. We come back to the issue of linkages later in the chapter.

Features of Positive Structural Transformation

In the mainstream view of structural change, positive economic structural transformation is assumed to be manifested by the following four phenomena:

1) A declining share of agriculture in gross domestic product (GDP) and employment
2) the rapid process of urbanisation as people migrate from rural to urban areas
3) the rise of a modern industrial and service sectors
4) demographic transition from high to low rates of births and deaths (see Timmer et al, 2012:1).

The role of agriculture in a transforming economy has sometimes been misunderstood because of the emphasis put on the declining share of agriculture in total output and labour force as an indicator of structural transformation. This has led to a situation where agriculture is given less attention based on the notion that its role in the economy should be declining over time (see Chitonge, 2016). The role of agriculture in industrialisation is discussed later in the chapter.

What Lies Beyond Services?

If understood as the shift in the sectoral composition of labour and output in an economy over time, structural transformation is an ongoing process as alluded to earlier, by the mere fact that sectoral proportions of the economy are constantly changing. As is often the case with economists "schooled in general equilibrium analysis," there is a tendency to present structural transformation in static terms, where the sectors assume fixed share in total output and employment (Krugman, 1987:41). Such views of structural transformation depict a linear and unidirectional process, framed in terms of "marching through the sectors", with structural transformation starting from agriculture, through manufacturing, ending with a large service sector, which is a dominant feature of post-industrial economies. But this understanding of structural transformation has not gone far in explaining the process of change in post-industrial societies where the process of change seems to come to a halt when these economies are dominated by services. Do services represent the ultimate sector beyond which there is no more room for further transformation? Is there anything beyond services? Are post-industrial economies expected to re-start the process from agrarian revolution through re-industrialisation again?

Most importantly, do the non-industrialised countries in Africa and elsewhere have to "march through" the sectors as the now industrialised and industrialising countries did? As evidence from Africa and other low-income countries shows, there may not be a single path to structural transformation after all. Different countries may go through different paths, as is the case now, when we are seeing a number of low-income countries transitioning to service-dominated economies without experiencing significant industrial growth (see Rodrik, 2015). Given this, the theory of economic structural transformation seems to suffer from the same weakness evident in the modernisation theory, which expects all countries to go through a linear path with predictable coordinates, determined by the level of per capita income.

Structural Transformation: Growth with DEPTH Perspective

For most countries in Africa, the challenge of structural change can be broadly assessed in terms of the *DEPTH deficit*. Instead of defining structural transformation in terms of sectoral share in total output and labour force, a broader approach that takes into account various dimensions of structural changes, induced by shifts in production and demand structure, is more helpful in understanding patterns of economic change over time.

The Africa Centre for Economic Transformation (ACET, 2014) adopted the DEPTH approach to understanding structural change. The DEPTH approach has five dimensions: *Diversification* of the economies, promotion of *Export* competitiveness, improving *Productivity* of labour (especially in the subsistence sector), upgrading and developing new *Technologies* in all sectors and finally, all these dimensions feed into the over-arching dimension of improving *Human* well-being. The first letters of the five elements of this approach make up the acronym *DEPTH*; derived from *diversification*, *export* promotion, *productivity* growth, *technology* advancement and improving *human* well-being.

While the word *depth* is important in the context of African economies where most countries could aptly be described as growing without *depth*, given the reliance on a narrow band of commodity for export, the individual letters that make up the word also carry significant meaning. For example, diversification is crucially important for African economies, which since independence have remained overly dependent on the export of a few commodities. What this means is that African countries lack *depth* in terms of their production and export structure. The lack of depth in most African countries is also manifested in the concentration of production in low value-added activities; high value-added activities which require "deepening" manufacturing capabilities are largely absent in most countries. In this regard, diversification of exports can only be achieved when industrial development deepens in the sense of building the capabilities to produce a wide range of manufactured products including consumer and capital goods.

Similarly, productivity growth is particularly important as African countries seek to deepen and broaden their industrial capabilities. Growth in productivity, particularly in agriculture, is critical at this moment given that majority of the people still work in the agricultural sector where productivity is awfully low (see Fox and Thomas, 2016; UNECA, 2016b). Technological advancement is also crucial if African economies are to have a chance to improve their competitiveness, especially in the manufacturing sector. In the context of the much touted *Fourth Industrial Revolution* driven by digitisation, developing the capacity to support the creation and use of new technologies in various sectors of the economy is an area that requires urgent attention in many countries seeking to successfully transform the structures of their economies.

Lastly, but most importantly, all the other dimensions of DEPTH should be tailored towards improving the most important factor in Africa's development strategy—human capital. Improving the well-being of Africans should provide a strong motivation for pursuing structural transformation. Progress on this will be made only if substantial advances in the other four dimensions mentioned earlier occur. Therefore, instead of being pre-occupied with whether the share of agriculture in GDP and labour force is declining or increasing, the shifting sectoral composition of labour and output should be analysed in terms of whether this is contributing to diversification, promoting export competitiveness, improving productivity, deepening technological capacity and the improvement of the welfare of all people. Understood from this angle, growing with DEPTH has always been, and still is, a challenge in many African countries.

Structural Transformation and Agriculture

Often, the structural transformation literature portrays the changes that occur as economies grow and develop, in terms of the "movement of labour out of less productive semi-subsistence agriculture…into the more productive sectors of manufacturing or services" (AfDB/OECD/UNDP/UNECA, 2013:14). This has frequently been interpreted to mean that in a dynamically growing economy, agriculture is a sector in secular decline. Linked to this is the popular view among economists that the declining share of agriculture in total output and employment in the economy should be singularly celebrated as evidence of structural transformation. Based on this interpretation of structural change, disastrous policy advice which neglects the agricultural sector has often been given by international experts. One might be forgiven for thinking that this view is no longer influential; to the contrary, this view is still prominent today even among eminent scholars and policy makers. The dominance of this view may partly explain the neglect of the agriculture sector in most African countries as noted in the preceding chapter, given the strong influence which international development experts have had on the African policy space.

Oftentimes, the phenomenon of declining share of agriculture in total output and employment is interpreted to mean absolute decline of the agricultural sector, when in actual fact the decline is relative to the share of other sectors, which grow faster than the agricultural sector. In other words, while the agricultural sector's share in the economy may be declining relative to the industrial and service sectors, it actually may be growing, but at a slower rate compared to growth in the other sectors (see Timmer et al, 2012). Thus, the agriculture sector need not contract or experience negative growth in a transforming economy. In most cases, where structural transformation has occurred, the agricultural sector continues to grow, though at lower rates compared to other sectors. What leads to the decline in the share of agriculture in total output is the fact that agriculture productivity grows at a slower rate than in the rest of the economy, and significantly lower than in manufacturing and the broader industrial sector (ibid). This is well elaborated by Mhone (2001:17) who diagrammatically illustrates the shifts in the sectoral share in total output and labour resulting from such changes.

The view that structural transformation is marked by the declining share of agriculture in total output and labour gives the impression that allocating resources to agriculture is like storing treasure in a sinking titanic. Contrary to the view of agriculture as a sector in secular decline, agriculture is important in the process of economic transformation especially at the beginning of the process when majority of the people derive their livelihood from subsistence farming, as is the case for most countries in Africa even today. This is a view which was widely held to be "axiomatic" among the pioneers of development economics (see Matsuyama, 1992). For example, Nurkse (1953:52–53), drawing from the English experience, argued that, "Everyone knows that the spectacular industrial revolution would not have been possible without the agricultural revolution that preceded it. The growth of industry would not have been possible without the turnip and other improvements in Agriculture." Arthur Lewis (1954), whose two-sector model has influenced the thinking around structural transformation, also acknowledged the significance of increasing productivity in agriculture (Lewis, 1954:433). The importance of agriculture is also evident in Rostow (1960:8) who observed that "revolutionary changes in agricultural productivity are an essential condition for successful take-off."

Structural Transformation Targets

Based on the view of transformation as a process where agriculture share in total output and employment declines while manufacturing share increases, it has become fashionable to set what are seen as appropriate sectoral share in total output, at a particular level of a country's national income. This view was first popularised by a UNIDO report during the 1980s (see UNIDO, 1980). Drawing from this view, it has been suggested that for high-income countries in Africa, the target should be to reduce agriculture share in total output to 3.3 percent, and for lower-middle and low-income countries, the aim should be to reduce agriculture-to-GDP ratio to 15.5 percent. As for manufacturing, the target is to increase manufacturing share in GDP to a minimum of 28 percent for high- and middle-income countries, and 24 percent for low-income countries (UNECA, 2012:72).

Seeing structural transformation from this angle leads to a situation where agriculture is negatively perceived, while in fact the sector has a strategic role in structural transformation, particularly during the early stages. The extreme opposite of the view that the role of agriculture should decline in a growing economy is the idea that poor countries should forget about industrial development; they should first of all focus on increasing productivity in agriculture to create the momentum for industrial growth. Henley (2012:26) exemplifies this view when he argues that, "aid agencies interested in reducing poverty and promoting growth—even industrial growth—in Africa might be well advised to forget about industry for the time being, and instead concentrate precisely on rural agricultural development…." A development strategy that focuses squarely on agriculture, ignoring growth in the industrial sector, cannot go far in promoting sustained and inclusive growth. The assumption under such a strategy is that agriculture growth will automatically stimulate the growth of industries, but the growth of industry anywhere has never been an automatic response; it has always been the result of a deliberate programme of action at the national level.

The Agriculture-Industry Linkage

While mainstream structural transformation theory tends to put more emphasis on industrial growth, particularly manufacturing, a sound industrial strategy should emphasise the importance of promoting the connection between and within sectors. The rationale behind this lies in the point that at the beginning of industrial development, expansion of the manufacturing sector depends heavily on a thriving agricultural sector. And this is because, as noted in chapters 3 and 8, productivity growth in agriculture creates suitable condition for the growth of the industrial sector from both the supply and demand side of the economy. From the supply side, a vibrant agriculture sector supplies the basic input used in the manufacturing of food, chemical, building material and other inputs in manufacturing production processes at the early stages of economic growth. From the demand side, a thriving agriculture sector provides the markets for manufactures, especially at the early stages when local manufacturing firms rely on the domestic markets to grow (Adelman, 1984). The linkages between agriculture and industry are therefore very important to understanding and in a strategy seeking to promote industrial development. In this sense promoting the growth of the agricultural sector has to be part of an integrated industrial strategy.

In countries with large proportions of the labour force in agriculture, it is quite clear that there can be no meaningful industrialisation without significant growth in productivity in the agriculture sector. As Nurkse (1953), Rostow (1960) and Lewis (1954) point out, growth in the agricultural sector has always been a basis for building a strong and viable industrial sector in all countries which we can today call successfully industrialisers. Johnson and Mellor (1961), for instance, argue that improving productivity in agriculture forms the foundation for broad-based structural transformation. Thus, any structural transformation strategy that neglects the agriculture sector can only achieve limited results, especially in countries with a large agrarian population. Ake (1981:100) articulated this point in the case of African countries when he argued that,

> Diversification of African economies will demand among other things heavy investment in agricultural extension services, in the development of new commodities and new techniques, in the importation of machinery, and in industrialisation. The chances of bringing this about are greatly reduced if the agricultural sector is too weak to reduce drastically the need for imported food, or increase the incomes of farmers….

On the other hand, a structural transformation strategy that neglects the growth of the industrial sector, particularly manufacturing will have limited success. There is now strong evidence showing that agriculture development cannot prosper in isolation, just as industrial development will not go far without a strong and diversified agricultural sector. Successful transformation of African economies would require paying attention to both sectors.

Historical evidence from the experience of a diverse set of countries supports the view that industrialising economies in their early stages rely on a dynamic agricultural sector as a launch-pad for industrial growth. Japan (1880–1910) and Russia (from 1924 onwards) used this strategy to accumulate more resources to finance industrial development needs (Lewis, 1954). It is also commonly observed that "East Asia's agrarian transformation served as the basis for economies to industrialise, paving the way for a more diversified base to emerge. Increased incomes for farmers created buoyant demand in rural areas for farm inputs, for processing and marketing services as well as for consumer goods and services" (UNECA, 2012:120). Sustained productivity growth in the agricultural sector is widely believed to have played a significant role in the rapid structural transformation of most Asian countries (Pingali, 1997).

Based on historical evidence, there is now wide agreement among analysts that the agriculture sector is the bedrock of structural transformation: "It is now largely accepted that growth in the agriculture sector which contributes to poverty reduction and makes internal demand more dynamic, has been the precondition for transforming economies that are now industrialised or undergoing industrialisation" (NEPAD, 2014:15).

Agriculture and Africa's Transformation

As noted in chapter 5, many African countries have since the time of independence been emphasising the importance of agriculture as the base on which to build a diversified, inclusive and sustainable economy. This is evidently clear in the first-generation NDPs discussed in Chapters 4 and 5, though in the actual allocation of resources and implementation of programmes, the agricultural sector has largely been over-looked in most countries. It is therefore surprising that while all the NDPs formulated during the 1960s and 1970s, consistently identified agriculture as a priority sector, the sector has remained undeveloped with declining productivity over time. Strong views of agriculture as a shrinking sector which we have discussed above could partly explain this disconnection. A successful industrial strategy in Africa will have to promote and nature the linkages between agriculture and industrial sectors. As long as the agricultural sector remains underdeveloped characterised by low productivity of labour, the dream of industrialising the country will be hard to realise. Even with the current hype and optimism around the FIR (Industrial Revolution (IR) 4.0), African countries would need to sort out the link between these two basic sectors if they are to have a chance of reaping the dividends of IR 4.0.

A review of data on African agriculture reveals that one of the features which has persisted from the time of independence across several countries is low levels of productivity in the sector. This is despite recurring commitment from African leaders, not just in the 1960s when they were drawing up their NDPs, but even recently as evident in the *Maputo Declaration* of 2003, to prioritise the sector.[2] Despite repeated commitments by African leaders to concentrate on the development of the agriculture sector, the sector has remained one of the most underdeveloped sectors in most African economies, a situation that has clearly constrained the development and growth of other sectors (see Timmer et al, 2012; UNECA, 2015). Outside of South Africa, Zimbabwe and Kenya, commercial agriculture production constitutes only a small section of the economy, often linked to the international export markets, with no connection to the rest of the economy. Even in countries largely dependent on agriculture for foreign exchange revenue such as Rwanda, Malawi, Madagascar, Uganda, Ethiopia and Burundi, commercial agriculture production is undertaken by a few agricultural enterprises, some of them state owned.

Majority of the farmers outside of the tiny commercial agricultural enclaves produce under highly constrained conditions in terms of access to inputs and services, as well as access to markets for their produce. In most countries where the small-scale and peasant farmers manage to produce some surplus for sale, they often struggle to find markets, resulting in most of them being discouraged to expand production beyond what is needed for sustenance.

Unfortunately, getting the agricultural sector into a high-productivity gear has been a perennial challenge for most countries in Africa since independence. Without doubt, this has been a huge clog in the industrialisation plan and the broader goal of structural transformation on the continent. As indicated earlier, the most apparent failure in this regard has been the inability to find an efficient way of utilising labour. Instead, labour is trapped in the low-productivity activities, mainly subsistence agriculture and urban informal sector, not primarily because that's where most people want to be, but because there are no alternative sources of livelihood or income elsewhere, including in the urban sector. For those who have moved from subsistence agriculture in search of more rewarding occupation, particularly in the urban areas, they often end up in the informal sector where productivity and income are not only low but precarious (Timmer et al, 2012; Fox and Thomas, 2016). This situation which has sometimes been described as a "mystery" given Africa's low levels of economic development (see Rodrik, 2014) is not a mystery at all if we decompose the labour dynamics over time.

The crucial question here, which many African countries have been grappling with for a long time, is, how does a country improve productivity in the subsistence agricultural sector? In the African context, this question is a critical one, and it amounts to asking how does a country develop or achieve sustained economic growth? Raising productivity in the agricultural sector has been and still remains at the centre of Africa's economic growth and industrial development challenge. Once the code for raising productivity growth sustainably in the agricultural sector is cracked, achieving sustainable and inclusive economic growth as well as industrialisation will only be a matter of time. On the other hand, realising sustainable economic development with broad-based welfare gains has been elusive in most countries primarily because of the failure to find a workable formula for stimulating productivity growth in the agricultural sector.

The Structure of African Economies

To get a sense of the challenges of structural transformation in African economies, this section looks at pattern of economic structural change in African economies. The starting point in this regard is the recognition made in the *Lagos Plan of Action* (LPA, 1980) that Africa is a richly endowed continent with a huge potential to build vibrant industrial sectors using its natural resources. The LPA (1980) was spot on when it observed that the lack of industrial development on the continent is a paradox, when one considers Africa's endowment:

> ...we are convinced that Africa's underdevelopment is not inevitable. Indeed, it is a paradox when one bears in mind the immense human and natural resources of the continent. In addition to its reservoir of human resources, our continent has 97 percent of world reserves of chrome, 85 percent of world reserves of platinum, 64 percent of world reserves of manganese, 25 percent of world reserves of uranium and 13 percent of world reserves of copper, without mentioning bauxite, nickel and lead; 20 percent of world hydro-electrical potential, 20 percent of traded oil in the world (if we exclude the United States and the USSR); 70 percent of world cocoa production; one-third of world coffee production, 50 percent of palm produce, to mention just a few (LPA, 1980:5).

It is indeed ironical that one of the most endowed continents on the planet has turned out to be the most impoverished region of the world! An International Study Group (ISG), coordinated by UNECA and the African Union, alludes to the fact that given that large tracts of the continent have not been surveyed yet, it is highly possible that huge reserves of natural resources remain unknown (UNECA/AU, 2011). An IMF (2013) report suggests that six African countries (Madagascar, Kenya, Uganda, Tanzania, Liberia and Guinea) have potential for oil and gas production, and there are suggestions that many more countries in Africa would eventually be classified as resource-rich (see IBIS, 2015)[3].

The natural resource fortunes of the continent are widely known just as the continent's impoverishment. The literature on economic development on the continent has tried to explain this irony by marshalling a number of factors such as resource curse, the negative effects of being in the tropics, ethnic fragmentation, corruption, poor policies, patrimonialism, effects of colonialism, the strong tendency among African leaders towards autocratic rule and prevalence of diseases such as malaria, Ebola etc., (see Chitonge, 2015). One of the factors less mentioned in these explanations, which is a crucial factor, is that the structure of African economies still intricately shaped by the colonial and neo-colonial power relations.

Unmasking the African Economic Paradox

As noted in Chapter 2, existing structures of African economies were set up during colonial rule, when their primary purpose was to supply raw materials to the industrialised colonial centres. It is therefore not surprising that that African economies are underpinned by an extroverted structure, which was primarily meant to benefit the countries where African raw materials were turned into finished products (Ake, 1981; Hountondji, 1997; Nabudere, 2006). In other words, because of the extroverted nature of African economies, African countries capture a tiny proportion of the value of the chrome, the platinum, the manganese, the bauxite, cocoa, coffee etc., they produce. This is primarily so because the high value-adding activities take place outside of the continent, where the commodities from Africa are processed, packaged, branded, bar-coded, labelled, stored and marketed. This debate goes back to the international division of labour debates discussed in Chapter 1.

At this point, critics might ask, but whose problem is it that African countries have specialised in the production and export of raw materials? The crucial point is to explain the African paradox by examining the structures through which the appropriation and expatriation of value from African natural and human resources is realised in historical and contemporary contexts. While this structure was perfectly justifiable under the colonial economic rationale, it does not make sense for African countries to continue operating under the same structures which is meant to benefit people outside Africa.

At the root of this is the failure of African states to disrupt the colonial economic logic by re-orienting African economies in such a way that Africa captures the largest value from its natural and human resources. As argued earlier, industrialisation offers a good opportunity for disrupting the colonial economic structure and logic because it would enable Africans to add and capture a higher value to the natural resources, and by so doing retain a larger share of the value generated from these resources. The benefits to the continent of disrupting the colonial economic structure are obvious, including the creation of adequate productive employment to reduce the currently high levels of under-employment and poverty, and the realisation of inclusive growth and sustainable economic development which does not damage the environment.

Enclavity: A Sign of Interrupted Structural Transformation

The IGS report mentioned earlier attributes the African economic paradox to the way African economies are structured. A central concept that is often used to analyse the colonial economic structure is enclavity, which is a persisting feature in most African economies event today. It reflects the lack of integration between the different parts of the economy, which is sometimes manifested by strong features of dualism and large productivity gaps between sectors. For the colonial economy, this made sense because dualism offered an opportunity for sustained high profit margins for international business firms operating on the continent and a strong grip on the political reins of power for the few colonial officials. Guy Mhone (2001) who is one of the few African scholars to apply the concept of enclavity to the analysis of African economies argues that, "economic dualism," which is a dominant feature in most African economies, is a clear manifestation of the persistence of the colonial economic logic.

Hundred years of colonial capitalism has resulted in economic structures which generate weak and highly unequal economic growth patterns and development outcomes. One of the clear outcomes of the enclave nature of African economies is high rates of under-employment (not open unemployment).

Under-employment is one of the enduring reminders of the challenges of economic structural transformation in Africa, presenting a huge drag on economic growth and development with high social and political costs. If we acknowledge, like the LPA cited above does, that one of Africa's important endowment is people, then the fact that large numbers of able-bodied Africans are unable to engage in productive activities implies that Africa is not efficiently utilising the most important resource in the economy. As it has been observed,

> The persistent and pervasiveness of under-employment is a fundamental problem for both economic and social reasons. From the point of view of economic efficiency, the fact that significant proportion of the labour force, or any resource for that matter, remains under-utilized must represent a constraint and a drag on economic growth and development. Indeed, the latter terms, "economic development" loses its meaning if economic growth does not entail the involvement of the majority in productive economic activities and the upliftment of their standards of living (Mhone, 2001:3).

In order for African countries to effectively use the resources in their economies, particularly labour, there is an urgent need to address the structural rigidities which impinge not just on labour absorption but also on productivity and growth. It is in this context that structural transformation and industrialisation in African economies should be seen as strategies aimed at finding a development path which can transcend past and current constraints.

Challenges of Perverse Structural Transformation

The challenge of the failure to generate the momentum for both agricultural development and industrialisation is manifested in a situation where labour is slowly moving out of agriculture in search of opportunities outside of the sector (McMillan and Harttgen, 2014), while at the same time, industrial growth has stagnated or declined in most countries (see Chapter 3). Employment in industry, and manufacturing in particular, only grew by a quarter of a percent between 1997 and 2012, while the labour force was growing at an average annual rate of 3 percent, over the same period. This has created a bulge in the urban informal sector where majority of the people leaving the agricultural sector end up (see Timmer et al, 2012; Fox and Thomas, 2016). The WEF (2017) estimates that between 15 and 20 million well-educated Africans will join the labour force every year for the next decade, yet the rate of creating employment is around 3.5 million, and most of these jobs are in the informal sector. This translates into a gross job creation ratio of between 17 and 23 percent; the net employment creation is likely to be much lower. With the low levels of employment creation, most of the youth entering the labour market find themselves in the urban informal sector where income is low and precarious.

Because of the steady growth of the urban informal sector over the past decade and half in most African countries, including countries with a relatively developed industrial sector such as South Africa, Mauritius, Cote d'Ivoire and Swaziland, the informal sector has become the largest creator of employment, although jobs in this sector are characterised by uncertainty and low wages (AEO, 2017). The expanding informal urban sector is attracting the attention of policy makers with some suggesting that the sector itself needs to be developed to ensure that it contributes to the creation of more productive employment than it currently does (UNIDO, 2016; AEO, 2017). But all indications are that this sector is currently dominated by non-wage work, with low and insecure income (Fox et al, 2013).

Thus, in terms of structural transformation, the challenge is that while the share of agriculture in total labour force has steadily declined in most countries, the sector still remains the main source of work for more than half of the population in 2015 (see Table 6.2).

Table 6.2: Labour Composition Trends by Sector by Region, 1960–2015.

	1960	1975	1990	2010	2015
Africa					
Agriculture	73	66	62	51	53.1
Industry	9	13	14	13	13.5
Mining	2	1	2	1	[0.8]
Manufacturing	5	8	9	7	[7.8]
Other Industry	3	4	4	4	[4.8]
Services	18	21	24	37	33.3
Asia					
Agriculture	48	43	32	21	29
Industry	19	23	26	23	24.4
Mining	1	1	1	0	[0.4]
Manufacturing	15	18	19	15	[14.9]
Other Industry	4	5	6	8	[9.1]
Services	33	34	42	56	46
Latin America					
Agriculture	47	34	25	14	14.2
Industry	21	24	24	22	21.3
Mining	2	1	1	1	[0.7]
Manufacturing	14	15	15	12	[12]
Other Industry	5	7	7	9	[8.3]
Services	32	42	51	64	64.4

Source: Author. Based on data from Timmer et al (2012) and the International Labour Organisation (ILO, 2018).

Note: The numbers in brackets in the last column show the breakdown of the industrial sector.

This situation is problematic because it means that more than half of the labour force is in the sector with the lowest productivity levels in the economy. While the decline of agriculture's share in total employment has been celebrated as an indication of an "African growth miracle" (McMillan and Harttgen, 2014), the challenge is that the labour moving out of agriculture is not going to sectors with high productivity; most of the people leaving the sector end up in low-productivity activities mainly in informal retail businesses (Fox et al, 2013). It is for this reason that formal wage employment on the continent has remained agonisingly low in many countries, averaging just 12 percent in 2016, with some countries such as Angola reporting only 9 percent, Burkina Faso and Niger reporting 6 and 5.5 percent of formal employment, respectively, and most of these are in the public sector (ILO, 2018).

Given this situation, it is evident that there are serious structural problems in most African economies which have made it difficult to generate significant numbers of productive jobs to absorb the growing labour force. Creating productive jobs is a solid foundation for spreading the benefits of the growing economy more widely and in an inclusive manner. Unless African countries rapidly transform the constraining economic structures, the labour question will persist and pose a major obstacle to both industrialisation and social stability. The challenge for African economies is that existing structural constraints are generating vicious circles which re-enforce and perpetuate under-development and features of enclavity.

Structural Transformation Trends in Africa

As noted above, economic structural transformation is commonly measured by the shifts in the sectoral composition of total labour and output over time. The rationale behind these indicators is that as economic growth progresses, the sectoral share in total output and labour force shifts, such that labour is gradually relocated from, mainly, agriculture to industry and services. In this model, it is expected that in a growing economy, the share of agriculture in both total output and labour force would decline over time. The rate of decline in the agricultural sector is determined by the growth of productivity in sectors outside agriculture. It has even been argued that the faster the rate of decline in agriculture's share in total output and labour, the faster the rate of structural change (see Timmer et al, 2012). As observed earlier, the declining agriculture share in total output and labour force is widely celebrated as a sign that the economy is turning a corner for the best; that the forces of growth are taking root and spreading widely. In the case of Africa where there are still many countries that are unable to produce enough food to meet local demand, it appears ironical that the falling of agriculture's share in national output and labour force should be celebrated as an indication of progress.

Structural Change: Labour Composition

With regard to sectoral shifts in labour composition, the two sector model is one of the dominant views. This view was put forward by Arthur Lewis (1954) in his famous two-sector model where the relocation of labour from the traditional (primarily subsistence agriculture) to modern (mainly industry, but capitalist agriculture as well) sector induces growth in labour productivity as the remaining labour in the traditional sector gets rationalised and perhaps works harder. Lewis (1954) made this statement on the assumption that the traditional sector has "surplus labour" (unlimited supply) in the sense that the marginal product of workers in the traditional sector was below their wage or income level. The practical implication of this is that many of the workers in the traditional sector were consuming above what they were producing due to the fact that the consumption of each person was socially determined by the prevailing living standards (i.e., by an institutional wage, see Ranis and Fei, 1961), and guaranteed through the social norms of sharing food and other basic requirements. In terms of labour supply, Lewis (1954) argued that most of these workers could be relocated from the traditional to the modern sector without decreasing productivity in the former sector. In this model the fact that labour can be relocated from the traditional to the modern sector without negatively affecting production in the former is argued as a sign of the existence of disguised unemployment or underemployment or surplus labour.

The main reason why the falling of agriculture share in total output and labour is celebrated as a positive development is that as labour moves from the traditional to the modern sector, it becomes more productive for two reasons. One is that before relocating to the modern sector, the labour in the traditional sector has low marginal productivity, sometimes assumed to be zero. Sen (1966) contends this view, arguing that although marginal productivity of labour in traditional agriculture tends to be low, it is impossible for it to be zero.

Although most commentators on the Two-Sector model attribute the view that marginal productivity of labour in the traditional sector is zero to Arthur Lewis (1954), it has been argued that this is a misinterpretation of Lewis; the correct interpretation of his model is that marginal productivity of labour in the traditional sector is "near zero," meaning very low (see Ranis, 2004). It is not necessary here to go into the debates about zero or near zero marginal productivity of labour in the traditional sector. The important point made by Arthur Lewis is that when labour with low marginal productivity is shifted to a modern sector where productivity is high, it contributes to the economy-wide productivity growth, as well as to the increase in wages, because wages in modern sector are higher than in the traditional sector.

In Lewis's (1954) model, wages in the modern sector were expected to be at least 30 percent higher in the initial phases of economic development. This wage differential is what triggers the movement of labour from traditional to modern sector, it is like a gradient exerting partial gravity, determined by the steepness of the slope. But it also reflects the difference in the marginal productivity of labour which justifies the wage differential between the two sectors. In other words, the movement of labour from the traditional to the modern sector should be seen as a positive development in as far as this represents a move from the low to high-productivity activity, resulting in the higher contribution to the economy and overall welfare.

But it is only under conditions where labour has moved from the low- to high productivity activities in the economy that the shift should be considered a positive development. In the two-sector model, the movement of labour from the traditional sector starts not because of what happens in this sector, but primarily because of the wage deferential between the traditional and the modern sector. Since, according to this model, it is only the higher wage in the modern sector that attracts labour from the traditional sector, the higher the wage deferential the faster the transfer rate, and the stronger the incentive to shift. It is important to note that this makes sense in a context where higher wage employment outside of the traditional sector exists. In the African context, where wage employment outside of the informal sector is lacking, the applicability of the model is highly questionable.

While the model includes the role of savings and the terms of trade between the two sectors in explaining the dynamics of structural transformation, it is ultimately the wage differential that is key to inducing the relocation of labour. Therefore, as soon as the wages between the two sectors are equalised, surplus labour is eliminated and the labour markets of two sectors merge into one labour market from which labour is sourced (Lewis, 1954).

There are of course questions about the assumptions on which this model is built and whether the model can help us understand the dynamics of economic changes occurring in Africa. It is not the intention of this chapter to go into the details of the Lewisian model of structural change, except to state that this has been one of the most influential models used to measure, analyse and track structural transformation.

Trends in Labour Shifts by Sector

Tracking the shifts in the sectoral composition of labour in Africa is not an easy exercise due to the challenge of lack of reliable and up-to-date employment data. But the overall trends are clear. Even if agriculture share in total employment and output has significantly declined since the 1960s, the agriculture sector still employs more than half of all the workforce (see Table 6.2 above). In this regard, Africa's agriculture share in total employment is highest in the developing countries, almost twice that of Asia and more than three times that of Latin America. Although employment share of the service sector has been increasing steadily, it is still the lowest among developing regions. It is also clear that productivity in agriculture has remained the lowest, although agriculture still accounts for the largest share of total employment. Mining, which has the highest productivity accounts for less than 1 percent of total employment (Table 6.3). Productivity in agriculture which is a sector with more than half of the labour force was only less than half of the economy-wide productivity.

Table 6.3: Employment and Productivity Trends by Sector, 1960–2017.*

	Employment by Sector (%)					Sectoral Productivity Relative to Total Productivity			
	1960	1975	1990	2010	2017	1960	1975	1990	2010
Agriculture	72.7	66	61.6	49.8	53.1	0.5	0.4	0.4	0.4
Industry	9.3	13.1	14.3	13.4	13.4	4.4	3.7	3.5	2.6
Mining	1.7	1.5	1.5	0.9	0.8	15.7	22.4	23.3	19.5
Manufacturing	4.7	7.8	8.9	8.3	7.7	2.5	2.8	2.4	1.6
Other Industries	3	3.8	3.9	4.2	4.9	8.5	5.8	5.3	2.9
Services	18	20.9	24.1	36.8	33.3	2.7	2.5	2.4	1.6
Distribution Services	8.2	9.5	11.4	20.1	3.5†	4.6	3.2	2.7	1.5
Market Services	8.8	10.3	12.9	23.5	2.4†	4.5	3.4	3	1.8
Financial and Business Services	0.6	0.8	1.5	3.4	2.6	6.1	8.9	10.4	8.1
Government Services	4.2	5	6.4	8.7	6.9	2.8	2.5	2.5	1.7

	Employment by Sector (%)					Sectoral Productivity Relative to Total Productivity			
	1960	1975	1990	2010	2017	1960	1975	1990	2010
Non-Market Services	9.2	10.6	11.2	13.3	12.5	1.8	1.7	1.8	1.3
Other Services	5.4	6.1	5.3	5.4	5.1	0.9	0.9	1	1

Source: Author. Based on data from Timmer et al, de Vries (2013), and the International Labour Organisation (ILO, 2018).

*Figures for 2017 are estimated from ILO (2018) data.

†The large difference between 2010 and 2017 could be due to the difference in the classification of activities between the two datasets.

From the data available, it is clear that "Labour is moving out of agriculture, [but] formal manufacturing industries are not the beneficiary. Urban migrants are being absorbed largely into services that are not particularly productive and into informal activities" (Rodrik, 2014:9). As noted earlier, in cases where labour moves from a low to low or lower productivity activity this does not represent a positive development. Such labour shifts do not contribute to positive structural transformation. Studies that have analysed structural transformation in Africa in recent years have stressed the point that while we have seen the share of agriculture in total labour force fall, it is important to examine where the labour moving out of agriculture is going before we can say whether the sectoral shifts in the composition of labour are indeed a positive development (McMillan and Rodrik, 2011; De Vries et al, 2015). Timmer et al (2012) show that because labour moved from high-productivity to lower-productivity activities, this has negatively impacted on Africa's growth dynamic, reducing it by 1.3 percentage points. If labour has been moving from lower- to higher-productivity activities, countries in Africa would have reported much higher growth rates and certainly more rapid decline in poverty rates (Page, 2015). If most people who are leaving the agriculture sector end up vending on the streets in urban areas with equally low or even lower and more precarious income than in subsistence agriculture, the overall declining share of agriculture in total labour force can be a deceptive indicator.

Perverse Labour Shifts

The challenge from the patterns of labour shifts observed on the continent is that the formal sector, particularly manufacturing, services and mining, where productivity is higher, has not expanded fast enough to absorb the labour relocating from agriculture. As illustrated in Chapter 3, employment in the manufacturing sector has actually been declining in almost half of the countries and has stagnated in many other countries. Fox and Thomas (2016) highlight the fact that while we have seen a significant decline in the share of agriculture in total labour force, labour moving from the agricultural sector (mainly subsistence farming) is relocating to the informal sector, dominated by retail trading and vending, which are characterised by low income and uncertainty. In this regard, it is important to pay attention to the destination of the labour moving from agriculture to understand structural transformation dynamics in Africa. If we compare trends in employment and productivity between sectors, it is sectors with high productivity (industry) that have the lowest share of employment, suggesting that Africa has not yet found a formula to efficiently allocate and use its available resources. Although agriculture employs more than half of the labour force, the share of an employee in the agriculture sector in total labour productivity was only 2.6 percent in 2015 compared to 67 percent for a worker in the industrial sector (Table 6.4).

Table 6.4: Trends in Productivity per Worker by Sector, 2000–2015 (in 2005 USD).

	2000	2005	2010	2015
Agriculture	390.10	426.68	336.17	356.71
Industry	5 796.52	5 925.15	6 572.73	9253.45
Services	2 584.02	2 527.89	3 818.07	4 160.39
	Sectoral Share in Total Productivity per Worker (%)			
	2000	**2005**	**2010**	**2015**
Agriculture	4.4	4.8	3.1	2.6
Industry	66.1	66.7	61.3	67.3
Services	29.5	28.5	35.6	30.1

Source: Author. Based on data from the World Development Indicators, 2018.

It is evident when we read Table 6.2 and 6.3 together that the challenge in most African countries is that productivity is higher in sectors with low levels of employment (less than 10 percent in manufacturing, less than 1 percent in mining, and less than 5 percent in utilities and construction, (See table 6.3). It is in sectors with the lowest productivity (agriculture) where there is a concentration of the labour force, and the share of this sector in total labour force seems to have increased in the last five years (Table 6.3). For instance, between 2010 and 2017, the share of agriculture in total labour force increased while the share in all the other sectors declined. It has been observed that "In 2010, labour productivity was 28 times higher in mining than in manufacturing (87 times higher than in agriculture). But mining employs less than 1% of the labour force" (AEO, 2017:163).

In a study ommi commissioned by the African Development Bank, McMillan and Harttgen (2014) try to track the movement of labour from agriculture, and they found that between 2000 and 2010, agriculture employment dropped by 10 percentage points. They also report that of the 10 percentage points, 2 went to the industrial sector, while the remaining ended up in the service sector, mainly retail trade and vending.[4] The 2013 African Economic Outlook which reviewed structural change in African economies confirms this when it observed that, "Most of jobs…are in the most unproductive sectors, with roughly three-quarters of the population in the two sector with below-average productivity namely, agriculture, and wholesale and retail trade" (AEO, 2013:20). McMillan and Rodrik (2011) observe that the large productivity gaps between sectors contribute to the low overall productivity observed in developing economies. They give an example of Malawi, where the average productivity in mining was estimated at 136 times higher than that of agriculture. They argue that if only half of Malawi's workers were employed in the mining sector, Malawi's labour productivity would be the same as that of the United States (ibid, 6). But unfortunately, Malawi only has a small portion (less than half a percent) of the workforce in mining, meaning that only this small portion is contributing meaningfully to total output growth; majority of the people in informal sector and subsistence agriculture are only contributing a tiny fraction of what they could be contributing had they been involved in more productive activities.

If these figures are anything to go by, they suggest that the momentum in the industrial sector has been low, such that labour leaving the agriculture sector is going mainly in to the sector with low productivity—services, particularly the informal trade and non-wage personal services.

In terms of structural transformation, this confirms the view that Africa has been experiencing perverse structural change, which is reflected in the growing levels of under-employment in the informal sector where people in most countries work (see Fox and Thomas, 2016). If the continent was experiencing positive transformation, we should see labour moving from the low- to higher-productivity activities. This would have resulted in rising overall productivity in these economies. In this sense, the failure to industrialise explains not just the challenges of structural transformation in most African economies, but also the persistently high levels of poverty and rising inequality at the time when most countries reported decent growth rates (see Page 2015).

Challenges of a Service-Led Growth Strategy

From the data presented above, it is clear that the service sector which has higher levels of productivity than agriculture (though it is only half of the industrial sector) is growing steadily and accounted for more than a third of total employment in 2015 (Table 6.2). While that looks like the possible option for Africa, when the productivity and employment rates in this sector are disaggregated, it becomes apparent that it is a small section of highly productive workers in highly skilled jobs such as real estates, business and legal services, banking, high-value tourism services, insurance etc., which are driving productivity levels in the service sector higher (see also Rodrik, 2014; Basbay, 2018). These activities, though expanding, are still small and account for a small fractions of the total labour force in the service sector (see Table 6.3).

Even if employment creation in the highly productive segments of the service sector (particularly real estate, financial and business services, and the higher end of tourism sector) were to expand faster, there is a question of skills levels which most of the people in the agriculture and informal sector may not have. This is the challenge that a service-led growth strategy in Africa faces; it would leave out majority of the people from participating in highly productive activities, and as such will fail to promote inclusive growth and rapid poverty reduction. To address this, African states would need to respond creatively to the challenge of skill upgrading.

Further, average productivity in the service sector can be quite misleading, given the high levels of heterogeneity in this sector in Africa. The service sector is quite broad including public services such as education, health care, community services; but also the private services such as retail trade (including street vending), wholesale, banking, telecommunication, tourism, hotel, transport, real estate services, etc. Outside of public services, the other subgroups of the service sector such as banking, insurance, real estate which are highly productive are still quite small, employing a small section of labour, and they are not really linked to the informal sector.

For example, a UNIDO (2016b:3a) report observes that the now growing financial sector in Africa "is positioning itself to lend to large companies and foreign investors, neglecting agriculture and local (especially rural) small and medium enterprises." Fox et al (2013) report that only 8 percent of workers in the service sector have wage employment. Although the service sector is growing, formal employment is still low since most of the people in the sector are concentrated in retail trade which is largely informal and self-employed. Fox and Thomas (2016) estimate that overall, 85 percent of employment in Africa is the informal sector dominated by household farms and small business retailing in urban areas.

Most of the people in the service sector are in the businesses services, mainly whole sale and retail, which in the African context needs to be carefully interpreted given that most of the jobs in the sector are non-wage-self-employment, and in cases where these jobs are wage employment, they are temporal in nature and highly vulnerable. Majority of the workers in the businesses services are actually self-employed informal workers, characterised by low productivity, except for a few medium enterprises. Even in the small enterprises which are doing well, their capacity to employ large numbers of people looking for productive work is limited. Although the service sector currently has low employment generation capacity and low productivity on average, it has higher productivity than agriculture (Table 6.4)

In order to understand the dynamics of structural change in Africa better, one needs to disaggregate what is generally referred to as the service sector and see what the composition of labour in this sector is. As illustrated above, the service sector has since the 1980s been the largest sector in all African economies in terms of its share in total output (see Table 6.1), larger than the industrial and agricultural sectors. In terms of structural transformation, this would not be problematic if productivity in the service sector was one of the highest or above the economy-wide productivity. Productivity in the service sector is certainly above that of agriculture, but below that of industry and the overall economy (see Table 6.4). The African Economic Outlook 2013 (AEO, 2013) estimates that productivity in the agricultural sector was only 36 percent of the average productivity in African economies, while productivity in the manufacturing sector was six times the average and in mining it was 60 times the average productivity. These figures are similar to what is reported in other studies (Timmer and de Vries, 2014 De Vries et al, 2015).

Such wide productivity gaps between sectors and between economic activities within sector are a common feature of underdevelopment and dualism. Large inter-sectoral productivity gaps are also a reflection of enclavity in the economy, where small but highly productive portions of the economy are surrounded by, often not connected to, the sea of low-productive activities (see Mhone, 2001). On the other hand, high-income countries are characterised by small sectoral productivity gaps, signalling a more efficient allocation and use of factors (including labour) as the different sectors compete for factors on the factor market.

The challenge for African countries is to get the larger sections of the labour force into activities where labour becomes more productive and contribute to generating higher income and faster poverty reduction for the majority. Moving labour to industries where productivity is higher has been widely acknowledged as the most effective way of raising over-productivity in an economy. In this regard, a growing manufacturing sector is seen as a crucial aspect of this dynamic primarily because of its higher potential for mass employment creation.

In many African countries, the absence of a dynamically growing and diversifying manufacturing sector is one of the major challenges. As data presented in this chapter show, it has been difficult over the past decades in most countries for the economy to create more job opportunities in the most productivity sectors of the economy. To the contrary, the most productive sectors such as mining and financial services account for a small portion of the labour force and this share is actually dropping over time (see Table 6.2).

Chitonge (2016:800) reports that in Zambia, even at the time when the copper industry was expanding in response to the high copper prices on the global market, the industry's share in total employment declined from 3.7 percent of total employment in 2005 to just over 1 percent in 2012, and this is in an economy where mining is a major economic activity. The total number of jobs in the mining sector fell from 154 515 in 2005 to 74 542 in 2012 (ibid). If one were to trace where the over-75 000 workers who exited the mining sector went, it is likely that majority of them went into self-employed retail trade where earnings are not only low but precarious. In this case, it would certainly not be a problem if the retail trade would be as productive as mining, but oftentimes that is not the case; the average productivity for the services sector, while above agriculture, is lower than the economy-wide average, especially in the case of the retail and distribution services.

If we take manufacturing which is often regarded as the engine of industrial growth, the employment levels have remained low compared to other developing countries (see Table 3.4). What is worrying is that employment share for manufacturing has remained stagnant, suggesting that it is not contributing to the creation of productive employment as it should. Recent estimates suggest that manufacturing share in total employment in 2015 was below the level in 1975, and the concern is that the levels are falling (see Table 6.3). Of the 54 countries in Africa, 31 have manufacturing employment share of less than 5 percent, with less than 1 percent in Chad, and 1.5 percent for Burkina Faso and Equatorial Guinea (see Table 3.5). It is not surprising therefore that vulnerable employment and working poor ratios in Africa have remained consistently high (see Figure 3.3).

The low wage employment levels that characterise most African countries account for the persistently higher levels of vulnerable employment. It is not surprising that vulnerable employment in Africa has remained high given the low productive-employment creation capacity in the region.

Table 6.5: Ratio of Vulnerable Employment by Region (2000–2016).

	Ratio of Vulnerable Employment by Region (%)						
	2000	**2005**	**2010**	**2011**	**2012**	**2013**	**2016**
Central and South Eastern Europe	22.6	21.3	20.1	19.7	19.3	19.2	29.7
East Asia	57.5	54.1	48.6	47.6	46.5	45.8	30.9
Latin America and the Caribbean	35.4	33.5	31.8	31.7	31.7	31.6	31.9
North Africa	39.1	40.8	36.3	36	35.8	35.6	32.4
South Asia	80.9	80.7	78.5	77.3	76.6	76.1	74.8
South East Asia and the Pacific	65.6	61.9	60.7	60.2	59.7	59	50.8
Sub-Saharan Africa	79.9	78	77.7	77.6	77.6	77.4	68.0
World	52.4	51.3	49.1	48.5	48	47.8	42.9
	Vulnerable Employment by Region (Millions)						
Central and South Eastern Europe	32.9	32.7	32.2	32.2	31.7	31.6	22.2
East Asia	430.7	425.4	392.7	388.2	382.6	379.2	276.1
Latin America and the Caribbean	74.7	78.8	83.1	84.7	86.7	88	91.2
North Africa	17.4	21.2	21.5	21.4	21.7	22.1	21.2
South Asia	411.5	469	475.9	573.6	472.5	480	511.4

	Ratio of Vulnerable Employment by Region (%)						
	2000	2005	2010	2011	2012	2013	2016
South East Asia and the Pacific	159.1	163	176.2	178.7	180.8	181.4	171.5
Sub-Saharan Africa	180.5	204.1	234.5	241.3	248.6	255.7	247.2
World	1,369.7	1,460	1,480.5	1,483.8	1,489.1	1,502.5	1,396.3
	Vulnerable Employment Growth by Region (%)						
	2000–05	2005–10	2010–13	2000–10	2000–13	2010–2016	
Central and South Eastern Europe	-0.6	-1.5	-1.9	-2.1	-4.0	-31.1	
East Asia	-1.2	-7.7	-3.4	-8.8	-12.0	-29.7	
Latin America and the Caribbean	5.5	5.5	5.9	11.2	17.8	9.7	
North Africa	21.8	1.4	2.8	23.6	27.0	-1.9	
South Asia	14.0	1.5	0.9	15.7	16.6	7.5	
South East Asia and the Pacific	2.5	8.1	3.0	10.7	14.0	-2.7	
Sub-Saharan Africa	13.1	14.9	9.0	29.9	41.7	5.4	
World	6.6	1.4	1.5	8.1	9.7	-5.7	

Source: Author. Based on data from the International Labour Organisation World Employment Social Outlook, 2016 and 2017.

While vulnerable employment declined in other developing regions of the world, it was growing in Africa between 2000 and 2016. The industrialisation challenge in this context is apparent.

Shifts in the Sectoral Composition of Output

The second common indicator, other than shifts in labour composition by sector, is the changes in the sectoral composition of output. If we look at the sectoral composition of output (Table 6.3) and labour (Table 6.1) over time, it is clear that shifts have occurred, some of them quite pronounced. In terms of output composition by sector, we see that agriculture share in total output has declined from almost 40 percent in the 1960s to about 16 percent in 2015, though this share rises between 2010 and 2015 (Table 6.1).

Although we see high levels of heterogeneity among countries, the general trend is that of declining agriculture-to-GDP ratio in most countries, especially starting from the mid-1990s. While we have countries such as Mauritius, South Africa, Libya, Equatorial Guinea, Gabon and Botswana where agriculture's share in total GDP is less than 5 percent, there are countries such as Somalia, Togo, Central African Republic, Ethiopia, Mali, Sierra Leone, Liberia, Niger, Guinea-Bissau and Burundi where agriculture's share is still over 40 percent (see Appendix I and II).

As observed earlier in this chapter, it is important to note that the reported decline in agriculture's share in GDP does not necessarily mean that agriculture GDP, in absolute terms, is falling. In some countries, it might be the case that absolute value added in agriculture has fallen over time. But in most countries the declining share of agriculture in total output is due to the fact that the agricultural sector is growing below the average output growth for the whole economy, and most definitely below the growth rates in the other sectors (industry and services). What this means is that even in situations where structural transformation is taking place as reflected by the fall in agriculture's share in total output, the sector continues to grow, but only slower than the average growth in the economy and certainly below the growth rate in the industrial and services sector (see also Timmer et al, 2012).

As illustrated in Appendix I and II, the agricultural sector has been experiencing steady decline in share of total value added. This can be explained largely by lack of productivity growth in the sector. Productivity in the industrial and service sectors has been growing faster than the agriculture sector for various reasons including the fact that the capital–labour ratio in industry, and to a certain extent services, tends to be higher. Chenery et al (1986) have argued that productivity in industry grows much faster than in agriculture not just because of the higher capital–labour ratio, but also because the industrial sector tends to accumulate and use new technology much more than the agricultural sector.

But for countries in the early stages of their economic growth and development process, the growth of the agricultural sector, even if it is slower than productivity growth in other sectors, has great potential to contribute to creating a foundation for an inclusive growth, and rapid fall in poverty rates. For this reason, industrial policies in African countries have to take into account the need to improve productivity in the agricultural sectors as the base for industrialisation.

Prospects of Structural Transformation in Africa

If we look at the manufacturing sector in particular, the failure to industrialise becomes even more apparent. While the contribution of the manufacturing sector to total output grew steadily from 1960 to about 1980s, we see a case of reversing the gains made in the earlier period in terms of industrial development. While some authors have used the terms de-industrialise to describe the period from the 1990s to the present (see Stein, 1994, Noorbakhsh and Paloni, 2000; Rodrik, 2015), the applicability of this term is debatable, given that most of the countries in Africa have not yet undergone industrialisation to any significant degree. However, it is clear that during the 1990s, the manufacturing sector, particularly, suffered heavy losses from which it has not yet recovered. In fact it has been suggested the larger share of industrial sector in total GDP which we have seen since 2005 is pushed up by the large extractive industry. If we take away the natural resource-based industries, the actual size of the industry is actually small (see Zamfir, 2016). This is partly why the value-added per capita of most African countries has remained low compared to countries in Asia and Latin America (see Table 3.6).

As noted at the beginning of this chapter, most discussions on structural transformation start from the assumption that as the economy grows, it will go through a process where the different sectors dominate economic activities at different times. In the initial phase, it is the agricultural sector which is the largest, in terms of both share in total output and in total employment. According to this view, the growth of the industrial sector sustains the growth of the agriculture through a backward linkage where the agricultural produce are used as inputs in the industrial sector, particularly manufacturing and construction. But the experience in most developing countries, as we have seen in the data for African countries, is that the services sector is expanding without any significant levels of industrialisation. Saikia (2011), drawing from the experience of India, observes that the tertiary sector expanded much faster than the secondary sector, growing from 34.2 percent in 1995 to 62.8 percent in 2007. Choudhury and Chatterjee (2015) also observed rapid expansion of the services sector while the industrial sector is growing at a much lower rate, a phenomenon which has referred to as the "services revolution," signifying that the services have become the dominant sector in the economy ahead of industry.

We have seen similar trends in the structure of most African economies where the services sector has become the dominant sector while the industrial sector has stagnated. In the African case, the average share of the services sector in the economy was estimated at 52 percent in 2015, which was almost twice the share of industry and five times the share of manufacturing (see Appendix I and II). This phenomenon is not adequately explained in the literature apart from putting a label that this is abnormal or premature de-industrialisation (Tregenna, 2016). One of the explanations offered so far is that the line between manufacturing and services has become blurred as technology develops (Manyika et al, 2012; Newman et al, 2016). For example, the designing of a new BMW 5 series, which in the earlier days was part of the manufacturing sector, is now out-sourced and often reported as a service and not part of the manufacturing value added.

But the magnitude of growth in the services sector cannot be just an industrial classification issue. Even if all the design and other services which used to be classified under manufacturing are accounted for, that will not affect much the shifts in the sectoral composition we are seeing in these economies. Therefore, it is not clear if the issue here is one of classification of economic activities or a fundamental shift in the way economies are organised and therefore requiring a new approach even to issues of structural transformation. There is need for an understanding of structural transformation which can accommodate the patterns of change we are seeing in developing countries. Buera and Kaboski (2009) have raised an empirical question on the same issue, but a much more theoretical discussion is needed to understand the implications of the observed trends in developing countries. Seeing the growth of the service sector before any significant levels of industrialisation occurs as a new phenomenon allows one to remain open to exploring the meaning of this development. But if the "service revolution" is looked at as an anomaly, it may block the efforts to take advantages of the opportunities this may offer.

In the case of African countries, it is apparent that even though at the moment the service sector is characterised by below-average productivity, it has great potential to pull other sectors from the top. One way in which the services sector can achieve this is through the inducement of a particular business practice and culture as businesses interact with others across sectors. For example, the various international franchise hotels which have been established in many parts of Africa in the last decade bring with them the international practice in terms of the requirement for services from suppliers. The strict service requirements from the suppliers can act as a push to adopt the international standards in the quality of services and goods that the local suppliers supply. With time, as local suppliers learn by doing, they can become competitive to the point that possibilities for entering the foreign markets may open up. One good example of this is Shoprite. This regional retail chain operates in 16 different African countries, and in some cases there is opportunity for local suppliers to supply products to the retail chain store. The strict requirement that Shoprite has put on suppliers has pushed the local suppliers to up their game as they strive to meet the required standards stated in the supplier contract. In this way, local companies have been able to create capacity to supply quality products to regional markets. For example Zambeef, which is a local Zambian meat producer, after working with Shoprite for some time, has now developed the capacity to supply Shoprite stores in Nigeria, Angola and Ghana. In this way the service sector has contributed to building capacity among local manufacturing firms. It is therefore clear that structural transformation should induce much broader shifts in society apart from the changes in the composition of GDP and labour force.

Notes

1. The five stages of economic growth that an economy is expected to go through start from i) traditional society, ii) to creating "precondition for take-off," and then iii) "take-off," followed by the iv) "drive to maturity" and the final stage being the v) "age of mass-consumption" (see Rostow, 1960).
2. In the *Maputo Declaration*, African leaders committed to spending 10 percent of their national budgets on improving agriculture production. In this declaration, African leaders pledged to "revitalise the agricultural sector including livestock, forestry and fisheries through special policies and strategies targeted at small scale and traditional farmers in rural areas and the creation of enabling conditions for private sector participation, with emphasis on human capacity development and the removal of constraints to agricultural production and marketing, including soil fertility, poor water management, inadequate infrastructure, pests and diseases. To this end, we agree to adopt sound policies for agricultural and rural development, and commit ourselves to allocating at least 10% of national budgetary resources for their implementation within five years" (AU, 2003).
3. In 2019, South Africa reported the discovery of huge natural gas reserves off shore.
4. The employment growth in manufacturing sector in this study contradicts the finding in Timmer et al (2012:3). who report that between 1995 and 2010, employment in manufacturing only grew by a quarter of a percentage.

References

Adelman, I. (1984). "Beyond Export Led Growth." *World Development*, Vol. 12, No. 9. 937–949.

African Centre for Economic Transformation (ACET, 2014). *Growth with Depth—2014 African Transformation Report*. Accra: African Centre for Economic Transformation.

African Development Bank/Organisation for Economic Cooperation and Development/United Nations Development Programme (AEO, 2013). *African Economic Outlook 2017: Keeping Pace*. Abidjan: AfDB/OECD/UNDP.

African Development Bank/Organisation for Economic Cooperation and Development/United Nations Development Programme (AEO, 2017). *African Economic Outlook 2017: Entrepreneurship and Industrialisation*. Abidjan: AfDB/OECD/UNDP.

African Union (AU, 2003). "Maputo Declaration." Assembly of the African Union, Second Ordinary Session, 10–12 July, 2003, Maputo, Mozambique.

Ake, C. (1981). *A Political Economy of Africa*. Lagos: Longman Nigeria.

Arbache, J. and Page, J. (2009). "How Fragile is Africa's Recent Growth?" Journal of African Economies, Vol. 19. 1–24.

Basbay, M. (2018). "Is Manufacturing Dead?" TRT World Research Centre Discussion Paper. London: TRT World. Available at https://researchcentre.trtworld.com/images/files/discussion_papers/IsManufacturingDead.pdf. Accessed 12/02/2019

Bates, R. H. (1981). *Markets and States in Tropical Africa: The Political Basis of Agricultural Policies*. Berkeley: University of California Press.

Bluestone, B. and Harrison, B. (1982). Deindustrialisation and Unemployment in America. New York: Basic Books.

Brixiova, Z. and Ndikumana, L. (2011). "Supporting Africa's Post-crisis Growth: The Role of Macroeconomic Policy." Political Economy Research Institute (PERI) Working Paper No. 54. University of Massachusetts Amherst.

Buera, F. and Kaboski, J. (2009). "Can Traditional Theories of Structural Change Fit the Data?" *Journal of European Economic Association*, Vol. 7, No. 2. 469–477.

Chenery, H., Robinson, S. and Syrquim, M. (1986). *Industrialisation and Growth: A Comparative Study*. Washington, DC: World Bank.

Chitonge, H. (2015). *Economic Growth and Development in Africa: Understanding Trends and Prospects*. New York/London: Routledge.

Chitonge, H. (2016). "Zambia at 50: The Persisting Challenges of Economic Structural Transformation." Development Southern Africa, DOI:10.1080/0376835X.2016.1231053.

Chitonge, H. (2018). "Trails of Incomplete Decolonisation in Africa: The Land Question and Economic Structural Transformation." *African Studies Monograph*, (Supplementary Issue) No. 57. 19–41.

Choudhury, P. and Chatterjee, B. (2015). "Inter-sectoral Linkage and Openness in India's Services Sector Growth." *Money and Finance* (November, 2015). 63–85.

De Vries, G., Timmer, M. and de Vries, K. (2015). "Structural Transformation in Africa: Static Gains, Dynamic Losses." *Journal of Development Studies*, Vol. 56, No. 6. 674–688.

Devarajan, S. and Fengler, W. (2012). "Is Africa's Recent Economic Growth Sustainable?" IFRI Note: Paris/Bruxelles: IFRI.

Dhin, H. (2014). *Light Manufacturing in Zambia: Job Creation and Prosperity in a Resource-based Economy*. New York: The World Bank.

Fox, L., Haines, C., Huerta-Munoz, J. and Thomas, A. (2013). "Africa's Got Work to Do: Employment Prospect in the New Century." International Monetary Fund (IMF) Working Paper 13/201.

Fox, L. and Thomas, A. (2016). "Africa's Got Work to Do: A Diagnostic of Youth Employment Challenges in Sub-Saharan Africa." *Journal of African Economies*, Vol. 25, No. 1. 16–36.

Henley, D. (2012). "The Agrarian Roots of Industrial Growth: Rural Development in South-East Asia and Sub-Saharan Africa." *Development Policy Review*, Vol. 30, No. (s1). 25–47.

Hirschman, O. A. (1958). *The Strategy of Economic Development*. New Haven: Yale University Press.

Hountondji, P. (1997). "Introduction: Centering Africa," in P. Hountondji (ed.) *Endogenous Knowledge: Research Trails*. Dakar: CODESRIA. 1–42.

IBIS (2015). *Natural Resource Watch Report on Sub-Saharan Africa*. Copenhagen: IBIS.

IMF (2013). "Boom, Burst or Prosperity? Managing Sub-Saharan Africa's Natural Resource Wealth.

International Labour Organisation (ILO 2018). *Labour Productivity: ILO Modelled Estimates* (ILOstat) available at http://www.ilo.org/ilostat/faces/oracle/webcenter/portalapp/pagehierarchy/Page3.jspx?MBI_ID=49 accessed 18/10/2018.

Johnson, B. and Mellor, W. J. (1961). "The Role of Agriculture in Economic Development." *American Economic Review*, Vol. 51, No. 4. 566–593.

Killick, T. (1980). "Trends in Development Economics and their Relevance to Africa." *Journal of Modern African Studies*, Vol. 18, No. 3. 367–386.

Killick, T. (1983). "Development Planning in Africa: Experiences, Weaknesses and Prescriptions." *Development Policy Review*, Vol. 1. No. 2. 47–76.

Krugman, P. (1987). "The Narrow Moving Band, the Dutch Disease, and the Competitive Consequences of Mrs. Thatcher." Journal of Economics, 27. 41–55.

Kuznets, S. (1966). *Modern Economic Growth: Rate Structure and Spread*. New Haven: Yale University Press.

Lewis, W. A. (1954). "Economic Development with Unlimited Supplies of Labour." *Manchester School*, Vol. 20. 139–191.

Manyika, J., Sinclair, J., Dobbs, R., Kassey, L., Mischke, J., Roxburgh, C., George, K., O'Halloran, D. and Ramaswamy, S. (2012). *Manufacturing the Future: The Next Era of Global Growth and Innovation*. Washington, DC: McKinsey Global Institute.

Mastuyama, K. (1992). "Agricultural Productivity, Comparative Advantage and Economic Growth." *Journal of Economic Theory*, Vol. 58, No. 2. 317–334.

McMillan, M. and Rodrik, D. (2011). "Globalisation, Structural Change and Productivity Growth." National Bureau of Economic Research (NBER) Working Paper No. 17143.

McMillan, M.t and Harttgen, K. (2014). "What's Driving the African Growth Miracle?" African Development Bank (AfDB) Working Paper No. 209. Tunis: AfDB.

Mhone, G. (2001). "Enclavity and Constrained Labour Absorptive Capacity in Southern African Economies." A paper prepared for the discussion at the UNRISD on The Need to Rethinking Development Economics, September 7–8, 2001, Cape Town South Africa.

Mkandaire, T. and Soludo, C. (1999). *Our Continent, Our Future: African Perspectives on Structural Adjustment.* Dakar: CODESRIA.

Mastuyama, K. (1992). "Agricultural Productivity, Comparative Advantage and Economic Growth." *Journal of Economic Theory*, Vol. 58. No.2. 317–334.

Nabudere, D. (2006). "Development Theories, Knowledge Production and Emancipatory Practice," in V. Padayach (ed.), *The Development Decade? Economic and Social Change in South Africa 1994–2004*. Pretoria: HSRC Press. 33–52.

Ndulu, B. and O'Connell, S. (2008). "Policy Plus: African Growth Performance, 1960–2000," in B. Ndulu, S. O'Connell, R. Bates, P. Collier and C. Soludo (eds.), *The Political Economy of Economic Growth in Africa 1960–2000*. Cambridge: Cambridge University Press. 1–75.

New Partnership for African Development (NEPAD, 2014). *Agriculture in Africa: Transformation and Outlook*. Johannesburg: NEPAD.

Newman, C., Page, J., Rand, J., Shimeles, A., Soderbom, M. and Tap, F. (2016). "The Pursuit of Industry: Policies and Outcomes," in C. Newman, J. Page, J. Rand, A. Shimeles, M. Soderbom and F. Tap (eds.), *Manufacturing Transformation: Comparative Studies in Industrial Development in Africa and Emerging Asia*. London: Oxford University Press. 1–24.

Noorbakhsh, F. and Paloni, A. (2000). "The De-Industrialisation Hypothesis, Structural Adjustment Programmes and the Sub-Saharan Dimension," in H. Jalilian, M. Tribe and J. Weiss (eds.), *Industrial Development and Policy in Africa: Issues of De-Industrialisation and Development Strategy*. Cheltenham: Edward Elgar. 107–129.

Nurkse, R. (1953). *Problems of Capital Formation in Underdeveloped Countries*. London: Basil Blackwell.

Olukoshi, A. (2004). "Democratisation, Gloabalisation and Effective Policy Making in Africa," in C. Soludo, O. Ogbu and H. Chang (eds.), *The Politics of Trade and Industrial Policy in Africa*. Trenton/Asmara: Africa World Press Inc. 43–73.

Oqubay, A. (2015). *Made in Africa: Industrial Policy in Ethiopia*. London: Oxford University Press.

Organisation of African Unity (LPA, 1980). *The Lagos Plan of Action for the Economic Development of African: 1980–2000*. Addis Ababa: OAU.

Page, J. (2012). "Aid, Structural Change and the Private Sector in Africa." United Nations University (UNU)/World Institute for Development Economic Research (WIDER) Working Paper No. 2012/21.

Page, J. (2015). "Structural Change and Africa's Poverty Puzzle," in L. Chandy, H. Kato and H. Kharas (eds.), *The Last Mile in Ending Extreme Poverty*. New York: Brooklyn Institute Press. 219–248.

Pingali, P. (1997). "From Subsistence to Commercial Production Systems: The Transformation of Asian Agriculture." *American Journal of Agricultural Economics*, Vol. 17, No. 2. 628–634.

Ranis, G. (2004). "Arthur Lewis's Contribution to development thinking and policy'. *Manchester School*, Vol. 72, No. 6. 712–723.

Ranis, G. and Fei, J. (1961). "A Theory of Economic Development." American *Economic Review*, Vol. 52, No. 4. 533–565.

Rodrik, D. (2014). "An African Miracle?" National Bureau of Economic Research (NBER) Working Paper Series No. 20188, Cambridge: NBER.

Rodrik, D. (2015). "Premature Deindustrialisation." National Bureau of Economic Research (NBER) Working Paper No. 20935. Available at: http://www.nber.org/papers/w20935. Accessed 16.09.2017.

Rostow, W. W. (1960). *Stages of Economic Growth: A Non-Communist Manifesto*. London: Cambridge University Press.

Saikia, D. (2011). "Analysing Inter-sectoral Linkages in India." *African Journal of Agricultural Research*, Vol. 6, No. 33. 6766–6775.

Sen, A. K. (1966). "Peasants and Dualism with or Without Surplus Labour." *The Journal of Political Economy*, Vol. 74, No. 5. 425–450.

Soludo, C. and Ogbu, O. (2004). "A Synthesis of Major Themes in the Political Economy of Trade and Industrialisation in Africa," in C. Soludo, O. Ogbu and H. Chang (eds.), *The Politics of Trade and Industrial Policy in Africa*. Trenton/Asmara: Africa World Press Inc. 1–42.

Stein, Howard (1994). "Theories of Institutions and Economic Reform in Africa." *World Development*, Vol. 22, No. 12. 1833–1849.

Timmer, P., McMillan, M., Badiane, O., Rodrik, D., Binswanger-Mkhize, H. and Wouterse, F. (2012). "Patterns of Growth and Structural Transformation in Africa: Trends and Lessons for Future Development Strategies." International Food Policy Research Institute (IFPRI) Thematic Research Note 02. West Africa Office.

Timmer, M., G. de Vries and K. de Vries (2014). Patterns of Structural Change in Developing Countries. Groningen Growth and Development Centre (GGDC) Working Paper No. 149.

Tregenna, F. (2009). "Characterising De-industrialisation: An Analysis of Changes in Manufacturing Employment and Output Internationally." *Cambridge Journal of Economics*, Vol. 33, No.4. 433–466.

Tregenna, F. (2016). "Deindustrialisation: An Issue for Both Developed and Developing Countries" in J. Weiss and M. Tribe (eds.), *Routledge Handbook of Industrialisation and Development*. London/New York: Routledge. 97–115.

United Nations Economic Commission for Africa (UNECA, 2012). *Economic Report on Africa 2012: Unleashing Africa's Potential as a Global Growth Pole*. Addis Ababa: UNECA.

United Nations Economic Commission for Africa (UNECA, 2015). *Report on Africa 2015: Industrialising Through Trade*. Addis Ababa: UNECA.

United Nations Economic Commission for Africa (UNECA, 2016b). *Economic Report on Africa 2016: Greening Africa's Industrialisation*. Addis Ababa: UNECA.

United Nations Economic Commission for Africa (UNECA, 2016a). Transformative Industrial Policy for Africa. Addis Ababa: Economic Commission for Africa.

United Nations Economic Commission for Africa and African Union (UNECA/AU, 2011). *Minerals and Africa's Development: International Study Group Report on Africa's Regimes*. Addis Ababa: ECA/AU.

United Nations Industrial Development Organisation (1980). World Industry Since 1960: Progress and Prospects. Vienna: UNIDO.

United Nations Industrial Development Organisation (UNIDO, 2016). *Industrialisation in Africa and Least Developed Countries: Booting Growth, Creating Jobs, Promoting Inclusiveness and Sustainability*. Vienna: UNIDO.

World Bank (2015). Africa's Pulse: An Analysis of Issues Shaping Africa's Economic Future. October 2015, Volume 15. Available at: https://openknowledge.worldbank.org/handle/10986/2272212/06/2016.

World Economic Forum (WEF, 2017). *The Future of Jobs and Skills in Africa: Preparing the Region for the Fourth Industrial Revolution*. Geneva: WEF.

Zamfir, Lionel (2016). Africa's Economic Growth: Taking off or Slowing Down? Brussels: European Parliament Research Services, PE573.891

· 7 ·

THE STATE AND INDUSTRIALISATION IN AFRICA

Introduction: The State as a Prime Mover of Industrialisation

One of the central themes which most of the chapters in this book have alluded to is that of the role of the state in industrial development. Whether one is talking about structural transformation, upgrading of industrial capabilities, transfer of technology, increasing productivity in agriculture or incentivising firms to promote industrial development, the state looms large across the ideological iron curtain. Experience of both early and late industrialisers clearly show that the state is a 'prime mover' of industrialisation. As noted in Chapter 4, the view that the state has an important role to play in the process of industrialisation is less contested today (see Wade, 1990; UNECA, 2012). What is highly contested is around what kind of role the state should play in the industrialisation process. For those who approach industrialisation from a neoclassical perspective, the state's role is expected to be limited to creating an environment in which markets can function efficiently. Analysts who adopt this framework argue that since markets are more efficient in the allocation of resources than the state, there is no need for industrial policy; markets should be enabled to function optimally. As Lall (2004) has argued, during the 1980s, it was widely believed that industrial policy was redundant and even harmful to the process of development.

On the other hand, there have been analysts who have maintained that the state has always played a central role in the industrialisation of now industrialised and industrialising countries (see Johnson, 1982; Wade, 1990; Amsden, 2001; Chang, 2003, UNECA, 2012; 2016a). Amsden (1989) drawing mainly from her study of industrialisation in East Asia argues that existing evidence strongly support the view that the state did not just intervene in economic activities to promote industrialisation but used every means available, including "rigging prices" and establishing state-owned manufacturing enterprises, to promote industrial growth. Analysts who support a stronger involvement of the state argue that in most less industrialised countries the challenges posed by low savings, low skills, dominance of commodities in the economy, small domestic markets and low capacity to absorb new technology warrants even a bigger role for the state (see Singer, 1950; Wade, 1990).

This debate on the role of the state in industrial development continues to influence industrial policies and strategies developed by African governments today. While the polarised feature of the debate has been present for a long time, there has been an emerging consensus that the role of the state in industrial development in Africa has been vindicated, after some strong anti-state ideology during the 1980s and 1990s (see Olukoshi, 2004; UNECA, 2012). Even if there is wider acceptance of the view that African states should play a central role in the industrialisation process, there are still voices that look at African states with suspicion, arguing that it is not just any kind of state that can deliver industrialisation. Analysts who support the involvement of the state in activities that promote industrial development, have argued that for the state to successfully promote industrialisation, it has to build strong capacity and commitment.

This chapter looks at the role of the state in promoting industrial development, focusing on African states, but drawing examples from a wide range of countries and regions of the world. The chapter focuses on the qualities of a state which enable nations to successfully drive the industrialisation agenda and realise the intended goals. Many analysts agree that most African states, over the years, have demonstrated the inability to intervene effectively to promote industrial development, in particular. In this regard, African states are widely seen to have failed to muster the energy and the will to decentre the colonial economic logic and structures. It is therefore important to look at what has been lacking in African states which has made it difficult for them to effectively implement the industrialisation strategies which many of them have outlined since independence as shown in chapters 4 and 5.

By reflecting on the experience of industrial development in Africa, the chapter looks at the question of what kind of state is required to promote industrialisation. Thus, the chapter is starting from the assumption that the state has an important role to play in the industrialisation of African economies. It is, however, argued in the chapter that not every state intervention in the economy leads to industrial development. As we have seen, many African countries intervened heavily in the economy prior to the commencement of SAPs, but this has not led to any significant industrialisation of the continent. If that is the case, then what kind of qualities should a state possess in order to promote and deliver industrial development? In answering this question, different views are presented in the chapter. One of the popular views proposed by many analysts is that for African states to effectively promote industrial development, they have to become "developmental states".

The Role of the State: The 'Pioneers' View

As noted above, the question of what role the state should play in the process of industrial development is one of the topics that has been hotly debated in development literature since the 1950s. After the *Great Depression*, when the *Keynesian Revolution* challenged the central tenets of neoclassical economics, the debate has since been largely binarised. On one side of the debate are those (mostly development economists) who believe that the state has a central role to play in the process of economic development in general. Examples include the pioneers of development economics such as Rosenstein-Rodan (1943), Nurkse (1953), Scitovsky (1954), Lewis (1954), Hirschman (1958), Singer (1950), Prebisch (1950). For these pioneers, the state was seen as the "prime mover" of economic growth and development, particularly in depressed areas where markets were underdeveloped or non-existent. On the other side of these debates are those who espouse neoclassical principles which emphasise the efficacy of markets. Among these are strong advocates for free market such as Fredrick Hayek (1945)[1] and Milton Friedman (1962)[2] who believed that the state has no role to play in economic activities other than to create an environment in which private actors can optimise their investments and productive activities. For those on this side of the debate, allowing the state to intervene in economic activities, beyond the minimum role of establishing effective public institutions and services which enable the private sector to thrive, amounts to introducing inefficiencies in an economy.

The influence that Keynesian analysis had on these debates, especially industrial development, is less known in the literature perhaps because Keynesian economics is sometimes seen as mere tinkering with neoclassical economics. But Keynes' emphasis on stimulating demand in the economy through various tools available to the state had greater influence on development strategies and prepared the way for views that support an active role of the state in the economy:

> By contradicting orthodox economics, Keynes had prepared the way for an alternative approach to economic problems. By assigning a larger role to the public sector, he had also prepared a case for discretionary national economic management. And public policy formation became a much more active force in national economies (Meier, 1984:14).

Hans Singer (1984: 277), reflecting on the development debates during the 1940s and 1950s, observes that "in some sense Keynes was the real creator of development economics insofar as he broke with 'mono-economics'—the view that economics consists of a body of universal truth applicable in all countries and in all conditions."

By emphasising a stronger role for the state in economic affairs, the early development economists challenged the neoclassical view that the market is the best institution to determine the allocation and use of resources in an economy. In terms of industrialisation, the neoclassical view did not recognise the role of policy (including industrial policy) in economic development since markets were believed to be efficient enough to do the job, if not better than the state. But the dominance of Keynesian economics after the Great Depression normalised state intervention to a point that not only did states formulate development policies (including industrial strategies), but they started to plan and strategise on how to promote and sustain economic growth. As Meier (1984:20) argues,

> Unlike the neoclassical economists who assumed a smoothly working market price system, some of the early development economists adopted a more structuralist approach to development problems. Structuralist analysis attempted to identify specific rigidities, lags, shortages and surpluses, low elasticities of supply and demand, and other characteristics of the structure of developing countries that affect economic adjustments and the choice of development policy.

Industrial policy has been a tool that most states have visibly utilised to affirm a stronger role in economic development. Industrialisation, as we have seen in Chapter 2, because it has been assigned a central role in promoting development in society, has been an arena where most states have been active in coordinating and directing the growth of various segments of the economy, not just the industrial sector. For countries that have successfully industrialised, this was achieved by deploying various state apparatuses through a carefully planned industrial strategy. As highlighted in chapters 4 and 5, most African states during the 1960s, were not only actively involved in coordinating investments in the economy, but established SOEs as a means to spearhead and quicken industrial growth. Indeed, industrialisation was widely believed to be a product of well-planned and coordinated state actions.

African States and Africa's Industrialisation

The disappointing outcome from the market-led approaches to industrialisation has led many African countries to rethink their strategies, and a number of them are now actively designing and implementing industrial policies (UNECA, 2015). However, many of these countries are finding it difficult to coordinate industrial policy with trade policy and the broader development strategy in sectors such as agriculture (ibid). The standard diagnostic for African countries' apparent struggle with coordinating and implementing industrial policy is that African states have weak capacity, weakened by two decades of structural adjustment, which resulted into the hollowing-out of the state, and significant reduction in institutional capacity and efficiency (Stein, 1994 Mkandawire, 2001; Githinji and Adesida, 2011).

While the World Bank and the IMF see the reforms implemented in Africa during the 1980s and 1990s to be paying off in terms of rebuilding state capacity (see World Bank, 2005, 2011), there is wide agreement among scholars that African states have not yet fully recovered from the shock therapy of the 1980s (Mkandawire and Soludo, 1999), such that at the moment they are still rebuilding the capacity to effectively coordinate industrial activities. Some analysts have even suggested that industrialisation continues to be elusive in the continent because of the inability of the state to effectively address market failures (see te Velde, 2013).

The Partnership Model

Although during the 1980s and 1990s, when neoliberal policy paradigm dominated the African policy landscape, the debate was restricted to what African states could do to create a business-friendly environment in which industrial development could occur, today the discussion seems to have shifted to a new consensus, which is that the state should partner with the private sector to deliver industrial development (Page, 2015). It is no longer a dichotomised approach of either the state or the private sector. Today, the state is given much more responsibility and space to play a leading role, and some African states are actively coordinating various industrial initiatives as illustrated in Chapter 10. This consensus is articulated more clearly in the *Economic Report on Africa* 2011, which looked at the role of the state in economic development:

> Advocating a stronger role for the state in development should neither be seen in terms of the old and tired debate of state versus market nor should it be understood that the private sector should not remain the engine of economic growth. This is because the issue is not whether the state—like the market or the private sector for that matter—should play a role in economic transformation and development but rather how to construct developmental states in Africa and how to strengthen their capacity and accountability to design and implement more effective development strategies and policies (UNECA, 2011:91).

UNECA, through its annual *Economic Report on Africa* (ERA), has regularly advocated for African states to play a stronger role in the process of industrialising the continent. But this endorsement of the state's role in industrial development is not unconditional. For African states to play an active role in promoting industrial development, they have to build capacity, by creating intuitions which can implement the outlined policies and strategies. Some authors have not hesitated to label this type of state a "developmental state," whose primary role is to define its developmental vision and implement it. The connection between a developmental state and industrialisation is discussed later in the chapter.

State-Business Alliance

The new development mainstream view has strongly endorsed the idea that the state should be in constant *dialogue* (not dictating to) with the private sector to promote a coherent development vision for the continent. Within the World Bank and other donor institutions, this idea has been articulated through the *Presidential Investors Advisory Councils* (PIACs), which are meant to promote good state–business relationships.[3] In a bid to promote state–business dialogue, the World Bank since 2008 has made allowance for governments in Africa and other developing countries to play a more active role in promoting industrial development by inviting private sector actors to actively participate in industrial policy formulation and implementation. For the World Bank, the emphasis has been on promoting an atmosphere where the public and private sectors see each other as partners in development.

It does not take Albert Einstein's wits to see that this is a polite way of asking the state to consult business at every stage of the policy process from formulation to implementation, and monitoring and evaluation. The strategy of promoting business participation in public policies is being implemented in a number of African countries through the PIACs as well as the Competitiveness Partnerships (CPs), which are aimed at promoting dialogue between the public and private sectors (Herzberg and Wright, 2006; Page, 2015). Through these platforms, it is hoped that a positive state–business relationship can be a catalyst for designing and implementing successful industrial strategies on the continent. The examples followed in these initiatives are largely drawn from the East Asian success stories (Page 2012).

During the early 1990s, it was already becoming clear among many analysts that the debate on industrial development was shifting from a dichotomised position of either the state or the market, to a view that accepted that both institutions had their role to play. Markets, through the discipline induced by competition, can assist firms to upgrade and remain alert to changing trends in customer preferences, technology, emerging niches and discovering new opportunities. Markets can induce this discipline in local firms if there are correct incentives for firms to learn and upgrade. The state, on the other hand, as Onis (1991) has observed, should be able to conceptualise the long-term development objectives and use the market to achieve these goals. Experience from countries which have successfully industrialised shows that they combined the strengths of markets with that of the state to successfully implement an industrialisation strategy with clear determination and vision.

Commentators have observed that if African countries are to realise their industrial growth potential, the state has to adopt a more aggressive and radical stance beyond the rituals of creating a business-friendly environment. Newman et al (2016) have, for instance, argued that the strategy of focusing on the low-hanging fruits of business policy reforms to attract investment, while important, will not lead to realising Africa's industrial development goal. They argue that what is needed over and above the efforts to create a business-friendly environment are aggressive industrial strategies which support local firms to build capacity and become competitive through learning to compete. While there is now wide agreement among scholars that the state has to play a more active role to realise the goal of industrial development, the critical question which often arise is: How does a country build such a state?

Features of an Industrial State

The Ability to Identify and Remain Committed to Long-Term National Goals and Insterests

To answer the question posed above, it is important to look at the role states are expected to play in bringing about industrial development. While examples from other countries can provide valuable lessons on what sort of capacities African states should aim to build in their quest for industrial development, they should seek to develop their own path and unique sets of state capabilities. Trying to replicate what other countries did is not likely to lead to any significant progress, because African states today are trying to industrialise under different domestic and international conditions (see Mkandawire, 2001; Naude, 2010). Further, the composition and nature of Africa states should be different from what obtained in countries which industrialised in the past. Therefore, while African countries can learn from what other countries did to achieve industrialisation, replication of the strategies undertaken by early industrialisers offers little prospect of succeeding. If there is a single lesson African states can learn from early industrialisers, it is that the state played defining roles.

Literature on industrialisation is replete with examples of states playing a variety of roles in promoting the growth of industries at different times. It has been asserted, for instance, that some states even spied on other states in order to build strong industrial capacity and advantage (see Chang, 2003). The fact that states commit espionage to build industrial capacity should not be surprising if states are situated in the international system where each state pursues (some aggressively) its own interest (see Chapter 1). This is why, industrialisation as an active process of creating dynamic comparative advantage should be driven by a central authority, which is unified in its pursuit of national self-interest. In the arena of international trade politics, it is clear that states look after their own interests. An honest acknowledgement of this came from Donald Trump in his *America First Speech* at the Asia Pacific Economic Cooperation (APEC) Summit in Vietnam, where he argued that,

> The current trade imbalance is not acceptable. From this day forward, we will compete on a fair and equal basis. We are not going to let the United States be taken advantage of anymore. I am always going to put America first the same way that I expect all of you in this room to put your countries first (Trump, 2017).

Here Trump is simply acknowledging something which all states do but the leaders pretend to be working together, when in actual fact, each pursues the interest of their respective states. Trump is asserting something which many industrialised nations believe and act on vigorously, but do not speak about openly.

In the earlier days of industrial development, the state used crude forms of intervention, which often served the interest of a small groups of farmers, merchants and industrialists. In England, for example, during the 18th century, the sheep and wool farmers lobbied the state to legislate against not only the importation of woollen clothing but also the export of raw sheep and wool. Adam Smith (2005 [1776]) who was a free trade advocate complained against the use of the state to protect the interests of a few business people against the public (consumers). But for the legislators who passed these laws, they were convinced that they did this to advance the industrial advantage of England (see Amsden, 1989). They believed that advancing the industrial advantage and capacity of the nation cemented national unity, strength and pride. It is strategies like these that the British government aggressively used to build a strong wool manufacturing industry that out-competed other rival nations like France and the United States, and later India (ibid). Chang (2003) describes how through the use of such protectionist strategies Britain and the United States too created formidable domestic industrial capacity, which could stand competition from their rivals. It was only after Britain had managed to create strong industrial capabilities to out-compete its rivals that it started to advocate for free trade (see also List, 1909).

Ability to Defy Static Comparative Advantage

In the case of Japan and the East Asian Newly Industrialised Countries (NICs), their success in building a strong and broad industrial base, between the 1960s and the 1990s, was not because they adhered to a free trade policy and religiously followed the contours of their static comparative advantage, but by flouting and defying the idea that Japan had no comparative advantage in steel industry and the manufacturing of cars. If Japan had strictly followed the contours of its static comparative advantage at that time, Toyota, Nissan and Mitsubishi, and other auto companies would not have emerged as major global players. In his account of the success of MITI in lifting Japan from an agrarian country to a world industrial power in just three decades, Johnson (1982) describes the several measures adopted by the government of Japan to build and boost domestic industrial capabilities. These ranged from foreign exchange controls, through the enactment of the *Foreign Capital Law of 1950* and the *Foreign Trade Control Law of 1949*, to the outright suppression of the importation of manufactured goods that competed with domestic manufactures. By means of state legislation and other strategies, the "MITI made every effort to suppress imports of finished goods," particularly those that competed with domestic manufactured goods. On the other hand, Japan zealously imported modern technology and machinery (Johnson, 1982:217). The MITI as a state department made strategic interventions not just by protecting local industries from cut-throat competition, but importantly by building capacity among the local manufacturers who, with time, developed adequate capability to compete with the big boys in the club. In realising this the state played a central role.

Ability to Provide "Secondary Public Goods"

The interesting part of the industrialisation story in many countries is that as industrialisation progressed, the state capacity to provide support to local firms grew as well. In this sense, industrialisation, while it is a product of strong state capacity, it in turn contributes to building stronger state capacity. States which have built capacity to support local manufacturing have performed well in terms of industrialisation, through the provision of what I am calling the *secondary public goods*. On the other hand, states that have succeeded in industrialising have strengthened their capacity to provide public goods in general. In the case of Japan, firms which the MITI assisted to upgrade their manufacturing capabilities were not all state-owned; they were private-owned companies as well. These companies (both private and public owned) performed well in terms of upgrading their manufacturing capabilities because of the support provided by the state. The state provided industrial support to private firms in the same way it provides the traditional public goods such as health, education and infrastructure, security, and law and order.

From the state's point of view, this was an essential element of the responsibilities of the state in the grand scheme of things, such that the support provided to manufacturing firms to promote industrialisation was largely treated as an indirect way of boosting the provision of primary or traditional public goods. Amsden (1989) in her account of South Korea's industrial development, and Wade's (1990) account of Taiwan's industrialisation strategy, find parallels with the Japanese industrial strategy, particularly the strategic interventions made by the state to build competitiveness among local firms. In pursuing such strategies, the state is not just creating an environment where firms can exploit their maximum potential, but it is propping up and guiding firms in a specific direction, along the path outlined in the industrial strategy and the development goals. Review of evidence in Japan and other Asian countries suggest that the state played a central role not just in creating an enabling environment, but by providing concrete and strategic support to private and public local manufacturing companies (Johnson, 1982).

In Africa, a good example of a state that has tried to provide secondary public goods to firms is Ethiopia. Oqubay (2015) describes how the Ethiopian government provided support to SOEs as well as private enterprises as a way of developing industrial capacity, which is largely seen as something that constitute public interest. Although he acknowledges that government interventions in the cement industry were not properly timed, Oqubay (2015:106) observes that,

> Government industrial policies have shaped the cement industry's development through direct and indirect interventions. Direct support including subsidised long-term investment loans, investment promotion incentives, and access to mining resources required as inputs. On the demand side, the government's large-scale housing and infrastructure development programme… became the prime mover of growth in the cement industry.

Here, we see a state that treats the growth of industry as something that can bring benefit to the public, and ensures that both public and private enterprises are provided with necessary support to build and strengthen industrial capabilities. When these industries succeed, the benefits to the country are many including rising employment, growing industrial capacity, increasing tax base and revenue, reduction of pressure on the current account through the expected decline in imports of consumer and intermediate goods, rising skills levels in the population as more people employed learn by doing. The list can be a long one. This is why providing support to the industrial sector should be seen as an investment in secondary public goods. For instance, in

Ethiopia, the growth of the cement industry had direct impact on the entire construction sector through backward and forward linkages such that between 2008 and 2012, the growing cement industry stimulated the growth of firms manufacturing building materials such as roofing materials, steel, plumbing materials, electrical etc., (ibid). This growth in the sector stimulated the growth of formal employment.

Capacity to Build New Ladders for Industrial Growth

By providing the secondary public goods such as the industrial extension services (IES), the state is actually doing more than just creating an investor-friendly environment. Creating a business-friendly environment is not sufficient to overcome the hurdles of industrialisation, especially for the late industrialisers who often face stiffer penalties for industrialising after others (see Felipe et al, 2017). To successfully industrialise, states in Africa should learn to play an active role in assisting local firms (both private and public) to overcome the hurdles which often act as barriers to upgrading industrial capabilities and creating competitiveness. Hurdles in the industrialisation of a country are sometimes created by the now industrialised countries who after achieving substantial industrial muscle decide to throw away the ladder which they used to build their industrial capacity. In a sense, one can't blame the early industrialisers for looking after their own interest as the 19th-century German economist Fredrich List rightly observes:

> It is a very common clever device that when anyone has attained the summit of greatness, he *kicks away the ladder* by which he has climbed up, in order to deprive others of the means of climbing up after him. Any nation which by means of protective duties and restrictions on navigation has raised her manufacturing power and her navigation to such a degree of development than no other nation can sustain free competition with her, can do nothing wiser than *to throw away these ladders* of her greatness to preach to other nations the benefits of free trade, and to declare in penitent tones that she has hitherto wandered in the paths of error, and has now for the first time succeeded in discovering the truth (List, 1909, emphasis added).

It seems that Trump's strategy of putting America first is not something new; it has been there since the creation of nation-states and states should not be blamed for looking after their interest; that's what they are supposed to do. The only share of blame that one can apportion to early industrialisers is that of being dishonest by claiming that they successfully industrialised by strictly adhering to the principles of free trade and comparative advantage. Historical accounts of how nations industrialised clearly show that early industrialisers used state apparatus to build their industrial ladders. When these states reached the summit they threw away the ladder as part of looking after their self-interest. As for the late industrialisers, their main task is to build their own ladders which they can use to climb to the top of the industrial pyramid. The secrete to industrialisation today is to realise that the ladders which countries that have already industrialised used to build their industrial capabilities have been thrown away, and the task is not to go and look for the old ladders; the task is to construct new ladders which can be used to climb to the industrial summit.

There are two important reasons why looking for the ladders used by the now industrialised or industrialising countries would most likely be a fruitless exercise. The first is that the industrial terrain has not remained the same in such a way that one could use the same ladders which were used 50 or 20 years ago. The texture and the slope of the industrial cliff have changed with time, thereby requiring new ladders to navigate its contours better. Naude (2010) has elaborated on some of the changes that have occurred since the 1990s, including the introduction of new international trade regimes as well as the structure of production now dominated by globally dispersed value chains, leading to minutely fragmented value chains across the globe. Sampath (2014) highlights the same point in the case of African countries where the policy space has consistently been narrowed by multilateral trade agreements and the nature of global manufacturing value chains. Navigating these spaces requires constructing new ladders, and African states, like the early industrialisers, have to play a critical role in stimulating the initiative as well as in the actual construction of the ladders. The second is that effective ladders are those that are constructed based on the vision of a county or region. It is only through this that countries can chart their own industrial path.

Capacity to Formulate and Implement Industrial Strategy

In a well-known study that reviewed the factors behind the rapid industrialisation of East Asian countries, the World Bank (1993) highlights two key factors. The first one which the study regards as an engine of growth is "private domestic investments," and the second is accumulation of human capital. While the study mentions other factors which contributed to the sustained growth reported in these economies since the 1960s, including a slow-down in population growth, sound macro-economic management, and effective administration, it acknowledges that the state did not just formulate policies which played an important role in the process of industrialisation, but actually intervened in the economy in strategic ways which violated the capitalist rationality of free trade and comparative advantage. The report observes that,

> Fundamentally sound development policy was a major ingredient in achieving rapid growth. Macroeconomic management was unusually good and macroeconomic performance unusually stable, providing the essential framework for private investment. Policies to increase the integrity of the banking system, and to make it more accessible to non-traditional savers, raised the levels of financial savings. Education policies that focused on primary and secondary schools generated rapid increases in labour force skills. Agricultural policies stressed productivity and did not tax the rural economy excessively. All the HPAEs [High Performing Asian Economies) kept price distortions within reasonable bounds and were open to foreign ideas and technology. But these fundamental policies do not tell the entire story. In most of these economies, in one form or another, *the government intervened systematically and through multiple channels-to foster development, and in some cases the development of specific industries*. Policy interventions took many forms: targeting and subsidizing credit to selected industries, keeping deposit rates low and maintaining ceilings on borrowing rates to increase profits and retained earnings, protecting domestic import substitutes, subsidizing declining industries, establish big and financially supporting government banks, making public investments in applied research, establishing firm- and industry-specific export markets, developing export marketing institutions, and sharing information widely between public and private sectors. …At least some of these interventions violate the dictum of establishing for the private sector a level playing field, a neutral incentives regime (World Bank, 1993:5–6, emphasis added).

In this extract, the active role that the state played in the industrialisation and development of East Asian economies is well-elaborated to allay any lingering doubts about whether the state did actually play a significant role.

From the passage above, the state went beyond the comfortable duties of formulating policies on education, agriculture and price regulation. We see an active and heavily intrusive state, bent not only on protecting infant industries through import substitution, but also dishing out subsidises to strategic firms and subsectors, and establishing some of the industrial enterprises through partnership with the private sector. Apart from that, it is also evident that the active state clearly identified and carefully defined an industrial development path and targets. If the description of how the East Asian countries grew in the above passage is anything close to the truth, one thing that is clear is that the state in these countries had a clear road map. From this, the state then marshalled its resources and institutions to realise the identified goals. Not only that, but we also see a state taking coordinated approach to development in such a way that the industrialisation strategy syncs with the agricultural, education and the tax policies, to create synergies not just in industry but in the entire economy and society at large. To successfully carry out these tasks, strong state capacity is a prerequisite. What makes the state in the example cited above effective is not the specific strategies adopted, but the clarity of vision and the commitment to achieving the set goals, including building state capacity along the way.

A Defiant but Disciplined Bureaucracy

Experience from the now industrialised countries shows that successful industrial development in these countries was achieved because of the strong awareness by state officials that the state had to provide conditional incentives for the private and public manufacturing firms to participate actively in realising the national industrial objectives. Through this strategy, the state demonstrated the ability to make the markets serve the broader goal of industrial expansion. To use Wade's (1990) phrase, the state succeeded in "taming markets." The experience of industrialised states in Asia provides a good example of effective states capable of defining and charting an industrial road map, mobilising and coordinating the support of key actors (including private sector) to implement the plan, often, by building alliances not just with business, but different sections of society. Experience suggests that no country has industrialised without an active state that coordinated the activities of different actors. It has thus been observed that,

> Key to rapid industrialization is a strong and autonomous state, providing directional thrust to the operation of the market mechanism. The market is guided by a conception of long-term national rationality of investment formulated by government officials. It is the "synergy" between the state and the market which provides the basis for outstanding development experience (Onis, 1991:110).

To direct the market in support of industrialisation requires a state with strong commitment to industrialisation. States which have no strong commitment to industrialisation end up being captured by the markets, instead of states taming markets and using them as instruments for building competitive capacity and advantage. In other words, an effective industrial state is essentially one that is *defiant* but also *disciplined*. The calibre of civil servants is crucial here.

Prepared to Weather the Stormy Ride

While there has been widespread tendency in the development and industrialisation literature to exalt the performance of the East Asian economies as the ideal examples for the less industrialised countries to emulate, it is important to note that it was not all smooth sailing for these states. The glorious portraits of the East Asian industrialised countries which are often flashed in most analyses of industrial development make them look less real, as if they were operating on another planet. The implementation of the industrial strategy and the broader development agenda required a lot of effort, commitment and perseverance when things did not go as planned. Onis (1991) observes that it was not easy for Asian states to enforce the strict discipline which was required to effectively run an industrial incentive programme. Getting the private sector to buy in to the industrial development strategy is not easy given the divergent interest between the public and private actors. For example, most East Asian states that have successfully manged to industrialise had to take a decision not to subsidise poorly managed firms, even if they were making profits or were politically connected. The state had to prescribe a set of measures of good management practices which firms on the industrial incentive programmes had to abide by and demonstrate that they were following the approved standards. This was done in an effort to incentivise firms to adopt the best practice as a way of building their competitive capacity.

Githinji and Adesida (2011) observe that these states had to force companies, both private and public, to upgrade the skills of their workers as well as the quality of their products, as part of the strategy of building competitiveness and the capacity to adapt to the changing markets. Johnson's (1982) account of Japan's rise to become a global industrial powerhouse, emphasise the point that the state had to deal with the difficult issue of the relationship between the bureaucracy and the privately owned firms in ensuring that they were all on board. The challenge of getting the private sector to buy into the industrial road map outlined by government officials emerged at an early stage of Japan's industrial policy. The state had to continuously find the best solution to the challenge. In the case of Japan, three strategies of self-control, state control and cooperation were used to deal with the challenge of eliciting compliance from the private sector. The corporation strategy sometimes entailed using *soft-power* to get the private firms to comply, and buy into the bigger agenda set by the state (see Johnson, 1982). Reflecting on the Ethiopian Experience, Oqubay (2015) highlights the same point arguing that little analysis has gone into examining the intricacies of implementing industrial policy sustainably, when this involves soliciting cooperation from various sections of society.

Apart from dealing with the internal challenges of ensuring discipline and compliance from both public and private firms, East Asian states had to deal with the international pressures, including the deliberate barriers created by the then industrialised countries in a bid to stem off competition. As List (1909) observed, industrialised countries often want to deprive less industrialised nations of the crucial tools for industrialisation. This reaction from industrialised countries is perfectly rational because they would not like to prop up countries that will compete with them (see Chang, 2003:24). They will try to keep the less industrialised countries below them as a way of protecting their interest. This sometimes involves outright bullying, treachery tactics and espionage to tilt the playing field in their favour. In some cases, industrialised nations oppose any strategy from the industrialising nations which might lead to catching up with them, in terms of what they produce by undercutting their static comparative advantage.

Any country embarking on an industrialisation project has to be prepared to deal with all the bullying and treacherous tactics which other nations, especially industrialised nations, might concoct. It would be politically naïve to think that Singapore and Germany would be celebrating Nigeria's advancement in robotics or 3-D printing. Nigeria and Madagascar need to anticipate the pressure from Germany and Singapore, and still be ready to compete and aim to surpass these industrial heavy-weights. This is not something that individual firms in Madagascar or Nigeria can achieve on their own; the states in these countries need to strategise and coordinate all the key actors. In the case of African countries that rely on aid, the donors may put pressure to force them to abandon radical industrial strategy by appealing to the idea that a poor African national should focus on labour-intensive activities in agriculture. Big nations often enforce this on small countries through bilateral agreements and support mechanisms. This is why any country that is seriously embarking on industrialisation has to be prepared to be defiant to the end, which might mean saying no to aid that runs contrary to the long-term plan that the state has earmarked. In this regard, African states face the hard choice between the immediate benefit of aid and the long-term cost of implementing a radical industrial policy, which may require a country to reject the short-termism which characterise most aid packages.

If Malawi decides that the country wants, in twenty years' time, to produce robots which can pick coffee beans or tea leaves on the slopes of Mount Mulanje, the state should marshal all the necessary resources (private and public investment) towards this goal. The government of Malawi should be able to mobilise and incentivise all the actors (public, private and donors) towards achieving this goal.

Plans for the Fourth Industrial Revolution (FIR)

The much talked about IR 4.0 has been developing silently over the last decade, with more progress being made in the last five years as computer capacity to store and process data increases. Although it is unpredictable how this revolution will unfold, one thing that is clear is that it is happening slowly in various sectors of society. Countries seeking to industrialise in the 21st century cannot overlook this nascent field of knowledge; it has to be part of the industrial strategy. Tapping into the opportunities presented by the IR 4.0, will not happen by chance or osmosis; countries have to plan and take strategic actions that can enable them not only to take advantage of the emerging opportunities, but also to navigate the challenges that this will engender in society. Most importantly, countries must identify which dimension of the FIR they seek to focus on as part of their industrial policy. We see many industrialised nations today making strategic decisions to position themselves in readiness for the FIR. For example, in 2017, the UK government set up an Industrial Strategy Challenge Fund meant to fund research and innovation in Artificial Intelligence (AI) (EIU, 2018:14). Similarly, the Japanese government established the Strategic Council for AI Technology (SCAIT) to coordinate and support all AI and robotics-related research and development centres in the country (ibid). We see a lot of countries around the world not just coordinating research, but encouraging and supporting various initiatives, by state and private sector, aimed at building capabilities to embrace IR 4.0. In Africa, Egypt provides an interesting case where the country in 2019 decided to establish a special faculty and an academy for Artificial Intelligence, the first in the world (Sawahel, 2019). All states which have made significant progress in industrial development have been actively involved in the research and the development of new technologies, and the intensity of the investment in research and development of technology has deepened, with industrialised nations seeking to outcompete each other.

In all this, it is evident that the state needs to be at the helm of the industrial strategy, directing, coordinating, mobilising as well as incentivising different actors, both in the public and private sectors.

Lessons for Late Industrialisers

In the current consensus on industrialisation, while there is some agreement that the main issue is not about whether the state should play a role or not, but about the strategy the state should adopt to promote industrialisation, there is also some lingering suspicion of the state as an inefficient actor whose role should be limited to creating an enabling environment for the private sector to thrive and in the process drive the industrialisation project. If the experience of the now industrialised countries has any lessons for the less-industrialised countries, two are obvious. The first is that industrialisation can only succeed when there is an effective and defiant state. The other is that the state's role should not just be restricted to rolling out a red carpet for business, especially foreign investors, but should be focused on guiding and coordinating the various decisions and actions which have significant implications for industrial development. The South African Industrial Policy Action Plan 2016–2019 articulates the role of the state well when it argues that the role of the state should be "steering but not Rowing" the ship as it were (DTI, 2016:6).

For example, private investors might all want to go into Information and Communication sector because that's where the profits are high, and the risks are low. If left uncoordinated, the country might end up with an oversubscribed ICT sector, a situation that may lead to imbalances if other sectors are not in a position to utilise the ICT facilities and services. An effective state should be able to say to the investors that the ICT sector is fully subscribed and encourage investors to go into the renewable energy sector or agro-processing, for example. To accomplish this task requires a disciplined state; a state that remains true to its vision and avoids being swayed into supporting narrow interests. In the literature on developmental states, this quality has been broadly referred to as *embedded autonomy* (see Evans, 1995). For the state to be able to accomplish this, it requires knowledge and a strong commitment to the vision of industrial development.

The state should have information about the required capacity to create sustained momentum in strategic sectors. It is only when the state has this adequate information that it will be able to plan for a long-term vision. This is a task which markets, especially in developing countries, have not been able to accomplish well. It is precisely because of such market failures that the state, even after considering the widespread phenomenon of state failure, is widely acknowledged to provide a better solution to the problem of investment coordination at a large scale. This is a point avidly made by the pioneers of development economics who succeeded in convincing many leaders of developing countries that the state is well-positioned to coordinate industrial strategic investments from various sources (see Rosenstein-Rodan, 1943; Nurkse, 1953).

The State as the Second-Best Option

However, as Chitonge (2015) has noted, the main reason for the pioneers' apparent faith in the state is not because they did not trust markets; their preference for the state was some sort of a "second best" option. Arthur Lewis who is one of the leading pioneers of development economics clarifies this when he argues that, "One reason why government is closer to the developing economy is that the market works less efficiently there than in the developed economy. So the government is constantly asked to rectify market error or market inequity" (Lewis, 1984:4). He further argues that,

> To say…[that the state should correct market failure] is not to imply that government action in the market always gives a better answer than the uncontrolled market, whether in allocation or distribution. [In LDCs] it is often the case that the imperfect solution of the market could be better than that of the government (ibid).

This idea that the state should intervene in the economy to correct market failure is sometimes referred to as the "Pigouvian paradigm," named after the 20th-century English economist Arthur Cecil Pigou. According to the Pigouvian view, the strategy of using the state to direct and coordinate economic development is preferred not because states are perceived to be better than markets; the state is preferred based on the view that a "developing country did not have a reliable market price system, that the supply of entrepreneurship was limited, and that large structural changes—not merely marginal adjustment, were needed" (Meier, 2001:14–15). In this sense, the option of allowing state intervention is clearly the second-best option; the first option is the market, the state is only called in when markets fail. Fortunately, in the real world, markets often fail. Given that market failures are a dominant feature not just in developing economies (see Stiglitz, 1992), the role of the state in promoting economic development should not be framed in terms of either the state or the market (UNECA 2012). Instead, the task should be to find a way that the state and private sector can complement each other. In the context of developing countries, defiant and disciplined states working with the private sector is the only feasible way to respond to the complex challenges of development (Singh, 1992).

China's rapid industrialisation and poverty reduction has reinforced the view that when a strong state directs, coordinates and takes an active role in economic activities of a country, the process of development is not only faster but more inclusive. In this view, the role of the state in fostering economic growth and industrial development is not just limited to that of being a watch-dog, reduced to enforcing contracts or rolling out the red carpet for investors. The state is increasingly expected to play a leading role in guiding and disciplining capital to fit in the broader scheme of economic growth and industrial development (Amsden, 1989). States which perform this role effectively are widely referred to as *developmental states*, whose main priority is development.

Developmental States

The term *developmental state* was first used in the study of Japan's experience of rapid industrialisation by Johnson (1982), but it has subsequently been applied to different states, especially the newly industrialised countries (NICs) in East Asia. In Africa, there has been a drawn-out debate about whether African states are developmental states or not. Critics, who are often in the majority, argue that most African countries do not exhibit any basic features of a developmental state primarily because they lack an effective and autonomous bureaucracy (Edigheji, 2005). It is often argued that African states lack government officials and politicians whose main priority is the development of their respective countries, that most countries have weak capacity to direct the actions of various actors in the economy towards the identified developmental goals (Chabal and Daloz, 1999). It is important to remember that there is no prototype developmental state against which to assess other states (see Onis, 1991). However, there are widely recognised features which define and differentiate a developmental state from other types of states. In other words, there is a common denominator which qualifies a state to be a developmental state. Here it will be useful to first briefly outline some of the fundamental features of a developmental state, and then try to see if any of these are noticeable in African states.

The Ideology of Developmentalism

One of the basic features of a developmental state that is widely believed to be the most important is that of being pre-occupied with development—that is, a state imbued with the ideology of developmentalism, a strong belief in development, defined as sustained broad-based improvement in the welfare of all the people in the country, not just the privileged few. This is often interpreted to mean that the state should see its essence or *raison d'être* as promoting development; a state whose first priority is to achieve development in the broader sense of the term. For example, Johnson (1982) argues that the Japanese state in the early 1920s identified development as its priority number one, and everything else including the "imperialism of the Pacific War" (which turned out to be a disaster) were all tailored to serve the goal of developing Japan. Mkandawire (2001:290) makes a similar point, arguing that "a developmental state is essentially one whose ideological underpinning is 'developmentalist' in that it conceives its 'mission' as that of ensuring economic development, usually interpreted to mean high rates of accumulation and industrialisation." In other words, a developmental state is one that is driven by a developmentalist ideology and agenda, everything else is done in the service of this goal.

Development in this context is understood to mean a rapid process of changing the economic structure of the country underpinned by widespread improvements in the welfare and standard of living of the people in the country. In short, development, in a developmental state, is understood as the attainment of rapid economic and social progress which evokes a collective sense of national pride among citizens. Thus, a developmental state does not aim at merely expanding total output in the economy; its mandate is broad-based development, one in which the majority of (if not all) the people share the dividends of the growing economy. This is why a developmental state's legitimacy is derived from its developmental outcomes. The performance of a developmental state is assessed by how broad the progress generated is spread to the people in the country. Chang (2010:82) brings out this feature more succinctly when he observes that, "a developmental state is one that derives political legitimacy from its record in economic development, which it tries to achieve mainly by means of selective industrial policy."[4] Notice that industrial development in both Mkandawire's (2001) and Chang's (2010) definition of a developmental state is seen as the central mission of a developmental state.

It is also important to note that the developmentalist ideology is not defined by the strategy used to realise the goal of economic growth and improved well-being of citizens. Whether the state decides to take the command economy approach or a mix of state and market strategy is of secondary importance. What matters is achieving the set developmental targets, especially broadening economic and social well-being of the people in the country. There can be debates about whether this or that route would be the most appropriate, but at the end of the day, the state will be judged by the 'fruits of its labour'. However, since in a developmental state there is a strong assumption that the state is in the driving seat of the development process, a developmental state, by definition, cannot adopt a pure market strategy to economic development, where the state's role is restricted to that of facilitating the smooth functioning of markets. A genuine developmental state should tame, discipline and exploit markets to achieve its intended goals. Seen from this angle, a developmental state must get its hands dirty; it must be in-charge.

Developmental State and Industrialisation

The second feature which characterises developmental states is broad-based industrialisation. As noted earlier, it is interesting that both Mkandawire (2001) and Chang (2010) include the achievement of rapid industrialisation as a defining feature of a developmental state. It is not by coincident that in the early development economics literature, there was a tendency to equate industrialisation with development, although this view is now being challenged in the context where the phenomenon of "service economies" is becoming common among less industrialised countries (Rodrick, 2015).[5] Associating development with industrialisation may be an old idea dating from the early days of development economics, but its centrality in the understanding of a development state is not accidental. Industrialisation, because it requires effective coordination and mobilisation, is a good test of the state's ability and capacity to design and implement strategies to achieve the defined goals. It is not by chance that all the states which have widely been acknowledged as developmental states experienced some form of industrialisation, some over a short period while others over an extended period of time.

In the past, developmental states were commonly associated with rapid industrialisation in which the state defined the goals and actively participated in realising them. In this sense, developmental states use industrial policy to achieve the goals they set. Even today when the role of industrialisation in promoting inclusive growth through mass employment generation is being questioned, it can be argued that industrialisation is still an important defining feature of a developmental state. Whether the progress is driven by an Agriculture Demand-Led Industrialisation (ADLI) or manufacturing-led, rapid growth of industrial activities remains the seal of broad-based development, a goal which a developmental state earnestly aspires to achieve.

Effective Institutions

The third common feature of a developmental state is the presence of effective public institutions. Sometimes this is depicted in terms of the capacity to define, design, coordinate and consistently implement strategies aimed at achieving the identified developmental goals. The measure of capacity in a developmental state includes the institutional, technical and administrative efficiency, which enable the state to carry out the outlined developmental plans or strategies. Evans (2010) drawing from Max Weber's conception of state bureaucracy emphasises the importance of meritocratic recruitment and long-term employment as key to creating effective bureaucracies. Meritocratic recruitment is important, "not only to promote competence but to give state employees a sense of *esprit de corps* and belief in the worthiness of their profession. Long term career rewards based on performance [keep] competent individuals from deserting the public service" (Evans, 2010: 45).

Similarly, in discussing developmental states, Mkandawire (2001) emphasises what he refers to as the *state-structure* aspect. This simply refers to the positioning of state institutions in such a way that they have sufficient autonomy to design and implement long-term economic policies aimed at realising the broader national objectives. An important feature of the developmental states in this regard is that state institutions and resources should not be used to serve narrow and short-term interests of the powerful groups in the country, be they private or public actors.

Evans (1995) describes the ability of the state bureaucracy to design and implement long-term developmental goals, without being captured by either politicians or big business, as *embedded autonomy*. Embedded autonomy means that state institutions have the capacity to resist the temptation of serving narrow, short-term, private interests, yet at the same time, these institutions are dedicated to realising the social and economic aspirations of the people. Johnson (1982) takes this as a challenge which any developmental state faces as it negotiates the relationship between the different actors in the economy: the bureaucracy, the politicians and the big guys in the private sector, including international players. It is the ability to navigate these knotted relations which determines whether the *state-structure* is autonomous or not. Again, examples from East Asia show that countries there developed strong autonomous bureaucracies (Amsden, 1989).

Intervention in the Name of Development

The fourth basic feature of a developmental state is that it is interventionist by nature. A developmental state always intervenes in economic affairs in the interest of the outlined development goals. Every state intervenes in the economic life of a country even those that have publicly adopted a market-oriented ideology. Johnson (1999) in his response to those who criticised him for praising what they thought were autocratic (undemocratic) regimes in East Asia argues that the notion of a developmental state often unsettles people especially those in English-speaking universities who do not fathom any deviation from the "orthodox" development paths experienced in the past. According to Johnson, what scares these people most in the concept of a developmental state is the affirmation of state intrusion in the economic life of a country and its people. Indeed intervening in the name of development is a central characteristic of a developmental state.

But, what distinguishes a developmental state's intervention in economic affairs from other states is that it does so only to further the chances of realising the outlined developmental goals. Intervening in the interest of development is a core mandate of a developmental state. The actions of a developmental state are expected to steer the economy and the country to a particular point, through a carefully thought-out strategy and plan of action. For example, when imported goods threaten to derail the realisation of creating local manufacturing capabilities to produce certain goods and services domestically, a developmental state may intervene by restricting the importation of certain goods or may intervene by providing appropriate incentives to stimulate capability growth and the improvement of technical ability in local firms. In a developmental state, this is not done to please certain powerful interest groups; such actions are taken to realise the broader goal of development.

Johnson (1982) describes how the Japanese state in the 1940s intervened in the banking sector to provide targeted financial support to manufacturing and other firms, which were identified as strategic in the industrial development plan. To ensure that the private sector understood and complied with the state-defined goals, the Japanese state, in some instances, assigned state officials to the boards of private corporations. All this was done not to serve the narrow interests of some politician or powerful business people, but in the service of the identified developmental objectives. This should not be read to mean that there was no pressure from various interest groups to extract rents from the state; such pressure is always there in any society. What sets a developmental state apart is its ability to resist the pressure, the ability to fend off any snares of capture by narrow interests. In other words, a developmental state keeps its eyes on the ball—national development.

Apart from the features discussed above, there are other characteristics which are often associated with a developmental state. For example, Edigheji (2005) and Mkandawire (2010) emphasise democracy as an important component of a developmental state, while Evans (2010) has stressed the importance of providing public goods as an essential element of a developmental state in the 21st century. Other authors mention a strong state with authoritarian approach as a vital feature of a developmental state, citing examples from East Asia, where some of the dictatorial regimes performed surprisingly well in terms of industrialising their countries (see Callaghy and Ravenhill, 1993).

Kim (2010) points out that the rapid economic development that occurred during the authoritarian regime in South Korea was the result of the state, at the beginning, using its "absolute autonomy" to dictate and direct industrial policy to private sector actors. But she argues that this strategy had its own limitations in that, with time, as the private sector grew and became more influential, it began to undermine the authoritarian directives by resisting to implement the orders and instead advocated for a transition to democratic governance. The growing opposition to military authoritarian rule among the general population led to the assassination of the military ruler (Major General Park Chung Hee) in 1979, and eventually the overthrow of the government. One of the main reasons for the success of the Korean military rule was not just the autonomy it enjoyed but the capacity developed in state institutions, which made it easier to communicate and monitor the directives.

Bureaucratic or Developmental State?

Within the development literature, the emphasis put on the role of the bureaucracy sometimes gives the impression that a bureaucratic state is the same as a developmental state. But the two are different in four critical ways. First, the bureaucratic state, seen in the Weberian sense, is mainly concerned with the application of the *rules and procedure* in the performance of public duties, which may not necessarily be developmental. Second, the bureaucratic state may not necessarily be guided by a developmentalist ideology; its main focus is the depersonalisation of state institutions and functions, with the ultimate aim of drawing a clear line between the *public* and *private*, between *office* and *family* matters. Once that separation is enforced, the bureaucratic state would have achieved its goal, which is not the case when it comes to a developmental state.

Third, a bureaucratic state is not necessarily defined by the goal of broad-based development; its main concern is the regulation of the entire state machinery in line with the prescribed rules, girded by a particular rationality, often the capitalist, post-industrial rationality. Thus, a bureaucratic state may be very effective in ensuring that the regulatory functions are performed to the letter, but this may not necessarily lead to broad-based progress in the economic and social life of the people.

Fourth, a bureaucratic state is usually a product of advanced industrial development processes, while a developmental state develops in pursuit of specific developmental goals, which includes industrialisation. Accordingly, while an efficient bureaucracy is an indispensable part of a developmental state, a bureaucratic state is not necessarily a developmental state. As Johnson (1982:306) has rightly observed, a developmental state must first be developmentally oriented, then it can be "a regulatory state, a welfare state, an equality state, or whatever other kind of functional state a society may wish to adopt." The pre-eminence of a developmental orientation is a critical defining feature of a developmental state.

No Prototype Developmental State

Regardless of the type of government, the features of a developmental state discussed above are commonly acknowledged to be central to a developmental state. It is however important to stress that there are no prototype developmental states or models; every developmental state responds to its specific challenges at a given time and, as such, it is futile to develop a blueprint developmental state. For this reason, copying models of a developmental state is like using old "ladders" to industrialise today. Unfortunately, not much can be expected from such a strategy. Evans (2010: 37) explains this, warning that copying and pasting the models from other context is likely to end in failure:

> There is no fixed, universal model of how to build a developmental state; 21st century developmental states will draw on examples from other regions and historical periods as well as on general theories of development, but unreflective imports of ready-made models are likely to fail. A "cookie cutter" approach to the construction of a developmental state—assuming that "one size fits all"—will fail in the same way

> that neoliberal one-size fits all, cookie cutter approaches to building effective markets have failed. Successful construction of a developmental state must be a continually reflexive "learning by doing" process.

On the question of whether other developing states can adopt the East Asian model of a developmental state, there has been almost a unanimous view that replication is not a feasible strategy.

Some of the reasons given include the fact that the global economic conditions which prevailed when the Asian developmental states successfully industrialised have changed, such that it would be difficult to use the same strategies today (see Mkandawire, 2001). Sampath (2014) makes a similar observation, arguing that there is no single path to constructing a developmental state, and it would be misguided to try and transport the East Asian developmental states to Africa because African states today are facing a different set of developmental challenges to those faced by the Asian economies from the 1960s to 1980s. As noted earlier, the strategy of looking for ladders used by the now industrialised countries is likely to end in disappointment, precisely because those ladders were constructed to climb different terrains, and as such may not be suitable for navigating the contours of industrial development today. This does not mean that late industrialisers cannot learn from the experience of early industrialisers, but it means that the old ladders may not be effective any more, hence the need to construct new ladders, based on the current industrial development challenges. The main issue for the "African state therefore, is to identify these challenges and to devise developmental responses" to address the challenges (Sampath, 2014:442).

Are There Developmental States in Africa?

Having looked at some of the fundamental features of a developmental state, it is now possible to address the question of whether there are developmental states or not in Africa. There is some agreement in the literature that from the early 1960s to the mid-1970s, many African states exhibited some rudimentary features of a developmental state as discussed above. Mkandawire (2001) for instance argues that during the 1960s and 1970s, many African states would have easily qualified as developmental states on the basis of their economic strategy and development performance. A specific example is the insatiable appetite exhibited by many African countries to industrialise (see Chapter 5). Githinji and Adesida (2011) make a similar observation arguing that the early post-colonial states in Africa were imbued with a strong developmentalist ideology, manifested in their quest to transform their societies within the shortest time possible.

Another feature of a developmental state which was apparent in the early post-colonial states in Africa is the state-led industrial strategy, underpinned by import substation industrialisation. As noted in Chapter 5, the earlier years of ISI achieved significant expansion of the industrial sector in many countries (see also Bates, 1981).[6] As highlighted earlier, many African states took a lead not only in designing development plans, but in the actual implementation of the programmes, by creating state-owned enterprises in strategic sectors, even in countries that did not openly adopt a planned economy approach. The importance attached to achieving social and economic development is evident in most NDPs developed in the first ten years of independence. For example, after acknowledging that the main purpose of formulating the first development plan was to increase the rate at which the country was achieving social and economic development, the Liberian government declared that,

> To this end we must devote all the resources of the nation, not only financial resources but equally human and administrative resources, to the coordinated and rational pursuit of our national goals. The policy and investment decisions that are at the heart of the planning process must be weighted in terms of their contribution towards increasing the rate of economic and social progress (Government of Liberia, 1967).

Most NDPs developed prior to the SAPs period contain statements suggesting strong intent on the part of the government to pursue developmental objectives. In most of these development plans, there was a clear sense that the state had the responsibility not only to draw up the plans, but to implement them.

It is also quite clear in most of the NDPs that African states were well aware that to be able to achieve these developmental objectives, they had to devote a significant amount of resources and effort towards the education of the people, most of whom, at independence, had not been to school. Githinji and Adesida (2011) observe that the issue of expanding access to education was crucial because on the eve of independence, enrolment ratios in French West Africa, Tanzania and Nigeria were 6, 10 and 16 percent, respectively, which reflects a low manpower capacity, and a strong indictment for the colonial regime as Berg (1964) has rightly observed. In this regard, Gilley's (2017:4) claim that one of the benefits of colonialism was "expanded education" amounts to a complete disregard of the evidence on the ground. The performance of colonial governments in Africa on social welfare for Africans had been dismal and there is evidence to support this in almost every country.

One of the reasons for the colonial state's dismal performance in Africa when it comes to the provision of public goods for Africans was the low capacity of the colonial states, especially in cases where indirect rule was adopted to deflect the administrative costs and responsibilities (see Mamdani, 1996). Mkandawire (2010) makes this point more emphatically arguing that the colonial state, outside of the settler colonies, had no capacity to provide social service such as education, health care and training of Africans:

> Although in the current revisionist history, the impression is given that Africans inherited strong states from erstwhile colonial masters, the fact is that the inherited colonial state was, in many parts of Africa, no more than a garrison stationed so as to protect trading outposts and the routes that the imperial order had set up. Only in the white settler colonies did the state have institutional capacity to provide extensive social services to the racially segregated society, and only in such cases did the state collect taxes that went beyond taxes on exports and poll taxes. With the expansion of demand on the state after independence, to meet the economic and social needs of the new nations and the exigencies of statehood, there was a rapid expansion of the state in both administrative capacity and reach (Mkandawire, 2010:62).

In social services, many post-colonial African states made significant progress, particularly in education and health care in the first decade of independence as part of their broader vision of development. Many countries during this period experienced positive economic growth and promising levels of industrialisation spearheaded by the state, with little contribution from the private sector. Thus, there is strong evidence to support the assertion that most African states prior to the 1980s manifested features of a developmental state. As noted above, a developmental state in Africa does not have to have a one-to-one match with those in East Asia or Europe for that matter (see Chang, 2010). What is essential in assessing developmental states is the presence of the intention and resolve to pursue developmental goals.

Hijacked and Vilified African States

In the developmental state literature, there is general agreement that the promising features of developmental states in Africa, which begun to emerge during the first decade of independence, were abruptly disrupted by two crucial events in the course of the 1970s and the 1980s. The first set of events was the two (first and second) oil crises in 1973 and 1979. The second incident, which was precipitated by the first, was the introduction of SAPs in most African countries during the early 1980s. The effects of SAPs on African economies and societies at large have been distilled in a large literature from different perspectives, and it is not my intention here to restate this well-known topic (see Stein, 1992, 2004; World Bank, 1994; Mosley et al, 1995; Lancaster, 1997; Mkandawire and Soludo, 1999; Olukoshi, 2004). These two events, it can be argued, reversed all the gains made since independence in many aspects including industrialisation.

One important area where SAPs had a significant impact was the weakening of capacity in African states to such a point that by the 1990s they became only shadows of what they were prior to the debt crises of the 1980s. SAPs weakened capacity of African states in three critical ways. First, the policy-making space was completely taken over by the World Bank and the IMF officials (Mkandawire and Soludo, 1999; Soludo and Ogbu, 2004). This was done with a blatant disregard of these institutions' own country representatives. UNECA (2011), for example, argues that by surrendering the basic element of national sovereignty (making of national policy) to advisers and consultants from the Bank and the IMF, African states were severely weakened to the point that they are still struggling to recover from this today. If anything, the weakening of African states has continued over time, resulting in most states not being able to drive their own agenda for development. This is particularly true when it comes to devising and implementing credible industrial strategies.

The elusive nature of industrial development in African is a clear reminder of the weak state capacity in most of the countries on the continent. Even if many countries are now developing industrial policies and strategies, the capacity to implement these strategies consistently remains low. With low capacity to implement their own policies, the prospects for industrial development remain low in many countries. As alluded to earlier, successful industrialisation has only occurred in countries where the state exhibited high capacity not just to design industrial strategies, but to implement them in a consistent manner. Concrete examples of low capacity and incoherence in implementing industrial policies and strategies are presented in Chapter 10 where the ability of African states to provide secondary public goods, particularly, the IES, is discussed.

The second significant way in which African states were weakened by SAPs was through the striping of the public sector in a bid to manage what was then seen as a bloated public service. The downsizing of the public service in Africa was supported by the argument that public service institutions were overstaffed and needed to be rationalised to improve efficiency and productivity. But the down-sizing of states in Africa left public institutions with low capacity to the extent that most countries struggled even to implement the programmes outlined in the SAPs themselves. The irony of this has been referred to, in the literature, as the orthodox paradox.[7] On this point, Mkandawire (2001) makes an interesting observation that the spaces left by the purged African states were expected to be filled by the private sector, NGOs and community organisations under the tutelage of international donors. But it only took a few years to realise that the state could not be replaced in any meaningful way by other formations. For this reason, the World Bank and other multilateral bodies started to bring back the state into development discourse, this time, though the *good governance* agenda, after realising that nothing much could be done if states are weak and with little capacity.

In terms of industrialisation, the massive retreat of the state led to a situation where industrial activities, which had picked up momentum during the 1970s, begun to slow down such that by the end of the 1990s Africa was said to have de-industrialised, with little manufacturing capacity (Stein, 1992; Jalilian and Weiss, 2000). Current figures on manufacturing value added (MVA) as a percentage of total export and MVA per capita when compared to earlier periods confirm the injunction that Africa lost most of its industrial capacity during SAPs, and most countries are yet to recover to the levels reached during the 1970s (see chapters 3 and 6). The fact that manufacturing capacity has declined at a time when the role of the state in the economy is reduced to that of rolling out a "red carpet" for foreign investors is not mere coincidence. The current low industrial momentum is an indication of the importance of a highly capacitated state in driving industrial development.

The third way in which SAPs weakened African states was through the rigid focus on stabilisation, liberalisation and privatisation, as the only valid way of inducing economic growth. The rigidness of this strategy made it impossible for African states to address and respond to other challenges such as declining state capacity. Githinji and Adesida (2011) argue that because of this narrow fixation on stabilisation, most African states found the policy space for considering the broader mandate of the state constrained, such that it became difficult to coordinate activities in different sectors. Individual sectors were literarily taken over by interested donors, and each of them was pulling in different directions. In the case of industrial development, which requires a well-coordinated approach, the outcomes from the donor-led strategy are obvious. Up to the present, most African states' role in the economy has been reduced to that of creating a market-friendly environment, a situation which has significantly reduced the prospect of industrial expansion and economic diversification. Stabilisation of the macro-economic environment is an important dimension of any industrial policy, but by itself it cannot generate the momentum for industrial growth. The pre-occupation with macroeconomic stabilisation which characterised economic policy during the 1980s and 1990s did more harm to industrial growth in most African countries.

Rebuilding Developmental States in Africa

As noted earlier, in terms of pushing ahead with industrial development, limiting the role of the state to that of creating an enabling environment for the private sector is not going to stimulate industrial development to any significant level (see also Newman et al, 2016). A more proactive state-led strategy is needed to revive the industrial vitality which has subsided in most African states since the early 1980s. But, instead of adopting a radical developmental strategy through an aggressive industrial policy, what we have seen in Africa are states busy pushing each other, to a point of causing a stampede, just to grab the top spot on the World Bank's *Doing Business Index* ranking, as if that is all that matters most (see Page, 2015; Chitonge, 2017).

Thus, at the moment, most African states do not exhibit basic features of a developmental state as elaborated above. It is difficult to find states in Africa whose main pre-occupation is development. Ethiopia and Rwanda come close to being outstanding examples of developmental states in Africa, defined by a clear and focused developmental ideology to which the state resources and institutions are directed. In the last three years, the two countries have been in the media as examples of how African countries should do development. But we are yet to see the Ethiopian and Rwandese governments build capacity in its public institutions to be able to carry out the outlined development programmes. As noted in Chapter 10, the Rwandese government, while it has clearly identified the industrial development goals, has not built the necessary capacity in the institutions which are expected to drive this project. Developmental states, as we have seen above, prioritise the building of capacity in key public institutions. Overall, we see few states in Africa vigorously intervening in the economy in the interest of industrial development, and we do not see many African states building capacity to achieve the identified developmental gaols.

Nationalist versus Developmentalist Agenda

One of the explanations given for the failure of African states to construct developmental states is that from the beginning African states did not embrace a developmentalist ideology; they instead adopted nationalism as the main ideology. Ake (1981, 1996), for instance, has argued that the commitment to pursuing broader developmental goals was not strong in most African states from the dawn of independence, including those states whose leaders openly proclaimed socialism as their guiding philosophy. Mkandawire (2001) expressed a similar view, though he qualifies this by arguing that a developmentalist ideology, logically, should have been supported by the philosophy of nationalism. In other words, a developmentalist ideology constituted a practical way of realising nationalism. The distinction made between a nationalist and a developmentalist agenda remains a hotly debated issue, and there are questions whether the two ideologies constitute two separate agendas. Ake's (1981) main contention is that because of a strong commitment to the ideology of nationalism, most African countries failed to make the difference between the two, and as such, the developmentalist ideology was watered down by giving priority to the nation-building project.

However, the evidence from many countries suggests that in the first decade of independence, many African governments embraced development in the broader sense of improving the welfare of citizens by providing basic social services and infrastructure which had been generally neglected during colonial rule. If we look at the budgetary allocations in most NDPs, there is a clear indication that at least two-fifths of the resources in the development plans were allocated to social services, mainly education, health and public infrastructure. In Nigeria, for example, the total allocation to social services and public infrastructure in the 1st NDP amounted to 65.7 percent of the plan's budget (see Republic of Nigeria, 1962). In Tanzania, public infrastructure and social services accounted for 44.3 percent in the 1st NDP, while in Ghana the share of social services and public infrastructure was 54.9 percent in the seven-year development plan. In Kenya, social services were allocated 46.8 percent of the total budget in the 1st NDP, excluding public infrastructure. While the allocations reflected in the NDPs may not have materialised in terms of the actual resources invested in these sectors, they, in principle, indicate the importance attached to the development of social services, and the significant progress made in many countries during the first decade of independence bears witness to this.

The subsequent failure to construct developmental states in Africa is sometimes blamed on the proliferation of development models, suggesting that there was no consistent policy which African states were following (see UNECA, 2011). The infiltration of these models (nine different models are recognised to have influenced development policy in Africa between 1960 and 2010, see UNECA, 2011:82) meant that the development process was largely influenced by people and ideas from outside the continent. Outside influence has continued even today in such a way that there is a large policy latitude accorded to development partners—mostly donors. In more recent times, the development partners have identified and focused on regulatory reforms aimed at making it easy for private sector to open businesses or obtain export permits. But the "low hanging fruits" (see Page, 2015:12) of regulatory reform contribute little to creating capacity in the industry sector. Clearly this can't be a strategy for re-structuring Africa's current comparative advantage. A much more aggressive and radical approach by African states is needed to defy the current static comparative disadvantage and create dynamic competitive advantage. A more radical approach is required to disrupt the colonial economic logic and its accompanying structures which remains dominant in most countries.

Industrialisation and Developmental State

The elusive industrial growth in Africa has also been attributed to the fact that the state which should play an important role in industrialisation is itself a product of industrial development. According to this view, it is not surprising that most African states exhibit weak industrial capacity. For example, Rodrick (2015) has argued that the modern state is itself a product of industrial development, and that lack of industrial development negatively affects the basic qualities of a modern state, including democracy, accountability and the capacity to mobilise resources towards achieving developmental goals. Applying this view to African countries, it can be argued that since industrialisation in most African states has been elusive, this might explain why most of these states have failed to construct stronger institutional and administrative capacities.

It is easy here to get into a circular argument about whether industrialisation leads to the emergence of modern states or the other way around. While historical evidence suggests that industrialisation leads to the strengthening of state capacity and institutions, there is also evidence that strong states not only predate but create the foundation for industrial development (Polanyi, 1944). It is perhaps true that a bureaucratic state emerges from sustained industrial growth, and as such, a bureaucratic state is largely a product of industrial development. In the case of a developmental state it is clear that such a state develops first and drives the process of industrialisation and not the other way around. Of course, in the process of industrial development, the developmental state itself can be transformed by the forces generated from the growing industrial sector and its effect on the rest of the economy. As noted in Chapter 2, sustained economic growth transforms the broader society not just the economic structure of a country. In this sense, the fact that industrial development in Africa has been weak should be one of the reasons why African states must be more developmentally oriented to create conditions suitable for rapid industrial development.

Overall, states in Africa have a lot of work to do to create conditions in which rapid industrialisation becomes possible on the continent. This would require more than just formulating industrial policies and strategies. It would require adopting a more aggressive approach to over-turn the current configuration of comparative advantage which puts African states in a disadvantaged position. Accomplishing this task will not be possible by trying to copy what other countries have done in the past. Surely, Africa's industrial policy can learn from what countries in East Asia and other places have done, but it will be futile to try and copy their strategies, for the simple reason that African countries today are facing a different set of challenges regarding industrial development. There are opportunities for being later industrialisers just as there are huge penalties associated with coming from behind.

If there is one area where African states should focus on in a bid to create a conducive environment for industrial growth, it is around the provision of what I have referred to as *secondary public goods*. These are essentially enablers of industrial development. Unlike the traditional public goods such as education, roads, public security and maintaining law and order, the secondary public goods constitute a set of carefully selected interventions aimed at supporting industrialisation. In other words, industrialisation should be seen as an indirect public good, just as the provision of public education, health care, social security and public infrastructure is. Supporting local firms through the provision of secondary public goods requires an active industrial policy that recognises the contribution which industrial growth makes to the traditional public goods, and to the general welfare of people in a country. Because of the different contexts in which countries need to deliver secondary public goods, it is not possible *ex ante* to compile a list of what these goods should be. In some contexts, this may constitute tax reforms which seek to give an advantage to domestic producers. In other cases, it might be financial support for informal producers to promote their capacity to enter the formal sector and participate in competitive markets. The fundamental issue is the way the state perceives these support instruments. We come back to the issues of the secondary public goods in Chapter 10 where the basics of industrialisation in Africa are discussed.

Notes

1. Friedrich Hayek was opposed to central planning and the concentration of power and ownership of property in the state. He argued:

   > Our generation has forgotten that the system of private property is the most important guarantee of freedom. It is only because the control of the means of production is divided among many people acting independently that we as individuals can decide what to do with ourselves (Hayek, 2001 [1945]:33).

2. In his famous Book, *Capitalism and Freedom*, Milton Friedman (1962), argues that centralised governments are not only a threat to individual freedom but also inhibit individual creativity and innovative abilities. In his preface he thus argues, "The great advances of civilization, whether in architecture or painting, in science or literature, in industry or agriculture, have never come from centralized government" (Friedman, 1962:11).
3. Page (2014) who reviewed the PIACs in Africa argues that the idea came from the former IMF managing director, Horst Koehler, and the former World Bank president, James Wolfensohn, who imported the concept from Asian countries.
4. Chang (2010) notes that this is a narrow definition of a developmental state that was only relevant in the context of the East Asian countries between 1950 and 1980.
5. Service economies are economies in which the service sector becomes the dominant sector in terms of its contribution to output without having experienced significant levels of industrialisation (see Amirapu and Subramanian, 2015; Choudhury and Chatterjee, 2015; Rodrick, 2015).
6. Bates (1981:71–73) in his book gives some figures of the number of industries which were established during the 1960 and 1970s in countries such as Kenya, Ghana, Tanzania and Zambia. For example, he reports that in 1969 there were 431 manufacturing establishments in Zambia, 356 in Ghana.

7. The paradox is that African states were asked to implement SAPs which require a substantial capacity to carry out the plans, while at the same time, the public service was being retrenched rendering the state incapable of implementing the proposed programme. Interestingly, the World Bank (1994) in one of its reports blames the poor outcome of the SAPs on the lack of capacity among African governments to implement the programmes (see Callaghy &Ravenhill, 1993).

References

Ake, Claude (1981). *A Political Economy of Africa*. Lagos: Longman Nigeria.

Ake, C. (1996). *Democracy and Development in Africa*. Washington D.C.: Brookings Institute.

Amirapu, A., and Subramanian, A. (2015). *Manufacturing or Services? An Indian Illustration of a Development Dilemma*. Washington, DC: Centre for Global Development and Peterson Institute.

Amsden, A. H. (1989). *Asia's Next Giant: South Korea and Late Industrialization*. New York: Oxford University Press.

Amsden, A. H. (2001). *The Rise of 'The Rest': Challenges to the West from the Late-Industrialising Economies*. London/New York: Oxford University Press.

Bates, Robert (1981). *Markets and States in Tropical Africa: The Political Basis of Agricultural Policies*. Berkeley: University of California Press.

Berg, E. (1964). "Socialism and Economic Development in Tropical Africa." *The Quarterly Journal of Economics*, Vol. 78, No. 4. 549–573.

Callaghy, T. and Ravenhill, J. (1993). "How Hemmed in? Lessons and Prospects of Africa's Response to Decline," in T. Callaghy and J. Ravenhill (eds.), *Hemmed in? Responses to Africa's Economic Decline*. New York: Colombia University Press. Chapter 13.

Chabal, P. and Daloz, J-P. (1999). *Africa Works: Disorder as Political Instrument*. London: James Currey.

Chang, H. (2003). "Kicking Away the Ladder: The 'Real' History of Free Trade." Foreign Policy in Focus (FPIF) Special Report. Available at: www.personal.ceu.hu/corliss/CDST_Course_Site/Readings_old_2012_files/Ha-Joon%20Chang%20-%20Kicking%20Away%20the%20Ladder-The%20"Real"%20History%20of%20Free%20Trade.pdf. Accessed 21.03.2015.

Chang, H. (2010). "How to 'do' a Developmental State: Political, Organisational and Human Resource Requirement for the Developmental State," in O. Edigheji (ed.), *Constructing a Developmental State in South Africa*. Cape Town: HSRC Press. 82–96.

Chitonge, H. (2015). *Economic Growth and Development in Africa: Understanding Trends and Prospects*. New York/London: Routledge.

Chitonge, Horman (2017) "Capitalism in Africa: Mutating Capitalist Relations and Formations." Review of African Political Economy, DOI: 10.1080/03056244.2017.1372280.

Choudhury, P. and Chatterjee, B. (2015). "Inter-sectoral Linkage and Openness in India's Services Sector Growth." *Money and Finance* (November, 2015). 63–85.

Department of Trade and Industry (DTI, 2016). *Industrial Policy Action Plan (IPAP) 2016/17–2018/19*. Pretoria: DTI.

Edigheji, O. (2005). "A Democratic Developmental State in Africa? A Concept Paper" Centre for Policy Studies, Research Paper No.105. Available at: www.cps.org.az. Accessed 27.04.2009.

Evans, P. (1995). *Embedded Autonomy: States and Industrial Transformation*. Princeton: Princeton University Press.

Evans, P. (2010). "Constructing the 21st Century Developmental State: Potentialities and Pitfalls," in O. Edigheji (ed.), *Constructing a Developmental State in South Africa*. Cape Town: HSRC Press. 37–58.

Ewusi, K. (1981). *The Process of Industrialisation in Ghana*. Accra: Institute of Statistics, Social and Economic Research, University of Ghana.

Felipe, J., Mehta, A. and Rhee, C. (2017). "Manufacturing Matters…But It's the Jobs that Counts." Asian Development Bank Paper Series, No. 420.

Friedman, M. (1962). *Capitalism and Freedom*. Chicago: Chicago University Press.

Gilley, B. (2017). "The Case for Colonialism." *Third World Quarterly*, DOI: 10.1080/01436597.2017.1369037

Githinji, Mwangi and Adesida, Olugbenga (2011). "Industrialisation, Exports and the Developmental State in Africa. The Case for Transformation." Economics Department Working Paper Series, University of Massachusetts-Amherst.

Hayek, F. (2001 [1945]). *The Road to Serfdom*. London: Institute of Economic Affairs/Reader's Digest.

Herzberg, B. and Wright, A. (2006). "Competitiveness Partnerships: Building and Maintaining Public-Private Dialogue to Improve the Investment Climate." Working Paper Series No. 3683, Washington, DC: World Bank.

Hirschman, O. A. (1958). *The Strategy of Economic Development*. New Haven: Yale University Press.

Jalilian, H. and Weiss, J. (2000). "De-industrialisation in Africa: Myths or Crisis," in H. Jalilian, M. Tribe and J. Weiss (eds.), *Industrial Development and Policy in Africa: Issues of De-Industrialisation and Development Strategy*. Cheltenham: Edward Elgar. 137–176.

Johnson, C. (1982). *MITI and the Japanese Miracle: The Growth of Industrial Policy*. Stanford: Stanford University Press.

Johnson, C. (1999). "The Developmental State: Odyssey of a Concept," in M. Woo-Cumings (ed.), *The Developmental State*. Ithaca: Cornell University Press. 32–60.

Killick, T. (1983). "Development Planning in Africa: Experiences, Weaknesses and Prescriptions." *Development Policy Review*, Vol. 1. No. 2. 47–76.

Kim, E. M. (2010). "Limits of the Authoritarian Developmental State of South Korea," in O. Edigheji (ed.), *Constructing a Developmental State in South Africa*. Cape Town: HSRC Press. 97–125.

Lall, S. (2004). "Selective Industrial and Trade Policies in Developing Countries: Theoretical and Empirical Issues," in C. Soludo, O. Ogbu and H. Chang (eds.), *The Politics of Trade and Industrial Policy in Africa*. Trenton/Asmara: Africa World Press Inc. 75–110.

Lancaster, C. (1997). "The World Bank in Africa Since 1980s: The Politics of Structural Adjustment Lending," in D. Kapur, J. Lewis and R. Webb (eds.), *The World Bank: Its First Half Century*. Washington: The Brookings Institution. 161–194.

Lewis W.A. (1954). "Economic Development with Unlimited Supplies of Labour." *Manchester School*, Vol. 20. 139–91.

Lewis, A. (1984). "The State of Development Theory." *The American Economic Review*, Vol. 74, No. 1. 1–10.

List, F. (1909). *The National System of Political Economy* (trans. by Sampson S. Lloyd). London: Longmans, Green & Co.

Mamdani, M. (1996). *Citizen and Subject: Contemporary Africa and the Legacy of Late Colonialism*. Princeton: Princeton University Press.

Meier, G. (1984). "The Formative Years," in G. Meier and D. Seers (eds.), *Pioneers in Development*. New York/London: Oxford University Press. 3–26.

Meier, G. (2001). "Introduction: The Old Generation of Development Economists and the New," in G. M. Meier and J. Stiglitz (eds.), *Frontiers of Development Economics: The Future in Perspective*. New York: Oxford University Press. 13–49.

Mkandawire, T. and Soludo, C. (1999). *Our Continent, Our Future: African Perspectives on Structural Adjustment*. Dakar: CODESRIA.

Mkandawire, T. (2001). "Thinking About the Developmental States in Africa." *Cambridge Journal of Economics*, Vo.25, No.3. 289–313.

Mkandawire, T. (2010). "From Maladjusted States to Democratic Developmental States in Africa," in O. Edigheji (ed.), *Constructing a Developmental State in South Africa*. Cape Town: HSRC Press. 59–81.

Mosley, P., Subasat, T. and Weeks, J. (1995). "Assessing Adjustment in Africa." *World Development*, Vol. 23, No. 9. 1459–1473.

Naude, W. (2010). "New Challenges for Industrial Policy." United Nations University (UNU)/World Institute for Development Economic Research (WIDER), Working Paper No. 2010/107.

Newman, C., Page, J., Rand, J., Shimeles, A., Soderbom, M. and Tarp, F. (2016). *Made in Africa: Learning to Compete in Industry*. Washington, DC: Brooking Institute Press.

Nurkse, R. (1953). *Problems of Capital Formation in Underdeveloped Countries*. London: Basil Blackwell.

Olukoshi, A. (2004). "Democratisation, Gloabalisation and Effective Policy Making in Africa," in C. Soludo, O. Ogbu and H. Chang (eds.), *The Politics of Trade and Industrial Policy in Africa*. Trenton/Asmara: Africa World Press Inc. 43–73.

Onis, Z. (1991). "The Logic of the Developmental States." *Comparative Politics*, Vol. 24, No. 1. 109–126.

Oqubay, A. (2015). *Made in Africa: Industrial Policy in Ethiopia*. London: Oxford University Press.

Page, J. (2012). "Aid, Structural Change and the Private Sector in Africa." United Nations University (UNU)/World Institute for Development Economic Research (WIDER) Working Paper No.2012/21.

Page, J. (2014). "Industrial Policy in Practice: Africa's Presidential Investors' Advisory Councils." WIDER Working Paper No. 2014/117.

Page, J. (2015). "Structural Change and Africa's Poverty Puzzle," in L. Chandy, H. Kato and H. Kharas (eds.), *The Last Mile in Ending Extreme Poverty*. New York: Brooklyn Institute Press. 219–248.

Polanyi, K. (1944). *The Great Transformation: The Political and Economic Origins of our Times*. Boston: Beacon Press.

Prebisch, R. (1950). *The Economic Development of Latin America and Its Principle Problems*. New York: United Nations Economic Commission for Latin America and Caribbean.

Republic of Liberia (1967). *Four Year Plan for Social and Economic Development 1967–1970*. Monrovia: RoL.

Republic of Nigeria (1962). *National Development Plan: 1962–1968*. Lagos: Ministry of Economic Development.

Rodrick, Dani (2015). "Pre-mature Deindustrialisation." National Bureau of Economic Research (NBER) Working Paper 20935.

Rosenstein-Rodan, P. N. (1943). "Problems of Industrialisation of Eastern and South-Eastern Europe." *Economic Journal*, Vol. 53, No. 210/211. 202–211.

Sampath, P. (2014). "Industrial Development for Africa: Trade Technology and the Role of the State." *African Journal of Science, Technology, Innovation and Development*, Vol. 6, No. 5. 439–453.

Scitovsky, T. (1954). "Two Concepts of External Economies." *Journal of Political Economy*, Vol. 62, No. 2. 143–151.

Sewahel, W. (2019). "First AI Faculty Unveiled at Global Forum Meeting." *University Wide New, Africa Edition*, April 05, 2019. Available at https://www.universityworldnews.com/post.php?story=20190405064313832 accessed 09/04/2019

Singer, W. H. (1950). "The Distribution of Gains Between Investing and Borrowing Countries." American Economic Review, Vol. 40, No. 2. 473–485.

Singer, W. H. (1984). "The Terms of Trade Controversy and the Evolution of Soft Financing: Early Years in the UN," in G. Meier (ed.), *Pioneers in Development*. New York: World Bank. 273–301.

Singh, A. (1992). "The Actual Crisis of Economic Development in the 1980s: An Alternative Policy Perspective for the Future," in K. Amitava Dutt and P. Kenneth Jameson (eds.), *New Directions in Development Economics*. Aldershot: Edward Elgar. 81–116.

Smith, A. (2005 [1776]). *An Inquiry into the Nature and Causes of the Wealth of Nations*. Pennsylvania: Pennsylvania State University Electronic Classics Series.

Soludo, C. and Ogbu, O. (2004). "A Synthesis of Major Themes in the Political Economy of Trade and Industrialisation in Africa," in C. Soludo, O. Ogbu and H. Chang (eds.), *The Politics of Trade and Industrial Policy in Africa*. Trenton/Asmara: Africa World Press Inc. 1–42.

Stein, Howard (1994). "Theories of Institutions and Economic Reform in Africa." *World Development*, Vol. 22, No. 12. 1833–1849.

Stein, H. (2004). "The World Bank and the IMF in Africa: Strategy and Routine in the Generation of a Failed Agenda." Centre for Afro-American and African Studies (CAAS),

University of Michigan. Available at: http://www.macua.org/Howard_Stein.pdf. Accessed 29.04.2009.

Stiglitz, Joseph (1992). "Alternative Tactics and Strategies for Economic Development," in K. Amitava Dutt and P. Kenneth Jameson (eds.), *New Directions in Development Economics*. Aldershot: Edward Elgar. 57–80.

te Velde, W. D. (2013). "State-Business Relations and Industrial Policy: Current Policy and Research Debates." Growth Research Programme (GRP) working Paper, UN-University/World Institute for Development Economics Research (UNU-WIDER).

The Economist Intelligent Unit (EIU, 2018). *Who is Ready for the Coming Wave of Automation? The Automation Readiness Index*. London: EIU.

Trump, D. (2017). "Remarks by President Trump at the APEC CEO Summit." Da Nang, Vietnam: U.S Embassy and Consulate in Vietnam. Available at: https://www.whitehouse.gov/briefings-statements/remarks-president-trump-apec-ceo-summit-da-nang-vietnam/. Accessed 04.03.2018.

United Nations Economic Commission for Africa (UNECA, 2011). *Economic Report on Africa 2011: Governing Development in Africa*. Addis Ababa: UNECA.

United Nations Economic Commission for Africa (UNECA, 2015). *Report on Africa 2015: Industrialising Through Trade*. Addis Ababa: UNECA

United Nations Economic Commission for Africa (UNECA, 2016a). Transformative Industrial Policy for Africa. Addis Ababa: Economic Commission for Africa.

Wade, R. (1990). *Governing the Market: Economic Theory and the Role of Government in East Asian Industrialization*. Princeton: Princeton University Press.

World Bank (1993). *The East Asian Miracle: Economic Growth and Public Policy*. Oxford: Oxford University Press.

World Bank (1994). *Adjustment in Africa: Reforms, Results and the Road Ahead*. New York. IBRD/World Bank.

World Bank (2005). *Building Effective States, Forging Engaged Societies. Report of the World Bank Task Force on Capacity and Development in Africa*. Washington, DC: The World Bank.

World Bank (2011). "Africa's Future and the World Bank's Support to It." Available at www.worldbank.org/africastrategy. Accessed 12.02.2012.

· 8 ·

INDUSTRIALISATION AND THE AGRARIAN QUESTION IN AFRICA

Introduction: The Land Industrialisation Connection

There is now an extensive body of literature which points to a critical role played by agrarian reforms in the successful industrialisation of East Asian economies. Many analysts who have considered the role of agrarian change in industrial development often make an indirect connection between land and industrialisation (see Mundle, 1985; World Bank, 1993; Pingali, 1997; Kay, 2002; Feizhou and Camille, 2009). The connection made is through the role of agriculture in industrial development. Using the example of Taiwan, the World Bank report makes a stronger case for the role agrarian reforms played in the Taiwanese industrial transformation:

> [The land reform] program fostered social and political stability and increased agricultural production. Greater agricultural output provided raw materials for exports and earned foreign exchange to fund imports of machinery, equipment, and industrial raw materials. These in turn helped to make possible subsequent export-led rapid development (World Bank, 1993:131).

In political economy approaches, agrarian reforms are expected to play an important role in accelerating capital accumulation by extracting the surplus from the agriculture sector, which is used to finance the growth of the industrial sector. But capital accumulation is just one important contribution that agrarian reform can make to industrial development. In cases where agrarian reforms are accompanied by substantial productivity growth in the agricultural sector, a broader momentum that supports industrialisation is often created through the rising demand for manufactured products. We have already briefly touched on this view in Chapter 6 in the context of structural transformation. Several scholars have argued that a strong and dynamic agricultural sector has always provided a foundation for sustainable industrialisation (Nurkse, 1953; Lewis, 1954; Adelman, 1984). Although these scholars did not discuss the issue of land and agrarian reform specifically, few would contend the view that land and agrarian issues have a direct bearing on the performance of the agricultural sector in general, which in turn impact on industrial development.

However, the debates on industrialisation have often focused on agriculture production in a way that gives the impression that industrialisation has nothing to do with agrarian issues. Because of this, many scholars make an indirect link between land and industrialisation; land and agrarian issues are only discussed tangentially in the industrial growth literature. In the massive literature on land and agrarian reform, there are only a couple of papers which have treated the land question as an important aspect which impacts on industrial development.[1] There is of course a wealth of papers drawing from Marxian political economy which have examined agrarian transition through various routes and forms of accumulation in the course of capitalist development (see, e.g., Byres, 1974, 1986; Griffin et al (GKI), 2002; Bernstein, 2004). But most of these do not make a direct connection between land and industrial development.

This chapter highlights the link between land and agrarian transformation, and industrialisation via agriculture, focusing on the African experience. The chapter looks at the various ways in which land and agrarian dynamics directly impact on industrial development in Africa. The chapter draws examples from different parts of the world to illustrate the influence that land and agrarian issues can have on industrialisation. It is argued in this chapter that the failure to resolve the land and agrarian question(s) in Africa is part of what accounts for the elusive industrialisation on the continent. The chapter looks at the key dimensions of the land as well as the agrarian questions to illustrate how these impact on industrialisation in Africa.

The Land and Agrarian Questions in Africa

In 2011 an American student in one of my postgraduate courses was very excited to hear about the stories of large-scale land acquisitions (land grabs as they are popularly known) in Africa by foreign companies and nations, which dominated media and academic discourse in the aftermath of the 2008/09 '*Great Recession*'. The main reason why she was excited about the land grab news is that she was convinced that this was the beginning of what she termed an *agrarian revolution* in Africa. In her view, the purchasing of land in Africa by investment funds, sovereign wealth funds and international agri-business firms presented a huge development opportunity for Africa. Her main argument was that the current land tenure system in Africa (largely dominated by customary land systems) is holding back economic progress and the improvement of peoples' lives, especially in rural areas.

This America student was of course not the first one to make this argument; a number of scholars and commentators on economic growth and development challenges in Africa have advanced similar arguments, identifying the persistence of traditional land tenure systems as one of the major barriers to development in Africa. For those who have been working on land tenure issues in Africa, this argument should be a familiar one. For example, the World Bank (1975), in its first land policy document, argued that Africa's failure to develop could be attributed to the absence of what the policy document called the "*Landlord Elite.*" According to this view, the *landlord elite* which in other regions was crucial in facilitating the absorption of modern technology, thereby promoting agrarian transformation, has not emerged in Africa. The World Bank's main argument during the 1970s was that customary tenure rights were vague and as such fail to stimulate the development and growth of land markets in rural Africa in particular. Based on this view, the World Bank (1975) expressed concern particularly over communal tenure, arguing that under the customary tenure system, land tenure is insecure and this affects investments and productivity generally. The recommendation was that in cases "where land is communally owned…the Bank would encourage subdivision" of the communally owned land into individual ownership as the most effective way of securing land rights (World Bank, 1975:14).

Individualising land was anticipated to unlock investment flows and growth in productivity in the rural sector. The thinking at that time was that customary tenure held back the prospect of increasing productivity in traditional agriculture (which in most African countries still constitute the largest share of the rural sector), primarily because of the supposed tenure insecurity associated with the customary land tenure systems. But during the 1990s, the World Bank abandoned the policy of pushing for individualisation of customary land rights; it instead opted for other means of securing land tenure rights, including the recognition of customary tenure rights through some form of documentation, individually and collectively (see Deininger and Binswanger, 1999).

Although approaching the same issue from a different angle, Goran Hyden (1983, 1986) embraced a similar view arguing that the African peasantry because he or she still enjoys uninterrupted access to the means of production (land) is blocking the unleashing of productive forces to transform African economies and societies. Hyden's argument focused on the idea that because most people under customary land engage in subsistence production, they fail to generate surplus value which can be extracted to provide capital for industrial growth. In other words, subsistence production does not promote capital accumulation which is a pre-requisite for industrialisation, mainly because subsistence producers are only interested in producing enough to feed their families; they are not interested in generating a surplus. According to Hyden (1983), since the African peasant is not primarily interested in using land to generate a surplus, this state of affairs has stifled the creation of surplus value, and consequently constrained the process of accumulating capital needed for the transformation of African economies.

In this sense, Hyden (1983) is trying to explain the weak (or lack of) industrialisation in Africa as a consequence of the unresolved agrarian question in Africa. He explains this using the idea that the African peasantry is not "captured" by either capitalist relations of production or the state through socialised production. More recently, Cox and Negi (2010) made a similar argument that because most of the "independent producers" in Africa have not been separated from the means of production to force them to sell their labour as the only means of survival, capitalism has not yet unleashed its transformative power on the continent. When capitalist productive and transformative forces are unleashed on Africa, they will start by breaking the bond between land and the African peasant.

Approaching the same issue from a totally different point of view, Johnson (1972, 2011) has argued that the prevalence of customary forms of tenure on the African continent is a barrier to economic progress and structural transformation. Though Johnson (2011) does not argue for a complete separation of the independent producers (small producers on customary land) from their land, he argues that customary tenure blocks the realisation of Africa's economic potential. His main concern regarding customary tenure is that the rights are not clearly assigned and this introduces high transaction costs which create inefficiency. Efficiency according to this view would be improved when customary land is individualised to give people clearer and, therefore, secure rights.

It is for this reason that those who believe that customary land tenure system is a barrier to economic and social progress in Africa were celebrating as land grabs intensified on the continent after the 2008/2009 *Great Recession*. They were celebrating because they believed that as more land is grabbed by international investors, this would result in the crucial separation of the peasantry from the land. In other words, the land grabs were celebrated because they signalled the beginning of the end of the African peasantry (Anseeuw et al, 2011). But one has to pause and ask, to what extent is the African peasant the barrier to realising Africa's economic potential? Attributing Africa's failure to transform its economic structure and societies to the subsistence producers on customary land sounds more like blaming the victim (Kasfire, 1986; Cliffe, 1987). This debate leads us to the agrarian question in Africa.

The Agrarian Question in Africa

Although the different views on land tenure in Africa come from different perspectives and recommend different approaches, they converge on the view that the customary land tenure system hinders the efficient use of the critical resource—land, which in turn impacts on productivity and the broader development process. Low productivity in the agriculture sector, as we have seen in Chapter 6, impacts on economic structural transformation, including industrialisation. Therefore, though these views on land do not directly address issues of industrialisation, their assertions ultimately touch on industrial development as shown later in this chapter.

Critics have challenged these views, arguing that customary land tenure is not the main problem in Africa's failed structural transformation (see Okoth-Ogendo, 1989; Shipton and Goheen, 1992; Bassett, 1993; Peters, 1994; Place, 2009). But for those who see customary land as the main factor in explaining Africa's apparent failure to realise its economic potential, the inability to resolve the land and agrarian question is cited as a major factor that accounts for much of Africa's weak industrial and economic performance. The solution they propose is simply to "free" the large number of independent producers (small farmers or peasants) from the land, assuming that more efficient, perhaps capitalist producers, would take over. Analysts who favour this approach advocate for the individualisation or formalisation of customary land rights, arguing that this would unleash economic forces which would increase productivity and income across African economies.

The quest for raising productivity in the agricultural sector and the need to find a formula which ensures that land is distributed fairly among the different groups of users remain at the centre of the agrarian question in Africa today (Moyo, 2004; 2008). These two dimensions (raising productivity and fair allocation of land customary land) constitute the core of the agrarian question in Africa, though there have been claims that in fact the *classic agrarian question of capital* does not exist anymore, even in the poorer countries of the Global South, including Africa. It has been argued, for instance, that what we have instead is an *agrarian question of labour* (see Bernstein, 2004).[2] The debate about whether the agrarian question has been resolved, like the debate on whether customary tenure is secure or not, is highly polarised, despite the claim that "an ideological divide has narrowed and disappeared" (Deininger and Binswanger, 1999:248).

In the case of Africa, which is the focus here, one would struggle to find evidence to support the view that the agrarian question has been successfully resolved. Regardless of whether one is speaking about the agrarian question of capital or labour, analysis of the current agrarian structure and conditions of production affirms the idea that the agrarian question remains unresolved in most parts of the continent. Examples include the high levels of employment in agriculture (particularly semi-subsistence producers), low productivity levels, high sectoral productivity differentials (see Table 6.4) and the dominant feature of dualism which is a classic sign of the absence of agrarian transformation. Many African scholars who work on the continent support the view that the agrarian question has not yet been resolved on the continent, citing the persistent challenges of food insecurity and the unresolved land tenure issues in customary areas as evidence (see Berry, 1984; Mafeje, 2003; Moyo, 2004, 2008).[3]

If resolving the agrarian question entails increased production of surplus and the accumulation of capital through productivity growth in the subsistence agricultural sector, few analysts would contend the view that the agrarian question in Africa is yet to be resolved. As noted earlier, the question of how to improve productivity in the smallholder and subsistence agricultural sector in Africa (which constitutes the largest share of the sector) remains a central question which touches on issues of productive employment, underemployment, enclavity, poverty reduction, sustained economic growth, structural transformation and industrial development (Chapter 6). It is indeed a question at the heart of the condition of underdevelopment on the continent. If the agrarian question was totally resolved, we would be seeing a different economic trajectory as well as social conditions on the continent.

The Land Question in Africa

Within the African agrarian question debates, some scholars have identified a set of issues which they separately refer to as the land question. Debates around the land question in Africa, as a separate set of issues, are framed around the different land dynamics between the former settler and non-settler colonies. Mafeje (2003), for example, argues that outside of the former settler colonies of South Africa, Algeria, Kenya, Zimbabwe, Namibia, and to a certain extent Swaziland, there is no land question. Mafeje (2003) goes further to argue that this is why most African governments did not see any urgency in formulating land reform policies; only agricultural policies were formulated to try and stimulate growth in agriculture production. To support the view that the land question in Africa does not exist outside of the former settler colonies, Mafeje (2003) cites the fact that 90 percent of the population in former non-settler colonies access land through customary tenure where everyone is guaranteed access to a piece of land by virtue of being a member of a community.

Several surveys from different sub-Saharan African countries have shown that more than 90 percent of the land rights enjoyed by African cultivators and pastoralists are generated through customary tenure (UNECA, 2005). This applies even to those cases where demographic pressure has reached critical proportions, for example, Rwanda, Burundi, Malawi and Togo.

> Membership in a given lineage or clan is still the major criterion for allocation of land. Recognition of certain clan domains makes it easy for lineages to maintain a steady pool of land and to control any influx of strangers, i.e., non-kinsmen. Likewise, the corporate land rights that lineage members have in common guard against alienation of land to outsiders. However, this does not mean that there is no exchange of land across lineage boundaries, but that a strong belief in the inalienability of land or in reversionary rights still persists. In the past this problem had been circumvented by loaning use of the land to needy strangers in exchange for an agreed price or portion of the produce, which is not tantamount to sale of land. This gave rise to the well-known phenomenon of migrant farmers in West Africa and in southern Uganda (Mafeje, 2003:4).

The point Mafeje (2003) is driving at is that access to land is not a central question where everyone has guaranteed rights in land, even in cases where land shortages, due to population pressure, are beginning to emerge. In other words, the land question does not arise in a context where the tenure system guarantees access for every member of the community, a feature which, according to Mafeje, still defines customary land tenure system.

In the paper cited above, Mafeje is responding to Mamdani's (1996) view that if the system is lineage-based, then it leads to the exclusion and discrimination of immigrants or those who do not belong to the lineage or ethnic group. Such a situation according to Mafeje is prevented by allowing outsiders to rent or borrow land from members of the lineage. In this sense, the system takes care of the land needs of everyone including strangers in such a way that there is no need for intrusive state actions, seeking to redistribute land. In Mafeje's (2003) view, while the customary tenure system is still functional in the former non-settler colonies, in the former settler colonies, where significant dispossession of the land of indigenous peoples occurred, the land question exists, precisely because the system resulted in highly unequal distribution of land, requiring the state to intervene to address the skewed land distribution patterns.

But Mafeje's view that the land question exists only in former settler colonies has been challenged as a narrow conception of the land question (see Moyo, 2008). Sam Moyo, for instance, has argued that,

> To assume that a land question in Africa can only arise out of a particular generic social formation, such as feudal and semi feudal tributary systems of land inequities or widespread settler colonial land expropriation, is to miss the salience of growing land concentration and inequality, and struggles to regain control over land (Moyo, 2004:1).

Critics argue that a broader conceptualisation of the land question should go beyond issues of access to land. The land question should include other dimensions such as gender disparities, tenure insecurity, inequality of access to and use of land along ethnic and class lines, as well as the question of citizenship in the current constitutional dispensation where people are free to settle in any part of the country they so wish, without being subjected to discrimination on the basis of ethnic ties. Apart from that, the validity of Mafeje's (2003) position that the customary land system guarantees access to land for every member of the community should be critically assessed on the basis of the evidence of the growing phenomenon of privatising customary land as land grabs become rampant across the continent. The growing phenomenon of land grabbing which takes different forms has led to increased contestation over land in most communities, especially those close to developed infrastructure (see Chitonge et al, 2017). This in a fundamental way has become a core component of the land question in Africa.

If the key element of the land question in Africa is about inequality and injustice in the way land is distributed, accessed, owned, controlled and used, then the land question cannot be restricted to the former settler colonies only. The view that the land question does not exist outside of the former settler colonies would be correct if we assume that customary land tenure system dispenses justice to every member of the community when it comes to accessing land. But that position is hard to defend in the current context where some of the traditional authorities who control customary land are alienating large tracts of land to non-residents including foreign investors, often at the expense of the poorer members of the community (Cotula et al, 2009).[4] Therefore, in as much as one would agree with Mafeje (2003) that there are different land dynamics between the former settler and non-settler colonies in Africa, the central features of the land question are evident in both, and a correct formulation of the land question cannot ignore the broader issues such as the gendered nature of access to and use of land in customary areas across Africa (Whitehead and Tsikata, 2003), the growing concentration of land ownership and the ensuing struggles over land (Moyo, 2010).

An adequate formulation of the land question should therefore be broadened to include concerns around the need to decolonise, not just the structure of land ownership (which has been the pre-occupation of the debates on the land question in Africa), but also the Eurocentric conception of land, which permeates Africa's land management and administrative systems.

The Land Question in Africa: A Legacy of Colonialism

Broadly, the land question in Africa can be framed as a by-product of colonialism, on one hand, and the failure of the post-independent African states to implement radical land reforms which would effectively address colonial legacies around land distribution, administration and conception, on the other. From this perspective, the land and agrarian transformation issues are also a concrete reminder of an incomplete decolonial project on the continent (see Chitonge, 2018). Mafeje (2003) is probably right in asserting that what we have seen so far in most African countries amounts to tinkering with the colonial social engineering around land. The land question, therefore, constitutes an important component of the unresolved agrarian question. It is part of the big failure to fully reboot the colonial system to release productive forces which can play significant roles in building industrial capacity. As Moyo (2010) observes, the piecemeal land reforms attempted so far have not resulted in inducing structural transformation through an aggressive accumulation plan.

In its broader formulation, the land question in Africa can be conceptualised in terms of inequality of ownership, access to and control over land. For instance, it has been argued that the land question and persistent rural poverty in Africa are fundamentally issues of social justice and equity (Moyo, 2004). Thus, the land question in Africa today requires a broader conceptual lens to capture the emerging trends including the need to unseat the deeply embedded European conception of land.

If the land question refers to the issues around access to, use, control and ownership of land, then there is a strong connection between the land and agrarian question in the sense that issues of access to, use and control over land impact on issues of how production is organised on the land. Evidently, the land question raises different, but related, sets of issues to the broader challenges related to agrarian transition. Both are connected to and influence industrial development through the mechanisms which promote or hinder diversification and structural change in African societies and economies. But before discussing the salient land and agrarian issues related to industrialisation in Africa today, it is essential to lay out the framework through which this relationship should be analysed.

Agrarian Transformation and Industrial Development

The link between agrarian transformation and industrial development, as noted above, is often indirectly made via agriculture. What has been extensively discussed in the agrarian political economy literature is the role of agrarian change in economic development in general, particularly the development of capitalism (see Byres, 1986; Bernstein, 2004; Moyo, 2008). One of the few analyses that have directly connected agrarian change to industrialisation is

Mundle's (1985) model of agrarian induced industrialisation. Kay's (2002) comparative study of East Asia and Latin America is another example of the few studies which have made a direct connection between agrarian transformation and industrial development. Although both did not specifically analyse the African conditions, their clear articulation of the connection can illuminate some of the issues specific to the African context. Mundle's (1985) analysis combines several perspectives, drawing insights from Keynes (the concept of aggregate demand); Adam Smith (the size of the Market); Joseph Schumpeter (the concept of entrepreneurial profits); Karl Marx (the concept of surplus value) and Arthur Lewis (the idea of relocating labour from traditional to the modern sector).

Organisation of Production and Agrarian Transformation

In Mundle's (1985) model of industrial development, the starting point is the idea that the way production is organised in the agriculture sector not only impacts industrial development, but determines the pace of industrialisation. The way agrarian production is organised in an economy constitutes the heart of the agrarian question, especially at the early stages of economic development. Because of its centrality, it is essential to grasp the role of agrarian change in industrial development. To illustrate that there are different ways of organising production in the agrarian sector, Mundle (1985) proposes three options, distinguished largely by who organises production, who does the actual production, and who appropriates the surplus. In one case, which he refers to as "*Type A*," production is organised by the *surplus producer*, while "gains in productivity" are appropriated by what he calls the "*surplus appropriator*." In *Type B* the *surplus appropriator* organises *production*, and the same person *appropriates* gains in productivity. In *Type C*, the surplus producers organises production, and at the same time appropriates the gains in productivity; here there is no expropriation of surplus value involved, the producer retains whatever surplus is generated in the production process.

While Mundle (1985) argues that these three are the only possible ways of organising agrarian production, it must be noted that there are other agrarian arrangements apart from the three outlined above. For example, there are many instances where the surplus appropriator is not directly involved in the actual production; he or she just receives payment for using his/her land, even in cases where the surplus producer organises production. There are other instances where surplus value is appropriated at two levels: at the level of the capitalist producer and at the level of the landowner, who leases out land to the capitalist farmer. In such an arrangement, although the producer of surplus is directly connected to the immediate appropriation, his surplus is diverted to the second layer of appropriator. In such situations, the surplus value is split into profit for the capitalist farmer and rent for the landowner. In today's situation where finance capital has infiltrated into agriculture production and assets, the agrarian framework is much more complicated than the simplified model which Mundle proposed.

Similarly, while Mundle (1985) asserts that the producers of surplus can either be wage labourers or peasants, there are arrangements in which the production of surplus is not restricted to the wage labourer or peasants, depending on how one defines the terms *peasant* and *surplus*. Surplus, especially used in the sense that he is using it as gains in productivity, can be generated by producers other than *wage labourers* and *peasants*. For example, cases of share cropping and labour tenancy may not accurately fit in the wage labour or peasant categories. In the African context, the situation can be even more complicated if land is borrowed without paying rent, as in the case of immigrants being given land in the community where they settle.

According to Mundle (1985) a typical example of Type A is the "landlord–peasant" arrangement, which dominated the feudal system, while Type B is a typical example of capitalist farming, where the capitalist farmer organises production but also appropriates the surplus. Type C is thought to be similar to Type A in that it involves the landlord–peasant relationship, only that in the former the "peasantry is cohesive and well-organised" to resist the appropriation of surplus. Type C is the closest arrangement that relates to the larger African context, with the big difference being that African producers, in a fundamental way, do not relate to anyone as the landlord. We come back to this point later in the chapter.

Preconditions for Successful Agrarian Transition

In the agrarian structure sketched above, it is important to note that controlling the means of production (land) determines not only how the surplus is handled, but also the rate of productivity and the size of the surplus produced. In capitalist farming systems (Type B), the surplus can be split into paying for rent (if the land is rented in), and net surplus kept for the capitalist farmer as profit. In cases where the capitalist farmer owns the land (as in the case of the freehold tenure system) he or she keeps the entire surplus generated. In such a situation, the process of accumulation is said to be faster and more definitive, since the surplus accrues to one class, and most importantly, it augments production capacity, which can increase productivity. In this model, the faster the accumulation of capital, the quicker is the process of industrial growth.

It is interesting to note that Mundle (1985), following Lewis (1954), recommends *Type B* arrangement as the best agrarian arrangement , which "sooner or later establishes the necessary condition for successful transition." The reason given for this is that the capitalist farmer has both the "means and the incentive to introduce innovation" which leads to growth in productivity. In other words, the momentum for transformation in capitalist agrarian arrangements is the ability to accumulate and re-invest capital, which leads to expanded production, and further enlargement of surplus production. In the case of *Type A*, where the peasant has no control over land, Mundle (1985:76) argues the surplus is entirely appropriated by the landlord and because of this, there is no "incentive to experiment with new ideas or introduce innovations to raise productivity," and as a consequence, this type of agrarian arrangement fails to establish the necessary condition for successful agrarian transformation.

In Mundle's (1985) model, it is assumed that when peasants are in control of the land there is no incentive to innovate and increase productivity. This sounds like familiar territory: communal ownership of land does not incentivise land user to invest, adopt new technology or try new methods of farming to raise productivity (see World Bank, 1975). In the case of *Type* C where the peasantry has managed to secure some level of independency from those who control the means of production (which might include the state, monarch or religious authorities in earlier days), Mundle (1985) argues that they have the incentive to try new things and innovate and therefore may establish the necessary precondition for successful transition, but their incentive is low because their previous surplus was appropriated before, leaving them with little capital to invest in mechanical innovation which is crucial to raising productivity.

What If There Are No Landlords?

While the model outlined above may capture the essence of the agrarian transition in Europe, it is important to note that applying this model to the African context, and perhaps other regions outside of Europe, may encounter several difficulties as is always the case when a model of agrarian transition, based on specific historical and material conditions, is transferred to a different context (see Mafeje, 2003). In Mundle's (1985) model, it is apparent that the characterisation of land relations or the way production is organised does not fit the African conditions where peasant–landlord relations never materialised in any substantial way, even today (see World Bank, 1975; Moyo, 2008). Although there is a suggestion made in the literature to attribute the role of landlord to traditional authorities (particularly chiefs and village heads), there is wide agreement among scholars that this is a misconception introduced through colonial machination, which is not supported by evidence of indigenous land relations in many African communities (see Colson, 1971; Okoth-Ogendo, 1989; Bassett, 1993; Mamdani, 1996; Agbosu, 2000; UNECA, 2005; Akuffo, 2009). Therefore in conceptualising the way agrarian production is organised, one must pay attention to the different land relations around which influence how production is structured.

In the African context, despite the several attempts to reform land relations, customary land relations have proved to be resilient yet flexible to changing conditions. All the three types of agrarian systems elaborated above fail to capture the dominant land relations in Africa's rural and peri-urban communities. Although there are capitalist forms of agriculture which are spreading in many African countries outside of the former settler colonies, the dominant land relations are characterised by customary land relations which do not constitute the landlord–peasant or tenant relations (see Mafeje, 2003). As elaborated later, producers under customary land tenure are not remitting a surplus to any landlord in any direct form. While it has been observed that most of the peasant farmers residing on customary land do not produce any significant surplus (Hyden, 1986), even in cases where they do, they do not remit any surplus through the landlord–peasant structure. So, when describing the transition mechanism one has to take into account the unique situation in which most independent producers in Africa operate.

Diverse Agrarian Paths

For some analysts (e.g., Cox and Negi, 2010), the very fact that Africa still has a large proportion of independent producers, with "free" access to and control of the means of production (land), is a reflection of failed agrarian transition, which, in turn, has affected economic structural transformation and industrialisation. According to this view, when compared with other regions, Africa still has the largest share of "independent producers" with access to and control over land. The weakness of the "failed transition thesis" is that it operates on the assumption that there is a single path to agrarian transformation (and economic development), which every region or country has to go through.

But historical evidence suggests that there are actually different paths to agrarian transition, such that we can talk about the *English Path*, the *Prussian path*, the *French Path*, the *American (US) Path*, the *Russian Path* etc, (see Byres, 1986). Given the unique material conditions and social formation in Africa, there is no justification to support the view that Africa's agrarian transition should look exactly like anything we have seen before. This was the grandiose fallacy of the modernisation theory which any credible analysis of how society changes over time will not struggle to expose. While it is important to understand other agrarian transition paths, to learn from them, it is crucial to be able to say how they differ from other paths.

From Agrarian to Industrial Transformation

When using Mundle's (1985) model of agrarian transition and how this shapes industrial development, it is important to note that he was attempting to illustrate a general mechanism through which agrarian transitions influence or connect to industrialisation. He describes the mechanism that connects agrarian transformation to industrialisation by means of what he calls the "double dependence" of industry on agriculture in a transitioning economy. By double dependence he is referring to the backward and forward inter-sectoral linkages between agriculture and industry. According to this view, in the earlier stages of economic transformation, where industrialisation is still in its formative stages, industry relies heavily on agriculture for both intermediate good used in the manufacturing production processes (which at the early stages is mainly dominated by food and agricultural commodity processing), as well as the market for its products (see Adelman, 1984). It is easy to grasp the forward link from agriculture to industry, but the backward linkages from industry to agriculture may not be so obvious.

To explain the dynamic of double dependence of industry on agriculture, Mundle (1985) thinks of the industrial sector, particularly the manufacturing sector, as an open economy which imports from as well as exports to the agriculture sector. What the manufacturing sector exports to the agricultural sector is constrained mainly by the size of the market in the agriculture sector, which in turn depends on the levels of income. If one assumes that the price effects are neutral, and income in agriculture rises, even if population in the short term remains constant, the demand for (mainly) consumer manufactured goods would raise as disposable income increases, thereby increasing aggregate demand for manufactured goods. Under these conditions, the manufacturing sector can export more goods to the agricultural sector. If supply of capital to the manufacturing sector is steady, the sector can expand its production in proportion to the size of the market, which is largely determined by both the productivity of labour and population in the agriculture sector. An important assumption which Mundle's model makes in this case is that the size of the market is determined by the level of income in the agricultural sector. In other words, the size of market in the agriculture sector is a binding constraint on the manufacturing sector. As such, the capacity for the manufacturing sector to expand depends on the income levels or productivity as well as population growth in the agricultural sector.

> As per capita income rises, the surplus income available for expenditure on manufactured items after meeting subsistence (food) requirement will rise. Since per capita income reflects the productivity of labour in the sector, we may say that the growth of the export market for manufactures depends on the rates of growth of population and productivity in agriculture (Mundle, 1985:58).

The issue of population growth is important in the model since the size of the market cannot grow faster to induce growth in the demand for manufactures in cases where the size of the population is small, even if income rises. There is also an assumption in the model that the inter-sectoral terms of trade between agriculture and industry do not shift in such a way that aggregate demand in both sectors remain the same. If the relative prices of the goods exchanged between the two sectors shift in either direction, it can have a different dynamic in terms of the size of the market. But because the model is assumed to be operating in a closed economy where the manufacturing sector is not exporting to external economies, the terms of trade and the size of the market are pretty much determined by the productivity and population growth in the agriculture sector. Mundle's (1985) argument for this is that since the manufacturing sector in transition economies is dominated by the production of consumer goods, mainly processed foods, it is plausible to assume that manufacturing firms produce only for the domestic market, which is largely the case in Africa as we have seen above. The key point that he is driving at is that the "pace for industrialisation is set by developments in agriculture since it is these developments which govern the growth of the market for the manufacturing industry" (Mundle, 1985:63). The developments in agriculture, particularly productivity and population growth, are in turn determined by the way production is organised as explained earlier. Ultimately, "an agrarian revolution is a necessary pre-condition for sustained industrialisation" (ibid, 77). Through this model, Mundle makes a direct link between the land and agrarian question and industrial development.

Timing of Agrarian Transformation

Kay (2002) advances a similar view in his comparative analysis of industrial development in Latin America and East Asia, arguing that the latter's industrial development performed far much better than the former, mainly due to the timing of agrarian reforms. Although Latin America had much bigger and advanced industrial capacity in the 1960s when East Asia started to industrialise, East Asian economies overtook Latin America in terms of spearheading industrialisation because they introduced agrarian reforms way before industrial development became a dominant sector in the economy (ibid). In the case of Latin America, agrarian reforms were only introduced after the industrialisation process was well under way. Commenting specifically on the Brazilian experience, Navaro (2009) observes that while agrarian reforms in Brazil began during the 1950s, the 1964 military takeover disrupted the implementation of the reforms until 1988, when new reforms were formulated, and implemented starting from the mid-1990s. He argues that agrarian reforms implemented in Brazil during the 1990s were envisioned to boost industrial capacity and competitiveness. However, Kay's (2002) main argument is that the timing of agrarian reforms is a central factor which accounts for the difference observed between East Asia and Latin America. In other words, the Latin American industrial strategy had a weak foundation since, according to Kay (2002), the industrial sector was not supported by a solid agrarian base. In Kay's argument, like Mundle's (1985), agriculture is the intervening variable, and the link to the land question is unambiguous. Both analysts see the land and agrarian question as pivotal to industrial development.

Agrarian Change and Agriculture-Led Industrialisation

The view that agrarian transformation is key to industrial development is central to the agriculture demand-led industrialisation (ADLI) strategy. The ADLI model makes a connection between land and industrialisation, albeit in an indirect way.[5] In his model, Adelman (1984) explores dynamics of industrialisation induced by the rise of internal demand for manufactured consumer goods, primarily by the agriculture producers who during the early stages of the development process constitute the largest section of society. When income among agriculture producers rises, it acts as an engine for industrial development and structural transformation through the growth in demand for manufactures. Adelman (1984) illustrates how rising productivity in agriculture sets in motion two fundamental forces of structural transformation. The first is the rise in income within the agricultural sector, either by more farmers receiving higher income for their produce or by the stabilising effect of increased agriculture production on general prices in the economy. The second dynamic, which follows from the first, is that as agricultural income rises, it creates demand for non-agricultural products both consumer and intermediate goods used in agricultural production, which come from the industrial (mainly manufacturing) sector.

The increasing demand for manufactured goods and services, as a result of the rising income among workers and famers in the agricultural sector, generates a momentum which induces increased production in the industrial and service sectors to meet the growing demand. This model draws its inspiration from the theory of inter-sectoral linkages which is discussed in Chapter 6.

In this sense, the ADLI model is built around strong linkage between agriculture and industrial sectors.

> That agriculture can have important linkage effects with manufacturing has been recognised for a long time. Most text book descriptions of the role of agriculture in economic development stress four functions of agriculture; these are provision of surplus for investment in manufacturing, a source of labour, a source of food and a source of demand linkages (Adelman, 1984:939).

At the initial stage of the transformation process, the agricultural sector leads the process of structural change by creating demand that stimulates growth in the industrial sector. As the linkages between the agricultural and industrial sector deepen, the industrial sector expands and diversifies, initially to meet the growing domestic demand, and after the domestic demand is exhausted, the sector then develops the capability to tap into the export market. In this sense, the ADLI model sees agriculture and industrial sectors as complementary sectors, which re-enforce each other as they grow. But the emphasis is on agricultural productivity growth:

> ... the ADLI strategy would stress the raising of agricultural productivity, especially that of medium-scale farmers, as a means of achieving industrialisation. It would accomplish the industrialisation goal by expanding internal demand for intermediate and consumer goods produced by domestic industry (ibid).

Based on this analysis, Adelman (1984) argues that sustained industrialisation through an export-led strategy is not a viable approach for late industrialisers because of the difficulties of breaking into the highly competitive export markets. Although he sees the growth of internal demand from the agriculture sector as key to industrialisation, he does not extend his analysis to issues of land and agrarian transition as Mundle (1985) does. He however observes, in passing, that the ADLI strategy may not yield the expected results if the land tenure issues are not addressed adequately (Adelman, 1984).

The other difference in Adelman's model is that the ADLI model would only be a viable strategy for industrial development in economies with large domestic demand, with a substantially diversified industrial base, which has adequate capacity to respond to growth in demand for a variety of goods. As such, the ADLI strategy works well in countries with large domestic markets, that is, countries with a large population, which in the case of Africa applies to a few countries such as Egypt, Ethiopia, Algeria, DRC, Nigeria, Tanzania, South Africa, Sudan, Uganda and Kenya. For the DRC and Uganda, the ADLI strategy may not be appropriate since the industrial capacity is quite low, and therefore the ability to respond to rapid growth in demand for consumer goods may be weak. In this sense, the ADLI strategy might be of limited application to many countries in Africa where the domestic markets are small and the industrial base is quite narrow as shown in Chapter 3.

However, Adelman (1984) makes two important caveats which are relevant to African countries. First, he prefers small-scale to large-scale farmers because they have: a) "large linkage effect" with other local industries; b) they have "large marginal propensity to consume" with a larger share of their consumption devoted to locally produced textile, clothing, footwear and simple consumer goods such as radios, bicycles, etc.; and c) they also "tend to invest heavily in building human capital, devoting a large share of their incremental income on education, thereby laying the foundations for increasing future productivity of both industry and agriculture" (Adelman, 1984:945).

Like Mundle's model, the emphasis in the ADLI model is on the level of income in the agriculture sector, which influences the demand for manufactured products in the early stages of industrialisation. This point is emphasised in Johnson and Mellor (1961) who firmly assert that the rising net income of the farming population acts as a stimulant for industrial development since this enlarges the market for manufactured goods. In other words, the key to sustainable industrial development is increasing productivity in the broader agriculture sector which in turn raises income for majority of the people in the sector. The low productivity in the agriculture sector which is prevalent in most African countries, particularly in the small/subsistence sector (see Chapter 6), has long been identified as a constraint which accounts for the elusiveness of industrialisation on the continent (UNECA, 2015). For a long time now, there have been suggestions to improve the productivity in the agriculture sector as a means of igniting economy-wide sustained growth. But raising productivity in the agricultural sector has proved to be an insurmountable challenge in many African countries, and this has continued from the time of independence (Uchendu, 1970). To a large extent, this constitutes the agrarian question in Africa.

The African Agrarian Transformation Challenge

The million dollar question in Africa is, if agriculture is so crucial to industrial development, then how does one raise productivity in the sector? There have been several suggestions made on how to achieve sustained productivity growth in the agricultural sector, including the use of modern methods of farming, the provision of extension services, the extension of basic infrastructure to rural areas, the provision of social services and a whole suit of strategies which during the 1970s were packaged as *rural development* (see Chapter 5). Johnson and Mellor (1961) recommended that the first step is to identify the key factors which constrain productivity growth in the agricultural sector and then devise interventions to address them. One of the factors they emphasised was the provision of complementary inputs:

> The low productivity of farm labour, land and other resources in the agricultural sector is largely due to the lack of certain complementary inputs of a technical, educational, and institutional nature. Under these circumstances a crucial requirement for devising an appropriate agricultural development program is to identify these complementary inputs, determine in what proportions they should be combined, and

establish priorities among programs designed to increase their availability (Johnson and Mellor, 1961:582).

It goes without saying that a suite of complementary inputs will vary from one context and time to another. But the fundamental point is to be able to diagnose the causes of low productivity properly by carefully considering the local conditions in which agriculture production is taking place. For this diagnostic to have credibility, it should be carried out in constant consultation with the farmers, especially those operating at the small-scale or subsistence level. What this means is that providing a set of complementary services put together in Washington D.C. or Sao Paulo, for that matter, is likely to have little impact in addressing the specific productivity growth constraints in the sector.

The set of interventions must be context specific, attacking the problem at its core, targeting the basic issues first. The sequencing of the productivity-enhancing interventions is critical since not all the challenges can be addressed at the same time. There have been suggestions that such interventions be phased in, starting with issues that create the precondition for agriculture growth, followed by interventions that deal with improving efficiency and labour-saving techniques(ibid).

Land Tenure, Productivity and Growth in Africa

Debates on how to increase productivity in the agricultural sector in Africa often boil down to issues of land tenure, an issue which is often framed as a constraint rather than an opportunity. As such, prescriptions for improving productivity in the agriculture sector have often included land tenure reform as a crucial factor. Policy recommendations for land tenure reform are supported by the argument that changing land tenure from communal to individual is likely to provide stronger incentives for investment, efficient use of the land, which can contribute to raising productivity in the agriculture sector. For example, Jonson and Mellor (1961:582) argued that, "Improvements in land tenure are likely to be the most essential requirement in Phase I since an unfavourable tenure situation may stifle the incentive for change even though the potential exists for large increases in output."

Examples from East Asian countries which achieved rapid industrialisation are often lined-up to support the idea that tenure reforms are the bedrock for agrarian transformation and, later on, industrial growth. Land tenure reform, particularly, the securing of land rights in rural areas, is often cited as one of the key factors that contributed to rapid industrial development in most countries in East Asia (see World Bank, 1975, 1993; Kay, 2002; UNECA, 2005; Moyo, 2010). Land reform in this view is seen as a means to create conditions for sustained industrial and economic development by improving productivity and efficiency in agriculture. Often in the discussion on agriculture development and land reform, there is a strong assumption that the state is willing and, most importantly, has the capacity to implement the programmes aimed at raising productivity in agriculture (see Platteau, 1996). But institutional capacity issues and the political dimensions of land reform programmes are often ignored in the design of interventions whether by donors or local technocrats. Consequently, the impact of these interventions over the years has been minimal, to say the least.

As noted in Chapter 6, despite several decades of trying to prop up productivity in the agriculture sector in Africa, through various programmes, the sector has remained at the bottom of the productivity ranking, with agriculture productivity being lowest among all the developing regions of the world, and it is declining (see Table 6.2). Griffin et al (2002) argue that in Africa where customary land is still prevalent, the push for individualising land tenure rights was supported by the view that communal tenure rights lead to inefficient use of land, which in turn affect productivity in the agriculture sector. As argued here, the evidence to support this view has remained largely weak, especially in Africa.

Is Customary Tenure the Problem?

The question of whether tenure issues affect productivity or not has been extensively debated in the literature on economic growth and development in Africa. The outcome of this debate remains inconclusive, whether one takes an empirical approach testing the hypothesis using various quantitative technique or considering historical and more anthropological evidence. As a result, there have been extended debates about whether the problem of low productivity in agriculture can be attributed to the fact that the larger portions of land on the continent are still under customary tenure.

While there is acknowledgement that there are other factors such as the failure to provide complementary support to small-scale farmers using land under customary tenure, the impact of customary land tenure features prominently as one of the factors that account for low productivity in the agricultural sector. As mentioned above, the prevalence of customary land tenure on the continent (some estimates suggest that up to 90 percent of land in Africa is under customary tenure, see Mafeje, 2003; UNECA, 2005) is often interpreted as a sign of failed or delayed agrarian transformation. This conclusion implies that there has been a failure to sufficiently introduce new technology to revolutionise production in Africa. This, in turn, is singularly cited as the main factor which accounts for the current low productivity in agriculture, affecting industrialisation and structural transformation.

The Customary Land Tenure and Productivity Debate

Arguments about the role of land tenure in increasing productivity in agriculture are sometimes linked to the view that Africa has not yet undergone meaningful agrarian transformation in which the productive potential of land is realised to create the basis for industrial development. According to this view, we should not be surprised that the continent has recorded weak industrial performance to date. This is often explained by the fact that the foundation for sustained industrial development has not yet been created by raising productivity and income in the agriculture sector. In these debates, sometimes the blame is squarely placed on the customary land tenure system which is seen as blocking agrarian revolution in Africa (see Johnson, 2011). As mentioned above, this is one reason why some analysts celebrated land grabs as an opportunity for agrarian revolution in Africa.

The reasons why customary land tenure is widely seen as a clog in the process of agrarian transformation are many, though the most prominent ones include the view that customary land tenure is insecure, and as such, it does not provide an incentive to the land user to invest in the land; that because of the "unclear" rights to land, investments have been low, leading to low productivity compared to land under individualised rights.

It has also been argued that customary land tenure, by virtue of ensuring that everyone has access to land, leads to inefficient allocation and use of the land, since it is not always the most efficient user of the land who gets the land. The other argument which is used to explain why customary tenure is widely seen as a barrier to agricultural productivity growth is that because the property rights are vague, it is difficult to use land as collateral to access credit. This is linked to the overriding argument that customary land tenure blocks the emergence of a land market which would unlock the potential of land, and contribute to economic growth and industrial development (World Bank, 1975). From these and other factors that are usually cited to explain low productivity in African agriculture, it is apparent that the core issues revolve around the customary land tenure system, particularly the nature of property rights, and it is therefore important to grasp the essence of this debate.

The Two Sides to the Debates

Broadly speaking, there have been two sides to the debate on land tenure and how this affects productivity in agriculture. On one side of the debate, there are analysts who argue that customary land tenure is problematic because of the informal and vague nature of rights, which constrain the flow of investments to the sector. Scholars such as Johnson (1972, 2011), Dorner (1972), Simpson (1976), De Soto (2000), Deininger (2003) share the common view that customary land does not provide sufficient security to promote investment and efficient use of land. The proponents of this view advocate for policies which promote formalisation of customary land rights (not necessarily titling). They support strategies that "can take customary land rights out of the realm of the informal lineage or community land ownership, to make them fully legal, formal and individual; measuring precisely the boundaries of claims, recording claims in a formal, state-administered land record system..." (see Attwood, 1990:659). These views were strongly supported and popularised by World Bank officials from the 1970s right into the mid-1990s. Many World Bank land experts argued that customary land tenure leads to inefficient use of land which, in turn, negatively impacts on economic growth and poverty reduction (Deininger and Binswanger, 1999).[6]

On the other side of the land tenure debate, scholars argue that land tenure is not the main factor that explains the low productivity in African agriculture (Shipton and Goheen, 1992; Bassett, 1993; Place, 2009). Several studies which have been conducted to establish if there is any discernible correlation between land tenure type and productivity have concluded that the evidence in the case of African countries is mixed at best, with often no clear relationship found (see Place and Hazel, 1993; Bassett, 1993; Migot-Adholla and Bruce, 1994; Smith, 2003; Place, 2009). Case studies on Ghana, Kenya, Rwanda, Burkina Faso, Senegal, Somalia and Uganda (Migot-Adholla and Bruce, 1994), Zambia (Smith, 2003) and Madagascar (Jacoby and Minten, 2007) find little or no evidence of a correlation between titling or individualised tenure and increased security, investment, access to credit or productivity. Place and Hazel's (1993) study conducted on Ghana, Kenya and Rwanda concludes that there is no evidence that tenure type affects input use, investment, access to credit, area cultivated or productivity.

Thus, the dominant policy prescriptions which emphasises titling as the first step towards a successful land and agrarian transformation do not seem to have a solid ground given that empirical evidence suggests that the key factors which inhibit productivity growth in agriculture is not primarily the type of tenure. The obsession among donors with formalisation of customary tenure is hard to explain in the context where formalisation and individualisation do not seem to be the main problem affecting productivity in African agriculture.

On the contrary, formalisation of customary tenure may be counterproductive given the inadequate state capacity to effectively accomplish the complex exercises of validating and enforcing land rights. What is crucial is to establish how people are using the land that they have access to and what factors constrain access and productive use of the land. Ironically, for many decades now, "many African governments have sought to replace customary land tenure system with a 'modern' system of property rights, based on state legislation, on European concepts of ownership and on land titling and registration" (Cotula et al, 2009:5). As a result the land reform policies in many African countries have largely ignored the evidence indicating that titling is actually not a panacea for development (Bruce and Dorner, 1982; Bassett, 1993).

A close analysis of evidence from small-scale farmers and other land users suggests that infrastructure, public services, input support, extension services and access to markets are some of the crucial factors that constrain productivity growth. If these constraints are addressed, even those on customary land will respond to the opportunities such a move creates. Without these enabling conditions, even if a person is given the most secure land rights, the contribution to raising agriculture productivity will remain insignificant. For instance secure rights to land in a place without roads, uncertain markets, agricultural services will contribute little to improving the life of the rights holder. Therefore, for majority of the people in rural Africa particularly, the key land and agrarian issue is creating the enabling conditions for them to use land more productively and sustainably. In most countries, majority of the small-scale farmers and land users complain about lack of inputs, access to product markets, equipment and agriculture services, and far less about issues of tenure insecurity.

Security of Tenure Is Not a Panacea

The controversy about tenure type and productivity is not so much about whether tenure security is important or not; there seems to be wide agreement on the importance of secure land tenure rights (Bruce and Migot-Adholla, 1994; Platteau, 1996; Chimhowu, 2006; Van den Brink et al, 2006). The controversy revolves around whether customary tenure is in fact insecure, and whether security of tenure impacts on land use, productivity and investment. The key questions is what constitutes tenure security? Critics have argued that "security" of tenure does not necessarily lie in having a piece of paper like a title deed (see Shipton and Goheen, 1992). Although many analysts acknowledge that security of tenure under customary system can be weak, especially for vulnerable groups such as widows, unmarried young women, migrants and the poor (Whitehead and Tsikata, 2003; Moyo, 2008), there is growing consensus that many forms of customary land tenure can guarantee secure access to and use of land. It has even been suggested that processes which intend to secure the rights of people on customary land often make them even more insecure. This is particularly true in the current context where land grabs by the urban elite and foreign investors have increased, leading to many members of rural and peri-urban communities losing their land as the process of formalising land intensifies (Cotula et al, 2009).

In a study that reviews the experience of Kenya's land titling and registration programme, it has been observed that

> whereas no evidence exists that agricultural production has increased by virtue of that programme, there are plenty of data to indicate that it [land titling and registration], in general, increased inequalities both structural and political-economic within the agrarian sector. Indeed it has led to the emergence of a relatively rich middle peasantry that enjoys much useful linkages with central bureaucracies (Okoth-Ogendo, 1993:269).

Other studies which have assessed the effects of formalisation of customary land in various African countries suggest that, in fact, the process of formalising customary land has often led to growing tenure insecurities among poorer local residents (see Bruce and Dorner, 1982; Shipton and Goheen, 1992; Adams, 2003; Peters, 2004; Place, 2009). In certain circumstances, formalisation of land can, in fact, lead to conflict due to "opportunistic behaviour" of some powerful members of the community or the elite who may attempt to amass land at the expense of the poor and voiceless.

> ... land registration creates increased insecurity for vulnerable parts of the population; it does not activate the land market, and if it does, it is mainly for speculative reasons; it does not bring about a reversal in land fragmentation nor does it improve land allocation; it does not in significant ways improve smallholders access to credit;

> and there is no significant correlation between land titling and increased agricultural yield (Havnevik, 1997:8).

Thus, while customary land rights may appear to be insecure, the ways meant to secure the land rights of people with land under customary tenure often lead to heightened insecurity among the poor.

With regard to the productivity and investment argument, a case study conducted among the rice-growing small-scale farmers in Madagascar reveals no significant relationship between titling and productivity or investment (Jacoby and Minten, 2007). As noted above, there are several other studies which have come to similar conclusions. Therefore, the "old consensus" that titling of land increases investment, productivity and efficient use of land needs to be evaluated in the light of emerging empirical evidence from different parts of Africa. Here, Johnson and Mellor's (1961) advice that the crucial issue in any strategy that seeks to raise productivity in the agricultural sector is to identify the factors that constrain productivity and address them, starting with the provision of complementary support whatever form this may take, is worth revisiting by African policy makers.

While some studies conducted in Asia and Latin America pick up some strong correlation between tenure type and productivity and access to credit, in sub-Saharan Africa, most studies fail to find any significant relationship:

> Whereas...studies in Asia, Latin America and Caribbean make a clear and consistence case for land registration as an economic proposition, the picture emanating from various studies in Africa has been mixed. A comparative study of ten rain-fed agriculture regions in Ghana, Rwanda and Kenya, based on farm surveys conducted during 1987–1988...found that land registration did not have a clear impact on productivity, land improvements or credit access in these areas (Feder and Nishio, 1999:35).

Part of the challenge of trying to test for a correlation between the type of tenure and productivity, investment, access to credit and input use is that what is being measured is actually not very clear. For example, what exactly does a correlation coefficient from a regression tell us about the relationship between tenure type and productivity? Apart from the theoretical issues around the challenges of establishing the relationship between tenure type and productivity, the scarcity of appropriate data in most cases lends such an exercise less credible, especially when it comes to complex issues of tenure and security which is largely a perception people have. Security of tenure, which may have an influence on investment decisions and eventually productivity, is largely a perception, which may have nothing to do with a piece of paper or document on which rights are stated. People living under customary tenure many have stronger belief that the land they are using is theirs and they have the right to pass it on to their children. On the other hand, a freehold land title holder may actually be more insecure if there is a policy to expropriate land; freehold title holder may be more insecure than someone on customary land.

Complexities of Land Tenure Security in Africa

Dominant policy views have tended to emphasise tenure security as the main challenge when it comes to agrarian transformation in Africa. As such, little attention is given to the question of how those who currently have access to land (with secure or insecure rights) are using the land. There is almost an implicit belief that land use is a function of the type of tenure rights one has. Certainly, land tenure security has an influential bearing on land use, but land use goes beyond tenure concerns. In most studies on land tenure cited above, while tenure security pops in various expressions by local people, it is secondary to the concerns about inputs, viable markets and rural infrastructure. To most people residing on customary land, issues of security of tenure is entirely academic; their main concern is around issues of how to use the land to ensure that there is enough food and income to provide for the family, including paying fees for children going to school.

The issue of tenure security which features so prominently in agrarian transformation debates in Africa is essentially about understanding the nature of customary land relations, an issue which has been difficult for most non-Africans to grasp (Bassett, 1993; Makunike, 2009). The larger part of the misunderstanding of customary tenure comes from using Western concepts to understand African land tenure relations (Meek, 1946; Okoth-Ogendo, 1989; Bassett, 1993; Agbosu, 2000; Akuffo, 2009). This problem was spotted by some of the early anthropologists who complained about the fact that most Europeans impose Western conceptions on African land tenure systems. Meek (1946) was one of the first to draw attention to the grave error that may result from such an approach:

> [A] frequent source of error has been a presupposition that native conceptions of ownership must be basically the same as those of Europeans. English terms such as "rent," or "lease" have been employed to denote practices which bear only a superficial resemblance to those denoted by these terms. The gift given to chiefs as admin-

istrators of land have been assumed to be "rent," and the chiefs to be "landlords." (Meek, 1946:11)

The main issue Meek (1946) is raising is not just a linguistic mismatch that results in a hermeneutical error; it speaks to a much deeper issue of trying to map the African cosmology on a European one, with a strong inclination and belief that the latter is the *norm* against which the former should be evaluated (see Mamdani, 1996). As one would expect, this creates misconceptions about the African land tenure system as something which is insecure, something incongruent with modernity, something static, etc. Understanding the intricate land relations in Africa has been difficult mainly because of the use of the concepts of absolute ownership and property (Bentsi-Enchill, 1965; Bassett, 1993), which are "loaded with the values of Western materialism" (Okoth-Ogendo, 1989:7). For example, it has been observed that the colonialist's pre-occupation with the notion of "private property" failed to "entertain the notion of multiple rights in land," resulting in serious distortion in their understanding of customary land tenure in Africa (Mamdani, 1996:139; see also Meinzen-Dick and Mwangi, 2008).

As Akuffo (2009) explains, the concept of land in traditional African societies was deeply embedded in the complex social relations which influenced access to land and the exercise of power over land. In most of these societies, a clear distinction was made between the *soil* (*solum*) and the things that grow on it: "there was a clear separation in African thought and law between the *solum* and any *manifestation*, such as crops, trees and buildings which symbolises human interaction with it" (Okoth-Ogendo, 1989:8 emphasis added). This separation is not present in the Dutch–Roman conception of land where the *solum* is fused together "with water and air in a compact, recording the claims of individuals rather than social labour upon it" (ibid).

What this difference in the conception of land highlights is that land ownership in the two systems means different things. While in the European system it was the norm for the individual to have exclusive rights to land, in the traditional African systems, ownership of the soil was only a reserve of the collective; only the things attached to the soil could be owned individually. The collective (which is often referred to as community) was understood broadly to include the past (ancestors), those living at the time and those yet to come (future generation).

This intergenerational conception of land ownership in Africa transcends the immediate imperatives of individual ownership of the *solum*, at any particular moment since the land was intricately connected to the past and the future, not just the present. This is why it was only the collective (community in the broader sense) that could own the land; no single individual, not even the chief had ownership rights to the *solum* (Okoth-Ogendo, 1989; Mamdani, 1996; Agbosu, 2000). Thus, when the concept of ownership is transported from its European context to the African context, it creates not only confusion, but tension and conflict as well:

> ... the transposition of Western (Roman-Dutch/civil law and Anglo-American) property concepts and terminology in the analyses of African processes is a veritable source of confusion. The characterisation of property concepts and legal relationships using Western analogies and paradigms is perhaps understandable but has nevertheless, led to an unnecessary degree of confusion with wholly negative practical consequences such as destructive litigation over land titles and land alienation (Akuffo, 2009:62).

The failure to distinguish between the two systems of land tenure is a clear example of the distortions imposed on African land tenure system, particularly the security of tenure, because this has to do with ownership and control over land. The fact that one system is privileged over another is a reflection of the hegemonic nature of the colonial project and its aftermath.

Land in Africa Is More Than Just a Means of Production

Although there have been extensive debates about how land in Africa needs to be treated as a valuable factor of production in the service of economic growth and structural transformation, it has to be remembered that land in Africa occupies a central place beyond being a means of production. The African Union *Framework and Guidelines on Land Policy in Africa* (AU/AfDB/ECA, 2010:8) captures this well when it argues that,

> To the vast majority of societies in Africa land is regarded not simply as an economic or environmental resource, but as a social, cultural and ontological resource. Land remains an important factor in the construction of social identity, the organisation of religious life and the production and reproduction of culture. The link across generations is ultimately defined by the complement of land resources which families, lineages and communities share and control.

Certainly, land in Africa has several other dimensions attached to it. It is not just another form of property like a house or a car. Because of this multidimensional nature of land in Africa, it permeates the entire African existence, providing a critical link between the material and the spiritual worlds, the past and the present (Akuffo, 2009). This multidimensional feature of land in Africa often makes land relations complex, in such a way that in "order to fully understand the social processes through which power over land is vested" one needs to "go beyond [the] man-land issues, which the doctrine of ownership implies, to encompass man-man relations, which create and determine power in land-based societies" (Okoth-Ogendo, 1989:9). As noted earlier, the land tenure systems in Africa conceive land not as a property belonging to a particular person (not even the king or chief), but as a "web of relationships" structured by cultural, traditional norms and practices (see Gluckman, 1969; Agbosu, 2000).

Further, the multidimensional nature of land places it at the centre of social and political formations in society. Land forms the basic feature of polities, be they states, nations, kingdoms, chiefdoms, villages or a mere settlements. As such, land defines, confines and forms the basis of identity for these formations and the people in them (Bentsi-Enchill, 1965; Uchendu, 1970). In this sense, land "is not only the physical dimension of a community but the spatial aspect of the polity" (Uchendu, 1970:478). There cannot be a polity without land; any form of polity is inherently rooted in and defined by a particular piece of land. The feature of being the spatial confines of a community gives land a central role in defining relations between not just polities, but also members within a particular polity. Consequently, control over this vital resource becomes an important feature of defining social and power relations for people in communities. In many societies, over the centuries, being able to lay claim to and control land has been a source of power, privilege, status and wealth (Bentsi-Enchill, 1965). In feudal societies particularly, land was,

> … the most important economic resource. It was the basic means of production. Hence its ownership and control carried with it the exercise of economic and political power over men. Thus, the feudal oligarchy, which claimed ownership over the bulk of the lands, regulated socially people's relations to the land as the basic means of production (Agbosu, 2000:3).

In Ugand it has been reported that "majority of land purchasers buy for social and political advantages, since owners of land have the right to sit on local councils, the first step on the political ladder" (Platteau, 1996:52).

But critics would argue that this is a traditional way of looking at land and it has contributed to the current failure to induce agrarian transition and industrial development on Africa. That granted, it could also be true that the unique nature of land in Africa may be an indication that the agrarian transformation will follow a significantly different path from what we have seen before.

Agrarian Reform, Industrialisation and Inclusive Growth: Connecting the Dots

The big question about the land and agrarian in Africa revolves around what type of land tenure will enhance agricultural productivity and contribute to industrial development, the creation of employment and reduction of poverty. The fact that this debate has continued is a good sign that issues of land are still treated as important aspects of the African growth equation. There is wide agreement in the literature that agrarian transformation, particularly land reform which makes land more equitably distributed with stable land management systems, contributes immensely to economic development in the early stages. Whether one follows Arthur Lewis' (1954) Two-Sector Model, Mundle's (1985) tripartite agrarian production model or Adelman's (1984) ADLI model, the land questions feature prominently as a critical starting point for dynamics that can support industrial growth. It is therefore important not to think of industrial growth as something isolated from the agrarian question. A comprehensive industrial policy in Africa cannot ignore agrarian issues and should take into account how these impact on industrial development. The tendency so far, especially among African scholars and policy makers alike, is to ignore the connections between land, agriculture and industrial development.

Given the centrality of land and agrarian transformation in African societies, there will always be contestations about how land resources should be managed to support production and structural transformation. Nonetheless, few will question the importance of land, especially in countries that are trying to industrialise. Although land issues are indirectly connected to industrial development, via agriculture, a successful industrial project will be baseless without addressing the land and agrarian question(s). To the extent that land relations influence agriculture production, land should be seen as an important factor in the process of industrialisation, especially in regions where majority of the people directly derive livelihoods from agriculture. As illustrated in Chapter 6, the agriculture sector in Africa still accounts for more than half of total employment, and in most non-resource-rich countries, agriculture can account for up to 80 percent of total employment (see ILO, 2017). In this context, the agrarian question is critically essential to any industrialisation strategy, and the African policy makers know very well that "transforming agriculture is a precondition for unleashing the continent's development potential" (UNECA, 2012:120).

Land and agriculture are crucial factors in Africa's sustainable development path for three reasons. First, growth in agriculture, as illustrated above, can improve Africa's income distribution, which has worsened in many countries at the end of the recent growth episode (WEF, 2017). As Chitonge (2015) illustrates, income inequality has been increasing in most countries, and it is in countries that reported the higher growth rates between 2000 and 2012 (Nigeria, Angola, Ethiopia, Ghana, Tanzania and Zambia) where income inequality has increased. The AfDB (2013) report also indicates that income inequality increased in most African countries at the time when growth rates were high, such that six out of the ten most unequal countries by income are not in Africa.

The main reason for this growing inequality at the time when most economies were experiencing decent growth rates is because majority of the people are not participating in the sectors where productivity is high and growing. Majority of the people, 51 percent in 2015, were working in agriculture where productivity and income were the lowest. It is only a small section of the population (estimated at just 15 percent, see ILO, 2017) in formal employment who capture and benefit from the growth reported in most countries. This is why it is critically important for African countries to focus on improving productivity in the agricultural sector as a starting point for industrial growth and structural transformation. It is clear that African economic growth rates would have been higher if income had been more equally distributed. More equally distributed income would enlarge domestic and provide further momentum in the growth of local industries.

The second reason is related to the first, and it is about inclusive growth, which is a theme that has prominently featured in recent analyses of African economies. Achieving inclusive growth is good for many reasons including social and political stability, sustainable local demand, steady accumulation of human capital, rapid reduction of poverty levels. All these provide a strong foundation for diversification in the economy as the demand base widens. At early stages of industrialisation when most firms are building the capacity to enter into export markets, the domestic market structure plays an important role in shaping the next stage of industrial growth. In this respect, having inclusive growth does not only expand the domestic market, but also provides resilience against external demand and price shocks. In the African context, since majority of people work in the agriculture sector, it is important that constraints on productivity growth are addressed adequately. While the importance of linkages between agriculture and industries in creating inclusive growth has been recognised in the literature, the role of agriculture growth in boosting local demand is often downplayed.

> The existence of a backward linkage between agriculture and industry via the home market in such transitional economies has been generally recognise ever since it was originally pointed out by Adam Smith toward the end of the eighteenth century.... However, the importance of agriculture as a market for manufacturing industry has usually been overshadowed by its alternative role as a source for mobilising surpluses of labour, food and fibre or savings for financing industrial growth (Mundle, 1985:89).

For economies at the early stages of industrial development, it is important to consolidate the linkage between agriculture and industry, but also to be aware of the double role that agriculture plays in promoting industrialisation: as a market for manufactured goods, but also as a source of accumulated capital and surplus labour.

As we have seen in the case of African economies during the 1970s which stressed the role of agriculture as a source of capital for industrialisation, failure to balance these crucial roles of agriculture can stymie both agriculture and industrial growth. To realise the dream of inclusive growth requires that the productivity of the majority of people in agriculture and the informal sectors is raised significantly, in line with the rising national income. Otherwise, those outside the formal sector employment, who are in the majority, will be left out of the growing economy and this can be not only a source of social and political tensions but also generate diseconomies via low domestic demand in the economy. Page (2015) has attributed the slow reduction in poverty in Africa to the fact that the growth has not spread beyond the highly productive mining and high skills services. Again, here agriculture and land are indispensable parts of this equation.

Thirdly, land and agriculture are critically important in the African strategy for economy growth and industrial development because of the strategic role agriculture can play in the processes of economic diversification. Adelman's (1984) emphasis on the growth of small-scale farmers offers feasible options for many African countries seeking to boost industrial growth by leveraging their potential in agriculture and related activities. As noted above, raising productivity within the agricultural sector can stimulate the growth of industry through the linkages between the two sectors before even tapping into export markets. This is why the agricultural–land nexus is so important in Africa that without resolving the issues around this, sustainable economy growth and industrialisation will remain subdued. In other words, there is a lot that hinges on the agricultural sector, and its poor performance has serious implications on the rest of society including food security, the growth of industrial activities and employment.

But the factors that contribute to the agriculture sector's poor performance go beyond tenure issues which are loudly fronted in the debates. The sector's persistently low productivity in Africa is due to a number of factors including poor infrastructure, inadequate access to inputs, low levels of extension services, poor access to markets, small domestic markets, low levels of skills and technology, which are mostly policy matters (see UNECA, 2012). Substantive improvements in productivity have been reported in cases where some of these constraints have been lifted or eased. One good example of this is the input support programme started in Malawi (spreading to Zambia, Mozambique, Zimbabwe and Swaziland) which saw massive improvements in food production of the local farmers who, prior to the input support programme,[7] were perpetually in need of food aid (see Chirwa, 2010). Productivity among the small farmers increased regardless of whether they were still on customary land or otherwise. Thus, while tenure reforms are important, they may not be the magic bullet to the challenge of increasing productivity in the agricultural sector in Africa.

Notes

1. One of the extensive discussions of land in the context of industrialisation is Kay's (2002) and (2009) papers. The other discussion is Mundle's (1985) paper in which he discusses how failed agrarian transformation imposes a barrier on industrialisation. Focusing particularly on Southern Africa, Sam Moyo (2010) also makes a direct link between the failure to radically transform the agrarian structure and the persistence of anaemic industrialisation in Africa.
2. What Bernstein (2004) means by the agrarian question of labour is the fragmentation and casualisation of labour throughout the world as increased labour productivity in agriculture and industry leads to what he calls the "employment crisis", whereby the labour released from agriculture is not being absorbed by industry as expected in the classic case of agrarian transition. Although this view originates from a totally different train of thought, it has some resemblance with Rodrik's (2015) view of premature de-industrialisation and the declining employment elasticity of industrial growth, not just in the industrialised countries, but in the non-industrial countries as well.

3. At the conference convened to celebrate the centenary of the *1913 Land Act in South Africa*, held at the University of Cape Town in 2013, Henry Bernstein honourably accepted that he might have been in error to conclude that the agrarian question in its classic form is no longer relevant, only the agrarian question of labour is.
4. See also Chitonge et al (2017) for an analysis of these dynamics in rural Zambia, and Obala and Mattingly (2013) for analysis on Kenya, and Ubink and Quan (2008) for analysis on Ghana.
5. See also Chapter 6 in this book, where ADLI is discussed in the context of structural transformation.
6. The World Bank position on formalisation of customary land rights has been evolving over time. Form the 1970s to the 1990s, the Bank supported the formalisation of land rights through individual titling and in some cases registration of customary land through a formal land market. But from the late 1990s, the Bank's position seems to have shifted to supporting the recognition of land rights through existing local institutions (Deininger and Binswanger, 1999; Cotula et al, 2009).
7. The programme was run by the Malawi government, and it involved providing seeds, fertiliser and extension services to poor farmers.

References

Adams, M. (2003). *Land Tenure Policy and Practice in Zambia: Issues Relating to the Development of the Agricultural Sector*. Zambia: Mokoro Ltd (for DFID).

Adelman, I. (1984). "Beyond Export Led Growth." *World Development*, Vol. 12, No. 9. 937–949.

African Development Bank (AfDB, 2013). Annual Development Effectiveness Review 2013: Towards Sustainable Growth for Africa. Available at: www.afdb.org. Accessed 23.10.2013.

African Union (AU), African Development Bank (AfDB), UN-Economic Commission for Africa (ECA). (AU/AfDB/UNEECA, 2010). *Framework and Guidelines on Land Policy in Africa.* Addis Ababa: AU-AfDB-UNECA.

Agbosu, K. L. (2000). "Land Law in Ghana: Contradiction Between Anglo-American and Customary Conceptions of Tenure and Practice." Land Tenure Centre Working Paper No. 33. University of Wisconsin.

Akuffo, K. (2009). "The Conception of Land Ownership in African Customary Law and Its Implications for Development." *African Journal of International and Comparative Law*, Vol. 17. 57–78.

Anseeuw, W., Ducastel, A. and Gabas, J. (2011). "The End of the African Peasantry? From Investment Funds and Finance Value-chains to Peasant Related Questions." A paper presented at the International Conference on *Global Land Grabbing*, 6–8 April, 2011, University of Sussex.

Attwood, D. (1990). "Land Registration in Africa: The Impact on Agricultural Production." *World Development*, Vol. 18, No. 5. 659–671.

Bassett, T. (1993). "Introduction: The Land Question and Agricultural Transformation in Sub-Saharan Africa," in T. Bassett and T. J. Crummey (eds.), *Land in African Agrarian Systems*. Wisconsin: University of Wisconsin Press. 1–27.

Bentsi-Enchill, K. (1965). "Do African Systems of Land Tenure Require a Special Terminology?" *Journal of African Law*, Vol. 9, No. 2. 114–39.

Bernstein, H. (2004). "'Changing Before Our Very Eyes: Agrarian Questions and the Politics of Land in Capitalism Today." *Journal of Agrarian Change*, Vol. 4, Nos. 1 and 2. 199–225.

Berry, S. (1984). "The Food Crisis and Agrarian Change in Africa." *African Studies Review*, Vol. 27, No. 2. 59–112.

Bruce, J. and Dorner, P. (1982). *Agricultural Land Tenure in Zambia: Perspectives, Problems and Opportunities*. LTC Research Paper, No. 76. Madison, WI: Land Tenure Center, University of Wisconsin.

Bruce, J. and Mighot-Adholla, S. E. (1994). *Searching for Land Tenure Security in Africa*. Washington, DC: World Bank.

Byres, J. T. (1986). "The Agrarian Question, Forms of Capitalist Agrarian Transition and the State: An Essay with Reference to Asia." *Social Scientist*, Vol. 14, No. 11/12. 3–67.

Chimhowu, A. (2006). "Tinkering on the Fringes? Redistributive Land Reforms and Chronic Poverty in Southern Africa." Chronic Poverty Research Centre Working Paper No. 58.

Chirwa, T. (2010). "Programme Evaluation of Agricultural Input Subsidies in Malawi Using Treatment Effects: Methods and Practicability Based on Propensity Scores." Munich Personal RePEc Archives (MPRA) Paper No. 21236. Available at: http://mpra.ub.uni-muenchen.de/21236. Accessed 12.03.2016.

Chitonge, H. (2015). "The Matthew Effect of Growth in Africa: The Case of Rising Inequality in the Midst of Sustained Growth." *African Journal of Social Science*, Vol. 5, No. 3. 1–20.

Chitonge, H. (2018). "Trails of Incomplete Decolonisation in Africa: The Land Question and Economic Structural Transformation." *African Studies Monograph*, Special Issue No. 57. 19–41.

Chitonge, H., Mfune, O., Kajoba, G., Umar, B., Banda, D. and Ntsebeza, L. (2017). "Silent Privatisation of Customary Land: Opportunities for a Few, Challenges for Many." *Social Dynamics*, Vol. 43, No. 1. 82–102.

Colson, E. (1971). "The Impact of Colonial Period on the Definition of Land Rights," in V. Turner (ed.), *Colonialism in Africa 1870–1960* (Vol. 3). Cambridge: Cambridge University Press. Chapter 6. 193–214.

Cotula, Lorenzo, Vermeulen, Sonja, Leonard, Rebecca & Keeley, James (2009). Land Grab or Development Opportunity? Agricultural Investment and International Land Deals in Africa. London/Rome: IIED/FAO/IFAD. Pp. 13–34

Cox, K. and Negi, R. (2010). "The State and the Question of Development in Sub-Saharan Africa." *Review of African Political Economy*, Vol. 37. Nos. 1 and 2. 71–85.

De Soto, H. (2000). *The Mystery of Capital*. New York: Basic Books.

Deininger, K. (2003). *Land Policies for Growth and Poverty Reduction*. New York: Oxford University Press.

Deininger, K. and Binswanger, H. (1999). "The Evolution of the World Bank's Land Policy: Principles, Experiences and Future Challenges." *The World Bank Research* Observer, Vol. 14, No. 2. 247–276.

Dorner, P. (1972). *Land Reform and Economic Development*. Harmondsworth: Penguin.

Feder, G. and Nishio, A. (1999). "The Benefits of Land Registration and Titling: Economic and Social Perspectives." *Land Use Policy*, Vol. 15, No. 1. 25–43.

Feizhou, Z. and Camille, B. (2009). "Land Reform Throughout the 20th Century in China," in H. Binswanger-Mkhize, C. Bourguignon and R. van den Brink (eds.), *Agricultural Land Redistribution: Towards a Greater Consensus*. Washington, DC: World Bank. 119–136.

Gluckman, M. (1969). "Property Rights and Status in African Traditional Law," in M. Gluckman (ed.), *Ideas and Procedures in African Traditional Law*. London: Oxford University Press. 252–273.

Griffin, K., Khan, A. and Ickowitz, A. (GKI, 2002). "Poverty and the Redistribution of Land." *Journal of Agrarian Change*, Vol. 2, No. 3. 279–330.

Havnevik, K. (1997). "Land Question in Sub-Saharan Africa," in Isaksson, Nils-Ivar (ed.), *Land Question in Sub-Saharan Africa*. Uppsala: Department of Rural Development Studies, Swedish University of Agricultural Sciences.

Hyden, Goran (1983). *No Shortcuts to Progress: African Development Management in Perspectives*. London/Nairobi: Heinemann.

Hyden, Goran (1986). "The Anomaly of the African Peasantry." *Development and Change*, Vol. 17, No. 3. 677–705.

International Labour Organisation (ILO, 2017). *World Employment Social Outlook 2017*. Geneva: ILO.

Jacoby, H. and Minten, B. (2007). "Is Land Titling in Sub-Saharan Africa Cost-Effective? Evidence from Madagascar." *The World Bank Economic Review*, Vol. 4, No. 3. 461–485.

Johnson, B. and Mellor, W. J. (1961). "The Role of Agriculture in Economic Development." *American Economic Review*, Vol. 51, No. 4. 566–593.

Johnson, O. (1972). "Economic Analysis, the Legal Framework and Land Tenure Systems." *Journal of Law and Economics*, Vol. 5, No. 1. 259–276.

Johnson, O. (2011). "Reforming the Customary Land Tenure System in Sierra Leone: A Proposal." International Growth Centre (IGC) Working Paper No. 11/0558. London School of Economics and Political Science.

Kasfir, N. (1986). "Are African Peasantry Self-sufficient? *Development and Change*, Vol 17 No. 2. 335–57.

Kay, C. (2002). "Why East Asia Overtook Latin America: Agrarian Reform, Industrialisation and Development." *Third World Quarterly*, Vol. 23, No. 6. 1073–1102.

Kay, C. (2009). "Development Strategy and Rural Development: Exploring Synergies, Eradicating Poverty." *Journal of Peasant Studies*, Vol. 36, No. 1. 103–137.

Lewis W.A. (1954). "Economic Development with Unlimited Supplies of Labour." *Manchester School*, Vol. 20. 139–91.

Lionel, C. (1987). "The Debate on the African Peasantries" *Development and Change*, Vol. 18. 625–35

Mafeje, A. (2003). "The Agrarian Question: Access to Land and Peasant Response in Sub-Saharan Africa." Civil Society and Social Movement Programme, Paper No. 6. United Nations Research Institute for Social Development (UNRISD, 2003).

Makunike, C. (2009). "Large-Scale Agricultural Investment in Africa: Points to Ponder," in K. Michael and L. Susan (eds.), *Land Grab: The Race for The Worlds Farmland*. Washington, DC: Woodrow Wilson International Centre for Scholars. 85–93.

Mamdani, M. (1996). *Citizen and Subject: Contemporary Africa and the legacy of Late Colonialism*. Princeton, NJ: Princeton University Press.

Meek, C. K. (1946). *Land Law and Custom in the Colonies*. London: Oxford University Press.

Meinzen-Dick, R. and Mwangi, E. (2008). "Cutting the Web of Interests: Pitfalls of Formalising Property Rights." *Land Use Policy*, Vol. 26. 36–43.

Migot-Adholla, E. and Bruce, J. W. (1994). "Introduction: Are Indigenous African Tenure Systems Insecure?" in J. W. Bruce and E. Migot-Adholla (eds.), Searching for Land Tenure Security in Africa. Washington, DC: World Bank. 1–14.

Moyo, S. (2004). "African Land Question, The State and Agrarian Transition: Contradictions of Neo-Liberal Land Reforms." Available at http://www.sarpn.org/documents/d0000692/P763-Moyo_Land_May2004.pdf accessed 06.03.15

Moyo, S. (2008). *African Land Questions, Agrarian Transition and the State: Contradictions of the Neo-liberal Land Reforms*. Dakar: CODESRIA.

Moyo, S. (2010). "The Agrarian Question and the Developmental State in Southern Africa," in O. Edigheji (ed.), *Constructing a Developmental State in South Africa*. Cape Town: HSRC Press. 285–314.

Mundle, S. (1985). "The Agrarian Barrier to Industrial Growth." *Journal of Development Studies*, Vol. 22, No. 1. 49–80.

Navaro, Z. (2009). "Expropriating Land in Brazil," in H. Binswanger-Mkhize, C. Bourguignon and R. van den Brink (eds.), *Agricultural Land Redistribution: Towards a Greater Consensus*. Washington, DC: World Bank. 267–290.

Nurkse, R. (1953). *Problems of Capital Formation in Underdeveloped Countries*. London: Basil Blackwell.

Obala, L. and Mattingly, M. (2013). "Ethnicity, Corruption and Violence in Urban Land Conflict in Kenya." *Urban Studies*, Vol. 20, No. 10, 1–17.

Okoth-Ogendo, H. W. O. (1989). "Some Issues of Theory in the Study of Tenure Relations in African Agriculture." *Journal of International African Institute*, Vol. 59, No. 1. 6–17.

Peters, P. (2004). "Inequality and Social Conflict over Land in Africa." *Journal of Agrarian Change*, Vol. 4, No. 3. 269–314.

Pingali, P, 1997. "From Subsistence to Commercial Production Systems: The Transformation of Asian Agriculture." *American Journal of Agricultural Economics*, 17(2). 628–634.

Place, F. (2009). "Land Tenure and Agricultural Productivity in Africa: A Comparative Analysis of the Economic Literature and Recent Policy Strategies and

Place, F. and Hazel, P. (1993). "Productivity Effects of Indigenous Land Tenure in Sub-Saharan Africa." American Journal of Agricultural Economics, Vol. 75, No.1. 10–19.

Platteau, J. (1996). "The Evolutionary Theory of Land Rights as Applied to Sub-Saharan Africa: A Critical Assessment." *Development* and *Change*, Vol. 27, No. 1. 29–86.

Rodrik, D. (2015). "Premature Deindustrialisation." National Bureau of Economic Research (NBER) Working Paper No. 20935. Available at: http://www.nber.org/papers/w20935. Accessed 16.09.2017.

Shipton, P. and Goheen, M. (1992). "Understanding African Land-Holding: Power and Meaning." *Journal of International African Institute*, Vol. 62, No. 3. 307–325.

Simpson, S. R. (1976). *Land Law and Registration*. Cambridge: Cambridge University.

Smith, R. (2003). "Land Tenure Reform in Africa: A Shift to the Defensive." *Progress in Development Studies*, Vol. 3, No. 3. 210–222.

Ubink, J. and Quan, J. (2008). "How to Combine Traditional and Modernity? Regulating Customary Land Management in Ghana." *Land Use Policy*, Vol. 25. 198–213.

Uchendu, V. (1970). "Impact of Changing Agricultural Technology on African Land Tenure." *Journal of Developing Areas*, Vol. 4, No. 4. 477–486.

United Nations Economic Commission for Africa (UNECA, 2005). Land Tenure Systems and their Impacts on Food Security and Sustainable Development in Africa. Addis Ababa: UNECA.

United Nations Economic Commission for Africa (UNECA, 2012). *Economic Report on Africa 2012: Unleashing Africa's Potential as a Global Growth Pole*. Addis Ababa: UNECA.

United Nations Economic Commission for Africa (UNECA, 2015). *Report on Africa 2015: Industrialising Through Trade*. Addis Ababa: UNECA.

United Nations Economic Commission for Africa (UNECA, 2016). *Economic Report on Africa 2016: Greening Africa's Industrialisation*. Addis Ababa: UNECA.

van den Brink, R., Thomas, G., Bruce, J. and Byamugisha, F. (2006). "Consensus, Confusion and Controversy: Selected Land Reform in Sub-Saharan Africa." Washington, DC: World Bank. Available at: www.worldbank.org. Accessed 13.02.2009.

Whitehead, A. and Tsikata, D. (2003). "Policy Discourse on Women's Land Rights in Sub-Saharan Africa: The Implications of the Return to the Customary." *Journal of Agrarian Change*, Vol. 3. Nos. 1 and 2. 67–112.

World Economic Forum (WEF, 2017). The Future of Jobs and Skills in Africa: Preparing the Region for the Fourth Industrial Revolution. Geneva: WEF.

World Bank (1975). Land Reform: Sector Policy Paper No. 440. Washington, DC: World Bank.

World Bank (1993). The East Asian Miracle: Economic Growth and Public Policy. Oxford: Oxford University Press.

· 9 ·

ENTREPRENEURSHIP AND INDUSTRIALISATION IN AFRICA

Can the Cheetah Generation Deliver?

Introduction: The Rise of African Cheetahs?

In the preceding chapters, we looked at the different aspects of the industrialisation story in Africa. We discussed what needs to be done to foster industrial growth, but little has been said about the agents of industrialisation in Africa today. Chapter 7 argues for building state institutions with the capability to implement the industrialisation strategy with the agility of the cheetah, but the state has to work with individuals and groups to mobilise resources and support from the general public. One group that has often played an important role in the industrial growth of many countries is entrepreneurs. In recent literature on African development, the current group of entrepreneurs is sometimes referred to as the *Cheetah Generation*, distinguished from the *Hippo Generation* (see Ayyiteh, 2005). We come back letter in the chapter to the significance of this distinction. However, although the entrepreneur is widely perceived as an important player in the process of industrial growth, this actor has surprisingly received less attention in the literature on industrial and economic growth. In recent years, many African governments have started to see entrepreneurs as important actors in the broader process of economic growth and industrial development, especially job creation.

The positive perception of entrepreneurship in Africa has emerged in the context of the growing challenge of job creation. In this context, the role of African entrepreneurs is slowly being acknowledged and valued not only because of the entrepreneurs' potential to contribute to job creation, but also their role in changing the mind-set of people in society. Although in recent times African entrepreneurs are increasingly regarded as important players in Africa's growth and industrial development strategy, little is known about this section of the African society. Information about the composition of African entrepreneurs, their relation to the broader African society, including the state, is scanty. If African societies are assigning an important role to entrepreneurs, then it is important to understand this segment of the African society, and its role in the process of industrial development on the continent. This chapter looks at entrepreneurship in Africa and its role in the industrialisation project on the continent.

The chapter focuses on understanding the context in which African entrepreneurs operate and the recent trends in this growing group. To understand the African entrepreneurs it is essential to locate them in social, economic and political milieu, which influence their growth and composition over time. Like any other entrepreneurs, the African entrepreneur operates in a particular social, cultural, political, economic and religious environment, which shapes what he or she does, and it is critical to understand this context in order to appreciate the role African entrepreneurs can play in the transformation of the broader society (see GEM, 2017). In this regard, the chapter seeks to highlight the importance of what I refer to as the *sociology of an African entrepreneur*, by specifically situating African entrepreneurs in the broader African social and economic context. Of particular importance in the construction of a sociology of African entrepreneurs is the question of whether the African entrepreneur can be at the forefront of industrial development in Africa. What sets an African entrepreneur apart, and what role can he or she play in industrialising the continent?

The chapter begins with a brief discussion of the factors that account for the apparent rise of public interest in entrepreneurship in Africa. A brief general discussion of who is an entrepreneur follows this. After this, a brief historical background to entrepreneurship in Africa is presented. This is followed by an overview of recent trends on African entrepreneurs, highlighting the differences between the current and past generations of entrepreneurs. This is followed by a discussion of the common features of African entrepreneurs, focusing on the unique characteristics, which distinguish them from entrepreneurs in other parts of the world. Following this is a discussion of the context in which African entrepreneurs operate. This context is an important aspect to understanding entrepreneurship and its role in Africa's industrial growth and development. The last part of the chapter attempts to highlight the importance of understanding the social milieu that shapes African entrepreneurs.

Entrepreneurship in Africa

Although there has been growing awareness and interest in African entrepreneurs in the last decade, it is important to note that entrepreneurship in Africa is not something new; Africa has never been short of entrepreneurs! However, in the last decade, there is a noticeable revival of interest in African entrepreneurs as noted above. This revival of interest in African entrepreneurs by the international media has been sparked by several factors[1] including the *Africa Rising narrative* (ARN), which attributes the alleged "Rising of Africa" to the emergence of a new class of African entrepreneurs and captains of industry—sometimes referred to as the *Cheetah Generation*. The story of a rising Africa has featured strongly in international media since 2011 when *The Economist* magazine reported that six of the ten fastest growing economies in the world between 2000 and 2010 were in Africa (see *Economist*, 2011). While there are several factors that are cited to support the view that Africa is rising, the emergence of a new crop of African business leaders and entrepreneurs is commonly believed to be one of the key factors (see Radelet, 2010a). This new generation of African entrepreneurs is said to be an independent class not relying on privileged access to state power and resources as was the case with entrepreneurs in the past; today's business classes in Africa are "making it" on their own (Rotberg, 2013).

The Cheetah Generation

In the ARN, those who doubt the existence of Africa's emerging captains of industry are often brushed aside as pessimists stuck in the 'old Africa.' The focus now has shifted to understanding the key features of the "new generation of African entrepreneurs" (McDade and Spring, 2005)— the "Cheetah Generation" (Ayitteh, 2005). For example, an online *Forbes* magazine, which profiles young African entrepreneurs, states that,

> There has never been a more inspired generation of young Africans. These builders, innovators and risk takers are fervent in their resolve to transform the continent. They are solving critical socio-economic problems, exporting African culture to the world, creating job opportunities for Africans, re-telling Africa's stories, and writing the future (Nsehe, 2014).

In trying to persuade everyone that this new generation of African entrepreneurs is different, several distinct features are cited as evidence. For example, the then Kenyan Minister of Industrialisation and Enterprise Development, Adam Mohammed, cited what he called a "mind-set" change among young Africans who are now increasingly thinking not as prospective *employees* but as *employers* (Obonyo, 2016:17).

Certainly, the last ten years have witnessed growing interest in African entrepreneurs. This growing interest comes from several sections of the African society, including African bureaucrats and senior state officials. On the part of African policy makers, the interest is mainly in the role African entrepreneurs can play in the broader process of economic growth, particularly the creation of jobs through the expansion of the industrial sector, with a strong focus on manufacturing. This growing interest by most African policy makers in African entrepreneurs is a direct outcome of several but closely related factors. First, the rapidly expanding urban informal sector, largely due to a steady exodus of labour from agriculture and rural areas in general (see McMillan and Harttgen, 2014),[2] which is absorbing a larger proportion of the emigrating labour force (Fox et al, 2013). Most of the people operating in the urban informal sector are self-employed, involved in some self-owned business ventures. Although most of these are classified as survivalist business ventures (GEM, 2012), they constitute a significant portion of the total labour force and cannot be ignored in any serious analysis of entrepreneurship in Africa. Of particular interest to policy makers is the fact that these self-run businesses are becoming a common alternative to wage employment for many people, and because this sector now is gradually overtaking agriculture as the source of livelihood, it is slowly attracting the interest of many government officials.

Entrepreneurship and Employment Creation

Second, and related to the first factor, formal wage employment has largely stagnated in most countries averaging just over 15 percent for the continent between 2000 and 2015, with employment in manufacturing and industry remaining flat for the larger part of the new millennium (see Chapter 6). The lack of formal wage employment has pushed many African governments to start looking for alternative ways of generating employment, and entrepreneurship is widely seen as a practical solution to the growing problems of unemployment and under-employment (Fox and Thomas, 2016). A McKinsey Global Institute (MGI) report argues that issues of entrepreneurship and industrialisation are featuring high on the agenda because of the pressure, on governments all over the world, to generate growth and productive employment in the aftermath of the *Great Recession* (Manyika et al, 2012). In fact, there is even a suggestion that the burgeoning small businesses and medium-size enterprises, including the survivalist ventures, if properly supported through various public interventions can contribute significantly to creating jobs as well as deepening industrial growth, especially in developing countries. Because of this, there is now growing attention given to entrepreneurship as a strategic node of activities not just for creation of employment opportunities but also for promoting innovation, growth of industrial capabilities and competitiveness (see AEO, 2017).

Unemployment and the Entrepreneurship Bulge in Africa

Third, because open unemployment is predominantly an urban youth phenomenon, the political risks associated with a highly educated yet unemployed urban youth has pushed a number of governments to embark on programmes which promote youth entrepreneurship, with most youths encouraged to start their own business ventures instead of waiting for a job (Filmer and Fox, 2014). Several countries in Africa now have youth entrepreneurship programmes, which seek to stimulate and sustain the entrepreneurial culture and the appetite among the youth to own a business. According to a recent survey conducted, 42 African countries have developed strategies and programmes to promote and support the growth of entrepreneurship (AEO, 2017). Most of these countries are promoting entrepreneurship though the SMEs, and by supporting SMEs many African governments aim to create employment and increase income (ibid). The GEM (2017) reports that African societies have the most positive attitude towards entrepreneurship, and a larger proportion of people in Africa believe that entrepreneurship is a good career path. This positive perception of entrepreneurship in Africa, which is the highest in the world, has been attributed to the shrinking of productive employment in the formal sector, leaving entrepreneurship as the most viable career path for many people, especially the youth (ibid).

Perceptions about Business Potential in Africa

The fourth factor that has contributed to the growing interest in entrepreneurship in Africa is the decent growth rates reported in most African countries over the last decade and half. The excitement sparked by relatively high growth rates in most African countries has given rise to the *Africa Rising Narrative (ARN)*, which has identified the emergence of a new generation of African entrepreneurs, sometimes referred to as the "*Cheetah generation*", to be one of the major contributing factors to Africa's higher growth rates in the new millennium. Within the ARN, there is a strong belief that entrepreneurs can play a positive role in promoting economic growth and industrial development in Africa primarily because of the innovative potential which entrepreneurship is believed to engender. There have been analysts advocating for an informal sector-led industrial growth strategy in Africa, with entrepreneurs seen as key actors (Elkan, 1988). A recent publication of the Africa Economic Outlook has also recommended that African governments should consider the strategic potential of SMEs in promoting industrial growth and poverty reduction, through the growth of entrepreneurship (AEO, 2017).

Hopes of Africa contributing significantly to gradually emerging *Industrial Revolution 4.0* (IR 4.O, Banga and te Velde, 2018) or simply the new industrial revolution (NIR, see UNIDO, 2016) are pinned on the African entrepreneurs who are at the frontier of adapting the new technology associated with the NIR including, automation, cloud computing, software development and telecommunication. African youth are reported to be interested in frontier technology such as automation, digitisation, nanotechnology, robotics, 3D printing, digitisation of financial services and related technologies, such as the M-Pesa technology[3] (AEO, 2017).

Although there is great expectation that the African youth entrepreneurs will play an important role in getting Africa ready for IR 4.0, it is not clear what technical capacities are being developed among African youth in terms of automation and digitisation. Apart from the innovative role expected from African entrepreneurs, there is also a strong belief that the African youth will increasingly play a more central role not just in the technological world but in politics, power brokering and social trend setting. Sometimes the African youth entrepreneurs have been aptly referred to as "social shifters" (see Durham, 2000).

Entrepreneurship: African Governments' Response to the Unemployment Challenge

Given the growing interest in entrepreneurship in Africa, several governments have introduced a number of programmes to promote the growth of entrepreneurship in general. For example, the government of Morocco, in its Industrial Acceleration Plan (API, this is the French acronym) 2014–2020, has identified specific measures such as training coaching, financing and digitalisation support to entrepreneurs (AEO, 2017). In Cote d'Ivoire, the government has specifically identified reducing start-up costs, improving infrastructure and creating an enabling legal framework as measures aimed at promoting the growth of entrepreneurship. In some countries such as Mozambique and Ethiopia, entrepreneurship has been introduced as a subject in secondary schools and technical training colleges (see Brixiova et al, 2015). Other countries have focused on setting up business incubators (BIs), accelerators, seed capital and start-up academies and tech-hubs, all of which are aimed at promoting the growth of entrepreneurship (AEO, 2017).[4] A survey conducted in 2015 found that 36 African countries have active BIs (ibid, 231). All these measures were absent just a couple of years ago, and their prevalence in many countries is a good indication of the growing interest, but also the high expectations built around entrepreneurship as an important activity in these countries. In the last five years alone, Africa has seen the growth of BIs, which now boasts about 300 BIs on the continent (see AEO, 2017:114).

Although what Africa's role in the FIR will be is seen to depend largely on how African governments position themselves in developing digitisation capacities (see Banga and te Velde, 2018), evidence on the ground suggests that African youth are going against all odds to equip themselves to play a significant role in the emerging digital economy. The response from most African governments, in this regard, is promising and if sustained can make a big difference. There are encouraging examples in software development in Kenya, and non-carbon-based auto engines in Uganda, South Africa and Nigeria. What happens to these stories depends much on what African governments do, in terms of providing what I am broadly referring to as *secondary public goods*, which are discussed in more detail in Chapter 10.

Who Is an Entrepreneur?

Although there is now rising interest in entrepreneurship in Africa, there are debates around who actually is an entrepreneur. In view of this, it is important to place the concept in its theoretical context. A full discussion of this topic is beyond the scope of this book; what this section does it to make a few general comments on the term *entrepreneur*, and the meaning it acquires in different contexts. As one would expect, the term *entrepreneur* can mean different things to different people, and there is considerable disagreement about who should be classified as an entrepreneur and who should not. In a discussion on industrialisation, there is even a stronger tendency to use one attribute (the size of a business venture) as the defining feature of an entrepreneur, an approach, which can be problematic in terms of identifying the broader characteristics of entrepreneurs, especially in Africa where this group is highly heterogeneous. Worse still, in the entrepreneurship literature, there is no consensus on the definition of who an entrepreneur is. Different analysts adopt different definitions such that there is a lack of consistency in the meaning assigned to this term (see Sharma and Chrisman, 2007). Because of the different ways in which the terms can be used, it is useful to state clearly the scope and meaning given to the term to avoid confusion.

Like many other commonly used terms, entrepreneurship is difficult to define accurately, precisely because the term has acquired wider usage and encompasses a wide range of actors. As Feinburg (1973) has observed, in the process of trying to define something, it often happens that the exercise of defining something results in making what is being defined appear mysterious. To avoid this pitfall it might be useful to find a set of basic features common to the category of entrepreneurs, and use these to delineate the meaning of the term. The danger with this approach is that it can lead to constructing a meaning that is either too inclusive to have any practical applicability or too restrictive that it becomes less useful to capture the heterogeneity that the term entails. But, in trying to come to some understanding of who an entrepreneur is, it might be useful to look at what exactly an entrepreneur does that sets him or her apart. Unfortunately, even with such an approach there is still a large band of grey area around what qualifies one as an entrepreneur.

The challenge of delineating an entrepreneur from other people is even more onerous in Africa where the scope of what entrepreneurship covers is quite wide. For example, should the person selling second-hand clothes on the roadside be classified as an entrepreneur in the same way as a person who makes wine from bananas for sale? Do these two people have anything in common? Such questions are difficult to resolve and often make the analysis of entrepreneurship more complicated. In the absence of a commonly agreed definition, analysts often make arbitrary decisions on who to include and exclude. While the lack of a common definition presents a difficulty in distinguishing entrepreneurs from non-entrepreneurs (see Spring and McDade, 1998), it has been observed that the absence of a common definition suggests that scholarship on this topic is still emerging, with the core concepts still being refined as this field of study grows (Sharma and Chrisman, 2007).

Important, yet an Elusive Character

Despite the absence of a common definition of an entrepreneur, entrepreneurship is widely acknowledged as an important component of economic development, and particularly industrialisation. Arthur Lewis is reported to have argued that "economic growth is bound to be slow unless there is an adequate supply of entrepreneurs looking out for new ideas, and willing to take the risk of introducing them" (cited in Amsden, 1989:78). Thomas Piketty (2015), although he is critical of entrepreneurs as largely constituting a rentier class, also acknowledges that entrepreneurship is an "indispensable force for economic development". Adelman (1984) asserts that the creation of the International Finance Corporation at the World Bank during the 1960s was motivated by the shortage of entrepreneurs in developing countries, and governments were encouraged to increase the training of entrepreneurs. From these ideas, it is quite clear that many societies have high expectation from entrepreneurs. Therefore, the deliberations about entrepreneurs should not just be about who should be included and excluded in this category. Entrepreneurship is fundamentally about the role of entrepreneurs, not only in economic growth and industrialisation, but in the broader transformation of society.

Ironically, as William Baumol (1968) observes, while entrepreneurship is widely acknowledged to be an important component of society, the entrepreneur has received less analytical attention as an economic agent:

> The entrepreneur is at the same time one of the most intriguing and one of the most elusive characters in the cast that constitute the subject of economic analysis. He has long been recognised as the apex of the hierarchy that determines the behavoir

> of the firm and thereby bears heavy responsibilities for the vitality of the free enterprise society. In the writings of the classical economists his appearance was frequent, though he remained a shadowy entity without clearly defined form and function. Only Schumpeter and, to some degree, Professor Knight succeeded in infusing him with life and in assigning to him a specific area of activity… (Baumol, 1968:64).

It is not clear why economic analysis has tended to treat the entrepreneur as if he or she is an entity that does not require analysis or understanding. Baumol was not alone in observing that the entrepreneur, though an important actor in society, has not received sufficient scholarly attention. Other analysts have made similar observations, arguing that while there is no doubt that an "entrepreneur contributes disproportionately to the economy of a nation… little has been done to isolate this individual for further analysis" (Carland et al, 2007:73).

This lack of scholarly attention given to entrepreneurs may account for the current lack of conceptual clarity regarding who an entrepreneur is. For instance, Schumpeter (1934) put the emphasis on two attributes as the defining feature of an entrepreneur: *organisational skills* (defining entrepreneurs as people who initiate new combinations of processes, input supply, products, markets, organisational forms etc.), and *innovation* (defining entrepreneurs as agents of change). But this understanding of entrepreneurship has been contested. Some scholars place the emphasis not on the ability to innovate and start something new, but on the ability to recognise and take advantage of an opportunity, as something which sets the entrepreneur apart from the rest (Chileshe, 1992; Holocombe, 1998; Gries and Naudé, 2010). Other analysts have argued that entrepreneurship need not result in the establishment of a new business (see Lighthelm, 2010:137). Thus, it seems as though "No one has been able to capture the 'beast' but everyone imagine what it looks like" (Spring and McDade, 1998:2).

What seems clear in the entrepreneurship literature is that entrepreneurs have received little scholarly attention when compared to other social and economic actors in society. We know quite a lot about politicians and managers as a class in society than we do about entrepreneurs in general. One of the common explanations offered is that entrepreneurship is often assumed to be an intricate part of any business venture, and therefore, it is rarely treated as a separate entity from business and management studies (Carland et al, 2007). Further, entrepreneurs are widely seen to be an integral part of the investor or business class broadly, such that scholars do not see the need to isolate them from the crowd of the business class. In a way, the malleability of entrepreneurs accounts for their elusiveness, making it difficult to distinguish them from other groups such as managers, innovators etc.

However, in recent years, there is a realisation that entrepreneurs cannot be taken for granted nor should they be lumped together with other groups. The entrepreneur is increasingly being perceived as someone with unique gifts which need to be natured and carefully studied to understand how he or she operates and what can be done to improve his or her contribution to society (UNCTAD, 2015). The importance of entrepreneurship is becoming more critical as the growing knowledge-based economy (KBE), riding on the digital revolution, opens up the possibility to innovate and create not only new tools and ideas, but also new circuits of value. The horizon of innovation has been greatly expanded in the last decade by the growth of technology, particularly the ability to handle and process large amounts of data, and with this, the opportunities for creating something new have exponentially increased. In the context of developing countries where employment growth has stagnated, the emphasis has shifted to promoting entrepreneurship as a means to reduce unemployment and underemployment, especially among the youth.

Entrepreneurship and Small and Medium Enterprises

In Africa, as noted earlier, part of the drive to promote entrepreneurship is also linked to the strategy for industrial development, and the youth are being encouraged to dream big and become important actors in the IR 4.0. For example, the 2017 African Economic Outlook (AEO), which explored the link between entrepreneurship and industrialisation has recommended that African countries' "new industrialisation strategies should … leverage Africa's booming entrepreneurship" (see AEO, 2017: 6). There is now growing recognition across the continent that the conventional way of industrialising through the large enterprises (usually foreign multinational companies) is not going to make much difference. It is rather the small and medium enterprises (SMEs) which are seen to have great potential to contribute to industrial development. The Action Plan for the *Accelerated Industrial Development for Africa* (AIDA), for example, has specifically identified the promotion of small and rural industries as a key to accelerating industrialisation, and the upgrading of entrepreneurial skills among the small-scale producers is widely believed to be vital to industrial growth (see AU, 2007).

Entrepreneurship as a Factor of Production

To highlight the importance of entrepreneurship, scholars and business people have both recognised entrepreneurship as a factor of production, which plays the important role of coordinating the way the other factors of production are combined (Klein, 2006). As a result, there are growing efforts since the mid-1990s to document and profile entrepreneurship trends globally through initiatives such as the Global Entrepreneurship Monitor (GEM). In addition, a number of detailed studies have been conducted to understand how to cultivate and sustain the entrepreneurial *ethos*, which is an important ingredient in the process of industrial development and the broader process of economic growth and social transformation (Gries and Naudé, 2010).

But still, even with this growing acknowledgement, much of the attention has been directed towards understanding the role of entrepreneurship as an activity and less on the actors and the environment in which they operate. For instance, the GEM report focuses on understanding the "influence of entrepreneurship on economic growth" (GEM, 2012:6), and much less on entrepreneurs as individuals in society.

Society's Perception of Entrepreneurs

Perhaps the little analytical attention given to entrepreneurs has affected the way they are perceived in society. In a recent paper, Naude (2013) makes the observation that scholars have often not only neglected analysis of this crucial protagonist, but have sometimes openly detested entrepreneurs. We also find a similar view in Piketty (2015) who, although admitting that entrepreneurs play a critical role in society, argues that many of them unscrupulously accumulate wealth and contribute immensely to growing inequality in terms of both income and wealth, globally. Entrepreneurs are often perceived as people bent on amassing wealth by any (including unscrupulous) means. In some societies, entrepreneurs are mistrusted because they are believed to manipulate production and other systems to maintain dominance in niche markets for years, and in some cases, for centuries as family businesses which are passed on from one generation to another.[5] Because of this, they are seen as people who disregard basic moral principles in their quest to succeed in business, and often conspire against the broader well-being of society.

It is perhaps this idea that entrepreneurs are people who are consumed by the desire to succeed in business, at any cost (super capitalist), which has made society suspicious and less interested in knowing this section of society. This view is articulated more strongly in African societies where successful entrepreneurs are believed to use supernatural powers to enhance their businesses. But this negative perception of entrepreneurs is controversial because some entrepreneurs, while they may manipulate prices and markets, and their activities directly exploit the entire society for decades, their new ideas or inventions make huge contributions to upgrading society in general. For instance, the Kenyan youth who developed the M-Pesa technology; while their businesses may be making money from poor families, at the same time, the service they developed has made it easy for people (including the poor) to transfer money. The ease with which money is transferred using the M-Pesa app contributes significantly to the well-being of many people in society. In the past, people would spend hours on treacherous roads and in long queues in banks, just to get 30 Kenya Shillings.

Further, not all entrepreneurs are motivated by the desire for profit; there are social entrepreneurs whose main goal is to bring new ideas that can improve the lives of ordinary people in society (see Rivera-Santos et al, 2015). These entrepreneurs create social investment funds or what is now known as "profit with a purpose" (see AEO, 2017).

Generally, the perceptions of entrepreneurs are changing as formal employment shrinks globally, and as interest in entrepreneurship, especially in developing countries where formal employment has remained low, grows. It is therefore not surprising that Africa has the most positive attitude towards entrepreneurship, with 77 percent of respondents indicating that entrepreneurs are respected in society and that entrepreneurship constitutes a respectable career path (GEM, 2017). Europe, as one would expect, reported the lowest score on how entrepreneurs are perceived, recording the lowest percentage of respondents who view entrepreneurship as an attractive career path (ibid).

Entrepreneurs and Social Change

However, the role of an entrepreneur has often been limited to the economic sphere, particularly creating jobs, promoting growth and competitiveness in the economy, increasing the pool of skills and creating and sustaining an entrepreneurial culture (McDade and Spring, 2005; Kritiko, 2014). But entrepreneurs can have much wider impact in society and contribute to broader processes of changes beyond the economic sphere. As Durham (2000) observes, entrepreneurs play an important role in the social, political and cultural dynamics in society, especially youth entrepreneurs who often set social trends by introducing new ideas, new ways of interacting, new services, new products. More recently, it has been recognised that entrepreneurs contribute more towards building good governance by promoting the culture of competitiveness. In Africa where the median age of entrepreneurs is 31, the vitality that young entrepreneurs bring can help create dynamism and optimism in society (see AEO, 2017). This optimism among the youth, if nurtured and supported well, can play a critical role in overcoming the comparative disadvantage that most African countries have when it comes to upgrading and developing industrial capacity and capabilities. Africa certainly needs the vitality and the militancy of youth entrepreneurs to defy the current configuration of comparative advantage.

Common Characteristics of Entrepreneurship

Since entrepreneurship is defined differently, it is not surprising that one finds different characteristics emphasised by different analysts as the defining features. In these circumstances, it is perhaps useful to look at the term in a less restrictive manner which allows one to talk about different types of entrepreneurs. The advantage of taking a broader approach in a field which is at its early stages of development is that it enables one to refine the concept as new evidence emerges from research (Sharma and Chrisman, 2007). Therefore, it might be useful to think of entrepreneurship as a continuum covering a wide range of activities and actors (Carland et al, 2007:76). Approaching entrepreneurship from this angle makes the terms more useful than adopting a more restrictive approach, based on a narrow range of attributes such as risk taking or innovativeness. A restrictive approach may not be appropriate to the African context where the range of entrepreneurs can be so wide that it becomes difficult to capture the reality on the ground (Rogerson, 2001).

However, within the wide range of features which people say are what sets entrepreneurs apart, it is possible to find a common set of features used by different analysts to define an entrepreneur, although it is important to keep in mind that most of these features are contested. In the entrepreneurship literature, which has actually grown significantly since the 1990s (see Parker, 2009), the ability to spot an opportunity and take action is often cited as one of the basic features common to all entrepreneurs. This can be broadened to mean that an entrepreneur is defined by the ability to recognise an opportunity and *act on it resolutely*. In other words, entrepreneurs are practical people; they are *doers*. They are usually people who are able to identify an opportunity to provide a service or introduce new products in a community or market and take action to actualise the opportunity (see AEO, 2017).

While many analysts take the ability to *spot* and take advantage of an opportunity as a fundamental feature of an entrepreneur, others emphasise the ability to take "calculated risk" as something that distinguishes an entrepreneur from other people (Marsden, 1990; Lighthelm, 2010). It is also widely acknowledged that entrepreneurs have a high risk tolerance. Chileshe (1992), for instance, argues that an entrepreneur is someone who is capable of overcoming the fear to take considerable risk. Often times, managerial skills are also seen as a core attribute of an entrepreneur, though this has been disputed, with some analysts arguing that a person who owns or runs an enterprise is not necessarily an entrepreneur (see Carland et al, 2007). It has been argued for instance that not all entrepreneurs are managers, and not all managers are entrepreneurs.

There is also some suggestion in the literature that a common feature that all entrepreneurs share is that of an exceptional work *ethic*, underpinned by the innovative drive and a passion for success. Applying this to Africa, it has been suggested that all entrepreneurs in Africa, "share the local… equivalent of the protestant ethic that was so important in Europe's nineteenth century economic development" (Elkan, 1988:173). There are other attributes which are widely seen as fundamental to the definition of an entrepreneur. For example, innovation is one attribute that is often associated with entrepreneurs in the Schumpeterian sense of the term. There has also been some degree of consensus around the view that entrepreneurs operate at different stages of the *entrepreneurship cycle*, and it is important to understand the cycle at which an entrepreneur is (Adrich and Martinez, 2007).[6]

In addition to the above, there is also some degree of consensus around the idea that entrepreneurs are people at the frontier of creating new ideas, new products, new ways of doing and organising business, new ways of seeing the world. For example, at the 2015 Global Entrepreneurship Summit (GES) held in Nairobi, Kenya, the then outgoing US President Barack Obama asserted that "entrepreneurship creates new jobs and new businesses, new ways of seeing the world—it is a spark of prosperity" (Obonyo, 2016:16). Similarly, "academics and policy makers agree that entrepreneurs, both young and old and the new business they establish, play a critical role in the development and well-being of their societies. As such, there is increasing appreciation and accounting for the role played by new and small businesses in an economy" (GEM, 2012:10).

In Africa there is an emerging belief that promoting entrepreneurship will contribute to the development of the continent, as entrepreneurs search for new opportunities while at the same time overcoming the barriers to innovate and generate new ideas. The 2017 AEO has emphasised the importance of peer learning, which entrepreneurship brings, as critical to the process of industrialising the continent (AEO, 2017). But the bigger question about the role of African entrepreneurs in contributing to industrial growth and development is around scale. The scale at which African entrepreneurs operate has to grow fast for Africa to make a mark on the industrial map of the globe.

Opportunity versus Survivalist Entrepreneurs

The literature in entrepreneurship makes a distinction between *opportunity* and *survivalist* entrepreneurs. It is often argued that only the former group (opportunity entrepreneurs) are the real entrepreneurs. For instance, there have been heated debates about whether the people who own food and clothing business ventures on the streets of African cities and towns should be regarded as entrepreneurs or not (Rogerson, 2001; McDade and Spring, 2005; Lighthelm, 2010; GEM, 2012). *Opportunity entrepreneurs* are seen as people "who pursue a business opportunity" while "*survivalist entrepreneurs*" are believed to be "those who are involved in an entrepreneurial endeavour because they have no other choice of work" (Lighthelm, 2010:137). Using the concepts of *opportunity* and *survivalism*, analysts often recognise only people who *spot and act* on an opportunity as entrepreneurs, since, according to this view, such people are not compelled by circumstances, as is the case with people engaged in survivalist ventures (ibid). Drawing from Vespers' categories of entrepreneurs, Carland et al (2007:78) make a similar argument that only enterprises which possess the four characteristics of: i) being able to introduce new goods (and probably services), b) introduce new methods of production, c) opening up new markets and d) industrial re-organisation should be categorised as entrepreneurial ventures. Anything else should not be confused with entrepreneurship.

But this approach to entrepreneurship would effectively exclude most small businesses, which often do not possess all or any of the characteristics listed above. This approach is problematic especially in Africa where an overwhelming majority of entrepreneurs are small and of a survivalist nature (Rogerson, 2001; GEM, 2012; Herrington and Kew, 2017). Further, the distinction between *opportunity* and *survivalist* may be spurious here. Someone could be driven by the necessity to survive, and as a result, recognises and takes advantage of an existing business opportunity. Such undertakings may not lead to re-organisation of industry or the introduction of new goods or services, but they do reflect a person's ability to recognise a business opportunity, and act on it. In this regard, applying the opportunity–necessity framework might be highly problematic in the African context.

More fundamentally, distinguishing entrepreneurs on the basis of *necessity* and *opportunity* may be conceptually superficial. It is possible that the same person motivated by *necessity* can have the capacity to spot and act on an *opportunity*, no matter how small. Similarly, all business ventures have an element of *necessity*, not necessarily the necessity to survive, but may be the strong prompting to succeed, to be self-employed, to be a business owner, etc. Necessity in this sense may actually drive someone to recognise and act on an opportunity. As long as necessity here is taken to mean an inner push to do something, there is always an element of *necessity* in acting on any business opportunity, regardless of scale. Therefore, if our concern in studying entrepreneurship is to identify the general characteristics of the various entrepreneurial activities, then scale and motive may not be valid grounds for distinguishing entrepreneurs. There can be business owners at a very small scale but with unique abilities to recognise a business opportunity wherever it exists. Surely, excluding such people on the grounds that they run an US$500 business or simply because that is the only thing they have to do to survive seems arbitrary. Does the mere fact that the person is operating at a very small scale (survivalist scale) mean that he or she is deprived of entrepreneurial qualities?

Not surprisingly, a number of studies on African entrepreneurs have entirely focused on what they call *productive entrepreneurs*, meaning those operating viable businesses (Brixiova and Ncube, 2013). For example, McDade and Spring's (2005:17) study decided to focus on medium- and large-scale entrepreneurs, arguing that most "research focuses on entrepreneurs who operate micro- and small-scale enterprises in the traditional informal and formal sector". In studies which have examined micro-business ventures in the informal sector, the owners of these undertakings are frequently considered as *survivalists, and not* entrepreneurs.

Despite the strong assertions of a rising Africa driven by, among other things, a growing class of African entrepreneurs (Radelet, 2010a), the bulk of entrepreneurial activities on the continent remain within the small-scale, survivalist range (GEM, 2012). In such a context, it may be analytically useful to disaggregate business ventures into different clusters to capture the wide spectrum of entrepreneurial activities. Similarly, this diverse landscape of entrepreneurship in Africa requires a framework which can capture the different types and sizes of business ventures. Understanding the diverse universe inhabited by African entrepreneurs can help policy makers begin to think of the possible role that each group can play in the process of industrialisation. For African governments to leverage the booming entrepreneurial spirit, it is crucial to have a clear understanding of what the various groups are in order to appreciate the contribution that each group can make towards the goal of industrialising the continent. Although there is no agreement about who an African entrepreneur is, there are common features which are associated with entrepreneurship in Africa.

Characteristics of African Entrepreneurs

It must be apparent by now that African entrepreneurs, like entrepreneurs in other parts of the world, come in different shapes, colours, sizes and ideological orientation. They are not a homogeneous group of people. As such, it is difficult to speak of an African entrepreneur in the singular. However, it is useful to identify some of the common characteristics of entrepreneurs in Africa, drawing from the social, economic and political milieu where they operate (Marsden, 1990). Here, I focus on features of African entrepreneurs which make them different from their European, Asian or Latin American counterparts. Although there has been little research conducted so far to provide some insights into what distinguishes an African entrepreneur from others, the few studies conducted so far have highlighted a number of common features, which are briefly discussed below.

Dominance of Informal Ventures

Studies conducted during the 1990s concluded that while there is no scarcity of entrepreneurs in Africa, majority of them operate in the informal sector. The AEO (2017) also reports that majority (more than half) of early-stage African entrepreneurs operate SMEs and are predominantly involved in the services sector, mainly retail, hotels and restaurant, with only 8 percent involved in manufacturing (AEO, 2017). Most of these ventures are one-person businesses, and some estimates suggest that only 2 percent of the entrepreneurs have 10 or more workers (McDade and Spring, 2005). These entrepreneurs establish business ventures in a wide range of activities including manufacturing of furniture, building accessories like door and window frames, sliding gates, water tanks, water tank stands; retail ventures ranging from selling food, medicine, new and second-hand clothes, vehicle repairs, public transport (taxis and minibuses), cosmetics and beauty services; micro-financing, construction, real estate and information and communication services.

One of the reasons why entrepreneurs in Africa and other developing countries concentrate in the services sector, particularly retail businesses and restaurants, is because these activities require low skills and low capital outlay to initiate. In other words, most African entrepreneurs set businesses in retail and hospitality sector, because the barriers to entry are low compared to other activities such as manufacturing and the information and communication sector which require not only large capital outlay but also a relatively high level of skills (GEM, 2017). While most of these entrepreneurs start their businesses with the hope of growing, it has been observed that majority of them remain small, at the survivalist level (GEM, 2012), and that many are not keen to formally register their business ventures due to the excessive regulation and high taxes (Sonobe et al, 2009). As a result, few of these entrepreneurs graduate from owning small businesses to large enterprises. Some estimates suggest that only 1 percent of enterprises transition from being micro to medium and large-scale ventures (see Rogerson, 2001:118).

If this is true, then for entrepreneurs to positively contribute to the goal of industrialising the continent, there is need to scale up the activities of most of these business ventures. The informal manufacturing sector particularly has great potential in many countries (see AEO, 2017). In the course of writing this book, I visited several small-scale manufacturing ventures in Kampala, Lusaka, Kigali and Soweto, and it is clear from the range of activities occurring in these places that the potential to upgrade some of these ventures is quite high, given the right incentive and support. As the world gears for an era of diminishing formal wage employment, African countries will have great deal of experience in this field, which they can take advantage of to promote alterative employment and income-generating strategies. The small-scale manufacturing ventures can play a significant role in adapting and promoting the growth of appropriate technology and learning by doing.

However, not all African entrepreneurs are locked in the small-scale, informal groove; there are many medium and large-scale multinational corporations owned and run by Africans. This is especially true in the last fifteen years when the internationalisation of African enterprises, as a result of the spread of *Africa to Africa* business (A2AB) initiatives, has taken root (Ngwu et al, 2016).

Lack of Start-Up Packages and Credit Facilities

The other feature that is common among African entrepreneurs is the well-studied factor of constrained access to credit and start-up capital in general. Most studies, which explored the issue among African entrepreneurs, report that most of them mention the lack of or inadequate access to capital as the main constraint. In Ethiopia, access to capital was one of the major constraints cited by most respondents (Brixiova and Ncube, 2013). Despite the establishment of the Youth Enterprise Funds (YEFs) as well as the Africa Guarantee Fund (AGF) for SMEs which operate in 35 countries (see AEO, 2017), access to capital, especially start-ups among the youth, is a binding constraint which is widely recognised across different countries (Brixiova et al, 2014). Lack of access to capital comes up often as a constraint to the development and growth of business enterprises because banks and other lending institutions have not yet embraced the small and micro-entrepreneurs, who often have to rely on their saving to get started and to grow. A UNIDO (2016) report observes that most of the large commercial banks globally have not yet developed products geared towards small businesses, largely because small businesses do not have conventional collateral. This is an area where selective policy intervention can have great impact if properly implemented.

Growing Numbers of Returnees

Another unique feature dominant among African entrepreneurs, especially the young business people, is the increasing number of young Africans returning from abroad to start business ventures on the continent, not necessarily in their country of origin. Many of these returnees have had experience of working in large corporations, some of them in managerial positions. These young entrepreneurs went to school abroad, and they have decided to come back and take advantage of the business opportunities they see in Africa. In a study conducted among members of the regional entrepreneurship network in

Africa, it was found that 85 percent of the members studied abroad but came back to start a business at home (McDade and Spring, 2005:23). Analysis of the *Forbes* magazine's list of 30 most promising young entrepreneurs in Africa in 2014 and 2016 also reveals a similar trend (Nsehe, 2016). George Ayitteh (2005) observes that most of the young entrepreneurs establishing new businesses in Africa are people who have studied abroad and have decided to return home because they have seen business opportunities which they are seeking to exploit.

However, it is important to note that this is at the higher end of the African entrepreneur pyramid; majority of the entrepreneurs in the informal sector are still characterised by low levels of education and skills, inadequate access to capital and lack of exposure to the frontiers of business ideas, beyond the confines of their local communities (Rogerson, 2001). Further, the growth of returnees is quite a recent phenomenon, which is associated with the changing perception of Africa, especially after the 2009 financial crisis when returns on investments in developed countries declined dramatically as interest rates plummeted to less than a percent in most industrialised countries. Many of the returnees do not just bring capital to start a business, they also bring a certain business culture, diverse business experiences and the skill of adapting a business venture to respond to changing consumer tastes and technologies. I remember interviewing a business public relations consultant in Lusaka, Zambia, about the role of the returnees and she indicated that one of the key distinguishing features of the returnees is that they bring a particular business culture, which they have learned from wherever they worked or did business before. However, anecdotal evidence suggests that not many of these returnees are actually setting up industrial ventures, particularly manufacturing; most of them are going into the information and communication sector as well as business consultancy. This is an area that requires empirical research to get some insight into the scale of the returnees and the areas where they are operating.

The Emergence of a Pan-African Entrepreneur

As entrepreneurship in African expands and become more professional, many African entrepreneurs are beginning to position themselves into operating beyond national borders. They are transforming the colonial boundaries by adopting a pan-African business orientation, which see Africa as a single market. What this pan-African entrepreneurial orientation has done is to create a sense of collective awareness, enabling entrepreneurs to share opportunities and the common challenges they face in different countries and business sectors. This is partly a result of the slowly deepening process of regional integration, which reduces the red tape around starting businesses in African countries.

A number of African entrepreneurs are taking initiative to organise themselves into business networks to take advantage of the business opportunities which the deepening of regional integration has created. A good example of this is the creation of regional entrepreneur networks during the 1990s—the African Enterprise Network (AEN).[7] These networks are facilitating the creation of a pan-African business outlook and approach among entrepreneurs who are now thinking more in terms of regional market opportunities, beyond the domestic market (Rogerson and Mushawemhuka, 2015; Obonyo, 2016). Members of these regional networks help each other on various issues including advice on how to set up business ventures in other countries. For example, a Ugandan network member disclosed during interviews that he "feels comfortable with his decision to venture into Zambia and Tanzania; he trusts the recommendation for prospective partners and advice about business conditions he received from network members in those countries…" (McDade and Spring, 2005:28).

This pan-African orientation among African entrepreneurs is boosted by the growing regional trading blocs such as COMESA, with 26 African member countries cutting across four regional economic communities, and the creation of the Africa Continental Free Trade Area (ACFTA) in 2018, is likely to enhance the growth of entrepreneurial activities across borders.

High Costs of Doing Business

The other unique feature about African entrepreneurs is that they face high costs at different levels. The costs can range from the time and money it takes to register a business, to high input and market access costs. The high logistical costs that many African entrepreneurs face are largely due to poor and inadequate infrastructure, which makes the transportation of inputs and products from and to markets relatively expensive (Goedhuys and Sleuwaegen, 2009). Logistical costs can be relatively high especially for small businesses, which operate below the scale needed to bring down the costs. For example, in 2011, one ton of cement costs US$53 in China, US$62 in Vietnam and US$92 in the USA, but costs US$223 in Nigeria, US$250 in Angola and US$170 in Ethiopia (see Oqubay, 2015:123). If you are an African entrepreneur dealing in cement products you are certainly facing a steep price cliff compared to counterparts who source cement from other parts. The issue of high costs applies in many other instances, not just cement.

Generations of African Entrepreneurs

As noted above, entrepreneurship is not something new in Africa; scholars have been studying entrepreneurship in Africa since the 1920s. There have been efforts in the past, during both the colonial and post-colonial periods, to analyse African entrepreneurs. But "much of what has been written about African entrepreneurship views it unfavourably" (Elkan, 1988:172). So the optimistic views and positive assessments of African entrepreneurs reported in the last decade is something which marks a recent shift in public opinion and perception. Perhaps this is because much of the stories about entrepreneurship is now being written by Africans themselves, including entrepreneurs, unlike in the past when most of the studies were done by non-Africans.

There are several reasons for the unfavourable assessments of African entrepreneurs in the past. One of the reasons is that an African capitalist class failed to emerge and steer-up the transformation of African economies and societies at large. In the past, those critical of African entrepreneurs argued that a genuine class of African entrepreneurs, imbued with the entrepreneurial spirit and ethos, did not emerge. What emerged was a class of "bureaucratic bourgeoisie" that relied mainly on privileged access to state power, resources and influence to support their private entrepreneurial activities (see Arrighi and Saul, 1968). Fanon (1963) had earlier made a similar critique arguing that what was emerging in the 1960s was not African captains of industry, but state bureaucrats who were only bent on replacing the white colonial officers. Given these views, it is important to see if the new generation of African entrepreneurs exhibits different qualities from what was observed in the past.

Absence of an Indigenous Capitalist Class

Goran Hyden (1983) has argued that one of the most important factors which account for the low levels of development and industrialisation on the African continent is that Africa has lacked a genuine indigenous capitalist class which could initiate the process of surplus production and accumulation. According to Hyden (1983), a foreign capitalist class which has dominated economic activities in Africa adopted a transitory posture, treating Africa as a place where money is made, but is kept elsewhere. As a result, the continent has always been a capital-scare region, relying on external capital, which only comes to make money that ends up elsewhere, and this has evolved into a vicious circle that has contributed to the inability to deepen and spread economic growth.

In recent years, this phenomenon has attracted the attention of policy makers at the continental level, who have highlighted the challenge of capital flight from Africa. A recent report by a High-Level Panel of experts, chaired by the former South African President Thabo Mbeki, reported that illicit outflows alone (excluding the legal outflows) amount to US$50 billion per annum (see AU/UNECA, 2015). While there are many factors which influence capital flight, the fact that most of the large companies operating in Africa are foreign contributes to the high rates of capital leaving the continent. If a large group of local entrepreneurs emerges, it would reduce the extent of capital flight as local capitalists may be more inclined to accumulate capital and keep it within the continent to finance industrial development and other economic activities.

One might argue that there are many Africans who have accumulated a lot of money but have chosen to keep it in the Swiss and Panama Bank accounts. It could be argued that this is because most of the people who accumulated this wealth were not genuine capitalists, they are generally bureaucratic bourgeoisies who are not infused with the entrepreneurial spirit; they have largely been looting state resources (see Arrighi and Saul, 1968). Genuine African entrepreneurs would keep and re-invest the money they make in the continent because this is a place where they work and live. Although the report by the High-Level Panel of Experts on illicit capital outflow from Africa has not attributed high levels of capital flight to the absence of an indigenous capitalist class, it does note that Africa is losing more capital than what comes in through FDI and ODI (official development assistance) combined (see AU/UNECA, 2015). In this regard, it would be interesting to examine if the now acclaimed "cheetah generation" is keeping the money accumulated in Africa. According to the factor endowment theory, the returns on capital in Africa ought to be higher because capital is a scarce factor relative to labour, and as such, Africa should be an attractive destination for capital because of the prospect for high returns (Krugman, 1987). But as we know, capital remains a scarce factor in Africa, and this could be attributed to the absence of a significant indigenous industrial entrepreneur class.

African Entrepreneurs in Colonial and Post-Colonial Periods

Although an entrepreneurial class has been part of the African social fabric for a long time, most of the African entrepreneurs during colonial rule were stifled by discriminatory rules and practices. A close examination of colonial rules and practices reveals that African entrepreneurs during colonialism were categorically prevented from rising to the top of the industrial sector; many were confined to retail and wholesale activities. The manufacturing sector was reserved for settlers and foreign investors during colonial rule and state-owned enterprises during the first two decades of independence.

To a large extent, the unfavourable perception of entrepreneurs in Africa in the past has to do with the enduring colonial biases which fuelled a vicious form Africa bashing. Such views have solidified into discourses which see Africans as people having no dreams beyond the immediate needs to survive. The prevalence of survivalist ventures on the continent is often cited to support the view that most Africans only think about surviving in the moment and have no concept of saving for tomorrow, which is crucial to the success of entrepreneurship (see Elkan, 1988). This negative perception of Africans is starkly expressed in a book that purports to understand Africans well:

> Many Africans, however, have little and see themselves potentially acquiring even less. Needing so much, they cannot think about being efficient. They want to garner what they can—in this sense they are certainly materialists—but they cannot and will not risk the little that they have on the chance of creating more. The image that comes to my mind is of a market woman alongside a road with her small stack of fruits or vegetables. I have often seen, across African cultures, such women stack and restack a few lemons, groundnuts, or green pepper, apparently savouring the value of the inventory and the prospect of garnering a few coins. This vendor is usually seated only a few feet from another woman who is selling the same lemons, doing the same rearranging. There is no apparent sense of competition—that is not the African way. And so African society avoids both the unpleasantness of competition and confrontation, and the attendant savings account! That African societies have developed in this way is easily understood, but such understanding does not make life more productive (Fredland, 2001:9–10).

The author is unmistakably clear that entrepreneurship is beyond the aspiration of Africans, and when we do not see much of it, we should not be surprised. For such critics, notions of a new generation of an African entrepreneur are just mere fantasy which should only be entertained by dreamers.

Starved by Colonial Scheming

The cynical view of African entrepreneurs dominant in some earlier accounts is challenged by Iliffe (1983) who argues that an African entrepreneurial class did in fact emerge, despite the various barriers put on its way, by both the colonial and post-colonial African states. Iliffe (1983) provides detailed historical evidence of many African entrepreneurs who established successful commercial ventures prior to colonial rule. Long and short distance merchant classes have been reported in West and East Africa, way before the contact with the West (see Amin, 1972). One example of a successful African entrepreneur class is the Giriama people in coastal Kenya, whose "enterprising younger family heads began to accumulate land and coconut palms at the expense of the less far-sighted" (Iliffe, 1983:48). In his study of entrepreneurship in West Africa, Bauer also found a thriving class of African entrepreneurs with a unique ascetic work ethic: "The general impression I formed was always the same", Bauer asserts; "exceptional effort, foresighted, resourcefulness, thrift and ability to perceive opportunity" (cited in Elkan, 1988:173). Similarly, in a study of Nigerian entrepreneurs, Swartz found the local people he studied to be "responsive to the possibility of gain and [ready] to pursue economic advantage vigorously and strenuously" (*ibid.*).

Iliffe (1983) cites many examples of enterprising African groups including members of the Jehovah's Witness in Zambia, Ayetoro in Nigeria, Bregbo in Ivory Coast, Giriama in Kenya, Sanusi Brotherhood in West Africa (particularly Niger), Reformed Tijaniyya Brotherhood in Nigeria, and Wahhabism in Burkina Faso (see Kilby, 1965). These religious groupings are said to have developed entrepreneurial spirit from the "belief that hard work and prosperity were demonstrations of faith and assurance of salvation" (Ilife, 1983:61). Strong entrepreneurial proclivities have also been reported among several African ethnic groups such as the Kikuyus in Kenya, the Luba in former Zaire, the Lala people in Zambia and the Hausa in Nigeria (ibid).

But the growth of most of these groups into an influential class of entrepreneurs was largely blocked by colonial racist tactics, some of which openly denied Africans the opportunity to undertake business ventures of any meaningful size. After independence, post-colonial African states, influenced by the colonial ideology that only foreign investors can establish and run successful industrial ventures in Africa, did little to promote the growth of local entrepreneurs. Despite the drive towards indigenisation that most African countries adopted (see Chapter 5), most local entrepreneurs were seen as a nuisance, an attitude that has continued among many African bureaucrats even today, largely manifested in the hard-line taken against local entrepreneurs when it comes to enforcing tax laws (see AEO, 2017).

On the basis of the colonial and post-colonial experience, it can be argued that most of these entrepreneurial efforts and passions were stymied in both periods. During colonial rule, the colonialists' strategy focused on restricting (in some cases completely eliminating) African competition against the settler business class. The impact of this on the growth of African entrepreneurship is often overlooked by those who see African entrepreneurs as inherently inept. What features more prominently in the narratives coloured with the racist and colonial ideology is that Africans just do not have it in their DNA to establish and run successful business ventures as the quotation from Fredland above clearly suggests. But a close look at the historical records shows that entrepreneurial spirit and effort among many Africans were restricted by the colonial policy which not only supported a settler business class but also devised ways to stifle African competition in important industrial and commercial ventures. Many enterprising Africans found themselves constrained by the laws which did not allow them to engage in certain business activities, especially those that directly competed with the commercial interests of settlers. In the agricultural sector, for instance, it has been reported that,

> Africans were systematically excluded from a number of colonial development schemes, and from producing export crops and improved cattle. British agricultural policy in Eastern Africa benefited European settlers, and discriminated against African farmers, prohibiting Kenyans from growing coffee, for example. Many peasant farmers were compelled to grow selected crops and to maintain roads (Nafziger, 1990:143).

There are several other examples in many African countries in which, during colonial or minority rule, policy was adopted to specifically prevent the emergence and growth of entrepreneurship among Africans. But, the stories one hears about African entrepreneurs are that they often lack the cardinal virtues of *thrift*, *self-discipline* and *diligence* (see Elkan, 1988). Contrary to these stories, as indicated above, many African entrepreneurs who established businesses in the past displayed a unique work ethic manifested by self-exploitation, particularly because many faced a harsh business environment during both the colonial and post-colonial periods. Even today, the African entrepreneurial environment is probably the toughest in the world, where one has to survive against all odds. African entrepreneurs face daunting challenges from harassment by state officials to poor infrastructure, high interest rates, the absence of start-up support and inadequate credit faculties. In this environment, African entrepreneurs have to "run while others walk", just to keep pace with those who operate in relative better environments (see Mkandawire, 2011).

African States and African Entrepreneurs

It is now widely recognised that the type and scope of entrepreneurship in a country is largely shaped by public policy and other strategies. This relates to the point made earlier in this chapter that entrepreneurs are shaped by the social, political, economic, cultural and religious context in which they operate. In this regard, what the state does or does not do can have huge impact on the type of entrepreneurship that develops in a particular country. In the case of Africa, it has been observed that over-extended states which emerged in many African countries during the 1970s negatively impacted on the size and quality of entrepreneurs. The establishment of state-owned enterprises in all sectors of the economy from agriculture marketing to passenger transport and retail chain stores is cited as one of the factors that dampened the entrepreneurial spirit. Marsden (1990), for instance, argues that the prevalence of SOEs in many African countries left little space for entrepreneurs to emerge and assert themselves as business leaders. According to this view, state ownership of means of production and other business ventures, together with tightly controlled licensing and regulation of industrial activities, constrained the growth of the entrepreneurial ethos and acumen.

> In countries where governments are dominant in every sphere of activity, whether through parastatal enterprises, through licensing and controls, or through obliging farmers to sell at prices set by statutory marketing boards, the possibility for gaining entrepreneurial experience are correspondingly reduced (Elkan, 1988:177).

Other than the strict state control, the development and growth of entrepreneurship has been hampered by the attitude of state officials towards local entrepreneurs. For some reason, most African bureaucrats seem to have a strong bias in favour of entrepreneurs and investors from outside the continent, particularly the West, and now the Chinese. Even in cases where local entrepreneurs and investors have more capital than their foreign counterparts, there is always a preference for a foreign investor. This is why, up until the current revival of interest in entrepreneurship, there was little done to promote and support the local entrepreneurs and investors. The current Presidential Investor Advisory Councils (PIACs) which have been established in several African countries to promote state–business dialogue have in most cases excluded local investors (see Page, 2014). There seems to be a strong belief that only money coming from outside the country can bring development. Although the attitude of public officials towards local entrepreneurs is slowly shifting (GEM, 2012), small local entrepreneurs often complain of being harassed by state officials, including the revenue collection agencies who are tough on the locals and extremely lenient with the foreign business operators (AEO, 2017).

It is only in the last decade when the challenge of creating jobs has become a persisting concern that entrepreneurs are looked upon favourably, with many African governments recognising their potential in alleviating the problems of unemployment, under-employment and growing inequality. Some analysts have argued that the dismantling of parastatals and the deregulation of the business environment has contributed to the current upsurge of entrepreneurship on the continent (McDade and Spring, 2005; Brixiova and Ncube, 2013). With specific reference to the role of a developmental state in promoting industrial development, an effective developmental state does not treat private entrepreneurs as a nuisance or opponent; it sees this group as a potential contributor to achieving its goal, and, as such, finds a way to channel the energies and resources of this group towards the identified national goals (see Amsden, 1989). The state–entrepreneur relationship is important during the early stages of industrial development, and a positive relationship between the two is a critical pillar of any successful industrial strategy (see Chapter 7). This requires state officials to appreciate the value of entrepreneurs in the long-term development plan.

Common African Beliefs about Entrepreneurship

It is not just the operation of the state that has affected the development of entrepreneurship in Africa. As noted earlier, societal views, about who an entrepreneur is and what he or she does, have also influenced the type and nature of entrepreneurs. It is for this reason that understanding an entrepreneur's role in society must go beyond the economic contribution they make. Current scholarship on entrepreneurship has not moved beyond the economic contribution entrepreneurs make in society, and this has affected the perception of entrepreneurs because their contribution to society is not fully accounted for. In Africa, the perception of an entrepreneur as someone bent on realising profit at any cost often evokes negative sentiments towards entrepreneurs. In the past, entrepreneurship was perceived negatively in most traditional African societies as something that destroyed the collective spirit, which is a dominant feature of most traditional African communities.

Many African communities, particularly in rural areas even today, deride entrepreneurship as something that promotes individualism, leads to a lack of concern for others, and slowly destroys the cherished communitarian values. Although this perception is said to be changing rapidly as more people see entrepreneurship as an attractive career path and as a source of employment (see GEM, 2017), entrepreneurship still carries some stigma. In many rural as well as urban African communities, successful entrepreneurs are commonly suspected of using *charms* or witchcraft to enhance their businesses. For example, it has been reported that,

> Many rural Rhodesians were said in the 1960s to believe that a successful trader must have buried the heart of a close relative under his counter. The Sukuma people of Northern Tanzania long ascribed the success of pioneer cotton farmers to the fact that they had made zombies work for them (Iliffe, 1983:54).

Such stories are still common, not just in rural areas. The xenophobic attacks against Rwandese-owned businesses in Lusaka, Zambia, in March 2016, have been attributed to the alleged ritual murders, purportedly committed by business owners to enhance the performance of their businesses. According to BBC News, the xenophobic attacks on Rwandese-owned shops in Lusaka were sparked by rumours circulating on social media, alleging that "Rwandans were behind ritual killings in Lusaka" and that "the body parts would be used as charms to ensure success in business" (BBC News, 19 April 2016). Such beliefs, if dominant, influence society's perception of entrepreneurs and this may affect the number of people who decide to engage in entrepreneurial activities (see Takyi-Asiedu, 1993). The 2012 GEM observes that,

> Beliefs about entrepreneurship play a very important role in influencing whether a potential entrepreneur actually starts a business. These beliefs are influenced by whether people see entrepreneurship as a good career choice, whether high status is given to entrepreneurs and what media attention is given to entrepreneurs (GEM, 2012:8).

Fortunately, public perception about entrepreneurship as people who engage in witchcraft or magic is reported to be weakening, such that entrepreneurship is now more favourably perceived in many African communities compared to other part of the world:

> In all SSA [sub-Saharan Africa] countries, without exception, entrepreneurship is seen as a good career choice; more so than in any other regions except Latin America and the Caribbean. In addition, both high status and good media attention is given to entrepreneurs, which is a good thing for the future and may explain the high levels of early-stage entrepreneurial activity in SSA countries (ibid).

The 2017 GEM also reports that positive perception of entrepreneurship as a good career path was highest in Africa in 2016.

> Africa is the region reporting the most positive attitudes towards entrepreneurship, with three quarters of working-age adults considering entrepreneurship a good career choice, while 77% believe that entrepreneurs are admired in their societies. In contrast, Latin America and the Caribbean reports the lowest proportion of adults believing that entrepreneurs are highly regarded (63%) while Europe has the lowest belief in entrepreneurship as a good career (58 percent) and the lowest media publicity for this activity (55 percent) (GEM, 2017).

The growing favourable attitude towards entrepreneurship in Africa can also be attributed to the fact that formal employment in the continent has been shrinking since the 1980s, and entrepreneurship is the only viable alternative for many people especially the youth. Self-employment businesses, where most people operate business ventures of all kinds and sizes, are becoming a common feature of the African urban fabric, and a major source of employment in most African countries (Sonobe et al, 2009; Gries and Naudé, 2010; Lighthelm, 2010; ILO, 2017).

The Role of African Entrepreneurs in Industrialising Africa

Economic growth theories, as observed earlier, have not accounted for the role of entrepreneurs in industrial development. Dries and Naude (2010) highlight this lacuna in the development literature when it comes to explaining the role of entrepreneurship in economic transformation and industrialisation in particular. The seeming absence of entrepreneurs in the growth theories and models may be accounted for by the view that entrepreneurs were often seen as part of the capitalist class and, as such, did not merit separate analysis. But, not all capitalists are entrepreneurs, in the same way that not all entrepreneurs are capitalists. As the role of an entrepreneur becomes more distinct from other economic agents, there is now growing awareness of the specific role entrepreneurship plays in industrial development. Consequently, the role of entrepreneurs in industrial development is becoming more distinct. This has led to specific attention being given to entrepreneurs as a separate analytical entity. In Africa, entrepreneurs are being valued for their potential to contribute to the broader transformation of African economies and societies through a number of channels. Below the commonly believed contributions which entrepreneurs can make towards promoting industrial development are discussed.

Potential to Upgrade Industrial Capabilities

A recent study of entrepreneurship in Africa found that there is growing awareness among policy makers in Africa that entrepreneurship has a critical role to play in the unfolding Industrial Revolution 4.0 (AEO, 2017). As a result of this growing awareness, entrepreneurship is gradually being perceived as an important factor which can influence industrial growth dynamics. As the awareness grows, the potential of entrepreneurs to contribute to industrial development is likely to become more apparent (ibid). Although only a small proportion of African entrepreneurs participate in manufacturing at the formal level, there is great potential to upgrade some of the informal manufacturing firms as domestic markets grow with the growing urban population and economies. The potential of informal manufacturers is evident in most large markets in African cities and towns, where a wide range of manufactured products are on sale, from furniture (home and office) to fabricated metal products including construction materials, crafts, clothing, and household goods such as pots, etc. This is a common feature that points to the fact that there is some form of manufacturing taking place in the informal sector, though at a small scale. The experience gained from these enterprises can be used to upgrade the manufacturing capacity and improve on the standards and quality of the products, as long as these ventures are adequately incentivised and supported to enable them upgrade.

This is where African states can play an instrumental role in facilitating the upgrade of the capabilities and skills, with the aim of improving the quality of the products. How many African states are positively engaging these informal manufacturers is not known. At the continental level, there are strong statements suggesting that African states should work with small business ventures to build industrial capacity and skills. For instance, the AIDA action programme identifies the informal manufacturers and the craft industries as strategic areas where skills can be developed (see AU, 2007). It has even been suggested that the potential for industrial development in Africa lies in the small manufacturing enterprises and not the big manufacturing firms as was the case among the early industrialisers.

The Power of Peer Learning

The other commonly identified role which entrepreneurs in Africa can play in promoting industrial development is learning though peers (see GEM, 2017). This is premised on the view that local actors find it easier to learn from their peers who operate in a similar business environment than from foreign-based firms. While this is similar to the *spill-over effects* approach associated with international trade, the local entrepreneurs can effect change through *peer learning*, which is said to be much easier for small-scale manufacturers than learning from big multinational corporations operating at a different scale. Small enterprises find it easier to learn from their peers who are doing similar things or operating under similar circumstances. In a situation where there are many small entrepreneurs, the learning process can be extensive, spreading to different sectors of the economy. All it takes is someone to introduce innovative ideas or products to initiate the Schumpeterian entrepreneurial momentum. The circle of learning from peers can grow bigger with time, and the capacity to introduce new ideas can be expanded and more entrepreneurs can learn from the leading firms, and eventually become leaders.

Growing the Local Innovation Capability

The capacity to introduce new ideas in the local economy grows when more firms participate in global value chains as suppliers and interact with international lead firms. The medium size and large local manufacturing firms can play an important role of being the link between the international manufacturing leaders and the informal manufacturers who often find it difficult to interact with the big international firms. Transfer of knowledge and technology often occurs through the medium and large firms, which act as a link between the international leaders in manufacturing and the small local firms. It has been observed that local manufacturing firms learn quite quickly such that the period for reaping the "entrepreneurial profits" is said to be short (AEO, 2017). The quicker learning among African firms has been attributed to the "cut and paste" approach which is rampant among small scale entrepreneurs.

During interviews with some of the local firms in Zambia and South Africa, there was a common complaint that small businesses often duplicate what they see others doing, as long as they can make some money. This is a common feature among most of the African entrepreneurs, who as soon as they see someone starting a new business, a million people would replicate the same idea or product as long as there is some money to be made. While this may discourage innovation since the rents for being innovative are small and quickly undercut by imitators, it can also spark the innovative spirit among a few leaders who introduce new ideas or products, and when their ideas spread to other firms, they start to look for new ideas. Through this chain of innovation, it is possible to cultivate the entrepreneurial spirit and develop the skills and capacity in the local economy. There are signs that a number of African entrepreneurs are putting high premium on introducing new ideas in the management of businesses as a way of responding to the rapidly changing consumption preferences and taste, as Africa undergoes rapid urbanisation. Entrepreneurs can play an important role in building local manufacturing capacity.

Growing a Culture of Saving for Start-Ups

The other commonly cited contribution which African entrepreneurs can make towards promoting industrial development in Africa is cultivating the culture of saving. Since most early-phase entrepreneurs face severe credit access constraints as highlighted above, majority of them finance their businesses from their own savings. Although these are often small compared to the large capital outlay required for industrial production (particularly manufacturing), the efforts made to save help to grow the culture of saving, which can contribute to building capital. As the entrepreneurial culture spread in the population, the capital constraint eases when a large number of those wishing to start their own businesses can actually draw from what they have saved. Of course, for upgrading and up-scaling, more capital would be needed, and once an enterprise has reached a scalable level, it is easier to access capital from more formal sources, including financial markets.

The contribution of entrepreneurs here lies in the fact that the initial capital raised by the individual business actors provides a base for experience and the foundation on which higher manufacturing capacity can be developed. The more such small self-financed entrepreneurs are in the economy, the higher the chance that some of them would upgrade into large-scale manufacturing.

Promoting Competitiveness

It is also often observed that entrepreneurship can contribute to industrial development by promoting competitiveness (see Amsden, 1989). If there are many entrepreneurs in a particular sector, they will all be seeking to outperform each other, and through this competition, competencies and efficiencies in firms and sectors can be developed. Developing competition is critical to industrial growth. Competition viewed from this angle can be a powerful force for inducing innovation and progress in building industrial capability. Lighthelm (2010), citing Potter, makes a similar observation that competition sometimes creates an advantage for the consumer as competing firms battle to outperform each other, with the competition often translating into the bid to offer competitive prices. Apart from this, there is a much broader positive outcome from a competitive environment, which is that it drives actors to be more creative. In this sense, Schumpeter's insight that competition leads to "creative destruction" is one of the critical roles entrepreneurship can play in industrial development, especially for countries with low levels of industrial development.

Although competition often leads to attrition of firms that are unable to establish a niche in their businesses, innovative thinking is induced through this mechanism. For the later industrialisers, the ability of firms to survive in the domestic market can be a good indication of a firm's ability to enter the manufacturing export market, where competition is even much stiffer. It would be difficult for local firms in less industrialised countries to be thrown into the deep end of international markets without having built the capacity to survive the risks this involves (see DTI, 2016). Competition among local entrepreneurs and their businesses can be used as a foundation to build efficient and resilient firms, with the capacity to adapt quickly to the pressures of global competition. Several countries which have successfully industrialised used the strategy of building the capacity of local firms through subsidy and infant industry measures as a means to build their competitive capacity, with the long-term plan of entering into export markets (see Wade, 1990; Amsden, 2001)

Building Human Capital through Serial Entrepreneurship

The other, perhaps more crucial contribution that entrepreneurs can make to industrial development is the accumulation of human capital. So far the best concept that captures the accumulation of human capital though entrepreneurship is Plehn-Dujowich's (2010) idea of "serial entrepreneurs". Plehn-Dujowich (2010) develops the concept of serial entrepreneur based on the view that entrepreneurs are often faced with three options, when a business venture is not doing well: a) abandon it and go into wage employment; b) close the poorly performing venture and start a new one; c) keep struggling with the underperforming venture. It is the second option that leads to serial entrepreneurship, and the positive contribution of this lies in the fact that a great deal of learning takes place in the process of closing one venture and starting another. The experience gained does not only improve the pool of human capital in a particular sector, but contributes to the creation of new firms, and in some cases, technical innovation in the Kaldorian sense of technological and capacity innovation. Brixiova et al (2015) stress this as an important factor in creating skills which play a vital role in the process of developing and building industrial capabilities.

A large pool of serial entrepreneurs can be a valuable resource in an economy. Serial entrepreneurs can provide opportunities for learning by doing which is crucial to the process of upgrading industrial capabilities and skills. When more entrepreneurs become serial entrepreneurs, they add to the pool of knowledge which constitutes human capital, in the broader sense of the term. A similar view was articulated by Arrow (1962) in his theory of *learning by doing*, except that in this case serial entrepreneurship refers to the practical knowledge developed around the dynamics of starting and sustaining business ventures. It must be emphasised however that the weight of human capital contribution depends on the activities in which the serial entrepreneur has been engaging. If most of the serial entrepreneurs are in small ventures such as street vending or petty trading, the value of human capital created will be low because of the low skills generated in these activities. Again, the state can play an active role in promoting particular sets of entrepreneurs in strategic areas, including those operating in the low- and medium-tech manufacturing ventures.

Can the Cheetah Generation Deliver?

The case for entrepreneurs playing an important role in Africa's industrial development process is perhaps clear by now. The question of course is: are African entrepreneurs playing this role? As noted above, in the past, African entrepreneurs were negatively perceived as a rent-seeking class, thriving on privileged access to state resources and power, and as such contributed little, if anything, to the industrial development of the continent. But, there seem to be a shift in the way African entrepreneurs are perceived today when a more positive perception seems to be emerging. This positive attitude towards entrepreneurship in Africa can be attributed to the now growing realisation that "Entrepreneurs are the ones who create new businesses, drive and shape innovation, speed up structural changes, introduce new competition and contribute to an economy's fiscal health" (GEM, 2012:16).

The positive view about entrepreneurship in Africa resonates strongly with the Africa Rising Narrative (ARN), which sees African entrepreneurs as the hope of Africa; that their growth in the continent will unleash not only forces of economic transformation, but also demand for good governance, social and political change, which creates the right condition for industrial development. This new generation of African entrepreneurs, on whose shoulders is placed the weight of driving and sustaining industrial development, is described as a shrewd group of Africans, bent on trying to make it against all odds:

> ....a new generation of smart, energetic, and entrepreneurial political, social, and economic leaders is emerging. They are African to the core, but with a globalized outlook that comes with the Internet and easy air travel. Many have lived and studied abroad. They are savvy, sharp, and entrepreneurial, capable of combining the best of both worlds (Radelet, 2010b).

The *Cheetah generation*, as the new entrepreneurs are sometimes referred to, is portrayed to be a brand of African elite that is hard working and intolerant of corruption and inefficiency:

> ....a new generation of young African graduates and professionals, who look at African issues and problems from a totally different perspective. They are the *cheetah generation*; Africa's new hope. They do not relate to the old colonialist paradigm, the slave trade, nor Africa's post-colonial nationalist leaders such as Kwame Nkrumah, Jomo Kenyatta, Kenneth Kaunda or Julius Nyerere. The *cheetahs* know that many of their current leaders are scandalously corrupt, their governments are hopelessly rotten, and commit flagitious human rights violations. They brook no nonsense about corruption, inefficiency, ineptitude, incompetence or buffoonery. They understand and stress transparency, accountability, human rights and good governance (Ayitteh, 2005).

This cheetah generation is different from the *hippo generation*, which has "miserably failed Africa and left a trail of horrendous devastation, chaos, instability, destruction and vapid corruption across Africa" (ibid).

However, the performance of the cheetah generation has not yet been subjected to any systematic analysis, particularly when it comes to industrial development. If African entrepreneurship is so central to the prospect of industrialising the continent, it is expedient to understand its composition, its philosophy, goals and mission. Such an understanding would be the basis for guiding public interventions aimed at directing attention to critical areas within the industrial policy.

The image of a cheetah as a fast, agile and strong animal is an attractive one, compared to that of a hippo. But there is need to learn more about these African cheetahs, how they operate, how they are different from the earlier generations (the hippos), and the way they perceive their role in the various African communities where they operate. This new generation of African entrepreneurs will not be able to play its role effectively if it is not adequately understood and natured to make its valuable contribution. Without a proper understanding of this new generation of African entrepreneurs it will be difficult to assign a role to the group. It is for this reason that a detailed study of these new actors and their roles constitutes an important research area, which requires the attention of scholars.

In Africa where formal employment has been shrinking or stagnating in many countries, more and more people are now starting businesses as a viable career option and a means of earning a living. This as we have seen has revived interest in entrepreneurship. As this interest in entrepreneurship grows, it brings with it the urgent need to understand entrepreneurs better. At this stage, the field of entrepreneurship has been described in the literature as an emerging research field, which is in the process of developing its own concepts, analytical framework and coherent theory (see Brixiova et al, 2015). To come to a better understanding of the various groups of African entrepreneurs, the social, cultural, economic, political and religious context which influence and shape what they do and are should be the starting point. In other words, an entrepreneur cannot be understood properly if analysed out of the broader context in which he or she operates. The task for researchers is to develop what I have referred to as a sociology of African entrepreneurs. We know enough of the economics of African entrepreneur, but little about the broader social dynamics in which they operate and how they relate to this milieu.

Constructing a Sociology of African Entrepreneurs

To locate the role entrepreneurs play (and can play) in the industrialisation project in Africa, it is important to understand the social context which shapes what they do and can do. This would require developing a sociology of African entrepreneurs. A justification for a sociology of African entrepreneurs is that it enables one to appreciate the broader dynamics of societal change beyond the economic dimensions associated with entrepreneurship. Although there have been several studies done in the last decade about African entrepreneurs (Ncube, 2005; Gelb et al, 2014; Baumol, 2010; Brixiova, and Ncube, 2013), these have not explored the social dimensions of entrepreneurship, particularly how African entrepreneurs relate to the broader society in which they operate. This area of study remains poorly researched, with scanty scholarly work to provide insights into what constitutes this group, the different sub-groups and how they navigate the African social, economic, cultural, religious and political milieu. So far, most of the studies which have been conducted have focused on the role African entrepreneurs (can) play in job creation, sustainable and inclusive growth, knowledge and technology transfer and industrial development broadly. Little attention has been given to understanding the defining attributes and the social context.

Up to this point, scholarship on African entrepreneurship, like the general scholarship on entrepreneurship, has largely focused on trying to understand the personal characteristics of outstanding entrepreneurs, ignoring the broader social forces which define and shape the spaces in which the entrepreneur creates, innovates, adapts and transforms (Adrich and Martinez, 2007). Although entrepreneurship scholarship is still developing into a distinct field of inquiry and more work needs to be done to distinguish this area of study from other fields (Adrich and Martinez, 2007; Lighthelm, 2010), there is now an urgent need to study not just the personal traits of entrepreneurs, but also the broader social forces which shape entrepreneurial activities in society. In the past, entrepreneurship scholarship, which was dominated by the personality and behavioural theorists, paid little attention to the context in which entrepreneurs operated. But from the 1980s, "entrepreneurship research [has] started to focus more on what entrepreneurs do rather than what their character traits are" (ibid, 138).

In this regard, there is still a huge gap in the scholarship, especially on African entrepreneurs as an analytical category. More work needs to be done regarding the specific social forces which influence what entrepreneurs do and how they relate to the broader society in Africa. To be able to do this, the scholarship has to move beyond the personality-based research to a more holistic approach which considers not just personal characteristics but also the environment in which entrepreneurs work. As Reivera-Santos and others have observed, "characteristics of the environment are likely to affect not only the possible emergence of social enterprises, but also many of the characteristics of these ventures" (Rivera-Santos et al, 2015:73). Adrich and Martinez (2007:294) make a similar observation that, "understanding entrepreneurial success requires that we consider the societal context in which entrepreneurs develop their efforts". In order to develop a richer understanding of entrepreneurs, the "individual, the organisation and the development context need to be studied" (Lighthelm, 2010:133).

From the existing knowledge, it appears that the African entrepreneurship scholarship needs a reorientation to understand the new class of African entrepreneurs about whom we know relatively little, other than the isolated cases of individual biographies of what Piketty (2015) refers to as the super-entrepreneurs, such as Aliko Dangote, Moise Katumbi, Tony Olumelo, Patrice Motsepe etc. The resurgence of interest in African entrepreneurs is obviously highlighting the need to develop a deeper understanding of this group of Africans and how they relate to the broader African society, and how they see their role in the urgent project of industrialising the continent.

A sociology of African entrepreneurs can shed more light on this group of Africans which is increasingly becoming important in public policy discourse on the continent. Such an endeavour will help understand systematically who the African entrepreneurs are, what sets them apart from the rest and what they can or cannot do. It was not the intention of this chapter to outline what a sociology of African entrepreneurs would look like; the main purpose here was to draw attention to the increasingly influential group of Africans—the new African entrepreneurs. The task at hand is to try and understand who an African entrepreneur is by locating him or her in the African context.

Notes

1. Some analysts attribute the rising interest in entrepreneurs to the growth and development momentum in emerging markets such as China, Brazil, India and other South East Asian countries (see Lighthelm, 2010). It has also been suggested that the shrinking of job opportunities in the formal sector has led to many people, especially the youth, to start establishing their own businesses and not to wait for someone to employ them (see GEM, 2012; Obonyo, 2016).
2. McMillan and Harttgen (2014) estimate that the share of agriculture in total labour force declined by 10 percentage points between 2000 and 2010, based on data from 24 African countries.

3. The M-Pesa is an electronic money transfer mechanism using mobile phone. The M-Pesa technology was invented in Kenya.
4. All these support mechanisms form what in this book have been referred to as the secondary public goods.
5. Piketty (2015) gives an example of Liliane Bettencourt, the owner of the multinational cosmetics company L'Oreal, who inherited the company from her parents.
6. Analysts who adopt the evolutionary approach to entrepreneurship studies argue that it is useful to think about entrepreneurship cycle as a process that has four phases: conception, gestation, infancy and adolescence (see Adrich and Martinez, 2007:295). Other analysts add the phases of maturity and exit from entrepreneurship as essential components of the cycle (see GEM, 2012:11).
7. The first AEN was the West African Enterprise Network (WAEN) in 1993 and the South African Enterprise Network (SAEN) and the East African Enterprise Network (EAEN) in 1998. These networks bring together entrepreneurs from different countries to share experiences and challenges, but also to lobby for policies which create a suitable environment for enterprises.

References

Adelman, I. (1984). "Beyond Export Led Growth." *World Development*, Vol. 12, No. 9. 937–949.

Adrich, H. and Martinez, M. (2007). "Many are Called, but Few are Chosen: An Evolutionary Perspective for the Study of Entrepreneurship," in A. Cuervo, D. Ribeiro and S. Roig (eds.), *Entrepreneurship: Concepts, Theory and Perspectives*. Berlin: Springer. 294–311.

African Union (AU, 2007). Action Plan for Accelerated Industrial Development of Africa. AU Conference of Ministers of Industry, 1st Extra-Ordinary Session, 24–27 September, Midrand, South Africa.

African Development Bank/Organisation for Economic Cooperation and Development/United Nations Development Programme (AEO, 2017). *African Economic Outlook 2017: Entrepreneurship and Industrialisation*. Abidjan: AfDB/OECD/UNDP.

African Union/United Nations Economic Commission for Africa (AU/UNECA, 2015). *Illicit Financial Flows: A Report of the High Level Panel on Illicit Financial Flows from Africa*. Addis Ababa: AU/ECA.

Amin, S. (1972). "Underdevelopment and Dependence in Black Africa: Historical Origin." *Journal of Peace Research*, Vol. 10, No. 2. 105–120.

Amsden, A. H. (1989). *Asia's Next Giant: South Korea and Late Industrialization*. New York: Oxford University Press.

Amsden, A. (2001). *The Rise of 'The Rest': Challenges to the West from the Late-Industrialising Economies*. London/New York: Oxford University Press.

Arrighi, G. and Saul, J. (1968). "Socialism and Economic Development in Tropical Africa." *Journal of Modern African Studies*, Vol. 6, No. 2. 141–169.

Arrow, K. (1962). "The Economic Implications of Learning by Doing." *Review of Economic Studies*, Vol. 29, No. 3. 155–173.

Ayitteh, G. (2005). "The Cheetah Generation: *Africa's New Hope*." Available at: https://freeafrica.org/wp-content/uploads/2014/02/The-Cheetah-Generation.pdf

Banga, K. and te Velde, D. W. (2018). "Digitisation and the Future of Manufacturing in Africa." Supporting Economic Transformation (SET) Working Paper. Available at: https://progs.odinet.org.uk/iedg/Economic%20Transformation/SharedDocuments/Future%20of%20manufacturing%20project/set.odi.org. Accessed 12.03.2018.

Baumol, W. (1968). "Entrepreneurship in Economic Theory." *American Economic Review*, Vol. 58, No. 2. 64–71.

Baumol, W. (2010). *The Micro-Theory of Innovative Entrepreneurship*. Princeton: Princeton University Press.

British Broadcasting Corporation (BBC, 2016). "Zambia Arrests Over Xenophobic Attacks in Lusaka." 19 April 2016.

Brixiovia, Z. and Ncube, M. (2013). "Entrepreneurship and the Business Environment in Africa: An Application to Ethiopia." IZA Discussion Paper No. 7553.

Brixiova, Z., Ncube, M. and Bicaba, Z. (2014). "Skills and Youth Entrepreneurship in Africa: Analysis with Evidence from Swaziland." African Development Bank Group, Working Paper No. 24.

Brixiova, Z., Ncube, M. and Bicaba, Z. (2015). "Skills and Youth Entrepreneurship in Africa: Analysis with Evidence from Swaziland." *World Development*, Vol. 67, No. 3. 11–26.

Carland, J., Hoy, F., Boulton, W. and Calarnd, J. (2007). "Differentiating Entrepreneurship from Small Business Owners: A Conceptualization," in A. Cuervo, D. Ribeiro and S. Roig (eds.), *Entrepreneurship: Concepts, Theory and Perspectives*. Berlin: Springer. 73–81.

Chileshe, J. (1992). *Nothing Wrong with Africa, Except* ... New Delhi: Viokas Publishing House.

Department of Trade and Industry (DTI, 2016). Industrial Policy Action Plan (IPAP) 2016/17–2018/19. Pretoria: DTI.

Durham, D. (2000). "Youth and the Social Imagination of in Africa: Introduction to Parts 1 and 2." *Anthropology Quarterly*, Vol. 73, No. 3. 113–120.

Elkan, W. (1988). "Entrepreneurs and Entrepreneurship in Africa." *Research Observer*, Vol. 3, No. 2. 171–188.

Fanon, F. (1963). *Wretched of the Earth*. New York. Groves Press.

Feinburg, J. (1973). *Social Philosophy*. Englewood Cliffs, NJ: Prentice-Hall.

Filmer and Fox (2014). *Overview: Youth Employment in Sub-Saharan Africa*. Washington, DC: World Bank.

Fox, L., Haines, C., Huerta-Munoz, J. and Thomas, A. (2013). "Africa's Got Work to Do: Employment Prospect in the New Century." International Monetary Fund (IMF) Working Paper 13/201.

Fox, L. and Thomas, A. (2016). "Africa's Got Work to Do: A Diagnostic of Youth Employment Challenges in Sub-Saharan Africa." *Journal of African Economies*, Vol. 25, No. 1. 16–36.

Fredland, R. A. (2001). *Understanding Africa: A Political Economy Perspective*. Chicago: Burnham Inc.

Gelb, A., Meyer, C. and Ramachandran, V. (2014). "Does Poor Mean Cheap? A Comparative Look at Africa's Industrial Labour Costs." Centre for Global Development (CGD) Working Paper No. 325, Washington, DC: CGD.

Global Entrepreneurship Monitor (GEM 2012). African Entrepreneurship: Sub-Saharan African Regional Report. International Development Research Centre, Canada.
Global Entrepreneurship Monitoring Association (GEM, 2017). *Global Entrepreneurship Monitor, 2016/2017*. Wellesley: GEMA.
Goedhuys, M. and Sleuwaegen, L. (2009). "High-Growth Entrepreneurial Firms in Africa: A Quantile Regression Approach." *Small Business Economics*, Vol. 34. 31–51.
Gries, T., and Naudé, W. A. (2010). "Entrepreneurship and Structural Economic Transformation". *Small Business Economics Journal*, Vol. 34, No. 1: 13–29.
Herrington, M. and Kew, P. (2017). *Global Entrepreneurship Monitor (GEM) 2016/17*. Wellesley: Global Entrepreneurship Research Association.
Holocombe, R. (1998). "Entrepreneurship and Economic Growth." *Quarterly Journal of Austrian Economics*, Vol. 1, No. 2. 45–62.
Hyden, G. (1983). *No Shortcuts to Progress: African Development Management in Perspectives*. London/Nairobi: Heinemann.
Iliffe, J. (1983). *The Emergence of African Capitalism*. London: Macmillan Press.
International Labour Organisation (ILO, 2017). *World Employment Social Outlook 2017*. Geneva: ILO.
Kilby, P. (1965). *African Enterprise: The Nigerian Bread Industry*. San Francisco: Institute for Contemporary Studies Press.
Klein, P. (2006). "Is Entrepreneurship a Factor of Production?" Available at: https://organisationsandmarkets.com/2006/14/is-entrepreneurship-a-factor-of-production/
Kritiko, A. (2014). "Entrepreneurs and their Impact on Jobs and Economic Growth." IZA World of Labour, doi: 10.15185/izawol.8.
Krugman, P. (1987). "The Narrow Moving Band, the Dutch Disease, and the Competitive Consequences of Mrs. Thatcher." *Journal of Economics*, Vol. 27. 41–55.
Lighthelm, A. A. (2010). "Entrepreneurship and Small Business Sustainability." *Southern African Business Review*, Vol. 14, No. 3. 131–154.
Manyika, J., Sinclair, J., Dobbs, R., Kassey, L., Mischke, J., Roxburgh, C., George, K., O'Halloran, D. and Ramaswamy, S. (2012). *Manufacturing the Future: The Next Era of Global Growth and Innovation*. Washington, DC: McKinsey Global Institute.
Marsden, K. (1990). *African Entrepreneurs: Pioneers of Development*. Washington, DC: International Finance Corporation, Discussion Paper No. 9.
McDade, B. and Spring, A. (2005). "The 'New Generation of African Entrepreneurs': Networking to Change the Climate for Business and Private Sector-led Development." Entrepreneurship and Regional Development, Vol. 17. 17–42.
McMillan, M. and Harttgen, K. (2014). "What is Driving the "African Growth Miracle?" African Development Bank (AfDB) Working Paper No. 209. Tunis, AfDB.
Mkandawire, T. (2011). "Running While Others Walk: Knowledge and the Challenge of Africa's Development." *African Development*, Vol. XXXVI, No. 2. 1–36.
Nafziger, W. (1990). "African Capitalism, Sate Power and Economic Development." *Journal of Modern African Studies*, Vol. 28, No. 1. 141–150.
Naude, W. (2010). "Promoting Entrepreneurship in Developing Countries: Policy Challenges." United Nations University Policy Brief No. 4, 2010.

Naude, W. (2013). "Entrepreneurship and Economic Development: Theory, Evidence and Policy." IZA, Working Paper No. 7507.

Ncube, N. (2005). "Economic Growth, Entrepreneurship and the Business Environment in Africa." Graduate School of Business, Working Paper No. 30, University of Witwatersrand, Johannesburg.

Ngwu, F., Adeleye, I. and Ogbechie, C. (2016). "Africa-to-Africa Internationalisation: Rhetoric, Reality and Risks of Intra-African Regional Expansion," in S. Nwankwo, K. Ibeh (eds.), *The Routledge Companionship to Business in Africa*. London/New York: Routledge. 9–28.

Nsehe, M. (2014). "30 Most Promising Young Entrepreneurs in Africa 2014." Available at: http://www.forbes.com/sites/mfonobongnsehe/2014/02/04/30-most-promising-young-entrepreneur-in-africa-2014. Accessed 28.05.2016.

Nsehe, M. (2016). "30 Most Promising Young Entrepreneurs in Africa 2016." Available at: https://www.forbes.com/sites/mfonobongnsehe/2016/04/25/30-most-promising-young-entrepreneurs-in-africa-2016/#48ec5b193f72. Accessed 28.05.2016.

Obonyo (2016). "Africa Looks to its Entrepreneurs." *Africa Renewal*, Vol. 30, No. 1. 16–17.

Page, J. (2014). "Industrial Policy in Practice: Africa's Presidential Investors' Advisory Councils." WIDER Working Paper No. 2014/117.

Parker, S. C. (2009). *Economics of Entrepreneurship*. Cambridge: Cambridge University Press.

Piketty, T. (2015). *Capital in the 21st Century*. Cambridge: Belknap Press of Harvard University Press.

Plehn-Dujowich, J. (2010). "A Theory of Serial Entrepreneurship." *Small Business Economy*, Vol. 35. 77–398.

Radelet, S. (2010a). *Emerging Africa: How 17 Countries Are Leading the Way*. Washington, DC: Brookings Institution Press.

Radelet, S. (2010b). "Success Stories from 'Emerging Africa.'" *Journal of Democracy*, Vol. 21, No. 4. 87–101.

Rivera-Santos, M., Holt, D., Littlewood, D. and Kolk, A. (2015). "Social Entrepreneurship in Sub-Saharan Africa." *Academy of Management Perspectives*, Vol. 29, No. 1. 72–91.

Rogerson, C. (2001). "In Search of the African Miracle: Debates on Successful Small Enterprise Development in Africa." *Habitat International*, Vol. 25. 115–142.

Rogerson, J. and Mushawemhuka, W. (2015). "Transnational Entrepreneurship in the Global South: Evidence from Southern Africa." *Bulletin of Geography*. Socio-economic Series No. 30. 135–146.

Rotberg, R. (2013). *Africa Emerges: Consummate Challenges, Abundant Opportunities*. Cambridge: Polity Press.

Schumpeter, J. (1934). *The Theory of Economic Development: An Inquiry into Profits, Capital, Credit, Interest and the Business Cycle*. Cambridge: Harvard University Press.

Sharma, P. and Chrisman, S. (2007). "Towards a Reconciliation of the Definition of Issues in the Field of Corporate Entrepreneurship," in A. Cuervo, D. Ribeiro and S. Roig (eds.), *Entrepreneurship: Concepts, Theory and Perspectives*. Berlin: Springer. 84–103.

Sonobe, T., Akoten, J. and Otsuka, K. (2009). "The Growth Process of Informal Entrepreneurship in Sub-Saharan Africa: A Case Study of Metalworking Cluster in Nairobi." *Small Business Economics*, Vol. 36, No. 3. 323–335.

Spring, A. and McDade, B. (1998). "Entrepreneurship in Africa: Traditional and Contemporary," in A. Spring and B. McDade (eds.), *African Entrepreneurship: Theory and Reality*. Gainesville: Florida University Press. 1–34.

Takyi-Asiedu, S. (1993). "Some Socio-Cultural Factors Retarding Entrepreneurship Activity in Sub-Saharan Africa." *Journal of Business Venturing*, Vol. 8. 91–98.

The Economist (2011). Africa Rising: The Hopeful Continent. December 3, 2011. Available at: http://www.economist.com/node/21541015.

United Nations Conference on Trade and Development (UNCTAD, 2015). "Promoting Entrepreneurship for Development. Note by UNCTAD Secretariat, Geneva, Switzerland.

United Nations Industrial Development Organisation (UNIDO, 2016). *Industrialisation in Africa and Least Developed Countries: Booting Growth, Creating Jobs, Promoting Inclusiveness and Sustainability*. Vienna: UNIDO.

Wade, R. (1990). *Economic Theory and the Role of Government in East Asian Industrialisation*. Princeton: Princeton University Press.

·10·

CONSTRUCTING PILLARS FOR AFRICA'S INDUSTRIALISATION IN THE 21ST CENTURY

Introduction: Back to the Basics

Discussions in the preceding chapters have highlighted the point that while efforts to industrialise the African continent have been ongoing for the past six decades, industrial development in Africa remains low. The 2017 World Manufacturing Report (UNIDO, 2017:15) indicates that Africa's share in global manufacturing value added (MVA) was only 1 percent, and 90 percent of these manufactures are resource-based. As shown in Chapter 3, manufacturing activities occurring on the continent are dominated by the processing of natural resources, using low and medium technology. The challenge with this production structure is that it locks countries in the low value addition segments of the global value chains. To change this, African countries will have to undertake radical restructuring of their economies.

As long as the commodity-based production structure persists addressing the challenges of poverty, underemployment, and rising inequality on the continent will continue to grow. As the former Japanese deputy minister of the MITI observed, heavy reliance on light industries makes it difficult to create adequate employment and to raise income and the standard of living of most people in a country (see Wade, 1990:25). These are precisely the challenges which most African countries are battling with: creating adequate productive employment and raising income among the poor, who are still the majority. As African countries seek to find a viable formula to address the persisting challenges of poverty and underemployment, the pressure to industrialise is intensifying in most countries.

The Political Imperative of Industrialisation in Africa

The pressure to industrialise has now become a political imperative in the sense that African politicians and governments are increasingly being assessed on their ability to create jobs as the employment situation on the continent becomes dire. Electorates in many countries are swayed by political parties which demonstrate that they are able to address the challenge of creating adequate jobs; this has now become a matter of bread and butter. With this, the pressure to industrialise is mounting specifically because of the weak employment growth and slow decline in poverty rates, especially during the period when most countries have experienced positive rates (see Page, 2015). An African Development Bank report estimates that currently African economies are creating 3 million formal jobs annually, while 10–12 million people enter the labour force each year (AfDB, 2017)[1]. Given the sluggish rate at which African economies are generating formal wage jobs versus the rate at which the labour force is growing, it is not surprising that the pressure to create jobs has become a major issue, and industrialisation is widely seen as one of the key solutions to this challenge.

Although there is an emerging view that the capacity of the industrial sector to create jobs has significantly reduced (Rodrik, 2015), there is a strong belief in Africa that industrialisation, in its broad sense, has great potential to address most of the development challenges on the continent, including creation of productive jobs (see UNECA, 2016). It is for this reason that many African governments are now directing attention towards finding effective strategies for expanding the industrial sector, particularly manufacturing.

Industrialising Africa: Past and Present Initiatives

The urgency on the part of African governments to address the challenge of industrial development is partly manifested in the number of industrial policy documents and strategies produced over the last decade, especially at the continental level.[2] Over the past decade and half, several initiatives at the continental level have been adopted starting with the *Alliance for Africa's Industrialisation* (AAI) in 2003, followed by the *Africa Productive Capacity Initiative* (APCI) in 2004; the *Accelerated Industrial Development for Africa* (AIDA) in 2007, the *Africa Agribusiness and Agro-industries Development Initiative* (3ADI), launched in 2010, and the most recent *Common African Position* (CAP) adopted in 2015. All these initiatives have a common emphasis on structural transformation, industrialisation and inclusive growth. Prior to these initiatives, there were earlier efforts by the Organisation of African Unity (OAU) during the 1980s to promote industrialisation on the continent, though most of these initiatives have not achieved much. Examples include the *first Industrial Development Decade for Africa* (IDDA I; from 1980 to 1990) and the *second Industrial Development Decade for Africa* (IDDA II; from 1993 to 2003).

At the national level, various countries have formulated industrial policies over the last decade, with most countries separating industrial from trade policies (see UNECA, 2015). In view of all these past and current strategies developed to promote industrial growth on the continent, it is apparent that the reason why industrialisation still remains elusive is not because of lack or inadequate policy; there are so many brilliant industrial policy documents at national, regional and continental level, such that if only 30 percent of what is said in those documents were to be implemented, we would be talking about an industrial revolution in Africa. The challenge lies in translating the ideas on paper into concrete actions on the ground. This is often a manifestation of the failure to take seriously the basic things which most African governments often overlook. In this regard there has been inadequate attention given to identifying and building the pillars of Africa's industrialisation.

This chapter looks at the basic things required to create conditions for industrial growth in Africa in the 21st century. Though most of these are simple and obvious things, they are vital to Africa's prospect of decentring the colonial economic structures and the logic behind it. The purpose of this chapter is not to prescribe how industrialisation should be approached; or to foretell how industrialisation will unfold in Africa (such an exercise will be merely speculative). The purpose is to highlight some of the basic things which are prerequisites to industrial development in Africa today. The observations made in this chapter are based on the long-run analysis of the constraints, but also the prospects for sustainable industrial development in Africa, taking into account the global context.

Building Blocks for Africa's Industrialisation

When thinking about industrialising the African continent today, it is imperative to locate the continent in today's and tomorrow's global context. The vast majority of the literature on industrialisation in Africa looks backwards, often holding the East Asian countries as the perfect example for African countries to emulate. As noted in Chapter 7, whereas African governments will do well to learn from the experience of countries that have succeeded in industrialising, replicating what these countries did is not a viable industrial strategy (Mkandawire, 2001; Evans, 2010). African countries will have to construct their own ladders to use to climb to the top of industrial pyramid. The starting point is to learn how to construct these ladders, after realising that borrowed or imitated ladder won't do the job, and no one other than African governments themselves can construct appropriate ladders for building industrial capacity and capabilities. When constructing such ladders, it is crucial to be aware that the instruments for industrialisation will be applied in the real world which includes events and barriers beyond the continent's control.

While the African industrial development context is unique, what is going on in other parts of the world undoubtedly has a strong influence on the industrial outcomes in Africa, and, as such, should be part of the discussion of the African industrial development strategy. One example of this is the emerging phenomenon of pre-mature de-industrialisation (see Dasgupta and Singh, 2006; Rodrik, 2015; Felipe et al, 2017). The implications of the observed changes in global industrial trends for Africa's industrial development need to be considered carefully in any industrial policy and strategy in order to come up with a realistic assessment of the prospects, the challenges and the opportunities. As Amirapu and Subramanian (2015) observe, while countries' and regions' industrial paths differ, a successful industrial strategy has to take into account international trends to locate a country or region's optimal path.

With specific reference to manufacturing, a McKinsey Global Institute report highlights several global changes which are re-shaping the global dynamics around manufacturing. The report identifies four key trends which include changing consumption patterns and customer preferences, specific skill shortages, faster technology and innovation dispersion and, most importantly for Africa, changing government policies which are now looking to support domestic manufacturing more aggressively than we have seen before (see Manyika et al, 2012). With regard to aggressive strategies for supporting local manufacturing firms, we have recently witnessed the growth of a vicious form of economic nationalism which has almost brought the world to the brink of a trade war (Trump, 2017). The big guys (China and USA) are the ones going for each other's throat.

What this means is that realistic hopes of industrialising the continent will have to be rooted in the size of the 'African domestic' market, especially during the early stages. In this regard, Africa has a huge advantage because of a sizeable population of about 1.4 billion people in 2020, which is expected to grow to more than 1.7 billion by 2030, and 2.5 billion by 2050. Even if there is only 15–20 percent of Africans with disposable income, the combined market size for manufactures in Africa is quite big. The strategy for Africa should be to rely on this massive and growing population and the huge and diverse natural resource endowment to build manufacturing capabilities that will be able to compete successful on the global stage.

The aggressive manufacturing stance being adopted in many countries, mainly industrialised countries, presents a huge challenge for African countries seeking to carve-out a share of the global market in manufactures. At the same time, this presents an opportunity for African governments to learn to aggressively support industrial activities in their respective countries and regions. It is through such strategies that African countries can restructure their economies and boost the share of manufacturing in total export, output and MVA per capita etc. To move Africa from being an outlier on many aspects of global industrial development including productivity in manufacturing and technology absorption to an important global player, would require taking radical steps to overturn the colonial economic logic and structures. Undoubtedly, the challenges and opportunities of industrialising Africa are huge. For African countries to take advantage of the existing opportunities, they must seriously consider and pay attention to a number of basic things some which are briefly discussed in this chapter. But before discussing the basic things, it is important to outline the challenge first.

The African Industrialisation Challenge

In the first televised US Presidential Inauguration in 1949, the 33rd US President Harry Truman boldly proclaimed to the world that, "For the first time in history, humanity possesses the knowledge and the skill to relieve the suffering of...people [living in misery]" (cited in Chandy et al, 2015:1). At the time Truman made this statement, half of the world population was living in what we would call today extreme poverty (below US$1.90 per day per capita in 2011 US$). In 2015 the ratio of the world's population living in extreme poverty dropped to just over 1 in ten people (11. 5 percent).[3] That is massive progress made at the global level since the Truman Speech 70 years ago. Much of this progress is accounted for by the rising income in East Asian economies, resulting in rapid decline in poverty rates in the last quarter of the 20th century.

For the African continent, although the proportion of people living in extreme poverty in 1949 was not known, the levels of extreme poverty remain high today, at over 40 percent of the population, accounting for almost half (48.6 percent) of all the people living in extreme poverty globally. The biggest challenge for Africa is that poverty is declining at a much slower pace compared to other regions of the world (see Table 10.1).

Table 10.1: Poverty Headcount Trends by Region (% @1.90/day/capita).

	1990	1993	1996	1999	2002	2005	2008	2011	2015
East Asia and Pacific	57	51.7	38.3	35.9	27.3	16.7	13.7	7.9	4.1
Europe and Central Asia	1.5	2.9	4.3	3.8	2.1	1.3	0.5	0.5	0.3
Latin America and Caribbean	12.2	11.9	10.5	11	10.2	7.3	5.4	4.6	4.3
Middle East and N. Africa	5.8	5.3	4.8	4.8	3.8	3	2.1	1.7	2
South Asia	54.1	52.1	48.6	45	44.1	38.3	34.1	24.5	18.1
Sub-Saharan Africa	56.6	60.9	59.7	59.3	57.1	52.8	49.7	46.8	40.9
World	**36.4**	**35.1**	**30.4**	**29.1**	**26.1**	**21.1**	**18.6**	**14.5**	**11.5**

Source: Author. Based on data from World Development Indicators (online databank).

There is a common view on what explains the slow decline in levels of poverty in Africa, which is that majority of the people in Africa have remained in low-productivity activities such that income trends for the majority have either stagnated or fallen over time. Page (2015) argues that poverty in most African countries would have fallen faster if more people shifted from agriculture to industrial and service sectors where productivity and income are generally higher. Other analysts come to a similar conclusion (see McMillan and Rodrik, 2011; Timmer et al, 2014; Page, 2015; Newman et al, 2016; Zamfir, 2016).

The challenge for Africa is that while many of the people who are still engaged in low-productivity activities would definitely like to move to activities where productivity and income are higher, there are not enough opportunities in the high-productivity sectors such as mining and financial services. This is why the question of creating more productive jobs has become a pressing issue for most African governments. So far, a workable strategy for generating adequate productive jobs on the continent has not yet been found. Perhaps it is time to look at alternative ways of making people more productive than the conventional approach of waiting for formal wage employment. Promoting entrepreneurship, a strategy which many African countries have now begun to seriously consider and promote, may be a game changer for the continent.

Trends in global employment are showing that formal employment globally is shrinking (Patnaik, 2017), and the formal employment gap has been growing over the past decade, reflecting the dwindling capacity in the global economy to create adequate productive employment and to improve the quality of jobs (see ILO, 2017). Low-income countries, such as those in Africa, are increasingly finding it difficult to generate sufficient jobs in the formal sector, and later on to improve the quality of existing jobs, giving rise to high proportions of vulnerable employment and working poor (see Table 6.5). The fact that majority of jobs in Africa are still in agriculture and the informal service sector is a clear indication of the enduring challenge arising from low levels of industrial development.

When the question of why so many people are stuck in low-productivity work in Africa is raised, it is often observed that this is largely because the growth of more productive (high-wage) jobs has not occurred to absorb the people in low-productivity activities. In other words, the explanations offered cite the lack of economic structural transformation, which is widely associated with a robust industrial growth, as the main reason for the persistently higher levels of poverty and low productivity in Africa (see ACET, 2014; UNECA, 2015; Fox and Thomas, 2016). The challenge is that although labour is evidently moving away from agriculture (see McMillan and Harttgen, 2014; Yeboah and Jayne, 2017), majority of the people are moving into low-productivity activities in the informal sector, particularly services, as elaborated in Chapter 6.

In trying to find the solution to this challenge, industrialisation is widely acknowledged as the most effective way of responding to Africa's war against low job creation and persisting high poverty rates. Without broad-based industrial development that can bring more people into highly productive activities, reducing poverty and creating inclusive and sustainably growing economies will remain elusive on the continent. A 2016 UNIDO report gives several reasons why Africa and other least developed countries (LDCs) need to industrialise, arguing that "without industrializing, it is unlikely that Africa and LDCs can meet the Sustainable Development Goal by 2030, particularly SDG 9 on industry, innovation and infrastructure" (UNIDO, 2016: 1).

The other reasons given to justify why Africa must industrialise are that achieving SDG on poverty and inclusive growth will not be possible without significant growth in the industrial sector. Creation of jobs to absorb the steadily growing labour force, especially the increasingly more educated youth, will certainly be more difficult without substantial levels of industrial expansion. In this sense, the issue in Africa is not about whether or not to industrialise, but more about how to achieve industrial growth that can enable the continent realise its potential for economic growth and improving the well-being of its peoples, especially those still living in extreme poverty.

Is Africa Prematurely Deindustrialising?

While there is strong optimism and confidence that industrialisation in Africa will provide the momentum for the continent to create conditions for inclusive economic growth, faster reduction in poverty levels, creation of more *real jobs*, and the promotion of sustainable development; global trends in industrial employment, manufacturing in particular, suggest that the capacity of the manufacturing sector to create mass employment is dwindling, even in less industrialised countries of Africa, South Asia and Latin America. This phenomenon, which in the literature has been referred to as pre-mature de-industrialisation, is reported to be taking root even in countries at low per capita income and lower levels of industrial development (Tregenna, 2009; 2016; Rodrik, 2015).

The now growing literature on pre-mature de-industrialisation is suggesting that it is increasingly becoming difficult for late industrialisers or LDCs to create mass employment through the growth of the manufacturing sector in particular (Dasgupta and Singh, 2006; Rodrik, 2015; Felipe et al, 2017).

Whereas in the past, countries that industrialised relied on the growing manufacturing sector to generate bulk employment and drive the process of structural transformation, creating the same labour dynamics in the manufacturing sector is becoming more challenging today.

Evidence reviewed suggests that manufacturing share in total employment is peaking at much lower levels of around 18 percent compared to the levels of 25–30 percent 3 decades ago. Dan Rodrik (2015) who is one of the leading scholars on de-industrialisation, in one of his papers, argues that although industrialisation in the past played an important role in transforming societies by creating the working class, the capitalist class, trade unions, political movements and professional associations which contributed to the deepening of democracy in the now industrialised countries, the role of manufacturing in creating these same dynamics today has diminished particularly because the employment share of the manufacturing sector has declined compared to the 1980s when most East Asian economies industrialised.

According to Rodrik (2015) this phenomenon which has been going on since the 1980s is characterised by the falling share of manufacturing in total employment and declining share of manufacturing in total output, except for a few countries in Asia. Rodrik (2015:3) argues that "In most of these countries, manufacturing began to shrink (or is on course for shrinking) at levels of income that are a fraction of those at which advanced economies started to de-industrialise. These developing countries are turning into service economies without having gone through a proper experience of industrialisation."

Using a different dataset and approach from Rodrik (2015), Felipe et al (2017) confirm the trend observed by Rodrik, concluding that current industrial development dynamics in many countries show that manufacturing share in total employment is peaking at lower levels than those reported among the earlier industrialisers. What this means is that the employment elasticity in the manufacturing sector in particular has declined, signifying that growth in the manufacturing sector is accompanied by few manufacturing jobs than was the case before.

The Filipe study also confirms that countries that are industrialising today start to de-industrialise at much lower per capita income level than the early industrialisers, and that the share of manufacturing in total employment is much lower today when compared to the experience of countries which industrialised before the 1980s. Felipe et al (2017) illustrate that while employment share in the early industrialisers peaked at between 25 and 30 percent (often exceeding 30 percent of total employment in some cases), the trend observed in the last fifteen years is that manufacturing employment is peaking below the 20 percent mark and rarely crosses the 18 percent mark, except for a few Asian economies. Tregenna (2016) also observes that while the phenomenon of deindustrialisation affected industrialised countries in the past, there is an observed trend showing that deindustrialisation is now affecting counties with very low per capita income.

The phenomenon of declining manufacturing share in total employment and output at much lower per capita income was also observed earlier in a study that examined the impact of industrial shifts on balance of payment in advanced economies (see Rowthorn and Coutts, 2004). Amirapu and Subramanian (2015) also find that the curve representing the relationship between manufacturing employment share and GDP per capita for different countries has been shifting downwards, confirming what has been observed in other studies that manufacturing employment share is peaking at lower levels of per capita income even in countries that are less industrialised

However, all these studies show that manufacturing share in total output has on average remained the same, suggesting that productivity is growing in the sector. The conclusion reached is that "it has become more difficult to achieve high manufacturing shares over time, and specifically, that today's late industrializing economies are unlikely to achieve the 18% manufacturing employment share threshold that all rich countries in our sample enjoyed" (Felipe et al, 2017:11).

A Penalty for Late Industrialisers

The implications of this phenomenon are that late industrialisers face a penalty and that for these countries to industrialise it will require more effort, commitment and careful selection of strategies to pursue. Dasgupta and Singh (2006) also show that for industrialised countries, manufacturing output grew more than the economy-wide growth rate between 1950 and 1973, and between 1973 and 1984. This situation has now been reversed, with the overall growth rate in the economy surpassing that of manufacturing output for all industrialised countries in the sample—suggesting the onset of de-industrialisation in the second period.[4] While Dasgupta and Singh (2006:6) argue that de-industrialisation may not necessarily reflect a pathological condition in an economy, especially if these changes are in response to the changing consumer taste and technological advances, they do note that it is however "a worrying sign when so many developing countries at low level of per capita income exhibit symptoms of deindustrialisation in terms of output and employment (in the sense of their respective shares either remaining constant or falling)."

While the de-industrialisation story is adequately explained in the structural transformation theory, which predicts that manufacturing share in both output and employment declines as an economy transitions from industrial-dominated to a service economy (Chenery et al, 1986; Syrquin and Chenery, 1989); the theory does not explain the pre-mature deindustrialisation when manufacturing employment is falling in economies with very low per capita income. In other words, there is no problem when this occurs to countries with high income per capita. It however becomes a real challenge when the manufacturing sector starts to lose momentum in economies which have low income per capita, and large population in agriculture and low productivity activities. This is when the situation becomes pathological; otherwise de-industrialisation is a 'normal' phase in a maturing industrial and in post-industrial societies (Tregenna, 2009).

Data presented in Chapter 3 on Africa seem to confirm this trend where manufacturing employment in most countries has either fallen or remained stagnant over the past two decades (see Table 3.5). In the African context, this poses many challenges and should force policy makers and analysts to think of other possible avenues for addressing the challenge of creating the much-needed mass employment.

What Accounts for Premature Deindustrialisation in Africa?

It is important here to point out that there are some analysts who contest the claim that manufacturing share in total employment is falling. The Economic Commission on Africa (UNECA) publication on industrial policy in Africa, for instance argues that, "Much of the apparent fall in the manufacturing sector's share of GDP in advanced economies is due to the decline in the prices of manufactured goods, relative to the prices of services. This is thanks to faster productivity growth in their production" (UNECA, 2016). Tregenna (2009) makes a similar point arguing that the decline in manufacturing share in total employment is largely attributed to the falling labour intensity of manufacturing, meaning that as productivity rises, manufacturing is needing less workers to produce the same or even more manufacturing products. Consequently, the apparent fall of manufacturing share in total output has sometimes been referred to as a *statistical illusion* or *artefact* (ibid).

Although there are various reasons and factors offered to account for the phenomenon of premature deindustrialisation and analysts may differ in what they see as the most important factor; what seems clear is that manufacturing share in both employment and output are peaking at levels much lower than what it used to be in the past. There is less dispute on that. But if pre-mature de-industrialisation is an established trend in all economies, what then explains its occurrence now?

There are several explanations offered. One of the most common view is that today, technological changes are resulting in rapid growth of "labour-saving" innovations than before, leading to less labour used as most manufacturing processes are increasingly relying on technology (Felipe et al, 2017; Tregenna, 2009; 2016). Put in a different way, manufacturing processes today are becoming more capital-intensive, requiring less labour than before. As the IR 4.0 takes root, with the growth of additive manufacturing using robotics and computer aided production, the capacity for the manufacturing sector to generate employment should be expected to fall even further (see EIU, 2018). Countries that are seeking to industrialise today must take this into account and have plans to address the challenges this brings.

Changing consumer taste has also been cited as a factor that explains the observed industrial dynamics. It has been estimated that due to automation, optimisation and other innovative techniques, manufacturing employment in industrialised countries fell by nearly 19 percent in just 8 years between 2000 and 2008, with the United States shedding 26 percent of manufacturing jobs followed by Japan at 21 percent between 1998 and 2008 (see Manyika et al, 2012:26). Part of this has been attributed to the growth of the digital economy, which is slowly taking root as the effects of the IR 4.0 spread in many economies, especially the highly industrialised countries (see Banga and te Velde, 2018; EIU, 2018).

The other explanation which has been offered is that productivity, in manufacturing particularly, is converging to the global mean much faster than before, such that there is stiffer competition for the market share in global manufacturing, especially for the industrialised countries which tend to have a high manufacturing wage compared to the LDCs. This, it is argued, has resulted in a situation where manufacturing is unconditionally converging, regardless of specific country conditions (see Rodrik, 2013). If manufacturing productivity is converging unconditionally, then the productivity advantage enjoyed by the industrialised countries should be quickly circumvented by the low-wage country with high concentration of semi-skilled and unskilled labour force. The evidence to support this, however, is scanty and not clear at the moment.

One of the reasons why manufacturing is said to be exhibiting strong tendencies of unconditional convergence is because of the quick technological dispersion which is a trend that is alleged to have occurred in the manufacturing sector particularly (see Manyika et al, 2012; Rodrik, 2013). Assuming that manufacturing technology is rapidly dispersed throughout the global economy, then it becomes difficult for industrialised countries to sustain their high wage manufacturing employment, a situation that may lead to the shift of manufacturing activities to the labour-abundant economies. The shift of manufacturing capacity from Western Europe to Asia, particularly China, is sometimes cited to support this view.

For developing countries, if manufacturing technology is widely dispersed, the competition from labour-abundant economies intensifies. The cost advantage enjoyed by high-income countries is undercut because of countries having access to the same manufacturing equipment, management styles and production organisation. This results in global manufacturing employment being shared between the major competing manufacturing economies. As more and more economies compete for manufacturing employment, the levels of manufacturing employment in each country drops, resulting in manufacturing employment peaking at much lower levels than seen before, when a few countries enjoyed the productivity advantage for a long time.

In this explanation, while higher wage levels are a disadvantage in industrialised countries, they are an advantage in low-income countries, with a large pool of low-wage workers. In this regard, the wage pressure is important in accounting for de-industrialisation in industrialised and industrialising economies, while the lack of competitiveness accounts for the low manufacturing employment elasticity in LDCs. For developing countries, the rapidly dispersing technology, and with it productivity growth, offers an opportunity to increase their share of manufacturing employment as long as these countries can get the basics right. However, it must be noted that competitiveness is not only a function of wages; there are other factors such as level of infrastructure development, availability of skilled labour and red tape, macroeconomic conditions which influence a firm's competitiveness.

Deindustrialisation in Africa?

While the de-industrialisation phenomenon is often presented as something new, it is in fact old news for most industrialised countries (see Rodrik, 2015). As economic development progresses, the relative share of employment and output shifts from manufacturing to services, mainly driven by the growing income elasticity of demand for services compared to manufacturing, as income rises in the general population (Syrquin and Chenery, 1989). A similar shift is seen in the transition from agriculture to industrial sector in the early stages of economic development (see Timmer et al, 2012). What is new, however, is the fact that countries with low levels of industrial development manifested in low per capita income are also experiencing falling manufacturing share in total employment even in economies with relatively abundant low-skilled and unskilled labour. In Africa, for instance, as shown in chapters 3 and 6, manufacturing employment in most countries is below 6 percent, and this has stagnated even at the time when most economies experienced high economic growth rates (see WEF, 2017).

But in the African context, it might be misleading to call this premature de-industrialisation because industrialisation has not occurred to any significant level that would merit the term de-industrialisation. The declining or stagnating manufacturing share in total employment which has been observed in a number of countries on the continent since the onset of SAPs can be aptly described as interrupted or failed industrialisation, rather than de-industrialisation. Part of the problem when it comes to conceptualising economic change, over time, is that there is a fixed approach to economic transformation as epitomised in the widely held view of "marching through the sector," leading to a hierarchal ranking of economic sectors, with manufacturing occupying the first rank followed by services and agriculture. While this might have been the case in the past, the current dynamics are pointing to a need to reconceptualise economic change in more flexible ways that allow sectoral analysis to shed more light on the broader economic trends occurring (see Buera and Kaboski, 2009; UNECA, 2016).

Often the analysis of structural transformation takes the experience of industrialised countries as the benchmark against which the less industrialised countries should be assessed (as evident in the term de-industrialisation), despite the conditions being quite different between the two (see Hirschman, 1958). The use of terms such as de-industrialisation in LDCs actually imposes the experience of industrialised countries on developing countries, which have not even experienced industrial expansion to justify the notion of de-industrialisation. The fact that manufacturing employment share in these economies is low and not growing should not be read as a sign that these economies have reached a turning point at which manufacturing potential to create jobs has petered off.

Certainly, industrialising a country today is more difficult than it was in the past, given the tight competition in the global market, despite the popular view that late industrialisers can catch up easily through technology transfer from the industrialised countries. But this suggests that the late industrialisers need to find their path based on a careful consideration of both local and global dynamics (Dasgupta and Singh, 2006). What LDCs should focus on is not the anxieties created by de-industrialisation, but on the opportunities that may exist in the current global context for their growth and industrial capacity building.

Countless Strategies, Little to Show

While there is almost consensus on the need for rapid industrialisation in Africa, there is also wide agreement that industrialising the continent has been challenging in the past and the prospects are not looking good, unless certain conditions are created (see UNECA, 2011; 2016). As we have seen in preceding chapters, there have been numerous efforts at the country as well as the regional and continental levels (especially in recent years) aimed at stimulating industrial development. Unfortunately, in the midst of all these initiatives, industrial activities on the continent have in real terms stagnated, mainly as a result of the failure to transform the economic structures established during colonial rule. Most African economies have continued to specialise in the supply of raw materials to the world, just as it was during colonial times. A report by the European Union observes that the top 5 exports in Africa accounted for 60 percent of total exports in 2015, and all of them were primary commodities (see Zamfir, 2016). The recent growth experienced in many countries was largely driven by the higher commodity prices on the global market between 2003 and 2015.

In terms of manufacturing share in total employment and output, recent trends suggest that the continent is still facing severe challenges when it comes to achieving dynamic and robust industrial growth. Several factors have been proposed to account for the elusive nature of industrial development in Africa, including that most countries on the continent have failed to structurally transform their economies, leaving many of them solely dependent on primary commodities for export (see AU, 2007). Other factors which have been highlighted include the failure to create strong institutions to coordinate and drive the process of industrialisation sustainably; the failure to implement industrial policy in countries where such policies exist; that most African countries have been trying to "copy and paste" industrial policies and strategies from other countries or regions; and that Africa has failed to promote stronger and positive public–private relations which is key to industrial development (see te Velde, 2013).

There are many other factors that one can cite to explain the weak industrial performance in most African economies. As illustrated below, so far, the emphasis has been on the failures to implement policy as the main challenge. There has been less attention given to issues of institutions and the environment in which they operate, such that policy failure is often analysed independently from the institutions and the local social, economic and political context. This is possibly a hang-over from the SAPs which saw poor policies as the only constraint to economic growth. While policies are important in understanding the context to industrial development in Africa, there are a number of basic things which have often been ignored perhaps because they are too obvious. But ignoring them is like starting a journey without knowing what means of travel one will use. Changing the industrial fortunes of Africa would require paying attention to some of the basic elements of industrial growth. Below some of the issues which are fundamental to creating conditions for sustainable industrial growth on the continent are briefly discussed.

Pillars for Industrial Development in Africa

Vigilant Industrial Policy

One of the basic facts about successful industrial development anywhere is that it requires the actors involved to be acutely aware that building a strong industrial sector is a product of deliberate, well-coordinated actions and long-term planning. This is even truer for late industrialisers as they face the disabling trends of pre-mature deindustrialisation. Being alert is so basic that we often take it for granted. But it is a crucial attribute of someone who is aware of the environment, aware of dangers, awake to any opportunities and in response takes appropriate action. Being awake also requires that one is attentive to changing situations and adjusts the course of action accordingly. All countries which have managed to industrialise demonstrate this basic attribute of being alert to risks and challenges as well as opportunities in the environment where they operate. Even during the first industrial revolution elements of planning, coordination and deliberate actions were crucial to the success of the national and individual efforts. Being vigilant is an important feature in the process of seeking to achieve industrialise growth, especially today.

Today when we speak about the Fourth Industrial Revolution (FIR), which is defined by hi-tech industrial activities such as Nano-technology, 3-D printing, robotics, blue and green economies, biotechnology, augmented reality, the imperative of coordination, planning have become indispensable. We have seen a number of industrialised countries spotting the opportunities as well as taking carefully crafted measures to lessen the negative impact of the forthcoming Industrial Revolution 4.0. For instance, many industrialised nations such as Japan, South Korea, Germany, USA, France UK, etc., mobilise million dollars to support initiative aimed at developing the digital capabilities (EIU, 2018:5). What this implies is that "someone" has to do the planning, the coordination and take deliberate action towards the identified industrial objective. Put in a different way, this means that genuine industrialisation cannot occur in an autopilot mode; someone has to be alert to the risks as well as the opportunities as they arise and be able to change course accordingly. This is crucial in the context where the state is providing support to stimulate industrial growth. The impact of the interventions have to be evaluated regularly to respond to changes in both the domestic and international environment as industrialisation progresses.

We find a good example of alertness in the way the Ethiopian government responded to the changes in the cement industry. When the country experienced cement shortages between 2005 and 2012, the government used various means to stimulate the expansion of cement production capacity while in the meantime stabilize the price of cement. The measures adopted included the easing of barriers to entry such as licensing procedure of new firms, collateral free loans, access to government construction tenders, direct import of cement, price controls, and cement allocations to critical projects (see Oqubay, 2015:126–127). Similarly, when high transport costs where constraining the growth of the sector, government purchased and distributed various heavy-duty machinery to different cement producers. These measures helped to contain the price of cement until the production capacity was able to match the demand in 2012 (ibid).

When the cement industry exhibited signs of excess capacity and lack of competitiveness, government "abandoned investment incentives and even prohibited the new FDI in the industry. The incentives may have outlasted their usefulness through time" (Ibid, 130). This is the type of agility that is needed to successfully implement industrial policy. What is key in this is that the institutions tasked with implementing industrial strategy should be alert and agile enough to change the course of actions whenever the situation on the ground requires a change of direction. There is no magic about this, it is a skill that is learnt in the course of implementing industrial policy and this is why learning by doing is so important.

Selective Industrial Strategy

A cursory review of the historical evidence on industrialisation from the earliest to the most recent industrialiser does confirm that no country industrialised by simply setting the processes in motion and let things run on their own. All countries in the past planned and decided on the kind of industrialisation they sought to achieve, often through selective intervention. The literature on industrialisation is quite clear that no country in the world has managed to industrialise without taking calculated plans and actions; all countries have marshalled different state institutions and resources to realise the broader goals of industrial development. In the case of East Asia, industrial development acquired the status of a national asset.

As Ha-Joon Chang has observed, it is dishonest to give the impression that early industrialisers achieved industrial expansion through free trade, justified by the principles of comparative advantages (see Lin and Chang, 2009). It is misleading to create the impression that early industrialisers strictly followed their static comparative advantage to achieve the level of industrialisation they did at their peak. "Contrary to the popular myth that depicts it as a country that first developed on the basis of market and free trade, Britain was an aggressive user, and in certain areas a pioneer, of activist policies intended to promote infant industries" (Chang, 2003:24). As the former MITI Japanese official observed, a country has to have a long-term plan on how to create comparative advantage even in areas where it currently does not have.

Arghiri Emmanuel (1972) in his book *Unequal Exchange* provides a rich historical account of how industrialised countries used protectionist policies to boost their local industries and consolidate their global market share in strategic manufacturing nodes. He documents the different periods which industrialised countries adopted and later abandoned principles of free trade, showing that protectionism has been the norm rather than the exception in most countries, including Britain that later took on the role of championing free trade:

> Year after year, decade after decade, the governments of every country in the world have practiced without interruption a policy of protection. This has gone on for centuries. The only break was the brief parenthesis of free trade that began for England in 1846 and ended completely in 1932... (Emmanuel, 1972:xiii)[5]

In fact, free trade policies were largely abandoned when the First World War began in 1914, as the global economic and financial systems were destabilised by the conflict (see Polanyi, 1944). Amsden (1989) makes a similar observation that the now industrialised countries did not successfully create their strong industrial capacity based on their comparative advantage; they relied on specially calculated interventions, including subsidising research and development (R&D) to boost technology and innovation, which enabled them to outcompete their competitors. She particularly emphasises the importance of assisting local firms (private or public) to learn how to compete by borrowing and adapting foreign technology (ibid). As noted in Chapter 7, no country has successfully industrialised without an effective state playing a central role.

In the context of this debate, the role of the state in performing the three basic functions (i.e., coordination, planning and calculated intervention/support) central to industrial development in the early stages is self-evident. The three functions constitute the essence of industrial policy (see Johnson, 1982). There cannot be industrial policy without the state playing an active role in guiding and coordinating the various actors on the industrial platform. It is this interventionist implication of industrial policy which made adherents of neoclassical theory scorn industrial policy as something that interferes with the smooth functioning of markets and by so doing brings inefficiency into an economy (see Adelman, 1984; Stein, 1994; UNECA, 2016).

Although neoclassical economists believe in the ability of markets to allocate, direct and coordinate investment activities in the industrial sector in such a way that the need for an industrial policy does not arise (see Wade, 1990; Lall, 2004), experience shows that no country industrialised relying on markets alone. Countries which have industrialised have relied on the state not only to enforcing property rights but also actively intervene to discipline and guide markets (Amsden, 1989). Rosenstein-Rodan (1943) and Nurkse (1953) as we have seen argued strongly that if left to the operation of the laissez faire system, developing countries cannot achieve their optimal industrial potential. Thus, for developing countries to achieve any meaningful level of industrialisation, it is necessary for the state to not only to formulate industrial policy and create an investor-friendly environment, but to actively direct, coordinate, support and discipline both capital and labour (see Amsden, 1989).

Creating Effective State Institutions

Although the debate about the role of the state in industrial development is far from over, few analysts would dispute the view that states in the past have played an active role in bringing about industrialisation. But as we have seen in Chapter 7, it is not just any kind of state that can deliver industrialisation; it is only states with specific attributes which can contribute to the process of industrialisation. In the case of most African countries where industrialisation has been elusive for the past six decades now, the basic condition for successful industrialisation is the building of capacity to make states more effective. When such states are created, planning, coordinating and deliberately intervening in the industrial development process becomes their raison d'être.

As noted in Chapter 5, it is not by coincidence that industrial performance in most African countries was relatively stronger during the time when most states were active through national planning and active participation in the economy by means of state-owned enterprises. Weak industrial performance coincides with the striping of state capacity during the implementation of SAPs, which effectively barred the state from intervening in the economy, restricting African states to enforcing property rights (see Mkandawire and Soludo, 1999; Noorbakhsh and Paloni, 2000). As it turned out, the stripping of African states went too far such that it jeopardised the implementation of SAP policies themselves. But it was realised subsequently that you need an effective state to implement any policy including the enforcement of property rights.

During SAPs, it was not just the withdraw of the state from undertaking economic activities that took centre stage, but African countries were advised to "specialise" according to their comparative advantage, which in this case meant continuing to produce commodities. The rationale was that countries that grow faster are those that follow their existing comparative advantage. But as experience has shown, concentrating on exploiting static comparative advantage prevents the most important goal of industrialisation, which is used to create industrial capacity, by learning to compete and develop competences in key industrial areas (see Kaldor, 1957; Amsden, 1989). Apart from forfeiting the opportunity to learn to compete, choosing to specialise in current static comparative advantage precluded most African countries from creating their long-term comparative advantage (see Dasgupta and Singh, 2006).

What SAPs did was effectively to do away with industrial policy, and by so doing, the planning, coordination and the necessary state actions required to defy static comparative advantage. Consequently, this prevented African countries from shaking off the mantle of disadvantage that comes from a rigid pursuit of static comparative advantage. Since the role of the state in a serious industrial strategy is to coordinate, plan and intervene in the economy, the fact that African state were ordered to stay away from the economy, explains why industrial development has remained elusive.

Without state action which has proved so crucial to the industrialisation process in many countries in the past, Africa's industrialisation plan was effectively reduced to the autopilot mode, with the state acting as a spectator. Left on their own, foreign investors, as expected, decided to put their money in commodity extraction, with little seepages into the industrial sectors. Again, the outcome is predictable. The progress made during the early post-colonial period, which recorded significant progress in initiating industrialisation, was quickly reversed by SAPs. Without any active role of the state, deliberate action required to stimulate and support the growth of industries in different sectors, especially manufacturing disappeared. Most African economies were without clearly identified long-term goals to guide economic activities.

Coordinated Policies and Strategies

The return of industrial policy on the development agenda in Africa, in the last decade and half, has highlighted the need for coordination and deliberate public action to direct the process of industrialisation to a particular end (UNECA, 2016). Several countries have now formulated first (and some like Uganda, Rwanda and Ghana, second)-generation industrial policies, which assign an active role to the state, beyond that of laying a red carpet for foreign investors. In the new industrial policies which a number of African countries have formulated, the role of the state is not just to woo investors, but also directing them to strategic investment nodes in the economy, in accordance with the identified priority areas.

There are encouraging examples from countries such as the Congo Republic, where a directorate specifically for industrial development has been established: Kenya, where the establishment of several export processing zones and the revival of the Industrial and Commercial Development Corporations have highlighted the importance of coordinating industrial strategy: Uganda, where a clear focus on developing the capabilities and skills of informal manufacturers is outlined: Morocco, where a national agency dedicated to the promotion of SMEs has been established: South Africa, where the industrial development corporation is being repositioned to provide support to local firms to stimulate industrial growth; and Rwanda where there are efforts to create institutions (such as the Rural SMEs Promotion Rwanda), to promote and support the growth of rural SMEs (see UNECA, 2014).

In most African states, there now seems to be a growing awareness that industrialisation will not happen unless the state takes a proactive role in coordinating the activities of different actors (including state entities) on the industrial platform. This is an important realisation without which industrialisation will remain elusive, especially today when achieving meaningful levels of industrial development requires well-calculated steps and unflinching commitment on the part of public actors to create the capacity in the economy to withstand stiffer international competition. Realising this basic feature of industrialisation is essential for all African countries seeking to industrialise because this awareness would inform and guide all the actions including the identification of industrial development priorities and targets.

Strong Institutional Capacity

For African states to coordinate, plan and effectively execute their outlined industrial strategies, developing the capacity in institutions tasked to undertake these crucial functions is essential. One of the commonly cited challenge when it comes to industrial development in Africa is the well-known fact that institutional capacity is low in most countries. While some analysts have argued that capable institutions are themselves a product of the process of industrialisation and development, such that weak institutional capacity is in itself a factor that explains weak industrial performance (see Rodrik, 2015), it can also be argued that institutional capabilities are built over time. Indeed effective bureaucracies in the Weberian sense are widely conceived to be offshoots of advanced industrial capitalism (see Weber [1911] 1968). But this view can easily lead us to a circular argument, where industrialisation depends on effective institutions, which should only emerge as an offshoot of industrialisation.

The question of what comes first, institutions with capacity or industrialisation, should not detain us here. The crucial point is the realisation that institutions capable of coordinating, identifying priority areas and taking deliberate, well-calculated actions are indispensable to a successful process of industrialisation. This is another basic element of industrial development in Africa and it is connected to the issue that industrialisation is always an outcome of planned, coordinated and deliberate action. The ability to plan and implement plans is a good reflection of a country's institutional capacity. In countries where institutions are weak with low capacity, implementation, particularly, coordination of strategies to stimulate industrial development, is expected to face serious challenges.

As noted earlier, most countries in Africa suffer from weak institutional capacity, and this is reflected in the fact that even if these countries which have formulated industrial policies, little is being implemented. Therefore, it is critical to consider the question of capacity in public institutions in any strategy for industrial development. Like comparative advantage, institutional capacity can be built where there is determination to achieve something. No country is born with capacity, capacity is created and for a particular purpose.

For any country to successfully execute an industrial strategy, suitable institutional capacity is essential. An industrial policy without effective institutions is like a car without a driver; no matter how good the policy insights and conclusions are, they amount to nothing if there are no channels through which they can be implemented. The Economic Report on Africa (UNECA, 2014) emphasises this point arguing that weak institutional capacity in most African countries is one of the major barriers to industrialisation. The report asserts that weak institutional structures and poor design have been at the root of Africa's industrial policy challenges throughout its post-independence history.

Weak institutional capacity has also been cited in most empirical growth studies on Africa, as a key challenge that hampers not just the implementation of policies, but also the design of appropriate policies to suit the African context (see Ndulu and O'Connell, 2008). What is surprising is that even if the fact that institutions in most African countries are known to be weak, with low capacity to implement the policies, there has been little attention in policy discussions to identify measures which can strengthen institutional capacity. For example, the World Bank (1994) assessment of the outcome of SAPs placed the blame solely on the failure by African governments to implement the recommended policies. Issues of institutional capacity were assumed to be part of the problem; and the impression created was that African governments sabotaged SAP. It was only later when the good governance agenda became mainstream that issues of institutional capacity began to attract policy attention.

In terms of industrial development, the history of industrialised countries, particularly the later industrialisers in Asia, attests to the fact that without effective institutions, industrial policy, no matter how good it may be, would achieve little. Effective institutions that can, first of all, identify key industries and firms to support, then provide relevant support, evaluate performance of supported firms and the institutions themselves regularly. Such institutions should have the capacity to monitor compliance of supported firms with the agreed principles and targets, and disciplining firms that fail to meet their targets. As Johnson (1982) and Amsden (1989) observe, in the case of Asia's late industrialisers, specific institutions were created to provide guidance and support aimed at realising the intended objectives.

It was not just a matter of creating institutions to drive the process of industrialisation. The crucial thing was that the institutions were sufficiently capacitated to enable them effectively carry out their mandate in their particular circumstances. From Japan, to Taiwan, Indonesia and Thailand, state institutions tasked with driving industrial development were provided with adequate incentives and resources to effectively carry out their missions, including the disciplining of firms that did not comply with the state directives (Wade, 1990). In all these countries, institutional capacity was created to enable the state agents to implement industrial strategy according to the plan. For example in Japan, at the beginning of the industrialisation process, subsidies were "dispensed according to the principle of reciprocity, in exchange for concrete performance standards with respect to output, exports, and eventually R&D" (Amsden, 1991:284). Sampath (2014) also observes that one of the pillars of the Asian industrial success was the ability to create institutions with the capacity to minimise the inherent industrial risks.

Oftentimes there is a sense of despair that weak institutions in Africa present insurmountable obstacles to industrialisation to such an extent that overcoming this challenge seems impossible. But if there is any lesson from history which African policymakers can learn, it is that effective institutions can be created if there is a strong appreciation by the leadership of the critical role such institutions play in realising the broader vision of a country. The danger is to try and duplicate the institutional set-up from other countries or regions just because these proved to be effective. The fact that a particular institutional arrangement succeeded in one place is not a guarantee that the same institutional set-up will produce similar positive results in an African country.

The likelihood of such institutional make-up producing similar results is small for the simple reason that the conditions under which institutions produce good results in Asia or Europe are different from those obtained in Africa. It is therefore important that when thinking about institutional set-up, while it is good to learn from experiences of other countries, local institutions should emerge out of the local conditions and needs, to be able to serve their intended purpose. In this regard, the call to avoid "blueprints" when designing and implementing industrial strategies cannot be over-emphasised (see UNECA, 2014:55).

Since institutions are crucial to the success of industrial policy, they need to be carefully thought out so that they can effectively contribute to realising the objectives outlined in industrial policy. The importance of institutions in the process of economic development was raised by the proponents of the New Institutional Economics (NIE) who observed that institutions other than markets have a crucial role to play in ensuring sustainable economic growth. Douglas North (1990), one of the main proponents of NIE,[6] maintained that economic performance is largely shaped by a set of local institutions to which economic actors respond. He further argued that the neoclassical theory's narrow focus on markets as the only important institution underestimates the role of other institutions in enhancing the functioning of markets. According to this view, "A set of political and economic institutions that provides low-cost transacting and credible commitment makes possible the efficient [functioning of] the factor and product markets underlying economic growth" (North, 1997:2).

A Right Mix of Institutions

In the context of industrial development where the state is expected to play a leading role in coordinating and shaping the process of industrialisation, the role of public institution is widely believed to be crucial. Several cross-country studies conducted during the 1990s, particularly Mauro's (1995), Knack and Keefer's (1995) and Evans and Rauch's (1999), reported a strong correlation between growth in general and the quality of public institutions. These studies provided strong empirical support for the idea that effective public institutions are central to economic growth. This is particularly true in the case of industrial development which, as we have seen, requires well-calculated interventions. Concepts such as a "fully institutionalised state," "political penetration" (Coleman, 1985), "embedded autonomy" and "internal coherence" (Evans, 1995) and "developmental state" (Johnson, 1982) are used to describe organisational and institutional arrangements within a country, essential to promoting sustained industrial development and economic growth.

Stein (1994) in the context of the intuitional reforms of the 1990s in Africa makes the observation that public institutions have a significant impact on innovation and the ability of firms to upgrade their production capacity and eventually strengthening their competitiveness. In the literature on industrialisation, there is no hesitation about the role public institutions play in promoting industrial development, though different approaches and contexts require different sets of institutions, and it is futile to prescribe in a vacuum the type of institutions which would be effective in promoting industrial development in all countries. Identifying the necessary set of institutions can only be an outcome of a careful review of the local context together with the objectives and targets of industrial development. Having said this, a general institutional framework can be a useful starting point in the process of creating effective institutions which can promote industrialisation.

Towards an Industrial Institutional Framework for Africa

Industrial Coordinating Body

Given the importance of capacity within institutions tasked with promoting industrial growth, an industrial institutional framework has to have three key components: an Industrial Policy and Coordinating Body (IPCB), an Industrial Services Agency (ISA) and a Quality Assurance Services body (QAS). In this framework, the IPCB can have the overall responsibility of overseeing the process of setting industrial goals and targets, and coordinating the activities of all stakeholders including the ISA and QAS. It should have a mandate to coordinate industrial activities, including ensuring that other actors are effectively fulfilling their mandates. A good example of such a body in Africa is Enterprise Mauritius (EM) which is an over-arching body for the industrial sector, created in 2006, whose main function is to promote coordination, coherence and synergies in the industrial sector (see UNECA, 2014:84).

EM was created as a result of a study concluding that the industrial sector lacked coordination and coherence and had duplication of roles scattered between different industrial sector entities. As a public–private venture, EM took over the responsibilities of overseeing industrial activities from the Mauritius Industrial Development Authority, which did not exercise the supervisory responsibilities adequately. As a body responsible for formulating industrial policy and strategies, EM is reported to be engaged in ongoing and extensive consultations with key role players, including the private sector before finalising policy and industrial targets. A former EM official reported that "the three leading private sector institutions namely JEC [Joint Economic Council], MCCI [Mauritius Chamber of Commerce and Industry] and MEXA [Mauritius Export Association] are all minority shareholders of the EM and hold directorship positions on the Board of EM and as such they participate fully in setting our goals" (cited in UNECA, 2014:84).

Similar structures that are slowly developing in other African countries include the Industrial Policy Councils, often chaired by senior government officials (sometimes the prime minister or the president as is the case in Uganda). Inviting a high-ranking politician to chair such initiatives has the advantage of creating traction as well as political support (see Page, 2014). On the other hand, this has the disadvantage of being seen as an activity for a particular party. The risks and the benefits here have to be considered carefully. In some countries (in Morocco, Rwanda, Uganda) the IPCs are connected to the Presidential Investors Advisory Council, and coordinate the investment activities and promote dialogues between business actors and the public sector. Examples of similar structures outside of Africa include the Economic Development Board (EDB) in Singapore, the Industrial Planning Committee (IPU) in Malaysia and the Industrial Development Bureau (IDB) in Taiwan.

What is common among all these different structures is the clear mandate to provide leadership and coordinate industrial activities of all role players. The effective coordination from a central body accounts for the highly successful industrial performance among East Asian economies, starting with Japan during the first half of the 20th century (see Johnson, 1999). While it is recommended not to replicate these institutions, the fundamental goal is to have a central body that coordinates the activities of other actors, a body that sets industrial goals and targets in full consultation with other stakeholders. With such structures it is possible to identify the priority areas and take deliberate actions towards meeting the identified goals. It must be mentioned here that some form of this kind of institution may already be in existence in some countries. What will be required in such cases is to streamline their work and clarify their role in industrial development.

> Policy coherence and alignment is crucial to ensure industrial policy's successful implementation. Hence, aligning economic policies (e.g, trade facilitation, competition policy, small business development, investment promotion and facilitation, higher education infrastructure development and macroeconomic policy) becomes critical, especially as some of these policies are driven and implemented by different agencies and government departments (TIPS, 2016:7).

Policy coherence is central to the success of any industrial strategy, and this cannot be achieved without a dedicated body to oversee that the different policies are talking to each other.

Industrial Extension Services Agency (IESA)

The work of the IPRB can be complemented by a more practically oriented body, responsible for the implementation of the industrial strategy, through direct interaction with firms and other actors. This body can be responsible for coordinating the provision of what is sometimes referred to as *industrial extension services*, with the primary aim of supporting local firms to upgrade and become competitive. Several key stakeholders such as financial institutions dedicated to supporting industrial development, institutions for skills upgrading and vocational training, organisations that support industrial activities including the promotion of SMEs, public and private agencies responsible for promoting investment, organisations that provide business and entrepreneurial services, research institutions that work on industrial matters should be part of this body.

The main purpose of IESA would be to ensure that a full suite of industrial services including financial advice, training and access to capital are provided to targeted firms and sectors. This should be part of the broader strategy to promote industrial development through selective industrial policy (see UNECA, 2016). A good example of a structure that provides this kind of services is the industrial extension services in Taiwan, which focuses on a range of services aimed at supporting industrial firms. The concept of industrial extension services is similar to the agricultural extension services. Like agricultural extension services, industrial extension services should aim at providing critical information to the small-scale industrial businesses as a way of assisting them to keep up with the latest trends in their respective fields. Many African countries are familiar with the provision of agricultural extension services, and good lessons can be drawn from that experience. As noted in Chapter 5, Kenya, in its second NDP, proposed to introduce industrial extension services to boost industrial production, modelled along the same lines as agricultural extension services.

In Taiwan, the focus of the industrial extension services was on providing services which promoted the linkages between local small and medium firms and multinational corporations as a way to speed up the upgrading of technological capacity among local manufacturing enterprises (see UNECA,

2014:66). The provision of enabling services should be institutionalised to promote sector-wide impact, as well as monitoring of the services and their effects on industrial development. In terms of the state's role, the provision of such services should be viewed as part of what I have referred to as the *secondary public goods* which are critical to achieving not just the industrial development goals but also other social and political objectives. The provision of secondary public goods should be a basic element of any industrialisation strategy in Africa.

Quality Assurance Agency

The third arm of the industrial institutional set-up should be a statutory body, whose main responsibility is to monitor the impact of industrial policies, but also to assess the compliance of the different actors with the broader industrial policy and targets. This is more of a monitoring and evaluation body tasked with assessing the outcome of interventions in an effort to identify the challenges, the constraints and how these can be effectively responded to in a systematic way. One of the findings of the UNECA study on industrialisation in Africa is that policy interventions are rarely monitored and evaluated, and because of this, industrial policies and strategies are not responsive to the changing environment in which they are being implemented (see UNECA, 2014). Monitoring and evaluating outcomes of industrial policy is a crucial part of creating a responsive and adaptive policy environment, which is a basic requirement for successful industrialisation. Regular assessment of strategies and their impact is crucial to ensuring that policy is adjusted to respond to various challenges as well as emerging opportunities in the course of implementing industrial strategy.

Case studies conducted in a number of countries in Africa suggest that lack of regular evaluation of policies and strategies has made most intervention non-responsive to the changing challenges of industrialisation. In some instances, changes to industrial policy are not guided by evidence from the realities on the ground (ibid). Lack of evaluation of programmes has also meant that industrial policies are arbitrarily changed, often with a short-term vision.

Some of the key actors that can be part of this body include the National Bureau of Standards, statistical office, the revenue services, the monitoring and evaluation department of the ministry of trade and industry, etc. The idea is to capture the result of policy interventions for the purposes of reviewing performance to guide subsequent interventions. The data which these bodies generate can be used to inform the process of redesigning and adjusting policy interventions to make them more effective. For example, the information from the Bureau of Standards about the quality of industrial products can be used to design interventions to assist designated firms to improve the quality of their products. This service can target those firms with great potential to enter into export markets. Similarly, in countries where a production subsidy is implemented, the information from such bodies can be used to assess the effect of the subsidy and whether the recipient has met the agreed conditions of the programme.

Experience from countries which have successfully industrialised suggest that they meticulously monitored and regularly evaluated compliance of firms, as well as the impact of specific interventions. Evaluation of programmes is meant to correct some of the unintended negative outcomes to make the interventions more effective. In the case of Asian economies, as noted earlier, compliance among participating firms was one of the conditions for being eligible to receive government support, and firms including banks which did not comply or meet the stipulated conditions were disciplined (Johnson, 1982; Amsden, 1991).

In Africa, monitoring and review of the interventions and strategies has always been the missing link. For instance the Kilimo Kwanza (Agriculture first) programme introduced in Tanzania in 2006 had never been evaluated 10 years after its commencement. Similarly, in Uganda the Presidential Investor Advisory Council has no mechanism for monitoring and assessing the outcome of the interventions (Page, 2014). Developing institutions with the capacity to assess and review the performance of policy and strategies is an indispensable ingredient of an effective industrial strategy. Without this crucial service, the industrial development project in Africa will continue to be only a dream.

Addressing the Institutions Capacity Deficit in Africa

But for these institutions to be able to carry out the envisioned task of driving the industrialisation project, they need to be capacitated. Lack of or weak institutional capacity makes it difficult for these institutions to perform their tasks effectively (see Githinji and Adesida, 2011; Sampath, 2014). But capacity has to be understood in the concrete conditions of each African country, taking into account the fact that capacity in institutions is a social, cultural and political construct. In other words institutional capacity is a product of the political, social, economic and cultural actions and decisions that local people and organisations make or ignore to make. It is not a given. As argued earlier, capacity in institutions can be created up to any level that key actors deem essential. In this sense, institutional capacity is largely a reflection of the level of priority attached to a particular institution. An institution that is highly valued is likely to be given the necessary support to build the required capacity for it to perform its functions better.

In South Africa for instance, there is a clear difference in levels of capacity between different state institutions, with the South African Revenue Services (SARS) enjoying the highest institutional capacity as far as performing its function is concerned. Arguably, this reflects the priority that the state attaches to this institution, to the extent that the institution is able to assemble the best available management and professional teams in the sector (at least the professionals who operate the institutions, but not so much the political appointees). Priority accorded to institutions is also reflected in the equipment, financial resources and broader public support provided. It is not by accident that some of the public institutions persistently suffer from weak intuitional capacity such that the services rendered are not efficiently and professionally delivered.

In several African countries, institutions which are responsible for promoting industrial development are reported to have low capacity, reflected in many ways such as low levels of skill and morale among officials, poor resources (human and financial), poor operating conditions and low political support. Yet these institutions are expected to accomplish the demanding task of coordinating and promoting industrial development. For example, while Rwanda has been widely lauded for creating institutions to drive the industrial development project, some of the institutions are poorly capacitated, making it difficult for these institutions to effectively perform their duties. A recent study revealed that the Rwanda Bureau of Standards (RBS), which has five divisions and 19 departments, is manned by only 138 staff, with an annual budget of about US$3.8 million in 2013. And yet,

> The RBS is expected to develop standards for all aspects of energy production and distribution, undertake certification for export markets and develop safety and environmental standards. On rural development, it is expected to work with local the government ministry to develop human settlement standards, to devise standards on irrigation and produce handling with the Ministry of Agriculture and to test material used in rural road construction. For productivity it is [expected] to develop information and communication technology standards with the Ministry of Information and Technology. It is also [expected] to work with Ministry of Youth and Employment to

> develop standardised products for youth training while also developing new manufacturing practices for SMEs to access export markets (UNECA, 2014:89).

Just looking at what is expected of the RBS and the resources (human and financial, without assessing the skill levels) available, the challenge of inadequate capacity is quite evident.

A similar story is reported in Kenya where the Kenya Industrial Property Institute (KIPI) is alleged to have limited institutional capacity required to carry out its mandate properly. One of the KIPI officials observed that, "There is lack of capacity in many areas, including infrastructure (such as adequate and reliable electricity, internet and communication resources) and facilities (such as machines) which limits its ability [to] discharge its duties. [Consequently] KIPI is limited in activities such as outreach, training and creating public awareness" (cited in ibid, 90).

In a study on the agro-processing sector in Zambia, similar challenges were reported by most of the managers who complained that the Zambia Bureau of Standards (ZBS) was unable even to test products imported, partly due to lack of capacity and partly because of corruption. There are several other examples that can be cited to illustrate the challenge of institutional capacity in most African countries. In terms of promoting sustainable industrial development on the continent, it is fundamental that these institutions are adequately capacitated as the foundation on which the industrial project can be built. As noted above, capacitating institutions is a matter of priority, and as such, not all institutions can receive the same weight. If industrialisation is seen as a critical area, then this should be reflected in the capacities created in the institutions tasked with driving the industrialisation venture. Since institutions that are established to promote industrialisation are either public or quasi-state institutions, creation of capacity in these organisations is a matter of political commitment and will. In view of this, creating political and public support for these institutions requires some kind of political alliance between different sections of society.

Provision of Secondary Public Goods

One of the basic preconditions for a successful industrialisation project in Africa, which is connected to the issue of institutional capacity discussed above, is that of making available what I call the *secondary public goods*. Here it is important to make a distinction between the conventional public goods or primary public goods such as national security, public health, public education, infrastructure, public parks, etc. The economic concept of public goods is defined by two characteristics: *non-rivalry* (an individual's consumption of the goods does not affect other people's opportunity to consume the same good) and *non-excludable* (an individual consumption of goods or services does not deny or exclude others). In the context of industrialisation, secondary public goods are *impure public goods* in the sense that they can be provided by the market, but because they have strong positive externalities or spill-over effects (higher social returns), the market will always under-supply these goods (Redding, 1999). A good example that has been widely explored in the empirical growth literature is that of Research and Development (R&D). Jones and Williams (1998), for instance, found that social returns to R&D are typically higher than the private returns. In this case, leaving R&D entirely to the market may result in the under-provision of R&D, given that the market will not price in the higher social returns, but will be guided by the private returns, which tend to be lower. This view was earlier used to justify state involvement in the industrialisation process since the spill-over effects of industrial activities would not be perfectly captured by private investors, and as such their incentive to invest would be lower (see Scitovsky, 1954; Rosenstein-Rodan, 1957). Scitovsky (1954) was convinced beyond any doubt that the social returns to industrial investments in developing countries where markets are missing or thin would even be greater in the initial stages of industrial development, and would therefore have larger societal positive impact.

Apart from R&D, there are a range of services which a state seeking to industrialise can classify as secondary public goods, largely because of their indirect effects on society. These services can be referred to as secondary public goods mainly because they are not directly producing benefits to the public like a police woman patrolling the streets; their benefit to the public is indirect. For instance, providing support to businesses to upgrade their production capacity and competitiveness can bring public benefits in several indirect ways. Some such services and goods include services that improve product quality, compiling information that gives an indication to local producers about their competitive ranking and how they can improve, services that help firms upgrade their production capabilities. Production subsidies, export facilitation services, product accreditation, standard certification, business start-up packages, business incubator facilities, focused industrial services targeted at specific economic zones are other examples. Most of these services can only be adequately provided by public institutions tasked with promoting industrial growth rather than by private actors who may not see the bigger picture or impact of their actions.

When local firms that are provided with these services upgrade and are able to enter export markets, their success can induce other local firms to learn from them, and as more firms learn, this can contribute to economic growth in terms of increased demand for labour as well as output. Further, as the upgraded firms enter export markets, they contribute to improving the balance of payment situation through their foreign currency earnings, which is important in most developing countries where export earnings are not only low but uncertain. The other indirect way through which secondary public goods may lead to increased public benefit is increased public revenue, which in turn increases as the number of successful firms and workers grows. With increased government revenue, the capacity to provide primary public goods such as infrastructure, training facilities in public institutions can be improved (Oqubay, 2015).

In this sense, secondary public goods and services should be seen as public investment to the extent that they have positive impact on the broader society. This view is acknowledged in the industrial action plan for South Africa where it is observed that given the broader benefit from domestic firms entering the export market, the state should be actively supporting these firms (DTI, 2016). But as noted earlier in this chapter, for these public investments to be effective, they have to be closely monitored and regularly reviewed so that they can achieve their intended objectives. It is pointless to provide a production subsidy to firms that are not yielding their expected results within the agreed time frames.

In most African countries, it is often argued that governments have no resources to provide such services to the industrial sector, when they are not able to adequately provide the primary public goods such as medicine and medical equipment in hospitals. But a long-term vision that seeks to expand the provision of primary public goods may as well start from the provision of secondary public goods which can create the capacity to provide primary public goods in the long run. What is essential is to see the expenditure on secondary public goods as an investment which is expected to yield some social return in the long run. As a public investment, it should be evaluated regularly to see if there are any justifiable returns. This should be the vision of an industrial strategy; there has never been successful industrialisation without a deliberate long-term plan, outlining where the country wants to be at a particular time in the future.

Striving to Create Dynamic Comparative Advantage

The other basic issue about industrialisation in African is that countries should recognise that comparative advantage is dynamic in nature and the focus should be on creating dynamic comparative advantage. Often, the literature on comparative advantage and free trade portrays the static view, such that the current comparative advantage of countries is presented as if it is cast in stones, a situation which has prevented many countries from learning to create new areas of comparative advantage by learning to build capabilities in completely new areas (Krugman, 1987). The need to look at comparative advantage as something that can be moulded into different capabilities is more clearly illustrated in Grossman and Helpman (1990) who show that comparative advantage can shift as countries specialise in producing a combination of different products and accumulating the necessary technology and skills. As the case of Japan cited in Chapter 1 shows, a country benefits more by striving to build industrial capacity even in those sectors where it currently does not comparative advantage. In fact the meaning of industrial policy is that a country concentrates its resources in what it sees as strategic areas, not because a country has comparative advantage, but because a country thinks that it is an important area to the broader national goals (UNECA, 2016).

Developing industrial capability through learning to compete and export is one of the fastest ways of learning to defy static comparative advantage and creating dynamic comparative advantage. African governments should not be deterred to explore learning how to create the capacity to compete in areas where they currently have no comparative advantage. Sticking to static comparative advantage implies that they will never change their position in the global configuration of production and international division of labour. For African countries, this would mean that they would remain suppliers of raw materials to the world, and the consequences of specialising in commodity production are well known in Africa. One of the most debilitating past experience in most African countries is the resignation to the idea that these countries' comparative advantage lies in commodities or labour-intensive activities (see Wood and Berge, 1997). In this regard, the biggest opportunity most African countries have missed is that of learning how to defy static and create dynamic comparative advantage. Here the fundamental idea is to realise that all countries create comparative advantage over time.

Navigating Premature Deindustrialisation

As alluded to earlier in this chapter, premature de-industrialisation is a phenomenon that has emerged strongly in the 21st century. The main challenge from premature de-industrialisation for later industrialisers is that countries that are seeking to industrialise today will find it much more difficult to create wealth and mass employment (see Rodrick, 2015; Felipe et al, 2017). Given this, it is important to see how this trend affects the prospects of industrialisation in Africa.

Sometimes, the declining share of manufacturing in total employment and output is framed as a matter of the changing classification of activities, with the lines between industry and services becoming blurred (Manyika et al, 2012; Newman et al, 2016). But the dynamics captured in the de-industrialisation phenomenon go beyond changing the classification of economic activities. The trends observed go to the heart of the theory of structural transformation, and they have to be explored in more detail to understand their impact on countries that are now embarking on industrial development. Available data show that employment elasticity of manufacturing growth has significantly fallen and this is reflected in the inability of economies world-wide to create adequate jobs, even in economies experiencing robust growth. We have seen this in most African countries where even if manufacturing share in total output remained the same, its employment share has declined (see Chapter 3). It is in the services sector (mainly retail and restaurants) where jobs are growing (Chapter 6).

Does this mean industrialisation should become less important in Africa's development agenda? Even if manufacturing does not have the strong employment generation capacity it used to have, it still remains an important factor in Africa's strategy of building inclusive economies. First, while the services sector seems promising, since that is where employment growth is occurring, the challenge is that the part of the service sector where jobs are being created is largely the informal services such as retail trade and household services, characterised by low income and more precarious employment (Fox et al, 2013; UNECA, 2016). As noted in Chapter 6, the configuration of economic activities will have little impact on reducing poverty and creating inclusive growth since most of the people moving into the service sector are engaging in low-productivity activities, and are not significantly contributing to and sharing in the growth.

Secondly, high-productive jobs in the services sector such as in banking, real estate, ICT, insurance, business service consultancy, design etc., require highly skilled personnel which excludes most Africans, given that the skills level in the population are low in most countries.

Third, the sections of the services sector with high productivity are not well-developed in most countries such that their capacity to create employment, even if there were adequately skilled people available, is small. Since employment in agriculture is stagnating and dwindling in many countries, for African countries to make a big dent on poverty and to create economies where more people can benefit from and contribute to growth, the growth of the industrial sector remains crucial. The prospects for such growth will largely depend on the decisions African governments will make regarding the basics of industrialisation discussed above. While global manufacturing trends are shifting such that it is much harder to generate jobs, industrial development remains important to Africa's sustainable growth and development prospect.

Notes

1. Most of the 3 million jobs created at actually in the informal sector, with formal wage employment averaging just less than 10 percent (ILO, 2017).
2. At the regional economic community (REC) level, the Southern Africa Development Community (SADC), the Economic Community of West African States (ECOWAS) and the East Africa Community (EAC) have all formulated and adopted regional industrial policies and strategies.
3. See the World Bank's World Development Indicators' online databank for details. The international poverty lines were adjusted from US$1.25 to US$1.90 per capita per day for extreme poverty and from US$2 per capita per day to US$3.10 for moderately poor in 2015.
4. The sample had only six industrialised countries: Japan, the United States, the UK, France, West Germany and Italy. If the figures on the growth rate in output for manufacturing and the broader economy are anything to go by, it is clear that the UK was de-industrialising much faster than the other economies in the period 1973–1984, followed by France and Japan (see Dasgupta and Singh, 2006:5).
5. Although free trade policies were widely adopted among industrial countries after 1846, they lasted for a short period in most countries, except England. For example, the United States abandoned free trade less than 20 years later in 1861 by implementing the *Morrill Tariff*, this was followed by France in 1871, Italy in 1877, Austria and Argentina in 1878, Canada in 1879, Australia in 1902 and Chile in 1916 (see Emmanuel, 1972:xiv).
6. The awarding of a Nobel Peace Prize in economics to Ronald Coase in 1991 and Douglass North in 1993 brought the ideas of NIE into the mainstream academic and research community.

References

Adelman, I. (1984). "Beyond Export Led Growth." *World Development*, Vol. 12, No. 9. 937–949.

African Centre for Economic Transformation (ACET, 2014). *Growth with Depth—African Transformation Report*. Accra: ACET. Available at: http://africantransformation.org/wcontent/uploads/2014/02/2014-african-transformation-report.pdf. Accessed 18.06.2016.

African Development Bank (AfDB, 2017). *Jobs for Youth in Africa: Strategy for Creating 25 Million Jobs and Equipping 50 Million Youth (2016–2025)*. Tunis: AfDB.

African Union (AU, 2007). "Action Plan for Accelerated Industrial Development of Africa." AU Conference of Ministers of Industry, 1st Extra-Ordinary Session, 24–27 September, Midrand, South Africa.

Amirapu, A. and Subramanian, A. (2015). "Manufacturing or Services: An Indian Illustration of a Development Dilemma." Centre for Global Development (CGD) Working Paper No. 409. Washington, DC: CGD.

Amsden, A. H. (1989). *Asia's Next Giant: South Korea and Later Industrialisation*. New York: Oxford University Press.

Amsden, A. H. (1991). "Diffusion of Development: The Late-Industrializing Model and Greater East Asia." *American Economic Review*, Vol. 18, No. 2. 281–286.

Banga, K. and te Velde, D. W. (2018). "Digitisation and the Future of Manufacturing in Africa." Supporting Economic Transformation (SET) Working Paper. Available at: https://progs.odinet.org.uk/iedg/Economic%20Transformation/SharedDocuments/Future%20of%20manufacturing%20project/set.odi.org. Accessed 12.03.2018.

Buera, F. and Kaboski, J. (2009). "Can Traditional Theories of Structural Transformation Fit the Data?" *Journal of Economic European Association*, Vol. 7, No. 2/3. 469–477.

Chandy, L., Kato, H. and Kharas, H. (2015). "From a Billion to Zero: Three Key Ingredients to End Extreme Poverty," in L. Chandy, H. Kato and H. Kharas (eds.), *The Last Mile in Ending Extreme Poverty*. New York: Brooklyn Institute Press. 1–33.

Chang, H. (2003). "Kicking away the Ladder: The 'Real' History of Free Trade." Foreign Policy in Focus (FPIF) Special Report. Available at: www.personal.ceu.hu/corliss/CDST_Course_Site/Readings_old_2012_files/Ha-Joon%20Chang%20-%20Kicking%20Away%20the%20Ladder-The%20"Real"%20History%20of%20Free%20Trade.pdf. Accessed 21.03.2015.

Chenery, H., Robinson, S. and Syrquim, M. (1986). *Industrialisation and Growth: A Comparative Study*. Washington, DC: World Bank.

Coleman, J. (1985). "The Concept of Political Penetration," in M. Twaddle (ed.), *Decolonisation in British Africa: A New Historiographical*. Debate. Copenhagen: University of Copenhagen.

Dasgupta, S. and Singh, A. (2006). "Manufacturing, Services and Premature Deindustrialisation in Developing Countries: A Kaldorian Analysis." United Nations University-World Institute for Development Economics Research (UNU-WIDER) Research Paper No. 2006/49. Helsinki: UNU-WIDER.

Department of Trade and Industry (DTI, 2016). Industrial Policy Action Plan (IPAP) 2016/17–2018/19. Pretoria: DTI.

Emmanuel, A. (1972). *Unequal Exchange: A Study of the Imperialism of Trade*. New York: Monthly Review Press.

Evans, P. (1995). Embedded Autonomy: States and Industrial Transformation. Princeton, NJ: Princeton University Press.

Evans, P. (2010). "Constructing the 21st Century Developmental State: Potentialities and Pitfalls," in O. Edigheji (ed.), *Constructing a Developmental State in South Africa*. Cape Town: HSRC Press. 37–58.

Evans, P. and Rauch, J. (1999). "Bureaucracy and Growth: A Cross-national Analysis of the Effects of the Weberian State Structures on Economic Growth." *American Sociological Review*, Vol. 64, No. 5. 748–765.

Felipe, J., Mehta, A. and Rhee, C. (2017). "Manufacturing Matters...But It's the Jobs that Counts." Asian Development Bank Paper Series, No. 420.

Fox, L., Haines, C., Huerta-Munoz, J. and Thomas, A. (2013). "Africa's Got Work to Do: Employment Prospect in the New Century." International Monetary Fund (IMF) Working Paper 13/201.

Fox, L. and Thomas, A. (2016). "Africa's Got Work to Do: A Diagnostic of Youth Employment Challenges in Sub-Saharan Africa." *Journal of African Economies*, Vol. 25, No. 1. 16–36.

Githinji, M. and Adesida, O. (2011). "Industrialisation, Exports and the Developmental State in Africa. The Case for Transformation." Economics Department Working Paper Series, University of Massachusetts-Amherst.

Grossman, G. and Helpman, E. (1990). "Comparative Advantage and Long-run Growth." *The American Economic Review*, Vol. 80, No. 4. 796–815.

Hirschman, O. Albert (1958). *The Strategy of Economic Development*. New Haven: Yale University Press.

Hirschman, O. Albert (1981). *Essays in Trespassing: Economics to Politics and Beyond*. Cambridge: Cambridge University Press.

International Labour Organisation (ILO, 2017). *World Employment Social Outlook: Trends 2017*. Geneva: ILO.

Johnson, C. (1982). *MITI and the Japanese Miracle: The Growth of Industrial Policy*. Stanford: Stanford University Press.

Johnson, C. (1999). "The Developmental State: Odyssey of a Concept," in M. Woo-Cumings (ed.), *The Developmental State*. Cornell, CA: Cornell University Press. 32–60.

Jones, C. and Williams, J. (1998). "Measuring the Social Returns to R & D." *Quarterly Journal of Economics*, Vol. 110. 1127–1170.

Kaldor, N. (1957). "A Model of Economic Growth." *Economic Journal*, Vol. 67, No. 268. 591–624.

Knack, S. and Keefer, P. (1995). "Institutions and Economic Performance: Cross-Country Tests Using Alternative Institutional Measures." *Economics and Politics*, Vol. 7, No. 3. 2007–2027.

Krugman, P. (1987). "The Narrow Moving Band, the Dutch Disease, and the Competitive Consequences of Mrs. Thatcher." *Journal of Economics*, vol. 27. 41–55.

Lall, S. (2004). "Selective Industrial and Trade Policies in Developing Countries: Theoretical and Empirical Issues," in C. Soludo, O. Ogbu and H. Chang (eds.), *The Politics of Trade and Industrial Policy in Africa*. Trenton/Asmara: Africa World Press Inc. 75–110.

Lewis, A. (1984). "The State of Development Theory," *The American Economic Review*, Vol. 74, No. 1. 1–10.

Lin, J. and Chang, H. (2009). "Should Industrial Policy in Developing Countries Conform to Comparative Advantage or Defy it? A Debate Between Justin Lin and Ha-Joon Chang." *Development Policy Review*, Vol. 27, No. 5. 483–502.

Manyika, J., Sinclair, J., Dobbs, R., Kassey, L., Mischke, J., Roxburgh, C., George, K., O'Halloran, D. and Ramaswamy, S. (2012). *Manufacturing the Future: The Next Era of Global Growth and Innovation*. Washington, DC: McKinsey Global Institute.

Mauro, P. (1995). "Corruption and Growth." *Quarterly Journal of Economics*, Vol. 110. 681–712.

McMillan, M. and Harttgen, K. (2014). "What is Driving the "African Growth Miracle?" African Development Bank (AfDB) Working Paper No. 209. Tunis, AfDB.

McMillan, M. and Rodrik, D. (2011). "Globalisation, Structural Change and Productivity Growth." National Bureau of Economic Research (NBER) Working Paper No. 17143.

Mkandawire, T. (2001). "Thinking About the Developmental States in Africa." *Cambridge Journal of Economics*, Vol. 25, No. 3. 289–313.

Mkandawire, T. and Soludo, C. (1999). *Our Continent, Our Future: African Perspectives on Structural Adjustment*. Dakar: CODESRIA.

Ndulu, B. and O'Connell, S. (2008). "Policy Plus: African Growth Performance, 1960–2000," in B. Ndulu, S. O'Connell, R. Bates, P. Collier and C. Soludo (eds.), *The Political Economy of Economic Growth in Africa 1960–2000*. Cambridge: Cambridge University Press. 1–75.

Newman, C., Page, J., Rand, J., Shimeles, A., Soderbom, M. and Tap, F. (2016). "The Pursuit of Industry: Policies and Outcomes" in C. Newman, J. Page, J. Rand, A. Shimeles, M. Soderbom and F. Tap (eds.), *Manufacturing Transformation: Comparative Studies in Industrial Development in Africa and Emerging Asia*. London: Oxford University Press. 1–24.

Noorbakhsh, F. and Paloni, A. (2000). "The De-Industrialisation Hypothesis, Structural Adjustment Programmes and the Sub-Saharan Dimension," in H. Jalilian, M. Tribe and J. Weiss (eds.), *Industrial Development and Policy in Africa: Issues of De-Industrialisation and Development Strategy*. Cheltenham: Edward Elgar. 107–129.

North, D. (1990). *Institutions, Institutional Change and Economic Performance*. Cambridge: Cambridge University Press.

North, D. (1997). "The Contribution of the New Institutional Economics to an Understanding of the Transitional Problem." *World Institute for Development Economics Research (WIDER)* Annual Lecture 1, Helsinki.

Nurkse, R. (1953). *Problems of Capital Formation in Underdeveloped Countries*. London: Basil Blackwell.

Oqubay, A. (2015). Made in Africa: Industrial Policy in Ethiopia. London: Oxford University Press.

Page, J. (2014). "Industrial Policy in Practice: Africa's Presidential Investors' Advisory Councils." WIDER Working Paper No. 2014/117.

Page, J. (2015). "Structural Change and Africa's Poverty Puzzle," in L. Chandy, H. Kato and H. Kharas (eds.), *The Last Mile in Ending Extreme Poverty*. New York: Brooklyn Institute Press. 219–248.

Patnaik, P. (2017). "Capitalism and Its Current Crisis." *Monthly Review*, Vol. 67, No. 8. 1–15.

Polanyi, Karl (1944). *The Great Transformation: The Political and Economic Origins of our Times*. Boston: Beacon Press.

Redding, S. (1999). "Dynamic Comparative Advantage and the Welfare Effects of Trade." *Oxford Economic Papers*, Vol. 51. 15–39.

Rodrik, D. (2013). "Unconditional Convergence in Manufacturing." *Quarterly Journal of Economics*, Vol. 128, No. 1. 165–204.

Rodrik, D. (2015). "Premature Deindustrialisation." National Bureau of Economic Research (NBER) Working Paper No.20935. Available at: http://www.nber.org/papers/w20935. Accessed 16.09.2017.

Rosenstein-Rodan, N. P. (1943). "Problems of Industrialisation of Eastern and South-Eastern Europe." *Economic Journal*, Vol. 53, No. 210/211. 202–211.

Rosenstein-Rodan, N. P. (1957). "Notes on the Theory of the Big Push." Economic Development Programme project C/57–25. Centre for International Studies. Cambridge: Massachusetts Institute of Technology.

Rowthorn, R. and Coutts, K. (2004). "Deindustrialisation and the Balance of Payments in Advanced Economies." *Cambridge Journal of Economics*, Vol. 27. 79–113.

Sampath, P. (2014). "Industrial Development for Africa: Trade Technology and the Role of the State." *African Journal of Science, Technology, Innovation and Development*, Vol. 6, No. 5. 439–453.

Scitovsky, T. (1954). "Two Concepts of External Economies." *Journal of Political Economy*, Vol. 62, No. 2. 143–151.

Stein, H. (1994). "Theories of Institutions and Economic Reform in Africa." *World Development*, Vol. 22, No. 12. 1833–1849.

Syrquin, M. and Chenery, H. B. (1989). "Three Decades of Industrialisation." *World Bank Economic Review*, Vol. 3, No. 2. 145–181.

te Velde, W. D. (2013). "State-Business Relations and Industrial Policy: Current Policy and Research Debates." Growth Research Programme (GRP) Working Paper, UN-University/World Institute for Development Economics Research (UNU-WIDER).

The Economist Intelligent Unit (EIU, 2018). *Who is Ready for the Coming Wave of Automation? The Automation Readiness Index*. London: EIU.

Timmer, P., McMillan, M., Badiane, O., Rodrik, D., Binswanger-Mkhize, H. and Wouterse, F. (2012). "Patterns of Growth and Structural Transformation in Africa: Trends and Lessons for Future Development Strategies." International Food Policy Research Institute (IFPRI) Thematic Research Note 02. West Africa Office.

Timmer, M., G. de Vries and K. de Vries (2014). Patterns of Structural Change in Developing Countries. Groningen Growth and Development Centre (GGDC) Working Paper No. 149.

Trade and Industrial Policy Strategies (TIPS, 2016). Analysis of Existing Industrial Policies and the State of Implementation in South Africa." Oneline resource available at https://

www.fes-southafrica.org/fileadmin/user_upload/TIPS_IP_REVIEW_FES-Revised_Final_Dec_2016_edit.pdf accessed 12.06.2017

Tregenna, F. (2009). "Characterising De-industrialisation: An Analysis of Changes in Manufacturing Employment and Output Internationally." *Cambridge Journal of Economics*, Vol. 33, No.4. 433–466.

Tregenna, F. (2016). "Deindustrialisation: An Issue for Both Developed and Developing Countries" in J. Weiss and M. Tribe (eds.), *Routledge Handbook of Industrialisation and Development*. London/New York: Routledge. 97–115.

Trump, D. (2017). "Remarks by President Trump at the APEC CEO Summit." Da Nang, Vietnam: U.S. Embassy and Consular in Vietnam. Available at: https://www.whitehouse.gov/briefings-statements/remarks-president-trump-apec-ceo-summit-da-nang-vietnam/. Accessed 04.03.2018.

United Nations Economic Commission for Africa (UNECA, 2011). *Report on Africa 2011: Governing Development in Africa—the Role of the State in Economic Transformation*. Addis Ababa: ECA.

United Nations Economic Commission for Africa (UNECA, 2014). *Report on Africa 2014: Dynamic Industrial Policy in Africa—Innovative Institutions, Effective Processes and Flexible Mechanisms*. Addis Ababa: UNECA.

United Nations Economic Commission for Africa (UNECA, 2015). *Report on Africa 2015: Industrialising Through Trade*. Addis Ababa: UNECA.

United Nations Economic Commission for Africa (UNECA, 2016). Transformative Industrial Policy for Africa. Addis Ababa: Economic Commission for Africa.

United Nations Industrial Development Organisation (UNIDO, 2016). Industrial Development Report 2016: The Role of Technology and Innovation in Inclusive and Sustainable Industrial Development. Vienna: UNIDO

United Nations Industrial Development Organisation (UNIDO, 2017). *World Manufacturing Production: Statistics for Quarter II, 2017*. Vienna: UNIDO.

Wade, R. (1990). *Economic Theory and the Role of Government in East Asian Industrialisation*. Princeton: Princeton University Press.

Weber, M. [1911] 1968. *Economy and Society* (edited by G. Roth & C. Wittich). New York: Bedminster.

Wood, A. and Berge, K. (1997). "Exporting Manufactures: Human Resources, Natural Resources, and Trade Policy." *Journal of Development Studies*, Vol. 34, No. 1. 35–59.

World Bank (1994). *Adjustment in Africa: Reforms, Results and the Road Ahead*. New York: IBRD/World Bank.

World Economic Forum (WEF, 2017). The Future of Jobs and Skills in Africa: Preparing the Region for the Fourth Industrial Revolution. Geneva: WEF.

Yeboah, K. F. and Thomas, Jayne S. (2017). "Africa's Evolving Employment Trends: Implications for Economic Transformation." *Africa Growth Institute*, Vol. 14, No. 1. 18–22. 1–25.

Zamfir, L. (2016). *Africa's Economic Growth: Taking off or Slowing Down?* Brussels: European Parliament Research Services, PE573.891.

APPENDIXES

Appendix 1: Trends in Output Composition by Sector (Resource-rich Countries), 1980–2015.*

	Agriculture					Industry					Services				
	1980	**1990**	**2000**	**2010**	**2015**	**1980**	**1990**	**2000**	**2010**	**2015**	**1980**	**1990**	**2000**	**2010**	**2015**
Algeria	8.5	11.4	9	6.9	**12.7**	57.7	48.2	58.1	62.1	**38.9**	33.8	40.5	32.9	31	**48.4**
Angola	…	17.9	9	9.8	**10.1**	…	40.9	72.1	59.9	**43.4**	…	41.2	22.3	30.2	**46.5**
Botswana	14.7	4.9	2.8	2.5	**2.4**	50.7	61	54.5	45	**33.1**	34.6	34.1	42.8	52.5	**64.4**
Cameroon	31.3	24.6	22.1	20.9	**22.8**	25.6	29.5	36	30.3	**28.5**	43.1	46	41.8	47.3	**48.7**
C. African Rep.	40	47.6	55	55.5	**45.5**	20.1	19.7	14.7	20.2	**15.1**	39.9	32.7	30.4	30.3	**39.4**
Chad	45	29.3	42.3	25.6	**29.6**	8.9	17.7	11.7	13.7	**10.8**	46	53	46.4	37.1	**38.6**
Dem. Rep. of the Congo	26.8	31	27.2	24.9	**20.1**	35	29	23.4	0.6	**42.5**	38.2	40	49.5	39.8	**37.4**
Equa. Guinea	…	61.6	8.6	4.6	**2.1**	…	10.6	87.7	92.5	**60.1**	…	27.8	3.8	3.8	**37.8**
Egypt	18.3	19.4	16.7	14	**11.3**	36.8	28.7	33.5	37.5	**36.2**	45	52	49.2	48.5	**52.5**
Gabon	6.8	7.3	6.7	4.1	**4.7**	60.4	43	60.4	59.4	**52.8**	32.8	49.7	32.9	36.5	**42.5**
Ghana	60.1	45.1	39.4	29.9	**21**	12.3	16.9	28.4	18.6	**27.6**	27.6	38.1	33.5	51.4	**50.3**
Mauritania	30.4	29.6	20.5	17.2	**27.7**	26	28.8	36.9	43.9	**28.6**	43.6	41.6	42.6	38.9	**43.7**
Mozambique	37.1	37.1	24	31.9	**25.2**	34.4	18.4	24.5	23.4	**21.6**	28.5	44.5	51.5	44.8	**62.3**
Namibia	11.2	11.7	11.8	7.5	**6.7**	55.8	38	28	19.6	**31**	33	50.3	60.2	72.9	**62.3**
Nigeria	…	…	…	…	**…**	…	…	52.2	41.5	**20.4**	…	…	21.8	23.6	**58.8**
Rep.. of the Congo	11.7	12.9	5.7	3.8	**7.7**	46.6	40.6	73	75.4	**56.1**	41.7	46.5	21.3	20.8	**36.2**

	Agriculture					Industry					Services				
	1980	1990	2000	2010	2015	1980	1990	2000	2010	2015	1980	1990	2000	2010	2015
Senegal	20.1	19.9	19.5	17.4	**17.5**	20.1	22.2	23.6	22.4	**23.4**	59.9	57.9	56.9	60.3	**59.1**
Sierra Leone	33	46.9	50.1	49	**61.3**	21.9	19.2	15.8	20.7	**4.8**	45	33.9	34.1	30.4	**32.5**
Sudan	32.9	40.6	36.9	35.4	**32**	...	15.3	17.2	33	**39.1**	53	44	45.9	43.3	**47.3**
South Africa	6.2	4.6	3.3	2.5	**2.3**	48.4	40.1	31.8	30.8	**29.2**	45.4	55.3	64.9	66.7	**68.5**
Tanzania	...	46	33.5	28.1	**31.5**	...	17.7	19.2	25.5	**26.4**	...	36.4	47.3	46.5	**42.2**
Tunisia	16.3	17.1	14.3	8	**11**	36	33.6	33	32.3	**27.2**	47.7	48.7	52.7	59.7	**61.8**
Zambia	15.1	20.6	22.3	9.2	**5.3**	42.1	51.3	25.3	26.8	**35.3**	42.8	28.1	52.4	53.6	**59.4**
Zimbabwe	15.7	16.5	25.3	25.3	**16**	11.8	29	33.1	20.4	**26.8**	24.7	55.3	50.4	54.3	**57.2**
Average	**23.6**	**25.7**	**20.3**	**16.8**	**17.4**	**36.4**	**31.0**	**38.5**	**37.0**	**32.6**	**41.2**	**43.3**	**41.2**	**42.7**	**50.1**

Source: Author. Based on data from the African Statistical Year Book (ASYB), various years.
*Ellipses indicate missing data.

Appendix 2: Trends in Output Composition by Sector (Non-resource-rich Countries), 1980–2015.*

	Agriculture					Industry					Services				
	1980	1990	2000	2010	2015	1980	1990	2000	2010	2015	1980	1990	2000	2010	2015
Benin	35.4	36.1	38.5	33.7	**23.1**	12.3	13.2	14.2	13.7	**25**	52.3	50.7	47.3	52.6	**51.9**
Cabo Verde	18.6	14.4	14.4	9.9	**9.7**	17	21.4	17.4	18	**20.5**	64.5	64.2	68.2	72.1	**69.8**
Comoros	34	41.4	39.9	48.4	**33.9**	13.2	8.3	11.7	11.4	**10.8**	52.8	50.3	48.5	39.9	**55.7**
Cote d'Ivoire	25.9	32.5	50	22.8	**22.1**	19.7	23.2	20.3	27.2	**31.7**	54.4	44.3	29.7	50	**46.2**

	Agriculture					Industry					Services				
	1980	1990	2000	2010	2015	1980	1990	2000	2010	2015	1980	1990	2000	2010	2015
Ethiopia	...	54.3	49.9	47.7	**39.2**	...	11.1	12.4	14.3	**17.7**	...	34.5	37.8	38	**43**
Gambia	30.9	29	26.8	28.5	**22.5**	14.9	13.1	9.2	12.3	**15.8**	54.3	57.9	64	59.3	**61.6**
Guinea	...	23.8	22.4	13	**20.8**	...	33.3	35.5	47.2	**28.9**	...	42.9	44.2	39.4	**50.3**
Kenya	32.6	29.5	33.1	25.2	**32.9**	20.9	19	17.5	19.8	**19.5**	46.6	51.4	49.4	48.2	**47.5**
Lesotho	24.6	25	11.6	8.6	**7.2**	26.5	34.4	28.5	31.9	**32**	48.9	40.7	59.9	59.5	**60.9**
Madagascar	30.1	28.6	28.4	28.2	**25.7**	16.1	12.8	15.6	12.2	**18.6**	53.9	58.6	56	56	**55.7**
Malawi	43.7	45	45.7	34	**27.5**	22.5	28.9	14.5	22.7	**16.3**	33.7	26.1	39.8	56.3	**56.2**
Mali	48.3	45.5	36.5	37.5	**40.4**	13.2	15.9	21	17	**19.8**	38.5	38.6	42.5	38.1	**39.8**
Mauritius	13.1	12.9	7	3.7	**3.5**	26.2	32.8	31	27	**21.7**	60.7	54.4	62.1	69.4	**74.8**
Morocco	18.5	18.3	15	15.4	**14.5**	31	33.4	29.2	29.7	**29.2**	50.5	48.3	55.8	55	**56.3**
Rwanda	45.9	32.6	39.7	32.2	**30.2**	21.6	24.6	14.5	15	**18.3**	32.6	42.8	45.8	52.8	**51.5**
Seychelles	6.8	4.8	2.9	2.9	**2.6**	2.5	15.6	16.3	31.2	**21.5**	14.3	77.5	78.9	65.9	**72.5**
Swaziland	22.7	10.4	12.2	12.2	**8**	8.4	30.2	43.2	44.1	**46.5**	39.1	47.1	46.5	43.7	**45.5**
Togo	27.5	33.8	37.6	37.6	**42.8**	24.8	24.5	22.5	19.6	**15.7**	27.2	47.7	43.7	42.7	**41.5**
Uganda	72	56.6	28.9	28.9	**24.3**	25.6	4.5	11.1	22.7	**25.5**	35.3	23.4	32.4	48.4	**50.3**
Average	**30.9**	**30.4**	**29.6**	**26.2**	**23.4**	**18.3**	**21.4**	**20.6**	**22.7**	**22.7**	**43.4**	**47.1**	**49.2**	**51.0**	**53.7**

Source: Author. Based on data from the African Statistical Year Book (ASYB), various years.

*Ellipses indicate missing data.

INDEX

A

B

C

D

E

F

G

H

I

J

K

L

M

N

O

P

Q

R

S

T

U

V

W

Y

Z

www.ingramcontent.com/pod-product-compliance
Ingram Content Group UK Ltd.
Pitfield, Milton Keynes, MK11 3LW, UK
UKHW021008120926
8556IPUK00028B/191

9 781433 165580